THEGREENGUIDE
Portugal Madeira
The Azores

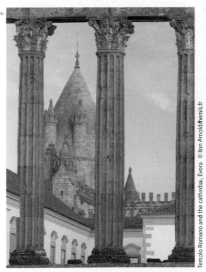

Templo Romano and the cathedral, Évora © Ion Arnold/hemis.fr

D0905800

MICHELIN

THE GREEN GUIDE **PORTUGAL MADEIRA THE AZORES**

Editorial Director	Cynthia Clayton Ochterbeck
Editor	Sophie Friedman
Principal Writers	Solveig Steinhardt, Daniel Mosseri
Production Manager	Natasha George
Cartography	Peter Wrenn
Picture Editor	Yoshimi Kanazawa
Interior Design	Chris Bell
Cover Design	Chris Bell, Christelle Le Déan
Layout	Natasha George

Contact Us	Michelin Travel and Lifestyle North America One Parkway South Greenville, SC 29615 USA travel.lifestyle@us.michelin.com Michelin Travel Partner Hannay House 39 Clarendon Road Watford, Herts WD17 1JA UK ✆01923 205240 travelpubsales@uk.michelin.com www.viamichelin.co.uk
Special Sales	For information regarding bulk sales, customized editions and premium sales, please contact us at: travel.lifestyle@us.michelin.com

HOW TO USE THIS GUIDE

PLANNING YOUR TRIP

The blue-tabbed PLANNING YOUR TRIP section gives you **ideas for your trip** and **practical information** to help you organize it. You'll find tours, practical information, a host of outdoor activities, a calendar of events, information on shopping, sightseeing, kids' activities and more.

INTRODUCTION

The orange-tabbed INTRODUCTION explores Portugal's **Nature** and geology. The **History** section spans the days of Phoenician settlement to the present. Another section highlights arts and crafts, art and architecture, literature and cinema, while **Portugal Today** delves into the modern-day country.

DISCOVERING

The green-tabbed DISCOVERING section features Principal Sights by region, showcasing the most interesting local **Sights**, **Walking Tours**, nearby **Excursions**, and detailed **Driving Tours**. Admission prices shown are normally for a single adult.

ADDRESSES

We've selected the best hotels, restaurants, cafés, shops, nightlife and entertainment to fit all budgets. See the Legend on the cover flap for an explanation of the price categories. See the back of the guide for an index of hotels and restaurants.

Sidebars

Throughout the guide you will find blue, orange and green-coloured text boxes with lively anecdotes, detailed history and background information.

😊 A Bit of Advice 😊

Green advice boxes found in this guide contain practical tips and handy information relevant to your visit or to a sight in the Discovering section.

STAR RATINGS★★★

Michelin has given star ratings for more than 100 years. If you're pressed for time, we recommend you visit the ★★★ or ★★ sights first:

★★★   **Worth a special journey**
★★   **Worth a detour**
★   **Interesting**

MAPS

🗺 Regional Driving Tours map, Principal Sights map.
🗺 Region maps.
🗺 Maps for major cities and villages.
🗺 Local tour maps.

All maps in this guide are oriented north, unless otherwise indicated by a directional arrow. The term "Local Map" refers to a map within the chapter or Tourism Region. A complete list of the maps found in the guide appears at the back of this book.

PLANNING YOUR TRIP

INTRODUCTION TO PORTUGAL

CONTENTS

DISCOVERING PORTUGAL

Welcome to Portugal, Madeira and the Azores

From fascinating UNESCO cities to remote fortress villages and beautiful golden sandy beaches backed by ochre cliffs, Portugal and its islands offer an eclectic mix of experiences, along with some delightful cuisine and excellent vinho verde and port wines.

LISBON AND THE LISBON REGION *(pp94–167)*

The capital of Portugal is an agreeable city to explore. Winding narrow alleyways in the old town, fascinating museums and the magnificent São Jorge castle and St Jerónimos Monastery mingle with the modern Parque das Nações with its huge Oceanario and Vasco da Gama Tower. It's a city that never sleeps – inviting restaurants, lively bars, trendy nightclubs in the Alcantara docks and soulful fado music carry on until dawn. Lively Estoril and Cascais, 30 minutes away by train, offer sunny beaches and championship golf courses. With its quirky palaces, glorious gardens, and cosy tea shops serving freshly baked *queijadas de Sintra* pastries, romantic Sintra, which Lord Byron called "Paradise on earth", hugs the rugged Serra de Sintra.

ALENTEJO *(pp168–195)*

Évora is situated at the heart of this region. The region's capital is a fine example of Portugal's 16C golden age with its plethora of richly decorated churches, medieval and Renaissance palaces and fascinating museums, many dating back 2 000 years. To the south lie vast, open golden plains, charming fortress villages and Beja, the capital of the southern Alentejo, with its flourishing markets selling local cheeses. The north is totally unspoiled, its fortified villages lying on the slopes of the São Mamede mountains, close to Spain. Plenty of outdoor adventure activities as well as tapestry museums, Baroque mansions and 13C castles keep the visitor amused. In summer, villages and spa towns come alive with festivals celebrating the region's local traditions and fine wines.

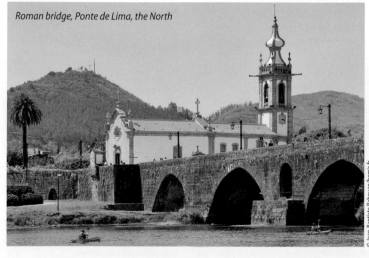

Roman bridge, Ponte de Lima, the North

© Jean-Baptiste Rabouan/hemis.fr

ALGARVE (pp196–221)

Portugal's southernmost playground enjoys a mild climate year-round. Sun-drenched sandy beaches backed by ochre cliffs, championship golf courses, busy holiday resorts such as Albufeira and Lagos and thriving markets line the coastline west of Faro. In the far west, the Atlantic coastline from Sagres to Aljezur near the southern Alentejo is more rugged and more spectacular, its rolling waves attracting surfers to miles of golden beaches. The eastern coastline towards Spain is quieter and, many would say, more authentic, the fishing ports of Olhão and Tavira being the liveliest with their first-rate seafood restaurants and fish markets. Inland, the mood cools in the majestic Monchique mountains where refreshing springs and fabulous views give way to forests of cork and tranquil white-washed villages.

CENTRO (pp222–285)

The heart of ancient Portugal, the Centro region is one where time has stood still. From fortified hilltop villages and mighty castles close to the border with Spain to the magnificent university city of Coimbra and the religious centre of Fátima in the west, the region offers a wealth of traditional customs and genuine hospitality. An ever-changing landscape of mountains and lush valleys in the Serra da Estrela National Park provides walkers, skiers and climbers the country's biggest outdoor playground.
Regional food specialities include the Queijo da Serra cheese.
Discover rock art dating back some 30 000 years at the Parque Arqueológico do Vale do Côa and 3C Roman ruins at Conímbriga. A necklace of white sandy beaches is strung along the Costa da Prata.

PORTO AND THE NORTH (pp286–339)

The gateway to an unmarred north, Porto is a melting pot of historic monuments, a charming UNESCO-listed World Heritage old town and bustling river-front where cruise ships and family-run restaurants ply their wares along the River Douro. On the south bank, Vila Nova de Gaia is a mix of trendy fusion restaurants and famous port wine lodges such as Taylor's, Dow and Sandeman. North of the city, the Costa Verde, Portugal's greenest and most northerly region, offers woodlands, the Peneda-Gerês national park, beautiful beaches, the Serra Amerela mountains, bustling markets at Ponte de Lima and Barcelos, *vinho verde,* and small villages where local customs and traditions are still followed. It has its fair share of remarkable palaces and castles, too, in Braga and Guimarães.

MADEIRA AND THE AZORES (pp340–405)

Stunningly beautiful and lush, Madeira's volcanic landscape is a delight. A subtropical climate provides an abundance of flowers and tropical fruits year-round. Two-thirds of the island is a national park (containing the laurisilva World Heritage Site), and the network of *levada* irrigation channels provides great walking trails. Cabo Girão, at 589m above the Atlantic, is the eighth highest seacliff in Europe. Capital Funchal is full of historic buildings and fine architecture, cobbled alleyways, shops, restaurants and museums. Neighbouring Porto Santo offers vast golden beaches, lots of water-sports and a quieter experience.
The nine islands of the Azores in the Mid-Atlantic are remote and untrammelled, their laid-back lifestyle offering a true get-away-from-it-all experience. Nine islands; nine ways of life; nine great experiences.

Algar Seco near Carvoeiro, Algarve
© Jon Arnold Images/hemis.fr

Michelin Driving Tours

1 LE MINHO
250km/155mi - 7 days
World Heritage Porto is the gateway to the meandering Douro and Portugal's greenest province. Stroll along Guimarães' medieval cobbled streets, visit the Archbishop's Palace in Braga for Baroque art and stock up on local delicacies at Ponte de Lima historic market before passing through ancient Viana do Castelo on your return drive all along a stunning coastline.

2 TRÁS-OS-MONTES AND VALE DO DOURO
500km/310mi - 7 days (without walks)
Steeply terraced vineyards, wine trails and villages time forgot provide a backdrop along the Douro. Visit medieval Vila Real with its ornate buildings and the fine Baroque Mateus Palace, famous for its fizzy rosé wine. Drive north and immerse yourself in folklore, Celtic bagpipes and picturesque villages. Visit Bragança's medieval battlements and palaces, and refresh yourself in the healing springs in Roman Chaves.

3 CENTRO AND BEIRA LITORAL
350km/217mi - 5 days
University town Coimbra is most impressive with its ornate buildings, monuments and *Sé Velha* (Old Cathedral), one of Portugal's oldest. Drive along the coastline with its wide sandy beaches bordered by dunes and pine groves, admiring Aveiro's pretty canals along the way. Drive through the Dão wine region to Viseu.

4 SERRA DA ESTRELA AND BEIRA BAIXA
350km/217mi - 5 days
High hills dominated by impressive stony outcrops and glorious views accompany the journey through the Serra da Estrela mountains to Guarda, Portugal's highest city.

5 HISTORIC WEST
450km/280mi - 5 days
Romantic Sintra, adored by Lord Byron for its fairytale castles, is a short drive from the seaside resort of Cascais. Driving north accesses the fishing town of Peniche and Óbidos with its narrow medieval streets. These are gateways to the pilgrimage routes of Alcobaça with its 12C monastery, and Fátima with its impressive Basilica of Nossa Senhora do Rosário. Stop off at Santarém on the drive back to Lisbon for superb views over the River Tagus.

6 TAGUS BASIN AND ALTO ALENTEJO
450km/280mi - 5 days
The River Tagus shapes the landscape north of Lisbon. Enjoy a tipple at a wine estate or visit the castles at Almourol or Marvã, Portugal's tallest, in the Mamede mountains. Admire Elvas' 14C walls and Évora on the way back to vibrant Lisbon.

7 ALENTEJO
400km/248mi - 5 days
Explore beautiful golden plains, ancient monuments, historic towns and sleepy villages. Royal Évora is a jewel with its splendid palaces, convents and 16C art. Nearby, ancient Monsaraz is a living museum with its castle, old houses and views over the Guadiana river. Beja's Roman walls are a treat to see.

8 ALGARVE
450km/280mi - 4 days
Drive west of Faro for lively seaside resorts Albufeira and Lagos and inviting sandy beaches. From Cabo de São Vicente to Aljezur, the rugged Atlantic coastline is spectacular, as are the mountains towards pretty Monchique, famous for its spring waters. Unspoiled villages, rolling hills and citrus groves beckon eastwards via rustic Alcoutim, elegant Tavira and the seafood capital, Olhão.

Driving tours

★★ **VALE DO DOURO** Name under which a route is described. See the index for the page number.

1. Le Minho : 250 km (7 days)
2. Trás-os-Montes et Vale do Douro : 500 km (7 days without hikes)
3. Centre and Beira Litoral : 350 km (5 days)
4. Serra da Estrela and Beira Baixa: 350 km (5 days)
5. Historic West : 450 km (5 days)
6. Tagus Basin and Alto Alentejo : 450 km (5 days)
7. Alentejo : 400 km (5 days)
8. Algarve : 450 km (4 days)

Harvesting at Quinta do Infantado near Pinhao, Douro valley

© Jon Arnold Images/hemis.fr

When and Where to Go

WHEN TO GO

Portugal has a relatively mild climate. However, the best time to visit the country depends on the region you wish to visit: the north is cooler than the south, and particularly in the mountains where winter can be harsh. In mid-summer the temperatures can rise pretty high (40°C) especially on the Algarve and in the interior, making it uncomfortable to those unaccustomed to such heat.

For a tour of the whole country, **spring** or **autumn** are the best seasons.

SPRING

Spring is the best time to visit the **south** of the country if you wish to avoid the heat of summer and the masses who flock to the beaches of the Algarve. It is also the season when the flowers, which adorn so many houses, come into full bloom and the countryside is green. Surfers will love spring on the blustery west coast. Late March and April (depending on the date of Easter) offer the added attractions of Holy Week festivities, especially in Braga.

SUMMER

The summer months are hot and dry inland, but in the coastal areas the heat is tempered by sea breezes. The **northern coast** (the Costa Verde) can have a few days of rain in mid-summer. Many *romarias*, festivals, feast days and sporting events take place during the summer months (◖*see CALENDAR OF EVENTS*) and of course, it's the best time to head for the beaches. Average sea temperatures are as follows: 16–19°C on the west coast; 21–23°C on the Algarve coast. Average summer temperatures for major towns and cities are: Porto – 20°C; Lisbon – 26°C; Évora – 29°C; Faro – 28°C.

AUTUMN

In the **north** with the chestnut trees and vineyards, the countryside takes on some lovely tints. The Douro and Dão valleys with their many vineyards become a hive of activity during the grape harvest (mid-September to mid-October). Autumn is also the ideal time to visit the Minho and Trás-os-Montes regions. Average temperatures in these two regions are 13°C and 8°C respectively (between October and December).

WINTER

Winter is a pleasant season to visit the Algarve coast, where swimming is possible from March to November (sea temperature: 17°C; air temperature: 18°C), the Costa de Estoril (sea temperature: 16°C; air temperature: 17°C), and, above all, Madeira and the Azores (sea and air temperature: 21°C), where winters are mild and sunny, though the odd day of drizzle is possible. The Algarve is transformed at the end of January when the almond trees start to blossom.

In winter, between January and March, skiers flock to the winter sports centres in the Serra da Estrela. Golfers can visit Portugal at almost any time of the year, particularly in the south where the winters are warm and often sunny. Around Lisbon, too, virtually the whole year is good for golf, though around Porto winters can be a little chilly.

WHERE TO GO

There is so much to do in Portugal – cities, palaces and other monuments, the culture trail, the vineyards, the beaches; surfing, paragliding, skydiving and golf for the sports-minded; shopping, museums, whale and dolphin watching, hiking the mountains, cycling, horse riding, and always the wonderful Portuguese food and wine – not forgetting port-tasting in and around Porto.

Lisbon, Portugal's capital, has more museums and monuments than anywhere else in the country and is ideal if you wish to get to know the cultural life of the country. Nearby, as a bonus, you will find the palaces of Sintra, Mafra and Queluz, all of them easily reached by a day trip and all well worth a visit. On the outskirts of Lisbon itself is the historically important centre of Belém, with its monastery, tower and museums (&see BELÉM).

For sun-worshippers, the Algarve in summer is hard to beat. By day there are water sports, sailing excursions, deep-sea fishing expeditions, diving and skydiving, or you could just soak up the sun on one of the glorious beaches or tiny coves. After dark, the entire coast comes alive with bars, restaurants and clubs catering for the evening pleasures of thousands of fun-loving visitors.

For something different try **Madeira** or the **Azores**. Diving, whale watching, walking and relaxing are the order of the day on both island groups.

Madeira is covered with flowers and forests, and the island has great botanical gardens where you'll find exotic plants from around the world. February to early April is a great time

Almond trees in blossom at the end of January, Loulé, Algarve.

© Jon Arnold Images/hemis.fr

Sete Cidades, São Miguel, the Azores

to visit, especially if you want to catch 'Carnaval', or go to the flower festival in April. Golf enthusiasts will find both Madeira and Porto Santo excellent, as well as for sea diving, sea-kayaking and whale and dolphin watching. The Azores are quiet, well away from bustling crowds. Volcanic, friendly and laid back, these islands, some of them hardly ever visited, are a haven of peace almost halfway across the Atlantic and on the main yacht route between Europe and the Caribbean. In Pico, the Azores have the highest mountain in Portugal, but they can be logistically difficult to visit if you want to include all nine islands, each so intrinsically different.

SHORT BREAKS

Short breaks are very popular and a couple of areas of Portugal are just made for this period of time. It is easy and relatively inexpensive to reach both Porto and Lisbon for a weekend.

Porto

Porto is a good place to get to know Portugal. It's a lively, hard-working city, but once the offices close, the inhabitants know how to enjoy themselves. The city itself has many monuments and museums; there is port-tasting in the great port lodges in Vila Nova de Gaia, just across the river Douro,

where you can learn about port and get to enjoy some special samples. The Ribeira river-front area has pulsating nightlife where you can join in the open-air party that seems to progress from one bar to the other all evening.

Lisbon

Lisbon makes an ideal destination for a long weekend. With its glittering array of designer shops and boutiques, you can spend almost an entire weekend shopping, particularly as many of the shopping malls stay open until 11pm. The Avenida de Liberdade has the high-quality names, but for something different, there's the flea-market in Alfama on Saturday mornings. For culture-vultures Lisbon has more museums and monuments than you could count – don't miss Belém with its famous tower, the Monument to the Discoveries; the world-famous Gulbenkian Museum, home to one of Europe's greatest art collections; the Park of Nations, built for Expo'98 but now housing a huge aquarium, several water gardens, a knowledge centre, a theatre, casino and a massive shopping centre – all connected by an overhead cable car. And with a Lisbon Card (*see LISBON),* you get free transport and free or reduced entry to most museums, art galleries and other attractions – many of which are free anyway on Sunday mornings.

FOOTBALL

Football fans frequently pop across to Lisbon just for a weekend during the season to watch Benfica, Sporting Lisbon or FC Porto. Getting tickets is easy, and with cheap flights and hotels, a weekend of football in Lisbon can work out to be less expensive than going to watch a top London team. The evening entertainment is fun, too, especially in the Bairro Alto district or along the river-front in the old dockyards, now converted into glitzy bars and clubs.

© Daniel Rodrigues/CC BY-NC-ND - Associação de Turismo do Porto e Norte, AR

RIVER CRUISING

Perhaps the most relaxing way to visit Portugal is a Douro valley river cruise. Lie back and indulge in all you want to eat and drink as you cruise along the glorious River Douro between steep hillsides lined with vineyards, soaking up the sun or enjoying a work-out in the fitness centre.

HORSE RIDING

For something more active, try a horse-riding expedition through the coastal and inland Alentejo, south of Lisbon, or the Algarve. Some competence is required, however.

SPAS

Many of the spas are natural, most of them dating back to Roman times. Spa-going was popular a century ago and is now back in fashion.

RELIGION

Being a predominantly Catholic country, Portugal has its fair share of churches, cathedrals, religious monuments, and museums dedicated to sacred art. Almost every village has its religious festivals to honour a saint. Semana Santa, the week leading up to Easter, is seriously observed in several places including Braga, the "spiritual" capital of Portugal. Another important aspect of religious life in Portugal is the pilgrimage to Fátima, the site of an apparition of the Virgin Mary in 1917. Thousands of pilgrims flock to this site each month, *(see CALENDAR OF EVENTS)*.

WORLD HERITAGE SITES

Lisbon Region
- p144 Cultural landscape of Sintra.
- p121 Monastery of the Hieronymites, and p123 Tower of Belém in Lisbon.

Alentejo
- p173 Garrison Border Town of Elvas and its Fortifications
- p179 Historical centre, Évora.

Centre
- p225 University of Coimbra
- p251 Monastery of Batalha.
- p257 Monastery of Alcobaça.
- p264 Convent of Christ, Tomar.

Porto and the North
- p247 Prehistoric Rock Art Sites in the Côa valley and Siega Verde.
- p297 Historical centre of Porto.
- p310 Historical centre Guimarães.
- p315 Bom Jesus do Monte
- p328 Alto Douro Wine Region.

Madeira
- p7 The laurisilva forest of Madeira

The Azores
- p385 Central Zone of the town of Angra do Heroísmo, Azores.
- p395 Landscape of Pico Island Vineyard Culture.

What to See and Do

OUTDOOR FUN

SAILING

There is ample opportunity for sailing in Portugal with its long coastline, the Tagus estuary and inland stretches of water. Many northern European yacht sailors stop at a Portuguese port as they sail round to the Mediterranean. In season it is possible to hire boats with or without crew. Apply to the Federação Portuguesa de Vela, Doca de Belém, 1300-082 Lisboa, ☎213 658 500; www.portugalvela.pt, though a better website (in English) is www.manorhouses.com/ports.

Coastlines where sailing is possible are marked by the symbol ⚓ on the Places to Stay map in this guide and on Michelin map 733. Marinas marked on Michelin map 733 have been selected for their facilities and infrastructure. ☻ Check weather bulletins before heading out to sea.

SURFING

Surfing is very popular in Portugal, especially along the west coast where the huge Atlantic waves come crashing in, often as high as 2m. The World Championships are held near Ericeira and there are several surf schools all along this part of the coast, right up to Peniche. There is also very good surfing at Praia do Guincho, near Estoril, and much farther south in the northern Algarve, near Carrapteira. You will find several surf schools and camps in most of these regions, and there is also one (which also caters for beginners) at Sagres. Surfing is also starting to become popular in Madeira at a number of locations.

DIVING

Diving is very popular along the Algarve, at Matosinhos near Porto where you can reach a German U-boat, in the Azores, and Madeira and Porto Santo, where there are several diving schools mainly in Funchal and Caniço de Baixo. A full dive with equipment hire will cost around €40-50. The limestone sea caves along the Algarve coast between Albufeira and Sagres are popular with scuba divers.

WATERPARKS

These parks are located mainly around Lisbon and in the Algarve (☝see ALGARVE). Further information can be obtained from tourist offices.

BEACHES

The symbol ⚐ on Michelin map 733 and on the Places to Stay map in this guide highlights the best beaches.

Watersport activities at Lagoa de Albufeira, Sesimbra near Lisbon

© Jon Arnold Images/hemis.fr

Diving in Madeira

© P.Banfi/WaterFrame/Getty Images

The Portuguese coastline is a series of beaches from north to south. The best known are the great sandy stretches of the **Algarve**, where both the climate and sea temperature (17°C in winter, 23°C in summer) are pleasant. The **Costa Dourada** between Cabo São Vicente and Setúbal is a more rugged coastline with tiny curves of sand at the foot of imposing cliffs and a colder and rougher sea (15°C in winter and 19°C in summer).

The **Costa de Lisboa** from Setúbal to Cabo da Roca includes the pleasant, well-sheltered beaches of the Serra de Arrábida, the great expanse of dunes of the Costa da Caparica south of the Tagus and the very crowded beaches of Cascais and Estoril, which are popular with Lisbonites.

The **Costa de Prata**, extending from Cabo da Roca to Aveiro, has flat sandy beaches. North of Nazaré the fishermen's boats can be seen high on the beaches. The **Costa Verde** from the Douro northwards to the Spanish border has fine sandy beaches backed inland with a green countryside. Many of Portugal's beaches are supervised, and it is important to heed the flags: red – it is forbidden to enter the sea even to paddle; yellow – no swimming; green – it is safe to paddle and swim; blue and white chequered – beach temporarily unsupervised.

Beware of strong currents, especially on the west coast where there are strong undercurrents.

FISHING

Freshwater Angling

This type of fishing is done mostly in the north for trout, salmon, barbel and shad (Rio Minho and the Douro) and in the numerous mountains of the Serra de Estrela (carp, barbel and trout). A fishing permit can be obtained from the Federação Portuguesa da Pesca Desportiva, Rua Eça de Queirós, n° 3 1°, 1050-095 Lisboa, ✆ 213 140 177, or 213 56 31 47; www.fppd.pt. Tourist Information Centres have the season's opening dates.

Sea Angling

In the north the catch usually includes skate, cod, dogfish and sea perch, while in the south Mediterranean species such as shark, tuna and swordfish are more common.

GOLF

The best time for golf is September to November, then March to June, although Portugal's mild climate enables golfers to play year-round. The country has a wide selection of courses to choose from, most of which are of championship standard. Green fees vary from about €50 to €200 and, on the Algarve at least, pre-booking is advised. Details of golf packages can be found on: www.portugalvirtual.pt and www.portugalgolf.pt.

Golf courses with the number of holes and their telephone numbers are listed in the *Michelin Guide Spain and Portugal* under the nearest town and are indicated on the Michelin Map 733 by the ⛳ symbol.

OTHER SPORTS

Spas

The country's numerous spas date from the 19C, and cater to people with a wide variety of ailments. The ⚕ symbol on the Places to Stay map in this guide and Michelin map 733 indicates some of the more important ones. For further information, contact Associação das Termas de Portugal, Avenida Miguel Bombarda, 110-2°, Dt°, 1050-167 Lisboa, ✆217 971 338; www.termasdeportugal.pt.

Bird Watching

Bird watching is very popular in Portugal, especially in the south of the country where many migratory birds can be observed at certain times of the year. Two comprehensive websites listing when and where various species are likely to be encountered are: www.birdinginportugal.com and www.visitportugalbirdwatching.com Madeira offers good conditions to birdwatchers, especially for vagrant bird species. Though there are only 47 breeding species to the islands, about half of them are endemic or subspecies (www.madeirabirds.com). The Azores archipelago has over 30 nesting bird species, and due to the islands' central position in the Atlantic you may also see a large number of migratory birds passing from America and Eurasia.

ACTIVITIES FOR KIDS 👫

In this guide, **sights of particular interest to children are indicated with a 👫 symbol. Some attractions may offer discount fees for children.**

🎧 *For specific activities in LISBON, see the chapter in Discovering Portugal.* The great attraction of Portugal for families is its relative compactness, and the range of activities and sights on offer. Hop on, hop off tours help with tired legs, if necessary, while the miniature tourist trains provide endless fascination for young minds.

CATERING TO CHILDREN

As family life is a very important factor in Portugal, you will find **hotels and restaurants** more than happy to cater for their younger visitors. Although they do not offer "children's menus" (except perhaps in some parts of the Algarve where foreign tourists outnumber the local population), you can always ask for a *"meia dose"* (half portion) which they will always be happy to provide. There are no restrictions about taking children into restaurants or bars, though you might want to use your own judgement in the case of the latter. Apart from the Algarve, most restaurants do not open much before 7.30pm for dinner.

For hotels and guesthouses, too, it is easy to get an extra bed or cot (*um berço*) put in a room at no extra cost – or perhaps a minimal charge. In other places discounts of 50 percent are not uncommon for children.

CHILDREN AND THE SUN

Sunshine in Portugal, especially in summer, is intense, and, especially between the hours of 11am and 3pm, you are advised to ensure that your child wears a hat, is covered sufficiently without being stifled, and has high factor suncream applied as appropriate.

ENTERTAINMENT

Portugal is wonderful for entertaining children. Places which may be fun for kids, are described in the relevant sights in the *Discovering Portugal* section, and you'll find many activities for children throughout this guide.

HIGHLIGHTS BY REGION

Lisbon Region

Visit the Oceanarium, Understanding Science Pavilion and Vasco da Gama tower at Nations Park; ride on a World War II tram; visit the Puppet Museum and Planetarium; swim at Parque Florestal de Monsanto; splash in the fountains at Jardin da Agua; visit the Toy Museum in Sintra and the Estoril beaches...take a ride on a horse-drawn carriage.

Alentejo

Explore the Great Discoveries at Vasco da Gama Palace in Évora; learn about the Romans at the Templo Romano; and for older children, visit the grisly Chapel of the Bones.

Centro

Visit Portugal dos Pequenitos, Coimbra; picnic in Buçaco Forest; take a cruise on Aveiro's canals; discover rock art at Vale do Coa Natural Park; swim in the lakes of the Serra de Estrela Natural Park; play on the São Marinho beach of Porto, Nazare.

Porto and The North

Take a boat trip along the River Douro; spot otters and badgers in the Peneda-Geres National Park; take the funicular to the top of Escadaria dos Cinto Sentidos in Braga; enjoy water-sports at the Cabedelo beach in Viana do Castelo.

Algarve

The Algarve is a great child-pleasing destination, arguably the best in Portugal, with endless beaches, zoos, water parks, horse-riding and boat trips. Explore sea caves at Ponta da Piedad near Lagos; have fun at the Krazy World and swim with dolphins at Zoomarine, both near Albufeira; spot herons on a Ria Formosa boat trip; or learn to surf at Praia do Amado near Carrapateira.

SHOPPING

HANDICRAFTS

Traditional Portuguese crafts will catch your eye, and the prices are attractive, too. From the north to the south, variety is found in the choice of colours and natural materials. In Viana do Castelo, look for hand-embroidered linen and cotton (tablecloths and napkins, shirts, aprons, etc) and the classic filigree jewellery in both silver and gold. Embroidered bedspreads are a good buy in Castelo Branco, as are the hand-made rugs from Arrailos, while many places offer ceramics (Caldas da Rainha, Coimbra etc) and pottery (Barcelos, Alentejo, Algarve). Woodworkers make decorative objects, kitchen utensils and toys, tinsmiths are famous for *almutelias*, the traditional recipients for olive oil, while glass-makers still continue their activity in Marinha Grande. *Azulejos* tiles are found everywhere, as are objects and kitchenware made of copper (including the typical *cataplana* from the Algarve).

FASHION

The big cities have many shops, particularly Lisbon where you will find everything from high-class brand-name fashion to "junk" in the flea-market. The international brand names for fashion (like Luis Vuitton, Armani, Trussardi, Burberry, Hugo Boss, Longchamp and Escada) are spread along Avenida da Liberdade in the centre of Lisbon, and also in discreet intimate malls behind the renovated façades of Chiado. Chiado also has several modern Portuguese designers selling their creations, so if you want something unique, this could be the place to come.

All big cities have shopping malls; in Lisbon the largest are Colombo, Galerias Monumental, Saldanha, Vasco da Gama, Amoreiras and El Corte Inglés. They are all open until 10pm or even 11pm, though not always on Sundays. Most of the smaller shops close for lunch from about 12.30pm to around 2.30pm or even later, but then stay open until around 8pm. Most smaller shops are closed on Sundays and in the less-visited areas of Portugal, on Saturday afternoons as well.

MARKETS

On Tuesdays and Saturdays the place to be is the Feira da Ladra (translates as Thieves' Market) on Campo de Santa Clara in Alfama, where you'll find all sorts of things you never realised you needed. Clothes, "antiques", pirated CDs and DVDs, jewellery of all descriptions, books, linens and much more. It opens at 8am so the earlier you get there the better. Obviously there will be some items that are not exactly genuine, but it's up to you what you buy. It pays to haggle. Be aware of the presence of pickpockets in the markets. Never have money waving around in your hand – it's too tempting for some people!

Lisbon and a few other towns also have street-vendors who sell a range of items, some genuine, some not. In Lisbon, especially in Bairro Alto at night, you will notice drugs being sold quite openly.

Most of the larger towns have weekly markets, some quite spectacular. Those in Évora, Loulé and Lemago are especially good. In the countryside they are more agricultural with local foods as the main attraction. If you want to have a picnic or if you are staying in self-catering accommodation, the markets will be the best place to buy food and wine. If you are in Lisbon, you should make a point of visiting the main market (opposite the Cais deo Sodré station near the Tagus); in Funchal visit the fish and flower market and in Setúbal the fruit and vegetable market.

Remember that when you return home, there are Customs regulations concerning how much you can bring back – and some foodstuffs are prohibited.

BOOKS
CONTEMPORARY PORTUGAL

Lisbon: Recipes from the heart of Portugal
by Rebecca Seals (Hardy Grant Books 2017)

Buying Property in Portugal
by Gabrielle Collison (Gabrielle Lea Publishing 2015)

Walking in Portugal by Bethan Davies/ Benjamin Cole (Pila Pala Press 2000)

Madeira's Natural History in a Nutshell by Paul Sziemer (Francisco Ribeiro & Filhos 2000)

Moving to Portugal by Louise and Ben Taylor (CreateSpace Independent Publishing Platform, 2012)

My Portugal: by chef Georges Mendes (Stewart, Tabori & Chang, 2014)

Walking in the Algarve by Julie Statham (Cicerone Press 2014)

Walking in Madeira by Paddy Dillon (Cicerone Press 2016)

HISTORY

Portuguese Seaborne Empire
by CR Boxer (Carcanet Press 1991)

Christopher Columbus and the Portuguese, 1476–1498 by Rebecca Catz (Greenwood Press 1993)

Wellington's Peninsular Victories
by Michael Glover (The Windrush Press 1996)

Portugal 1715–1808 by David Francis (Tamesis Books 1976)

The Pope's Elephant by Silvio A Bedini (Carcanet Press 1997)

A Concise History of Portugal
by David Birmingham (Cambridge University Press 1993)

Portugal: A Companion History by Jose Hermano Saraiva (author), Ian Robertson (editor), Ursula Fonss (translator) (Carcanet Press 1997)

In Search of Modern Portugal, the Revolution and its Consequences by Lawrence S Graham, Douglas L. Wheeler (University of Wisconsin Press 1983)

The Making of Portuguese Democracy by Kenneth Maxwell (CUP 1997)

The Journal of a Voyage to Lisbon by
    Henry Fielding, T Keymer (ed)
    (Penguin Books 1989)
They Went to Portugal Too by Rose
    Macaulay (Carcanet Press 1990)
*Journey to Portugal: In Pursuit of
    Portugal's History and Culture*
    by Jose Saramago (Harvest
    Books 2002)
Portugal: A Traveller's History
    by Harold Livermore (Boydell
    Press 2004)
*A History of Portugal and the
    Portuguese Empire from Beginnings
    to 1807* by A R Disney (Cambridge
    University Press 2009)
The Portuguese: A modern history by
    Barry Hatton (Signal Books 2011)
*Conquerors: How Portugal seized the
    Indian Ocean and forged the First
    Global Empire* by Roger Crowley (Faber
    and Faber, 2015)
*Unorthodox Kin: Portuguese Marranos
    and the Global Search for Belonging*
    by Naomi Leite (University of
    California Press, 2017)

ART AND ARCHITECTURE

The Age of the Baroque in Portugal
    by Jay A Levenson (ed) (National
    Gallery of Art 1993)
The Fires of Excellence by Miles Danby,
    Matthew Weinreb (Garnet
    Publishing 1996)
Portuguese Gardens by Helder Carita,
    Homem Cardoso (Antique
    Collectors' Club 1991)
Gardens of Spain and Portugal by
    Barbara Segall (Mitchell
    Beazley 1999)
Landscapes of the Azores by Andreas
    Stieglitz (Sunflower Books 1992)

PROSE AND POETRY

The Lusiads
    by Luiz de Camões, WC Atkinson
    (translator) (Penguin Books 1952)
Selected Poems
    by Fernando Pessoa, J Griffin
    (translator) (Penguin Books 1996)
Always Astonished: Selected Prose
    by Fernando Pessoa, E Honig
    (translator) (City Lights Books
    1988)
Travels in My Homeland by Almeida
    Garrett (Peter Owen 1986)

FILMS

Portugal produces many films, almost
always in Portuguese, sometimes with
subtitles.

*Letters From Fontainhas: A Trilogy
(1997), (2000), (2006)* directed by
    Pedro Costa.
    Set in the slums of Lisbon's
    Fontainhas district, "Ossos" tells
    the story of a suicidal teenage girl
    who makes the mistake of trusting
    the care of her newborn child to its
    father. In "Vanda's Room", a drug-
    addicted woman's self-destructive
    behaviors is representative of the
    impoverished community around
    her. "Colossal Youth" focuses on
    the life of an elderly man who
    relates to his neighbours as he
    might his own children.
Testamento (1997) directed by
    Francisco Manzo.
    The director's first film is based
    on a novel by author Germano
    Almeida which examines life and
    the choices one makes. Shot in the
    Cape Verdean city of Mindelo off

Portuguese Film Festivals

Portugal hosts a number of cinema
and film festivals throughout the
year, such as:

Sept: **Portugal International
Film Festival** (Porto) www.
portugalfilmfestival.com. Feb/
Mar: **Fantasporto** (Porto); www.
fantasporto.com Apr: **Caminhos
do Cinema Português** (Coimbra);
www.caminhos.info Jun: **Festróia
Festival Internacional de
Cinema de Tróia** (Setúbal); www.
festroia.pt
Sept: **Lisbon Gay & Lesbian Film
Festival** (Lisbon); queerlisboa.pt

the coast of West Africa, the film focuses on the death of a wealthy businessman whose secrets which unfold amaze everyone.

Abraham's Valley (1993) directed by Manoel de Oliveira.
A beautiful woman in a loveless marriage with a wealthy doctor has affairs with others but still cannot find spiritual fulfillment.

Dead Man's Memories (2003) directed by Markus Heltschel.
This whodunit focuses on a music student from Vienna who travels around Lisbon and the murder of an archeologist .

O Fantasma (2000) directed by Joao Pedro Rodrigues
Refuse collector Sergio's surfacing desires for a male motorcycle owner on Lisbon's streets are rebuffed and unleash his darkest impulses.

The Convent (1995) directed by Manoel de Oliveira. An American professor arrives with his wife, Helene, at a Portuguese convent where he expects to find the documents needed to prove his theory that Shakespeare was born in Spain not in England.

The Ornithologist (2016) directed by João Pedro Rodrigues. Swept away by rapids while looking for black storks, ornithologist Fernando, must find his way out of the forest and through all manner of bizarre, sometimes creepy encounters.

Calendar of Events

PORTUGAL

SPRING

Ovar — Carnival: procession of floats.

Torres Vedras — Carnival: procession of floats. www.cm-tvedras.pt.

Loulé — Carnival and Almond Gatherers' Fair. www.portobayevents.com.

Barcelos — Festival of Crosses, Pottery Fair and folk dancing.

Sesimbra — Festival in honour of Our Lord Jesus of the Wounds: fishermen's festival dating from the 16C. Procession early May.

Vila Franca do Lima — Rose Festival: Mordomias procession in which the mistress of the house bears on her head a tray of flowers arranged to represent one of the many provincial coats of arms.

Fátima — First great pilgrimage. Candlelight procession at 9.30pm on the 12th and International Mass on the 13th. These take place every evening on the 12th and 13th of every month until October.

Leiria — Fair and agricultural machinery exhibition with town festival on 22 May (processions, celebrations etc).

Matosinhos — Pilgrimage in honour of the Senhor of Matosinhos: folk dancing.

SUMMER

Ponte de Lima (June-October) — International Garden Festival, dedicated to a different topic every year. www.festivaldejardins. cm-pontedelima.pt.

Santarém — National Agricultural Show: folklore.

Lisbon — Popular saints' festival.

Vila Real — St Anthony's Festival: procession, fireworks. St Anthony's Festival from 6–17 June.

Braga — St John's Midsummer Festival.

Largo de São Carlos - Lisboa (3 weeks in July) — The "Festival ao Largo" (Festival in the square) brings art into the street, offering free performances including classical music, ballet and theatre. www.festivalaolargo.pt.

Vila do Conde — Lacemakers' procession.

Coimbra (2 weeks in July, in even-numbered years) — Festivities of the Holy Queen. Performances, exhibitions, gastronomy, craft fairs, sporting competitions and entertainment. www.visitcentro.com.

Estoril — International Handicrafts Fair: Portugal's oldest handicraft fair. www.visitcascais.com.

Cabedelo - Vila Nova de Gaia (mid-July) — Marés Vivas Festival. Apart from the music, which is being performed at a beautiful natural spot very close to the beaches, the Marés Vivas Festival is also concerned with nature and the environment. http://maresvivas.meo.pt.

Vila Franca de Xira — Festival of the Red Waistcoats.

Setúbal — St James' Fair: bullfights and folk groups.

AgitÁgueda (3 weeks in July)— The Agitágueda Festival brings a lot of colour and animation to this city.

Porto Covo and Sines (July) — World Music Festival. www.fmm.com.pt.

Aveiro — The Ria Festival with a competition for the best decorated prow

Guimarães — St Walter's Festival: fair, decorated streets, giants procession.

Quinta das Lágrimas - Coimbra (mid-end July)— An eclectic festival offering public exposure to all kinds of artistic expression. www.festivaldasartes.com.

SUMMER: Popular saints' festival, Lisbon

© Alain Evrard/Imagestate/Tips Images

Miranda do Douro — St Barbara's Festival: dance of the Pauliteiros.

Óbidos (July–August) — Medieval market, where everything is sold from medieval costumes to traditional home-made medical remedies. http://mercadomedievalobidos.pt.

Santa Maria da Feira (July–August) — Every year in the month of August, Santa Maria da Feira once again becomes a medieval town. www.viagemmedieval.com.

Barragem de Póvoa e Meadas - Castelo de Vide (August) — Andanças is an International Traditional Dance and Music Festival, held annually. www.andancas.net.

Days of the Week

While Monday in Portuguese is the second day of the week (segunda-feira), Tuesday the third (terça-feira), Wednesday the fourth (quarta-feira), Thursday the fifth (quinta-feira) and Friday the sixth (sexta-feira), Sunday, the first day of the week, remains that of the Lord (domingo) and Saturday, the seventh, the sabbath (sábado).

This denomination is believed to have originated in the 6C when São Martinho, Bishop of Braga, took the Christians to task for using the traditional calendar dating from the time of the Chaldeans and thereby dedicating each day to a pagan divinity: the Sun, the Moon, Mars, Mercury, Jupiter, Venus and Saturn.

Zambujeira do Mar (August) — The Sudoeste (Southwest) Festival is the biggest summer festival of music in Portugal. http://sudoeste.meo.pt.

Idanha-a-Nova (August) — **Boom Festival**: A biennial festival, held during full moon in August, and dedicated to independent and artistic culture. www.boomfestival.org.

Silves (August) — **Medieval Fair**: Over a nine-day period, Silves (capital of the Algarve during the Arab occupation) returns to its golden age in a historical recreation of the Christian Reconquest era.

AUTUMN

Palmela — Grape Harvest Festival: benediction of the grapes, running of the bulls through the streets, fireworks.

Mirando do Douro — Pilgrimage in honour of Our Lady of Nazo at Póva *(11km/7mi north)*: a fair precedes the pilgrimage and a festival ends the celebrations.

Viseu (August into September) — Feira de São Mateus; this fair dates to medieval times and now includes lmusic, folklore, handicraft, gastronomy and entertainment. www.visitcentro.com.

Vila Franca de Xira— Fair of handicrafts, running of the bulls through the streets, touradas.

Santarém (October-November) — National Gastronomy Fair. www.festivalnacionalde gastronomia.pt.

Castro Verde — October Fair which goes back to the 17C: agricultural show and handicrafts.

Golegã (November) — National Horse Fair and the Feast of St Martin: benediction of the horses, a tradition dating back to the 17C. One of Portugal's most traditional fairs. http://fnc.cm-golega.pt.

Lisbon and Estoril (November) — Film Festival celebrates cinema as an artistic creation. www.leffest.com.

WINTER

Porto (February-March) — International Film Festival **Fantasporto** celebrates the best in cinema, plus top sci-fi, fantasy, films and experimental projects. www.fantasporto.com.

MADEIRA

SPRING

Funchal (February) — Madeira Carnival: street party.

Funchal (April/May) — Madeira Flower Festival, and Wall of Hope Ceremony. www.visitmadeira.pt.

Funchal (April) — Literary Festival. www.festivalliterariodamadeira.pt.

Funchal (April) — Film Festival, an international independent film festival inspired by nature. www.madeirafilmfestival.com.

Ponto do Sol — Aqui Acolá Festival of music, sculpture, theatre, cinema, photography and ethnography. www.festivalaquiacola.com.

Funchal (May) — Classic Car Revival Exhibition, featuring old and vintage vehicles exhisting in Madeira. www.visitfunchal.pt

Santana (May) — Lemon Festival, paying homage to the main local product.

Jardim da Serra — Cherry Festival: a wide range of sports and leisure activities culminating in a parade in a tribute to the harvesting of cherries.

SUMMER

Funchal (June) — Madeira Atlantic Festival, with emphasis on pyromusical shows; the Atlantic Roots Festival and the Regional Arts Week. www.visitmadeira.pt.

Funchal — Fica na Cidade (Stay in Town): musical and stand-up comedy performances promoting food and local traditions.

APRIL/MAY: Madeira Flower Festival

© Francisco Correia/Associação de Promoção da Madeira

Funchal — Sé Festivities: traditional Madeiran celebrations.
Santana — 24-hours Dancing and Folklore Festival.
Monte — The Monte Festival.
Funchal and various locations (July) — Classic Car Rally.
Funchal and various locations (August) — Madeira Wine Rally, for those curious or passionate about motorsports.
Funchal (end of July) — Rally Vinho da Madeira, the European Rally Championship. www.ralivm.com.

AUTUMN

Funchal, and **Estreito de Câmara de Lobos** (end August into September) — **Madeira Wine Fest**...a perfect excuse to visit Madeira. www.visitmadeira.pt.
Porto Santo (September) —
Columbus Festival: A festival to remind people of Columbus' time in the Madeira Archipelago. www.visitmadeira.pt.

WINTER

Funchal (December-early January) — New Year in Madeira: see Funchal illuminated by a thousand lights. www.visitmadeira.pt

THE AZORES

SUMMER

Porto Formoso (August) — Azors Burning Summer: An environment-themed international music festival. www.azoresburningsummer.com
Santa Maria (August) — Festival Maré de Agosto: International Festival of Music. www.maredeagosto.com.
São Miguel (July) — **Festival Walk&Talk Azores:** public art, featuring established contemporary art names and new talents. www.walktalkazores.org.
São Miguel (September) — **SATA Airlines Azores Islands Pro** surfing exhibitions. www.azoresislandspro.com.

AUTUMN

Angra do Heroísmo - Terceira (October) — **AngraJazz:** one of the leading jazz festivals in Portugal, featuring well-known North American and European jazz musicians. www.angrajazz.com.
São Miguel (late October) — **Wine in Azores:** a promotional fair of Portuguese wines. www.wineinazores.com.

Know Before You Go

USEFUL WEBSITES

www.visitportugal.com – The official Portugese tourism website with a wealth of well-presented information on everything from themed itineraries to upcoming events to where to stay and eat.

www.portugal-live.net – A good website for those looking for hotels in particular, plus lots of information on tourist sights.

www.portugal.com – A commercial site for booking restaurants and hotels; good suggestions for holiday programmes.

www.madeira-web.com – A comprehensive tourism destination guide.

www.visitmadeira.pt – The official website for Madeira tourism.

www.madeira-tourist.com – Another comprehensive website with good links to help you find accommodation, restaurants, etc.

www.visitazores.com – Official Tourism Website of the Azores

www.azores.com – Comprehensive information about the Azores, getting there and around.

www.azoreschoice.com – Very efficient UK-based company able to book everything you are likely to need; island specialists since 1998.

TOURIST OFFICES
LOCAL TOURIST OFFICES
Tourist Information Centres
All Portuguese towns have a Tourist Information centre, known as Posto or Comissão de Turismo or simply Turismo, marked on Michelin town maps with an 🄸.

INTERNATIONAL VISITORS
FOREIGN EMBASSIES AND CONSULATES IN PORTUGAL

British Embassy and Consulate
- Rua São Bernardo, 33, 1249-082, Lisbon ☎213 924 000.

British Consulates:
- Av da Boavista, 3072 4100-120 Oporto. ☎226 184 789.
- Rua Domingos Rebelo, 43A, 9500-234 Ponta Delgada, S. Miguel, Azores. ☎296 628 175.
- Avenida de Zarco 2, CP 417 9000-956 Funchal, Madeira, ☎291 212 860-867.

American Embassy
Avenida das Forças Armadas, 133C, 1600-081 Lisbon.
☎217 273 300.

Canadian Embassy and Consulate
Avenida da Liberdaade 198-200, 3rd Floor, 1269-121 Lisbon.
☎213 164 600.

Embassy of Ireland
Avenida da Liberdade 200, 4th floor, 1250-147 Lisbon.
☎213 308 200.

ENTRY REQUIREMENTS
Visitors must have a passport valid for their entire trip. British, Irish and US passport holders need no visa to stay for up to 90 days. For visits of less than 90 days, a passport valid for at least three months after the end of their stay is necessary for visitors from Australia, Canada, the USA and a number of other countries.
Others, and those planning to stay longer than 90 days, should enquire at a Portuguese consulate.
Under the terms of the Convention Implementing the Schengen

© Assiciação de Promoção da Madeira

Madeira Airport

Agreement, flights between Schengen states are considered to be internal flights and passengers do not need to obtain another visa.

CUSTOMS REGULATIONS

UK citizens can apply for a Customs guide for travellers: http://customs.hmrc.gov.uk.

There are no limits on the amount of duty and/or tax paid alcohol and tobacco that you can bring back into the UK as long as they are for your own use or gifts and are transported by you.

If you are bringing in alcohol or tobacco goods and UK Customs have reason to suspect they may be for a commercial purpose, an officer may ask you questions and make checks. Similar restrictions apply to travellers to Portugal arriving from EU countries.

HEALTH

If you require medical assistance contact the nearest doctor's office or emergency room. Except in rural areas, medical centers generally have English-speaking staff.

Hospital emergency services should be used only in serious situations (serious injury, poisoning, burns, infarction, thromboses, breathing difficulties, etc.).

British citizens should apply for the **European Health Insurance Card**, either online (www.ehic.org.uk) or at a post office, to obtain free or low-cost treatment in the EU. *Following the exist of the UK from the EU, it is not clear at the time of writing how these arrangements will be affected, if at all.* The card can be obtained from the NHS, Newcastle-upon-Tyne, either by post (forms available at Post Offices), by phone ℘0845 606 2030, or at www.ehic.org.uk.

Medical insurance is advisable. Since medical insurance is not always valid outside the US, American travellers are advised to take out supplementary medical insurance with specific overseas coverage.

Pharmacies are open weekdays 9am to 1pm and 3pm to 7pm, Saturdays 9am to 1pm. All prescription drugs taken into Portugal, Madeira or the Azores should be clearly labelled; it is recommended to carry a copy of prescriptions. All visitors should also be insured for uncovered medical expenses, lost luggage, theft, etc.

ACCESSIBILITY ♿

Many of the sights and places listed in this guide are accessible to visitors with special needs. Sights marked with the ♿symbol have wheelchair access, but it is advisable to telephone prior to your visit to re-check. Portugal's main airports and train stations have ramps and lifts. The railway operator, CP-Comboios de Portugal, offers a service called SIM, short for Integrated Mobility Service, that can be contacted by calling +351 707 208 746, open 24 hours a day. The service allows Special Needs Customers to obtain information (in Portuguese) about accessibility on board trains and at stations as well as assistance during their journey and when boarding and alighting. Public transport vehicles usually have reserved spaces for people with special needs although not all may be accessible to wheelchair users. Newer trams in Lisbon are becoming more wheelchair friendly, but the old yellow type have no facilities. Access is improving, though, as Portugal signed up for the European City and People with Disabilities initiative. **Holiday Care** (www.holidaycare.org.uk) has further information.

Taxis adapted for use by passengers with reduced mobility operate in a number of Portuguese cities, including Lisbon, Faro and Oporto, and on Madeira to a lesser extent.

Accessible beaches: almost 200 maritime and river beaches are accessible for persons with restricted mobility. These beaches are identified with a white flag, including the respective symbol, and have reserved parking areas, pedestrian access, beach walkways and adapted toilet facilities.

Getting There and Getting Around

BY PLANE

Various airlines operate services to the international airports in Portugal (Lisbon, Porto, Faro and Funchal). British Airways and TAP Air Portugal operate daily flights from London to Lisbon, Porto and Faro. There are also budget flights between the UK and Portugal, including services by Monarch, easyJet, Jet2.com and Ryanair. SATA flies direct from the UK to the Azores, others operate via Lisbon. There are several direct flights between London or Manchester and Funchal (Madeira).

- **TAP Portugal**
  www.flytap.com
- **British Airways**
  ☎ 808 200 125
  www.britishairways.com

- ◆ **easyJet**
  www.easyjet.com
- ◆ **Jet2.com**
  www.jet2.com
- ◆ **Ryanair**
  www.ryanair.com

INTERNAL FLIGHTS

TAP Air Portugal operates flights from Lisbon and Porto to Madeira (Funchal) and from Lisbon to the Azores (Ponta Delgado on São Miguel). Local airlines operate inter-island flights in the Azores. Internal flights are the most practical way of travelling from the north to south.

Major airports – Lisbon, Porto, Faro, Funchal and Porto Santo (on Madeira); Ponta Delgada, Santa Maria and Terceira (in the Azores).

- ◆ **TAP Air Portugal**
  Praça do Marquês do Pombal, 3A, Lisboa. ☎ 707 205 700
  www.flytap.com.

- **Azores Airlines**
  ✆ 707 227 282
  www.azoresairlines.pt/en

BY SHIP

There are no direct ferry services between Britain and Portugal. However, there are car-ferry services between Plymouth and Portsmouth and Santander (Spain) and from Portsmouth to Bilbao (Spain) two to three times a week; journey time: 24hr (www.brittany-ferries.co.uk). Distances from Santander are 827km/517mi to Lisbon, 640km/400mi to Porto and 1 016km/635mi to Faro.

© DANITA DELIMONT STOCK/age fotostock

Rossio train station, Lisbon

Across the Channel then on through France and Spain

Although a long journey by road, it is possible to use the Channel Tunnel or cross-Channel services and then drive. The distance to Lisbon by road when you have landed from the car ferry or taken the Channel Tunnel is about 1 985km/1 240mi. The most direct route is via Le Mans, Tours, Bordeaux, then San Sebastián, Burgos, Salamanca and Coimbra to Lisbon.

BY TRAIN

It is possible to travel to Portugal from the UK by train (through France and Spain), although it is a long trip and possibly more expensive than flying, albeit a most pleasant way to travel. You would have to travel from London to Paris to Barcelona, then on to Madrid, and from there you'd pick up an overnight train to Lisbon. The total journey would take 13 hours 45 from London to Madrid and then the following evening, the overnight train from Madrid to Lisbon is a further 10 hours 30 minutes.

PORTUGUESE RAILWAYS

Caminhos de Ferro Portugueses (CP) has a rail network linking major cities and an inter-city service. The *rápidos* or express trains are fast. The *directos* or inter-city trains are slower, make more stops and have both first- and second-class compartments.

There is a range of discounts available covering multiple journeys, advance purchase, discounts for children and a 7-day weekly pass offering unlimited travel on urban trains.

For further information, ✆ 707 210 220; www.cp.pt (including online chat).

BY COACH/BUS

Fairly regular coach services to Portugal are operated from London (Victoria Coach Station) by **Eurolines**, a consortium of coach operators in conjunction with National Express. To the main destinations they operate year-round, but other cities are served only on a seasonal basis. The journey to Lisbon (Sete Reos) takes a couple of days (www.eurolines.co.uk). Another coach line operating from London to Lisbon is **Flixbus**. www.flixbus.com. **Intercentro** also operates international routes to and from Portugal (London only in the UK). ✆ 707 200 512; www.internorte.pt.

GETTING AROUND BY COACH

Portugal's national coach network (Rede Nacional de Expressos) is extensive and covers all parts of the country. For information, contact: Terminal Rodoviário de Sete Rios, Praça Marechal Humberto Delgado, Estrada das Laranjeiras, 1500-423 Lisbon. ✆ 707 22 33 44; www.rede-expressos.pt.

BY CAR
DOCUMENTS

Nationals of EU countries driving their own vehicles require:

- personal ID
- valid driving licence
- insurance certificate
- the registration papers and log-book, or equivalent, and
- a national identification plate of the approved size

Third party insurance is compulsory in Portugal. Special breakdown and get-you-home packages are a good idea. If the driver of the vehicle is not accompanied by the owner, he or she should have written permission from the owner to drive in Portugal.

DRIVING IN PORTUGAL

The minimum driving age is 18. Traffic drives on the right. Unless otherwise indicated, vehicles coming from the right have priority in squares and at intersections. At junctions with roundabouts, vehicles already on the roundabout have right of way.
It is compulsory for the front-seat passengers to wear seat belts.
The drink-driving rules in Portugal are very strict: one small beer can put you over the limit. Be very careful.
The rules of the road are the same in Portugal as in other European countries, and Portugal uses the international road sign system.
Portuguese road network:
Portugal has an excellent road network composed of Motorways, Main Trunk Routes, Complementary Trunk Routes, Main (National) Roads and Secondary (Municipal) Roads.
There are two types of motorways, of which there are more than 500km/370mi:

- **traditional motorways** with toll booths, where payment is made either in cash or by bank card. These motorways also have a Via Verde (green channel), intended for use solely by those with an electronic device identifying their vehicle, which they have previously acquired at one of the respective sales outlets (www.viaverde.pt).
- **motorways** that have an exclusively electronic toll system, where tolls are collected by exclusively electronic means. As vehicles pass through the toll gates, they are picked up by electronic detectors placed at the entry to the channels, which are identified with the words "Electronic toll only".

For information about the roads covered by this system and the respective forms of payment, consult www.portugaltolls.com. Tolls are also payable on many bridges.
Madeira has a couple of high-speed motorway-like roads (*via rapida*), on which it is obligatory to have headlights on at all times.
Maximum speed limits are:
120kph/75mph on motorways (*auto-estrada*); **90kph/56mph** on dual carriageways (*estrada com faixas de rodagem separades);*
90kph/56mph on other roads;
50kph/31mph in built-up areas.

BREAKDOWN SERVICE

The Portuguese Automobile Club (Automóvel Club de Portugal), Rua Rosa Araújo 24-26, 1250-195 Lisbon, ☎808 222 222, offers members of equivalent international organisations medical, legal and breakdown assistance. www.acp.pt. But UK residents would find it just as convenient to arrange European Breakdown Cover through there own motoring organisation.

PETROL/GASOLINE

Diesel and unleaded petrol (*gasolina sem chumbo*) are generally available throughout the country. Credit cards are accepted in most petrol stations, but visitors are strongly advised to have other means of payment with them. Petrol stations are generally open from 7am–midnight, although some open 24hr a day, and an increasing number have pay-at-the-pump facilities.

CAR RENTAL

The major car rental firms have offices in all large towns. Cars may be hired from airports, main stations and large hotels. The minimum age to qualify for car rental is 18 though insurance is higher for under-25s. When renting a car, be very careful where you park and don't trust anyone who tries to direct you to "private parking". Illegally parked cars are often towed and it will cost at least €120 to get it back, plus the parking fine.

Car hire and holders of UK driving licences

In 2015, changes to the UK Driving License came into force which mean that details of fines, penalty points and restrictions are now only held electronically.

This change will affect you if you turn up at Portuguese airport, for example, to pick up a hire car, because you are going to have to make arrangements for the hire company to be able to access your online driving record by means of a DVLA-issued pass code, should they wish to.

The pass code number, however, can be used only once; so if this isn't set up before you get to the hire company desk you may face delays. Moreover, the code is valid for 21 days only and then lapses, so you will need internet access if trying to hire a car while already in Portugal.

The new system allows you to download a summary of your licence record, which can be printed or shared. To log into the system you will need to know your National Insurance number and postcode, so take them with you in case you need to log in to the DVLA website while abroad. To access your online driver record you need the last eight digits of your driving licence, plus the special pass code. You can view your licence at www.gov.uk/view-driving-licence. You will also be able to call the DVLA and give permission for your driving record to be checked verbally.

ROUTE PLANNING

www.travelguide.michelin.com
Available on the Internet, this service offers various routes to drive, distances between towns and cities, as well as details of restaurants, hotels and bars. It also offers detailed information on must-see towns, regions and tourist sights such as stunning Évora and romantic Sintra, suggests Michelin tourist routes such as Secret Lisbon, and includes useful information to tourists and drivers.

See Companion publications, p 417.

Where to Stay and Eat

WHERE TO STAY

The extent of accommodation throughout Portugal, Madeira and the Azores is both diverse and considerable, many of which are able to offer meals and a range of services. **Many cities have introduceds a tourist tax. In Algarve, this tax is currently €1.5/night, and in Lisbon and Porto it is €2, applicable for a maximum of seven nights for all tourists older than 12.**

HOTELS

The number of 'conventional' hotels is considerable, classified from 1-star to 5-star depending on location and the quality of facilities.

APARTHOTELS

These hotel apartments are classified from 1-star to 5-star, and make an ideal choice for tourists who want greater independence, but still wishing to enjoy all the services of a hotel.

POUSADAS

Quite different from a regular hotel, the state-owned *pousadas* are marked by ⌂ on the Places to Stay map in this

Pousada do Palácio de Estói, Algarve

guide and on the Michelin map 733. Special mention should be made of around 30 Portuguese *pousadas*, most of which are extremely comfortable, restored historic monuments (castles, palaces and monasteries) in beautiful sites or excursion centres.

The *pousadas* are very popular and usually full, so it is always wise to book in advance.

For further information, check the website: www.pousadas.pt/en.

Michelin Guide

The Michelin Guide Spain and Portugal is revised annually and is an indispensable complement to this guide, with information on hotels and restaurants including category, price, degree of comfort and setting. Towns underlined in red on the Michelin map 733 are listed in the current edition of the Michelin Guide Spain & Portugal with a choice of hotels and restaurants.

The Portuguese Tourist Board also publishes a list with hotel categories ranging from one-star to five-star establishments. In Portugal, hotel prices are inclusive of VAT and the price of breakfast is almost always included in the cost of the room.

ESTALAGEMS

Similar to *pousadas*, *estalagems* are often in refurbished historic buildings, but they are privately owned.

QUINTAS

In Portuguese 'quinta' originally meant a farm and house let out at a rent of one-fifth of its produce, from Latin *quintus*, 'one fifth'. Today, in the case of Madeira in particular, the term refers to former colonial manor houses now converted to luxury hotels enclosed within their own grounds; smaller versions are known as 'quintanhas'.

RESIDÊNCIAS

Residências are comfortable guesthouses almost on par with some hotels, but they do not serve meals.

PENSÕES

Pensões are modest guesthouses.

SOLARES DE PORTUGAL

Solares de Portugal are privately-owned stately manor houses, elegant country homes and rustic farmhouses. Sometimes they are properties that were in decline, but are now restored to their former glory and are open to guests who are treated as part of the family. They are usually of considerable historic interest, and many are 17C and 18C houses still in the ownership of the descendants of the founding family.

For this type of stylish rural tourism, contact **Solares de Portugal** (Turismo de Habitação); ℘258 742 827, www.solaresdeportugal.pt/en.

COUNTRY HOUSES

Casas no campo are country houses or villas restored for rural tourism. Renovated in style, they are geared towards upmarket travellers, and offer exclusive facilities such as a private pool or private gardens. ℘924 757 829; www.casasnocampo.net.

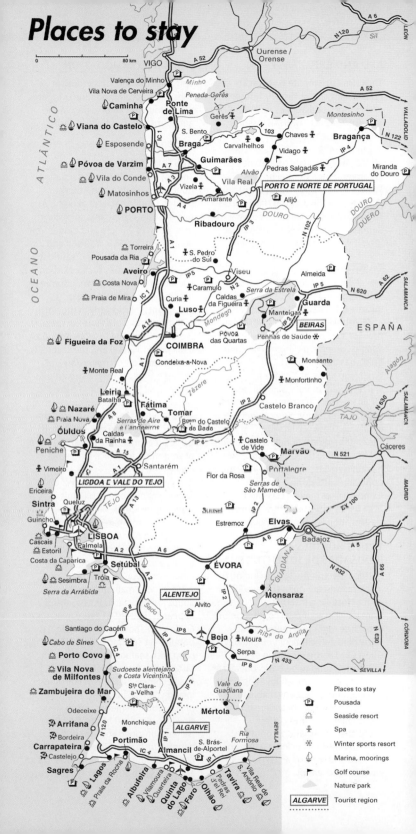

BED AND BREAKFAST

The term **Turismo de Habitação (TH)** usually covers historic houses and manors, and applies to cultural tourism. Contact TURIHAB, Associação do Turismo de Habitação, Praça da République, 4990-062 Ponte de Lima, ✆258 741 672, www.turihab.pt. For accommodation in rural houses, **Turismo no Espaço Rural (TER)**, apply to CENTER (Central Nacional de Turismo de Espaço Rural), Praça da República, 4990-062 Ponte de Lima. ✆258 931 750; www.center.pt/en.

CAMPING

See △ sign on Michelin map 733.
In Portugal independent camping outside official sites is not allowed. Local tourist information centres can provide a list of official campsites. The *Roteiro Campista (Camping Portugal)* guide has details of all campsites. When you arrive at a campsite, you will be asked for your passport and for an international camping carnet, which is obligatory. You can get details on these carnets from the Fédération Internationale de Camping et Caravanning (FICC): www.ficc.org. It is advisable to book in advance for popular resorts during summer. Camping sites may be classified from 3-star to 5-star, although such classification is not mandatory.

YOUTH HOSTELS (POUSADAS DE JUVENTUDE)

Portugal's youth hostels (including 6 in the Azores) are open to travellers with a Hostelling International Card (contact HI in your own country before departure regarding membership: www.hihostels.com), or you can buy a Guest Card at the reception desk. The hostels tend to be basic, but all are well located, and most have cooking facilities and lounges available to guests. Be advised that some rural hostels have an 11pm curfew. For further information, contact MOVIJOVEM, Rua Lúcio de Azevedo, 27, 1600-140 Lisbon. ✆217 232 100, www.movijovem.pt.

FARM ACCOMMODATION

This form of agricultural tourism consists of accommodation on a farm, where tourists can take part in the agricultural work if they so wish.

WHERE TO EAT
RESTAURANTS

The Portuguese keep similar dining hours to the British and Americans, though tend to eat later at night. As a general rule, restaurants serve lunch from noon to 2.30pm and dinner from about 7pm onwards. You will find many restaurants closed on Sunday nights, even in cities such as Lisbon (although not the Algarve in summer). In some of the more popular restaurants, particularly in the north of Portugal, two prices are written by the same item. The first price denotes a full portion *(dose)* and the second is for the half portion *(meia dose)*.

Hors-d'œuvres are often served prior to the meal (cheese, cured ham, spicy sausage, olives, tuna and croquettes) and are added to the bill. In Madeira and the Azores, you will be offered garlic bread *(bolo de caco)* at the start of your meal, for which a nominal charge will be made.

It is customary to leave a tip of about 10 percent of the total bill unless service is included.

While it is rare (apart, perhaps, from parts of the Algarve where the tourist trade is sizeable) to find a children's menu, you can buy half portions *(meia dose)* – or, if you are not too hungry, you can get a main dish to share. Soups are popular in Portugal and appear at the start of every main meal. *Caldo verde* (potato and cabbage) is popular yet seafood *acorda* (bread soup with seafood) is an acquired taste. Fish is found everywhere, but has become expensive of late, and inland you will find goat, kid, suckling pig or rabbit on menus, often stewed slowly in wine and herbs. *Bacalhau* (salted, sun-dried codfish) is the national dish. You will see rows of codfish drying in shop windows. It's an acquired taste but the Portuguese are skilled at serving it countless ways – gratin (with cheese), pataniscas (fried patties) or stuffed with smoked ham. Meat and fish *cataplanas* – thick stews served in a copper dish (the cataplana) – are available on every menu in the Algarve, but not widely available in either Madeira or the Azores.

😊 Be aware that seemingly simple lunchtime meals, in Madeira especially, often come accompanied by boiled potatoes, salad, mixed vegetables and sometimes rice, in addition to what is already on your plate.

A large variety of pastries, cakes, tarts and buns is available from *confeitarias, casas de chá* (tearooms), pastelarias and cafés.

In terms of fine dining, Portugal is not especially over-endowed, and such 'starred' restaurants as there are will be found in the Algarve and Douro regions. There are two starred restaurant in Madeira, but quite a few where the food and service is of a high standard. Bib Gourmand restaurants, whoever, are well represented, but mainly in Portugal.

Mercado da Ribeira Nova, Lisbon

© C. Bouvet/Michelin

Useful Words and Phrases

Common Words

	Translation
Bank; exchange	Banco; câmbio
Boat	Barco
Bus; tram	Autocarro; Eléctrico
Car	Carro
Car park	Parque de estacionamento
Chemist	Farmácia
Customs	Alfândega
District	Bairro
Doctor	Médico
Entrance; exit	Entrada; saída
Expensive	Caro
Good afternoon	Boa tarde
Good morning	Bom dia
Goodbye	Adeus
Guide	Guia
Bus stop	Paragem
I beg your pardon	Desculpe
Information	informações
Large; small	Grande; Pequeno
letter; postcard	Carta; Postal
Letter-box	Caixa de correio
Light	Luz
Madam	Minha senhora
Miss	Menina
At what time..?	A que hora..?
Much; little	Muito; Pouco
How much..?	Quanto custa..?
Noon	Meio-dia
Road works	Obras
Petrol; oil	Gasolina; óleo
Danger	Perigo
Please	(se) Faz favor
Prohibited	Prohibido
Post office; Stamp	Correio; Selo
River; Stream	Rio; Ribeira
Ruins	Ruínas
Sir	Senhor

Square	Largo; Praça
Station; Train	Estação; Comboio
Street; Avenue	Rue; Avenida
Thank you (said by a man) (said by a woman)	Obrigado Obrigada
Today	Hoje
Toll	Portagem
Tomorrow morning	Amanhã de manhã
Tomorrow evening	Amanhã à tarde
To the left	à esquerda
To the right	à direita
Town; Quarter	Cidade
Where; When	Onde? Quando?
Yes; No	Sim; Não
Where is?	Onde é..?
The road to..?	A estrada para..?
At what time..?	A que hora..?
How much..?	Quanto custa..?
Road works	Obras
Danger	Perigo
Prohibited	Prohibido

Sightseeing

	Translation
Abbey	Abadia
Reservoir	Albufeira
Town Centre	Centro da cidade
Dam	Barragem
Town hall	Câmara municipal
Chapel	Capela
House	Casa
Castle, itadel	Castelo
Fountain	Chafariz
Key	Chave
Prehistoric city	Citânia
Convent	Convento
Monastery	Mosteiro
Cross; Calvary	Cruz; Cruzeiro
Escada	Stairs, Steps
Excavações	Excavations
Closed, Open	Fechado, Aberto
Church	Igreja
Island	Ilha
Site	Local

Wood	Mata
Market, Fair	Mercado, Feira
Belvedere	Miradouro
Palace, Castle	Paço, Palácio
Park	Parque
Harbour, Port	Porto
Beach	Praia
Country Property	Quinta
Cathedral	Sé
Century	Século
Manor-house	Solar
Tapestry	Tapete; Tapeçaria
Treasure; Treasury	Tesouro
Tower	Torre
Keep	Torre de menagem
Tomb	Túmulo
View, Panorama	Vista
Apply to...	Dirigir-se a...
May one visit?	Pode-se visitar?

Dining

Note: for more detailed restaurant terminology consult the *Michelin Guide Spain & Portugal*.

	Translation
Açucar	Sugar
Água; Copo	Water; Glass
Almoço	Breakfast
Azeite	Olive Oil
Café com leite	Coffee with milk
Carne	Meat
Cerveja	Beer
Conta	Bill
Copo	Glass
Ementa, Carta	Menu
Faca	Knife
Fresco	Cold, Chilled
Garfo	Fork
Garrafa	Bottle
Gelo	Ice-cream
Jantar, Ceia	Dinner
Leite	Milk
Lista	Menu (à la Carte)
Óleo	Peanut Oil

Pão	Bread
Peixe	Fish
Pequeno	Small
Pimenta, Sal	Pepper, Salt
Prato Do Dia	Dish Of The Day
Sumo De Fruta	Fruit Juice
Vinho Branco/Tinto	White/Red Wine

Typical Dishes

Açorda de Mariscos
Bread soup with clams and prawns, mixed with garlic, eggs, coriander and spices

Amêijoas à Bulhão Pato
Small clams cooked in olive oil, garlic and coriander

Arroz de Marisco Rice with clams, shrimp, mussels and coriander

Bacalhau Cod

Cabrito Roast goat

Caldeirada Spicy fish and seafood stew

Caldo verde Potato and cabbage stew

Canja de Galinha Chicken bouillon with rice and hard egg yolks

Carne de porco à Alentajana
Diced pork in olive oil, garlic and coriander sauce, served with potatoes and small clams

Cataplana Steamed seafood or meat traditionally served in a copper dish

Chouriço Smoked sausage

Cozido Pot roast with meat, sausage and vegetables

Cataplana

© StockFood/hemis.fr

Feijoada Beans prepared with pork, cabbage and sausage

Frango na púcara Chicken casserole with port and almonds

Gaspacho Cold vegetable soup

Leitão assado Grilled suckling pig, served hot or cold

Pastéis de nata Puff pastry with egg custard filling

Presunto Smoked ham

Salpicão Spicy smoked ham

Sopa à Alentajana Garlic and bread soup, served with a poached egg and coriander

Sopa de Feijão verde
Green bean soup

Sopa de Grão Chickpea soup

Sopa de Legumes Vegetable soup

Sopa de Marisco Seafood soup

Sopa de Peixe Fish soup

Basic Information

BUSINESS HOURS

MONUMENTS, MUSEUMS AND CHURCHES

Monuments and museums are generally open from 9.30–10am to 12.30pm and then from 2pm to 6pm. Many are closed on Mondays. Some churches are open only for Mass early in the morning or in the evening. Most have free entry Sunday morning until 2pm. For more detailed information, please consult the admission times and charges in the *Discovering Portugal* section.

SHOPS

Shops generally open weekdays 9am/10am to 7pm, although some close for lunch from 1pm to 3pm (some department stores stay open during the lunch hour). Most shops are closed on Saturday afternoons and most all day Sunday. Shopping centres are the exception as they are open every day of the week from 10am to 11pm. Street markets are normally on

Tuesdays, Thursdays or Saturdays and start early, about 8am.

ENTERTAINMENT

Evening performances begin about 9.30pm and *fados* at about 10.30pm. Most trendy bars and clubs do not open until 11pm. They stay open until 2am or 4am at weekends. Many are closed Sunday night.

COMMUNICATIONS

TELEPHONES

In public telephone booths, coins and phonecards are widely used, the latter sold in MEO shops, post offices and some kiosks and news-stands (*tabacarias*). Some phone boxes also accept credit card payments. International calls may be made from modern phone boxes or from post offices; in bars and hotels be prepared to pay more than the going rate. For **international calls** dial: 00 + 44 for the United Kingdom; 00 + 353 for Ireland; 00 + 1 for the US and Canada followed by the area code (omitting the first zero) and then the recipient's number. To call from abroad to Portugal, it is necessary to dial the international access code 00 and the country code 351.

CELL/MOBILE PHONES

Coverage for most mobile phones is good in the main parts of Portugal, but in Madeira and the Azores, and inland Portugal (particularly the natural parks and mountains), it may be difficult to receive a signal. Your own network will be able to advise you which partners they use in Portugal. There are three network service providers: TMN, MEO and Optimus, that have roaming agreements with most international mobile phone companies and provide users with a good coverage nationwide.

INTERNET

Al hotels and many bars, cafés, and restaurants have WiFi, usually free for guests.

ELECTRICITY

The electric current is 220 volts/50Hz. Plugs are two-pin. You can get adapters at most main airports, electrical stores and souvenir shops.

EMERGENCIES

112 - In an emergency, dial 112 anywhere in Portugal. If you lose your credit card (or have it stolen), you should call the issuing office immediately. The phone numbers should be kept somewhere safe, separate from the credit card itself. Always have a copy of the numbers and date of expiry. A photocopy of the ID page on your passport will also be a good thing to carry with you. There is a lot of petty theft in tourist areas such as Lisbon and the Algarve; mostly opportunistic rather than violent. Do not keep money in your back or top pockets, and keep hold of your bags.

MEDIA

NEWSPAPERS

The main Portuguese newspapers are the following: *O Diário de Notícias, O Correio da Manhã,* and *O Público.* Porto has its own daily newspaper, *O Jornal de Notícias.* Weekly publications include *O Expresso,* which has the widest readership, *O Seminário, O Independente* and *O Jornal.*

RADIO

Like the UK, Portugal has dozens of local radio stations, many with non-stop music. Nationwide, the biggest is Antenna 1 with a good mix of golden oldies, Portuguese music and news (in Portuguese). Antenna 2 is the classical music station; Antenna 3 is the station for alternative music and the promotion of Portuguese bands.

MONEY

Portugal is part of the Euro zone. Euro notes come in denominations of €5, €10, €20, €50, €100, €200 and €500. Beware of accepting notes of high value (€200 and €500) as these are a favourite of counterfeiters. Most shops and all taxis will refuse any note larger than €100.

Transport and circulation of money: Travellers who enter or leave the EU carrying amounts with them equal to or higher than €10,000, should declare this amount to the Customs authorities.

CURRENCY EXCHANGE AND CREDIT CARDS

Banks, airports and some stations have exchange offices. Commissions vary, so check before cashing.

All major credit cards (American Express, Diners Club, Visa and MasterCard) are accepted but always check in advance.

MULTIBANCO is a national network of automatic cash dispensers that accept international credit and debit cards and enable cash withdrawal 24 hours a day.

Banks are generally open Mondays to Fridays 8.30am to 3pm. These times are subject to change, especially in summer. Most banks have cash dispensers (ATMs), which accept international credit cards. In many out-of-the-way places, particularly inland and in the north, you will find that ATMs are very rare and that most smaller places with accommodation do *not* accept credit cards. Take cash with you.

REDUCED RATES

In Lisbon, if you are staying a few days you should invest in the **Lisbon Card** which permits the use of all public transport facilities in the city and trains between Lisbon and Sintra or Cascais, and offers free entrance or discounts in monuments, museums or tourism circuits. The prices are €20 for 24 hours, €34 for 48 hours and €42 for 72 hours. www.visitlisboa.com and lisboacard.org.

POST OFFICES (CORREIOS)

Post offices are open Monday to Friday, 9am to 6pm. Central and airport offices have extended opening hours and may be open on Saturdays and in some cases on Sundays.

Stamps are sold in post offices and vending-machines in the streets. Many post offices have the Netpost service that on payment allows access to personal email and the Internet. More detailed information about opening hours and services available at each office can be found on www.ctt.pt.

The **Michelin Guide Spain & Portugal** gives the post code for every town covered. Letter boxes and phone booths are red in colour.

SMOKING

Smoking is banned in many public places in Portugal, though owners of bars and restaurants, with a floor area of less than 100m², may choose whether to allow smoking on their premises: if they do, the area must have a good ventilation system, and may not amount to more than 30% of the total area. Smoking is not permitted on public transport.

TEMPERATURE AND MEASUREMENT

Portugal uses the metric system: distances in kilometres (km), temperatures in Celsius. Roughly speaking 85°F = 30°C and in speed 48kph = 30mph; 80kph = 50mph and 112kph = 70mph.

TIME

Mainland Portugal is the same as Greenwich Mean Time, although summer time is used so the time is always the same as the UK. Madeira is the same as mainland Portugal, but the Azores are always 1hr behind (summer time is observed).

TIPPING

The bill is usually inclusive of service charges. An extra tip, about 5%–10%, can be left for special service. The same is the usual amount given to taxi drivers, and about €2 per bag for hotel porters.

*Stonework depicting Amália Rodrigues
by Alexandre Farto (aka Vhils) and
Ruben Alves, Alfama, Lisbon*

© Jon Arnold Images/hemis.fr

INTRODUCTION TO PORTUGAL

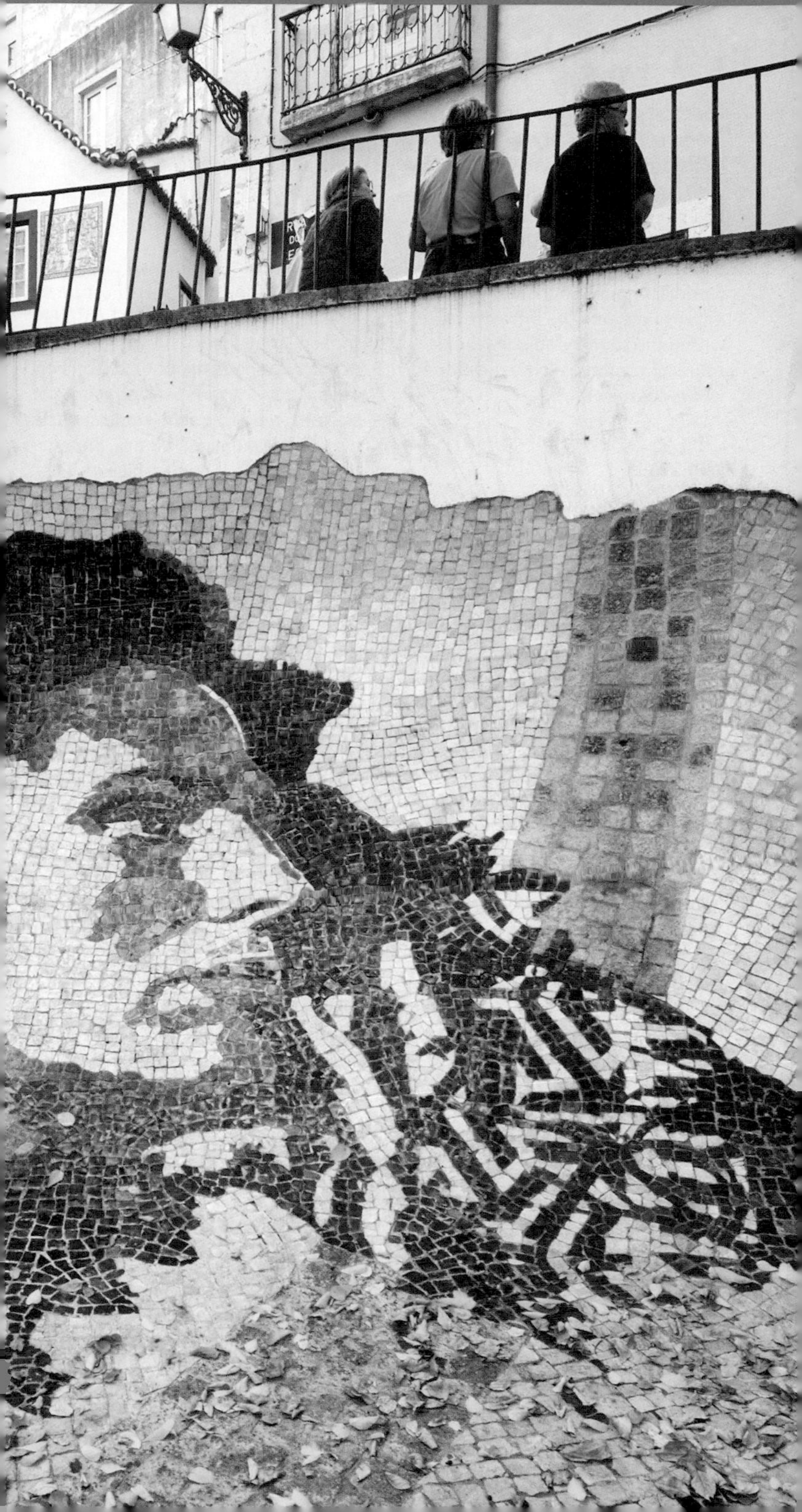

Portugal Today

Portugal's accession to the European Economic Community in 1986 transformed the country's economy, with large inflows of direct foreign investment. It has become a vital part of the European Union and continues to play its part in the world economy. Tourism is of great importance, and the infrastructure within the country, so crucial to tourism, continues to be developed and modernised.

21ST CENTURY PORTUGAL

LIFESTYLE

The Portuguese enjoy a good standard of living and fairly relaxed lifestyle away from the main cities. The cost of living is reasonable compared to some other European destinations although prices have risen of late. The pace of life in the far south and north, particularly in the Algarve and Alentejo, is slower than the rest of the country. The south enjoys a hotter and dryer climate.

Madeira is becoming increasingly dependent on tourism, and in 2015 was voted the World's Leading Island Destination by the World Travel Awards. The lifestyle here is also relaxed, easy-going but up-beat. The Azores in comparison have a culture that reflects a lifestyle where it was necessary to be both independent and yet mutually supportive. Tourism here is developing steadily, but there is much room for progress. The culture is an engaging mix of agricultural, whaling, military and wine growing people.

RELIGION

The majority of Portuguese are Catholics, but the Portuguese constitution guarantees religious freedom and there are a number of different religions in Portugal.

LANGUAGE

One of the Latin languages, Portuguese is the third most spoken European language and the fifth most natively spoken language in the world, being the native tongue of about 220 million people. Portuguese-speaking countries are scattered all over the world and it is the official language in Brazil, Mozambique, Angola, Guinea-Bissau, East Timor, Equatorial Guinea, Cape Verde, and São Tomé and Príncipe.

English is widely spoken throughout Portugal and Madeira especially in the cities and holiday areas, as are French, German and Spanish. In the Azores, outside the tourist areas, English and other languages, while in use, are a little less in evidence. But this is increasing all the time.

MEDIA

Portugal's commercial TV stations command a lion's share of the viewing audience from the public broadcaster. Public TV services are operated by RTP and the commercial channels by SIC. Multichannel TV via cable, satellite and digital terrestrial reaches more than two million homes. There are some 300 local and regional commercial radio stations plus four daily national newspapers and three English-language weekly newspapers.

The Portuguese Flag

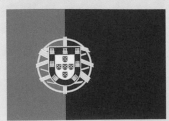

The green vertical stripe at the hoist and red stripe in the fly are divided by an armillary sphere bearing the Portuguese coat of arms. The sphere supports a white shield with five blue shields, each with five white disks symbolising Christ's wounds. The seven yellow castles represent the strongholds retaken from the Moors.

Praça do Comércio, Lisbon

© John Warburton-Lee/Photononstop

GOVERNMENT

Portugal has been a Republic since the overthrow of the monarchy in 1910. The **Constitution**, promulgated in 1976, brought in a semi-presidential form of government. **Executive power** is held by the **President of the Republic** who is directly elected for a five-year term. The president appoints the **Prime Minister**, who represents the Parliamentary majority, and, on his suggestion, the rest of the government. The revised Constitution of 1982 has limited the president's powers although he retains the right to veto laws approved by straight majority vote in the Assembly. **Legislative power** is held by a single Chamber of 230 members who are elected for four years, and is the representative assembly of all Portuguese citizens.

The archipelagos of **Madeira** and the **Azores** are Autonomous Regions with their own Regional Government and Regional Assembly. This is justified by their geographic particularities and based on their populations' wish for self-government. The Assembly is elected by universal suffrage. The President of the Republic appoints a **Minister of the Republic** for each of the autonomous regions, who then appoints a **Regional Government President**.

ADMINISTRATIVE ORGANISATION

The old historical provinces of the Minho, Trás-os-Montes, Douro, Beiras (Alta, Baixa and Litoral), Ribatejo, Estremadura, Alentejo and Algarve no longer fulfil an administrative role but still denote the main regions of the country. Portugal's present administrative organisation is as follows:

Distritos: There are 18 districts in mainland Portugal, three in the Azores and one in Madeira. Health, education and finance are managed at district level.

Concelhos: These councils represent municipal authority. There are 305 in all. A *concelho* is similar to a district borough or a canton. Each one has a town hall or *Paço do Concelho* and an executive committee or *Câmara Municipal* led by a president who acts as mayor. Both the president and the municipal assembly are elected by universal suffrage every four years.

Lastly, each *concelho* consists of several **freguesias**, the smallest administrative unit, some of which represent a village, and others a district. There are about 4 200 *freguesias* in Portugal, responsible for keeping public records, civil status, the upkeep of natural heritage, and organising festivals and events.

ECONOMY

At the time of the 1974 Carnation Revolution, Portugal had fallen behind many of its European neighbours. Lack of investment in the country's industry and infrastructure under the Salazar regime was the cause, even though Portugal had significant gold reserves originating mainly from its mining concerns in its former colonies. Traditional activities, such as agriculture and fishing, still formed the basis of the country's economy until its membership in the European Economic Community in 1986, which marked a transitional point in Portugal's development, thanks in part to EEC aid. In 2011 Portugal requested a 78 billion euro bailout package from the European Union to stabilise its public finances, a measure necessary after decades of government overspending and a top heavy civil service.

Today, Portugal remains one of the world's largest producers of wine and the leading producer of cork. Other industries include shoe, textile and paper production, car manufacturing, metallurgy and mechanical engineering. Tourism is still very important, and increasingly so.

Arts and Crafts

Portugal's arts and crafts are remarkably varied and unpretentious. The weekly markets held in most towns give a good idea of the skill of Portuguese craftsmanship.

CERAMICS AND POTTERY

There are many village potters *(olarios)* producing domestic and decorative earthenware which varies in shape and colour according to the region.

In Barcelos, pots are glazed, colours bright with ornamentation consisting of leaves, stems and flowers; handsome multicoloured cockerels are also made locally. Around Coimbra, the colour used is green with brown and yellow overtones and the decoration is more geometric.

The potters of Caldas da Rainha use bright green and produce items with surprising shapes. Continuing the tradition set up by Rafael Bordalo Pinheiro (&see LISBON, Museu Rafael Bordalo Pinheiro), water jugs, salad bowls and plates are all heavily adorned with leaves, flowers and animals. In Alcobaça and Cruz da Légua the potters work with more classical designs, distinguishing their ware by the variety of blues they use in its decoration.

In the Upper Alentejo (in Redondo, Estremoz and Nisa) the clay is encrusted with shining quartz particles or marble chips; in the Algarve amphorae are still made based on Greek and Roman models, while in Tras-os-Montes the potters damp down their ovens at the end of the firing to give the ware a black colour.

LACE

Lace is made virtually only along the coast. The decorative motifs used are fir cones and flowers, trefoils at Viano do Castelo where the lace looks more like tulle, and seaweed, shells and fish at Vila do Conde.

Famous Markets & Fairs

Barcelos: Pottery fair on Thursday mornings.
São Pedro de Sintra: Antiques fair on the second and fourth Sunday of the month.
Estremoz: Pottery market on Saturdays.
Estoril: Handicraft fair (Feira do Artesonato) in July and August.
Santarém: Agricultural fair in October.
Golega: Horse fair in November.

© DRT Madeira

Madeira enbroidery

EMBROIDERY

Madeira's embroidery is particularly impressive and well-known, although mainland Portugal also produces shawls, tablecloths and bedspreads, and there is a small industry producing embroidery in the Azores, notably on São Miguel. The best-known bedspreads *(colchas)* are from Castelo Branco and are embroidered with silk on linen. The tradition is a long-standing one, the work pains taking.

FILIGREE WORK

The working by hand of gold or silver wire which reached its height in the reign of King João V (1706–50) is still held in high regard in Portugal.

The chief centre is the small town of Gondomar not far from Oporto. Delicate, intricate jewellery in the shape of hearts, crosses, guitars and, above all, caravels (sailing ships) is fashioned from this extremely pliable wire. In the Minho, filigree earrings and brooches are worn to set off the regional costume.

WEAVING AND CARPET-MAKING

Hand weaving still flourishes in some mountain villages. Lengths of heavy frieze are woven on old looms to make capes and tippets. Guimarães specialises in bedspreads and curtains in rough cloth bordered with classical motifs in bright colours. The hemp or linen-based carpets embroidered in wool at Arraiolos are the best known of their type and have simpler designs.

WOODWORK

In the Alentejo many items made of wood, including trays, chairs and cupboards, are painted with brightly-coloured, naive motifs.

Painted whitewood is an important feature of traditional Portuguese handicraft and may be seen all over the country. Examples include ox yokes (the most famous being in the Barcelos region), painted carts (in the Alentejo and the Algarve) and carved and painted fishing boats (in the Ria de Aveiro and on many of the country's beaches).

BASKETWORK

Rushes, willows and rye straw are all used to make decorative and utilitarian wickerwork baskets. Pack saddles may be seen in Trás-os-Montes with twin pairs of deep baskets on either side.

CORK

Wherever the cork oak grows (particularly in the Alentejo and the Algarve), a local craft has developed, making cork boxes, key rings, belts, bags and hundreds of other creations.

Cuisine

Traditional Portuguese meals are copious and wholesome. The menu can consist of several dishes, usually prepared with olive oil and flavoured with aromatic herbs such as rosemary and bay leaves. Eggs play an important part in Portuguese food, being used in soups and often to accompany fish and meat dishes. Rice, for which the Portuguese developed a liking following their voyages to Asia, is an ingredient in numerous traditional dishes. Fried potatoes are also commonly served.

SOUPS

Soup is served at most meals. Among the many varieties are *canja de galinha*, chicken soup with rice, *sopa de peixe*, fish soup, *sopa de marisco*, seafood soup, *sopa de coelho*, rabbit soup, and *sopa de grão*, chickpea soup.

The most famous is the Minho **caldo verde** which is served north of the Mondego. This dish consists of a mashed potato base to which finely shredded green Galician cabbage is added; lastly olive oil and slices of black pudding, *tora,* are mixed in. Bread soups or **açordas** are to be found in all regions, those of the Alentejo having many variations such as the *sopa de coentros* made with coriander leaves, olive oil, garlic and bread, with a poached egg on top.

In the south, **gaspacho**, a soup of tomatoes, onions, cucumbers and chillies seasoned with garlic and vinegar, is served cold with croutons.

FISH AND SEAFOOD

Fish is a basic element of Portuguese cuisine. Cod, **bacalhau**, is the most common fish, particularly in the north, though there are issues involved with the dwindling stocks of cod in the Atlantic and surrounding areas. There are, it is said, 365 ways of preparing it (©*see recipe for Bacalhau à Brás left).*

Many other fish, however, are to be found in some part or other of the country: the aroma of grilled sardines wafts the streets of every coastal town; many types of fish are put into the **caldeirada** or stew made by fishermen on the beach. You will get tuna fillets in the Algarve, river lampreys and salmon beside the Minho and shad beside the Tagus. Seafood *(mariscos)* including octopus is plentiful. Shellfish are delicious and varied especially in the Algarve where a special copper vessel, a *cataplana,* is used to cook clams and sausages spiced with herbs. Limpets (*lapas*) are especially popular in Madeira, usually as a starter; they tend to be grilled in garlic butter and are rather chewy but provide excellent protein.

Crayfish *(lagosta)* prepared in the Peniche way, or steamed, are rightly famous, but in the deep waters of the Atlantic around Madeira and the Azores, bear in mind that any seafood that normally crawls about on the seabed, e.g. lobster, langoustines, etc. is likely to be imported and therefore more expensive.

MEAT AND GAME

Apart from pork and game, Portuguese meat is often very ordinary. Pork is cooked and served in a variety of ways. The **leitão assado**, or roast sucklingpig, of Mealhada (north of Coimbra) is delicious.

Meat from various parts of the pig can also be found in stews, in **linguiça** or smoked pigs' tongue sausages, in smoked pork fillets, *paio,* and in smoked ham, *presunto,* at Chaves and Lamego. Ham and sausages are added to the **cozido à Portuguesa**, a hotpot of beef, vegetables, potatoes and rice, also to the local tripe prepared in the Oporto way, *dobrada,* a dish of pig or beef tripe cooked with haricot beans.

Pork in the Alentejo way, or **carne de porco à Alentejana**, is pork marinated in wine, garnished with clams. Other meat is mostly minced and consumed as meat balls, although lamb and kid are sometimes roasted or served on skewers.

CHEESES

Cheeses are made all over Portugal with several special varieties being made in the Azores. It is possible to visit a num-

Bacalhau

© PierreOlivierClementMantion/iStock

A "faithful friend"

Cod *(bacalhau)* has played an important role in Portugal's maritime history, and is such a standby in family dining that it is commonly known as the "faithful friend". Fished in the cold, far-off waters of Newfoundland, it had to be salted to preserve it until the fishing fleet returned home. The dish was popular in Portugal and other Roman Catholic countries because of the many days on which the Church forbade the eating of meat. Emblematic of Portuguese cooking, a delicacy enjoyed by fishermen and peasants alike, cod is enjoyed throughout the country, particularly served as fish balls. In Porto in the north, you will see rows and rows of large, white salted codfish drying in lines in shop windows all over the city With the collapse of cod stocks and dismantling of the cod fleet, *bacalhau* has become expensive, especially around Christmas time, as it features in traditional dishes of the holiday season. **Bacalhau à Brás**, a cod recipe which originates from Lisbon, is now served the length and breadth of Portugal. Accompany it with two wines from the north of the country – the white *vinho verde* (green wine) or the light and slightly sparkling Mateus rosé produced at the Mateus Palace in the Douro valley. The Douro river valley is the oldest demarcated wine region and a UNESCO World Heritage Site. *Vinho verde* is produced at Ponte de Lima in the heart of a rich farming region

Ingredients for 4 people:
500g (about 1lb) of cod
500g of potatoes such as Maris Piper
3 medium-sized onions
5 eggs, lightly beaten
2 cloves of garlic
4 tablespoons of oil
Chopped parsley, black olives, salt and pepper

- Soak the cod overnight, changing the water several times.
- Shred the cod, taking care to remove the skin and any bones.
- Slice the onions into thin rings.
- Cut the potatoes into matchsticks; fry them and set aside.
- Heat the oil in a frying pan with the onions and garlic and cook until golden. Then add the cod. Leave on the heat for 5min, add the potatoes. Season with salt and pepper and add the beaten eggs and mix well. Remove from the heat before the eggs solidify into an omelette. Serve hot with parsley and black olives.

Pasteis de nata at Pastéis de Belém, Lisbon

© Robert Harding/hemis.fr

ber of cheese producers, many of which are small-scale cottage industries where you will get a personal tour as well as the opportunity to try (and hopefully buy) some of the often hand-made product. Ewes' milk cheese should be tried between October and May, notably the *Queijo da Serra da Estrela*, the *Queijo de Castelo Branco* and the creamy *Queijo de Azeitão* as well as goats' milk cheeses such as the *cabreiro*, the *rabaçal* from the Pombal region and the small soft white cheeses or *quejinhos* from Tomar, often served as an hors d'œuvre as is the fresh goat's cheese, *Queijo fresco*.

DESSERTS

Portugal has an infinite variety of cakes and pastries. Nearly all recipes include eggs and come in most instances from old specialities prepared in convents such as the **Toucinho-do-Céu**, **Barriga-de-Freira** and **Queijadas de Sintra**, with almonds and fresh sheep's milk. The dessert most frequently seen on menus is the **pudim flan**, a sort of crème caramel, or the creamier **leite-creme**. Rice pudding, **arroz doce**, sprinkled with cinnamon is often served at festive meals. In the Algarve, the local figs *(figos)* and almonds *(amêndoas)* are made into the most appetising sweetmeats and tidbits. A particularly delicious pastry is the **pasteis de nata**, a small custard tart sprinkled with cinnamon.

Wine

Portugal is the seventh largest wine-producer in the world and has a rich variety of wines, including the world famous Port and, although not quite as popular as it once was but still important, Madeira. The wines bought locally or enjoyed in a restaurant are of good quality, reasonably priced, suitable for all occasions and deserve to be better known. Significantly, Portugal has two wine producing regions protected by UNESCO as World Heritage: the Douro Valley Wine Region (*Douro Vinhateiro*) and Pico Island Wine Region (*Ilha do Pico Vinhateira*).

PORT

The vines of the Upper Douro and its tributaries produce a generous wine which is shipped from the city that gave it its name (Oporto) only after it has matured.

THE ENGLISH

In the 14C, some of the wines produced in the Lamego region were already being exported to England. In the 17C, the Portuguese granted the English trading rights in exchange for their help against the Spanish. By the end of the 17C, once the port process had been developed, some Englishmen acquired country estates *(quintas)* in the Douro valley and began making wine. Through the **Methuen Treaty** (1703) the English crown obtained the monopoly of the Portuguese wine trade. However in 1756, to combat this English invasion, King Dom José I and the Marquis of Pombal founded the **Company of the Wines of the Upper Douro** (*Companhia Geral da Agricultura dos Vinhos do Alto Douro*) which fixed the price for all exported port. The following year the company defined the area in which port vines could be grown. Various English companies were set up, among them Cockburn, Campbell, Offley, Harris, Sandeman, Dow, Graham etc. The Portuguese followed suit in 1830 with their own companies with names like Ferreira and Ramos Pinto. In 1868 phylloxera raged throughout the region but the vineyards were rapidly rehabilitated – many of the vineyards were grafted from phylloxera-resistant American stocks – and "vintage" port was being produced by the end of the 19C.

VINEYARDS

The area defined by law in 1757 for the cultivation of vines covers 240 000ha of which a tenth consists of vineyards that stretch for about sixty miles along the Douro to the Spanish border. The approximate centre is situated at Pinhão. There are more than 25 000 vineyard owners. Port's inestimable quality is due to the exceptional conditions under which the grapes are grown and ripened – hot summers, cold winters, and schist soil – and the processing of the fruit when harvested. The vines grow on steep terraces overlooking the Douro, a striking picture not only from an aesthetic point of view but also in terms of the extraordinary amount of work involved.

MAKING PORT

The grape harvest takes place in late September. Men carry the bunches of grapes in wickerwork baskets on their backs. The cut grapes go into the press where mechanical crushing has taken the place of human treading which, with its songs and rhythmic tunes, was so

highly picturesque. The must is sealed off during fermentation which reduces the sugar content to the right amount, then brandy – from Douro grapes – is added to stop the fermentation and to stabilise the sugar. In the spring the wine is taken by lorry and train to Vila Nova de Gaia. Up until a few years ago it was transported 150km/90mi along the Douro to Oporto in picturesque sailing craft known as *barcelos rebelos*. Some of these boats may be seen at Pinhão and Vila Nova da Gaia.

The wine is stored with the 58 port wine companies that have set up in Vila Nova da Gaia and matures in huge casks or, more commonly, in vats containing up to 1 000hl. It is then decanted into 535-litre barrels *(pipes)* in which the porous nature of the wood augments the ageing process. The Wine Institute (Instituto do Vinho do Porto) sets the rules and controls the quality.

TYPES OF PORT

Port, which is red or white according to the colour of the grapes from which it is made, has many subtleties – it can be dry, medium or sweet.

The variety of port also depends upon the way it is made. Port aged in casks matures through oxidation and turns a beautiful amber colour; port aged in the bottle matures by reduction and is a dark red colour. The alcohol content is about 20%.

Vintage ports are selected from the best wines of a particularly fine year and are bottled after two years in casks. They then mature in the bottle for at least ten

Terraced vineyards near Pinhão, Douro Valley

© Olimpio Fantuz/Sime/Photononstop

years or more before being served. Since 1974 all Vintage Port must be bottled in Portugal.

White port or **Branco** is less well known than the reds. It is a fortified wine made from white grapes. Dry or extra dry, it makes a good apéritif.

Blended ports are red ports made from different vintages from different years. The blending and ageing differ according to the quality required. They include:

- **Tinto**, the most common, which is young, vigorous, distinctly coloured and fruity.
- **Tinto-Alourado** or **Ruby**, which is older, yet rich in colour, fruity and sweet and is the result of the blending of different vintages from different years.
- **Alourado** or **Tawny** is blended with different vintages from different years and ages in wooden casks. Its colour turns to a brownish gold as it ages. It should be drunk soon after it is bottled.
- **Alourado-Claro** or **Light Tawny** is the culmination of the former.

BUYING AND SERVING

White port, which should be drunk chilled and is best served as an aperitif, is the least expensive, followed by the reds (**Ruby** and **Tawny**). Very good quality Tawny ports will provide an indication of their age on the label (10, 20, 30 or more years spent in the barrel).

Next come the ports which bear their vintage date *(colheita)*; they have been made with wines from the same year. The best and most expensive are **Vintage ports** and **Late Bottled Vintage Ports (L.B.V.)**. The former are made with wine from an exceptionally good year and are bottled after two to three years; likewise, the latter are made with wine from the same vineyard and are bottled after four to six years. These can be kept for many years provided that they are laid down horizontally and are stored at a suitable temperature. Vintage port should be served in a carafe and drunk quickly, preferably on the day the bottle is opened. All ports, with the exception of the whites, are a perfect accompaniment to game, hams, foie gras, cheeses, dried fruit etc. For additional information on port, contact the Instituto do Vinho in Oporto (www.ivdp.pt) which, in association with other official organisations, particularly the Port Wine Route association in Peso da Régua and the region's tourist offices, has created a Port Wine Route within the official Douro region. The itinerary passes through numerous sites, including estates, **co-operatives** and wine information centres, providing visitors with an ideal opportunity to discover the beautiful landscapes of the region and to taste its most famous product. Since 1963 the French have replaced the English as the largest importers of port.

WINE

Several regions in Portugal produce perfectly respectable wines that can be enjoyed in restaurants. One can ask for the *vinho da casa*, usually the local wine.

Madeira – Madeira wine, which deserves to be more widely celebrated, has always been particularly popular with the English. *See MADEIRA*.

Vinho Verde – *Vinho Verde* from the Minho and the Lower Douro valleys can be white (tendency to gold) or deep red. Its name, "green wine" comes from its early grape harvest and short fermentation period which gives the wine a low alcohol content (8% to 11%) and makes it light and sparkling with a distinct bouquet and what might be described as a very slightly bitter flavour. It is best enjoyed young and chilled. It is an ideal aperitif and is a perfect accompaniment to salads and both fish and seafood. The most renowned *vinho verde* is produced from the Alvarinho grape, which enables the wine to be kept longer than wine produced from other grape varieties.

Dão – Vines growing on the granite slopes of the Dão valley produce a fresh white wine as well as a sweet red wine with a velvety texture and a heady bouquet which most closely resembles Bordeaux *crus*. *Quinta* wines are the equivalent of French *château* wines.

Bairrada – This very old vine-growing region produces a robust, fragrant red, as well as a natural sparkling wine which goes wonderfully well with roast suckling pig.

Colares – The vines grow in a sandy topsoil over a bed of clay in the Serra de Sintra. The robust, velvety, dark red wine has been famous since the 13C.

Bucelas – Bucelas is a dry, somewhat acidic straw-coloured white wine produced from vineyards on the banks of the Trancão, a tributary of the Tagus.

TABLE WINES

The Ribatejo vineyards produce good everyday wines: full bodied reds from the Cartaxo region and whites from Chamusca, Almeirim and Alpiarça on the far bank of the Tagus.

Also worth trying are the wines of Torres Vedras, Alcobaça, Lafões and Agueda, and the Pinhel and Mateus rosés.

In the Alentejo, full-bodied reds such as Reguengos, Borba and Redondo predominate. The one exception to this is the white Vidigueira wine.

In the Algarve, a small amount of wine is still produced in Lagoa, home to the country's oldest **co-operative**.

Although **Madeira** is famous for its eponymous fortified wine, there is an increasing endeavour in the production

Vineyards divided by walls made of lava rocks, Pico Island, Azores

© font83/iStock

WINES AND REGIONAL SPECIALITIES

- Wine-producing regions
- *Bucelas* Major vineyards

of table wines from new and established wine producers on the island that are well worth trying, and which will only get better as the vines improve. These include blends such as Quinta do Moledo (merlot with cabernet sauvignon), and Beira da Quinta (verdelho and ansburger), while the Atlantis and Seiçal rosé wines deserve attention.

DESSERT WINES

Setúbal moscatel from the chalky clay slopes of the Serra da Arrábida is a generous fruity wine which acquires a particularly pleasant taste with age.

Fruity amber-coloured Carcavelos is drunk as an apéritif as well as a dessert wine.

SPIRITS

The wide variety of Portuguese brandies includes *ginginha*, cherry brandy from Alcobaça, *medronho*, arbutus berry brandy and *brandimel*, honey brandy from the Algarve. *Bagaço* or *bagaceira*, a grape marc, served chilled, is the most widely drunk.

History

Portugal was part of the Iberian Peninsula until the 11C.
The earliest people were of Celtic orgin, but were overrun, in succession, by the Greeks, Carthaginians, Romans, Visigoths and in 711, the Moors, who remained in control for several centuries. Portugal's first attempt at independence came in 1065, though Spain regained control. In 1143, the country finally emerged as an independent kingdom.

ORIGINS

9C–7C BCE The Greeks and the Phoenicians establish trading posts on the coasts of the Iberian Peninsula, inhabited in the west by Lusitanian tribes, originally a Celtiberian population.

3C–2C BCE The Carthaginians master the country; the Romans intervene (Second Punic War) and take over the administration of Lusitania, so named by Augustus.
Viriate, chief of the Lusitanians, organises resistance and is assassinated in 139 BCE.

5C AD The Suevi (Swabians) and Visigoths occupy most of the Iberian Peninsula.

MOORISH OCCUPATION

711 The Moorish invasion from North Africa.

8C–9C The Christian war of **Reconquest** of the Iberian Peninsula begins at Covadonga in Asturias, led by Pelayo in 718. By the 9C, the region of Portucale, north of the Mondego, has been liberated.

THE KINGDOM FOUNDED

In 1087, Alfonso VI, King of Castile and León, undertakes the reconquest of present-day Castilla-La Mancha. He calls upon several French knights, including Henry of Burgundy, descendant of the French king Hugues Capet, and his cousin Raymond of Burgundy.
When the Moors are vanquished, Alfonso offers his daughters in marriage to the princes. Urraca, heir to the throne, marries Raymond; Tareja (Teresa) buys the county of Portucale, stretching between the Minho and Douro rivers, as her dowry to **Henry of Burgundy** in 1095. Henry thus becomes Count of Portugal.
Henry dies in 1114; Queen Tareja becomes regent pending the coming of age of her son **Afonso Henriques**. But in 1128 the latter forces his mother to relinquish her power (*see GUIMA-RÃES)*; in 1139 he breaks the bonds of vassalage imposed upon him by Alfonso VII of Castile and proclaims himself King of Portugal under the name Afonso I; Castile finally agrees in 1143.
Afonso Henriques continues the reconquest and after the victory at Ourique (1139) takes Santarém and then Lisbon (1147) with the aid of the Second Crusade's fleet.
The capture of Faro in 1249 marks the end of Moorish occupation.

BURGUNDIAN DYNASTY (1128–1383) – WARS WITH CASTILE

1279–1325 King Dinis I founds the University of Coimbra and establishes Portuguese, a dialect of the Oporto region, as the official language.

1369–83 Taking advantage of the trouble in Castile, Fernando I attempts to enlarge his kingdom; in failing he proposes the marriage of his only daughter, Beatriz, to the King of Castile, Juan I.

13 June 1373 First Treaty of Alliance with England (signed in London).

AVIS DYNASTY (1385–1578) – THE GREAT DISCOVERIES

(*see The Great Discoveries section*)

1385 Upon Fernando I's death in 1383, his son-in-law Juan of Castile claims the succession;

Detail of 15C miniature depicting Battle of Aljubarrota

© BL/Robana/age fotostock

but João, bastard brother of the late king and Grand Master of the Order of Avis is acclaimed to rule; the **Cortes** in Coimbra proclaims him King of Portugal under the name **João I**.
Seven days later, on 14 August, Juan of Castile confronts João of Avis at the **Battle of Aljubarrota** but fails.
To celebrate his victory, João builds the monastery at Batalha. He marries Philippa of Lancaster, thus sealing the alliance with England that is to last throughout Portugal's history.

1386 Treaty of Windsor with England.

1415 The **capture of Ceuta** in Morocco by João I and his sons, including **Prince Henry**, puts an end to attacks on the Portuguese coast by Barbary pirates and marks the beginning of Portuguese expansion.

1420–44 Settlement of the Madeira archipelago begins in 1420 and that of the Azores in 1444.

1481–95 **João II**, known as the Perfect Prince, promotes maritime exploration; however, he mistakenly rejects Christopher Columbus' project. During his reign Bartolomeu

Dias rounds the Cape of Good Hope (1488) and the **Treaty of Tordesillas** is signed (1494), dividing the New World into two spheres of influence, the Portuguese and the Castilian.

1492 Christopher Columbus discovers America.

1495–1521 Reign of **Manuel I**. In order to marry Isabel, daughter of the Catholic Monarchs of Spain, he expels the Jews in 1497 and Portugal loses a great many traders, bankers and learned men. **Vasco da Gama** discovers the sea route to India in 1498 and **Pedro Álvares Cabral** lands in Brazil in 1500. **Magellan**'s expedition from 1519–22 is the first to circumnavigate the world.

August 1578 **Sebastião I** is killed (see box p55) and succeeded by his great uncle and former regent, **Henrique I**, a pious man, whose reign lasts two years and ends without heir.

1580 Three of Henrique's cousins lay claim to the crown: **Dom António**, Prior of Crato, the **Duchess of Bragança** and the King of Spain, **Philip II**, son of the Infante, Isabel. The Prior of Crato seeks support in the Azores (see The AZORES).

Sebastião I, the "Regretted" 1554–1578

Dom Sebastião came to the throne in 1557 at the age of three. He was educated by a Jesuit priest who instilled in him the old-fashioned values of chivalry, which his romantic, proud nature was prone to exacerbate. He believed that a mission had been conferred upon him: namely, to conquer Africa from the Moorish infidels. In 1578, having made the decision to fulfil his destiny, he set sail for Morocco along with 17 000 men and the finest of Portuguese nobility. However, with his soldiers poorly prepared and encumbered by their stately armour under a ruthless sun, his dream was to end in brutal fashion in the muddy reaches of the Malhazin river at Alcácer Quibir, where half of his armada was to die and the other half to be taken prisoner. His body was never found. The Spanish domination that followed encouraged the development of **Sebastianism**, which transformed the young king into a long-awaited Messiah to save Portugal, thus enriching the Portuguese soul with yet another type of nostalgic longing (saudade).

Philip II sends the Duke of Alba in November 1580 to claim Portugal by force. Lisbon soon falls and Philip is elected king.

SPANISH DOMINATION (1580–1640)

1580 Philip II of Spain invades Portugal and is proclaimed king Felipe I. Spanish domination lasts 60 years.

1 Dec 1640 Uprising against the Spanish; the war of restoration of Portuguese supremacy ensues. Duke João of Bragança takes the title João IV of Portugal; the **Bragança family** remain as the ruling dynasty until 1910.

1668 Spain recognises Portugal's independence.

THE 18C

1683–1706 Pedro II on the throne.

1703 Britain and Portugal sign the Methuen Treaty and a trade treaty facilitating the shipping of port to England.

1706–50 The reign of **João V**, the Magnanimous, is one of untold magnificence – sustained by riches from Brazil – in keeping with the luxurious tastes of a king of the Baroque period. The

The Earthquake of 1755 by João Glama, Museu Nacional de Arte Antiga, Lisbon

finest testimony to the period is the monastery at Mafra *(see MAFRA)*.

1 Nov 1755   An earthquake destroys Lisbon.

1750–77   **José I** reigns assisted by his minister, the **Marquis of Pombal**. Through the latter's policies, Portugal becomes a model of enlightened despotism. Pombal expels the Jesuits in 1759.

THE NAPOLEONIC WARS

Portugal joins the first continental coalition against Revolutionary France in 1793. In 1796 Spain leaves the Convention and allies itself to France. Spain invades Portugal in 1801, when Portugal refuses to renounce its alliance with England; the resulting conflict is known as the **War of the Oranges**. To ensure a strict application of the blockade on Britain, Napoleon invades Portugal, but his commanders have little success in a country supported by English troops under the command of Wellesley. The future **Duke of Wellington** prefers guerrilla tactics and finally forces the French from the Peninsula. Portugal suffers violence and depredations at the hands of both armies with a long-term effect on the politics of the country. **General William Carr** (1768–1854) is assigned to take command of the British forces in Portugal. With the king in Brazil (until 1821), Carr takes full advantage of his power. Named Viscount of Beresford following a string of victories resulting in the **Sinatra Accord** (which allows French soldiers to return home), Carr is appointed regent by the absent **João VI**. By 1821 Beresford's tyranny provokes a conspiracy by liberal forces. He flees the country and in 1822 the same liberals obliged João to accept a liberal constitution.

THE DOWNFALL OF THE MONARCHY

1828–34   **Civil War between liberals and absolutists**. In 1822 Brazil is proclaimed independent and Pedro IV, older son of João VI, becomes Emperor Pedro I of Brazil. In 1826, on his death Pedro I retains the Brazilian throne and leaves the throne of Portugal to his daughter **Maria II**. Dom Pedro's brother Miguel, who has been appointed regent, champions the cause for an absolute monarchy and lays claim to the crown, which he eventually obtains in 1828. A bitter struggle ensues between the absolutists and the liberal supporters of Dom Pedro. Aided by the English, Dom Pedro returns to Portugal to reinstate his daughter on the throne in 1834; the Évoramonte Convention puts an end to the Civil War. In 1836 Maria II marries Prince Ferdinand of Saxe-Coburg-Gotha, who becomes king-consort.

1855–90   In spite of political restlessness during the reigns of **Pedro V** (1855–61), **Luís I** (1861–89) and **Carlos I** (1889–1908), a third Portuguese empire is reconstituted in Angola and Mozambique. The British Ultimatum ends endeavours by the Governor, **Serpa Pinto**, to set up a territorial belt linking Angola and Mozambique.

1899   Treaty of Windsor under which Portugal pledges to allow the movement of British forces through its colony of Mozambique during the Anglo-Boer war.

1 Feb 1908   Assassination in Lisbon of King Carlos I and the Crown Prince. Queen Amélia manages to save her youngest son who succeeds to the throne as **Manuel II**.

5 Oct 1910   Abdication of Manuel II, Proclamation of the Republic.

THE REPUBLIC

1910–33   The Republic cannot restore order. Entering the war against Germany in 1916

Portuguese Royal Succession

This chart is selective; it traces the affiliation of reigning monarchs with their regnal dates, their consorts and other people mentioned in the guide.

Henry of Burgundy m. Tareja of Castile

House of Burgundy

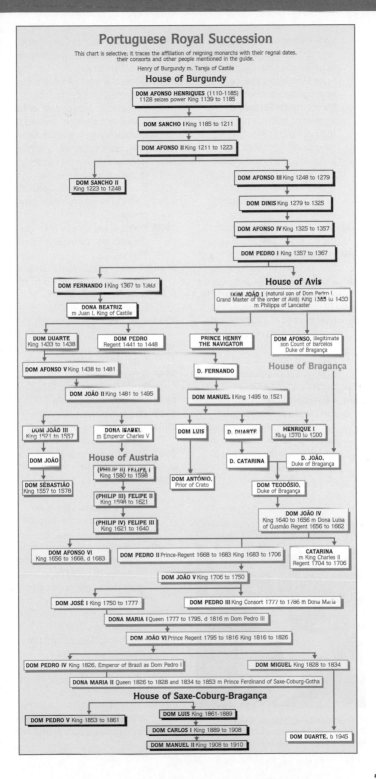

DOM AFONSO HENRIQUES (1110-1185)
1128 seizes power King 1139 to 1185

DOM SANCHO I King 1185 to 1211

DOM AFONSO II King 1211 to 1223

DOM SANCHO II King 1223 to 1248

DOM AFONSO III King 1248 to 1279

DOM DINIS King 1279 to 1325

DOM AFONSO IV King 1325 to 1357

DOM PEDRO I King 1357 to 1367

House of Avis

DOM FERNANDO I King 1367 to 1383

DONA BEATRIZ m Juan I, King of Castile

DOM JOÃO I (natural son of Dom Pedro I) Grand Master of the order of Avis) King 1385 to 1433 m Philippa of Lancaster

DOM DUARTE King 1433 to 1438

DOM PEDRO Regent 1441 to 1448

PRINCE HENRY THE NAVIGATOR

DOM AFONSO, illegitimate son Count of Barcelos Duke of Bragança

DOM AFONSO V King 1438 to 1481

D. FERNANDO

House of Bragança

DOM JOÃO II King 1481 to 1495

DOM MANUEL I King 1495 to 1521

DOM JOÃO III King 1521 to 1557

DONA ISABEL m Emperor Charles V

DOM LUIS

D. DUARTE

HENRIQUE I King 1370 to 1300

DOM JOÃO

House of Austria

(PHILIP II) FELIPE I King 1580 to 1598

DOM ANTÓNIO, Prior of Crato

D. CATARINA

D. JOÃO, Duke of Bragança

DOM SÉBASTIÃO King 1557 to 1578

(PHILIP III) FELIPE II King 1598 to 1621

DOM TEODÓSIO, Duke of Bragança

(PHILIP IV) FELIPE III King 1621 to 1640

DOM JOÃO IV King 1640 to 1656 m Dona Luisa of Gusmão Regent 1656 to 1662

DOM AFONSO VI King 1656 to 1668, d 1683

DOM PEDRO II Prince-Regent 1668 to 1683 King 1683 to 1706

CATARINA m King Charles II Regent 1704 to 1706

DOM JOÃO V King 1706 to 1750

DOM JOSÉ I King 1750 to 1777

DOM PEDRO III King Consort 1777 to 1786 m Dona Maria

DONA MARIA I Queen 1777 to 1795, d 1816 m Dom Pedro III

DOM JOÃO VI Prince Regent 1795 to 1816 King 1816 to 1826

DOM PEDRO IV King 1826, Emperor of Brazil as Dom Pedro I

DOM MIGUEL King 1828 to 1834

DONA MARIA II Queen 1826 to 1828 and 1834 to 1853 m Prince Ferdinand of Saxe-Coburg-Gotha

House of Saxe-Coburg-Bragança

DOM PEDRO V King 1853 to 1861

DOM LUIS King 1861-1889

DOM CARLOS I King 1889 to 1908

DOM DUARTE, b 1945

DOM MANUEL II King 1908 to 1910

and sending troops to France only aggravates the domestic situation. General Carmona calls upon Oliveira Salazar, professor of economics at Coimbra University. **Dr Salazar** is appointed Minister of Finance, then in 1932, Prime Minister. He restores economic and political stability but in 1933 promulgates the Constitution of the New State instituting a corporative and dictatorial regime.

1939–45 Portugal remains neutral during World War II.

1949 Portugal is one of the founding members of NATO.

1961 India annexes Goa, a Portuguese territory since 1515.

1968–70 Salazar, whose accident near the end of 1968 prevents him from taking part in affairs of state, dies in July 1970. His successor, Caetano, continues a ruinous and unpopular anti-guerrilla war in Africa.

1974 Carnation Revolution (Revolução dos Cravos): the Armed Forces Movement, led by General Spínola, seizes power on April 25. Independence of Guinea-Bissau.

António de Oliveira Salazar (1889-1970) Portuguese professor and politician who served as Prime Minister of Portugal, 1941

© World History Archive/Ann Ronan Collection/age fotostock

1975 Independence of Cape Verde Islands, Mozambique, Angola and São Tomé.

1976 General António Ramalho Eanes is elected President of the Republic. Independence of East Timor. Autonomy is granted to Macau, Madeira and the Azores.

1980 The conservative party wins the general election. Sá Carneiro forms a government, but dies in a plane crash. General Eanes's presidential mandate is renewed.

1986 Portugal becomes a member of the EEC. Mário Soares is elected President.

March 1986 600 years of friendship between Britain and Portugal celebrated with Queen Elizabeth II's state visit.

1991 Mário Soares is re-elected president.

1994 Lisbon chosen as European Capital of Culture.

1996 Jorge Sampaio elected President of the Republic.

1998 Lisbon hosts **Expo'98**.

1999 The euro is the new currency.

2001 Socialists win elections and Sampaio becomes Premier.

2002 Social Democrat José Barroso becomes leader.

2004 Barroso resigns. Social Democrat Pedro de Santana Lopes becomes Premier. Portugal hosts the Euro '04 football championships.

2005 Socialists sweep to victory. José Pinto de Sousa becomes Premier. Droughts and forest fires devastate large parts of the country.

2006 Centre-right Cavaçao Silva elected President.

2007 Portugal takes over the Presidency of Europe. The Lisbon Treaty, binding the nations of Europe closer together, is signed.

2010 Government announces package of austerity measures to reduce budget deficit, and introduces a law that permits same-sex marriages.

2011 The EU and IMF agree to a 78b.euro bailout on condition of severe cuts.

2012 Hundreds of thousands go on strike at government's austerity measures. Guimarães is European Capital of Culture.

2013 Prime Minister Passos Coelho survives a vote of no confidence.

2014 Portugal exits international bailout without obtaining back-up credit.

2015 Govt. allows descendants of Jews expelled from the country centuries ago to claim citizenship.

2015 Socialist leader Antonio Costa forms centre-left government.

2016 Independent Marcelo Rebelo de Sousa is elected president, addressing the country's economic imbalances.

2018 Finance Minister Mário Centeno elected president of the Europgroup.

2019 Fiscal consolidation continues: Moody's changes Portugal's rating from stable to positive.

Great Discoveries

On 25 July 1415, some 200 ships under the command of Dom João I and his three sons, including Prince Henry, set sail from Lisbon. The capture of Ceuta in Morocco ended attacks by Barbary pirates, resulting in Portuguese control of the Straits of Gibraltar. The Portuguese also hoped that the expedition would reward them with gold and slaves from the Sudan.

At the end of the Middle Ages wealth lay in the hands of the Moors and Venetians, who monopolised the spice and perfume trade brought overland from the Orient to the Mediterranean. To bypass these intermediaries, a sea route had to be found, and Henry the Navigator was to devote his life to this dream.

THE SAGRES SCHOOL

Prince Henry the Navigator (1394–1460) retired to the Sagres promontory together with cosmographers, cartographers and navigators to try and work out a sea route from Europe to India. **Madeira** was discovered in 1419 by João Gonçalves Zarco and Tristão Vaz Teixeira, the **Azores** in 1427 (supposedly by Diogo de Silves), and in 1434 **Gil**

Eanes rounded **Cape Bojador**, then the farthest point known to western man. Each time they discovered new land the mariners erected a **padrão**, a cairn surmounted by a cross and the arms of Portugal, to mark their presence. Prince Henry inspired new methods of colonisation by setting up **trading posts** *(feitoras)*, exchanges and banks. These offices, set up and run by private individuals, sometimes fostered the development of towns independent of the local powers, such as Goa. Companies were created to control trade in a particular commodity, for which the monopoly rights were often acquired. There were also **deeds of gift**, usually of land, to ships' captains with the proviso that the area be developed. Henry died in 1460, but the stage was set.

NEW TERRITORIES

The major discoveries were made during the reigns of João II and Manuel I who were both grand nephews of Henry the Navigator. **Diogo Cão** reached the mouth of the Congo in 1482 and the whole coast of Angola then came under Portuguese control. In 1488 **Bartolomeu Dias** rounded the Cape of Storms, which was immediately rechristened the Cape of Good Hope by Dom João II. A few years earlier **Christopher Columbus**, a Genoese navigator with a Portuguese wife, had the idea of

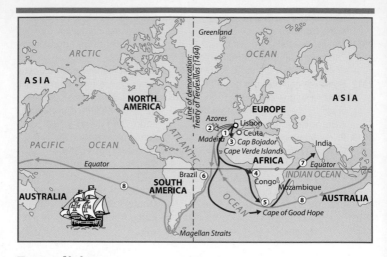

Expeditions (1419–1522)

1 1419—Madeira
Two captains of Prince Henry the Navigator, João Gonçalves Zarco and Tristão Vaz Teixaira, were driven by a storm to the island they called Porto Santo. When, later, an expedition came to populate the island, they discovered Madeira and took possession on behalf of the Portuguese crown.

2 1427—The Azores
Portuguese explorer Diogo da Silves, accidentally came upon the island of Santa Maria (the southernmost island in the archipelago) in 1427. Subsequent explorers found São Miguel and then Terçeira, which means third in Portuguese.

3 1434—Cape Bojador
The discovery of a passable route around the African headland by explorer Gil Eanes was considered a real breakthrough for traders en route to Africa and later India. This was Eanes' second attempt, having failed previously in 1433.

4 1482—Congo River Mouth
Diogo Cão was the first European to discover the mouth of the Congo. For almost 400 years the course of the river remained unknown until the 1860s.

5 1488—Cape of Good Hope
Bartolomeu Dias led this voyage along the west coastline of Africa to discover how far south the African continent extended and whether it would be possible to round the continent and open up trading routes to the east.

6 1500—Brazil
Pedro Álvares Cabral became the first European to discover this South American country, although this is contested. A fleet of 13 ships and 1 500 men left Lisbon on 9 March and Cabral landed on the coast of Brazil on 22 April. Three days later the entire fleet sailed into Porto Seguro.

7 1498—Mozambique and India
Vasco da Gama set sail on 8 July 1497 with three ships. He rounded the Cape of Good Hope and sailed north, stopping along the coast of Africa. He arrived in Calicut on the southwest coast of India on 20 May 1498.

8 1522—Magellan circumnavigation
Ferdinand Magellan's expedition was the first to sail from the Atlantic Ocean into the Pacific Ocean and the first to circumnavigate the earth. Of the 237 men who set out on five ships, only 18 completed the voyage. Magellan himself did not complete the entire voyage, being killed during the Battle of Mactan in the Philippines.

Monument of Discoveries in Belém, Lisbon

© Jean-Heintz/hemis.fr

sailing to India by a westerly route. His proposals, rebuffed in Lisbon, found favour with the Catholic Monarchs and in 1492 he discovered the New World. In 1494, under the **Treaty of Tordesillas** and with the Pope's approval, the Kings of Portugal and Castile divided the newly discovered and as yet undiscovered territories of the world between them: all lands west of a meridian 370 sea leagues west of the Cape Verde Islands were to belong to Castile, all east to Portugal. The position of the dividing meridian has led some historians to speculate as to whether Portugal knew of the existence of Brazil even before its official discovery by **Pedro Álvares Cabral** in 1500.

The exploration of the African coast by the Portuguese continued. On 8 July 1497, a fleet of four ships commanded by Admiral **Vasco da Gama** sailed from Lisbon with the commission to reach India by way of the sea route round the Cape. By March 1498 Vasco da Gama had reached Mozambique and on 20 May he landed in Calicut (Kozhicode, southern India): the sea route to India had been discovered. This epic voyage was later sung in **The Lusiads** (*Os Lusíadas*) by the poet Camões.

In 1501 **Gaspar Corte Real** discovered Newfoundland, but King Manuel was interested primarily in Asia. Within a few years the Portuguese had explored the coastlines of Asia. By 1515 they were in control of the Indian Ocean, thanks to fortified outposts like Goa, which had been established by **Afonso de Albuquerque** in 1510.

It was, however, on behalf of the King of Spain that the Portuguese **Fernão**

© DEA PICTURE LIBRARY/age fotostock

Portrait of Vasco da Gama, Museu de Marinha, Lisbon

de Magalhães (Magellan) set out in 1519 and landed in India in 1521. Though he was assassinated by the natives of the Philippines, one of his vessels continued the journey to become the first to circumnavigate the world in 1522.

In 1517 King Manuel I sent an ambassador to **China** but this proved a failure and it was not until 1554 that the Portuguese were able to trade with Canton and make contact with Macau.

In 1542 the Portuguese arrived in Japan where they caused political upheaval by introducing firearms. The Jesuits, whose Society of Jesus had been founded in 1540, became very active there and by 1581 there were almost 150 000 Christians.

The Discoveries had a huge impact on western civilization. New products – the sweet potato, maize, tobacco, cocoa and indigo – were introduced to Europe; gold from Africa and America flooded in through the Tagus. Portugal and Spain became great powers.

A DIFFERENT WORLD

The sea faring age and Europe's discovery of new lands and civilizations disrupted every sphere of global society. in Europe, the discovery of the existence of formerly unknown peoples posed religious problems: did the men of the New World have a soul and were they marked by original sin? These doubts presaged the Reformation and the development of the critical approach led to the advancement of modern science.

Emerging trade empires began to thrive on cheap manual labour, bringing about history's most ignominious period of international slave trading.

EVANESCENT RICHES

Portugal overspent its strength; many went overseas and the population halved from two to one million; riches encouraged idlers and adventurers; land was not tilled, wheat and rye had to be imported; crafts and skills were lost while the cost of living rose steeply. Gold was exchanged for goods until little remained. Two years later Portugal came under Spanish control.

Art and Architecture

ORIGINS

Portugal's prehistoric sites range from the megaliths around Évora and the rock engravings in the Vale do Côa. Highlights of the Iron Age include ruins in Citânia de Briteiros, and the Roman remains at Conímbriga, Tróia and Évora. There are also small pre-Romanesque churches that recall the different architectural influences that swept across the Iberian peninsula from the north and the east. These influences include Visigothic (Igreja de São Pedro de Balsemão near Lamego and Igreja de Santo Amaro in Beja), Mozarabic (Capela de São Pedro de Lourosa in Oliveira do Hospital) and Byzantine (Capela de São Frutuoso near Braga).

MIDDLE AGES (11C–15C)
ROMANESQUE ART

The Romanesque influence arrived in Portugal in the 11C. Brought from France by Burgundian knights and monks, it retained many French traits. Nevertheless, the influence of Santiago de Compostela, particularly in northern Portugal, produced a style more Galician than French, which was further enhanced through the use of granite. Monuments have a massive and rough appearance with capitals that show the granite's resistance to the mason's chisel.

Cathedrals were rebuilt at the same time as local fortified castles and often resemble them. The cathedrals in Coimbra, Lisbon, Évora, Oporto and Braga are good examples. Country churches, built later, sometimes have richly carved main

RATES – Chevet of Igreja de São Pedro (12C–13C)

This church is typical of the Portuguese Romanesque style and is part of the remains of a monastery founded by Henry of Burgundy for the monks of Cluny.

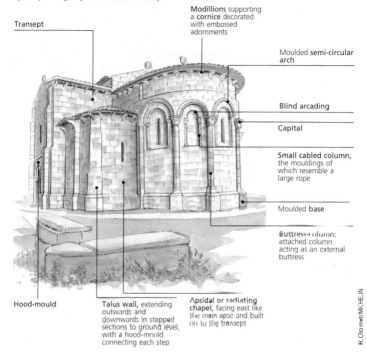

Transept

Modillions supporting a **cornice** decorated with embossed adornments

Moulded **semi-circular arch**

Blind arcading

Capital

Small cabled column, the mouldings of which resemble a large rope

Moulded **base**

Buttress-column: attached column acting as an external buttress

Hood-mould

Talus wall, extending outwards and downwards in stepped sections to ground level, with a hood-mould connecting each step

Apsidal or radiating chapel, facing east like the main apse and built on to the transept

H. Chomet/MICHELIN

doorways. Interior design frequently including pointed arches and even groined vaulting, was often transformed by Manueline or Baroque additions.

GOTHIC ART

While the Romanesque style blossomed in chapels and cathedrals in the north, Gothic architecture developed most vigorously at the end of the 13C in Coimbra and Lisbon in the form of large monasteries. The churches, designed with a nave and two corresponding aisles with polygonal apses and apsidal chapels, retain the proportions and simplicity of the Romanesque style.

The Mosteiro de Alcobaça served as a model for the 14C cloisters of the cathedrals in Coimbra, Lisbon and Évora. Flamboyant Gothic found its perfect expression in the **Mosteiro da Batalha** even though this edifice was only completed in the Manueline period.

Sculpture – Gothic sculpture developed in the 14C for the adornment of tombs, but barely featured as decoration on tympana and doorways. Capitals and cornices were ornamented only with geometric or plant motifs with the exception of a few stylised animals or occasional human forms (capitals in the Mosteiro de Celas in Coimbra). Funerary art flowered in three centres, Lisbon, Évora and Coimbra from where, under the influence of **Master Pero**, it spread into northern Portugal, principally to Oporto, Lamego, Oliveira do Hospital and São João de Tarouca.

The most beautiful tombs, those of Inês de Castro and Dom Pedro in the Mosteiro de Alcobaça, were carved from limestone. Coimbra's influence continued into the 15C under **João Afonso** and **Diogo Pires the Elder**.

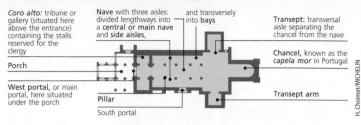

LISBON – Ground plan of Igreja de Santa Maria (Mosteiro dos Jerónimos), Belém

This church is a **hall-church** (the nave is the same height as the aisles; when these have different heights a distinction is made between the central nave and the aisles).

Coro alto: tribune or gallery (situated here above the entrance) containing the stalls reserved for the clergy

Porch

West portal, or main portal, here situated under the porch

Nave with three aisles: divided lengthways into a central or main nave and side aisles,

and transversely into **bays**

Pillar

South portal

Transept: transversal aisle separating the chancel from the nave

Chancel, known as the *capela mor* in Portugal

Transept arm

H. Choimet/MICHELIN

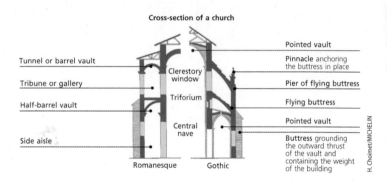

Cross-section of a church

Tunnel or barrel vault

Tribune or gallery

Half-barrel vault

Side aisle

Clerestory window

Triforium

Central nave

Pointed vault

Pinnacle anchoring the buttress in place

Pier of flying buttress

Flying buttress

Pointed vault

Buttress grounding the outward thrust of the vault and containing the weight of the building

Romanesque   Gothic

H. Choimet/MICHELIN

A second centre developed at Batalha inspired by **Master Huguet** (tombs of Dom João I and Philippa of Lancaster).

MILITARY ARCHITECTURE

The Portuguese, in the wars first against the Moors and then the Spanish, built castles. The first examples mark the successive stages of the **Reconquest**, the second, from 13C to the 17C, guard the major routes of communication. Most of these castles, built in the Middle Ages, are similar, double perimeter walls circling a keep or *Torre de Menagem*, crowned with pyramid capped merlons. Heavily fortified gates and innovative stonework are features borrowed from Moorish architecture.

MANUELINE PERIOD (1490–1520)

The Manueline style marks the transition from Gothic to Renaissance in Portugal; its name recalls its appearance during

the reign of Manuel I. Despite the brevity of the period in which it developed, the Manueline style's undeniable originality has given it major importance in all aspects of Portuguese art. It reflects the passion, which inspired all of Portugal at the time, for the sea and of faraway territories which had just been discovered, and manifests the strength and riches accumulating on the banks of the Tagus.

ARCHITECTURE

Churches remained Gothic in their general plan, in the height of their columns and network vaulting – but novelty and movement appeared in the way columns were twisted to form spirals; triumphal arches were adorned with mouldings in the form of nautical cables; ribs of plain pointed arched vaulting were given heavy liernes in round or square relief; these, in their turn, were transformed by further ornamentation into four-pointed stars or were supplemented by deco-

BATALHA – Monastery: Capela do Fundador (15C)

The chapel housing the tombs of João I, his wife Philippa of Lancaster, and their sons, including Henry the Navigator, is a magnificent example of Flamboyant Gothic architecture. It is a square room crowned with an octagonal two-storey lantern and a ribbed vault shaped like an eight-pointed star.

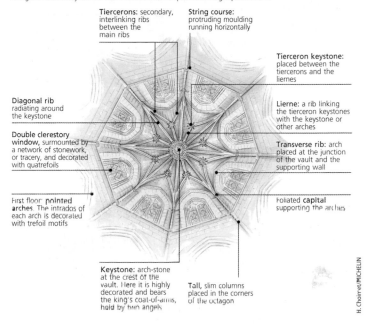

Tiercerons: secondary, interlinking ribs between the main ribs

String course: protruding moulding running horizontally

Tierceron keystone: placed between the tiercerons and the liernes

Diagonal rib radiating around the keystone

Lierne: a rib linking the tierceron keystones with the keystone or other arches

Double clerestory window, surmounted by a network of stonework, or tracery, and decorated with quatrefoils

Transverse rib: arch placed at the junction of the vault and the supporting wall

First floor: pointed arches. The intrados of each arch is decorated with trefoil motifs

Foliated capital supporting the arches

Keystone: arch-stone at the crest of the vault. Here it is highly decorated and bears the king's coat-of-arms, held by two angels

Tall, slim columns placed in the corners of the octagon

H. Choiret/MICHELIN

ÓBIDOS – Castle (13C-14C)

The fortress built by the Moors on the site of a Luso-Roman hillfort was considerably modified after the reconquest of Óbidos. However, Arab influence is still evident, particularly in the pyramidal shape of the merlons on the Dom Ferdinand Tower and in the absence of architectural features such as machicolations on the 42ft/13m-high walls.

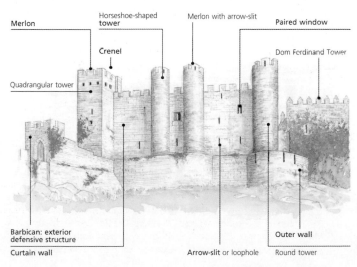

Merlon

Horseshoe-shaped tower

Merlon with arrow-slit

Paired window

Crenel

Dom Ferdinand Tower

Quadrangular tower

Barbican: exterior defensive structure

Outer wall

Curtain wall

Arrow-slit or loophole

Round tower

H. Choiret/MICHELIN

Domestic Architecture

Algarve

R. Corbel

Portugal has a number of different styles of traditional housing; these are most apparent in the Alentejo and the Algarve.

The North – The most popular building material is granite. Houses are massive with tiled roofs. As chimneys are very small or even non-existent, the smoke has to escape through gaps in the roof, the doorway or the windows. The outside stairway leads to a stone balcony or veranda large enough to be used as a living room.

Alentejo

R. Corbel

On country estates in the Douro valley, simple cottages stand alongside elegant manor-houses *(solares)*, which are often whitewashed.

The Centre: Estremadura and Beira Litoral – The limestone used in the region's houses adds a pleasant touch to their appearance. The façades are often ornamented with cornices and stucco; outside staircases have disappeared.

Alentejo – The houses, built to shelter the inhabitants from the summer glare and heat, are low-lying single storey structures with whitewashed walls and small doors and windows. Nevertheless, the winters are so harsh that huge square or cylindrical chimneys are a local feature. Building materials vary according to the region: usually *taipa* (dried clay), or adobe (mud mixed with cut straw and dried in the sun), which was used in Moorish times. Bricks are used for decorative features, for chimneys, crenellations and verandahs, while around Estremoz marble is common.

Minho

R. Corbel/MICHELIN

Madeira

R. Corbel

The Algarve – The white houses squat low, several juxtaposed cubes making up each dwelling. The white flat-roofed houses in Olhão and Fuseta resemble the villages of North Africa. Very occasionally the terrace is replaced by a four-sided peaked roof, *telhado de tesoura*, which some attribute to a Chinese influence. Peaked roofs are mostly to be seen in Faro, Tavira and Santa Luzia. Chimneys are slender and elegant, gracefully pierced, painted white or built of brick laid in decorative patterns, crowned with a ball, a finial, a vase, or an ornament of some kind.

Madeira and the Azores – In Madeira, traditional mountain dwellings have a thatched roof with two eaves that descend right down to the ground, thus covering the whole house. The main door on the front of the house is flanked by two small windows, with an occasional third one above it. All these openings are set into the wall with colourful surrounds. Houses in the Azores are similar to those in the Algarve, offering a reminder of the islands' first inhabitants. The Empires (*Impérios*) of the Holy Ghost are brightly-coloured original buildings, similar in style to chapels, which have large windows and are used to house objects for the worship of the Holy Ghost.

Typical Features

Pavements – Throughout the country and even in Madeira and the Azores, pavements and squares are paved with beautifully patterned compositions of alternating blocks of black basalt, golden sandstone, white limestone and grey granite. These are known as **empedrados**.

Windmills (Moinhos) – There were about 2 000 windmills in Portugal several years ago but most have now been abandoned and are in ruins. They may still be seen on hilltops around Nazaré, Óbidos and Viana do Castelo. The most common, the Mediterranean, is a cylindrical tower built of stone or hard-packed clay supporting a turning conical roof bearing a mast with four triangular sails.

Stone monuments (Padrões) – These public monuments, memorials bearing the cross and the arms of Portugal, were erected by Portuguese explorers when they reached new lands. They may be seen in former colonies and in Madeira and the Azores.

© Ion Arnold Images/hemis.fr

Empedrados in front of the cathedral, Elvas

Windmill in Sesimbra, Setúbal

© José Elias/Bigstockphoto.com

Manueline style window of the Convento do Cristo, Tomar

FREIXO DE ESPADA-À-CINTA – South porch of the church

The small parish church is attributed to Boytac and displays the main characteristics of the **Manueline style**: twisted columns interspersed with rings, vegetal decoration and spiral pinnacles. This decoration, an extension of the Mudéjar style, is not unlike the Plateresque style found in Spain. In this church, the style is only evident on the portals, but it later became more popular and could also be found inside buildings and on façades.

Spiral **pinnacle**

Vegetal decoration

Engaged twisted columns framing the composition

Pier or jamb shaft: decorated lateral pier of an opening

Archivolt: comprising a series of arched mouldings

Rounded arch: here the three rounded arches are extradosed

Rings dividing the columns

Footing

Pedestal

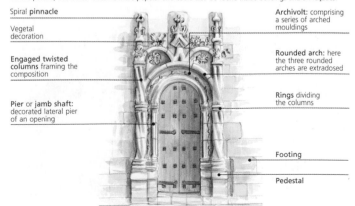

Mudéjar influence (13C-16C)

After the Christian Reconquest an artistic style developed in the Iberian peninsula which borrowed certain decorative features from Islamic art and which became known as Mudéjar, the name given to Muslims who had remained under Christian rule. In Portugal this influence is particularly noticeable in the Évora region, where King Manuel I had a palace built, of which only one pavilion remains.

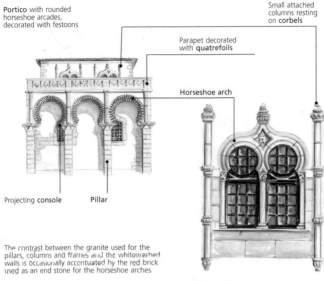

Portico with rounded horseshoe arcades, decorated with festoons

Small attached columns resting on **corbels**

Parapet decorated with **quatrefoils**

Horseshoe arch

Projecting **console**   Pillar

The contrast between the granite used for the pillars, columns and frames and the whitewashed walls is occasionally accentuated by the red brick used as an end stone for the horseshoe arches

Paired windows under rounded horseshoe arches with a curved moulded frame

H. Holmet/MICHELIN

rative cables occasionally intertwined into mariners' knots. The contour of the vaulting itself evolved, flattening out and resting on arches supported on consoles. The height of the aisles was increased, so giving rise to true hall-churches.

SCULPTURE

The Manueline style shows its character in the form of decoration. Windows, doorways, rose windows and balustrades are covered with sprigs of laurel leaves, poppy heads, roses, corn cobs, acorns, oak leaves, artichokes, cardoons, pearls, scales, ropes, anchors, terrestrial globes, armillary spheres and lastly the Cross of the Order of Christ, which forms a part of every decorative scheme.

ARTISTS

Diogo de Boytac was responsible for the first Manueline buildings, the Igreja do Convento de Jesus at Setúbal, and the cathedral *(sé)* at Guarda. He also contributed to the construction of the Mosteiro dos Jerónimos in Belém, Lisbon, the Igreja do Mosteiro da Santa Cruz in Coimbra and the Mosteiro da Batalha. His artistry lay in magnificent complication: twisted columns, of which he was the master, were covered with overlapping laurel leaves, scales and rings; doorways, which were a major element in Manueline art, stood in a rectangular setting bordered by turned columns crowned with spiralled pinnacles; in the centre of the whole or above it stood the Manueline emblems of the shield, the Cross of the Order of Christ and the armillary sphere.

Mateus Fernandes, whose art was distinctly influenced by the elegance

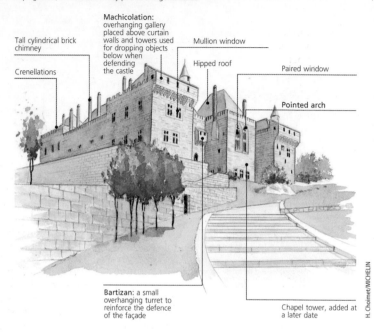

GUIMARÃES – Paço dos Duques de Bragança (15C)

Built by the first Duke of Bragança, the palace has been restored to its original appearance and bears traces of both Norman and Burgundian influence. Its defensive character can be seen in the huge corner towers, crenels and covered machicolations. It prefigures the buildings dating from the Renaissance period with their sloping roofs, numerous chimney pots and large windows.

Machicolation: overhanging gallery placed above curtain walls and towers used for dropping objects below when defending the castle

Tall cylindrical brick chimney

Crenellations

Mullion window

Hipped roof

Paired window

Pointed arch

Bartizan: a small overhanging turret to reinforce the defence of the façade

Chapel tower, added at a later date

H. Choimet/MICHELIN

of Flamboyant Gothic, brought a Manueline touch to Batalha. Decoration, which he usually designed as an infinitely repeating plant, geometric or calligraphic motif, takes precedence over volume – the doorway to the Capelas Imperfeitas (Unfinished Chapels) at Batalha is outstanding for the exuberance of its decoration.

Diogo de Arruda was the most original Manueline artist. He designed the famous and marvellously inventive Tomar window. Nautical themes were a positive obsession with this artist.

Francisco de Arruda was the architect of Lisbon's Torre de Belém. He rejected the decorative excesses of his brother, preferring the simplicity of Gothic design embellished with Moorish motifs.

The Arruda brothers were recognised equally as the "master architects of the Alentejo", where they displayed their skill in combining the Manueline style

with Moorish themes which gave rise to an entirely new style, the **Luso-Moorish**. This design is characterised by the horseshoe arch adorned with delicate mouldings. Most of the seigneurial mansions and castles in the Alentejo, as well as the royal palaces in Sintra and Lisbon, bear the stamp of this style.

Simultaneously, as Manueline architecture was reaching its peak at the end of the 15C, Portuguese sculpture came under Flemish influence due to **Olivier de Gand** and **Jean d'Ypres** – their masterpiece is the carved wooden altarpiece in Coimbra's Sé Velha. **Diogo Pires the Younger** followed, adopting Manueline themes in his work, the best example of which is the font in the Mosteiro de Leça do Bailio (1515).

In the early 16C artists came from Galicia and Biscay to work in northern Portugal. There they helped build the churches at Caminha, Braga, Vila do Conde and Viana do Castelo. The obvious influences in their work are Flamboyant and Spanish Plateresque. From 1517 onwards, two Biscayan artists, **João** and **Diogo de Castilho** worked successively in Lisbon, Tomar and Coimbra. Their art, which had much of the Plateresque style in it, became integrated in the Manueline style (Mosteiro dos Jerónimos).

PAINTING 1450–1550
THE PRIMITIVES (1450–1505)

Early painters were influenced by Flemish art, introduced into Portugal partly through close commercial ties between Lisbon and the Low Countries.

Only **Nuno Gonçalves**, author of the famous **São Vicente polyptych** (*see Museu de Arte Antiga, Lisbon*) remained truly original, not least in the way the picture's composition evoked a tapestry more than a painting. Unfortunately none of his other works are known except for the cartouches for the Arzila and Tangier tapestries which hang in the Collegiate Church of Pastrana in Spain. A group of "masters", including the **Master of Sardoal**, left many works that may be seen throughout the country's museums in the sections on Portuguese Primitives. Among the Flemish painters who came to Portugal, **Francisco Henriques** and **Carlos Frei** stand out for their rich use of colour.

THE MANUELINE PAINTERS (1505–50)

The Manueline painters created a true Portuguese School of painting which was characterised by delicacy of design, beauty and accuracy of colour, realism in the composition of the backgrounds, life-size human figures and an expressive naturalism in the portrayal of people's faces tempered, however, with a certain idealism. The major artists in the school worked in either Viseu or Lisbon. The **Viseu School** was headed by **Vasco Fernandes**, known as Grão (Great) Vasco, whose early works, including the altarpiece at Lamego, reveal Flemish influence. His later work showed more originality and a richness of colour. **Gaspar Vaz**, whose works can be seen in the Igreja São João de Tarouca, began painting at the Lisbon School, but painted his best pictures at Viseu.

The **Lisbon School** – established around **Jorge Afonso**, painter for King Manuel I – saw the development of several very talented artists:

♦ **Cristóvão de Figueiredo** who uses black and grey in portraiture.

♦ **Garcia Fernandes**, painter of sacred art, notably altarpieces.

♦ **Gregório Lopes**, who excelled in backgrounds which present contemporary Portuguese life.

THE RENAISSANCE

The Renaissance style, which retained its essential Italian and French characteristics in Portugal, spread – particularly in sculpture – from Coimbra, where several French artists had settled.

Nicolas Chanterene, whose style remained entirely faithful to the principles of the Italian Renaissance, undertook the decoration of the north door of the Mosteiro dos Jerónimos in Belém before becoming the master sculptor of the Coimbra School. The pulpit in the Igreja da Santa Cruz in Coimbra is his masterpiece. **Jean de Rouen** excelled in altarpieces and low reliefs, as may be seen in the Mosteiro de Celas in Coimbra. **Houdart** succeeded Nicolas Chanterene in 1530 at Coimbra as grand mas-

Detail of Infant panel of Saint Vincent polyptych attributed to Nuno Gonçalves, Museu Nacional de Arte Antiga, Lisbon

© Luísa Oliveira/José Paulo Ruas/Direção-Geral do Património Cultural/ Arquivo de Documentação Fotográfica

Azulejos

Ever since the 15C the *azulejo* has been a component of the different styles of Portuguese architecture that have followed one another through the centuries. There is some controversy as to the etymological origin of the word *azulejo*; some say it comes from *azul* meaning blue, others that it in fact derives from the Arabic *az-zulay* or *al zuleich* which means a smooth piece of terra-cotta.

Origin

The first *azulejos* came from Andalucía in Spain where they were used as decoration in alcázars and palaces. They were introduced into Portugal by King Manuel I who, having been dazzled by the Alhambra in Granada, decided to have his Sintra palace decorated with these rich ceramic tiles. *Azulejos* at that time took the form of alicatados, pieces of monochrome glazed earthenware cut and assembled into geometric patterns. The process was superseded by that of the corda seca in which a fine oil and manganese strip were used to separate the different enamels, and when fired, blackened to form an outline for the various motifs. Another method for separating the motifs was known as aresta and consisted of drawing ridges in the clay itself. In the 16C, the Italian Francesco Nicoloso introduced the Italian majolica technique, in which the terra-cotta was covered with a layer of white enamel which could then be coloured. *Azulejos* thus developed into another type of artistic medium with a wide range of decorative possibilities. The Portuguese created a standard square with 14cm/5.5in sides and opened their own workshops in Lisbon.

Renaissance and Mannerist styles

Towards the middle of the 16C Flemish influence took precedence over Spanish, and more complex *azulejo* panels were used to decorate churches; the transept in the Igreja São Roque in Lisbon is a good example. *Azulejos* were in great demand for decorating summer houses and gardens. The finest examples may be seen at Quinta da Bacalhoa and date from 1565. They consist of wonderful multicoloured panels with an Italian majolica-ware quality, which illustrate allegories of great rivers. The panel of Nossa Senhora da Vida, in the Museu do Azulejo in Lisbon, dates from the same period.

Polychrome panel, Palácio dos Marqueses da Fronteira, Lisbon

© Mark Edward Smith/Tips Images

17C

Portugal entered a period of austerity under Spanish domination. In order to decorate church walls without incurring great expense, simple monochrome tiles were used and placed in geometric patterns. The Igreja de Marvila in Santarém is a fine example. A style known as *tapete*, a sort of tile-carpet or tapestry, was developed, repeated in blocks of four, 16 or 36 tiles, which resembled oriental hangings on account of their geometric or floral patterns.

The restoration of the monarchy was followed by a period of great creative development. There was a return to figurative motifs on panels with illustrations of mythological scenes or caricatures of contemporary society life. Traditional blues and yellows were enhanced by greens and purples; there are

Detail of 18C panel depicting Lisbon before the 1755 earthquake, Museo Nacional do Azulejo, Lisbon

© Krzysztof Dydynski/Getty Images

fine examples at the Palácio dos Marqueses da Fronteira in Lisbon. Little by little, multicoloured tiles gave way to cobalt blue motifs on a white enamel background as may be seen in the Victory Room of the Palácio dos Marqueses da Fronteira.

18C

Tiles in the 18C were almost exclusively blue and white. This fashion developed from Chinese porcelain, popular at the time of the Great Discoveries. *Azulejos* were decorated by true artists and masters including **António Pereira**, **Manuel dos Santos** and especially **António de Oliveira Bernardes** and his son **Policarpo**. Their works include the Capela dos Remédios in Peniche, the Igreja de São Lourenço in Almansil and the Forte de São Filipe in Setúbal.

The reign of João V (1706–50) was characterised by magnificence, with gold from Brazil funding all manner of extravagance. The taste of the day was for dramatic effect which expressed itself particularly well in *azulejos*. Panels became veritable pictures, with surrounds of intermingling festoons, tassels, fluttering angels and pilasters – the **Baroque style** in full bloom. The main artists at the time were **Bartolomeu Antunes** and **Nicolau de Freitas**.

Igreja de São Lourenço, Almansil, Algarve

© Joae Fuste Raga/age fotostock

The second half of the 18C was marked by the **Rocaille style** (rock and shell motifs). There was also a return to polychromy with yellow, brown and purple being the dominant colours; painting became more delicate; smaller motifs were popular and frames were decorated with scrolls, plant motifs and shells as may be seen at the Palácio de Queluz. The opening of the Fábrica Real de Cerâmica in Rato in 1767 meant that *azulejos* could be manufactured in great quantity. The **neo-Classical style** was framed by garlands, pilasters and urns.

ter of statuary. His sculptures are easily recognisable for their realism.

The advance in architecture, which came later than in the other arts, was brought about by native Portuguese: **Miguel de Arruda** introduced a classical note to Batalha after 1533; **Diogo de Torralva** completed the Convento de Cristo in Tomar; **Afonso Álvares** began the transition to classical design by giving buildings a monumental simplicity.

CLASSICAL ART

The classical period saw the triumph of the Jesuit style with **Filippo Terzi**, an Italian architect who arrived in Portugal in 1576, and **Baltazar Álvares** (1550–1624); churches became rectangular in plan and were built without transepts, ambulatories or apses.

Painting came under Spanish influence and produced only two major artists: **Domingos Vieira** (1600–78), whose portraits are vividly alive, and Josefa de Ayala, known as **Josefa de Óbidos**

(1634–84). A feeling for classical composition is apparent in the work of the gold and silversmiths of the period. The 17C was marked by the Indo-Portuguese style of furniture, typified by marquetry secretaries, rare woods and ivory.

BAROQUE ART (LATE 17C–18C)

The Baroque style, which owes its name to the Portuguese word *barroco* – a rough pearl – corresponds to the spirit of the Counter Reformation.

ARCHITECTURE

Baroque architecture abandoned the symmetry of the classical style and sought movement, volume, a sense of depth through the use of curved lines and an impression of grandeur. The beginning of Baroque architecture coincided with the end of Spanish domination. In the 17C, architecture took on an austere and simple appearance under **João Nunes Tinoco** and **João Turiano**,

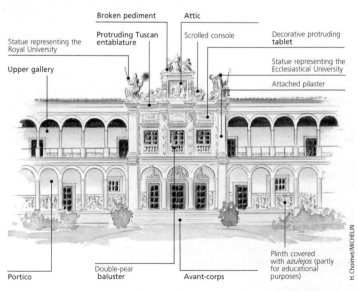

ÉVORA – Cloisters of the old university (16C)

The former Jesuit university (Antiga Universidade dos Jesuitas) was inspired by the Italian Renaissance. The central triple-bayed avant-corps, flanked by attached pilasters topped by statues, leads to the Sala das Actas (Hall of Acts). Above the central bay a crowned attic ornamented with an escutcheon bears a broken pediment decorated with a group of sculptures. Note the rounded arcades supported by slender columns and a pedestal in the upper gallery and by columns in the portico.

Broken pediment — Attic

Protruding Tuscan entablature — Scrolled console — Decorative protruding tablet

Statue representing the Royal University

Statue representing the Ecclesiastical University

Attached pilaster

Upper gallery

Plinth covered with *azulejos* (partly for educational purposes)

Portico — Double-pear baluster — Avant-corps

H. Cholmet/MICHELIN

LISBON – Praça do Comércio (18C)

After the earthquake on 1 November 1755, the Marquis of Pombal decided to demolish and rebuild the Baixa district. Between Terreiro do Paço, renamed Praça do Comércio, and the Rossio, he created a district built on a grid plan, with streets intersecting at right angles where all the buildings had three floors and where just a few decorative features distinguished one street from the next. This new style, partly inspired by the city's architectural past, became known as the **Pombaline style**.

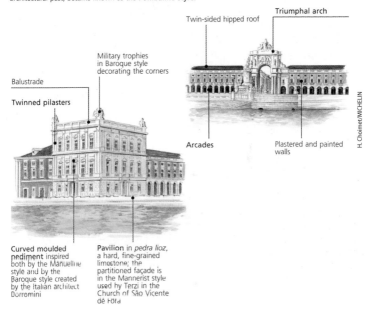

Twin-sided hipped roof

Triumphal arch

Military trophies in Baroque style decorating the corners

Balustrade

Twinned pilasters

Arcades

Plastered and painted walls

H. Choimet/MICHELIN

Curved moulded pediment inspired both by the Manueline style and by the Baroque style created by the Italian architect Borromini

Pavilion in *pedra lioz*, a hard, fine-grained limestone; the partitioned façade is in the Mannerist style used by Terzi in the Church of São Vicente de Fora

but from the end of the century onwards façades became alive with angels, garlands and the interplay of curving lines, particularly at Braga. The architect **Joao Antunes** advocated an octagonal plan for religious buildings (Igreja da Santa Engrácia in Lisbon). In the 18C King João V invited foreign artists to Portugal. The German **Friedrich Ludwig** and the Hungarian **Mardel**, both trained in the Italian School, brought a monumental style, best seen in the Mosteiro de Mafra. True Baroque architecture developed in the north and can be seen in both religious and civic buildings (Igreja de Bom Jesus near Braga and Solar de Mateus near Vila Real), where the whitewashed façades contrast with the pilasters and cornices which frame them. In Oporto, **Nicolau Nasoni**, of Italian origin, adorned façades with floral motifs, palm leaves and swags, while in Braga, architecture bordered on Rococo in style (Palácio do Raio in Braga, Igreja de Santa Maria Madalena in Falperra).

DECORATION

Azulejos and *Talha Dourada* were popular forms of decoration, the latter being the Portuguese name for the heavily gilded wood used in the adornment of church interiors, including, from 1650 onwards, high altarpieces which were first carved before being gilded. In the 17C altarpieces resembled doorways; on either side of the altar, surrounded by a stepped throne, twisted columns rose up while the screen itself was covered in decorative motifs in high relief including vines, bunches of grapes, birds and cherubim.

Altarpieces in the 18C were often out of proportion, invading the ceiling and the chancel walls. Entablatures with broken pediments crowned columns against which stood atlantes or other statues. Altarpieces were also surmounted by baldaquins.

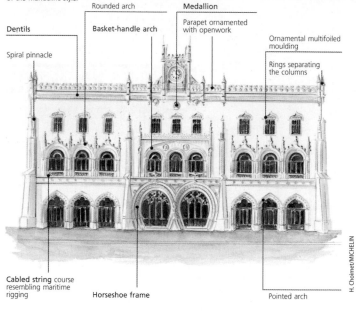

LISBON – Main railway station, Praça do Rossio (19C)

Built in 1886-87 by José Luis Monteiro, the façade of this building, a beautiful example of the neo-Manueline style, conceals an iron structure. The harmony of the three sections on the first floor is achieved through slender polygonal columns which rest on the sloping retaining walls of the ground floor. The crowning aedicule above houses a clock. The decorative elements used (cabling, rings and spiral pinnacles) are typical of the Manueline style.

Dentils

Spiral pinnacle

Rounded arch

Basket-handle arch

Medallion

Parapet ornamented with openwork

Ornamental multifoiled moulding

Rings separating the columns

Cabled string course resembling maritime rigging

Horseshoe frame

Pointed arch

H. Choimet/MICHELIN

STATUARY

Many statues, generally in wood, were to be found on the altarpieces that decorated the churches. In the 18C, statuary largely followed foreign schools: at Mafra, the Italian **Giusti** and his colleagues instructed many Portuguese sculptors, among them **Machado de Castro**; in Braga, Coimbra and Oporto, **Laprade** represented the French School; at Arouca, the Portuguese **Jacinto Vieira** gave his carvings a very personal, lively style. The idea of the Baroque cribs (*presépios*), that can be seen in many churches, originate from southern Italy. In Portugal they are more naive but not without artistic merit. The figures in terracotta are often by **Machado de Castro, Manuel Teixeira** or **António Ferreira**. The talent of the Baroque sculptors is also evident in the many fountains found throughout Portugal especially in the Minho region.

The monumental staircase of Bom Jesus near Braga is made up of a series of fountains in the Rococo style.

PAINTING

Painting is represented by **Vieira Lusitano** (1699–1783) and **Domingos António de Sequeira** (1768–1837), the latter a remarkable portraitist, whose works can be found in the royal palaces at Mafra, Ajuda and Lisbon.

Lusitano's mature work is in the Italian late Baroque manner, which he had absorbed during his studies in Rome.

LATE 18C–19C
ARCHITECTURE

The second half of the 18C saw a return to the classical style, seen in the work of **Mateus Vicente** (1747–86 – Palácio Real in Queluz), **Carlos da Cruz Amarante** (Igreja de Bom Jesus), and the Lisbon architects, particularly **Eugénio dos**

MAFRA – Basilica (18C)

This basilica is a masterpiece of 18C Portuguese architecture, which is heavily influenced by Italian neo-Classicism and German Baroque. It took its inspiration from Saint Peter's in the Vatican and the Gesù Church in Rome.

Twinned transverse arch which supports the barrel vault, decorated with caissons

Triangular pediment decorated with a group of sculptures (Christ crucified, the Glory and two angels in adoration)

Rounded arch decorated with flowerets

Pendentive: a concave triangle connecting the surface of the dome and the walls

Cornice with a hood-mould underlined by dentils between two moulded strips

Lunette: part of a barrel vault which does not extend as far as the keystone and which opens out the upper sections of a bay

Corner piece

Tuscan capital

Pink marble **frieze**

Architrave with two **fasciae** (banding edged with fillets) crowned with a moulded strip

Organ

Overhanging organ loft

Twinned **pilasters** adorned with fluting

Composite capital

String course running horizontally along the capitals

Pink marble **columns** framing the high altar

Retable or altarpiece

Communion table

Triforium

H. Cholmet/MICHELIN

Ballroom wing, Palácio Nacional de Queluz

© JoseIgnacioSoto/iStock

Santos who created the Pombal style. In the late 19C when the Romantic movement favoured a revival of former styles, Portugal developed the neo-Manueline, an evocation of the period of the Great Discoveries exemplified by the Castelo da Pena in Sintra, the Palace-Hotel in Buçaco and the Estação do Rossio in Lisbon. At the time *azulejos* were being used to decorate entire house façades.

SCULPTURE

Soares dos Reis (1847–89) tried to portray the Portuguese *saudade* or nostalgia in sculpture; his pupil, **Teixeira Lopes** (1866–1918), revealed an elegant technique, particularly when portraying children's heads.

PAINTING

Portuguese painters discovered the naturalistic approach from the Barbizon school in France.

Two painters, **Silva Porto** (1850–93) and **Marquês de Oliveira** (1853–1927) followed the Naturalist movement, while **Malhoa** (1855–1933), the painter of popular festivals, and **Henrique Pousão** (1859–84) were closer to Impressionism; **Sousa Pinto** (1856–1939) excelled as a pastel artist and **Columbano Bordalo Pinheiro** (1857–1929) achieved distinction with his portraits and still-life paintings.

20C
ARCHITECTURE

The influence of Art Nouveau may be seen in buildings in Lisbon, Coimbra and Leira, while one of the finest examples of Art Deco
in Portugal is the Casa de Serralves in Oporto. In the 1930s, the architect **Raúl Lino** built the Casa dos Patudos in Alpiarça, near Santarém. However, it was only in the 1950s that a noticeable development in housing came about which may be seen in council houses, garden cities and buildings like the Museu Gulbenkian in Lisbon.

The Oporto School of architecture stands out for the modernism it advocates with internationally known architects such as **Fernando Távora** (1923–2005) and **Álvaro Siza** (b.1933) who was commissioned to restore the Chiado quarter in Lisbon after it was partly destroyed by fire in 1988. The main architectural event in Lisbon in the 1980s was the construction of the post-modern Torres das Amoreiras designed by **Tomás Taveira**.

SCULPTURE

Francisco Franco (1885–1955) held great sway over the official sculpture of the period, including the commemorative monuments so popular under Salazar. More recently, **João Cutileiro** has come to prominence with his original collection of statues (Dom Sebastião in Lagos, and Camões in Cascais), while **José Pedro Croft** (stonework), **Rui Sanches** (woodwork) and **Rui Chafes** (metal) are all contemporary artists who adhere to a more conceptual style of sculpture (installations).

PAINTING

In the early 20C Portuguese painting mainly stuck to Naturalism; only a few artists diverged to follow the general trend; **Amadeo de Souza Cardoso** (1887–1918), a friend of Modigliani, worked in Paris assimilating the lessons of Cézanne and found his true expression first in Cubism then in a highly coloured variant of Expressionism; his friend **Santa Rita** (1889–1918), who died unexpectedly, made a great contribution to the Portuguese Futurist movement but destroyed much of his work. **Almada Negreiros** (1889–1970) was influenced by Cubism while at the same time remaining a classical draughtsman. He was also a poet and playwright. He painted the large frescoes in Lisbon's harbour stations in 1945 and 1948. **Maria Helena Vieira da Silva** (1908–92), who moved to Paris in 1928, derived her art from the Paris School, although in her space paintings the *azulejo* influence may be seen.

Among the best known contemporary painters are **Paula Rego** (b.1935), who draws upon Op-Art, **Júlio Pomar**, Lourdes Castro, **José de Guimarães** and, more recently, Julião Sarmento, Pedro Cabrita Reis, Alberto Carneiro (installations), Pedro Calapez (abstraction and volumetric forms), Álvaro Lapa, Pedro Portugal, Pedro Casquiero (abstraction), Graça Morais and Pedro Proença (allegorical images).

ARCHITECTURAL TERMS

(Cadeiral: words in bold italics are in Portuguese or Spanish)

Adufa: A protective lattice screen made of small strips of wood arranged on the outside of windows.

Ajimez: a paired window or opening.

Apse: the generally rounded end of a church behind the altar. The exterior is called the east end.

Altar Mor: the high altar.

Armillary sphere: a globe made up of hoops to show the motions of the heavenly bodies. As the emblem of King Manuel I, it is often portrayed in Manueline art.

Artesonado: a marquetry ceiling in which raised fillets outline honeycomb-like cells in the shape of stars. This particular decoration, which first appeared under the Almohads, was popular throughout the Iberian Peninsula in the 15C and 16C.

Windows with adufa screens, Algarve

©Hani Alex Latif/iStock

Detail of empedrado, Praça do Rossio, Lisbon

Atlas (or **telamon**): support in the form of a carved male figure.

Atrium: a forecourt or open central courtyard in a Roman house.

Azulejos: glazed, patterned, ceramic tiles (*see p 72*).

Bastion: a projecting part of a fortification built at the angle of, or against the line of, a wall.

Cadeiral: the choir stalls in a church.

Campanile: a bell-tower, often detached from the church.

Chicane: a zig-zag passageway.

Chrisma: the monogram of Christ, formed by the Greek capital letters *khi* (X) and *rhô* (P), the first two letters of the word Christos.

Churrigueresque: in the style of the Churrigueras, an 18C family of Spanish architects. Richly ornate Baroque decoration.

Citânia: a term used to describe the ruins of former Roman or pre-Roman settlements on the Iberian Peninsula.

Coro: the part of a chancel containing the stalls and used by canons and other members of the clergy.

Cupola (or **dome**): curved roof, most often hemispherical, crowning the top of a building.

Empedrado: a typical surface covering for Portuguese pavements and streets made from stones of various types and colours to create attractive designs.

Entablature: beam member made up of the architrave, frieze and cornice.

Foliage (or **foliated scrolls**): sculptural or painted ornamentation depicting foliage, often in the form of a frieze.

Gable: the decorative, triangular upper portion of a wall which supports a pitched roof.

Glacis: an embankment sloping gently down from a fort.

Grotesque: (from *grotta* or *grotto* in Italian); a fantastic or incongruous ornament used in the Renaissance.

Hypocaust: a space under a floor in a Roman house where hot air or furnace gases were used for heating.

Impluvium: a square basin in the atrium of a Roman house for collecting rain water.

Jacente: a funerary statue.

Judiaria: an old Jewish quarter.

Lantern: the part of a dome which opens laterally.

Lavabo: a fountain basin in cloisters used by monks for their ablutions.

Levada: Irrigation channels used to provide water.

Lombard arches: a decorative device in Romanesque architecture consisting of small slightly projecting blind arcades linking vertical bands.

Modillion: a small console supporting a cornice.

Moucharaby: a wooden lattice-work screen placed in front of a window.

Mouraria: a former Moorish district.

Mozarabic: the work of Christians living under Moorish rule after 711. On being persecuted in the 9C, they sought refuge in Christian areas bringing with them Moorish artistic traditions.

Mudéjar: the work of Muslims who remained under Christian rule following the Reconquest. It is used to describe work reminiscent of Moorish characteristics which was undertaken between the 13C and 16C.

Padrão: a stone monument erected by the Portuguese to denote possession of lands they discovered.

Peristyle: a row of columns surrounding a court, garden or façade.

Plateresque: a style that originated in Spain in the 16C and is derived from the word *plata* (silver); it is used to describe finely carved decoration inspired by the work of silversmiths.

Predella: the lower part of a retable.

Púlpito: a pulpit.

Retable: an altarpiece; marble, stone or wood decoration for an altar.

Rinceau: used in painting and sculpture. An ornamental motif of scrolling foliage, usually vine.

Rococo: a late-Baroque style of decoration with asymmetrical patterns involving scroll-work, shell motifs.

Sé: a cathedral or episcopal seat; from the Latin *sedes* meaning seat.

Stucco: a type of moulding mix consisting mainly of plaster.

Tree of Jesse: a genealogical tree showing Christ's descent from Jesse through his son David.

Literature

While remaining open to outside influences which are quickly and successfully assimilated, Portuguese literature is nonetheless original and reflects the lyrical and nostalgic spirit – the famous *saudade* of the people, as in the *fado*. Poetry has always held a privileged position with the monumental work of Camões as a figurehead.

THE MIDDLE AGES

The earliest known Portuguese literature dates from the late 12C with the poetry of the troubadours, influenced by Provençal lyricism. There were **Cantigas de Amor** for male voices, the more popular **Cantigas de Amigo** and the satirical **Cantigas de Escárnio e Maldizer** which were collected in anthologies or *cancioneiros*. The most famous of these, the *Cancioneiro Geral,* compiled by the Spaniard Garcia de Resende in the 16C, covered all the poetry written in Portuguese and Castilian over more than a century. King Dinis I, a poet himself, imposed the official use of Portuguese in the 13C. Dom Pedro was the major literary figure of the 14C. However, **Fernao Lopes** (born c.1380–1390), the chronicler of Portuguese kings and queens (*Chronicles of Dom Pedro, Dom Fernando, Dom João I and Dom Dinis)*, is considered *the* great name in medieval literature.

THE RENAISSANCE

The 16C introduced humanism and a revival of poetry and dramatic art which can be seen at its best in works by **Francisco Sá de Miranda** (1485–1558), **Bernardim Ribeiro** (1500–52), author of the famous novel *Child and Damsel (Menina et Moça)*, **António Ferreira** (1528–69) in his *Lusitanian Poems (Poemas Lusitanos)* and *Castro*, and especially **Gil Vicente** (1470–1536), a great dramatist whose 44 plays painted a satirical picture of Portuguese society in the early 16C.

So we ploughed our way through waters where none save Portuguese had ever sailed before. To our left were the hills and towns of Morocco, the abode once of the giant Antaeus; land to our right there was none for certain, though report spoke of it. And now our course took us into regions and past islands already discovered by the great Prince Henrique.

Luís de Camões
The Lusiads, Canto V

The greatest figure of the period, however, remains **Luís de Camões** or Camoens (1524–80) who, having demonstrated his virtuosity of verse in *The Lyric (A Lírica)*, shows himself to be the poet of the Great Discoveries in his vast portrait of *The Lusiads (Os Lusíadas*, 1572), which relates the epic voyage of Vasco da Gama in a similar way to the *Odyssey*. He led an adventurous life, which took him to Morocco (where he lost an eye) and to Goa.

CLASSICISM

During the 60 years of Spanish domination, Portuguese literature was confined to the Academies in Lisbon and the provinces; Baroque affectation prevailed, but at the same time "Sebastianism" developed, a belief in the return of King Sebastião and the restoration of the country's independence. Much of the literary output consisted of chronicles and travel narratives including work by **Fernão Mendes Pinto** (1509–83) who wrote *Peregrination (Peregrinação)*. The Jesuit **António Vieira** (1608–97) revealed the growing personality of the immense colony of Brazil in his sermons and letters as a missionary.

18C

The Age of Enlightenment was represented in Portugal by scholars, historians and philosophers. Theatre and poetry came under French influence. **Manuel MB do Bocage** (1765–1805), of French descent, was the great lyric and satirical poet of this century.

19C

Romanticism took a firm hold thanks to **Almeida Garrett** (1799–1854), who was not only a poet (*Fallen Leaves – Fôlhas Caídas* and *Flores Sem Fructo*) and master of a whole generation of poets, but also a theatre reformer, playwright *(Frei Luís de Sousa)* and novelist *(Travels in My Homeland – Viagens na Minha Terra)*. The century's other outstanding poets included **António F de Castilho** *(Amor e Melancolia)* and **João de Deus**. **Alexandre Herculano** (1810–77) introduced the historical novel and his *História de Portugal* was a great success. Among fellow historians, mention should be made of **Oliveira Martins**. The transition to realism came about with work by **Camilo Castelo Branco** (1825–90) whose best-known novel *Fatal Love (Amor de Perdição)* gives an account of society at the time. The end of Romanticism was signalled by the work of the Azorian **Antero de Quental** (1842–91), whose *Odes Modernas* were an instrument of social unrest. **Eça de Queirós** (1845–1900), a diplomat and a novelist, made a critique of the morals of his day through his works *(Cousin Bazilis, The Maias, Barbaric Prose, The Sin of Father Amaro (O Primo Basílio, Os Maias, Prosas Bárbaras, O Crime do Padre Amaro)*. **Guerra Junqueiro** (1850–1923) wrote satirical and controversial poems.

CONTEMPORARY AUTHORS

Fernando Pessoa (1888–1935), a complex and precursory genius, revived Portuguese poetry by using different names and personae, among them Ricardo Reis, Álvaro de Campos, Alberto Caeiro and Bernardo Soares,

Fado

There are many theories about the origin of the *fado*: a monotonous chant that derived from the troubadour songs of the Middle Ages, or, a song with Moorish or Afro-Brazilian roots.

The *fado* first appeared in Portugal in the late 18C in the form of sentimental sailors' songs. It developed in the early 19C during the troubled times of the Napoleonic Wars, English domination and the independence of Brazil. These circumstances explain the popular response to the song, with its serious subject matter, usually the forces of destiny (the name *fado* is said to come from the Latin *fatum:* destiny) or human passions. It became popular in Lisbon in 1820 with the singer **Maria Severa**. In 1833 the first *fado* houses *(casas de fado)* opened and the song took on its present form. By the end of the century it had become a literary genre and the great poets and writers of the day tried their hand at it. A *fastida* figure began to appear in novels, wandering from *fado* house to *fado* house, sitting in a cloud of smoke, drinking and, eyes half-closed, listening to nostalgic tunes. At the beginning of the 20C the fado served as a means for critics to voice their ideological quarrels. The singer **Amália Rodriguez**, who died in 1999, brought the *fado* international fame, so much so that it has become the symbol of Portugal and its *saudade*.

Cristina Branco

© Oscar Gonzalez/WENN.com/age fotostock

Unfortunatley for Carlos do Carmo, another famous fado singer, Rodriguez's fame rather overshadowed his, so he remained a national, rather than international star. A singer in the Lisbon Song genre, he became one of the most prominent singers to commemorate freedom during the Lisbon uprising of 1974.

One of the most popular fado stars today is Cristina Branco, a musician who has focused on the poems from which major fado lyrics have been taken.

Her contemporary, Marisa dos Reis Nunes is strongly influenced by the musical rythms of Brazil where she lived with her family before returning to Portugal. Her music is infused with a strong Brazilian-beat undertone.

Singing and playing the fado

The singer *(fadista)*, often a woman, is accompanied by one or two instrumentalists. The Portuguese guitar *(guitarra)* differs from the Spanish *(viola)* in having twelve strings as opposed to six, and is thus a more subtle instrument. The *fadista*, who is often dressed in black, stands straight, head thrown back, eyes half closed, and sings out in a strong, often deep, voice. The effect is very beautiful, moving and captivating.

The Lisbon *fado*, which can be heard in restaurants in the city's old quarters, more closely resembles the original *fado* form than the Coimbra version. This latter, which is gradually dying out, is sung only by men, dressed in large black student capes. The subject matter is generally about students' love affairs with working-class women.

which enabled him to express himself in different styles. His *Book of Disquietude (Livro do Desassossego)* was published forty years after his death. Among his contemporaries and successors mention should be made of his friend **Mario de Sá Carneiro**, who committed suicide at the age of 26 leaving some very fine poems, **José Régio** *(Poems of God and the Devil – Poesias de Deus e do Diabo)*, **Natália Correia**, **António Ramos Rosa** and **Herberto Helder**. Among the main novelists are **Fernando Namora** *(The Wheat and the Chaff – O Trigo e O Joio)*, **Ferreira de Castro** (1898–1974), who drew upon his experiences during a long stay in Brazil *(The Jungle* and *The Mission – A Selva, A Missão)*, **Carlos de Oliveira** (1921–81), who wrote about life in small villages *(Uma Abelha na Chuva)*, **Manuel Texeira Gomes** *(Letters with No Moral – Cartas sem nenhuma moral)*, **Urbano T. Rodrigues** *(Bastards of the Sun – Bastardos do Sol)*, **Agustina Bessa Luís** *(The Sibyl – A Sibila* and *Fanny Owen)*, as well as regionalist authors like **Aquilino Ribeiro** and **Miguel Torga**. **Vergílio**

Ferreira first wrote neo-realistic novels before adopting a very personal style in which he tackles existential problems *(Aparição)*.

Over the last few decades Portuguese literature has undergone a veritable revival with writers such as **José Cardoso Pires** *(Ballad of Dog's Beach – Balada da Praia dos Cães)*, **Lídia Jorge** *(A Costa dos murmúrios, Notícia da Cidade Silvestre)*, **Vitorino Nemésio** and his beautiful novel *Mau Tempo no Canal* which takes place in the Azores, **António Lobo Antunes** *(South of Nowhere* and *An Explanation of the Birds – O Cús de Judas, Explicação dos Pássaros)*, **Sofia de Melo Breyner**, whose work s mainly poetical and in a similar vein to **Nuno Júdice** *(Theory of Sentiment, A Field in the Depths of Time)*, and Nobel Prize-winner **José Saramago** (1922–2010), who mixed all the great legends and figures of Portuguese history, including João V and Fernando Pessoa in his novels *(Memorial do Convento, The Year of the Death of Ricardo Reis, The Gospel According to Jesus Christ)*.

Mention should also be made of the philosopher **Eduardo Lourenço** *(O Labirinto da Saudade)*, **Eugénio de Andrade**, a major, prolific post-war poet, **Almeida Faria** who writes about memory, exile and nostalgia, and **Maria Judite de Carvalho** who is continuing her demanding work *(Os Armários Vazios)*.

The former Portuguese colonies, particularly Brazil, contribute greatly to Lusitanian literature with authors such as **Jorge Amado**, José Lins do Rego etc. Angola also has a tradition of great storytellers and poets such as Luandino Vieira *(Velhas Estórias, Nós os de Makuiusu)*, Pepetela *(As Aventuras de Ngunga)* and José Eduardo Águalusa *(A Nação Crioula, A Estação da Chuva)*, as has Mozambique, with Mia Couto *(A Varanda do Frangipani, Contos do Nascer da Terra)* and Luís Carlos Patraquim *(Litemburgo Blues)*. In Cape Verde the philologist Baltazar Lopes *(Chiquinho)* and the storyteller Manuel Lopes *(Os Flagelados do Vento Leste)* bear witness to the literary wealth of these West African islands.

Nobel Laureate

Born in 1922 in Azinhaga, near Santarém, **José Saramago** lived in Lisbon from the age of three. He worked in a number of jobs (mechanic, draughtsman, social security employee, editor, translator, journalist) before publishing his first novel *(Terra do Pecado)* in 1947. He then worked for a publishing house and was the literary critic for the *Seara Nova* magazine. His second book, *Os Poemas Possíveis*, was published in 1966, although his great literary success came in the 1980s with *Memorial do Convento* (1982), which retraces the construction of the Mafra monastery, *The Year of the Death of Ricardo Reis* (1984), *The Stone Raft* (1986), *History of the Siege of Lisbon* (1989) and *The Gospel According to Jesus Christ* (1991). He died in June 2010.

Romarias

Romarias are religious festivals held in honour of a saint. The most important are in northern Portugal, particularly in the Minho. Small *romarias* in mountain chapels last one day, but the larger ones in towns can last several days. Some groups, such as the fishermen of Póvoa de Varzim, hold their own *romarias*.

Romaria in Viana do Castelo, Minho

Collections

A few days prior to the festival the organisers make a collection. Gifts in kind are collected in baskets decked with flowers and garlands and are then auctioned. The collections, which mark the start of the festivities, are enlivened by players such as the *gaitero* or bagpiper, the *fogueteiro* or firework lighter and, in the Alentejo, the *tamborileiro* or tambourine player. Streets are carpeted with flowers.

The candle (Círio)

The most important part of the religious ceremony is the solemn bearing of a candle, from which the name *círio* has evolved to describe the focal point of the *romaria*. The candle is borne on a flower-decked cart; behind, led by the *gaitero*, follows a procession accompanying the statue of a saint or the Virgin covered in garlands, lace and flowers. The procession circles the sanctuary two or three times accompanied by music and fire-crackers. The candle is set down near the altar and the faithful advance to kiss the feet of the saint.

The "Saints of Intercession"

To win special favour from certain saints, believers perform acts of penance such as going round the sanctuary on their knees. The traditional worship of the **Holy Ghost** is particularly deep-rooted in the Azores and Brazil. The famous festival *(Festa dos Tabuleiros)* in Tomar, founded in the 14C by Holy Ghost brotherhoods, continues to this day.

Festa dos Tabuleiros, Tomar, Ribatejo

Cinema

Portugal produces a large number of films primarily for the Portuguese-speaking market. Few films are translated into English, however, or have subtitles, but are popular among Portuguese-speaking communities.

During the 1930s and 1940s the development of Portuguese cinema was marked by popular-based themes, rural films and moralistic comedies with leading actors such as Beatriz Costa and António Silva. The ideology of the Salazar regime then began to dominate with the almost-official producer António Lopes Ribeiro. From the 1950s onwards, directors became a fundamental part of Portuguese cinema, which became known for its creativity and independence, while the 1960s were marked by the exodus of young Portuguese to France and Great Britain to study cinema. The best known directors of the time were **Paulo Rocha**, who was Jean Renoir's assistant, **Fernando Lopes** (*Belarmino*) and **António de Macedo** (*Domingo à tarde*). Paulo Rocha distinguished himself in 1963 with *The Green Years* (Verdes Anos) which made a break with films under the dictatorship and was the precursor for the "Cinema Novo" (New Cinema) movement, the equivalent of "New Wave" in France. He then went on to film in Japan (*The Island of Loves – A Ilha dos Amores* and *The Mountains of the Moon – As Montanhas da Lua*). Many directors returned to Portugal after the Carnation Revolution to make films with a militant, political bent, such as *O Recado*, which was produced during the dictatorship by **José Fonseca e Costa**. Other important directors of the period include **António Reis** (*Jaime*), **António Pedro de Vasconcelos** (*O lugar do Morto*) and **Lauro António** (*A manhã Submersa*).

The new generation of directors in the 1980s and 1990s imparted a certain artistic quality to Portuguese cinema. These directors set themselves apart by their great originality and include names such as **Joaquim Pinto**, **João**

The Language

Portuguese is a Romantic language originating from Latin. Although the syntax and etymology are similar to Castilian, the pronunciation is totally different, being closer to French for letters such as j, c, z, ç and ch, but dissimilar in the way, for example, that 's' is pronounced as 'sh', and in the pronounciation of nasals and sibilants. With a very rich and expressive vocabulary, Portuguese lends itself very well to poetry and *fado*.

Mário Grilo (*O Processo do Rei, Longe da Vista*), **João Botelho** (*A Portuguese Farewell – Um Adeus Portugûes, Three Palm Trees – Três Palmeiras* and *Tráfico*), **João César Monteiro** (*Recollections of the Yellow House – Recordações da Casa Amarela* and *God's Comedy – A Comédia de Deus*), **Pedro Costa** (*O Sangue, A Casa da Lava* and *Ossos*) and **Teresa Vilaverde** (*Os Mutantes*).

Portuguese cinema is dominated abroad by the extraordinary personality of **Manoel de Oliveira**, born in 1908. His early films were dedicated to his home town, Oporto, where he filmed from 1931 onwards. Later he turned to more imaginary themes and mainly drew upon Portuguese literature with works by Camilo Castelo Branco (*Fatal Love – Amor de Perdição* and *The Day of Despair – O Dia do Desespero*), and Agustina Bessa Luís (*Francisca*, adapted from *Fanny Owen*, which he co-wrote), as well as a number of Italian works such as Dante's *Divine Comedy*. French literature also provided him with inspiration, including *Le Soulier de Satin* by Paul Claudel, *Valley of Abraham (Vale Abraão*), inspired by Flaubert's *Madame Bovary*, and *La Lettre*, an adaptation of *La Princesse de Clèves* by Madame de Lafayette, and winner of the Prix du Jury at the 1999 Cannes Film Festival. Luís Miguel Cintra and Leonor Silva are actors who have frequently figured in his films, as have international stars such as Catherine Deneuve and John Malkovitch (*The Convent*), Michel Piccoli and Irène Papas (*Party*), and Chiara Mastroianni (*La Lettre*).

Nature

Portugal has a wide variety of landscapes, from the mountainous northeast to the flatter areas near the coast and in the south. The continental part of the country, southwest of the Iberian peninsula, occupies a relatively small area. Generally speaking, the altitude decreases from the Spanish border towards the Atlantic and from north to south; the Tagus (Tejo) divides a mountainous region in the north from an area of plateaux and plains in the south. The archipelagos of Madeira and the Azores out in the Atlantic are a distant volcanic arena, enriched by a variety of flowers, geology and history.

GEOLOGICAL FORMATION

In the Primary Era the north of Portugal was affected by Hercynian folding which resulted in the emergence of hard granite and shale mountain ranges. These were worn down in the Secondary Era to form a vast plateau out of which rose erosion-resistant heights such as the Serra de São Mamede. In the Tertiary Era, the raising of the Alps and Pyrenean folding led to a brutal upheaval of the plateau, dislocating it into a series of small massifs such as the Serra do Marão and Serra da Estrela. The massifs were separated by fissures near which emerged thermal and mineral springs and, especially in the north, metal deposits. The upheavals were accompanied in some cases by eruptions of a volcanic nature which formed ranges such as the Serra de Sintra and Serra de Monchique. It was at this point that the Tagus and Sado basins were formed and the coastal plains folded into the low ranges of the Serra de Aire, Serra do Caldeirão and Serra da Arrábida. This zone of faults in the earth's crust is still subject to geological disturbance as shown in the earthquake which destroyed Lisbon in 1755 and even more recent tremors. The coastline became less indented in the Quaternary Era through erosion of the Estremadura and Alentejo cliffs and alluvial accumulation in the Aveiro and Sines areas.

RELIEF

The Cantabrian Cordillera extends westwards into Portugal, north of the Douro, where it takes the form of massive mountain ranges separated by heavily eroded valleys.

Between the Douro and the Tagus, the Castilian sierras extend into Portugal as particularly high relief. Monte da Torre in the Serra da Estrela is Portugal's highest mainland peak (1 993m). The Mondego and a valleys surround the ridge. South of the Tagus lies a plateau that drops towards the sea. Its vast horizons are barely interrupted by the minor rises of

Serra da Estrela

© Maurício Abreu/John Warburton-Lee/Photononstop

the Serra de Monchique and Serra do Caldeirão.

The 837km/520mi of coast offer incredible variety, with beaches of fine sand sheltered by rock cliffs, creeks, and promontories such as Cabo Carvoeiro, Cabo Espichel and Cabo de São Vicente. Wide estuaries are occupied by the country's main ports: Oporto on the Douro, Lisbon on the Tagus and Setúbal on the Sado. Fishing harbours like Portimão have developed in bays, or, as with Peniche and Lagos, in the protection of headlands. However, most of the coast consists of flat sandy areas sometimes lined by offshore bars as in the eastern offshore Algarve and along Ria de Aveiro.

REGIONS AND LANDSCAPE

The areas described below correspond to the old historical provinces which closely reflect the country's natural regions. Portugal's present administrative divisions, known as districts, are also given.

THE NORTH

The old provinces of the Minho and Douro are green and heavily cultivated while the inland regions of Trás-os-Montes, Beira Alta and Beira Baixa are bleaker and drier.

The Minho (Districts: Braga and Viana do Castelo) and the Douro (District: Porto)

The region is part of the tourist area around Oporto and Northern Portugal. The greater part of the Minho and Douro provinces consists of granite hills covered with dense vegetation. The exceptions to these are the bare summits of the Serra do Gerês, Serra do Soajo and Serra do Marão, which make up the Parque Nacional da Peneda-Gerês, and are strewn with rocky scree.

The fields, enclosed by hedges and climbing vines, sometimes produce two crops a year. Vineyards, orchards and meadows contribute to the rural economy. Olive, apple and sometimes orange trees grow on the sunniest slopes. Main roads tend to follow lush river valleys like those of the Lima and the Vez. The region, with Porto (in Portuguese, Oporto) as capital, is an active one and has more than a quarter of Portugal's population.

Trás-os-Montes (Districts: Bragança and Vila Real)

Trás-os-Montes means "beyond the mountains". True to its name, this province of high plateaus relieved by rocky crests and deeply cut valleys, stretches out beyond the Serra da Marão and Serra do Gerês. The moorland plateaux, dominated by bare summits and covered with stunted vegetation, are used for sheep grazing. Remote villages merge into the landscape. The more populous river basins around Chaves, Mirandela and Bragança, with their flourishing fruit trees, vines, maize and vegetables, seem like oases in the bleak countryside.

The Alto Douro region in the south contrasts with the rest of the province by its relative fertility. The edges of the plateaux and the slopes down to the Douro and the Tua have been terraced so that olive, fig and almond trees can be grown, and particularly the famous vine that produces the grapes for port wine and *vinho verde*.

The Beira Alta (Districts: Guarda and Viseu) and Beira Baixa (District: Castelo Branco)

This region, the most mountainous in Portugal, is geographically a westward extension of the Spanish Cordillera Central. The landscape consists of a succession of raised rock masses and down-faulted basins. The mountains, of which the principal ranges are the Serra da Estrela and Serra da Lousã, have thickly wooded slopes crowned with rocky summits. Occasional reservoirs fill the sites of ancient glaciary corries or gorges hollowed out of the quartz.

The greater part of the population lives in the Mondego and Zêzere valleys. The Mondego valley, a vast eroded corridor and a main communications route, is rich arable land; with vines extending up hillsides in the vineyards of the Dâo region. The Upper Zêzere valley, known

as the Cova da Beira, specialises more in livestock, wheras
the main town, Covilhã, has
an important wool industry.

THE CENTRE

The Beira Littoral (Districts: Coimbra and Aveiro)

This low lying region, cut by
many water courses, corresponds approximately to the
lower valleys of the Vouga, the
Mondego and the Lis.

There are rice fields in the
irrigated areas around Soure
and Aveiro. The coast consists
of long straight beaches and
sand dunes anchored by vast
pinewoods such as Pinhal
de Leiria and Pinhal do Urso,
while at Aveiro, the *ria* or
lagoon provides an original
touch to the scenery. Inland,
the cottage gardens of wheat
and maize are bordered by
orchards and vines.

There are some beautiful
forests, including Mata do
Buçaco. The region's two main
centres are Coimbra with its
famous university and Aveiro
with its *ria* and salt-pans.

PROVINCES AND DISTRICTS

○ Braga   District boundaries and capitals

MINHO   The old provinces

Estremadura (Districts: Leiria, Lisboa and Setúbal)

In the past, this was the southern limit of
the lands reconquered from the Moors,
hence the name Estremadura which
means extremity. Today, the region,
which includes the Lisbon area, contains
a third of the country's population.

Between Nazaré and Setúbal the countryside is gently undulating. Villages of
single storey houses are surrounded by
fields of wheat and maize. Olives, vines
and fruit trees grow between clumps of
pine and eucalyptus.

Along the coast, where tall cliffs and
sandy beaches alternate, there are many
fishing villages. The Serra de Sintra is a
pleasant wooded range near Lisbon,
while the Serra da Arrábida, south of

the Tagus, provides shelter for small
seaside resorts.

The region's activities are centred on
Lisbon, the political, administrative,
financial and commercial capital.

The Ribatejo (District: Santarém)

The Riba do Tejo, or banks of the Tagus,
is an alluvial plain formed in the Tertiary
and Quaternary Eras. On the hills along
the north bank farmers cultivate olives,
vines and vegetables. The terraces along
the south bank grow wheat and olives.
The plain is covered with rice fields, market gardens and acres of grassland for
rearing horses and fighting bulls. The
region, with its main centre in Santarém,

is renowned for its Portuguese-style bullfights known as *touradas*.

THE SOUTH

The Alentejo (Districts: Beja, Évora and Portalegre)

The Alentejo, meaning beyond the Tagus (*Além Tejo*), covers nearly a third of Portugal. It is a vast flat plain, except for the Serra de São Mamede. There is almost no natural vegetation. However, in spite of the difficulties of irrigation, the land is seldom left fallow. The Alentejo, Portugal's granary, is also the region of the cork oak, the ilex (holm oak) and the olive tree; in addition plums are grown around Vendas Novas and Elvas, while sheep and herds of black pigs are still reared on the poorer land. The vast stretches of open countryside dotted with old villages make this one of Portugal's more attractive regions.

Traditionally, the region has been one of huge estates centred on a *monte* or large remote whitewashed farmhouse, built on a rise. The other local inhabitants live in villages of low houses with big chimneys. The situation changed after the Carnation Revolution when the land reform of July 1975 split up the estates into smaller **co-operatives**. As this has not been very successful, there has been a return to medium and large scale properties.

The coast is generally uninviting, although several seaside resorts are beginning to develop. There are few harbours apart from Sines, which is well-equipped.

There are no large towns; Évora with about 50 000 inhabitants, acts as the regional capital but lives mainly from tourism.

The Algarve (District: Faro)

Portugal's southernmost province takes its name from the Arabic *El Gharb* meaning "west" for this was in fact the most westerly region conquered by the Moors. The Algarve, separated from the Alentejo by shale hills, is like a garden: flowers grow alongside crops and beneath fruit trees, allowing one to see geraniums, camellias and oleanders,

cotton, rice and sugar cane as well as carobs, figs and almonds. Many cottage gardens are surrounded by hedges of aloes *(agaves)*. The villages have brightly whitewashed houses with decorative chimneys. To the west rises a mountain range of volcanic rock, the Serra de Monchique, covered in lush vegetation. The coast is very sandy. The *Sotavento* stretch east of Faro is protected by off-shore sandbanks, while the *Barlavento* section to the west consists of beaches backed by high cliffs which form an impressive promontory at Cabo de São Vicente.

Over the last few years the Algarve has undergone extensive tourist development, sometimes to the detriment of traditional activities such as fishing, canning, horticulture and the cork industry. Most of the small fishing villages have become vast seaside resorts. The main towns are Faro, Lagos and Portimão.

PARKS AND RESERVES

There are several conservation areas in Portugal to protect the beauty of the landscape and local flora and fauna.

NATIONAL PARK

Portugal's only national park is **Peneda-Gerês** (72 000ha) in the north (*see Parque Nacional da PENEDA-GERÊS*). Its rare habitats of mixed forest, groves, peat bogs and bushes provide food and shelter for, among others, wild goat, squirrel, adder, brown bear, pine marten, golden eagle, eagle owl and honey buzzard.

NATURE RESERVES

Among Portugal's specially protected areas are the nature reserves of **Montesinho** near Bragança, **Douro Internacional** in a grandiose setting of natural beauty, **Alvão** near Vila Real, and **Serra da Estrela**. Near Fátima are the nature reserves of **Serra de Aire** and **Serra dos Candeeiros**, which form a beautiful limestone landscape with many caves, **Sintra-Cascais**, nestled between the ocean and surrounding forest, **Serra da Arrábida**, **Serra de São Mamede**, the **Guadiana valley** alongside the river of

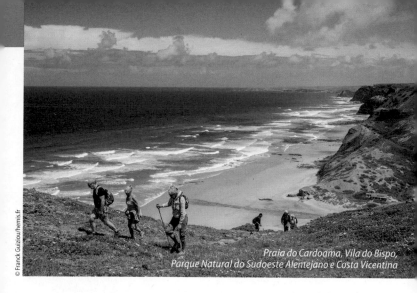

Praia do Cardoama, Vila do Bispo, Parque Natural do Sudoeste Alentejano e Costa Vicentina

the same name, **Sudoeste Alentejano and Costa Vicentina**, and **Ria Formosa** (18 400ha), an ecosystem which is home to a variety of rare sea birds. All these nature reserves are in mountainous regions with the exception of the last two, situated in the Algarve, where the aim is to protect coastal areas from the harm caused by mass tourism and the rapid erosion of this coastline.

CONSERVATION AREAS

Many areas have been singled out for the protection of their flora and fauna. Among them are mountainous regions like **Serra de Malcata**, swamps such as **Paúl de Arzila** and **Paúl do Boquilobo** and river estuaries which have a particularly rich birdlife, including the **Tagus estuary**, the **Sado estuary** and **Sapal de Castro Marim-Vila Real de Santo António** in the Guadiana estuary.

Dune areas, including the **São Jacinto dunes** in Ria de Aveiro and those on the **Berlenga islands** off the coast of Peniche, have also been designated as conservation areas.

Most of the beauty spots in Madeira and the Azores are now classified as conservation areas (*see MADEIRA and the AZORES*).

PROTECTED LANDSCAPES

Some of Portugal's coastal areas have been declared protected landscapes to prevent uncontrolled building development. They include **Esposende** (440ha) and the **Costa da Caparica** as well as South Western Alentejo, Arrabida, and a number of other listed sites around the country.

VEGETATION

The diversity of plants in Portugal is a visual reminder of the contrasts in climate and types of soil found here. The **robur** and **tauzin oak**, together with **chestnuts**, birches and maples, grow on the wet peaks over 500m. South of the Tagus and in the Upper Douro valley where summers are very dry, there are dense woods of **ilex** (holm oak) and **cork oak**, which grow beside heaths and moorlands sparsely covered with cistus, lavender, rosemary and thyme. Cork oaks are particularly abundant in the Alentejo. Portugal is the world's leading cork producer.

Eucalyptus mainly grows along the coast together with **maritime pines** and umbrella pines, which form vast forests beside the beaches near Leiria, Coimbra and Aveiro. Aleppo pines dominate in the Serra da Estrela. Eucalyptus and pines are being planted on ever-increasing areas of land.

Mediterranean plant species acclimatise well in the Algarve, where one may see **aloes** *(agaves)*, as well as **carob**, **almond**, **fig**, **orange** and **olive** trees.

Alto Alentejo countryside with cork trees in spring
© Robert George Young/Getty Images

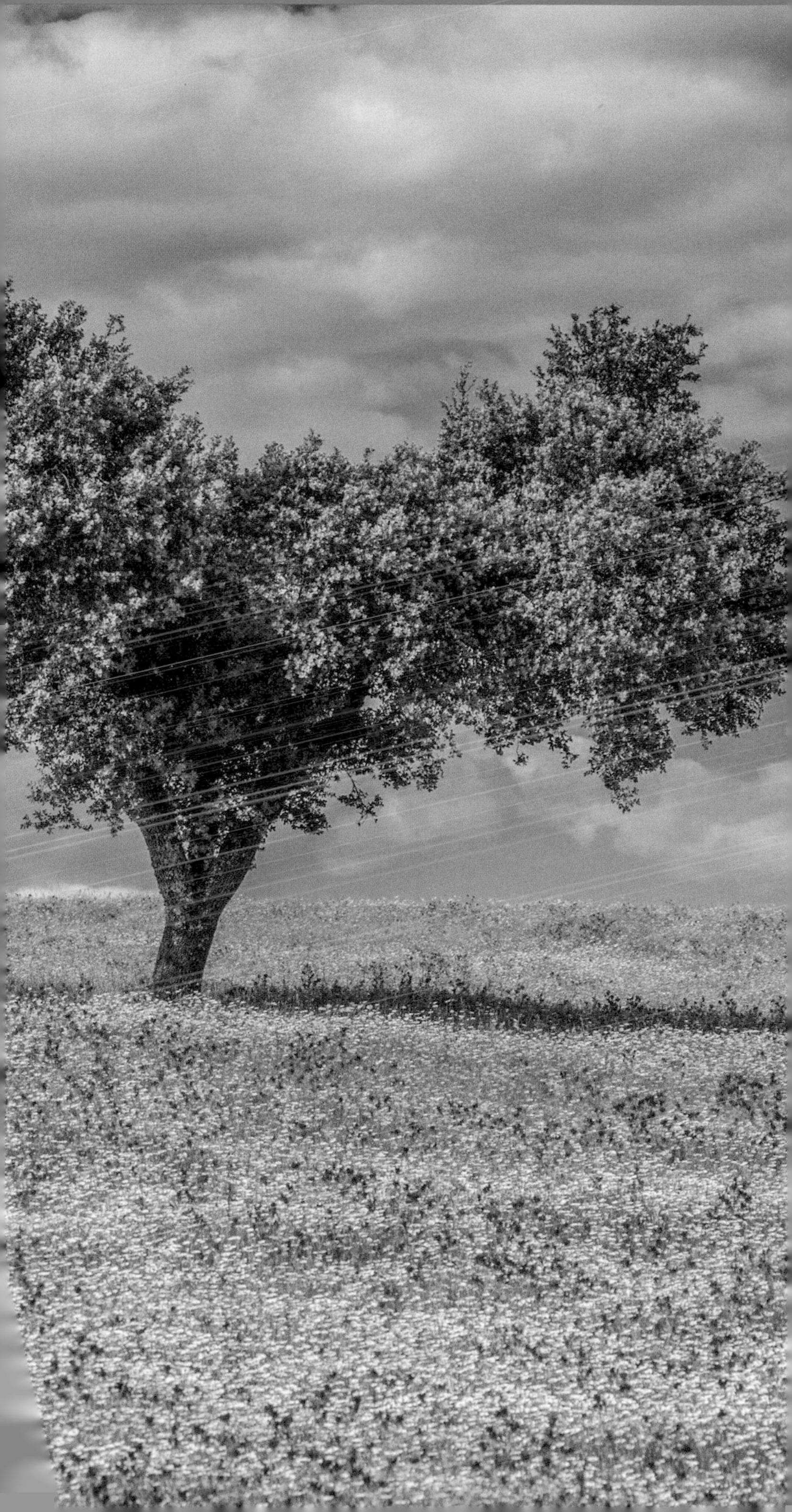

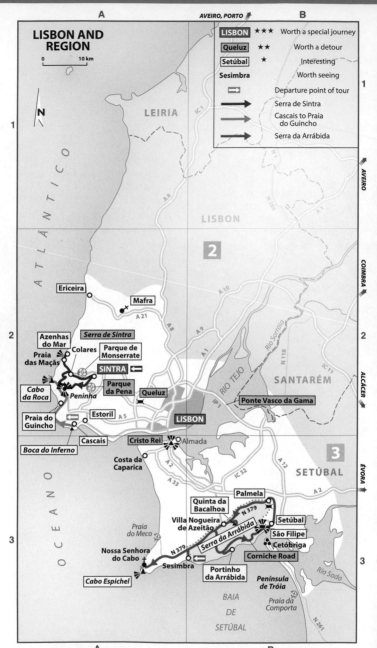

LISBON AND REGION

0 ___ 10 km

LISBON ★★★ Worth a special journey
Queluz ★★ Worth a detour
Setúbal ★ Interesting
Sesimbra Worth seeing
⇨ Departure point of tour
→ Serra de Sintra
→ Cascais to Praia do Guincho
→ Serra da Arrábida

AVEIRO, PORTO

LEIRIA

LISBON

SANTARÉM

AVEIRO
COIMBRA
ALCÁCER
ÉVORA

Ericeira
Mafra
Serra de Sintra
Azenhas do Mar
Colares
Praia das Maçãs
Parque de Monserrate
SINTRA ⇦
Cabo da Roca
Peninha
Parque da Pena
Queluz
Praia do Guincho
Estoril
LISBON
Cascais
Boca do Inferno
Cristo Rei
Almada
Costa da Caparica
Ponte Vasco da Gama
SETÚBAL
Praia do Meco
Palmela
Quinta da Bacalhoa
Villa Nogueira de Azeitão
Setúbal
Serra da Arrábida
São Filipe
Cetóbriga
Corniche Road
Nossa Senhora do Cabo
Sesimbra
Portinho da Arrábida
Península de Tróia
Cabo Espichel
Praia da Comporta
BAIA DE SETÚBAL

ATLÂNTICO
OCEANO

RIO TEJO
Rio Sorraia
Rio Sado

Lisbon and its Region

» Lisbon★★★   p95
» Lisbon Region   p143

The capital of Portugal stands midway between the north and south, on the Atlantic at the mouth of the Tagus. At the time of the Great Discoveries, Lisbon, according to the Portuguese poet Camões, was the "princess of the world… before whom even the ocean bows".

The City

The old town was built on the northern shore of the 'Straw Sea', as the bulge in the Tagus River (Tejo) was called on account of the golden reflections of the sun at this spot. Lisbon (Lisboa) has a jumbled skyline, its buildings dotted over seven hills offering wonderfully varied views. The attraction of the city lies in its light, its pastel ochres, pinks, blues and greens, and the mosaic paving on its streets and squares – the small black and white paving-stones made of limestone and basalt known as *empedrados*. With its maze of narrow streets, alleys and steps in the old quarters, its magnificent vistas along wide avenues and its lively harbour and exotic gardens, Lisbon is a delightful city to explore.

Like any modern city, Lisbon is an eclectic mix of old and new, and construction and reconstruction works are always going on. Lisbon is doing its best to extend a modern urban mass transit system (the metro is excellent) while maintaining its original character. The choice of Lisbon as the site for Expo'98 resulted in a large scale rebuilding pro-

Highlights

1 Ride the **trams**. Numbers E15 and E28 visit main sights (p100)

2 Take the **elevador de Santa Justa** for a bird's-eye view (p107)

3 View the exquisite *azulejos* at the **Palácio dos Marqueses de Fronteira** (p127)

4 Enjoy the *pasteis de nata* at **Confeitaria Nacional** (p140)

5 Listen to haunting **fado** at one of Alfama's top restaurants (p138)

gramme along the Tagus, particularly at the Olivais docks, near the exhibition site, now a major tourist attraction and shopping centre. The Santo Amaro, Santos and Alcântara docks have their leisure facilities that include bars, restaurants and discos.

Museums and other attractions abound, and Lisbon's restaurants provide wonderful traditional meals, though many

City in twilight viewed from Mouraria, 25 de Abril bridge over the Tagus in the background

© Magdalena Paluchowska/Shutterstock

Alfama during the festival of Santo António

© Jon Arnold Images/hemis.fr

modern chefs are using new methods, and the city still retains its 'tea shops' – almost a relic from another age.

Above all, it must be said that Lisbon is probably one of the friendliest capitals in Europe.

Four days might be about right to soak up the atmosphere without cultural overload. Spend a day out along the coast (take the railway that runs right along the sea-wall) to Cascais (⟲ *see CASCAIS*). Or go the other way, across the Vasco da Gama bridge to Setúbal. And don't forget visit Sintra with its handsome palace and cosy town centre. Close by is the exquisite Palace of Queluz. All these places are easily reachable by public transport from Lisbon.

The Beginning

Lisbon, so legend has it, was founded by Ulysses, but exactly where that claim comes from no-one really knows. It was, though, the Phoenicians who, in 1200 BCE, landed here on their seaborne travels and named it "serene harbour" – a haven of peace and calm water after the rough water of the Atlantic once they had passed through what is now the Straits of Gibraltar.

It soon became a regular stopping point on the route to northern Europe for traders from the Mediterranean: Greeks, Carthaginians and eventually Romans, who conquered the city in 138. Subsequently, it was under Barbarian rule and then Moorish from 714 when it was given the name Lissabona. Not until 1147 did King Dom Alfonso retake the city for the Portuguese after a four-month siege aided by mainly British mercenaries on their way to and from the Crusades. It did not become the capital of Portugal – that honour was given to Coimbra – until 1255, when Dom Afonso III chose Lisbon as the seat of his government.

Age of the Great Discoveries

Lisbon benefited from the riches that accumulated after the voyages of Vasco da Gama to the Indies in 1497–1499 and the discovery of Brazil (and its gold) by Pedro Álvares Cabral in 1500. New trade routes developed; merchants flocked to Lisbon, which was packed with small traders buying and selling gold, silver, spices, ivory, silks, precious stones and rare woods. Monuments, including the Mosteiro dos Jerónimos and Torre de Belém, were built and no expense was spared in decorating them. The ornamentation of these buildings, always inspired by the sea, became known as the Manueline style after King Manuel.

The Earthquake

On 1 November 1755 at about 9.30am, just as much of the population was at Mass, the town was shaken by an exceptionally violent earth tremor: churches, palaces and houses collapsed; fire spread; survivors rushed to take refuge in the Tagus, but a huge wave came upstream, breaking over and destroying the lower town. Lisbon's riches were

Rua Augusta Arch, Baixa

© Sohadiszno/IStock

engulfed. At least two large aftershocks did more damage; estimates suggest that as many as 90 000 people died out of a total population then of about 270 000. The devastation was not just confined to the city; many towns as far away as the Algarve were destroyed.

The King, Dom João I, escaped as did his minister, Sebastião de Carvalho e Melo, the future **Marquis of Pombal**. The minister immediately began the rebuilding of Lisbon to plans in a style utterly revolutionary for the period. The straight wide avenues and the plain and stylised houses to be seen in the Baixa today are Pombal's legacy.

In November 1807, Napoléon's troops took the city, remaining for four years. In 1908 the King Dom Carlos and his son were assassinated in the Praça do Comércio, and an era of republican revolution took hold. Another high-profile assassination, that of the President, Sidónio Pais, shook the city in 1918.

Lisbon remained neutral during World War II, though the place was teeming with spies and exiles.

The Carnation Revolution

At 4.30am on 25 April 1974, Portuguese radio broadcast a message from the command of the Movement of the rmed Forces (Movimento das Forças madas) calling upon the population eep calm and remain indoors. Thus n the *coup d'état* led by General io de Spínola against the regime zar and his successor Caetano.

Spínola's take-over was virtually bloodless and his soldiers, with a red carnation stuck in the barrel of their rifles, were acclaimed by the citizens of Lisbon, who surged onto the Praça do Comércio.

Lisbon Today

Lisbon is a delightful city with numerous focal points that can all be admired from the Tagus. Modern though the city is, its 18C layout and many 18C buildings add to its charm. The Praça do Comércio encompasses a maze-like network of streets in the Baixa district, which is the lower part of town extending towards Rossio: the Praça dos Restauradores and the Avenida da Liberdade, the city's main boulevard, are lined with trees. In Baixa, the Lisboa Story Centre offers a great introduction to the city. On the hill to the right stands the imposing Castelo São Jorge surrounded by the ancient districts of Alfama and Mouraria, while the hill to the left houses the city's commercial area of Chiado, with the working-class residential areas of Bairro Alto and Madragoa beyond. Then you reach the slightly more refined areas of Lapa, Alcântara and Belém. The areas along the Tagus have been taken over by nightclubs, restaurants and bars, turning this old industrial area into a thriving, lively community.

Despite the rush and bustle, Lisbon remains perhaps the friendliest capital city in Europe.

OVERVIEW

Population: City: 550 000; Greater Lisbon: 2.8 million (2018). **Michelin Map:** 733. **Kids:** The Lisboa Story Centre, which takes you on an audio-visual journey through the history of the city, the Oceanarium with its intriguing marine life, the Calouste Gulbenkian Planetarium, the Museum of the Marionettes (puppets) and, of course, the Zoo.

USEFUL INFORMATION

Main Tourist Board Office – Palácio Foz, Praça dos Restauradores (Rossio) *213 463 314. Open daily 9am–8pm.* **Lisbon Welcome Centre** – Praça do Comércio (entrance Rua do Arsenal). *210 312 800. www.visitlisboa.com. Open 9am–8pm.* The centre includes a tourist information office, a fashion boutique, an auditorium, art gallery, café and a food shop. Internet access. **Ask Me** – In the summer several of these little kiosks dot the city centre at main tourist sites; they are handy for maps and local tips.

LISBON CARD – CARTÃO LISBOA

The Lisbon Card (www.lisboacard.org) is very useful if you are planning to stay a few days in the city. The card gives you a complimentary tourist guide full of helpful city info; unlimited travel on public transport (bus, tram, metro and funicular) together with free or reduced entry to 26 museums, monuments and World Heritage Sites (including the Lisboa Story Centre, the Monastery at Belém and the Palace at Sintra), as well as travel to Sintra and Cascais by rail. **Prices:** adult/child (ages 4–15): €20/€13 (24hr); €34/€19 (48hr); €42/€22.50 (72hr). Available for sale at the airport, tourism offices and online. The Lisboa Card is valid for a full calendar year after its purchase date (in case you want to postpone your trip), and is validated only on its first use. The card also gives deals and discounts on visits, tours, shopping and nightlife.

Emergency Phone Numbers
✚ **Emergency Services – 112**
✚ **24-hour Medical Emergency 211 301 075**, www.qualihealth.eu
✚ **Tourist Police 213 421 623/34**
Other Useful Phone Numbers
Telephone enquiries – *118
Railways – *707 201 220; www.cp.pt
Lisbon Airport – *218 413 500; www.aeroportolisboa.pt
Useful Websites: www.golisbon.com www.visitlisboa.com

PICKPOCKETS – Tourists are fair game for pickpockets and other petty criminals in Lisbon, as in all big cities. The good thing is that violence is hardly ever resorted to in such encounters. These thieves, normally working in twos or threes, are opportunistic. Never carry money in a rear or top pocket, never have your handbag open and never leave a handbag, purse or wallet out on a desk, table-top or even on the floor beneath your legs in a restaurant. If you get credit cards out to pay in a store, hold on to everything at all times. Be aware of pickpockets on buses and metro – they tend to "crowd" you. It only takes a second for a petty thief to disrupt your holiday and leave you feeling helpless and distressed.

GETTING THERE AND GETTING AROUND

AIRPORT – The airport, also commonly referred to as the Portela Airport, due to its location nearby Portela, lies about 7km/4.2mi north of the city centre. The **metro**'s red line now services the airport to and from the city centre (*see metro map on inside back cover*). A few **bus lines** (Aerobus no. 1 & 2) run from the airport to the city (#1 to Rossio, #2 to Cais do Sodré, close to Praça do Comércio) with service from 8am–9pm, departures every 20min. *2͏͏ 503 225. There are also local buse͏ but they're slower and less relia͏

Taxis from the airport to downtown cost around ⊛€15, with a surcharge for luggage. There is a surcharge after midnight as well. Ask beforehand – the fare should certainly not be more than about €20 to a city centre hotel. Allow 30–40min for the trip by bus, more at peak periods.

🕙 Only use licensed taxis, and always agree the taxi fare with your driver before leaving the airport.

The tourist office inside the airport will sell you prepaid taxi vouchers to your hotel, though watch out for surcharges. A taxi voucher costs around €25, which includes a surcharge for luggage, but this is significantly more than simply getting in a taxi and paying the driver.

RAIL STATIONS – Cais do Sodré – Services about every 20min to Estoril and Cascais. Journey takes about 40min to Cascais.
Santa Apolónia – Services to the north of Portugal and international (Paris).
Rossio – Suburban trains to the northwest and Sintra. Trains for Sintra leave about every 10min. Journey takes approximately 35min. Last train 11pm.
Sul e Suesta – For services to Alentejo and the Algarve via the ferry that provides access to the station at Barreiro.
Oriente – Superb intermodal station (metro, bus, train) with services to the north, connecting with trains for Santa Apolónia and Sintra.

BY BOAT – The *cacilheiros*, which serve the towns on the opposite banks of the Tagus, offer an opportunity to cruise on the river. Throughout the day boats depart about every 15min. Tickets are on sale from machines at the stations.
🚢 **Estação Fluvial do Terreiro do Paço** – For Montijo, Seixal, Barreiro and trains to Alentejo and the Algarve. Also the departure point for Tagus river cruises.

🚢 **Estação do Cais do Sodré** – Serves Cacilhas and Almada.
🚢 **Estação de Belém** – Services to Brandão and Trafaria.
🚢 **Estação Fluvial do Parque das Nações** – Services to Barreiro.

BY CAR – Since Lisbon is a busy and compact city it is normally better to use public transport. By day the traffic is quite heavy, particularly in the older quarters in the centre where the streets are narrow and very congested. Parking spaces are scarce, although you will find some large underground car parks, but they are not cheap. Public transport is the easiest option.
If you do need to rent a car (maybe for a trip outside the city), there are several car rental agencies at the airport and also scattered around the city. If you have any problems, ask your hotel concierge. Only the larger hotels will have parking spaces overnight; if you park on the street you may have to move the car fairly early. Never leave valuables in your car.

BY TAXI – A good way of getting round Lisbon, taxis are plentiful and less expensive than you might think – certainly less than in any comparable city in Europe. Most of them are beige in colour, and the price is shown on meters, at least within Lisbon. Outside the city centre, fares are calculated on a per kilometre rate, though if you go farther afield, you can negotiate a price.

ON FOOT –The best way to discover Lisbon and its various neighbourhoods (Baixa, Avenida da Liberdade, Chiado/Bairro Alta and Alfama) is on foot, or on the tram, using the lifts *(👆see Funiculars/Elevadores p100)* where possible. Parts of the city are quite hilly, so it helps to be in reasonably good physical shape.

BY METRO – Metro stations are shown on the map on the inside back cover. The network comprises four lines:
- Blue (Baixa-Chiado/Amadora Este)
- Red (Odivelas/Rato)
- Green (Cais do Sodré/Telheiras)
- Yellow (Oriente/Alameda).

The metro operates from 6.30am until 1am. A few metro stations are user-friendly for those with disabilities: *www.metrolisboa.pt.*

Several stations are decorated with *azulejos* by well-known Portuguese artists. Worth a special mention are Cidade Universitária (Vieira da Silva), Alto dos Moinhos (Júlio Pomar), Campo Grande (Eduardo Nery) Marqués de Pombal (Menez) and Baixa-Chiado (Álvaro Sizo Vieira).

Tickets – Metro tickets cost ∞€1.50 per journey, but it's much cheaper (€0.50 per journey) to buy a Viva Viagem card – this is an electronic card on which you put money that is then deducted as you travel (like the Oyster card in London). If you are planning on doing a lot of travelling, buy the 24-hour ticket for €6.40, which is valid for 24 hours after validation on the entire Metro and Carris networks. Or you can use your Lisbon Card (*see p98)*), which is also valid on public transport. *www. metrolisboa.pt.* ☏ *213 500 115.* See the metro map on the inside back cover.

FUNICULARS/ELEVADORES – Lisbon has several lifts within the city:
- Elevador da Bica: R. de S. Paulo/ Largo do Calhariz;
- Elevador da Glória : Restauradores/ São Pedro de Alcântara;
- Elevador do Lavra (the oldest): Largo da Anunciação/R. da Câmara Pestana;
- Elevador de S. Justa: .de Santa Justa (to viewpoint).

They each cost ∞€3.80–€5.30 or you can use your Lisbon Card. www. carris.pt.

BY BUS – Principal routes: No. 45 (Prior Velho/Cais do Sodré); No. 83 (Portela/Cais de Sodré); No. 46 (Est. Sta. Apolónia/Damaia); No. 15 (Cais do Sodré/Sete Rios); No. 43 (Praça Figueira/Buraca).

BY TRAM (Elétricos) – The old tramways are one of the charms of Lisbon as well as being one of the best ways to see the city and avoid climbing its hills! The old yellow bone-shaker trams are being replaced by newer models that are more user-friendly and comfortable. Of five possible routes, two lines in particular serve a number of monuments and museums:

No. E15: provides a useful link from central Lisbon to the Belem District: Praça da Figueira/Algés – Praça do Comércio – Mosteiro dos Jerónimos – Museu Nacional de Arqueológia – Museu da Marinha – Discoveries Monument – Tower of Belém;

No. E28: cuts through the Alfama district: São Vicente de Fora church – Museum of Decorative Arts – São Jorge castle – Cathedral – Baixa – Chiado museum – Largo do Chiado – São Bento – Basilica d'Estrela.

TIMES AND COSTS – Bus and trams adhere to a regular timetable between 6am and 1am with a frequency of between 11–15min until around 9.30pm. A small network of night buses operate until 5am. Most of

Elevador da Bica

© André Gonçalves/age fotostock

these night buses leave from the Cais do Sodré station.

The funiculars stop between 9pm and 12am/4.30am (Glória).

Tickets: A single Lisbon tram ticket costs €3 and can be purchased onboard from either the driver or the ticket machines (Note that the machines only accept coins). However, as with Metro tickets, a much better option is to use the Viva Viagem pre-paid ticket, which makes a single tram journey cost only €1.45. You can buy individual tickets on the bus or tram, but if you are staying a few days in Lisbon, it makes sense to buy a **Lisbon Card** (♿ see p98).

♿ **Accessibility** – Buses and trams in Lisbon are not user-friendly for disabled travellers, but there is a door-to-door minibus service (available for the same price as regular public transport) for those with special needs. It is, however, essential to make a reservation not less than two days in advance. ☎ 213 613 141, www.carris.pt/en/reduced-mobility/ (line open 7am–midnight).

CITY TOURS

A very good way to see any city that is new to you is an organised tour, either hop-on-hop-off or a regular tour. Lisbon has both.

Yellow Bus Tours (www.yellowbus tours.com) offer the official bus or river tours of the city at a variety of prices. The Tagus Tour takes you to Belém, departing from Praça da Figueira and passing many significant historical sights and monuments.

If you prefer to be on the water, take a Tagus River Cruise (*Yellow Boat Tour*) past Saint Jorge Castle, the Sé Cathedral and the April 25th Bridge. After the stop made in Cacilhas you will have the opportunity to climb to the Cristo Rei Sanctuary.

Tours for You (Rua do Pólo Norte; ☎ 213 904 208; www.toursforyou.pt) in half-day city tours and longer

Vasco da Gama Shopping Centre, Parque das Nações

© StockPhotosArt.com/iStock

tours farther afield, as well as private half-day or full-day days, overnight guided tours, self-drive independent tours and VIP Experiences.

PARQUE DAS NAÇÕES
♿ See Map I, pp102-103)

Parque das Nações (Park of Nations) was the site of Expo 98 and has since been transformed into an ultra modern side of traditional Lisbon. The park borders the River Tagus estuary and is a popular tourist area. Within the park is an oceanarium, a cable car, the Vasco da Gama shopping centre, a museum (the Pavilion of Knowledge), Lisbon's casino, the 15km Vasco da Gama bridge (once Europe's longest bridge) and other attractions with a water theme. At night there is a strip of restaurants, bars and nightclubs and is regarded as one of Lisbon's best areas for a night out.

Cable Car – runs through the park just above the banks of the Tagus, affording a fine view over the Vasco da Gama bridge and in the evening, of the sunset over the river. Operates daily 11am–7pm; ⛟ €6 (return), €4 one-way.

The Parque das Nações is easy to reach from any location in Lisbon as it is served by the Gare do Oriente station. *www.telecabinelisboa.pt.*

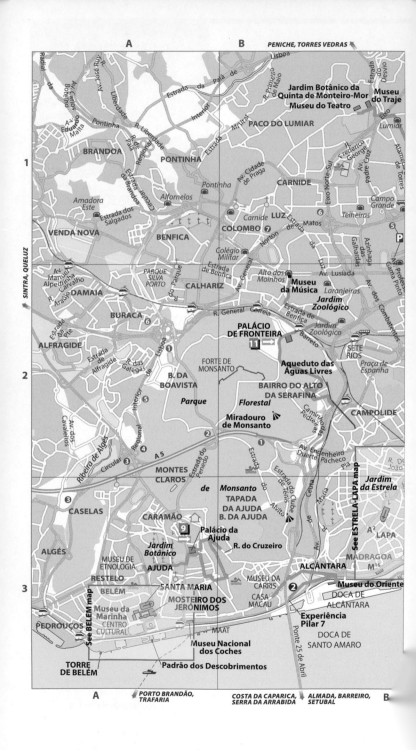

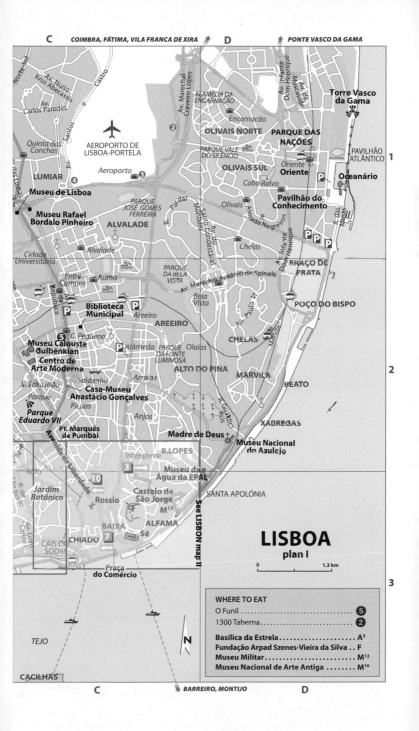

Av. Nuno Krus Abecassis
Norte-Sul
Castro
Av. Carlos Paredes
Santos

Av. Marechal Craveiro Lopes

ALAMEDA DA ENCARNAÇÃO

Av. Infante Dom Henrique

Torre Vasco da Gama

Quinta das Conchas

AEROPORTO DE LISBOA-PORTELA

Encarnação

OLIVAIS NORTE

PARQUE DAS NAÇÕES

PAVILHÃO ATLÂNTICO   **1**

Aeroporto

PARQUE VALE DO SILÊNCIO

OLIVAIS SUL

Oriente

Oriente

P

Oceanário

LUMIAR

Museu de Lisboa

Cabo Ruivo

Museu Rafael Bordalo Pinheiro

PARQUE JOSÉ GOMES FERREIRA

Olivais

Pavilhão do Conhecimento

ALVALADE

Paial

Santo Monteiro

Alameda Negreiros

Av. Infante Dom Henrique

P P P

Cidade Universitária

Alvalade

Chelas

BRAÇO DE PRATA

Entre Campos

Roma

PARQUE DA BELA VISTA

Av. Marechal António de Spínola

Bela Vista

POÇO DO BISPO

Biblioteca Municipal

P

Areeiro

AREEIRO

P

C. Pequeno

CHELAS

2

Museu Calouste Gulbenkian

P

Alameda

PARQUE DA FONTE LUMINOSA

Olaias

Centro de Arte Moderna

Saldanha

ALTO DO PINA

S. Sebastião

Parque

Arroios

MARVILA

BEATO

Casa-Museu Anastácio Gonçalves

Picoas

Parque Eduardo VII

Anjos

XADREGAS

Pr. Marquês de Pombal

Madre de Deus

Museu Nacional do Azulejo

Avenida da Liberdade

Intendente

B.LOPES

Jardim Botânico

Museu da Água da EPAL

SANTA APOLÓNIA

Rossio

Castelo de São Jorge

M13

Av. Dom Carlos

CAIS DO SODRÉ

CHIADO

BAIXA

Sé

ALFAMA

See LISBON map II

3

LISBOA
plan I

0 ————— 1.3 km

Praça do Comércio

TEJO

N

CACILHAS

WHERE TO EAT	
O Funil	**5**
1300 Taberna	**2**

Basílica da Estrela .... A²
Fundação Arpad Szenes-Vieira da Silva .. F
Museu Militar M13
Museu Nacional de Arte Antiga M16

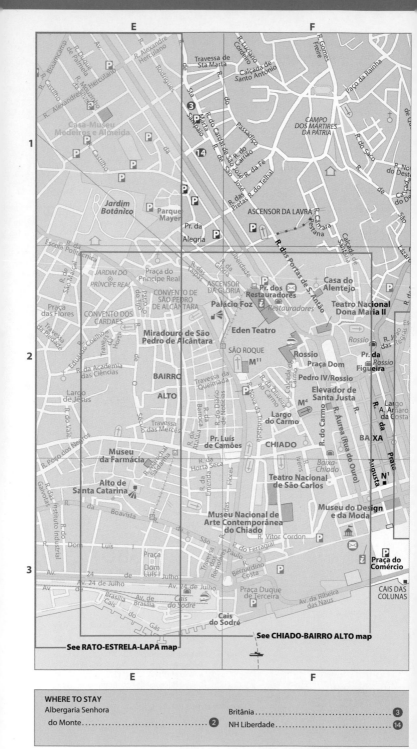

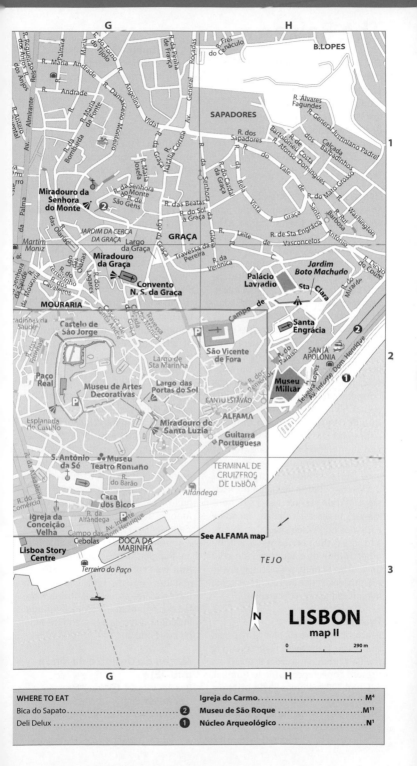

WHERE TO EAT		Igreja do Carmo	M⁴
Bica do Sapato	❷	Museu de São Roque	M¹¹
Deli Delux	❶	Núcleo Arqueológico	N¹

The Baixa★★

This part of the city, which was completely devastated by the earthquake and tsunami in 1755, was rebuilt to plans laid down by the Marquis of Pombal. Start at Praça dos Restauradores, just to the north of Rossio. On the elegant Praça do Comércio is the Lisboa Story Centre.

🕐 **Timing:** *Map II*. Walking, this itinerary should take you 2–3 hours, but don't rush.

SIGHTS

Praça dos Restauradores

The square owes its name to the men who, in 1640, led the revolt against the Spanish and proclaimed the independence of Portugal. The fine red roughcast façade on the west of the square belongs to the **Palácio Foz**, built in the 18C in Italianesque style by an Italian architect. Today it houses Lisbon's Tourist Information Centre *(Posto de Turismo)*. Next door is the **Éden Teatro**, designed by Cassiano Branco in 1937, now a hotel. Part of its Art Deco façade and its monumental staircase remain from the original building. Avenida da Liberdade runs northeast off the square to the Parque Eduardo VII. Parallel to the avenue is **Rua das Portas de Santo Antão**, a pedestrian street with cinemas, cafés and shops. The **Casa do Alentejo** at No. 58 has an unusual Moorish courtyard and a restaurant with abundant *azulejo* decoration. **Estação do Rossio**, the train station, has a 19C neo-Manueline, almost Italianate, **façade★** with wide horseshoe-shaped openings, and serves the town of Sintra, among others. Although stations might not be on your list of must-see places, it is well worth a look, inside and out. It has some magnificent *azulejo* decoration.

Praça do Rossio★

Praça Dom Pedro IV, popularly called the Rossio, is the lively main square of the Baixa that dates from the 13C. Its present appearance is due to Pombal: 18C and 19C buildings line it on three sides, the ground floors being given over to cafés such as the famous **Nicola** with its Art Deco façade, and small shops that have kept their decoration from the beginning of the century. Among these are the tobacconists near Nicola with *azulejos* by Rafael Bordalo Pinheiro, and the corner shop that serves *ginginha*, the well-known cherry liqueur, off Largo de São Domingos, next to a milliners dating from the late 19C.

The north side of the square is bordered by the **Teatro Nacional Dona Maria II**, built in 1840 on the site of the former Palace of the Inquisition. The façade is adorned with a statue of Gil Vicente, the father of Portuguese theatre. In the middle of the square, between the Baroque fountains, is the bronze statue of Dom Pedro IV, after whom the square is named and who was crowned Pedro I, Emperor of Brazil.

Parallel to the Rossio and to the east is the **Praça da Figueira**, a square of Classical buildings with an equestrian statue of Dom João I in the centre.

South of the square, the grid of Baixa streets, some pedestrianised, forms Lisbon's main shopping district. The streets running south between the Rossio and Praça do Comércio are named after the guilds that originally practised there. Among them are Rua dos Correeiros (Saddlers' Street) and Rua dos Sapateiros (Cobblers' Street). The three main streets are Rua do Ouro (Goldsmiths' Street), **Rua da Prata** (Silversmiths' Street), and **Rua Augusta**, at the end of which there is a large arch with statues of some famous figures from Portugal's history, including Vasco da Gama and the Marquis de Pombal.

Museu do Design e da Moda (MUDE)★

Rua Augusta, 24. 🕐*Closed for renovations until 2022; check website for latest information. During the renovations, the museum's many exhibitions and shows are taking place* outdoors around the country (MUDE online). *218 886 117. www.mude.pt.* Housed in a former bank, this museum displays the collection of Francisco Capelo, who has assembled works here from the Museu de Arte Moderna in Sintra. The collection comprises creations by more than 200 fashion designers as well as furniture and objects indicative of design aesthetics from 1937 to the present. The old bank vault downstairs is worth seeing.

Elevador de Santa Justa★

May–Oct 7:30am–10:45pm; Nov–Apr 7:30am–9pm. €5 (acquired on-board, valid for 2 trips, includes access to viewpoint); viewpoint access only €1.50. The lift was built in 1901 by Raoul Mesnier de Ponsard, a Portuguese engineer of French origin who was influenced by Gustave Eiffel. It gives direct access to Chiado. From the upper platform, 32m above the street, there is a good **view★** of the Rossio and the Baixa.

Rua do Ouro (or Rua Áurea)

In the 15C and 16C, this street was the city's gold trading; today it is lined with banks, jewellers and goldsmiths, and there are vendors selling water, snacks and items like sunglasses. One very interesting diversion in the Baixa is a trip below the streets into the **Núcleo Arqueológico**, which reveals 2 500 years of Lisbon's history (*Mon–Sat 10am–noon and 2–5pm, Sun, public holidays. Entry is via the Millennium BCP building on Rua dos Correeiros. *211 131 004.*).

Praça do Comércio★★

The finest square in Lisbon (also known as **Terreiro do Paço**) is the site where the Royal Palace once stood, facing the Straw Sea (*Mar da Palha*). The palace was destroyed by the earthquake. The square was designed as a whole and is an excellent example of the Pombaline style. It measures 192m long by 177m wide and is lined on three sides by Classical buildings with tall arcades supporting two upper storeys with red façades. A 19C Baroque triumphal arch forms a backdrop to the equestrian statue of King José I. This statue by the late 18C sculptor Machado de Castro is cast in bronze and is the reason for the square's also being known as Black Horse Square. On 1 February 1908, King Carlos I and his heir, Prince Luís Felipe, were assassinated on the square.

Southeast of the square, Lisbon's South Station, **Estação do Sul e Sueste** (*estação fluvial on plan*), is decorated with *azulejo* panels of towns in the Alentejo and the Algarve. Passengers embark here by ferry to the railway station on the opposite shore of the Tagus for destinations to the south and southeast of Portugal.

♟ Lisboa Story Centre★

*Terreiro do Paço 78 –81. 10am–8pm. Closed 25 Dec. €7, child, 6–15 €4.50. *211 941 099. www.lisboastorycentre.pt.* On the east side of the square is a fun, hands-on visitor attraction, the Lisboa Story Centre, which offers a fun way to learn about the city's history in an hour. Dramatic re-creations of Lisbon's most important historical events, such as the Great Earthquake of 1755, are presented in a playful and interactive manner, using a mixture of elaborate sets, multimedia and sensory experiences. The myths and realities of this ancient city are also explored.

Igreja da Conceição Velha

The **south side★** of the transept, the only remains of the original church, which collapsed in the earthquake of 1755, is a fine example of the Manueline style. The carving on the tympanum shows Our Lady of Compassion sheltering with her cloak, Pope Leo X, Dom Manuel, Dona Leonor, bishops and others.

Casa dos Bicos

This **House of Facets**, faced with diamond-shaped bosses, once formed part of a 16C palace, damaged in the 1755 earthquake. It belonged to the son of Afonso de Albuquerque, the viceroy of India. It lost its entire top floor, but it was rebuilt in 1982. Inside, the marble staircase stands out against the black walls.

Chiado★

The name Chiado applies not only to **Largo do Chiado** but also to a whole district of which the main streets, Rua Garrett and Rua do Carmo, link the Rossio to Praça Luís de Camões. The **Santa Justa** lift ascends to the area struck by fire on 25 August 1988. The four blocks of buildings damaged were mainly shops, including the *Grandella* department store (since replaced by the *Printemps* store) and the famous *Ferrari* tearoom. Some 2 000 people lost their jobs as a result of this tragedy, though no lives were lost. The rehabilitation of the area was overseen by well-known Portuguese architect Álvaro Siza, who put forward a resolutely classical plan to rebuild and safeguard the façades of the buildings, and to transform their interiors into patios, elegant shops and café terraces.

SIGHTS

Museu Arqueológico do Carmo★

Largo do Carmo, Ruínas do Convento do Carmo. ◑*May–Sept Mon–Sat 10am–7pm (closes 6pm Oct–Apr).* ◑*1 Jan, 1 May and 25 Dec.* ◉€5. ✆213 478 629. *www.museuarqueologicodocarmo.pt.* Once through the doorway of the Carmelite Church, which was almost totally destroyed during the 1755 earthquake,

© efesenko/iStock

A Brasileira, Rua Garrett

◑ **Timing:** *Map IV.* Allow 2h30 for this area.

the visitor is struck by the atmospheric aura of the ruins and the silence.
Today, the ruins of the late 14C Gothic church built by Constable Nuno Álvares Pereira, house an archaeological museum. Among the collections are Bronze Age pottery, marble low reliefs, an Egyptian and two Peruvian mummies, Romanesque and Gothic tombs (including the recumbent statue of Fernão Sanchez, illegitimate son of Dom Dinis) and Spanish Arabic *azulejos*.

Rua do Carmo and Rua Garrett★

These elegant streets with their old-fashioned storefronts are renowned for their book shops, patisseries and cafés. The most famous of the latter is the **Brasileira**, once frequented by the poet Fernando Pessoa whose centenary was celebrated in 1988. A bronze statue of the poet stands on the terrace.

Museu Nacional do Chiado★

Rua Serpa Pinto, 4. ◑*Tue–Sun 10am–6pm.* ◉€4.50 *(free 1st Sun of each month).* ✆213 432 148. *www.museuartecontemporanea.pt.* The building, originally a 13C abbey, was transformed into a contemporary arts museum in 1911. Following the 1988 fire, it was refurbished by the French architect Jean-Michel Wilmotte.
The museum, which is beautifully lit and laid out, displays an exhibit of predominantly Portuguese paintings, drawings and sculpture from the period between 1850 and 1950. The first floor is devoted to French sculpture, including Rodin's *Bronze Age* and Canto da Maia's *Adam and Eve*. Soares dos Reis' sculpture *O Desterrado (The Exile)* stands out among the works on the second floor. Various periods are represented: the **Romantic**, **Naturalist** (*A Charneca de Belas* by Silva Porto, *Concerto de Amadores* by Columbano, and *A Beira-Mar* by José Malhoa)

and **Modernist** (*Tristezas* by Amadeo de Souza-Cardoso, *O Bailarico no Bairro* by Mário Eloy, *Nú* by Eduardo Viana, and the drawing *A Sesta* by Almada Negreiros), and a small collection of **Symbolist** and **neo-Realist** works.

Teatro Nacional de São Carlos
Rua Serpa Pinto, 9. ☎213 253 000. www.tnsc.pt.
A venue for regular concerts, ballet and opera, this lavish theatre is situated in an area overlooking the Tagus. It was built in 1793 in Neoclassical style; its façade was inspired by the San Carlo theatre in Naples. Rich in gold and red velvet, the interior is worth a visit.

Praça Luís de Camões
Luís de Camões is regarded as Portugal's top poet, famed for his love sonnets and plays. He was well educated and attended the University in Coimbra, where he began his writing. After a few mishaps and a time in prison, he was sent as an army officer to Goa (where his father had died many years before) and then to Macau, where, despite losing one eye, he wrote *The Lusiads*, his

greatest poem. He also chronicled the voyages of his colleagues in this new part of the world, including his own shipwreck, in which his Chinese lover died. He returned to Portugal and died in Lisbon in 1580, aged 56.
The square, with a statue of the great poet at its centre, was one of the stages for the revolution on 25 April 1974. The square is the transition zone between the Chiado and the Bairro Alto.

Rua da Misericórdia
The street is part of the Praça Camões and borders the Bairro Alto quarter to the west of Chiado.

Museu da Farmacia★ (Pharmacy Museum)
Rua Marechal Saldanha, 1. ⒸOpen Daily 10am–7pm. ⊗€6.50. ☎213 400 680/88. www.museudafarmacia.pt.
This museum is housed in a palace dating from 1870, and contains more than 14 000 objects from all over the world; pharmacies dating from the 15C to 19C are represented, including a Chinese pharmacy from Macao that was functioning there until 1996.

Bairro Alto★

This picturesque working-class area dating from the 16C has kept its character in spite of becoming the centre for trendy fashion houses, designers, restaurants, and *fado* venues. The main shopping streets are **Rua do Diário de Notícias** and **Rua de Atalaia**. Don't miss sunsets over the Tagus from the **Alto de Santa Catarina★** belvedere with its statue of Adamostor, the giant who was transformed into the Cape of Storms (Cape of Good Hope).

SIGHTS
Museu de São Roque★
Largo Trindade Coelho. ⒸOct–Mar Mon 2–6pm, Tue–Sun 10am–6pm; Apr–Sept Mon 2–7pm, Tue–Wed 10am–7pm, Thu 10am–8pm. w/e 10am–7pm.

▷ **Location:** *Map IV.* The narrow 17C streets of the "upper town" are high above the central city to the west of the Baixa.
Ⓒ **Timing:** 2 hours are sufficient to explore the sights; at night, you may wish to spend longer bar-hopping around the cobbled streets to the west of Rua de Misericórdia.

Ⓒ*1 Jan, Easter Sunday, 1 May and 25 Dec. ⊗€2.50. ☎213 235 421. www.museu-saoroque.com.*
The Museum and Church of São Roque are both part of the former Professed-House of São Roque, the main Jesuit

Evening in Bairro Alto

© Patrice Hauser/hemis.fr

building in Portugal until the 18C. Construction of the church started in 1567. Throughout the 17C and first half of the 18C, it was embellished by numerous artists, creating the exuberant **interior**★ it has today. The ceiling, painted by Francisco Venegas and Amaro do Vale in *trompe l'oeil* style, has scenes that allude to the Eucharist and is the only one of its kind in Lisbon. The Chapel of Saint Roch has *azulejos* by Francisco de Matos, a masterpiece of late 16C European ceramics, and a painting depicting the *Apparition of the Angel to Saint Roch* by Gaspar Dias. The most astonishing masterpiece is the **Capela de São João Baptista**★★ (Chapel of St John the Baptist), commissioned by King John V in 1742. It was made entirely in Rome, where it was designed by Luigi Vanvitelli and Nicola Salvi, blessed by Pope Benedict XIV and then shipped to Lisbon. It's completely crafted in precious or semi-precious materials, such as lapis lazuli (columns and altar), amethyst (altar), alabaster (pilasters), porphyry (steps) or Carrara marble (sculptures), while the wall panels are made in minuscule mosaics.

The **museum** houses treasures from the Chapel of St John the Baptist, including Italian liturgical **vestments**★ in silk or lamé embroidered in gold, and the metalwork collection that the king commissioned for the chapel, unique in its kind.

This collection is one of the largest reliquary amassings in Europe, and includes Eastern art, and Mannerist and Baroque Portuguese painting and sculpture. As a whole, it's one of the most important sacred art collections in Portugal.

Miradouro de São Pedro de Alcântara★

The belvedere takes the form of a pleasant garden suspended like a balcony over the lower town, with a wide **view**★★ of the Baixa, the Tagus and Castelo de São Jorge on the hill opposite *(viewing table)*.

▶ The Calçada da Gloria funicular descends to Praça dos Restauradores.

Jardim Botânico (Botanical Gardens)

Entry via the old Faculty of Science, Rua Escola Politécnica 58, or via Rua da Algeria. ◯*Apr-Sept 9am-8pm, Oct-Mar 9am-5pm.* ◯*Closed 1 Jan, 25 Dec.* ✆€3. 𝄞*213 921 802.*
www.museus.ulisboa.pt

This beautiful garden, established in 1873 to further the study of plants and part of the Academy of Sciences, is one of the most respected in Europe for its collection of subtropical flora, much of it brought from what were at the time Portugal's overseas territories.

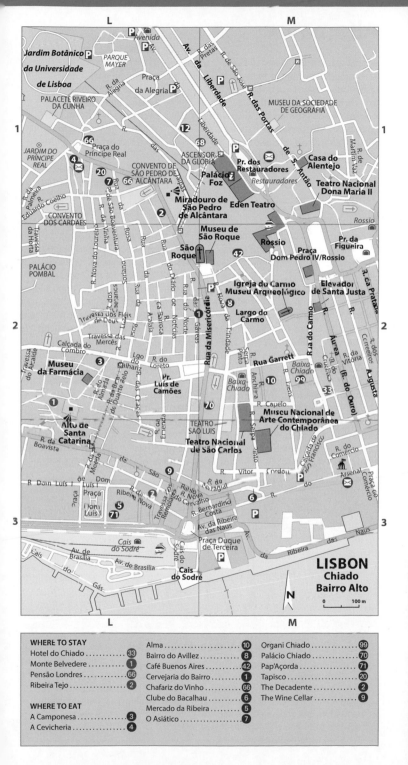

LISBON
Chiado
Bairro Alto

N

0 ——————— 100 m

WHERE TO STAY				Alma	10		Organi Chiado	99
Hotel do Chiado	33			Bairro do Avillez	8		Palácio Chiado	70
Monte Belvedere	1			Café Buenos Aires	42		Pap'Açorda	71
Pensão Londres	66			Cervejaria do Bairro	1		Tapisco	20
Ribeira Tejo	2			Chafariz do Vinho	66		The Decadente	2
				Clube do Bacalhau	6		The Wine Cellar	9
WHERE TO EAT				Mercado da Ribeira	5			
A Camponesa	3			O Asiático	7			
A Cevicheria	4							

Alfama★★

Alfama was largely spared in the earthquake, a symbol of hope to Lisbonites. Today it is a bustling, lively area of houses fronted by wrought-iron balconies bursting with flowers, and decorated with *azulejos* representing The Virgin and St Anthony (patron saint of Lisbon).

●● WALKING TOUR

Sé (Cathedral)★★

Largo da Sé 1100-585. ⏱*Daily 9am–7pm (cloisters 10am–5pm).* ⏱*Closed public holidays.* ✆*Cathedral free; cloisters €2.50.* 📞*218 866 752.*
www.patriarcado-lisboa.pt.

Lisbon's cathedral *(sé)*, like those of Oporto, Coimbra and Évora, was once a fortress, as can be observed from the two towers flanking the façade and its battlements. It was built in the Romanesque style in the late 12C, shortly after Afonso Henriques had captured the town with the aid of the Crusaders. The architects, it is believed, were the Frenchmen Robert and Bernard who designed Coimbra Cathedral. Remodelling followed the earthquake of 1755 when the chancel collapsed. Much of its

⏱ **Timing:** Map pp114-115. The most pleasant way to see Alfama is simply to wander through the district, preferably in the morning when the market is open. The walking route marked on the map follows the order in which the sites of the quarter are described. Allow half a day for this neighbourhood.

former Romanesque appeal can be seen on the façade and in the nave, although Gothic features and the remodelling of the 17C and 18C are still apparent.

In the **interior**, the nave, supported by wide arches and groined vaulting, is in plain Romanesque style. An elegant triforium runs above the aisles and the transept. The Gothic Bartolomeu Joanes Chapel, off the north aisle, contains a terra-cotta crib by Machado de Castro. The chancel, with its groined vaulting, was rebuilt in the 18C, but the ambulatory, pierced with lancet windows, kept the earlier Gothic style of the 14C when it was remodelled. The third chapel on the south side contains the 14C **Gothic tombs★** of Lopo Fernandes Pacheco,

© peresanz/iStock

Ponte Vasco da Gama★★

This magnificent road bridge was built across the Tagus between 1995 and 1998. It is 18km/11mi long, 10km/6mi of which passes over water. At its lowest point, the bridge has the illusion of balancing directly on the Tagus. This superb feat of engineering is made up of several sections supported on pillars, some of which rise to 150m and are buried to a depth of 95m. The superstructure's height varies from 14m to 30m to enable ships to pass beneath it.

companion in arms to King Afonso IV, and his wife. Note the fine Romanesque wrought-iron **grille**★ enclosing a chapel near the entrance to the cloisters.

The **cloisters** are in the late 13C style of Cistercian Gothic: the lower gallery is supported alternately by massive buttresses and Gothic arches, above which are star-shaped oculi. The chapterhouse contains the tomb of Lisbon's first bishop. Excavations in the garden of the cloisters have led to the discovery of vestiges from the Phoenician (8C BCE) and Roman periods, as well as the ruins of a former mosque (9C and 10C).

Treasury★

Access to the treasury on the right, near the entrance to the cathedral.

A staircase leads to rooms displaying magnificent vestments, reliquaries and gold and silver plate. The impressive 18C chapter room contains the **King Dom José I monstrance**, richly decorated with 4 120 precious stones.

Not far from the cathedral stands the **Igreja de Santo António da Sé**, which was built in 1812 on the site of the house in which St Anthony of Padua (1195–1231), known to the city's inhabitants as Saint Anthony of Lisbon, was born. He is Lisbon's patron saint and a small museum, the **Museu Antoniano**, (○*Tue–Sun 10am–6pm;* ○*public holidays;* ☎*218 860 447)*, testifies to his popularity.

Miradouro de Santa Luzia★

A small terrace near the Igreja de Santa Luzia has been laid out as a lookout point on the remains of the old Arab fortifications. It affords an excellent **view**★★ of the Tagus, the harbour and, just below, the Alfama quarter, a maze of alleys from which rise the belfries of São Miguel and São Estêvão.

The outer walls of the Igreja de Santa Luzia are covered with small panels of *azulejos*, one of which shows Praça do Comércio and another Lisbon's capture by the Crusaders and the death of Martim Moniz in the Castelo de São Jorge.

Azulejos covering a wall marking the south edge of the square show a general view of Lisbon.

Largo das Portas do Sol★

The Sun Gateway was one of the seven gates into the Arab city. The square, situated on the other side of the Church of Santa Luzia, has a small esplanade that offers a lovely **view**★★ over the rooftops, São Vicente de Fora and the river.

Museu Artes Decorativas Portuguesas★★ – Fundação Ricardo do Espírito Santo Silva (FRESS)

Largo das Portas do Sol, 2. ○*Wed–Mon 10am–5pm.* ○*1 Jan, 1 May and 25 Dec.* ◈€4. ☎*218 814 600. www.fress.pt.*

The former palace of the Counts of Azurara (17C) and the fine collections it contains were bequeathed to the city of Lisbon by Ricardo Espírito Santo Silva. Portugal's most important **furniture collection** is housed here, with valuable wooden Portuguese, French and English furniture dating from the 16C to the 19C. Bedrooms, dining rooms, function rooms, music salons and dressing rooms from different eras have been reconstructed in their original forms. Wall hangings, silver, porcelain, ceramics and books complete the touch of authenticity. The museum brings to life the Lisbon of the 17C and 18C through a series of small, intimate rooms decorated with *azulejos* and frescoes on three floors. Level 4 *(second floor)* is quite elegant, while Level 3 displays interiors with a plainer, yet no less handsome, decorative touch. The Portuguese and Indo-Portuguese furniture is particularly interesting; there are also collections of silver, Chinese porcelain and several tapestries from the 16C and 18C.

○ Starting from Largo das Portas do Sol, take the steps down from **Rua Norberto de Araújo**, which are supported on one side by the Moorish town wall.

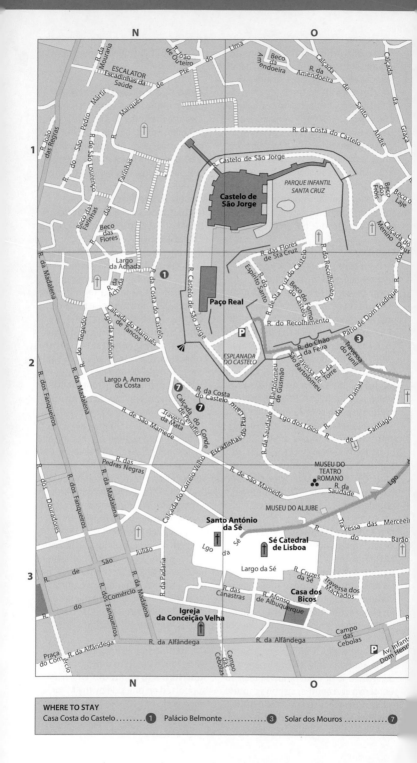

WHERE TO STAY

Casa Costa do Castelo.........**1**   Palácio Belmonte.............**3**   Solar dos Mouros.............**7**

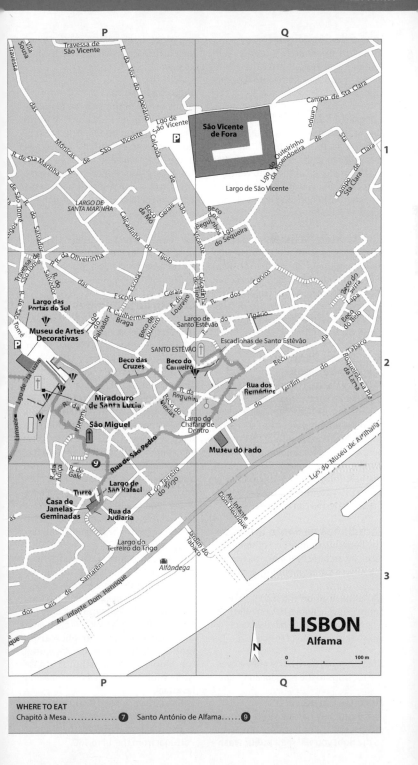

LISBON
Alfama

N

0   100 m

WHERE TO EAT
Chapitô à Mesa .... **7**   Santo António de Alfama...... **9**

Igreja de São Miguel

Although the church is medieval in origin, it was rebuilt after the earthquake. It contains some fine Baroque woodwork.

Largo de São Rafael

On the west side of this small square, which is surrounded by 17C houses, there still stand the remains of a **tower** that formed part of the Arab wall and later the defences of Christian Lisbon until the 14C, when King Fernando had a new wall built.

Rua da Judiaria (Jewish Quarter)

In this street stands a 16C **house** with paired windows, above the fortification of the old Arab wall. It was custmary, under Moorish occupation, for the Jewish community to live outside the city walls, and here you can see the juxtaposition of the two.

Rua de São Pedro and Rua dos Remédios

These are the busiest trading streets in the Alfama, lined with small shops and taverns. Rua de São Pedro is at its liveliest in the morning when its fish market is held. At the top of Rua dos Remédios, note on the left-hand side the Manueline door on the Igreja do Santo Espírito. Farther along, at No. 2 Calçadinha de Santo Estêvão, another doorway from the same period can be seen.

Escadinhas de Santo Estêvão★

The harmonious interplay of stairs, terrace and architecture make this one of the Alfama's most picturesque spots.

▷ As you head behind the Igreja de Santo Estêvão, note a balcony and a panel of *azulejos*. Climb the stairs which skirt the side of the church.

At the top you have a fine **view★** over the rooftops to the harbour and Tagus.

Beco de Carneiro

This extremely narrow street has very steep steps. At the bottom of the street to the right you will see a **public washing place**. Look behind you for a fine view of the façade of the Igreja de Santo Estêvão.

Beco das Cruzes

At the corner of this street and Rua de Regueira stands an 18C house of which the overhanging upper floors are supported by carved corbels. Above one of the doors a panel of *azulejos* shows the Virgin of Conception; from the same spot there is a view up the alley to the place where it is crossed by an arch surmounted by a cross.

▷ Take Beco de Santa Helena back up to Largo das Portas do Sol. Take Travessa de Santa Luzia, which leads to the castle.

Castelo de São Jorge★★

🕐 *Open daily 9am–9pm (Nov–Feb until 6pm).* ⌛€10. *Guided tours daily 10:30am, 1pm and 4pm.* 🕐 *Closed 1 Jan, 1 May, 24–25 Dec, 31 Dec.* ✆ *218 800 620. http://castelodesaojorge.pt/en*

The castle stands high above the city in a remarkable position. Built by the Visigoths in the 5C, enlarged by the Moors in the 9C and then modified during the reign of Afonso Henriques, it has since been turned into a shaded flower garden. After passing through the outer wall you reach the former parade ground from which there is a magnificent **view★★★** of the Tagus. Activities for children are held here on Sundays, such as actors in period costume performing and displaying weapons.

The castle's 10 towers are linked by huge battlemented walls. Once through the barbican at the castle entrance, steps lead to the parapet walk and the towers that provide **viewpoints** over the town. In the north wall there is a door where the Portuguese knight **Martim Moniz** lost his life as he prevented the Moors from shutting the gate while Afonso Henriques was making his attack.

The Royal Palace, **Paço Real**, built on the site of a former Arab palace, was used as the royal residence by the kings of Portugal from the 14 to 16C.

The museum displays archaeological finds from the castle.

NEAR THE ALFAMA
The following sights can be reached by tram No. E28.

Campo de Santa Clara★
The square between the churches of São Vicente and Santa Engrácia is the setting on Tuesdays and Saturdays for the **Feira da Ladra**, a colourful flea market. On the northern side of the square stands the graceful 18C **Palácio Lavradio**.

Mouraria, Graça, Santa Apolónia

Mouraria, one of Lisbon's oldest districts, is associated with fado, which has been heard here since the 19C. Legendary fadista Maria Severa lived here. Graça is a popular residential district, where several villas from the 19C can still be seen. It is situated on the hill to the north of the city, overlooking the Alfama and easily reached from Alfama's top end. Santa Apolónia has the city's oldest railway station, dating from 1886.

SIGHTS
Miradouro da Senhora do Monte★★
This vantage point offers an extensive **view★★★** over Lisbon (the best, without doubt) and in particular over the Castelo de São Jorge and the Mouraria quarter. The chapel next to the belvedere dates from 1796, although its origins can be traced back to 1147, the year of Lisbon's reconquest.

Mosteiro de São Vicente de Fora
Largo de São Vicente. ◷Tue–Sat 8am–6pm. ◷ 1 Jan, Easter Sun and 25 Dec. ☞€5. ℘218 810 500.

The small **Jardim Boto Machado** offers a haven of peace and tranquillity amid its exotic plants.

Igreja de Santa Engrácia★
National Pantheon, Campo de Santa Clara. ◷Tue–Sun 10am–5pm.
Begun in the 17C, the Baroque church was never completed. In the form of a Greek cross, it is surmounted by a cupola added in 1966. The interior features slabs of polished marble. The National Pantheon houses the cenotaphs (though not necessarily the tombs) of great Portuguese men and women, including Prince Henry the Navigator.

> ◷ **Timing:** *Map II.* Allow half a day to stroll around this area, taking in the views and the relaxing ambience.

This monastery church was built by the Italian architect Phillippe Terzi between 1582 and 1627. From the rooftop are incredible **views★** of the city below. The interior, covered with a fine coffered vault, is outstanding for the simplicity of its lines. On the south side of the church, the **cloisters** have walls covered in 18C *azulejos★* illustrating the *Fables* of La Fontaine. Galleries lead to the former monks' refectory which, after the reign of Dom João IV, was transformed into a pantheon for the House of Bragança. Interesting exhibits that change regularly are worth checking out. The church's museum (◷*daily 10am–6pm* ☞€5. *www.patriarcado-lisboa.pt)* is organized around four sections and houses the largest collection of azulejo tiles under one roof.

Igreja and Convento de Nossa Senhora da Graça
This imposing religious complex on the Graça hill dominates the city. The church and convent were founded in the 13C, but have been rebuilt a few times, particularly after the earthquake in 1755.

Note the bell-tower from 1738 next to the convent doorway. The interior is Baroque and contains fine 17C and 18C *azulejos*.

Opposite the church, a belvedere offers an extensive **view★** over the city.

Museu Nacional do Azulejo★★

Rua da Madre de Deus 4. Take the No. 104 or 105 bus from Praça do Comércio; it is down near the river-front.

🕐*Tue–Sun 10am–6pm.* ⊛€5. ℘218 100 340. www.museudoazulejo.gov.pt.

Despite its rather unattractive location near the waterfront and the old docks, this fascinating museum is housed in the **Madre de Deus Convent**, an absolutely magnificent building and arguably one of the best in Lisbon. It contains a wonderful collection of *azulejos*, the exotically painted Hispano-Moorish tiles dating back to the 15C. Wherever you go in Portugal you cannot escape *azulejos,* and this is a good opportunity to find out something about them. The galleries on the ground floor are arranged around the cloisters and contain *azulejos* brought in from Seville in the 15C. Particularly noteworthy is the altarpiece of Nossa Senhora da Vida (1580) depicting a Nativity scene. The highlight of the museum, in the cloisters, is a blue and white composition of 1 300 tiles, 23m in length, of Lisbon's cityscape that was produced in 1738, prior to the earthquake.

Leaving the cloisters and entering the **church★★**, you come through the low choir, whose walls with their 16C Seville *azulejos* have been preserved. The 18C church and in particular the Baroque altar are resplendent with gilded woodwork. The nave has a coffered vault with panels depicting scenes from the life of the Virgin. Other paintings depict the lives of St Clare and St Francis.

In the **chapter-house★** are ceiling panels painted with portraits from the 16C and 17C of King João III and his Queen, Catherine of Austria, attributed to Cristóvão Lopes.

Over the Tagus

Take a ferry to the south bank of the River Tagus to Almada and you will be rewarded with the best view of the city of Lisbon. More outstanding views are from the castle, the funicular of the Boca do Vento (Mouth of the Wind), and the statue of Cristo Rei (Christ the King).

SIGHTS
Cacilhas

Reached by ferry from Cais do Sodré pier, Cacilhas is best known for its local beer houses. Walk along the wharves (1km/0.6mi) to an elevator that climbs to the top of the cliff terrace overlooking the Tagus. The Casa da Cerca is a contemporary art centre.

🕐 **Timing:** Take a day and join a **boat trip**. The trips give a good view of Lisbon and its surroundings and the harbour where, in addition to the commercial traffic, Venetian style barges with large triangular sails may sometimes be seen. The crossing of the estuary in one of the regular ferries makes a pleasant trip as well as giving fine **views★★** of the city. Approaching Lisbon by boat at Terreiro do Paço (Praça do Comércio) is a wonderful experience, providing the visitor with the feeling of having entered the very heart of the city.

Cova do Vapor

Access by ferry from the station Belém towards Trafaria.
Follow the coastal path from Trafaria past huge silos along the Tagus to this small fishing port *(30min)*. Windsurfers often sail offshore.

Cristo Rei (Christ the King)★★

♿ *See also COSTA DA CAPARICA.*
3.5km/2mi from the south toll gate of the 25 de Abril suspension bridge, turn left at motorway exit 1 towards Almada. Follow signs; leave car in car park near the monument. ⊙*Daily from 9.30am until 6.15pm in winter, 6.30pm Mon–Fri in summer and 7pm at weekends.* ⊛€5. ☎212 751 000. www.cristorei.pt.
This enormous statue of Christ in Majesty, which can be seen from the Lisbon side of the river but is on the opposite shore, was erected in 1959 to thank God for having spared Portugal during World War II. Although the country was officially neutral, there was always a threat that it might become involved. Thankfully it did not, though Allied aircraft

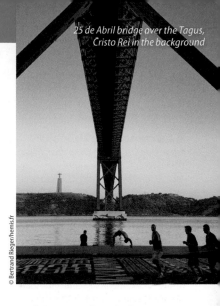

25 de Abril bridge over the Tagus, Cristo Rei in the background

© Bertrand Rieger/hemis.fr

used the Azores for refuelling on their way across the Atlantic.
It is a slightly smaller replica of the statue of Christ the Redeemer in Rio de Janeiro. From the pedestal *(access by lift, plus 74 steps)* which is 79.3m above ground level and 104m over the Tagus, there is a **panoramic view★★** of the Tagus estuary, Lisbon and the plain to the south as far as Setúbal.

Parque das Nações★

The park's site, which hosted Expo'98, is spread out along the Tagus to the east of the city. With its breezy oceanfront setting and futuristic architecture, it makes a pleasant change from the narrow lanes and old buildings of the centre. There are plenty of bars, restaurants, gardens and shops. The Oceanário is a large aquarium, one of the best in Europe. On the grounds of the casino are 20 or so works by contemporary Portuguese and international artists, including João Cutileiro, in the Passeio das Tágides; an immense iron oxide-coated steel sculpture by Jorge Vieira; stone paving by Fernando Conduto; works by Pedro Cabrita

⊙ **Timing:** An entire day is best. The easiest way to arrive is by metro, at the modern Oriente station.
▷ **Location:** *MAP I. See Getting There p98–99* for details of transport within the park.

Reis and Pedro Calapez; and stone paving by Pedro Proença. A superb panorama of the River Tagus and city can be had from the Torre Vasco da Gama and cable car.

SIGHTS
Estação do Oriente★

This intermodal complex houses a railway station, metro, suburban and a regional bus terminal. It was designed by the Spanish architect Santiago Calatrava and is covered by a strong yet delicate steel and glass structure that provides the building with an abundance of natural light.

👥 Oceanário de Lisboa★★

Esplanada D. Carlos I - Doca dos Olivais. 🕐*Daily Apr–Oct 10am–8pm; Nov–Mar 10am–7pm (last entry 1h before closing).* 💶€19 (child, 4–12, €13) – online discounts. 📞218 917 002. www.oceanario.pt.

Designed by the American architect Peter Chermayeff, this huge aquarium has five main tanks providing an introduction to the natural habitats of the Arctic, Indian, Pacific and Atlantic Oceans. In total more than 15 000 marine animals and fish and 250 species of plants are exhibited here.

The main tank displays grouper, rays, different species of shark and shoals of mackerel; the Antarctica shows the acrobatic feats of cormorants and penguins; and the Pacific features sea-otters.

👥 Pavilhão do Conhecimento Ciência Viva (Understanding Science)

Alameda dos Oceanos. 🕐*Tue–Fri, 10am–6pm, Sat–Sun and public holidays 10am–7pm.* 💶€9 (child, 3–11 €6, 12–17 €7, discounts available). 📞218 917 100. www.pavconhecimento.pt.

Many interactive exhibits explaining science and its place in our life fill this ever-changing exhibition. This is a great place for children.

Torre Vasco da Gama

This tower, situated at the far end of the park, has great views of the Tagus and surrounding areas.

Other facilities include a panoramic restaurant, bars, nightclub and a large shopping centre that stays open until 11pm.

The **Jardin da Água** 👥 section of the park area is a fun and leisure area with a water-based theme. Many statues can be found among the fountains and jets of water.

The attractive **Jardim Garcia da Orta** in front of the Olivais dock, along the Tagus, reflects regions visited by the Portuguese during the period of the Great Discoveries. On summer nights concerts are held on the Praça Sony, at the Palco da Doca, in the Pavilhão Atlântico and in the numerous bars and restaurants.

SOUTH OF THE PARK
Museu Militar

Largo Museu da Artilharia, 1100 - 468 Lisboa 1100. 🕐*Tue–Sun 10am–7pm.* 🕐*Public holidays.* 💶€3, free Sunday mornings. 📞218 842 330. www.exercito.pt.

This former 18C arsenal on the banks of the Tagus has preserved its outstanding woodwork as well as *azulejos* and interesting **ceilings★** mainly illustrating battle scenes.

Models, paintings and in particular numerous weapons from the 16C to the late 19C, some manufactured on the spot, recall Portugal's military past. The museum claims to have the largest collection of artillery in the world.

👥 Museu da Marioneta (Puppet Museum)

Rua da Esperança, 146 (Convento das Bernardos). 🕐*Tue–Sun 10am–6pm.* 🕐*1 Jan, 1 May, 24–25 and 31 Dec.* 💶€5, child €2.50 (13–25 y.o. Under-13s free). 📞213 942 810.

www.museudamarioneta.pt.

Located in a beautiful 18C Cistercian monastery, this fascinating museum has traditional puppet shows at certain times by the São Lourenço company, as well as many older examples of puppets. On display are shadow puppets from Turkey, string puppets from Indonesia, Punch-and-Judy puppets and Plasticine Wallace & Gromit-style models, with an explanation of how they are moulded. Children's activities are provided in Portuguese and English.

Docks

The docks area along the river was formerly occupied by warehouses, but has been transformed into a fashionable district with bars, restaurants and discos.

Belém★★

It was from the harbour at Belém (Portuguese for Bethlehem) that sailing ships set forth on their brave journeys in search of hitherto unknown lands and continents.

🐾 WALKING TOUR
Starting from Praça do Comércio, either drive alongside the Tagus or take tram No. E15 to Belém.

Mosteiro dos Jerónimos★★★
Praça do Império. 🕐*May–Sept Tue–Sun 10am–6.30pm; Oct–Apr Tue–Sun 10am–5.30pm.* 🕐*1 Jan, Easter Sunday, 1 May, 25 Dec.* ✎€10. *www.mosteirojeronimos.gov.pt.*
In 1502, on the site of a former hermitage founded by Prince Henry the Navigator, King Dom Manuel undertook to build this magnificent Hieronymite monastery, considered to be the jewel of Manueline art. This style of art glorified the Great Discoveries, in this case that of Vasco da Gama who, on his return from the Indies, had moored his caravels in Restelo harbour near Belém. The architects of the monastery, benefitting from the riches then pouring into Lisbon from these overseas expeditions, were able to immerse themselves in an ambitious, large-scale work. The Gothic

⏱ **Timing:** Allow at least half a day.

style adopted by the Frenchman Boytac until his death in 1517 was modified by his successors who added ornamentation typical of the Manueline style with its diverse influences: João de Castilho, of Spanish origin, added a Plateresque form to the decoration, Nicolas Chanterene emphasised the Renaissance element, while Diogo de Torralva and Jérôme de Rouen, at the end of the 16C, brought in a Classical note.
The Monastery is now a UNESCO World Heritage Site.

Igreja de Santa Maria★★★
🕐*Same hours as the monastery.*
The **south door**, the work of Boytac and João de Castilho, combines a mass of gables, pinnacles and niches filled with statues. Crowning all is a canopy surmounted by the Cross of the Order of the Knights of Christ.
The **west door**, sheltered beneath the 19C porch that leads to the cloisters, is by Nicolas Chanterene and is adorned with fine statues, particularly those of King Manuel and Queen Maria. Represented above the doorway are the Annunciation, the Nativity and the Adoration of the Magi.

Cloister, Mosteiro dos Jerónimos

© miialev/iStock

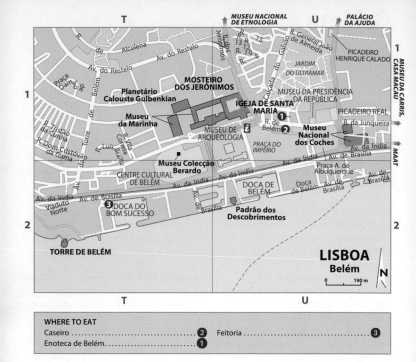

WHERE TO EAT

Caseiro .... ❷	Feitoria .... ❸
Enoteca de Belém .... ❶	

The **interior** is outstanding for the intricate beauty of the stonework, carved throughout in great detail but never obscuring the architectural lines, as for instance, in the network **vaulting★★** of equal height over the nave and aisles. This vaulting withstood the 1755 earthquake. The decoration on the pillars and the vaulting over the transept crossing are by João de Castilho.

The transepts are Baroque, designed by Jérôme de Rouen, and contain the tombs of several princes. In the chancel, reconstructed in the Classical period, are the tombs of Dom Manuel I and Dom João III, with their queens. Beneath the gallery of the *coro alto* at the entrance to the church are the neo-Manueline tombs of Vasco da Gama and the great poet and chronicler of the discoveries, Luís de Camões, whose recumbent figure wears a crown of laurel leaves.

Cloisters★★★

🕐 *Same times as the monastery.*
This masterpiece of Manueline art is fantastically rich in sculpture. The stone is at its most beautiful when it takes on the golden tint of the late afternoon sun. The cloisters, forming a hollow square of which each side measures 55m, are two storeys high. The ground level galleries with groined vaulting by Boytac have wide arches with tracery resting upon slender columns, and Late Gothic and Renaissance decoration carved into the massive thickness of the walls.

Look out for a simple monument here containing the remains of the poet Fernando Pessoa.

The chapter-house contains the tomb of the writer Alexandre Herculano.

A staircase leads to the church's **coro alto** with another view of the vaulting. The graceful Renaissance stalls carved out of maple are by Diogo de Carça.

Museu da Marinha★★

Opposite the Centro Cultural de Belém.
🕐 *May–Sept 10am–6pm (until 5pm the rest of the year).* 🕐 *1 Jan, Easter Sunday, 1 May and 25 Dec.* ⊕ €5. *http://ccm. marinha.pt.*

This museum, containing a remarkable collection of **models★★★** of seafaring craft over the centuries, is located on both sides of the esplanade of the **Calouste Gulbenkian planetarium** in two separate buildings: the west wing of the Mosteiro dos Jerónimos and the modern Pavilhão das Galeotas.

Once through the entrance, take the stairs in front of the door on the right.

The Sala da Marinha de Recreio, a room dedicated to pleasure craft on the upper floor, includes a small collection of models of 18C and 19C yachts. The Sala da Marinha Mercante (Merchant Navy Room) recalls the history of merchant shipping in Portugal, with exhibits such as the *Santa Maria* and the *Infante Dom Henrique*, which transported soldiers to the colonies, and the *Nelva* oil tanker. The Sala da Construção Naval at the far end takes an informative look at naval construction techniques.

Main Building

Giant sandstone statues of historical figures (including Henry the Navigator) and ancient cannon can be seen in the entrance hall. On the ground floor there is an immense room devoted to the Great Discoveries and the Navy, from the 15C to the 18C, with maps and magnificent models of sailing ships, caravels and frigates, including the 18C vessel, the *Príncipe da Beira*.

There are displays of figureheads and navigational instruments such as 15C astrolabes. Warships of the 19C and 20C can also be seen (small-scale models of gunboats, frigates and corvettes, and modern submarines) as well as a fishing fleet (the Henrique Seixas Collection) with models of various boats that used to fish in the estuaries or along the coast: a *muleta* from Seixal with its many sails, a *calão* from the Algarve, a *galeão* from Nazaré. Models of boats used for river navigation include frigates of the Tagus and *rabelos* of the Douro.

In the last room there is a reconstruction of the royal stateroom of the yacht *Amélia* (late 19C).

👥 Planetário Calouste Gulbenkian (Planetarium)

Praça do Império, Belém. ⏰*Tue–Fri, Sun 10:30am–noon & 1:30–5pm, Sat 1.30–5pm.* 💶*€5, child, 4–12 €2.50.* 📞*213 620 002.*

A special show looking at Portugal's starry skies, an imaginary voyage through the planetary system, a trip to the moon, a journey across the polar region, various films, plus eclipses of the sun and the moon – these are just some of the audio-visual adventures on offer here.

Museu Coleção Berardo★★

Praça do Império. ⏰*Daily 10am–7pm (24 and 31 Dec 10am–2.30pm; 1 Jan noon–7pm).* 💶*€5, child, 7–18 €2.50, Sat free entry.* ⏰*Closed 25 Dec.* 📞*213 612 878. www.museuberardo.pt.*

Housed in the heart of the cultural centre, this exceptional collection of modern and contemporary art, courtesy of Madeiran millionaire Joe Berardo, represents all the principal art movements of the 20C and 21C. Most of the big names in modern art are here, including Marcel Duchamp *(Bottle Dryer)*, Picasso, Dali *(White Aphrodisiac Telephone)*, Max Ernst, Mondrian, Francis Bacon, Man Ray, Jackson Pollock, Andy Warhol and Keith Haring, among others.

Padrão dos Descobrimentos (Monument of Discoveries)

Av. Brasília. ⏰ *Mar–Sept 10am–7pm; Oct–Feb Tue–Sun 10am–6pm.* ⏰*Closed 1 Jan, 1 May and 25 Dec.* 💶*€5.* 📞*213 031 950. www.padraodosdescobrimentos.pt.*

The 52m Monument to the Great Discoveries by the sculptor Leopoldo de Almeida was erected in 1960 beside the Tagus on the 500th anniversary of the death of Prince Henry the Navigator. It represents the prow of a ship with the prince pointing the way to a crowd of important figures.

Torre de Belém★★★

⏰*Open Tue–Sun May–Sept 10am–6.30pm; Oct–Apr 10am–5.30pm.* ⏰*Closed 1 Jan, Easter Sunday, 1 May*

Torre de Belém

© Tuul et Bruno Morandi/hemis.fr

and 25 Dec. ⊕€6, under 12s free. www.
torrebelem.gov.pt.

This elegant Manueline tower was built between 1515 and 1519 in the middle of the Tagus to defend the river mouth and the Mosteiro dos Jerónimos. Today, as the river altered course during the earthquake in 1755, and with further silting up since then, it stands on the north shore. It is an architectural gem; the Romanesque-Gothic structure is adorned with loggias like those in Venice, and small domes like those in Morocco where the tower's architect, Francisco de Arruda, had travelled. The tower is five storeys high ending in a terrace. On the ground floor are openings through which prisoners were thrown into the dungeons below. It looks particularly spectacular at night when fully floodlit. To be honest, it is possible to see it all from off-site without paying the entrance fee. ⊕

Palácio Nacional da Ajuda★ (Ajuda National Palace)

Largo da Ajuda. ○*Thu–Tue 10am–6pm.* ○*1 Jan, Easter Sunday, 1 May and 25 Dec.* ⊕€5; combined ticket with National Coach Museum: ⊕€12). ☎213 637 095. www.palacioajuda.gov.pt.

This former royal palace (18C–19C) to the north of Belém was built after the earthquake, yet never completed. However, it was renovated in 2019, with the addition of two wings. One of them will host the Royal Tresaure Museum, which includes the rich collection of crown jewels. The Museum is scheduled to open in late 2020. It was the residence of the Portuguese monarchs, Dom Luís and Dona Maria Pia from 1862 onwards. Its two floors offer a succession of rooms with painted ceilings and an interior richly filled with furniture, tapestries, statues and decorative objects from the 20C.

At the top of the Calçada da Ajuda is the **Jardim Botânico da Ajuda** (○*Nov-Mar, Apr-Oct 10am-5pm, May-Sept 10am-6pm & to 8pm on weekends and hols.* ⊕€2). The Palácio was renovated in 2019 and two wings were added. One of them will host the Royal Tresaure Museum, which includes the rich collection of crown jewels. The Museum is scheduled to open in late 2020.

Museu Nacional dos Coches★★ (National Coach Museum)

Praça Afonso de Albuquerque. ○*Tue–Sun 10am–8pm.* ⊕€8 (combined ticket with Adjuda National Palace: ⊕€12). ☎210 732 319. www.museudoscoches.gov.pt.

In the former riding stables of the Royal Palace, this is a fascinating collection of coaches dating back to the 17C. The oldest coach, with a mirrored ceiling, was used by Filipe II to tour Portugal in 1619. Each coach is magnificent.

One of the most outstanding examples has gilded figures on the tailgate. Another, used by Louis XIV, has cherubs, and another was built for Portugal's ambassador to Pope Clement XI.

North Lisbon

In this neighbourhood, criss-crossed with wide straight avenues laid out in the 19C, beautiful Art Nouveau houses sit alongside modern concrete buildings of glass.

AROUND AVENIDA DA LIBERDADE

Avenida da Liberdade★

The Avenida da Liberdade is the most majestic of Lisbon's avenues. On either side, late 19C buildings and more recent constructions house hotels and offices. The pavements are covered in black and white mosaics. To the north, the Avenida leads to the **Praça do Marquês de Pombal**, Lisbon's nerve centre, where several wide avenues converge. In the centre of this circular "square" stands a monument to the Marquis of Pombal.

▷ Take Avenida Fontes Pereira de Melo then Avenida António Augusto de Aguiar on the left.

Parque Eduardo VII★

This formal landscaped park, crowning Avenida da Liberdade, was named after King Edward VII of England on the occasion of his visit to Lisbon in 1902. There is a magnificent **vista★** from the upper end of the park of the Baixa district and the Tagus, dominated on either side by the castle and the Bairro Alto hills.

Estufa Fria★

🕐 Open daily Apr– Sept 10am–7pm; Oct–Mar 9am–5pm. 🕐 Closed 1 Jan, 1 May and 25 Dec. ☞ €3.10. ℘ 218 170 996. estufafria.cm-lisboa.pt.
Wooden shutters in this Cold Greenhouse provide protection from the extremes of summer heat and winter cold. The exotic plants displayed grow beside fishponds or cooling waterfalls near small grottoes.

GULBENKIAN FOUNDATION

Just north of the Parque Eduardo VII.
One of Europe's great unsung galleries, Lisbon's Gulbenkian is home to the private collection of **Calouste Gul-**

🕐 **Timing:** Map I. Allow a day.

benkian, an Armenian oil magnate who donated his magnificent haul of European and Asian art to his adopted country. His keenness for collecting started at an early age with the acquisition of a few old coins, and was to lead to the creation of an outstanding collection of works of art over a period of 40 years. On his death in 1955, Gulbenkian bequeathed his immense fortune to Portugal, where he had lived for many years. A year later the Calouste Gulbenkian Foundation was set up, a private institution that runs its own museums, an orchestra, a ballet company and a choir.
The foundation's headquarters, set in beautiful gardens, consist of a complex of modern buildings that house the Gulbenkian Museum, the Modern Art Centre, four multi-purpose lecture halls, of which one is open-air, a conference centre, two large galleries for art exhibitions and a library with 152,000 books.

Museu Calouste Gulbenkian★★★

Av. de Rema. 🕐 Daily except Tue 10am–6pm. 🕐 1 Jan, Easter Sun, 1 May, 24–25 Dec. ☞ €10 (€14 incl. special exhibitions), 12.5. ℘ 217 823 000. www.gulbenkian.pt.
The museum was especially designed for the Gulbenkian collections, which consist of selected exhibits of great value and beauty. They are particularly rich in Oriental and European art. The lower floor displays contemporary art.

Ancient Art

The Ancient art section is represented by works from Egypt (an alabaster bowl about 2 700 years old; a stone statuette of "Judge Bes"; a bronze sun-boat; and a silver-gilt mask for a mummy dating from the 30th Dynasty), the Graeco-Roman world (a superb 5C BCE Attic crater; jewellery; the head of a woman attributed to Phidias; iridescent Roman vases; and a magnificent collection of gold and silver coins) and Mesopotamia (9C BCE Assyrian stele and a Parthian urn).

Near Eastern Art

The finest pieces in the vast Near Eastern art collection are the pottery and carpets. The sumptuous woollen and silk carpets, mainly Persian from the 16C and 17C and the shimmering Prusa velvets from Turkey are especially exquisite. The pottery (12C–18C), silk costumes and lamps from the mosque of Alep are as finely worked as Persian miniatures. There are also collections of poetry, Korans and Armenian manuscripts.

Far Eastern Art

Far Eastern art, primarily Chinese, is represented by magnificent porcelain (a 14C Taoist bowl; a 17C vase of the hundred birds) and "rough stones" (an 18C green nephrite bowl); Japanese exhibits including prints and a selection of lacquerware from the 18C and 19C.

European Art

The European art section begins with **medieval religious art**, carved **ivories**, illuminated manuscripts and books of hours. A section on **15C, 16C** and **17C painting** and **sculpture** follows: The *Presentation at the Temple* by the German artist **Stephan Lochner** was one of Gulbenkian's first acquisitions. The Flemish and Dutch schools are well represented with a *St Joseph* by **Van der Weyden**, an admirable *Annunciation* by **Dirk Bouts**, a magnificent *Old Man* by **Rembrandt** and a masterly *Portrait of Helen Fourment* by **Rubens**. From the Italian school there is a delightful *Portrait of a Young Woman* attributed to **Ghirlandaio**.

The 18C French school of painting, famous for its portraits and festive scenes, is represented here by **Lancret** *(Fête Galante)*, **Hubert Robert** *(Gardens of Versailles)*, **Quentin de la Tour** *(Portrait of Mademoiselle Sallé* and *Portrait of Duval de l'Epinoy)*, and **Nicolas de Largillière** *(Portrait of M. et Mme. Thomas-Germain)*.

Among the sculptures is **Diana** in white marble by Houdon. English painting of the 18C includes works by **Gainsborough** *(Portrait of Mrs. Lowndes-Stone)*, **Romney** *(Portrait of Miss Constable)*, **Turner** *(Quillebœuf)* and **Thomas Lawrence**.

A gallery on the Venetian apprentice of Canaletto, **Francesco Guardi**, is hung with some of his large and impressive scenes of Venice.

The 19C French school is represented by **Henri Fantin-Latour** *(La Lecture)* the Impressionists, including **Manet** *(Boy with Cherries* and *Blowing Bubbles)*, **Degas** *(Self-portrait)*, and **Renoir** *(Portrait of Mme. Claude Monet)*, a number of canvases by **Corot** *(Bridge at Mantes,*

Museu Calouste Gulbenkian

© Axiom/hemis.fr

Willows), as well as a fine collection of bronzes *(Spring)* and marble sculptures *(Benedictions)* by **Rodin**.

In the last room there is an extraordinary collection of works and jewels from the Art Nouveau period by the French decorative artist **René Lalique** (1860–1945).

Centro de Arte Moderna★★

Rua Dr. Nicolau de Bettencourt.
🕐*Daily except Tue 10am–6pm.* 🚫*1 Jan, Easter Sun, 1 May, 24–25 Dec.* €10. 🕿217 823 000. www.gulbenkian.pt.

The centre, which was built by the British architect Sir Leslie Martin in 1983, has a roomy design in which plants have been incorporated, giving the impression of a screen of greenery. It houses modern works by Portuguese artists from 1910 to the present. Among the artists represented are Vieira da Silva, Amadeo Souza-Cardoso, Almada Negreiros and Julio Pomar. Several sculptures, including the *Reclining Woman* by **Henry Moore**, are exhibited in the gardens surrounding the centre.

ADDITIONAL SIGHTS

Igreja de Nossa Senhora de Fátima

This modern church is adorned with **stained-glass windows★** by Almada Negreiros.

Biblioteca Municipal

The library is housed in the 16C Galveias Palace opposite the neo-Moorish **bull ring** at Campo Pequeno.

Palácio dos Marqueses de Fronteira★★★

Take the metro to Sete Rios, followed by a 20min walk along Rua das Furnas and Rua São Domingo de Benfica.
🔍*Guided tours (~45min) Jun–Sept, Mon–Sat 10.30am, 11am, 11.30am, 12.30pm; Oct–May, Mon–Sat 11am, noon. Gardens open Mon–Fri 2pm–6.30pm, Sat 10am–1pm.* 🚫*Public holidays.* €11 (gardens only €3, audioguide €3).
🕿217 782 023. www.fronteira-alorna.pt.
The palace, to the north of the Parque de Monsanto near Benfica, was built as a hunting lodge by João Mascarenhas, the first Marquis of Fronteira, in 1670. While a strong Italian Renaissance influence is apparent, particularly in the layout of the gardens, the palace is one of the most beautiful Portuguese creations with its *azulejos★★* of outstanding quality and variety.

Inside the palace, the *azulejos* in the Victory Room depict the main events in the War of Restoration, in which the first Marquis of Fronteira distinguished himself. The dining room is adorned with 17C Delft tiles, the first to be imported into Portugal.

Outside, on the terraces and in the gardens, every conceivable flat surface has been decorated with small ceramic tiles. Some depict country scenes of the seasons and work in the fields; others illustrate more stately, solemn subjects like the 12 horsemen in the Kings' Gallery, which are reflected in a pool.

127

🚶‍♂️ Jardim Zoológico★★

Metro: Sete Rios. ⏰*Daily Apr–Sept 10am–8pm (until 6pm Oct–Mar).* ✆€22, (child, 3–11, €14.50). ✆217 232 900. www.zoo.pt.

The park, which is both a lovely garden and a zoo, is laid out in the 26ha of the Parque das Laranjeiras, incorporating the rose-coloured palace of the Counts of Farrobo, to the right of the entrance. The lower part includes the rose garden, a variety of other flowers, and enclosures for the 2 500 animals, many of which are exotic species. The highlights are the dolphin show (11am, 3pm and 5pm, except 5pm in winter) and the sea lion's feeding at 10.30am and 2pm. Other attractions include a children's farm, reptile house, cable car and a miniature train.

Museu Rafael Bordalo Pinheiro

Campo Grande, 382. Metro: Campo Grande. ⏰*Tue–Sun 10am–6pm.* ⏰*Closed public holidays.* ✆€3. ✆218 818 540. http://museubordalopinheiro.pt.

The museum, which stands across the Campo Grande from the Museu da Cidade, contains collections of drawings, caricatures and particularly **ceramics★** by Rafael Bordalo Pinheiro (1846–1905). He was a prolific artist and, together with his brother and sister, had some influence on social life in Lisbon at the end of the 19C.

Museu Nacional do Traje★ (National Museum of Costume)

Largo Julio de Castilho, Lumiar. ⏰*Tue-Sun 10am–6pm,* ⏰*1 Jan, Easter Sunday, 1 May, 13 Jun and 24–25 Dec.* ✆€4 (€6 if combined with Museu Nacional do Teatro). ✆217 567 620. www.museudotraje.pt.

The graceful palace of the Marquis of Angeja holds outstanding costume exhibits. The well-presented collections bring a whole era, or a town or profession, to life, through the art of dress.

Museu Nacional do Teatro

Strestrada do Lumiar. ⏰*Tue–Sun 10am–6pm.* ⏰*Closed 1 Jan, Easter Sunday, 1 May, 13 Jun and 25 Dec.* ✆€4, combined ticket with Museu Nacional do Traje €6. ✆217 567 410. www.museudoteatroedanca.gov.pt.

Housed in the palace of Monteiro-Mor, which was rebuilt after a fire, this small museum holds temporary exhibitions on drama-related themes.

Below the palace, the attractive **Jardim Botânico do Monteiro-Mor** (⏰open Tue–Sun 10am–6pm; ⏰closed 1 Jan, Easter Sunday, 1 May and 25 Dec; ✆€3), with their pools and a rich variety of plants, lie in a wild, hilly setting.

Amoreiras

This district lies to the west of Parque Eduardo VII and borders the Parque Florestal de Monsanto, Lisbon's answer the Parisian Bois de Boulogne. It is dominated by the Torres das Amoreiras and the Aqueduto das Águas Livres. The name recalls the mulberry trees that existed here to produce silkworms used in the manufacture of silk.

⏰ **Timing:** *Map I.* Allow at least half a day.

SIGHTS

Torres das Amoreiras

The famous pink, grey and black post-modern towers designed by the architect Tomás Taveira were completed in 1983 and house Lisbon's first shopping centre. They are situated close to one of the entrances to the city and can be seen from afar. They comprise three floors, and contain offices, luxury apartments, restaurants and plenty of shops.

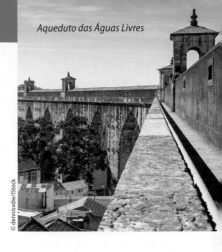

Aqueduto das Águas Livres

© dennisvdw/iStock

Aqueduto das Águas Livres★

The aqueduct built between 1731 and 1799 (*see Museu da Água*) measures a total of 58km/36mi, including all its ramifications. It is a system for collecting and transporting water using gravity, and has enjoyed National Monument status since 1910 and considered to be a remarkable work of hydraulics engineering. Thirty-four of its arches stride across the Alcântara valley. The tallest is 65m high with a span of 29m.

Museu da Água★

Rua do Alviela 12. ⏱*Tue–Sat 10am–5.30pm.* ⏱*Public holidays.* ⬚*€4 (under-12s free).* ☏*218 100 215. www.museudaagua.epal.pt.*

The museum traces the history of water supply to Lisbon and more particularly of the Aguas Livres (Free Water) project drawn up by the engineer Manuel de Maia. Attempts to bring water to Lisbon from springs at the foot of the Serra de Sintra had begun in 1571, but it wasn't until 1732 that the aqueduct was started (although unfinished the aqueduct finally started to carry water in 1748). The water ran into the Mão d'Água des Amoreiras reservoir and was then channelled to the town's fountains and pipes. In 1880 the third link in the chain, the Barbadinhos pumping station, was built. The combined system supplied the town with water for almost 250 years until 1967.

♣♣ Parque Florestal de Monsanto★ (Monsanto Forest Park)

⏱*24hr.* ☏*218 170 552.*

This hilly, wooded park of 900ha is dissected by roads providing panoramic **views**★ of Lisbon, particularly from the Monsanto belvederes. The park contains several small parks that are ideal for children: the Parque Alvito has plenty of games and a swimming pool for children ages 3–14 years; and the Parque dos Índios, for children ages 4–12 years, one of the most popular playgrounds in Lisbon for youngsters.

ADDITIONAL SIGHTS

Casa-Museu Anastácio Gonçalves

Av. 5 de Outubro. ⏱*Open Tue–Sun 10am–1pm & 2–6pm.* ⏱*Closed 1 Jan, Easter Sunday, 1 May,13 Jun, 24 and 25 Dec.* ⬚*€3.* ☏*213 540 823. blogdacmag.blogspot.com/.*

This museum is housed in two villas formerly owned by the artist José Malhoa, and more recently by Dr Anastácio Gonçalves, a great patron of the arts and a friend of Gulbenkian. The first part of the museum is used to display temporary exhibitions predominantly devoted to early 20C Portuguese artists (modernists such as Columbano, Eduardo Viana, Amadeo de Souza Cardoso, Vieira da Silva and Mário Eloy, and naturalists including Silva Porto and Sousa Pinto). The permanent collection comprises ancient Chinese porcelain, furniture, textiles and jewellery, as well as an interesting set of drawings by Almada Negreiros.

Museu da Música★

⏱*Open Mon–Sat 10am–6pm.* ⬚*€3.* ☏*217 710 990. www.museunacionaldamusica.pt.*

The small museum, located inside the Alto dos Moinhos metro station, contains a wide variety of musical instruments and publications from the 16C–20C, including a set of Baroque harpsichords and a large collection of string and wind instruments.

Rato, Estrela, Lapa and Alcântara

To the west of the Bairro Alto district lies hilly and residential Rato and Estrela, where the Basilica da Estrela, Palacio de Sao Bento and Jardim da Estrella park are the main attractions. Lapa, to the south, is home to embassies and upper-class houses. Alcântara, on the banks of the Tagus, was revitalised some years back when numerous bars and restaurants were opened in and around the old docks.

SIGHTS

Basílica da Estrela★

The white Baroque edifice was built at the end of the 18C. Inside, the transept crossing is covered by a fine **cupola** topped by a lantern tower. Note also a Christmas crib with life-size figures carved by Machado de Castro.

The **Jardim da Estrela★★** opposite the basilica is one of the most beautiful gardens in Lisbon with its varied display of exotic plants and trees.

> 🕐 **Timing:** Allow at least half a day.

Casa Fernando Pessoa★

Rua Coelho da Rocha, 16. 🕐*Mon–Sat 10am–6pm.* 🕐*Closed 1 Jan, 1 May and 25 Dec.* ✆€3. ☎213 913 270. http:// casafernandopessoa.pt. Closed for renovations until mid-2020.*

This house, where the poet Fernando Pessoa spent the last 15 years of his life, has been refurbished and now serves as a cultural centre specialising in Portuguese poetry as well as an exhibition centre for painting and sculpture. The works of Pessoa and his archives are also assembled here. He is regarded as Portugal's greatest 20C poet, a true Modernist in his thinking and writing. The majority of his work was published posthumously after his death in 1935 of cirrhosis at the age of 46.

Fundação Arpad Szenes – Vieira da Silva★

🕐*Tue–Sun 10am–6pm.* 🕐*Public holidays.* ✆€5. ☎213 880 044. www.fasvs.pt.*

This foundation is located on one side of the leafy Praça das Amoreiras, next to the Águas Livres aqueduct. It is a fine 18C

Adoration of Saint Vincent, Museu Nacional de Arte Antiga

1 St Vincent
2 King Afonso V
3 Prince João, future João II
4 Prince Henry the Navigator
5 Queen Isabel
6 Isabella of Aragon, her mother
7 Nuno Gonçalves

8 Prince Fernando
9 Knights
10 The Archbishop of Lisbon accompanied by two canons
11 The Chronicler, Gomes Eanes de Azurara
12 Cistercians from Alcobaça
13 Fishermen and navigators

14 Fernando, Second Duke of Bragança
15 Fernando, his oldest son
16 João, his youngest son
17 A Moorish knight
18 A cleric proffering St Vincent's skull
19 A Jew
20 A beggar before the saint's coffin

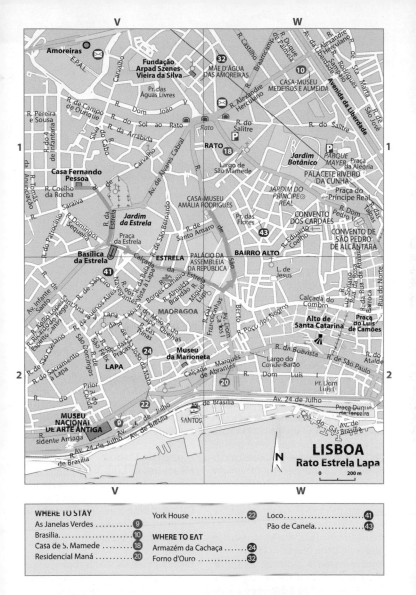

workshop that has been remodelled in a sober, elegant manner. **Maria Helena Vieira da Silva** (1908–92), who lived a great part of her life in Paris with the artist Arpad Szenes, is one of Portugal's most famous 20C artists. The museum displays a small collection of works by the artists, as well as works donated by collectors and institutions.

Museu Nacional de Arte Antiga (National Museum of Ancient Art)★★★

Rua das Janelas Verdes. ◐Tue–Sun 10am–6pm; Tue 2pm–6pm. ◑1 Jan, Easter Sunday, 1 May and 25 Dec. ◉€6. ℘213 912 800. www. museudearteantiga.pt. The jewelry section is currently closed for renovations. The Museum of Ancient Art, housed in the 17C palace of the Counts of Alvor and in an annexe built in 1940, has an outstanding collection of paintings, sculptures and decorative arts from

Detail of Japanese folding screens (1593-1601) attributed to Kano Naizen, Museu Nacional de Arte Antiga

the 12C to the early 19C, reflecting the history of Portugal.

The main wealth of the museum lies in the Portuguese Primitives, of which the major work is the **polyptych★★★** of the **Adoration of St Vincent** (*see illustration and key above),* painted between 1460 and 1470 by Nuno Gonçalves. The panels of this previously unknown work were discovered in an attic in the monastery of São Vicente da Fora in 1882.

The masterly **Annunciation★** by Frei Carlos (1523), is a remarkable example of Luso-Flemish painting. Among other Portuguese works are the *Cook Triptych* by Grão Vasco and the *Martyrdom of the Eleven Thousand Virgins* from the Igreja da Madre de Deus. It is an unsigned work showing the arrival in Portugal of the relics of Santa Auta that were given by the Holy Roman Emperor Maximilian I to his cousin Dona Leonor in 1509.

Notable among the paintings from other European schools is the extraordinary **Temptation of St Anthony★★★** by Hieronymus Bosch.

Mention should also be made of the *Virgin and Child* by Memling, *St Jerome* by Dürer, *Virgin, Child and Saints* by Hans Holbein the Elder and the **Twelve Apostles★** by Zurbarán.

One of the rooms contains precious **Nambans** or **Japanese folding screens★★** showing the arrival of the Portuguese on the island of Tane-ga-Shima in 1543. The Japanese called the Portuguese *Namban-jin* meaning barbarians from the south (they had approached Japan from the south) and

the art that ensued came to be known as Namban.

There is also a rich collection of gold and silver plate, the finest of which is the **monstrance from the Mosteiro de Belém** (1506) attributed to Gil Vicente who, it is believed, made it from gold brought from the Indies by Vasco da Gama. The newer section of the museum houses the **chapel★** from the former Carmelite Convent of Santa Alberto, outstanding for its gilded woodwork and its 16C–18C *azulejos.*

Museu de Lisboa (Museum of Lisbon)

Campo Grande, 245, across from the Museu Pinheiro. ◯*Tue–Sun 10am–6pm.* ◯*Public holidays.* ◉*€3.* ☏*217 513 200. www.museudelisboa.pt. Ground floor currently closed for renovations, check website.*

The city's museum stands above Campo Grande (a bit too close to the motorway interchange) in the graceful 18C Palácio Pimenta built during Dom João V's reign. The different stages in the history of Lisbon may be traced through Roman, Visigothic, Arab and medieval remains held in five different locations: Palácio Pimenta, Santo António, Teatro Romano, Casa dos Bicos and Torreão Poente.

The emblem of the city, a caravel transporting the body of St Vincent guided by ravens, can be seen on the many coats of arms displayed.

A model of Lisbon in the early 18C gives an idea of the city before the earthquake as do the *azulejos* of Terreiro do Paço square showing the Royal Palace still in place. The palace kitchens are adorned with *azulejos* of country scenes. The first floor is devoted to ceramics and engravings of Lisbon. Note the famous *Fado* canvas by Malhoa.

ADDITIONAL SIGHTS
Experiência Pilar 7★★
(Bridge Museum and Viewing Platform)
Av. da Índia, Pilar 7 da Ponte 25 de Abril. Ⓞ*daily 10am–8pm (Jan–Mar until 6pm).* Ⓞ*25 Dec.* ⏾*€6.* ☏*211 1117880.* *www.visitlisboa.com*
This interactive exhibition about the bridge and its history walks visitors through the first phases of its construction, using virtual reality and multimedia effects. The tour ends with an elevator ride inside the bridge's pillar and up to a viewing platform that offers a great view of the city and river.

Museu do Oriente★★★
(The Orient Museum)
Av. Brasília, Doca de Alcântara Norte. Ⓞ*Tue–Sun 10am–6pm (Fri until 10pm).* Ⓞ*1 Jan, 25 Dec.* ⏾*€6 (free Fri evening).* ☏*213 585 200. www.museudooriente.pt.*
Inaugurated in 2008 along with the transformation of the **Alcântara docks**, this cultural gem of the Fundação Oriente is installed within former cold-storage facilities for warehousing cod. This outstanding museum is dedicated to **Asian art** and objects. Many artefacts in the collection reflect Portugal's extensive travels to the Far East during the country's heyday of sea-faring exploration, and its long contact and trade with Asia.
Well-represented in the exhibit galleries are 17C and 18C Chinese ceramics and porcelain, Japanese screens, Indo-Portuguese furniture, textiles, paintings and silverware.
The remarkable 13 000-piece **Kwon On Collection** represents important performing-arts traditions in music, theatre and religious and secular festivals; on display are such items as musical instruments, costumes, shadow puppets and masks.

Temporary exhibitions are also mounted by the museum. A research centre, an auditorium and a café (*10am–6pm*) restaurant (*noon–3pm*) are also on the premises.

ADDRESSES

🏠 STAY
The Baixa area is fairly quiet at night though you will need to go a little way for restaurants; Rossio can be livelier though the side streets are calmer, but café life goes on until about 1am; Bairro Alto and Chiado are the nightlife districts and can be noisy until 4am; Alfama is fairly residential and a good choice if you want quiet nights. It is obviously wise to pre-book, especially from June to September. *Note: not all addresses provide breakfast, and those that do may make an additional charge for it.*

BAIXA

Residência Nova Avenida – *Rua Santo António da Glória, 87.* ☏*213 423 689. 25 rooms.* Beautiful house decorated with tiles, and balconies. Single rooms (with shower and toilet), some with TV, high ceilings and impeccably clean. Six family rooms.

Vistas de Lisboa – *Rua dos Douradores, 178.* ☏*218 867 256. 16 rooms.* Housed in a historical building, Vistas de Lisboa offers both shared, dormitory-style rooms and private double rooms with bathrooms. Most rooms have a balcony and the décor is colorful and modern. There's also a communal kitchen.

Norte Guesthouse – *Rua dos Douradores, 159.* ☏*218 878 941. 34 rooms.* Rooms are simple but very clean and the staff is friendly. Not all have private bathrooms, so make sure to ask in advance. Great value for money and very central and convenient location.

City Center Guest House – *Rua Augusta 188, 1 Andar.* ☏*213 470 327. www.citycenterhostel.net. 5 rooms.* Centrally located in a lovely pedestrian area, this Guest House offers bright, no-frill rooms (not all en-suite) with balconies. There is also a shared kitchen and a dining area.

Pensão Geres – *Calçada do Garcia, 6.* ☏*215 958 3687. www.pensaogeres.com. 53 rooms.* A very well maintained and tastefully decorated pension on the first and second floors of an old house. Rooms vary in size, with shower or bath, most with a nice view.

🍽 **Pensão Praça da Figueira** –*Travessa nova de São Domingos, 9-2 °. ☏213 426 757. www.pensaopracadafigueira.com. 8 rooms.* Located in Lisbon's historic area of Baixa Pombalina, this friendly guesthouse is in a pedestrianised street. The 3rd and 4th floors are not accessible by elevator. Rooms are comfortable, though some do not have their own private bathroom. Good value for money.

🍽🛏 **Pensão Varandas** – *Rua dos Bacalhoeiros, 8-2° (next to the Casa dos Bicos, at the edge of Alfama). ☏218 870 519. 4 rooms. Breakfast not included.* A decent pension located on the second floor of a building overlooking a pleasant square at the foot of Alfama, near Terreiro do Paço station and Santa Apolónia. All rooms are equipped with shower-cabin, and all have a balcony overlooking the square or the river.

🍽🛏 **Lisbon Downtown** – *Rua dos Fanqueiros, 262. ☏925 609 314 12 rooms* A tastefully furnished hotel with historical details such as azulejos and wooden floors combined with modern furniture. Each room has a kettle, breakfast is good, and there's a shared kitchen for those who wish to cook a meal. Third floor without elevator.

🍽🛏 **Grande Pensão Residencial Alcobia** – *Poço Do Borratem 15. ☏218 844 150. 42 rooms. www.grandepensao residencialalcobia.com.* Very central hotel housed in a 5-storey historical building with views on Castelo de São Jorge. All rooms are air conditioned and have a modern décor. Rental cars and bikes available at the reception.

🍽🛏 **Inn Rossio** – *Rua 1° de Dezembro, 73. ☏213 474 976. www.innrossio.com. 49 rooms.* Near the Rossio station. All rooms have wooden floors and simple furnishings which include a wardrobe or chest of drawers. WiFi.

🍽🛏 **Residêncial Florescente** – *Rua Portas de Santo Antão 99. ☏213 426 609. www.residencialflorescente.com. 68 rooms.* A pleasant hotel with friendly staff, WiFi, a lift and clean rooms. Good value. Well situated near Avda da Liberdade and plenty of restaurants.

🍽🛏 **VIP Executive Eden Aparthotel** – *Praça dos Restauradores, 24. ☏213 216 600. www.viphotels.com.* This former

theatre was converted to an "apart-hotel", with 75 studios (1–2 people) and 59 apartments (2 rooms for 4 people). Rent by the week or day, all fully equipped with kitchenette. Small swimming pool next to the bar on the panoramic terrace, and atrium with palm trees.

🍽🛏 **Metropole** – *Praça de Pedro, 30. ☏213 219 030. www.almeidahotels.pt 36 rooms.* Very well located in the busy Rossio square (noisy until 1am), the Metropole has comfortable rooms in an early 20C building, some with castle views. Bedrooms decorated with original 1920's Art Déco or Art Nouveau furnishings.

CHIADO

🍽 **Pensão Estrela do Mondego** – *Calçada do Carmo, 25 2°. ☏213 461 133. 11 rooms.* The rooms of this small *pensão*, next to the Rossio station, are comfortable and clean, and have air-conditioning. Tiny bathrooms with just a shower cubicle. Some rooms overlook the station so the area at night is not exactly quiet. Budget-friendly.

🍽🛏 **Martinhal** – *Rua das Flores 44. ☏210 029 600. www.martinhal.com. 37 suites.* The best base in Lisbon for families with young children. Big suites with super comfortable beds and ample space for the entire brood. Hotel provides everything, down to cookies, milk, and laundry detergent.

🍽🛏 **Hotel do Chiado** – *R. Nova do Almada, 114. ☏213 256 100. www. hoteldochiado.com. 40 rooms.* 🅿. Located above the Armazéns do Chiado retail gallery, this hotel, designed by the celebrated architect Álvaro Siza, is decorated with great taste in a Portuguese-Asian style. The rooms have every modern comfort and magnificent views over the Tagus, the castle and the city.

BAIRRO ALTO

🍽 **Residencial Camoes** – *Travessa do Poço da Cidade, ☏213 467 510. 16 rooms.* Housed in a renovated 16th-century building, Camoes offers small, simple rooms, not all en-suite, on the third floor with no elevator. There are fans for the warmer nights, and breakfast is good. Decent value for money.

🍽🛏 **Pensão Londres** – *Rua Dom Pedro V. 53, 1. ☏213 462 203. www.pensao londres.com.pt. 36 rooms.* This *pensão* occupies four floors of a handsome

Casa de São Mamede

© Casa de São Mamede

building on the edge of the Bairro Alto, Lisbon's pulsating night-life district, so don't go to bed too early. Certain rooms have original ceilings and good views of the Castelo São Jorge. A clean and well-maintained establishment offering reasonable rates in a good location.

⊖⊜🅂 **Casa de S. Mamede** – *Rua da Escola Politécnica, 159. ☎213 963 166. 28 rooms.* This charming hotel sits in an 18C mansion and still has a family feel to it, with *azulejos* and early 20C furniture. It really is in an ideal location, among the antique shops, close to the Principe Real and the botanical gardens and one of the top choices for discerning visitors.

ALFAMA

⊖ **Pensão São João da Praça** – *Rua de São João da Praça 97. ☎218 862 591. 15 rooms.* Immediately next to the cathedral (busy by day, quiet by night) this is a nice hotel at budget prices, though not all rooms are en suite. In a lovely building with character. There is another, more expensive hotel next door – don't confuse them.

⊖ **Pensão Flor dos Cavaleiros** – *Rua dos Cavaleiros, 58. ☎218 872 286. 20 rooms.* The rooms are simple but clean, and the building has not been renovated in a long time, but the location is excellent, right in the heart of Alfama and close to all transportation.

⊖⊜ **Casa Costa do Castelo** – *Rua Costa do Castelo, 54. ☎218 822 678. www.c-c-castelo.com. 5 rooms.* Below the esplanade of the castle, this house is surrounded by a terraced garden

planted with vines, orange and lemon trees. The four double rooms and one suite are bright and nicely decorated (wooden floors, rockers and Turkish kilims), but are on the fourth floor with no lift. A hearty breakfast is served in the conservatory. Beautiful views.

⊖⊜🅂🅂 **Solar dos Mouros** – *Rua do Milagre de Santo António, 6. ☎218 854 940. www.solardosmouroslisboa.com. 13 rooms.* Note: the hotel has no lift/elevator and no handicapped access/facilities. Built on an old Arab wall, the house belongs to a painter, Luís Lemos, whose abstract paintings and private collection hang around the walls. Ultra-spacious rooms, overlooking the castle and the Tagus, are decorated with statues, African masks, designer furniture, rare books and collectible lamps. All rooms are equipped with a hi-fi system, minibar and safe. A little Zen garden lies at the bottom of the hotel.

⊖⊜🅂🅂 **Solar do Castelo** – *Rua das Cozinhas, 2. ☎218 806 050. www.solardocastelo.com. 14 rooms.* Within the walls of St George's castle, this small mansion built on the site of the former Alcaçova Palace has been renovated with a beautiful interior and patio with fountain where guests can take their breakfast. The rooms, standard or superior, are all pleasant and sunny, decorated in neutral tones. The hotel has an electric car to pick up guests at the castle gate. Excellent service.

⊖⊜🅂🅂 **Palácio Belmonte** – *Páteo D. Fradique, 14. ☎218 816 600. www.palaciobelmonte.com. 10 suites from*

€450 to €3000 per night. 🏊. A hotel built in a 17C palace, perched on the highest point of the hill by the castle and renovated in a Franco-Portuguese style, this is one of the best. Nearly 4 000 blue-and-white Portuguese tiles from the 1700s cover the walls. Private terraces with all suites and a black-marble pool await you if you have time to make use of them. If you really want to celebrate, try the Himalaya Suite with a 360° bird's-eye view over the city.

BELÉM AND AJUDA

⊜⊜ **Residencial Setubalense** – R. de Belém, 28. ℘213 636 639. www. setubalense.pt. 30 rooms. For those who prefer to stay in a quiet, calm and elegant part of the city, away from the bustle of the centre, this little *pensão* is ideal, close to the Mosteiro dos Jerónimos. A beautiful pink-coloured façade and with rooms that are simple and comfortable.

NORTH LISBON

⊜ **Parque de Campismo** – Estrada da Circunvalação (west of the park). ℘217 628 200. www.lisboacamping.com. In the midst of pines, there is a well-equipped bar, restaurant, laundry, tennis, pool and food available. Spaces for tents and caravans plus 70 comfortable bungalows. A bit noisy and garbage collection sometimes random.

⊜ **Pousada de Juventude** – Rua Andrade Corvo, 46 (Saldanha). ℘213 532 696. 41 rooms. www.pousadajuventude.pt. Behind the Sheraton hotel, this youth hostel is clean and well kept. Double rooms with or without toilets, dormitories of 4 or 6 people.

⊜⊜⊜ **Hotel Dom Sancho I** – Av. da Liberdade, 202. ℘213 513 160. www.domsancho.com. 40 rooms. An impeccably maintained hotel, in an 18C building, with friendly staff. The rooms are outdated, but spacious and comfortable, and there is a nice buffet breakfast.

⊜⊜⊜⊜ **NH Liberdade** – Av. de Liberdade, 180B. ℘213 514 060. www. nh-hoteles.pt. 83 rooms. 🏊📛. Lovers of refinement cannot afford to miss this elegant, ultra-modern hotel just off Lisbon's main street, in the small Tivoli Forum. On the roof is a pool and a terrace with wonderful panoramic views over the city and the Tagus. The rooms are decorated in minimalist style. Very chic!

⊜⊜⊜⊜ **As Janelas Verdes** – Rua das Janelas Verdes, 47, Lapa. ℘213 968 143. www.asjanelasverdes.com. 29 rooms. Located just a few steps from the Museu de Arte Antiga, this beautiful 18C mansion has been transformed into a welcoming and comfortable boutique hotel, decorated with the personal touch. The rooms are not large and do look out over the busy street, so are not always quiet. At the back of the hotel a lovely terrace/patio is the ideal place for breakfast in the open in the summer months.

⊜⊜⊜⊜ **Four Seasons Ritz Hotel** – Rua Rodrigo da Fonseca, 88. ℘213 811 400. www.fourseasons.com/lisbon. 282 rooms. The interior of this imposing building on the edge of Edward VII Park is a mixture of Art Deco and Louis XVI style, comprising coloured marble, hundreds of works of art and fabulous tapestries. There is a splendid spa on the top floor, a fitness centre and the service is impeccable. Arguably Lisbon's premier luxury hotel, and located in the heart of the city.

⊜⊜⊜⊜ **Lisboa Plaza** – Travessa do Salitre 7 (close to Avenida da Liberdade). ℘213 218 218. www.lisbonplazahotel.com. 112 rooms. This beautiful hotel from the neo-Classic 1950s features creamy marble and tasteful furniture. Pretty rooms with bathroom. Parking, elevator, WiFi. Hearty breakfast.

RATO, ESTRELA, LAPA AND ALCÂNTRA

⊜ **Brasília** – Rua Alexandre Herculano, 29. ℘213 149213. 4 rooms. No breakfast. Just steps from the Avenida da Liberdade and Marquês do Pombal, this small guesthouse in an apartment offers a quiet, intimate atmosphere, single rooms (with or without shower). Plenty of charm and good value for money.

⊜ **Lisbon Budget Inn** – Calçada da Estrela 144. ℘964 865 415. 7 rooms. Just a few minutes away from the Basilica de Estrela, this hotel is situated in a typical Portuguese building and features historic details, ancient wooden floors, and a lovely inner courtyard. The rooms have simple furnishings, air conditioning, and a relaxed atmosphere. Self-catered apartments also available. Extra charge for internet use in the rooms.

⊜⊜ **Maná** – Calçada Marquês de Abrantes, 97. ℘213 900 394. 17 rooms. In a quiet area, near the Museu de Arte

Antiga and the nightlife of Santos, this is a beautiful well renovated house. The rooms, many of which appear as small suites are equipped with refrigerators and are elegant, even if the decoration is not always in the best taste. Choose rooms which overlook the garden or with views over the Tagus.

⊖⊜⊜⊜ **Albergaria Senhora do Monte** – *Calçada do Monte, 39.* ℘*218 866 002. www.albergariasenhoradomonte. com. 28 rooms.* Perched on the highest hill of Lisbon, this hotel has panoramic views, parking, lift and panoramic bar and terrace. Décor is a bit dated, but the rooms are comfortable and spacious. The junior suites have large private terraces with sun loungers.

⊖⊜⊜⊜ **York House** – *R. das Janelas Verdes, 33, Lapa.* ℘*213 962 435. www.yorkhouselisboa.com. 32 rooms.* Lisbon's best known historic inn has every modern comfort, yet with an atmosphere of relaxed calm as befits the 17C Carmelite convent in which it is housed. The rooms overlooking the street are best avoided, as this is the heart of the nightlife district. The handsome dining room looks onto a cobblestone courtyard. ⊛ The inn's location near the Museu de Arte Antiga is ideal for visiting Lisbon on foot.

⑨/**EAT**

Throughout the city, the quality of food is high particularly in La Baixa and the narrow streets of the Bairra Alto, where you will find a cluster of good restaurants, offering everything from Japanese fare to excellent seafood and the most traditional of Portuguese "tasca" restaurant-taverns serving dishes such as Alentejo black pork. The Chiado offers an eclectic mix of lively, cheaper cafés, Art Deco restaurants and terraces frequented by workers and students and offering local Portuguese dishes. Alfama's family-run restaurants are often secreted away beneath the castle, their menus featuring the catch of the day at reasonable prices. This working-class district and Mouraria are the best places to listen to fado while enjoying a meal but beware the tourist traps. You will find cafés serving *bica* (espresso) and delicious *pastéis de nata* (egg custard tarts) all over the city. Stop off and enjoy one as the locals frequently do.

BAIXA

⊖ **To B.** – *Rua Capelo, 24,* ℘*213 471 046. http://www.to-burger.com.* give This quality burger restaurant provides a broad variety of meat types, breads, and condiments including veggie burgers, which are not so common in Lisbon. Ideal for a quick lunch.

⊖⊜ **Casa do Alentejo** – *Rua Portas de Santo Antao, 58.* ℘*213 405 140. www. casadoalentejo.com.pt.* Built in the late 17C, the former palace of Alverca opens onto a Moorish, richly decorated patio. A marble staircase serves the lounges and the restaurant whose walls are lined with glazed tiles depicting themes of fields in the Alentejo. The food, which is hearty and rustic, includes daily specials and a variety of classics like pork with clams and *migas* from the Alentejo (fried bread in lard). Sunday afternoon dance to the orchestra. Avoid very busy days (the quality of the food suffers sometimes). Reservations recommended at night.

⊖⊜⊜ **Olivier Avenida** – *Hotel Tivoli Jardim, Rua Júlio César.* ℘*213 174 105. http://avenida.olivier.pt. Closed Sun.* Excellent gourmet cuisine, cosy dining and good service in the heart of cosmopolitan Lisbon. Dishes may include seared duck foie gras, shaved black pork with mango chutney and raspberry vinaigrette, duck breast with port and vegetable flan, or rack of lamb Provençal. The tasting menu is a good way to experience the variety of flavours on offer without spending too much. The wine list is excellent.

⊖⊜⊜⊜ **Gambrinus** – *Rua Portas de Santo Antão, 23.* ℘*213 421 466. www. gambrinuslisboa.com.* One of the best fish restaurants in the city. Here you will find a refined cuisine served in a décor of dark wood and brown leather. Dishes include an excellent fish soup, fried sole, bar en croute, turbot with hollandaise sauce, fried octopus, oysters and caviar from Iran. Service at the bar by the entrance is less formal.

CHIADO

⊖ **Alpendre** – *Rua Augusto Rosa, 32–4 (near the cathedral).* ℘*218 862 421. Closed Sun.* This typical Portuguese restaurant offers a generous kitchen based on grilled fish, seafood and pork. Spacious restaurant and very efficient staff.

☺ **Cantina das Freiras** – *Travessa do Ferragial 1, 3rd Floor (corner of Rua Vitor Cordon).* ℘*213 240 910.* Students of Fine Arts and office workers jostle each noon in this self-service restaurant. From the terrace, there is a view over the Tagus Bridge and the 25 April bridge. The affordable menu will delight small budgets and big appetites.

☺ **Leitaria Académica** – *Largo do Carmo, 1.* ℘*213 469 092. Closed Sun.* The sunny terrace, facing the church of Carmo, is frequented by students of the faculty nearby. Exquisite little old room, with moulded ceilings and painted floral tiles. Simple dishes (chicken or grilled squid, fish fillets), good and cheap. The perfect place for lunch.

☺☺ **Café Buenos Aires** – *Calçada do Duque, 31-B.* ℘*213 420 739. www. cafebuenosaires.pt. Closed Sun.*
An Argentinian coffee shop and restaurant with old wooden tables, where the waitresses, dressed in black, serve while dancing to the music of the tango. Warm and rather bohemian. The terrace, overlooking the castle, is appreciable. On the menu: meat of the pampas, wtih especially good steaks (unsurprisingly), warm goat's cheese salad, tagliatelle with mushrooms and gourmet sandwiches. And for dessert, a delicious chocolate fondant.

☺☺ **Cervejaria Trindade** – *Rua Nova da Trindade, 20-C.* ℘*213 423 506. www.cervejariatrindade.pt. Open to 1.30am on Fri–Sat. Closed bank holidays.* This brewery founded in 1836 is in the refectory of a former convent, the oldest and most beautiful in Portugal. Tiles representing the four seasons line the vaulted great room. The restaurant brews until late in the evening. The service is always friendly and the food, except seafood, somewhat variable.

☺☺ **Mercado da Ribeira (Time Out Market)**– *Av. 24 de Julho, 49.* ℘*213 951 274. timeoutmarket.com.* Run by what's-on mag Time Out, this 40-stall market serves everything from delicious square pizza slices to contemporary Portuguese fare, like grilled octopus. Good souvenirs at A Vida Portuguesa. Clean bathrooms. Free WiFi.

☺☺ **Sacramento** – *Calçada do Sacramento, 40–46.* ℘*213 420 572. Closed Sun.* In the former annex of the Confeitaria Nacional (Praça da Figueira) this bright, contemporary restaurant,

wine bar and café is spread over several levels, with live jazz on Saturday evening. Tapas, cold and hot dishes as well as some Portuguese and Mediterranean dishes.

☺☺☺☺ **Tavares** – *Rua da Misericordia, 37.* ℘*213 421 112. www.restaurantetavares. net. Closed Sun and Mon.* This famous restaurant, the equivalent of Maxim's de Paris, was founded in 1784 and decorated with gilded woodwork, mirrors, crystal chandeliers and red velvet chairs.

BAIRRO ALTO

☺ **Tapa Bucho** – *Rua dos Mouros, 19.* ℘*914 566 392. Closed Sun.* This fun restaurant combines the Spanish *tapas* tradition with Portuguese *petiscos*, which are small dishes made to share. Specialties include squid, cod, and different types of potatoes and eggs.

☺ **Restaurante Sucolento** – *Rua do Instituto Industrial, 7.* ℘*211 993 084. Closed Sun.* A colorful and friendly restaurant serving a variety of meat dishes including pork ribs and steak, all very reasonably priced. All dishes have a Portuguese touch, and are served with rice, cous cous, or salad.

☺☺ **Antigo Primeiro de Maio** – *Rua da Atalaia, 8.* ℘*213 426 840. Closed Sat lunch and Sun.* Traditional Portuguese cuisine: grilled sole, rabbit with clams, suckling pig. The setting is pleasant and service courteous and prompt. Good quality food at fair prices. A sure bet.

ALFAMA

☺ **Café da Garagem** – *Rua Costa do Castelo, 75.* ℘*218 854 190. Open Tue–Sun 5pm–midnight.* Located behind the castle, this is a small café serving vegetarian food and fish dishes combined with an independent theatre. It often hosts performances by English actors, poetry readings and avant-garde performances. The association that manages the place also has programmes to fight against social exclusion of youths from the suburbs. WiFi available.

☺☺ **Barracão de Alfama** – *Rua de Sao Pedro, 16.* ℘*218 866 359.* Near the Museum of Fado, the president of the Restaurant Association of Portugal cooks up some excellent fresh fish at really cheap prices: cod with cream, grilled turbot, bouillabaisse, steak swordfish, sole or sea bream, according to what's available at market. The restaurant is very busy at noon with locals. There are a few tables located outside.

Mestre André – *Calçadinha de Santo Estêvão, 6. ☎218 866 232. Closed Mon.* The menu is more elaborate than average, serving dishes such as breaded veal in the style of Sintra, and almond chicken livers. The host provides a convivial and lively atmosphere.

Santo António de Alfama – *Beco Sao Miguel, 7. ☎218 881 328. http://siteantonio.com.* A large hall decorated with portraits of film stars in black and white was enough to make this a trendy restaurant in Alfama, where fashion aficionados and press congregate. Menu combines sweet and sour (duck in orange sauce, breaded brie with raspberry compote), plus tapas, salads and pasta. Reservations recommended at night.

Chapitô à Mesa – *Rua Costo do Castelo, 1. ☎218 875 077. Closed Sat–Sun lunch.* This modern restaurant offers fabulous views over the city, especially when illuminated at night. The menu consists mainly of vegetarian dishes (casseroles) and fish (turbot in caper sauce, sole Florentine, salmon fillets). Intimate and romantic. Reservations recommended.

Bica do Sapato – *Avenida Infante Dom Henrique, Armazém B, Doca do Jardim do Tabaco. ☎218 810 320. www.bicadosapato.com.* This popular Alfama restaurant belongs to Manuel Reis, charismatic figure of the restaurant scene in Lisbon, and American actor John Malkovich. On the ground floor, the restaurant serves high quality Portuguese cuisine plus there is a sushi bar (evenings). All in a sumptuous, retro-futuristic setting. Designer furniture from the private collection of Manuel Reis. Terrace is on the Tagus. Prices are high.

MOURARIA, GRAÇA AND SANTA APOLONIA

Zé da Mouraria – *Rua João do Outeiro, 24. ☎218 865 436. Closed Sun.* In a maze of streets at the foot of the Mouraria hill, close to Martim Moniz Square, this authentic cantina, without a sign, serves home cooking that is generous and tasty. Go at lunchtime when the place is filled with workers.

Cantinho do Aziz –*Rua de São Lourenço, 5. ☎218 876 472. www.cantinhodoaziz.com.* This colorful eatery brings the flavors of the former Portuguese colony of Mozambique to the Mouraria neigborhood, with spicy meat and fish dishes, coconut rice, and curry. Great deals at lunch time.

DeliDelux – *Avenida Infante Dom Henrique, Armazém B, Loja, 8. ☎218 862 070, www.delidelux.pt.* This deli, where you can find good Italian, French and Portuguese products, has an intimate and sunny terrace, perfect for escaping the hustle of the city. Snacks are genuine quality and served at any time: carpaccio of tomatoes, asparagus with scrambled eggs, fudge. Popular at weekends for brunch.

Via Graça – *Rua Damesceno Monteiro 9B. ☎218 870 830. www.restauranteviagraca.com. Closed Sat–Sun lunch.* Situated below the Belvedere of Nossa Senhora do Monte, this sophisticated restaurant, decorated in contemporary style, offers superb views of Castelo São Jorge and the city centre.

BELÉM AND AJUDA

Caseiro – *Rua Belém, 35. ☎213 638 803. http://caseirorestaurante.com. Closed Sun and Aug.* An eclectic décor in which onions, garlic and banknotes from around the world hang from the walls. Typical Portuguese cuisine.

OVER THE TAGUS

Ponto Final – *Cais do Ginjal, 72, Cacilhas (from the landing stage, turn to right immediately and go along to the end of the quays, a 15min walk). ☎212 760 743. Closed Tue.* You have the feeling that you are at the end of the world here with the whole of Lisbon laid out before you. Come here in the evening to look at Lisbon by night. You dine on a jetty out over the Tagus itself. Delicious traditional cuisine – grilled meat, fish and simmered rice *(carapauzinhos con arroz de tomate, pataniscas com arroz de feijão)*. Excellent wine list; friendly, magical ambience.

NORTH LISBON

Os Tibetanos – *Rua do Salitre, 117. ☎213 142 038. http://tibetanos.com/en. Reservations recommended. Closed Sun, public holidays.* This small restaurant, slightly tucked away, is near the botanical garden and serves tasty Tibetan-inspired vegetarian cuisine at very reasonable prices. Pleasant ambience.

O Funil – *Avenida Elias Garcia, 82A. ☎210 968 912. www.ofunil.pt. Closed Sun and bank holidays.* The cod dish prepared in "Funil" style is one of the specialities of this elegant restaurant. Excellent wine list.

⊜⊜ Cervejaria Ramiro – *Avenida Almirante Reis, 1. ☎218 851 024. www. cervejariaramiro.pt. Closed Mon, 1 May and in August*. For over 50 years, this institution attracts Lisboan lovers of fresh seafood. A mixed clientele enjoys garlic prawns, crabs, oysters and other shellfish, accompanied by a small Vinho Verde. Friendly service, good value for money.

⊜⊜⊜⊜ Varanda – *Rua Rodrigo da Fonseca, 88. ☎213 811 400. www. hotel-mundial.pt*. Run by French chef Pascal Meynard, the Four Seasons Ritz restaurant offers arguably the best dining experience in Lisbon. Gourmet Méditerranean cuisine of fish, grilled meats, vegetables and olive oil. Reservations recommended.

TAKING A BREAK

Lisbon is known for its delightful pastry shops and cafés and you can either take a break mid-morning or mid-afternoon to enjoy life the Lisbon way. One tradition in Lisbon is the *pastéis de nata* (egg custard tarts) that are eaten either with a coffee or with a small, cold glass of beer. With all the walking you'll do, you'll soon work off the calories.

Café Nicola – *Praça Dom Pedro IV, 25. ☎213 460 579. www.nicola.pt*. A Lisbon landmark steeped in history. It was here that the first Portuguese women dared to put an end to the exclusively male

character of the city's cafés by coming out for coffee.

Confeitaria Nacional – *Praça da Figueira, 18B. ☎213 424 470. www. confeitarianacional.com. Closed Sun Oct– Apr*. This old pastry shop (1829) is one of the best in Lisbon. A huge choice of pastries and traditional sweets.

Pastelaria Mexicana – *Avenida Guerra Junqueiro, 30C. ☎218 486 117. www. mexicana.pt*. Don't let the name fool you. This pastelaria is 100% Portuguese and has been a family business since the 1940s, as testified by the charming retro look. Sit down and order some of the staples of Portuguese pastry art and one of their local coffee specialties.

Pastelaria Aloma – *Rua Francisco Metrass, 67. ☎213 963 797. www. pastelariaaloma.com*. Award-winning pastelaria selling some of the best pastéis de nata in all of Lisbon, but locals also come here for some of the other sweets, such as the *tartelete de amêndoa* or the *bola de berlim*, or for the savory *queijadas*.

Alcântara Café – *Rua Maria Luisa Holstein, 15. ☎917 568 554. www.alcantaracafe.com*. This brasserie-style café-restaurant is situated in an old factory. A young, elegant and fashionable ambience in amazing industrial-baroque décor. Attracts the trendy crowd.

A Brasileira – *Rua Garrett, 120. ☎213 469 541. Open daily 8am–2am*. A well-known café with a literary tradition. Artists, fashion designers, tourists and residents all meet in this legendary establishment.

NIGHTLIFE

The clubs in Lisbon come in two categories – the trendy, noisy disco variety for the young, and the more refined bar-clubs. Many clubs and late bars do not open before about 10 or 11pm, and no serious clubber would be seen out before midnight. They tend to finish late, with 4am being the witching hour. The Baixa is fairly quiet with a couple of late bars, the most famous of which is **Ginginha do Rossio** (*Largo de São Domingos, 8; daily*) known for its *ginginha* (cherry brandy).

Café No Chiado (*Largo do Picadeiro; daily*) sits next to the San Carlos theatre and is the place where, it is claimed, you can taste the best mango mousse in the world. Well, at least in Lisbon.

😊 What's On? 😊

For details of all entertainment in Lisbon, look at the street posters or in one of the free magazines/ papers on offer. *L'Agenda Cultural* is a monthly publication with a schedule of all cultural events in Lisbon. It's available free from main tourist offices, hotels and on kiosks throughout the capital. Another publication, in English and Portuguese, is called *Follow Me Lisboa* with lists of shows and events: also available free from most tourist attractions.

You can buy tickets at kiosks in *Praça dos Restauradores*, or on *R. de São Mamede, 30 – Principe Real*.

In the **Bairro Alto** area, the real heart of the nightclub area, you will find **Hot Club Portugal** *(Praça da Alegria, 48; www.hcp. pt),* the oldest jazz club in Lisbon. Many internationally renowned acts perform here on Fridays and Saturdays.

Alfama has the **Bar das Imagens/Costa Do Castelo** *(Calçada Marqués de Tancos, 1-1B; closed Jan and Feb).* Halfway up the hill towards the castle, this bar has a wonderful view out over the city and the 25 de Abril bridge. It combines two bars in one: a traditional bar and a terrace bar with DJ.

Lux Frágil *(Av. Infante D. Henrique, Armazém A, Cais da Pedra in Santa Apolónia; closed Sun-Wed).* Created by the former owner of the legendary Frágil, Lux is currently one of the hottest venues in the city, housed in an old warehouse opposite Santa Apolónia railway station.

FADO

You cannot visit Lisbon without listening to **fado**, the traditional music that tells of love and often disaster. Fado is traditionally sung by women (though there are some fine male singers) and the *fadistas* are the pop stars of Portugal. The best places to see fado are in the working-class districts such as Alfama, normally fairly late on a Thursday to Saturday evening. Many fado clubs cater to tourists, many of which include a meal (though not always the very best dining) with the show. They rarely begin before 9pm. Most are closed on Sundays.

Adega do Ribatejo – *Rua Diário Notícias, 23.* ☎*213 468 343. Daily.* One of the venues with the most authentic *fado* and a lively, friendly atmosphere.

O Faia – *Rua Barroca, 54/56.* ☎*213 426 742. Closed Sun.* Authentic Lisbon *fado* in a district where *fado* is the traditional form of expression.

CONCERTS

LA BAIXA

Coliseu dos Recreios – *Rua das Portas de Sto. Antão, 96.* ☎*213 240 580. www. coliseulisboa.com.* A huge auditorium, first opened in 1890, which holds operas, concerts and shows of all kinds.

CHIADO

Teatro Nacional de S. Carlos – *Largo de S. Carlos.* ☎*213 253 000. www.tnsc.pt.* Opera, ballet and classical concerts.

BELÉM

Centro Cultural de Belém – *Praça do Império.* ☎*213 612 400. www.ccb.pt.* Hosts lots of concerts and exhibitions.

Comuna Teatro de Pesquisa – *Praça de Espanha.* ☎*217 221 770.* A traditional programme of theatre, plus a bistro-style café-theatre for contemporary music concerts (rock, jazz, music from around the world) every Sun at 10pm.

The Lisbon Players – *Rua da Estrela, 10, Estrela.* ☎*213 961 946. www.lisbon players.com.pt.* A group of amateur playwrights organising plays and operas in English with audience participation.

Escola Portuguesa de Arte Equestre – *Palácio Nacional de Queluz (Łsee QUELUZ).* ☎*214 358 915. www.cavalonet.com. Shows Wed 10:30am May–Oct (except Aug).* The school, which keeps alive the tradition of Portuguese equestrian art, particularly with Lusitanian thoroughbreds, was founded by King João V at the end of the 18C.

SHOPPING

Lisbon is probably Western Europe's least expensive capital, and you'll find some great bargains as well as the normal international brand names – *Luis Vuitton, Armani, Trussardi, Burberry, Hugo Boss, Longchamp* and *Escada* – whose prices are pretty standard worldwide. Many of these international brand names are on the famous Avenida da Liberdade, but if you want lesser-known but interesting Portuguese designers, at prices that might be more acceptable, go to the Bairro Alto and Chiado districts. Bairro Alto is popular with the alternative fashion set, with club and streetwear shops. Most of those only open after a late lunch and continue well into the night so if you go there in the morning you'll find them closed.

Rua Augusta is situated in the Baixa, one of the busiest quarters of Lisbon. Closed to traffic, this pedestrian-only street offers a great variety of shopping options with European chain-stores like Zara, Mango or H&M, but you'll also find peddlers selling all sorts of things from neck-scarves to jewellery, from shoes to hand-made bags.

A very trendy area for shoppers these days is Principe Real, about 10 minutes away from Bairro Alto and filled with designer ateliers, art galleries, and

Mercado da Ribeira Nova

modern cafès mixing Portuguese tradition with a cosmopolitan, up-and-coming feel. More generally, some of the best bargains in Lisbon are leather, with purses, handbags and shoes being good value. Look for antique hand-painted tiles, distinctive regional ceramics and textiles such as tablecloths and embroidery, and don't forget that all gold sold in Portugal is at least 19.2 carat and is one of the best buys in the country. In the Baixa in particular you will still find streets with names that indicate the work of their original inhabitants, Prata (Silver), Ouro (Gold) and Ferreiros (Blacksmiths).

There are plenty of **shopping centres** throughout the city. The biggest ones are at Colombo, Galerias Monumental, Saldanha, Vasco da Gama, Armazens

Feira da Ladra

do Chiado, Amoreiras and El Corte Inglés. Most of them have cinemas, gyms, restaurants as well and are open from about 10am to 11pm. There is also the Freeport Outlet Shopping, the biggest outlet in Europe, where you can find everything you may need. Many international brands offer discounts up to 50 percent throughout the year. There are a couple of huge street markets, the biggest being the **Feira da Ladra** (translates as Thieves' Market) all day Sat and Tue morning, on Campo de Santa Clara, Alfama, where you'll find all sorts of things you never realised you needed. Arrive early if you want to avoid the crowds, and watch out for pickpockets.

Mercado da Ribeira Nova – *Av. 24 de Julho. Closed Sun.* Wonderful food market where colours, smells and the sales pitch of its vendors all blend together.

Feira de Carcavelos – *In the centre of Carcavelos 21km/13mi west of Lisbon on the Estoril road. Thu morning.* Inexpensive clothes market selling seconds with minor – and often barely discernable – defects. A number of well-known French and British brand names are often on sale here, particularly cotton goods.

Also consider – **Feira de Sintra** – *Largo de São Pedro à Sintra –2nd and 4th Sun/month, all day.* This large market in one of Sintra's squares sells the same goods as most other markets, plus plants and animals. Around the square you will also find small craft and antique stalls.

The Lisbon region is a bountiful mix of bustling seaside resorts, romantic UNESCO towns, fairy-tale palaces and rugged, rolling countryside. Estoril, a fashionable seaside resort with a glitzy casino, and Cascais, a former fishing village, are situated on the coast road 35-40km/22-25mi west of Lisbon. Inland, Sintra nestles on the north slope of the rugged Serra de Sintra, which extends down to the surfing coastline. South of Lisbon, across the Vasco da Gama bridge, Setúbal sits among the foothills of the Serra da Arrabida on the north bank of the Sado estuary. The Serra da Arrábida natural park lies between Sesimbra and Setúbal.

Sintra

Lord Byron called Sintra "Paradise on earth" – and the description of this romantic and picturesque UNESCO World Heritage Site is just as fitting today.

Located in the lush hills of the granite Serra among wooded ravines and fresh water springs, Sintra is a melting pot of grand and eccentric palaces, glorious gardens, cosy tea shops and fascinating museums and markets. For six centuries the town was the favourite summer residence of the Portuguese royal family. Visit the National Palace, complete with its distinctive conical chimneys, before heading out to the peaceful Serra de Sintra, where the quirky Pena Palace remains much as it was when the royal family lived there in the 19C.

A wonderful way to experience the serra is to take the restored tram that runs from Sintra all the way to the rugged coastline. It ends at the sheer Cabo da Roca, or Cape Rock, mainland Europe's most westerly point.

Estoril

An hour's bus ride away are the bustling seaside resorts of Estoril and neighbouring Cascais. Estoril is the more fashionable of the two, with its glitzy casino and cabaret shows, palm-lined avenues, tropical gardens of exotic trees and plants, and sporting events such as horse racing, surfing and tennis. The Estoril Open tennis championship is held here every year, and dozens of top championship golf courses dot the area. Two of the region's most impressive monuments are Mafra Palace and Monastery – 40km/25mi northwest of Lisbon – and the 18C Royal Palace of Quelez,

located between the capital and Sintra. Inspired by Versailles, the sumptuous palace gardens are an invitation to stroll around its refreshing pools, statues and Rococo facades.

Setúbal and Serra da Arrábida

South of Lisbon is the fishing port of Setúbal, which is famous for Moscatel wine and orange marmalade. Visit the Quinta da Bacalhoa, which produces mandarins from its ornamental kitchen garden and fabulous wine.

From Setúbal, take the ancient ferry across the Sado to Troia, an immense strip of fine sand, dunes and pines.

A couple of miles inland, close to Lisbon, is the pretty whitewashed town of Palmela, built in tiers on the northern slope of the Serra da Arrábida. Have lunch at the castle, now partly converted into a *pousada*, which has a wonderful restaurant open to non-residents.

The Serra da Arrábida is a pleasant place to drive around. Stop off at Sesimbra, a popular beach resort and deep-sea fishing centre, famous for swordfish.

Sintra★★★

Only half an hour from Lisbon, Sintra, up against the north slope of the *serra*, is a haven of peace and greenery. For six centuries the town was the favourite summer residence of the kings of Portugal. In the 19C several English Romantic poets, including Lord Byron, stayed here. Three different areas make up the town of Sintra: the old town (*Vila Velha*), grouped round the royal palace, the modern town (Estefânia), and the former village of São Pedro, famous for its market of secondhand goods held on the second and fourth Sundays of each month. Sintra's popularity, particularly during weekends, is reflected in the old town's many antique and craft shops, smart boutiques, restaurants, and tearooms where one may sample the local gastronomic speciality: delicious small tarts known as *queijadas*.

THE TOWN

Sintra is a popular tourist destination as well as home to a good-size population of its own. Reachable by train from Lisbon in about 30 minutes, it makes for an ideal day out from the capital, though many people choose to stay in one of its charming hotels for a few nights. This cultural landscape of Sintra is a UNESCO World Heritage Site.

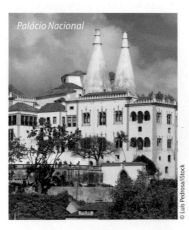

Palácio Nacional

© Luis Pedrosa/iStock

- ▸ **Population:** 387 000.
- ♿ **Map:** p141.
- 🚻 **Info:** Praça da República; ℘219 231 157; www.sintra-portugal.com.
- ▸ **Location:** 25km/15.5mi northeast of Lisbon.
- 👥 **Kids:** The toy museum (Museu do Brinquedo).
- 🕐 **Timing:** Allow a couple of days to explore the region.
- 🅿 **Parking:** Difficult in the centre, especially at weekends.
- 👁 **Don't Miss:** The royal palace; the Palaces at Mafra and Queluz, as well as the Cabo da Roca, the westernmost point of mainland Europe.

Palácio Nacional★★

🕐*Daily 9.30am–7pm.* 🕐*1 Jan and 25 Dec.* ✍€10 (child, 6–17, €8.50. *Discounts available for combined tickets).* ℘219 237 300. *www.parquesdesintra.pt.*
The palace's irregular structure is due to the additions made during different periods; the central part was erected by Dom João I at the end of the 14C and the wings by Dom Manuel I early in the 16C. Apart from the two tall conical chimneys, the paired Moorish-style *(ajimeces)* and Manueline windows are the most striking features of the exterior.
The interior is remarkable for its decoration of 16C and 17C **azulejos★★**; the finest embellish the dining room or Arabic Hall (Sala dos Árabes), the chapel and the Sirens' Hall (Sala das Sereias). The **Sala dos Brasões** (Armoury), which is square, is covered with a **ceiling★★** in the form of a dome on squinches. The dome itself consists of coffers painted with the coats of arms of Portuguese nobles of the early 16C – the missing blazon is that of the Coelho family who conspired against Dom João II.
The **Sala das Pegas** (Magpie or Reading Room) has a ceiling painted in the

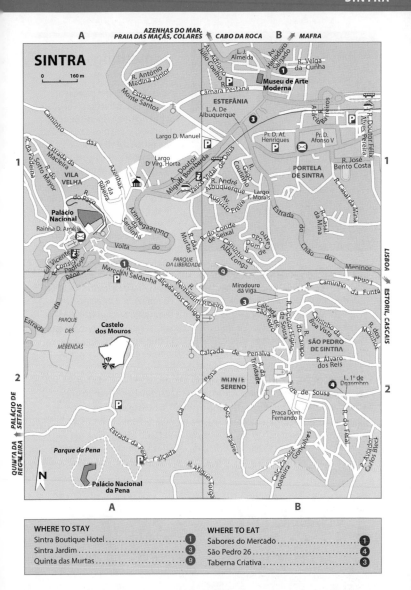

SINTRA

0 ——— 160 m

WHERE TO STAY

Sintra Boutique Hotel	❶
Sintra Jardim	❸
Quinta das Murtas	❾

WHERE TO EAT

Sabores do Mercado	❶
São Pedro 26	❹
Taberna Criativa	❸

GETTING THERE

The easiest, fastest and most environmentally friendly way of getting to Sintra is by train from Lisboa-Rossio. From Sintra station there is a bus to the centre of the old town. Trains run every 10–15min and the journey takes 35min. With the **Lisboa Card** the train is free. Alternatively, take a bus from the centre of Cascais – it is much slower as the bus stops at many places along the way, but it will drop you in the centre of Sintra, close to Pena Palace.

Travesseiro

© Garuti/Dreamstime.com

Something Sweet

Sintra's wonderful palaces are not its only attraction. For years it has boasted a long-standing tradition in pastries and sweets, the recipes of which have remained a closely guarded secret since the Middle Ages.

The most famous of them all is the *queijadas de Sintra*: thin and flaky pastry cases filled with fresh cheese, flour, egg yolks, sugar syrup and cinnamon. They are quite delicious.

They originated at the Queijadas da Sapa Bakery, now also a delightful tea shop situated near the town entrance close to the main bus stop. Try one with a pot of tea or a bica (espresso coffee) on the café terrace that overlooks the conical chimneys of the Palacio Real.

Over the years a number of different versions have been produced in the area, but the original recipe remains a closely guarded secret by artisans. So famous are these pastries that the historic family establishments that produce them have formed their own association to keep standards high, the Associacão das Antigas Fabricas das Queijadas de Sintra.

The original Queijadas de Sintra are easily recognised by their hand-wrapped artisan paper packages that come in rolls of approximately seven pastries.

The town of Mafra produces a version made with marzipan called *fradinhos*.

Piriquita, another of Sintra's oldest pastry shops, makes another Sintra speciality, *travesseiros*. Puff pastry shells are filled with a mixture of egg and almond; the best way to enjoy them is hot and fresh from the oven. Another delight made in the vicinity of Sintra is the delicious *fofos de Belas*, small sponge cakes filled with cream and sprinkled with sugar.

Queijadas de Sintra

© rfranca/iStock

17C with magpies holding in their beaks a rose inscribed with the words: *por bem* – for good – words pronounced by Dom João I when his queen caught him about to kiss one of her ladies-in-waiting. To put an end to the gossip the king had as many magpies painted on the ceiling as there were ladies at court. Don't miss the kitchens with their chimneys rising to the sky.

Museu de Arte Moderna★ (Colecção Berardo)

⏱ *Winter: Tue–Fri 10am–6pm. Sat & Sun noon–6pm. Summer: 10am–8pm Tue–Fri, 2–6pm Sat & Sun.* ⊛€3. ℘*219 248 170. www.cm-sintra.pt.*

Housed in the town's former casino near the train station, the museum holds the valuable private collection of the benefactor J Berardo. It features works from the second half of the 20C, and represents the avant-garde artistic trends that developed after 1945.

The exhibits, which are shown on a rotating basis, include works by Dubuffet (the oldest on display), Gilbert & George, David Hockney, Jeff Koons, Joan Mitchele, Richter, Rosenquist, Tom Wesselmann and Andy Warhol. The museum also has a café, a bookshop and a gift shop.

Quinta da Regaleira★★

Rua Barbosa da Bocage, on the road to Steais, 800m from the village centre. ⏱ *Apr–Sept 10am–8pm; Nov–Jan 10am–5:30pm. Oct, Feb, Mar 10am–6:30pm.* ⏱ *1 Jan, 25 Dec.* ⊛€6. ℘*219 106 650. www.regaleira.pt.*

On the site of a 17C *quinta* (farmhouse) just five minutes' walk from the town, Carvalho Monteiro (1848–1920), a successful businessman (the palace is known as Palace of Monterio the Millionaire) adopted an esoteric lifestyle and had this eclectic mix of buildings erected, notably in Gothic, Manueline or Renaissance style. You enter by a revolving stone door and then go through a tunnel that comes out by a lake.

There are beautiful gardens here full of unexpected treasures: various styles of monument, chapels, statues (many of which have religious or mythological overtones, or refer to freemasonry). Notable are the **gruta de Leda** (grotto of Leda), the **Capela da Santíssima Trinidade** and the **tour da Realeira**.

ADDRESSES

🏠 STAY

⊜⊜🛏 **Hotel Sintra Jardim** – *Travessa dos Avelares, 12.* ℘*219 230 738. http://hotelsintrajardim.pt. 15 rooms.* ⬛🅿
This elegant 19C building – a former summer retreat for a rich family based in Lisbon – is convenient for the historic centre, being just 800 metres away, but is in a residential area so it is pleasantly quiet. Large bathrooms and a lush garden.

⊜⊜🛏 **Quinta das Murtas** – *Rua Eduardo Van Zeller, 4.* ℘*219 240 246. www. quintasmurtas.pt. Closed early Jan - mid-Feb. 20 rooms.* ⬛ 🅿. This pretty pink house furnished with Venetian mirrors and antiques offers pleasantly spacious rooms. It's a romantic and peaceful place to stay.

⊜⊜🛏🛏 **Palácio de Seteais** – *Rua Barbosa do Bocage, 8.* ℘*219 233 200. www.tivolihotels.com/en. 30 rooms.* ⬛ 🅿
This elegant 18C palace is where the Convention of Sintra was signed in 1808. Nowadays the hotel, with its magnificent grounds, is considered one of Portugal's finest lodgings. Rooms are richly decorated with magnificent paintings, luxurious carpets and frescos of rare beauty.

🍴 EAT

⊖ **Metamorphosis** – *Rua Joao de Deus 41–45.* ℘*219 244573.* The shredded cod, roasted squid, shrimp risottos, and chicken with beer are all delicious and artfully served at this lovely restaurant. Portions are big and vegetarians won't leave hungry.

⊖ **Fábrica das Queijadas da Sapa** – *Volta do Duche, 12.* ℘*219 230 493. Queijadas* are the traditional pastries from Sintra made with eggs, *fromage frais* and cinnamon. This pastry company, founded in 1786, has a small tearoom with a fine view overlooking the royal palace in which to enjoy famous local delicacies with tea.

Palácio Nacional da Pena

© Pierre Jacques/hemis.fr

Serra de Sintra★★

The Serra de Sintra is a lovely area west of Sintra, with convents, palaces, castles and parks. Rugged in parts, it is very inviting for visitors, and the beach resorts on the coast are quite good, one being the location for the World Bodysurfing Championships. The restored Sintra Tram now runs down to the coast from Sintra, making an easy way to travel.

🚗 DRIVING TOUR

PARQUE DA PENA★★

🕐Daily Apr–Oct 9.30am–8pm; Nov–Mar 10am–6pm. 🕐1 Jan and 25 Dec. ⊜€7.50 (the combination ticket includes the palace ⊜€14. Further discounts available for combined tickets including more attractions). 📞219 237 300. www. parquesdesintra.pt.

South of Sintra the Parque da Pena covers 200ha on the granite slopes of the Serra de Sintra; the park is planted with rare species of trees, and there are several lakes and fountains. It is best visited on foot to fully appreciate its great charm, but the motorist can gently drive along the small roads that cross it, or at least go to the top of the two culminating points; the Palácio da Pena stands on one, and the Cruz Alta (High Cross) on the other.

⚓ **Map:** p149.
🛈 **Info:** Parque Natural de Sintra-Cascais, Rua Gago Coutinho, Sintra; 📞219 247 200. www.parquedesintra.pt.
▶ **Location:** Runs to the west of Sintra as far as the coast.
👪 **Kids:** Cabo da Roca; the Sintra tram makes for a great ride.
🕐 **Timing:** A day at least to include lunch at one of the beaches.
🅿 **Parking:** Parking is available at most tourist sights.
👁 **Don't Miss:** Moorish Castle; Pena Palace; Capuchin Convent; Cabo da Roca.

▶ Leave Sintra to the south, on the road to Pena.

After skirting the Estalagem dos Cavaleiros, where Lord Byron planned his narrative poem *Childe Harold*, the road rises in a series of hairpin bends.

▶ At the crossroads with the N 247-3, turn left to Pena.

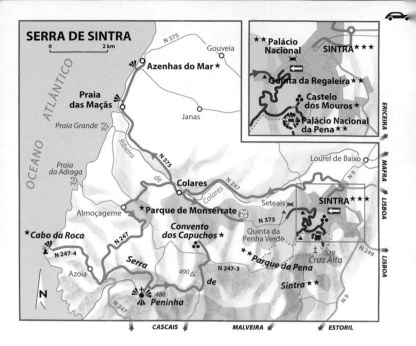

🏯 Castelo dos Mouros★

*30min round trip on foot from the car
park.* 🕐*Daily Apr–Oct 9.30am–8pm;
Nov–Mar 10am–6pm.* ✆€8. *Further
discounts available for combined tickets
including more attractions.* ℘219 237
300. www.parquesdesintra.pt.

The Moorish Castle, built in the 8C or 9C,
still has a battlemented perimeter wall
guarded by four towers and a ruined
Romanesque chapel. From the tower,
which is climbed by a series of staircases,
there is a fine **view★** of Sintra and its palace, the Atlantic coast and the Castelo
da Pena.

◗ Go through the wrought-iron gate
at the entrance to the Parque da Pena
and leave the car in the car park.

Palácio Nacional da Pena★★

🕐*Daily Apr–Oct 9.30am–7pm; Nov–Mar
10am–6pm. Guided tours daily 10.30am
and 2.30pm.* 🕐*1 Jan and 25 Dec.* ✆€14
*palace and park, further discounts if you
combine with more attractions).* ℘219 237
͓. www.parquesdesintra.pt.

͓palace, perched on one of the high-
͓eaks of the range, was built by Ferdinand (ℹ️*see box p150*) in the middle of
the 19C around a former Hieronymite
monastery dating from the 16C. Its
eccentric architecture evokes some
of Ludwig II of Bavaria's castles – with
domes, towers, ramparts and a drawbridge that was never designed to
draw – although it predates them by
30 years. It is a pastiche in which several styles merge with varying degrees
of success: Moorish, Gothic, Manueline,
Renaissance and Baroque. A drawbridge
leads through a Moorish doorway to the
palace courtyard where the remains of
the monastery, the Manueline cloisters
and the chapel – with an alabaster altar
by Nicolas Chanterene – are decorated
with *azulejos*. From the terraces there
are good **views★★** over the Atlantic
coast to the Tagus.

AROUND THE SERRA★

30km/18.6mi. About 3hr.

◗ Leave Sintra on the road towards
Pena then turn onto the N 247-3
towards Cabo da Roca.

Cabo da Roca

© lavendertime/iStock

After several kilometres, a 16C **Capuchin monastery**★ appears amid a striking landscape of jumbled rocks. The monks' cells were cut out of the living rock and the walls lined with cork, the best insulator against cold back then.

▷ Head towards Peninha along the road opposite the monastery.

Peninha

The **panorama**★★ from the chapel terrace includes the vast beach of Praia do Guincho in the foreground. From here you can go directly to Cabo da Roca by heading towards Azóia.

Cabo da Roca★

The Serra da Sintra ends in a sheer cliff, the Cabo da Roca or Cape Rock, nearly 140m above the sea. This is mainland Europe's most westerly point.

▷ Return to N 247: continue to Colares.

Colares

Colares is an attractive town known for its red and white table wines.

From here continue northwards to **Azenhas do Mar**★ *(6km/3.7mi)* via the resort of **Praia das Maçãs**. The approach to Azenhas do Mar gives a general view of the town's **setting**★, with its houses rising in tiers up a jagged cliff above the Atlantic.

▷ From Colares return to Sintra on the N 375. This narrow road offers superb views of the surrounding hills as it winds its way through the lush landscape.

Parque de Monserrate★

◷*Daily Apr–Oct 9.30am–8pm; Nov–Mar 10am–6pm.* ◷*1 Jan, 25 Dec.* ✆*€8. Discounts available for combined tickets.* ✆*219 237 300. www.parquesdesintra.pt.*
The landscape **park**★ surrounding the neo-Oriental palace was built by Sir Francis Cook (based on the design of Brighton Pavilion, though the dome is modelled on the Duomo in Florence) in the 19C.

The Artist King

Prince **Ferdinand of Saxe-Coburg-Gotha** (1816–85), nephew of the Belgian king, Léopold I, married Queen Maria II, widow of Duke Auguste of Beauharnais-Leuchtenberg, the grandson of the Empress Josephine, in 1836. Upon the birth of Crown Prince Pedro in 1837, he received the honorary title of Ferdinand II of Portugal. Intelligent and diplomatic, modern and liberal, Ferdinand was Regent of Portugal from 1853 to 1855 and was offered the Spanish throne in 1870. He was a highly cultured man who devoted himself to etching, ceramics and watercolours. President of the Royal Academy of Science and Fine Arts and a patron of Coimbra University, he purchased the ruined monastery of Nossa Senhora da Pena in 1838 and built around it a magnificent palace.

Ferdinand was also a Grand Master of the Order of the Rosy Cross and his château is rich in alchemical symbols. Here, Ferdinand and his second wife, Elisa Hensler, a singer of Swiss origin, received the greatest artists of the day. Richard Strauss said of the palace, where he stayed and which prefigured the castles of Ludwig II of Bavaria: "The gardens... are the gardens of Klingsor, and above them is the castle of the Holy Grail".

Palácio and Convento de Mafra★

Ericeira

The Royal Convent of Mafra, later renamed the National Palace of Mafra, stands some 40km/25mi northwest of Lisbon. Its impressive size and mix of Baroque and Italian Renaissance styles, in which marble proliferates, testify to the rich reign of its builder, King João V. It has often been compared to the Escorial in Spain.

  Michelin Map: 733; Michelin Atlas Spain & Portugal p58 (P 2).

  Info: ✆261 810 550. www.palaciomafra.pt.

  Location: 40km/25mi northwest of Lisbon: take the A 8 then N 116.

  Timing: Spend a full morning in the palace, then have lunch in the gardens or on the coast at nearby Ericeira.

  Don't Miss: The Basilica and the library in the Palace.

A BIT OF HISTORY

King João V, who, having no children after three years of marriage, vowed to build a monastery if God would grant him an heir. A daughter, Barbara, was born, later to become Queen of Spain. Work began in 1717 with 50 000 workers and artisans under a German architect, though the plans were drawn up by a group of Roman artists under the direction of the Marquis de Fontes, Portugal's ambassador to the Holy See.

Originally planned for just 13 monks, it ended up housing 300, together with the entire royal family (and their considerable staff).

Part of the palace is used as a military academy, so visits are permitted only as part of a guided tour, in various languages.

MAFRA SCHOOL

While the monastery was under construction, João V took advantage of the presence of so many foreign artists at Mafra to found a school of sculpture. The first principal was the Italian, Alessandro Giusti, and among the teachers were such men as José Almeida, Giovanni Antonio of Padua, who carved the main statues in the cathedral at Évora and particularly, **Joaquim Machado de Castro** (1731–1822).

The total number of students who ttended this school is unknown, but produced several generations of Por-

tuguese sculptors. Their work spread far and wide and a great many works of sacred art from this renowned school can be found throughout Europe.

VISIT

🕐 *Palace: 9am–5:30pm; Basilica: 9.30am–1pm, 2–5:30pm.* 🕐*1 Jan, Easter Sunday, 1 May and 25 Dec.* ⊗€6. *www. palaciomafra.gov.pt.* The visit to Mafra includes the **palace**, the **monastery** and the **basilica**. There are also extensive gardens (⊛*see Tapada Nacional de Mafra*).

The 220m long façade of the complex is flanked at either end by Germanic-style wings surmounted by bulbous domes. The basilica stands in the centre of the façade.

Basílica★★

The basilica, with its flanking wings, is built of mock marble, its façade breaking the monotony of the main face by its whiteness and Baroque decoration. The towers (68m tall) are joined by a double row of columns; niches high up contain Carrara marble statues of St Dominic and St Francis and below of St Clare and St Elizabeth of Hungary. The church **interior** is strikingly elegant in its proportions and in the marble ornamentation. The rounded vaulting rests upon fluted pilasters which divide the lateral chapels, each of which con-

Inside the basilica, Palácio Nacional de Mafra
© StockPhotosArt/iStock

tains statues and an altarpiece in white marble with a low-relief carved by sculptors from the Mafra School. The jasper and marble altarpieces in the transept chapels and the chancel pediment are also by the Mafra School. Note especially the fine marble altarpiece of the Virgin and Child in the chapel off the north aisle and the sacristy and lavabo where marble of every description may be seen. Four delicately worked arches at the transept crossing support a magnificent rose and white marble **cupola★**, which rises to a height of 70m. The bronze candelabra and six fine organs dating from 1807 are also remarkable. The bell towers contain no less than 92 bells ordered from a Flemish bellmaker. The initial order was for 50 but when this was queried Dom João doubled the order and paid in advance!

Palace and Monastery

The guided tour proceeds through a museum of comparative sculpture, the monks' infirmary (with its beds on wheels so that sick monks could still be wheeled into Mass), the pharmacy, the kitchens and a museum of sacred art. The palace reached the height of its opulence at the start of the 19C and on the second floor, the extensive royal apartments form a long succession of galleries, with the Queen's Pavilion at one end and the King's at the other. The ceilings are painted and the rooms have been refurnished with reproductions of the originals, most of which

were taken to Brazil by Dom João VI in 1807 when he fled into exile.

The grandiose and harmoniously proportioned **Audience Room** (Sala da Bênção) gives onto the basilica. It was from this gallery with its columns and mouldings faced with coloured marble, that the royal family attended mass. The bust of Dom João V is by the Italian master, Alessandro Giusti.

The **Sala dos Troféus** (Trophy Room), is almost shocking to modern eyes and sensibilities with its furniture made from boars' heads, antlers and upholstered in deerskin.

The highlight (as in the Escorial) is the impressive Rococo **library★** *(biblioteca)*, 83.6m long, beautifully illuminated and containing more than 35 000 bound books in many languages. They are kept in mint condition by a colony of small bats which, each night, fly about devouring any insects that might fancy nibbling a book!

Tapada Nacional de Mafra

🕐 *Daily May–Oct 9:30am–6pm; Nov–Apr 9am–5pm.* ✆ *261 814 240. www.tapadademafra.pt. There is a road-train that takes you round if you do not wish to walk* ✺ *€12, though weekdays it is normally reserved for groups of visiting school children. www.tapadademafra.pt.*

The gardens, about 7km/4.3mi north of the palace, were originally designed as hunting grounds for the royal family and you are likely to see deer and wild boar (some people still hunt here, but mainly to control animal populations) and are totally enclosed by walls. The trails, either for walking or cycling, do cover some beautiful landscape. There is also a carriage museum, a wildlife museum and plenty of space for picnics.

EXCURSION

Ericeira★

On the west coast about 53km/33mi north west of Lisbon. 🄿 *Parking can be difficult in the old town; it's free near the market.*

Ericeira is a lively seaside resort perched on a cliff facing the Atlantic. It has preserved its old quarter around the church, its maze of alleyways and its picturesque fishing harbour. The area around the parish church is also worth a visit. Its nearby beaches are renowned world-wide for their surfing.

Ericeira was, until the 19C, a major port, though since then it has declined and its sea trade these days consists of little more than fishing boats. However, the quality of its seafood and the restaurants that dot the old town centre and the promenades lining its beaches, are renowned far and wide. The centre of the town, based round the **Praça da República**, is mainly pedestrianised and has dozens of bars, restaurants and shops around it. The main street, **Rua Dr Eduardo Burnay**, leads from the square to the main beach near the fishing harbour.

It was from this harbour that the last Portuguese King, Dom Manuel II, sailed into exile on 5 October 1910, while the Republic was being proclaimed in Lisbon. Alerted by his staff that a mob was on its way from Lisbon after the proclamation of a Republic, he hurriedly left his palace at Mafra and sailed south to Gibraltar and the safety of the Royal Navy. He was taken to England, where he lived out his exile.

The best **beaches** are to the north and south and have become extremely popular with surfers. So much so, in fact, that the World Surfing Championships have been held here, on the **Praia da Ribeira d'Ilhas**, the beach about 3km/1.8mi north of the town. Several surf camps and schools have been set up and are at their busiest in spring and autumn when the sea is rougher.

In the summer it's calm, hot and lovely, and although many Lisboetas spend their holidays or weekends here (and many apartments have sprung up along the sea road), there is still plenty of room on the wide and glorious beaches. Praia do Norte and Praia do São Sebastião, the latter just round the headland, are also worth a visit and are slightly less busy.

A further option is to go 2km/1.2mi south to Foz de Lizandro, where river bathing is safe and calm.

Ericeira seafront

© moedas1/iStock

Ericeira has plenty of hotels and *pensões* and rates can be competitive, apart from the height of summer (July, August) when, unless you have a reservation you might struggle to find a room.

Restaurants are plentiful and renowned for their quality and there are plenty of bars and cafés. Most of the nightlife is out of town though a few bars are clustered along the Praça dos Navegantes close to the Praia do Sul.

Ericeira is very handy for nearby Mafra with its wonderful palace and gardens with walking and cycling trails (🄲*see MAFRA)* and also for the UNESCO World Heritage Site town of Sintra (🄲*see SINTRA)* with its fairy-tale palaces and charming tea shops.

Cascais★

Praia do Guincho

Cascais is both a traditional fishing port and a bustling holiday resort, with its pleasant pedestrian streets lined with shops and restaurants. Popular with international visitors and Portuguese alike, it is just 20 minutes by train from Lisbon.

TOWN

In medieval times, Cascais relied on its fishing and agriculture industries, providing Lisbon with produce by the 13C. Tourism came to Cascais in 1870 when the court moved here for the summer to escape the heat of Lisbon. With the court came a tradition of elegance and fine architecture. The **royal palace**, or former citadel, sits on the promontory which protects the bay on the southwest. Part of it is now an official residence of the Head of State, while most of the building is a five star hotel.

Museu-Biblioteca dos Condes de Castro Guimarães

🕐*Tue–Sun 10am–6pm* 🚫*Public holidays.* 💶€4. 📞214 815 308.

On the coast road, this 19C nobleman's residence has a large collection of 17C Portuguese and Indo-Portuguese furniture and *azulejos*, 18C and 19C Portuguese gold and silversmith work and pottery, 18C bronzes, carpets and Chinese vases and many valuable books, the most valuable of which is an illustrated 16C *Chronicles of D. Afonso*

▶ **Population:** 234 000.
♿ **Michelin Map:** 733.
🇮 **Info:** Praça 05 de Outubro, Cascais 912-034214 www.visitcascais.com.
▶ **Location:** About 30km/18.6mi west along the coast from Lisbon.
🕐 **Timing:** It's the place to stay at least for a weekend, with a lively atmosphere and interesting museums. Make sure you visit the beaches here and in Estoril.
🅿 **Parking:** Not too difficult, apart from Friday and Saturday evenings.
👁 **Don't Miss:** The old town hall square, which is lively; Boca do Inferno.

Henriques and has a drawing of pre-earthquake Lisbon. Nearby is the **Casa de Santa Maria** (🕐*Tue–Sun 10am–6pm;* 💶€5. 📞214 815 383), another lovely house displaying a rich collection of tiles. Beyond the house, at the end of the promontory, an 18C lighthouse has a **museum** (Farol Museu de Santa Marta, 🕐*open Wed–Sun 10:30am–noon & 2:30–5pm;*💶€5 incl. Casa de S. Maria).

The art museum **Casa Historias Paula Rego** (🕐*open daily except Mon 10am–6pm;*💶€5. 📞214 826 970; www.casa-dashistoriaspaularego.com) displays works by the artist Paula Rego and her husband Victor Willing.

Windsurfing at Praia do Guincho

© silkfactory/iStock

Seafront, Cascais

© P. Kaczynski/mauritius images/age fotostock

🚗 DRIVING TOUR

Cascais to Praia do Guincho★

8km/5mi heading west on the coast road. About 30min.

On leaving Cascais, pass the former royal palace on the left. A restaurant with a few pines marks the site of the **Boca do Inferno★** abyss, formed by marine erosion. The sea, entering under a rock arch, booms and crashes in stormy weather. The road continues as a *corniche* above the sea, offering views of the wild coast. Beyond Cabo Raso (small fort), where the road turns off towards the Serra de Sintra, stretches of sand pounded by rough seas can be seen between the rocky points before you come to **Praia do Guincho★**. This immense beach is backed by windswept dunes and a small fort; the imposing headland, Cabo da Roca, can be seen. This is a popular spot for surfing, kitesurfing and windsurfing. The strong undercurrents make it dangerous for inexperienced surfers.

Rent bikes in the city centre and cycle to Guincho beach (available from outside the train station, in front of the Paula Rego Museum and near the entrance to the Casa da Guia Comercial Complex).

ADDRESSES

🏨 STAY

⊜⊜⊜ **Hotel Baia** – *Passeio D. Luis I.* ☎*214 831 033. www.hotelbaia.com. 113 rooms.* A modern seafront hotel with a rooftop pool, good restaurant and some balcony rooms.

⊜⊜⊜ **Martinhal Cascais** – *Quinta da Marinha, Rua do Clube.* ☎*211 149 900. www.martinhal.com. 72 rooms.* A waterfront family paradise with big, homey rooms, dynamite playground and kids club. Great food and drink.

🍴 EAT

⊜⊜ **Jardim dos Frangos** – *Av. Com da Grande Guerra 68.* ☎*214 861 717. www.jardimdosfrangos.com.* The place for chicken, indoors or outside on the pavement terrace. Service can be peremptory, but the prices are good, and locals always come back for more.

⊜⊜ **Dom Pedro I** *Beco dos Inválidos 32.* ☎*214 833 734.* A tiny restaurant with tiled walls and traditional furnishings serving local fish dishes including various cod recipes. Try one of their bacalhau recipes, or their traditional desserts.

GOLF

Golfers have two very good courses to choose from on the outskirts of Cascais. In the grounds of the Quinta da Marinha hotel is an excellent 18-hole course with some very challenging holes.

A short walking distance away is **Oitavos**: a links course laid out in traditional fashion – nine out, nine back. It runs straight out towards Cabo da Roca, the most westerly point of mainland Europe. The region has five other courses close by, all within 30 minutes' drive. Contact: www.clubgolfestoril.com.

Estoril★

Estoril has developed into a refined and attractive beach and winter resort, favoured by a mild climate and a temperature that averages 12°C in winter. It lies on the sea road linking Lisbon and Cascais, a point on the Costa de Estoril that is famous for its luminous skies. Formerly a small village known to a few for the healing properties of its waters, Estoril now attracts an elegant international circle who come for the resort's entertainments (golf, casino and sea fishing), its sporting events (horse-racing and regattas), its pleasant location facing Cascais bay, its park of tropical and exotic plants and trees, palm-lined avenues, beaches of fine sand and its highly successful festivals (Festival of the Sea in late August).

▸ **Population:** 29 000.
⌚ **Michelin Map:** 733; town plan in the *Michelin Guide Spain* and *Portugal*.
ℹ **Info:** Largo Cidade Vitória – Cascais, 2750-642 Cascais. ℘912 034 214; www.visitcascais.com.
▷ **Location:** On the coast road about 35km/21.7mi west of Lisbon.
👥 **Kids:** They'll love the beach.
🕐 **Timing:** A day trip is fine, though there is plenty to do if you are based here.
🅿 **Parking:** Can be very difficult. The casino has a large car park.
✿ **Don't Miss:** The casino with its shows each night; the golf if you play.

RESORT

Estoril was once a sedate and refined resort reserved for the well-heeled. It tries to maintain this image, largely succeeding despite the influx of tourism, attracted by its wonderful beach and, at night, its **casino**, with spectacular cabaret shows. It was in this casino that Ian Fleming, in the last days of World War II, prowled around tracking Dusko Popov, a Yugoslav double-agent.

From this experience came the novel-turned-film *Casino Royale*. Graham Greene, another intelligence officer-turned-novelist, was also a frequent visitor in those days when the area around Lisbon teemed with exiles, spies and sundry ne'er-do-wells.

The casino stands in a large palm-lined square whose gardens are maintained to a very high standard. As well as the cabaret shows there are obviously gaming rooms and several shops, though an unusual attraction is a very good art gallery, in which, each October, the International Naïve Painting Salon holds its show, the largest in Iberia.

During the summer there is a nightly crafts market outside the casino, from 6pm to midnight.

Estoril is also known for the quality of its nearby **golf courses**, which include Oitavos, a relatively new course (www.oitavosdunes.com) that is expensive but spectacular, running out to Cabo da Roca, the westernmost part of mainland Portugal; Quinta da Marinha, based in the eponymous hotel, Penha Longa and designed by Robert Trent Jones Junior with its spectacular fourth hole, where you can see as far as the Lisbon bridge and the sea; and the oldest course in Portugal, Estoril GC, which dates back to 1945.

Other golf courses worthy of note in the area are the Lisbon Sports Club, the second oldest club in Portugal; Belas, an American-style course designed by Rocky Roquemore with its narrow fairways, steep bunkers and severely undulating greens; and the much flater course, Quinta da Beloura, which opened in 1994 among oak trees, pines, cedar and magnolia.

For more informaion, contact www.estorilgolfcoast.com.

Setúbal★

and Around

Setúbal, situated in the foothills of the Serra da Arrábida on the north bank of the wide Sado estuary, is an industrial town, port and tourist centre. It has an old quarter with narrow alleys that contrast sharply with the wide avenues of the modern town. The town's Moscatel wine and orange marmalade are popular.

THE PORT

The town has a variety of commercial activities; salt marshes; car and truck assembly; chemicals; fish canning and agriculture.

Setúbal is Portugal's third port after Lisbon and Porto. It consists of a fishing port (sardines) with a fleet of about 2 000 boats, a marina and port.

▶ **Population:** 91 000.
Ⓒ **Map:** Below.
🅘 **Info:** Tv. Frei Gaspar 10, Setúbal; ℰ265 009 933. www.visitlisboa.com.
Ⓒ **Location:** Cross the Vasco da Gamal bridge from Lisbon and keep going south. It will take almost an hour from central Lisbon.
Ⓒ **Timing:** Pretty much a whole day or few days, with an afternoon trip to Troia. Take the ancient ferry across the Sado to Troia.
🅟 **Parking:** No problems.
🅓 **Don't Miss:** The Church of Jesus, the São Filipe castle, paintings in the museum and the market.

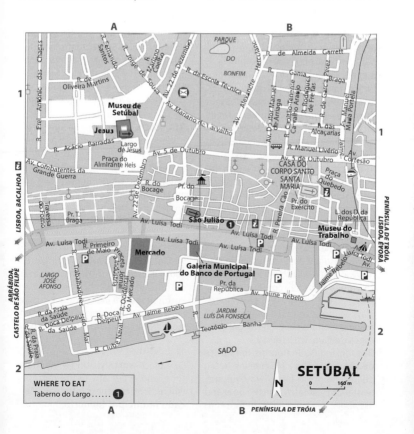

WHERE TO EAT

Taberno do Largo ...... ❶

Igreja de Jesus

© JEAphoto/Fotolia.com

CHURCHES

It is worth seeing two of the town's churches. The first, the **Igreja de Jesus★** *(currently closed for restoration until summer 2020)*, was constructed of Arrábida marble in 1491, to the design of the architect Boytac (also responsible for the Mosteiro dos Jerónimos at Belém). This is the first example of a building with Manueline decoration. It is late-Gothic, judging by its Flamboyant doorway – twin doors with bracketed arches framed in ringed columns – and its three lines of vaulting of equal height which make it into a hall-church.

In the church's Gothic cloisters, the **Museu de Setúbal** (⊘ *currently closed for restoration, check website; ℘265 537 890; www.mun-setubal.pt*), houses a large collection of 15C and 16C Portuguese Primitives. All these **paintings★** are said to be by the anonymous artist known as the Master of the Setúbal Altarpiece, now thought to have been Jorge Afonso. The lower galleries contain 15C–18C *azulejos* and there are also stained-glass windows from the church as well as some glorious paintings by Gregório Lopes that are rich in detail.

Overlooking Pr. do Bocage, the **Igreja de São Julião** has a Masnueline trefoil door in its north face. Two columns, twisted like cables, frame the door and rise above it in a moulding before ending in pinnacles. Inside, beautiful 18C *azulejos* depict the life of St Julian.

MUSEUMS

The collection of Portugeuse Primitives kept in the Museu de Setúbal (⊘ *opposite*) is probably Setúbal's pre-eminent collection, but the town has other small museums that celebrate its maritime history.

The **Museu de Arqueologia e Etnografia** (⊘ *Tue–Sat 9am–12.30pm, 2–5.30pm; ⊘Public holidays and Sat in Aug; ℘265 239 365, www.maeds.amrs.pt)* is a small museum that reflects Setúbal's role as a fishing port. Here you will find prehistoric objects, Luso-Roman coins and mosaics, folk art, crafts, costumes and models of boats.

The **Museu do Trabalho Michel Giacometti** (⊘ *Jun–mid-Sept Tue–Fri 9.30am–6pm, Sat 3–6pm; mid-Sept–May Tue–Fri 9.30am–6pm, Sat–Sun 2–6pm; ℘265 537 880)* is a fascinating little museum in an old fish-canning factory, which explores Portuguese rural life over the years. Its main feature is a complete 1920s grocery store, transplanted from central Lisbon.

THE MARKET

One place worth visiting if you have time, and especially in the morning when it is at its busiest, is the vast **Mercado Municipal** (municipal market)

Manuel Maria Barbosa du Bocage

Manuel Maria Barbosa du Bocage was born in Setúbal in 1765. A prodigy, he began writing verse as a child and at age 14 left school and decamped for Lisbon where he joined the Navy, though spent most of his time chasing girls. Postings to Brazil, Goa, India and China followed, though he deserted and took to writing satire. His return to Lisbon brought him into contact with other "radicals" and into conflict with the authorities and he spent some time incarcerated in various prisons, though often recanted to gain his liberty. Unable to make much money he lived a mainly bohemian life, though his work was, and still is, highly popular in Portugal. In 1805 he died from syphilis. A monument was erected to him in Setúbal in 1871.

which overflows with fresh fish, vegetables, flowers and anything else you can think of. It makes for an interesting diversion and is close to the pedestrianised town centre.

ADDITIONAL SIGHTS
Castelo São Filipe★

Take Av. Luísa Todi to the west then follow the signs to the pousada.

The fortress overlooking the town has been partially converted into one of Portugal's most beautiful *pousadas*. It was built in 1590 on the orders of King Philip II of Spain to prevent the English from establishing themselves in Tróia. Cross a covered passage to a chapel with 18C *azulejos* attributed to Policarpo de Oliveira Bernardes which illustrate the life of St Philip. A wide **panorama★** from the top of the ramparts looks out over

the Sado estuary, the Troia peninsula, and on a clear day you can see as far as Lisbon. It is possible to stay at the *pousada (www.pousadas.pt)* and the restaurant is open each evening for non-residents.

Península de Tróia

Cross the Sado estuary by the ancient ferry (10min – departures every 30min from Setúbal) and continue 4km/2.5mi from the pier; or approach by road from Setubal on the N10, N5, IC1 and N253-1.)

The Tróia peninsula, an immense strip of fine sand across the Sado estuary, lined with dunes and pine, was intended to be developed as a major resort, but apart from a magnificent golf course nothing much happened as early developments sank in the sand. You reach the **Roman ruins at Cetóbriga**. Some of the

Clock tower of Castelo São Filipe

© PhotoLocation Ltd/Travel Pictures

Cabo Espichel
© Inacio pires/Fotolia.com

remains of an important Roman town destroyed by the sea in the early 5C have been excavated in a pleasant site beside the Sado lagoon. They include an installation for salting fish, a sepulchral vault, the remains of a temple decorated with frescoes, and some baths.

EXCURSIONS
Costa da Caparica
On the opposite side of the Tagus from Lisbon. Allow a day if venturing out here from Lisbon. Don't miss the statue of Christ – Cristo Rei. 👥 *Kids will enjoy the area's beaches.*

The Costa da Caparica is the nearest seaside resort to Lisbon on the southern shore of the Tagus. With its vast beaches, which are less polluted than those on the northern shore, it is one of the most popular weekend spots with Lisbonites (*Lisboetas*). The resort is constantly being developed parallel to the ocean and the ridge of sand dunes that protects it from the wind. In season, a **small train** runs along the coast for 11km/6.8mi, giving access to the immensely long beach. Fishing boats, their prows adorned with a painted star or eye, may still be seen bringing in their nets helped by holidaymakers.

The vast Rio-like statue of **Cristo Rei**★★ dominates the Tagus and can be seen from Lisbon as well. You can visit (🕐 *open 9.30am–6.30pm; www. cristorei.pt*) and take the lift to the top, 80m above ground from where you have a magnificent view as far as Sintra. The other reason to go to Caparica is to laze on the beach, though surfers and windsurfers find this a great place. There is a little road-train that is well worth a ride and stops at dozens of places along the coast, each of them different in character, from family-orientated to nudist sunbathing to a gay community. Choose the right stop carefully!

Quinta da Bacalhôa★
The Quinta da Bacalhôa is on the N 10 as you leave Vila Fresca de Azitão heading towards Setúbal, opposite the bus station. An hour should be just right to visit the Quinta. Take an extra hour or two to visit nearby Cabo Espichel and its fantastic views over the vast Atlantic.

This seigneurial residence, built at the end of the 15C and remodelled in the early 16C by the son of Afonso de Albuquerque, Viceroy of India, has both Renaissance and Moorish styles and rich *azulejo*★ decoration. These days, the Quinta is a huge estate dotted with vineyards that produce various types of Portuguese wines. Check the website (*www.bacalhoa.pt*) for winery tours.

In the manor house a graceful loggia giving onto the gardens is adorned with polychrome *azulejo* panels depicting allegories of great rivers, including the Douro, Nile, Danube and Euphrates. The **gardens** (👁 *guided visits Tue–Sat 9am–5pm;* 🕐 *closed public holidays;* 📞 *212 198 060; www.bacalhoa.pt*) were inspired by the style current in 16C France. An ornamental kitchen garden, where mandarins and walnut trees, bamboo and cinerarias grow, ends at an attractive pavilion and ornamental pool. The walls inside the pavilion are decora with Spanish artists with geometrical patterns but the most impressive panel is the Florentine-style depiction of **Susannah and the Elders★**, the oldest figurative panel in Portugal (1565).

Cabo Espichel★

Cape Espichel lies at the tip of the Seúbal Peninsula. Allow around an hour to visit here. Don't miss the views from the cliff.

Cabo Espichel (Cape Espichel), at the southern tip of the Serra da Arrábida, is a true World's End, beaten continuously by violent winds. The cliff drops a sheer 100m to the sea. It was off this cape that Dom Fuas Roupinho vanquished the enemy in 1180 in a brilliant victory at sea, when Portuguese sailors succeeded in capturing several enemy ships. The remains of the Santuário de Nossa Senhora do Cabo have been a popular pilgrimage centre ever since the 13C, though the buildings we can see today were erected by pilgrims in the 18C.

Cabo Espichel is remote, wild and desolate, with very little left of what was once an arcaded pilgrimage and lodgings. Today they are totally run-down and look more like a former prison. The reason for coming here is to see the wonderful views out over the Atlantic from the edge of the imposing cliffs. You can easily see why the place has been used as a location for several films. Dinosaurs' footprints have been found close by.

In the crumbling late-17C **Santuário de Nossa Senhora do Cabo** you will find a Classical architectural style and Baroque interior.

Palmela★

Just a couple of miles inland from Setúbal, close to Lisbon. Don't miss the castle and the church, and the local ambience.

This pretty white town is built in tiers on the northern slope of the Serra da Arrábida at the foot of a mound crowned by a large castle which became the seat of the Order of St James in 1423. Palmela lies at the heart of one of Portugal's richest wine growing regions, growing the Periquita variety of grape.

The **castle★** (*follow the signs to the pousada, leave your car in the outer yard;* ○*open daily with the exception of one part of the castle, which opens from 8am–6pm, 8pm in summer;* ℘*212 331 580*), now partly converted into a *pousada* (and with a restaurant open to non-residents), was originally Moorish. Part of it is occupied by the Church and Monastery of St James, erected in the 15C by the Knights of St James. The views are magnificent, looking out over the Sado estuary and even as far as Lisbon. The Bishop of Évora died a painful death in the dungeon here, punishment for his part in a conspiracy against King João II. The church, the **Igreja de São Pedro**, dates from the 18C. The interior is entirely lined with *azulejos★* depicting scenes from the life of St Peter; outstanding are those in the south aisle illustrating the miraculous catch of fish, Christ walking on the waters, as well as the crucifixion of St Peter.

ADDRESSES

🏨 STAY

▭◍🛏 **Hotel Solaris** – *Praça Marquis de Pombal 12.* ℘*265 541 770. www solarishotel.pt. 36 rooms.* 🅿. This hotel has good views overlooking the square. Some rooms have balconies, and all have free cable internet access. There is WiFi in the reception area.

🍴 EAT

▭◍ **Taberna Típica O Pescador II** – *Tv. Álvaro Anes 8.* ℘*265 533 369. Closed Tue.* Big portions of simple fare: seafood grilled, fried, or in broth, with chips, rice and salad.

▭◍ **Antoniu's** – *R Trabalhadores do Mar 33.* ℘*265 523 706. https:// restauranteantonius.wordpress.com.* Long established and long popular, one of the best places for seafood in town.

▭◍🛏 **Perola da Mourisca** – *R. da Baía do Sado 9.* ℘*265 793 689.Closed Tue.* Wonderfully fresh seafood grilled and in soups. Meat and chips for those who want it. Heavenly house-made bread is perfect for sopping up mussel sauce.

Serra da Arrábida★

The Serra da Arrábida rises and falls over the southern part of the Setúbal peninsula, covering 35km/21.7mi between Cabo Espichel and Palmela. The line of hills is made up of the ends of Secondary Era limestone deposits, pushed back, broken and buried beneath more recent deposits, and which reappear on the north side of the Tagus abutting the Sintra Massif. The Parque Natural da Arrábida, which covers 10 800ha between Sesimbra and Setúbal, was created to protect the local scenery and architecture.

🚗 DRIVING TOUR

ROUND TRIP FROM SESIMBRA
77km/47.8mi. About 4hr.

This small range of mountains is a mere 6km/3.7mi wide. The **southern side** slopes down to the ocean, ending in cliffs 500m high. The indented coastline, with its array of colours, is more reminiscent of the Mediterranean than the Atlantic. The **northern side**, with a more rounded relief, has a landscape of vineyards, orchards and olive groves and, on poorer ground, its original brush and pine woods.

Sesimbra
Mid-afternoon is the best time to arrive. Stay for dinner in one of the restaurants along the seashore. Don't miss the old town on a warm evening with the smell of fish cooking. 🅿 No problems apart from the tiny village centre at night.
Sesimbra occupies a pleasant site in an inlet at the foot of the southern slope of the Serra da Arrábida. Its beach is popular with Lisbonites. Sesimbra is a centre for deep-sea fishing for swordfish. These sports provide a counterpoint to the more traditional fishing activities which remain the town's main industry.

⌖ **Map:** Opposite.

🛈 **Info:** *Ask me Arrábida:* Tv. Frei Gaspar 10, Setúbal ☎ 265 009 9930.

▷ **Location:** Cross the Vasco da Gama bridge from Lisbon and just keep going towards Setúbal.

👥 **Kids:** The Oceanographic Museum in Portinho da Arrábida.

🕐 **Timing:** Allow a day.

The small fishing harbour has grown into an important seaside resort but has nonetheless preserved its atmosphere, seen best in its steep streets leading down to the sea. Along these picturesque alleyways you'll see washing hanging out to dry. The many restaurants along the shore serve grilled fish and seafood. The **beach** is alive with holidaymakers at weekends and in summer. The rest of the time it reverts to fishermen who may be seen mending their lines and nets on either side of **Fortim de Santiago** (fort).

The fishing boats bring in sardines, eel, bream and shellfish every morning and evening and several boats take visitors out deep-sea fishing. The **castle**, on the crest of a bare ridge, occupies a first-class defensive position which the first King of Portugal, Afonso Henriques, captured from the Moors in 1165. From its crenellated walls surrounding the cemetery there are fine **views★** of Sesimbra and its harbour.

▷ After Santana, the N 379 to the right winds between hills enlivened by orange trees and windmills.
2.5km/1.5mi before Vila Nogueira de Azeitão, turn right on N 379-1 towards Arrábida.

After a brief run through olive groves and vineyards, the road begins a winding climb through dense vegetation. The sea is visible far below.

▷ Follow the signs to Portinho.

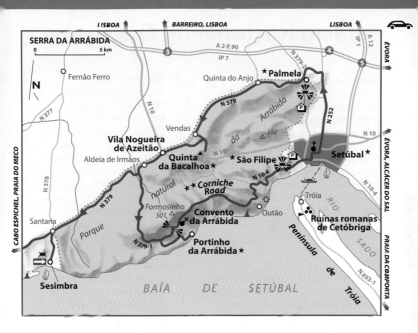

Portinho da Arrábida★

The bay of Portinho da Arrábida, at the foot of the *serra*, forms an even curve, edged by a semicircular beach of fine white sand that is very popular at weekends. At the entrance to the village, the **Forte de Nossa Senhora da Arrábida**, built in the 17C as a protection against pirates, now houses a small **Museu Oceanográfico** ♠♣ (☉Tue–Fri 10am–4pm, Sat 3–6pm; ☉Public holidays; ⊗€3,50 ☏212 189 791) with fine displays of sponges and various marine species. Steps lead from the left of the fort entrance down to a cave.

◗ Continue along the N 379-1, leaving the lower corniche road on the right.

Corniche Road★★

The Corniche road *(estrada de escarpa)* follows a section of the mountain crestline with views of both the northern and southern slopes. On the left there is a view of Monte Formosinho (499m) the *serra's* highest peak, and on the right of Portinho and the Sado estuary. Below, in the foreground, abutting on a cliff overlooking the sea, stands the **Convento da Arrábida**, founded by Franciscans in 1542. Prior to this, on

the site where the Old Convent now stands, was the Chapel of Remembrance, a place of many pilgrimages.

Setúbal★
⚓ *See Setúbal.*

◗ Leave Setúbal heading north on the N 252 and, before the motorway, take the N 379 to the left. You then reach **Palmela★** (⚓*See PALMELA).* The N 379 runs near Bacalhoa (on the N 10 opposite the Rodoviária Nacional bus station), which can be reached from Vendas on the left, before you reach **Quinta da Bacalhôa★**. The N 10 passes through vineyards and orchards to Vila Nogueira de Azeitão.

Vila Nogueira de Azeitão

Set amidst beautiful *quintas*, this town is famous for its moscatel wine. The main street is bordered with lovely Baroque fountains and the graceful buildings and gardens of the **Casa Vitícola José Maria de Fonseca**, a firm which has been making moscatel wine since 1834.

◗ Return to Sesimbra on the N 379 via Santana.

Palácio Nacional de Queluz★★

Lisbon

The **Royal Palace of Queluz**, between Sintra and Lisbon, takes the visitor right back into the heart of the 18C. In the formal gardens adorned with pools and statues, overlooked by pastel-coloured Rococo façades with their many windows, one almost expects to come upon a romantic scene from a painting by Watteau. Although Inspired by Versailles, the Queluz Palace is smaller in proportion, making it more intimate.

A BIT OF HISTORY

At the end of the 16C, the land belonged to the Marquis of Castelo Rodrigo, who had a hunting lodge here. After the restoration of the monarchy and Dom João IV's accession to the throne, the property was confiscated and several years later, in 1654, became the residence of the *Infantes*. Dom Pedro (1717–86), son of Dom João V and the future Dom Pedro III, was the first *infante* to show a real interest in the estate and decided to build a palace.

From 1747 to 1758, the Portuguese architect Mateus Vicente de Oliveira built the main façade in a washed-pink stone as well as the wing that would later contain the Throne Room. While the overall style of the palace is Rococo, architectural differences between the three periods are apparent.

 ⚹ **Michelin Map:** 733; Michelin Atlas Spain & Portugal p58 (P 2).

Info: ✆214 343 860. ⏱9am–7pm. ⊘1 Jan, Good Fri, Easter Sunday, 1 May, 29 Jun and 25 Dec. ✆€10, children ages 5–18 €8.50. Further discounts if you buy combined tickets. www.parquesdesintra.pt.

▶ **Location:** 21km/13mi west of Lisbon and 16km/10mi east of Sintra.

👪 **Kids:** They'll enjoy eating in the original kitchens, now a restaurant called Cozinha Velha (daily, lunch and dinner; ✆214 356 158).

⏱ **Timing:** A full morning, or afternoon, but have lunch as well.

🅿 **Parking:** Not difficult except at very busy times (summer weekends).

👁 **Don't Miss:** Pedro IV's bedroom and the gardens (included in ticket price).

VISIT

Palace

See times and charges in **Info***, above.*
The sumptuous **Sala do Trono**★ (Throne Room), recalls the Hall of Mir-

---

A Victim of the Revolution

This palace, built as a place of celebration, was also the setting for the dramatic life of **Maria I**. Maria was pious almost to the point of superstition and considered the death of her uncle and husband Pedro III in 1786 to be a warning of the misfortune that was to afflict her family and people. The loss in 1788 of two of her children, Crown Prince Josef, who died at the age of 27, and the Infanta Maria-Anna, who was married to the son of the Spanish king, in less than two months, merely confirmed her premonitions. Her feelings of melancholy were increased by the death of her confessor soon after. She became so disturbed by the outbreak of the French Revolution that by 1791 she was already showing the first signs of dementia. Her second son, João, governed in her name and took the title of Regent in 1799. When French troops invaded Portugal, João took his mother to Brazil, where she died, still Portugal's reigning sovereign, in 1816.

© Michael Howard/4Corners/Sime/Photononstop

rors in Versailles. Magnificent Venetian crystal chandeliers hang from the ceiling decorated with allegorical Illustrations and supported on caryatids.

Just beyond, the Music Chamber has a portrait of Queen Maria above the grand piano. This space is the place where the queen's orchestra performed operas and concerts.

Also noteworthy is the royal bedroom, a square room with stunning murals of Cervantes' "Don Quixote," a domed ceiling, and a floor decorated in exotic woods giving it a circular appearance.

The **Sala dos Azulejos** is so called on account of the wonderful multi-coloured 18C *azulejos* depicting landscapes of China and Brazil. The Sala da Guarda Real (Royal Guard Room) contains a fine 18C Arraiolos carpet.

The **Sala dos Embaixadores** (Ambassadors' Hall), where visiting diplomats and statesmen were received during the 19C, decorated with marble and mirrors, has a painted ceiling of a concert at the court of King Dom José and diverse mythological motifs.

Beyond the Queen's Boudoir and sitting room, French Rococo in style, is the Sculpture Room, though the only item on display is an earthenware bust of Maria. Then comes the **Sala Don Quixote**, which was used as Pedro IV's bedroom and where eight columns support a circular ceiling with paintings of Cervantes' hero decorating the walls.

In the **Sala das Merendas** (Tea Room), embellished with gilded woodwork, are several 18C paintings of royal picnics.

If, after having seen how the Kings lived, you want to live like a king, part of the palace (the building formerly used by the Royal Guard of the Court) has been converted into a *pousada* offering luxurious rooms for the night. It has an attractive interior design and also serves exquisite cuisine in its original kitchens (**Cozinha Velha**), now a restaurant where you can have lunch or dinner (℘214 356 158; 12.30–3pm, 7.30–10.30pm. www.pousadas.pt). The kitchens have retained the old stone chimney, arches, and vaulted ceiling, and the restaurant is particularly known for its desserts, many of which are based on ancient convent recipes.

Gardens

The sumptuous gardens were designed by the French architect J.B. Robillon in the style of the 17C French landscape gardener, Le Nôtre. Individual attractions include the Amphitrite basin. The walls of the **Grand Canal** are covered in 18C *azulejos* of between which flows the Jamor river. In the past the royal family went boating along the canal. Note the façade of the Robillon wing, fronted by a magnificent **Lion Staircase★** (Escadaria dos Leões), which is extended by a beautiful colonnade.

Vila Franca de Xira

and Around

This industrial town on the west bank of the Tagus, inland from Lisbon, is known for its festivals and bullfights. The city comes alive, particularly in July, at the time of the Festival of the **Colete Encarnado**, the *campinos'* "red waistcoat" festival, with its picturesque processions of *campinos* and bulls running loose through the streets. Folk dancing, bullfights, open-air feasts and the occasional regatta on the Tagus complete the festivities.

▶ **Population:** 140 000.
  Michelin Map: 733
▯ **Info:** Rua Alves Redol, n.º 7; ☎263 285 605.
▶ **Location:** Follow the Tagus (and A1) inland from Lisbon until it narrows about 35km/21.7mi northeast.
◑ **Timing:** No more than half a day will allow you to see all you need.
⊛ **Don't Miss:** The belvedere at Monte.

VISIT

In the fertile plains, or *lezírias* (alluvial plains) that surround the town, the *campinos* (Ribatejo cowboys) keep watch on the horses and bulls that are bred there. Vila Franca's **Museu Municipal** (*R. Serpa Pinto 65, ↻ open Tue–Sun 9:30am–12.30pm, 2–5:30pm; ☎263 280 350; hours*) explores the many aspects of the region's history and traditions. The main building is housed in an 18C residence, but the exhibition continues in different locations, including a traditional boat offering trips on the Tagus river,

Fishing on the Tagus

©zulufriend/iStock

a church (Igreja de Santo Martir), and the Núcleo Museológico de Alverca do Ribatejo, devoted to the region's rural aspects, such as bullfighting, the raising and training of horses, and more.

EXCURSIONS

Alverca do Ribatejo

8km/5mi southwest on N 1, then follow signs to the Museu do Ar.

A hangar at the military aerodrome has been converted into an aviation museum, the **Museu do Ar** (*◑Tue–Sun 10am–5pm; ◑1 Jan, Easter Sunday, 24–25 Dec; ⊛€3; ☎219 678 984; www.museudoar.pt.* The history of Portuguese aviation is retraced through a collection of photographs, archives and genuine old planes and replicas such as the Blériot XI, the 1908 Demoiselle XX, which was piloted by the Brazilian Santos-Dumont, and the 1920 Santa Cruz flying boat which was the first to cross the South Atlantic.

Miradouro de Monte Gordo

3km/1.8mi to the north on the Rua António Lucio Baptista, passing under the motorway, and then onto a surfaced road which climbs steeply.

From the belvedere between two windmills at the top of the hill there is a **panoramic view** to the west and north over the hills covered with woods and vineyards; to the east over the Ribatejo plain; and to the south over the first two islands in the river's estuary.

Lusitanian horse

The Lusitanian thoroughbred was already known to humans during the Upper Palaeolithic period, as shown by engravings on rocks in the Côa valley. It has been ridden for almost 5 000 years and is the world's oldest saddle horse. Its spirited, yet docile temperament, its agility, strength and courage have made this particular breed the battle horse par excellence. Since the Middle Ages in Portugal, the nobility used the Lusitanian horse during times of war, preparing it for battle by pitting it against Iberian bulls. Although the Portuguese School of Equestrian Art was created in the 18C, Portuguese riders of today still wear the same ceremonial dress and the horses the same

© Stefano Scata/age fotostock

equipment as in the past. These features combine to create an equestrian show of rare beauty, in which the rider and horse execute highly complex manoeuvres in perfect harmony, with a lightness and agility that do justice to the "son of the wind" nickname given to this magnificent breed.

Centro Equestre da Lezíria Grande – *3km/1.8mi from the centre of Vila Franca on the N 1 towards Carregado. ☎263 285 160. www.celg.pt. Closed Mon.* This equestrian centre is devoted to the native Lusitanian horse. It was established by the great equestrian master Luis Valença, who taught Portuguese equestrian art to riders from around the world. The names of the centre's most famous horses are engraved on *azulejos* above their individual stables. A high level of horsemanship is required to be taught here, although visitors can eat at the pleasant restaurant *(open lunchtime)*

Centro Equestre do Morgado Lusitano – *Quinta da Portela, 2615 Alverca do Ribatejo. ☎219 936 520. www.morgadolusitano.pt. Closed Mon.* This centre breeds Lusitanian horses and trains experienced riders. It also presents a magnificent show of Portuguese equestrian art using 18C traditional costumes and harnesses.

© H. Kuczka/age fotostock

Alentejo

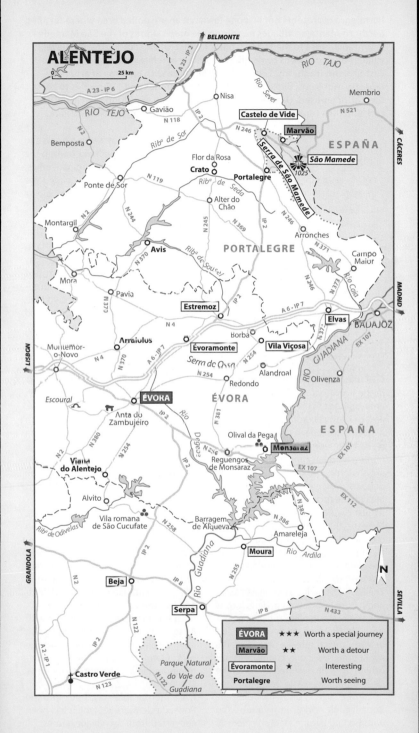

ALENTEJO

0   25 km

ÉVORA	★★★ Worth a special journey
Marvão	★★ Worth a detour
Évoramonte	★ Interesting
Portalegre	Worth seeing

Portalegre represents not just one town but an unspoiled area where fortified northern Alentejan villages huddle on the green slopes of the São Mamede mountains, close to the Spanish border. Peaceful and scenic, the medieval villages and spa towns come alive in summer when festivals celebrate local customs and traditions. Tourism is low key here with an array of art and tapestry museums, Baroque mansions and churches and 13C castles to keep the visitor amused. Outdoor enthusiasts will enjoy exploring the vast plains, cork and pine forests, and the rugged Serra de São Mamede Natural Park.

Highlights

1 Marvel at tapestries replicating works of art in **Portalegre** (p171)

2 Taste invigorating mineral spring water at **Castelo de Vide** (p172)

3 Climb the ramparts of **Marvao castle** at sunset (p175)

4 Walk to the top of **São Mamede** (1 025m) for stunning views (p175)

5 Trek the **Fresco Route** to discover the best Portuguese murals (p176)

Natural Splendour

In the northeast Alentejo, close to the Spanish border, the vast barren plains and oak forests gradually give way to a rocky landscape in the majestic Serra de São Mamede natural park.

Impressive quartz and granite boulders are sculpted into unusual shapes and deep fissures, creating their own carvings on the rock face.

At just over 1 000m, the mighty São Mamede, the highest point, towers over the mountain range. Make your way to the top for amazing panoramic views of the Alentejo plains on the one side and the Spanish sierras on the other.

The 30 000ha park is a national treasure and nature lover's dream. Here, forests of oak, chestnut, olive and pine neighbour cherry trees, gorse, broom, and heather, their fragrance perfuming the air. At times, your only company as you drive along the deserted roads will be deer, otter, foxes, wild boar and some of Europe's rarest birds, including the Bonelli eagle and Griffon vulture. You will also find Europe's largest colony of

bats here. Take your walking boots and enjoy one of five walking trails in the area. Pick up a map at the park office, in Portalegre *(Rua General Conde Jorge Avilez, 22)* or Castelo de Vide *(Rua de Santo Amaro, 22–25)*.

Cities and Culture

Roman Portalegre, the capital of Haut-Alentejo, is a great place to spend a day or two exploring its small museums and cathedral (sé). Situated on the southern slopes of the Serra, this town built its wealth on the textiles, tapestry and silk industries, which still flourish today, along with the cork trade.This wealth is reflected in its graceful Renaissance and Baroque mansions and monuments, such as the Church of São Lourenço (St. Laurence) in the old city. The Franciscan order also established a presence here, most notably in the Convents of São Francisco (St. Francis) and Santa Clara (Saint Claire).

The strategic importance of this region as a defence against invaders can be seen in the numerous fortified towns with their castles and ramparts that are dotted among the vast plains. Stop off for a *bica* (strong coffee like an espresso) at Avis, Castelo de Vide, Elvas, and medieval Marvao – the 360-degree panoramic view alone would be reason enough to visit this mountain-top village. A candidate for the World Heritage list, the town is one of Portugal's most spectacular fortified villages, with its steep and narrow lanes leading to a magnificent 13C castle rising from the rock. Clamber onto the walls, battlements and towers for impressive views at sunset.

For a memorable stay, book into the Pousada de Marvao, which has been converted from two village houses.

Portalegre

and Around

Portalegre is an important town close to the Spanish frontier. The ruins of the town's fortified castle, built by King Dinis I in 1290, are still visible, and the bustling town makes an ideal stop-over. It has a history of tapestry-making and cork manufacture. Portalegre is the starting point for an excursion in the Serra de São Mamede.

▶ **Population:** 24 000.
⚅ **Map:** p169.
🛈 **Info:** Rua Guilhermo Gomes Fernandes. ℘245 307 445. www.cm-portalegre.pt
◗ **Location:** About 105km/ 65mi northeast of Évora, in Alentejo.
◷ **Timing:** A good half day, though worth an overnight stop.
🅿 **Parking:** In the Praça de República (fee).
◉ **Don't Miss:** Summer evening spectacles in the Praça de República.

SIGHTS

Museu José Régio

◷*Winter: Tue–Sun 9am–12:30pm, 2–5pm. Summer: 9:30am–1pm, 2:30–6pm.* ◷*Public holidays.* ◉€2.10. ℘245 307 535. www.cm-portalegre.pt.

The collection of art assembled by the poet José Régio (1901–69) is the most interesting part of the museum, which is installed in the house where he lived: about 400 crucifixes date from the 16C to 19C. There are also naïve statuettes of St Anthony, and lots of ceramics from Coimbra.

Museu da Tapeçaria Guy Fino

◷*Winter: 9am–12:30pm, 1:30–5pm. Summer: Tue–Sun 9am–1pm, 2:30–6pm.* ◉€2. ℘245 307 530.

This small museum is housed in the former San Sebastian College in the lower town. Home to fascinating creations of tapestry from the last century, it includes a selection of the 5 000 different colours of wool used in copying major works of art.

Museu Municipal

◷*Winter: Tue–Sun 9am–12:30pm, 1:30–5pm. Summer: 9:30am–1pm, 2:30–6pm.* ◷*Public holidays.* ◉€2.50. ℘245 307 525.

Occupying the former diocesan seminary, the museum contains a rich collection of sacred art: a Spanish *Pietà* in gilded wood dating from the end of the 15C, a 16C altarpiece in polychrome terracotta, a magnificent 17C tabernacle in ebony, four ivory high reliefs (18C Italian School), an 18C ivory crucifix and 16C gold and silver plate.

EXCURSIONS

Avis

Michelin Map: 733.

The first glimpse of Avis comes as a welcome sight as you cross the Alentejo plateau, covered mostly with cork oaks and olive trees. The town, about midway between Évora and Portalegre, has kept traces of its early fortifications and overlooks the confluence of the Seda and Avis rivers, now submerged below the waters of the reservoir serving the

Cathedral (Sé)

The 18C façade has distinctive marble columns. The interior is from the 16C.

The second chapel on the right has a beautiful altarpiece illustrated with the life of the Virgin. The sacristy walls are covered in *azulejos*.

Walking around the town itself, you should take time to look particularly at the **Rua 19 de Junho**, which is lined with late Renaissance and Baroque mansions, and have a coffee in one of the pavement cafés in the **Rossio**, the main square with its lovely fountain – the heart of Portalegre.

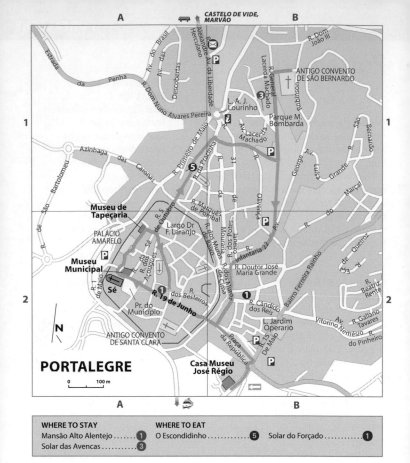

CASTELO DE VIDE,
MARVÃO

A | B

1

2

PORTALEGRE

0   100 m

N

A | B

WHERE TO STAY	WHERE TO EAT	
Mansão Alto Alentejo . . . . ❶	O Escondidinho . . . . ❺	Solar do Forçado . . . . ❶
Solar das Avencas . . . . ❸		

Maranhão power station, 15km/9.3mi downstream.

The N 243 from the south offers the best **view★** of the town. Ramparts, a few medieval towers and the church of the Convento de São Bento, rebuilt in the 17C, stand witness today of the city's brilliant past.

It was here, at the beginning of the 13C, that the military order founded in 1147 by Afonso Henriques to fight the Moors became geographically established. The oldest order of chivalry in Europe bore several names and followed the rules of several other orders before finally becoming the Order of St Benedict of Avis. It prospered in the Tagus region until 1789.

Avis was also the cradle of the dynasty that was to reign over Portugal from 1385 to 1580. On 7 August 1385 João (bastard son of Pedro I), Grand Master of the Order of Avis, was proclaimed king

under the name **João I**. In February 1387 he married Philippa of Lancaster.

You will probably want only to stop here en route, for a coffee perhaps and maybe an hour or so to rest.

Castelo de Vide★

20km/12mi north of Portalegre.

⌖Local map see Serra de SÃO MAMEDE.

The village of Castelo de Vide lies at the foot of its castle, which stands perched on an elongated foothill of the Serra de São Mamede just to the north of Portalegre, and close to the Spanish border. It owes its attraction to old whitewashed houses stepped high up the hillside along winding alleys brilliant with flowers. The town is also a spa; its waters are allegedly beneficial for various ailments. Visit the Jewish Quarter and Synagogue while you are here. About a half day is all you will need to see everything.

Mosteiro de Flor da Rosa, Crato

© johncopland/iStock

From the top of the **keep** in the **castle** (🕐 *the castle is always open; the keep is open 9am–12.30pm, 2–5.30pm; 10am–7pm in summer*), there is a good **view★** of the town.

Also visit the **Praça de Dom Pedro V**, where you will see the Igreja de Santa Maria opposite two 17C buildings, the Baroque Palácio da Torre and the Santo Amaro Hospital. The 13C Sinagoga is the oldest building in town, set in the old alleyways of the Judairia, the Jewish Quarter.

Crato

About 20km/12.4mi due west of Portalegre. As early as 1350, Crato became the seat of a priory for the Order of the Knights Hospitallers of St John of Jerusalem, which later became the Order of the Knights of Malta. The title of Grand Prior of Crato was bestowed until the late 16C. In 1356 the command of the knights' residence was transferred to the monastery-fortress in the neighbouring village of Flor da Rosa; Crato, however, retained its role as a priory. Although Crato's castle was burned in 1662 by Don Juan of Austria, several old houses and the Varanda do Grão Prior (balcony) can still be seen.

The **Mosteiro de Flor da Rosa★** (👓*entrance is free; ask for key at pousada reception*) was a monastery-fortress of the Order of the Knights of Malta. Built in 1356, it forms a compact group of fortified buildings within a crenellated perimeter wall. The **church★** on the right has been extremely well restored; the simplicity of its lines and the height of its nave are outstanding. The small flower-decked cloisters in the centre are robust in design but are given an overall elegance by their graceful Late Gothic network vaulting.

Elvas★

Elvas is an impressive fortification still surrounded by its ramparts, only 19km/11.8mi from the Spanish citadel of Badajoz. The town was not liberated by the Christians from the Moorish occupation until 1229, almost 100 years later than Lisbon. Elvas subsequently resisted many assaults by the Spanish until 1580 when it was attacked by Philip II's troops. Today Elvas is a charming little frontier town with cafés and restaurants in its main square. Famous for its markets, it makes a perfect interlude to an otherwise busy schedule.

The Elvas **fortifications★★** (Muralhas, 👓*open 10am–6pm Tue–Sun, to 5pm in winter,* ✆*268 625 228*), renovated in 2018 and now a UNESCO World Heritage Site, are the most accomplished example of 17C military architecture in Portugal. Fortified gates, moats, curtain walls, bastions and glacis form a remarkable defensive group completed to the south and north by the 17C Santa Luzia and the 18C Graça forts, each perched on a hill. Constructed from 1498 to 1622, the **Aqueduto da Amoreira★**(aqueduct)

Elvas fortifications

© Jacobo Hernández/age fotostock

begins 7.5km/4.6mi southwest of the town and still brings water.

The **cathedral** *(sé)*, originally Gothic, was rebuilt in the 16C by Francisco de Arruda in the Manueline style. The interior, whose pillars were decorated in the Manueline period, contains an 18C chancel faced entirely with marble. On Largo de Santa Clara, the Renaissance style **Igreja Nossa Senhora da Consolação★** (Church of Our Lady of Consolation) was built in the 16C. Its interior, covered by a cupola resting on eight painted columns, is decorated with 17C multi-coloured *azulejos★*. The pulpit, supported by a marble column, has a 16C wrought-iron balustrade. The **Castle of Elvas** (◷*Mon–Fri 9:30am–1pm, 2:30pm–5:30pm;* ◷*1 Jan, Easter Sunday, 1 May and 25 Dec.* ⊛€1.50 to walk the battlements) was constructed by the Moors and reinforced in the 14C and 16C. From the top of the ramparts there is a view of the town, its fortifications and the surrounding countryside scattered with olive trees and isolated farmsteads.

ADDRESSES

🛏 STAY

🛏**Pensao S. Pedro** – *Rua da Mouraria, 14.* ℘*245 031 770. http://pensaosaopedro. weebly.com. 14 rooms.* Sister to the previous pension, it is located in an alleyway running parallel. The rooms are identical, some with small balcony overlooking the garden.

🛏🛏**Mansão Alto Alentejo** – *Rua 19 Junho, 59.* ℘*245 202 290. www.mansaoalto alentejo.com.pt. 12 rooms.* In the centre of the old town, in a steep lane leading to the cathedral, this hotel is a bit dated, but its charm and comfort are intact. Terrace and garden are a bonus.

🛏🛏🍽**Rossio Hotel** – *Rua 31 de Janeiro, 6.* ℘*245 082 218. www.rossiohotel.com. 15 rooms and 3 suites.* Contemporary hotel in the heart of the historical city centre. The rooms are comfortable and quiet and the service is helpful and friendly.

🛏🛏**Solar das Avencas** – *Parque Miguel Bombarda, 11.* ℘*245 201 028. 5 rooms.* An attractive 18C house decorated at the front with an ancestral coat of arms. The ambience is smart, overflowing with antique furniture, china, sofas, embroidery and religious images. The rooms are full of character.

🍴 EAT

🍽**Casa Capote** – *Rua 19 de Junho, 56.* ℘*245 092 312. Closed Sun.* Near the pension Alentejo, this tasca (tavern) attracts drinkers to the bar and diners to its simple restaurant. Dishes are calorie-rich and inexpensive.

🍽🍽**O Tarro** – *Avenida Movimento das Forças Armadas.* ℘*961 508 899. Closed 2:30-7pm and Mon.* At the bottom of a garden behind the Rossio, this nice cafeteria has a lovely view over the park and serves a good menu of the day at reasonable prices.

🍽🍽**O Escondidinho** – *Travessa das Cruzes, 1–3.* ℘*967 419 084. Closed Sun.* A pretty tavern, "founded in 1952," says the boss. On the menu is dogfish soup, cod and potatoes with grilled sardines. The desserts are a real treat: try the pineapple mousse or mango and orange tart

Serra de São Mamede★

and Around

The Serra de São Mamede is a small oasis of greenery in an arid and stony region; its altitude (at its highest point: 1 025m) and the impermeable soil combine to provide sufficient humidity for a dense and varied vegetation. The triangular-shaped massif is composed of hard rock that has resisted erosion.

🚗 **DRIVING TOUR**

73km/45mi. About 2hr 30min.

▷ Leave Portalegre to the east; then turn northwards.

After leaving Portalegre the road rises through woods, with views back over Portalegre. On the entire route there are ample opportunities to stop and walk. The tourist office in Portalegre has a series of pamphlets and maps that will assist you.

▷ Continue on to São Mamede.

⚓ **Michelin Map:** 733.
🏛 **Info:** Rua General Jorge Conde de Avilez, Portalegre; ℘245 203 631.
▷ **Location:** Near the town of Portalegre, close to the Spanish frontier, directly inland from Óbidos.
🕐 **Timing:** You could spend a night in Portalegre and travel this area for a couple of days, no more.

São Mamede

São Mamede is the highest point here, rising to 1 025m. From the summit a vast **panorama★** extends south over the Alentejo, west and north over the Serra de São Mamede and east over the Spanish *sierras*.

▷ Return to the main road and continue on to Marvão.

Marvão★★

⚓*Local map see Serra de SÃO MAMEDE*
The hilltop village is still totally enclosed by its defensive walls and makes a great place to stop for a couple of hours. The castle and the views from the ramparts are particularly worth seeing.

Marvão

© Jon Arnold Images/hemis.fr

© TMAX/Fotolia.com

The Fresco Route

The Rota do Fresco (fresco route), created by the towns of Alvito, Cuba, Vidigueira, Viana do Alentejo and Portel, is a marvellous opportunity to discover the noteworthy frescos and murals that decorate the churches, monasteries and chapels of this region. Pick up a brochure outlining the 114km/70mi circuit at the Portalegre tourist office or in churches.

Most of the frescos that date from the 15C to 17C are well-preserved religious paintings often depicting realistic religious moments and colourful events in history.

The frescos in the Ermida de São Brás (17C) at Vila Frades near Vidigueira show figures of saints and a scene illustrating the beheading of St. Cucufate by the Moors. On the south wall of the Church do Carmo in Cuba is a beautiful representation of St. Christopher carrying the child Jesus. The Mother Church (16C) in Alvito, with its battlements and gargoyles at the foot of the altar, has a fine 17C fresco called *The Lamentations of the Marys*. Nearby, the Chapel of São Sebastião, built in Mudejar style, features a ribbed vault entirely covered with frescos of angel musicians.

© TMAX/Fotolia.com

A few kilometres farther on, the chapel in Passos de Vila Nova da Barony has good examples from the early 17C that include a fresco showing the Last Supper.

Don't miss the richly ornamented dome at the Santuário Nossa Senhora de Aires near Viana do Alentejo, itself an imposing edification of the Rococo 18C. Pilgrimages are held here in September.

If the tour has increased your appetite for more, visit the Church of São Lourenço in the old city of Portelegre and the Convents of São Francisco and Santa Clara, established by the Franciscan order, which based itself here.

Marvão is a fortified medieval village on the Serra de São Mamede near the Spanish border. This outstanding **site★★** played a major part in the Portuguese Civil War in 1833.

The 13C **Igreja de Santa Maria** at the foot of the castle now houses the **Museu Municipal**, which displays Roman stelae, old maps of Marvão and other artefacts.

The late 13C **castle★** was remodelled in the 17C. It consists of a series of perimeter walls dominated by a square keep. Go through the first fortified gate and immediately to the right take the stairs that lead down to a **cistern★**. Ten wide arches are reflected in the water.

A second fortified gate leads into the first courtyard, where the parapet affords fine **views★** of the village stretching out below.

In the second courtyard, take the stairs to the right up to the parapet walk and follow it around to the keep. Impressive **views★★** give a good idea of the various walls and particularly of the crenellated towers built on the overhanging rocks. The vast **panorama★★** extends all the way to the jagged mountain ranges of Spain in the east, the Castelo Branco region and Serra da Estrela as well as the Serra de São Mamede.

Wash house, Castelo de Vide

© StockPhotosArt/iStockphoto.com

Castelo de Vide★
See CASTELO DE VIDE.

Castelo de Vide has a lovely little village square and the ruins of an old castle. Be sure to see its columned wash house. Close by rises the **Monte da Penha**, another high mountain (700m) with glorious views over the surrounding countryside. It is a stony massif, but fascinating to behold. Take your camera.

▷ Return to Portalegre on the Carreiras corniche road.

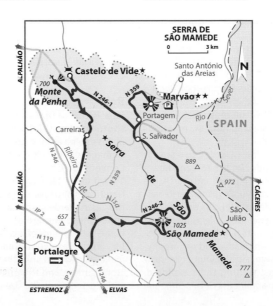

Évora, the capital of the Alentejo, stands in the centre of the region some 130km/81mi from Lisbon and south of the Tagus River (Rio Tejo). The city is one of the finest celebrations of Portugal's 16C golden age, its plethora of ornate churches, palaces and museums testament to the region's power and influence. It is surrounded by vast golden plains that are home to many bird species and fortress villages. Beja is the capital of the southern Alentejo, a beautiful arid region north of the Algarve and west of Spain. In Roman times it was the regional capital under Julius Caesar.

Highlights

1 Chill out in the **Praça do Giraldo**, a tranquil place to people watch (p179)

2 Walk around grisly **Capela dos Ossos** (Chapel of the Bones) (p185)

3 Buy a carpet in **Arraiolos**, made here since the 17C (p185)

4 Climb to the top of **Évoramonte** castle for an epic panorama (p190)

5 Bird-watch in the vast plains of **Castro Verde** (p195)

Évora

A UNESCO World Heritage Site, the historic centre of Évora is the jewel in the Alentejo's crown. You will see glimpses of the city's 2 000 year history at every turn – the Roman walls and museums, Renaissance fountains and ornate ducal palaces, Moorish courtyards, Gothic doorways and turrets, and richly decorated churches and convents. The 16C was a golden age for the city when artists and scholars from Europe flocked here to make their mark. You will see their work at the university and the ornate palaces, churches, mansions and convents.

Among the finest are the Convento dos Loios, founded in the 15C and now a *pousada* (historic hotel) and church. The University of Evora's 16C Italian Renaissance Students' Cloisters are adorned with amazing 18C *azulejos* representing the subjects taught there: physics, history, mathematics and philosophy. The old town has a labyrinth of narrow streets just waiting to be explored. Stop off to admire the Gothic cathedral with its Romanesque influences, the palaces of the Dukes of Cadaval and the Counts of Basto, the Diana Roman temple and the chilling Capela dos Ossos (Chapel of the Bones), whose walls and pillars are faced with the bones and skulls of 5 000 people. Take your camera.

Village and Castles

Once you have had your fill of culture, there are lots of charming villages and castles to explore nearby.

Arraiolos is famous for its fine wool carpets; Estremoz is known for Alentejan pottery, which can be bought at the Saturday market. Sleepy Viana do Alentejo has an interesting church behind its castle; while Estremoz, with its 17C ramparts, has several good museums including the Capela da Rainha Santa Isabel, whose chapel walls are covered with *azulejos* depicting scenes from the life of Queen Saint Isabel of Aragon.

Fortified Évoramonte has a remarkable setting on top of a hill, while Vila Vicosa boasts a fine ducal palace, once the seat of the Dukes of Braganca.

Beja

Beja is the capital of the beautiful southern Alentejo, whose golden plains extend as far as the eye can see. Highlights in Beja include the Antigo Conveno da Conceicao, founded in 1459, and the 13C castle.

Nature and bird lovers should not miss the Castro Verde, a special protection zone whose vast golden plains are home to thousands of local and migratory birds. Take your binoculars and make an effort to spot the Alentejan stone curlew, and the great bustard, which can grow to the size of a turkey.

Évora★★★

and Around

A walled town since Roman times, Évora is attractively Moorish in character with alleyways cut by arches, brilliant white houses, flower-decked terraces, openwork balconies and tiled patios. From its rich past, Évora retains several medieval and Renaissance palaces and mansions, which, in themselves, provide a panoply of Portuguese architecture. They are at their most impressive at night (floodlit during the summer from 9pm to midnight), standing out against a starry sky. Today the town is an important agricultural market and the base for several dependent crafts and industries (cork, woollen carpets, leather and painted furniture).

▶ **Population:** 57 000.
◔ **Map:** p180–181.
🛈 **Info:** Praça do Giraldo; ☎266 777 071.
◔ **Location:** Along the A6, about 132km/82mi east of Lisbon.
🧑‍🧒 **Kids:** The Vasco da Gama palace with its history of the Great Discoveries.
◔ **Timing:** Tourist buses from Lisbon arrive about 11am. You might like to get there earlier – spend a day. It's quiet in the evenings too.
🅿 **Parking:** Park outside the town where parking is free and unrestricted.
◔ **Don't Miss:** The university, the Roman temple and the cathedral.

OLD TOWN
(Cidade Velha)

Praça do Giraldo

The bustling town centre is a vast square partly bordered by arcades. An 18C marble fountain by Afonso Álvares stands on the site of a former triumphal Roman arch. Several little streets and alleys lead off the square, including the famed **Rua 5 de Outubro**, a narrow street lined with houses with wrought-iron balconies, as well as arts and crafts shops; no. 28 has a niche decorated with *azulejos*.

Cathedral★★

◔*Daily 9am–5pm.* ⊕€2.50 (church and cloisters), €3.50 (roof, cloisters and cathedral). ☎266 759 330.
The cathedral was built in the late 12C in the Transitional Gothic style on the site of a former mosque. While it has Romanesque characteristics, the cathedral was completed under Gothic influence.
The **exterior**'s plain granite façade is flanked by two massive towers crowned by conical spires added in the 16C. The tower on the right consists of several turrets similar to those on the Romanesque lantern-tower over the transept.

The main doorway is decorated with figures of the Apostles supported by consoles. The sculptures were probably carved in the late 13C by French artists. In the **interior**★ the large nave, with broken barrel vaulting, has an elegant triforium. To the left, on a Baroque altar, is a 15C multicoloured stone statue of the Virgin with Child; opposite is a 16C statue, in gilded wood, of the Angel Gabriel attributed to Olivier of Ghent. A fine octagonal **dome**★ on squinches, from which hangs a chandelier, stands above the transept crossing. The arms of the transept are lit by two Gothic rose windows: the north one shows the Morning Star and the south the Mystic Rose.

In the north transept the Renaissance archway to a chapel is decorated with a marble sculpture by Nicolas Chanterene. The south transept contains the tomb of the 16C humanist André de Resende. The chancel was remodelled in the 18C by Friederich Ludwig, architect of the monastery at Mafra. The **Cadeiras do coro★ (choir stalls)**, made of oak, were carved in the Renaissance period by Flemish artists. They are decorated with sacred and secular motifs; note in

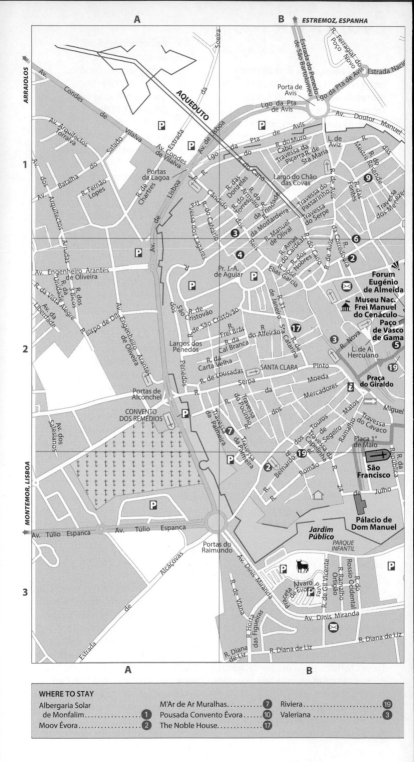

ESTREMOZ, ESPANHA

WHERE TO STAY

Albergaria Solar de Monfalim .... ❶	M'Ar de Ar Muralhas .... ❼
Moov Évora .... ❷	Pousada Convento Évora ...... ❿
	The Noble House .... ⓱

Riviera .... ⓳
Valeriana .... ❸

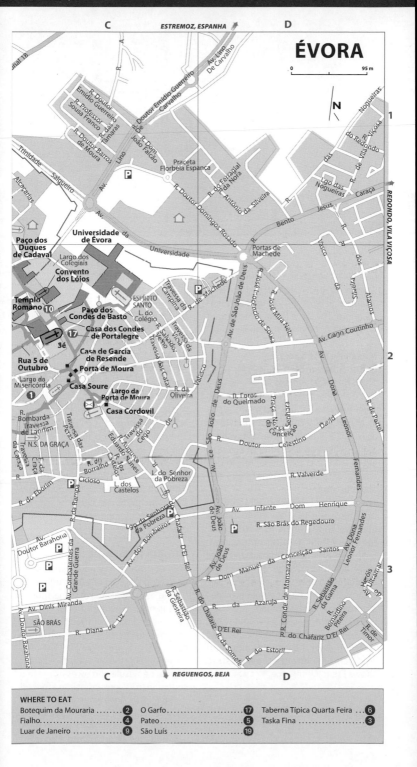

ÉVORA

0   95 m

N

ESTREMOZ, ESPANHA

REDONDO, VILA VIÇOSA

REGUENGOS, BEJA

Paço dos Duques de Cadaval

Universidade de Évora

Largo dos Colegiais

Convento dos Lóios

Templo Romano

Paço dos Condes de Basto

Casa dos Condes de Portalegre

Casa de Garcia de Resende

Rua 5 de Outubro

Porta de Moura

Largo da Misericórdia

Casa Soure

Largo da Porta de Moura

Casa Córdovil

Sé

Portas de Machede

ESPÍRITO SANTO

L. do Colégio

N.S. DA GRAÇA

L. do Senhor da Pobreza

L. dos Castelos

SÃO BRÁS

WHERE TO EAT

Botequim da Mouraria .... ❷	O Garfo .... ⓱	Taberna Típica Quarta Feira ... ❻
Fialho........................ ❹	Pateo .... ❺	Taska Fina .... ❸
Luar de Janeiro .... ❾	São Luís .... ⓳	

181

Templo Romano, the spires of the cathedral in the right background

particular the scenes on the lower panels showing peasants at their daily tasks (grape-picking, pig-sticking and sheep-shearing). The large Renaissance organ is thought to be the oldest in Europe.

Museu de Arte Sacra★
⏰ *Tue–Sun 9am–5pm (winter closed 12:30-2pm)* ⏰ *1 Jan and 24–25 Dec.* ⊜ *€4.50 incl. cathedral.* ℘ *266 759 330.*
This museum contains vestments, a collection of ecclesiastical plates, including an ivory 13C French **figure-triptych★★** of the Virgin, and a 17C reliquary cross of St Lenho in silver gilt and multicoloured enamel decorated with more than 1 000 precious stones.

The **Gothic cloisters★**, which were built between 1322 and 1340, have a massive appearance, further accentuated by their granite composition, despite the elegance of rounded bays with radiating tracery. Statues of the Evangelists stand in each of the four corners. The southwest corner provides a good view of the Romanesque belfry. An adjoining chapel contains the 14C tomb of the founder-bishop and 14C statues of the Angel Gabriel and a polychrome Virgin, whose posture shows French influence.

Casas Pintadas★
⏰ *Mon–Sat 10am–6pm (to 7pm in summer). Ring the bell for entry. Min 5. people for guided tours.* ⊜ *€1, €3 (tour)* ℘ *266 703 327.*
This mansion, which was once thought to have been built by Vasco da Gama and is the former palace of the Inquisition, contains fabulous **wall paintings** from the second half of the 16C detailing mythological creatures such as dragons and sirens and other exotic scenes. The building itself is impressive with cloisters, arcades and a chapel.
Known as the Casas Pintadas, the building is part of the **Fórum Eugénio de Almeida** (⏰ *Tue–Sun 10am–6pm.* ⏰ *25 Dec, 1 Jan.* ℘ *266 748 350. www.fea.pt)* a centre for contemporary art and culture opened in 2013.

Templo Romano★
This Corinthian-style Roman temple erected in the 2C is often thought of as having been dedicated to Diana, though that is now considered unlikely. The capitals and bases of the columns are of Estremoz marble; the 14 Corinthian column shafts are of granite. The temple is probably the best preserved in the Iberian peninsula and owes its present condition to its conversion into a fortress in the Middle Ages when it was walled up, after which it was used as a prison and later as an abattoir (having been restored only about a century ago).

Convento dos Lóios★

The Dos Lóios or St Eligius monastery, dedicated to St John the Evangelist, was founded in the 15C. It is now a lovely hotel (www.pousadas.pt), with nice restaurant in the cloisters. The church façade was remodelled after the earthquake of 1755 with the exception of the porch, which protects a Flamboyant Gothic doorway. The nave, with lierne and tierceron vaulting, is lined with beautiful *azulejos* (1711) by António de Oliveira Bernardes, depicting the life of St Laurence Justinian, patriarch of Venice, whose writings influenced the Lóios monks. Two grilles in the pavement enable the castle's cistern, on the left, and an ossuary, on the right, to be seen.

Conventual buildings

The conventual buildings have been converted into a *pousada* (www.pousadas.pt). The chapter-house **door★** has outstanding architectural elegance and is a good example of the composite Luso-Moorish style, the crowning piece over the doorway and the piers topped by pinnacles that serve as a framework to the door are Gothic inspired; the columns are twisted and Manueline in style. The twin bays with horseshoe arches are, like the capitals, reminiscent of Moorish design.

Palacio Cadaval

◷*Daily 10am–8pm.* ◷*Public holidays.* ☞€3 (€5 combined ticket with the church of the Covento dos Lóios). ✆967 979 763. www.palaciocadaval.com

The **Palace of the Dukes of Cadaval** is protected by two crenelled towers and has a façade that was remodelled in the 17C. It was given by King João I to his councillor, Martim Afonso de Melo, *alcalde* of Évora, in 1390. Kings João III and João V also lived within its walls at different periods.

The Dukes of Cadaval's **art gallery** contains a collection of historic documents about the Cadaval family and two fine Flemish commemorative plaques in bronze, dating from the late 15C. Contemporary events are also regularly hosted here.

▷ Retrace your steps to the street between the Convento dos Lóios and the Museu Regional. Turn left into the street running perpendicular to the east end of the cathedral.

Paço dos Condes de Basto

The Palace of the Counts of Basto was built over the remains of the Roman wall including the Sertório Tower. The Gothic palace's main front has several paired Mudéjar windows.

▷ Return to the east end of the cathedral and continue round.

Museu Nacional Frei Manuel do Cenáculo

◷*Tue–Sun 9.30am–5.30pm. In winter, 10am–6pm.* ◷*1 Jan, Easter Sunday, 1 May and 25 Dec.* ☞€3, free 1st Sun of month. ✆266 730 480. www.museudevora.pt.

Located in the former archbishop's palace (16C), this museum displays significant archaeological artefacts found in the area (from the Neolithic, Bronze and Iron ages to the Roman era), and a fine collection of 16–18C paintings and sculptures taken from buildings destroyed in the dissolution of the monasteries.

The **Casa de Garcia de Resende** is a 16C house in which the humanist Garcia de Resende (1470–1536) is said to have lived. Manueline decoration adorns the three sets of paired windows on the first floor.

The **Porta de Moura** gateway with its two towers formed part of the medieval town fortifications. A niche at the foot of the left tower contains a crucifix.

The picturesque **Largo da Porta de Moura** square is divided into two parts. On the larger of the two, in the centre, stands a Renaissance **fountain★** that consists of a column surmounted by a white marble sphere. On the west side, steps descend to the church of the

Several lovely houses border the square: the 16C **Casa Cordovil** on the south side has an elegant loggia with twin arcades, festooned horseshoe arches and Moorish capitals, and a crenelled roof surmounted by a conical spire. On the west side, steps descend to the church of the former Carmelite Convent which has a Baroque **doorway**. On the east side are the Law Courts, in a modern building. The 15C **Casa Soure** was formerly a part of the palace of the Infante Dom Luis. The Manueline façade has a gallery of rounded arches crowned by a conical spire.

◯ Head toward Largo da Graça by way of Travessa da Caraça.

Igreja de São Francisco

This early 16C church is preceded by a portico pierced by rounded, pointed and horseshoe arches, and crowned with battlements and conical pinnacles. The Manueline doorway is surmounted by a pelican and an armillary sphere, the emblems of João II and King Manuel. The **interior★**, with ribbed vaulting, is surprisingly wide. The chancel contains two galleries, on the right, Renaissance, on the left, Baroque. The former chapter-house is furnished with a balustrade of fluted marble and turned-ebony columns. Covering to the walls, *azulejos* depict scenes from the Passion.

◯ Take the door to the left of the balustrade in the former chapter-house.

Capela dos Ossos (Chapel of Bones)★
◯Open 9am–6:30pm (until 5pm in winter). ☞€5. ✆266 704 521.
This macabre ossuary chapel was built in the 16C by a Franciscan to induce meditation by his fellow men. The bones and skulls of 5 000 people have been used to face the walls and pillars.

Jardim Público

The public gardens lie just to the south of the Igreja de São Francisco. Part of the 16C **Palácio de Dom Manuel** and the ruins of another 16C palace still stand in the gardens. The Dom Manuel palace was built by the Avis dynasty in a curious mixture of Gothic, Manueline, neo-Moorish and Renaissance styles, but all that remains of it now is the Gallery of Ladies. It is thought that it was here that Vasco da Gama received his orders before setting off to discover the sea route to India. Note the paired windows with horseshoe arches in the Luso-Moorish style.

ADDITIONAL SIGHTS
Fortifications★

Traces of the 1C Roman wall, reinforced by the Visigoths in the 7C, can be seen between the Paços dos Duques de Cadaval and dos Condes de Basto (Largo dos Colegiais). The 14C medieval wall marks the town limits to the north and west. The 17C fortifications now form the boundary of the public gardens to the south.

Universidade de Évora★
◯Mon–Fri 9am–7pm (until 8pm in Aug), Sat 9am–1pm. ◯Public holidays. www.uevora.pt.
The university occupies the former Jesuit University (Antiga Universidade dos Jesuitas); the building's inner courtyard is of particular interest.
Buildings in the 16C Italian Renaissance style surround what is known as the main **Students' Cloisters★** (Claustro Geral dos Estudos) with its arched gallery. Facing the entrance, the pediment over the portico to the Sala das Actas (Hall of Acts) is decorated with statues personalising the royal and the ecclesiastical universities.
The classrooms opening onto the gallery are adorned with 18C *azulejos* representing the subjects taught here: physics, history, philosophy, mathematics.

Aqueduto da Água de Prata

The "Aqueduct of Silver Water" was completed in 1530 to bring clean water into the town. Below its huge arches, particularly at its end on Rua do Como, shops and restaurants have been established, giving a self-contained village feel to the area.

EXCURSIONS
Arraiolos
22km/14mi north of Évora.
This charming village, perched on a hill in the great Alentejo plain has long been famous for its wool carpets. The 14C

Claustro Geral dos Estudos,
Universidade de Évora

© miralex/iStock

castle *(partially restored)* dominates the narrow streets of white-walled houses, and offers a fine view of the village and olive groves beyond. The **Convento dos Lóios** has been converted into a *pousada*. In the second half of the 17C, a small industry was established in the Arraiolos region, manufacturing hemp and linen carpets that were then embroidered with wool and used as chest and wall coverings.

Arraiolos carpets first followed Indian and Persian designs with animal figures and plant motifs, but later the Oriental patterns and colourings were abandoned in favour of more popular, regional themes. They can be found on sale in the village in several shops; the carpets range in price from €75 to more than €2 500.

Viana do Alentejo

31km/19mi west, by N 114.

This sleepy agricultural town in the vast Alentejo plain, away from the main roads, hides an interesting church behind its castle walls. The castle's ramparts have fortified walls flanked at each corner by a tower with a pepperpot roof surrounding the pentagonal edifice. The entrance porch is adorned with worn capitals decorated with animals, including tortoises and lions.

Church

The church façade has a fine Manueline doorway: a slender twisted column serves as the supporting pier for twin arches framed by two candlestick shaped pilasters; it also supports the tympanum, which is decorated with stylised flowers and the cross of the Order of Christ in a medallion surmounted by the Portuguese coat of arms: a gable formed by a twisted cable ends in a type of pinnacle flanked by two armillary spheres. The interior, which is Romanesque, is outstanding for its size. The walls are decorated at their base with 17C *azulejos*. A particularly fine crucifix can also be seen in the chancel.

Estremoz★

Approached from the south, the old town appears perched on a hill overlooking the bright whitewashed houses of the modern town below. Estremoz, standing in a region of marble quarries, is a pleasant town, still possessing its 17C ramparts and dominated by its medieval castle. It is well known for Alentejo pottery, which can be seen at the Saturday market in the *rossio* (main square).

Torre de Menagem

The keep has now been converted into one of the most famous *pousadas* in Portugal. It was built in the 13C and is crowned with small pyramid-shaped merlons and flanked in its upper part by galleries supported on consoles.

Torre de Menagem, Estremoz

© LuA~s GraAa/iStock

Capela da Rainha Santa Isabel

🕒*Open Tue–Sun 9am–12:30pm,
2–5.30pm.* 🕒*Public holidays.*

The chapel walls are covered with beautiful *azulejos* depicting scenes from the life of **Queen Saint Isabel of Aragon**, wife of King Dinis. The Miracle of the Roses scene is the most delightful: in it, the queen, surprised by the king as she is carrying bread to distribute to the poor, opens the pleats of her skirt to banish her husband's suspicions: only rose petals fall out. Excellent café in the former jail.

Sala de Audiência de Dom Dinis

🕒*Tue–Sun 9am–12.30pm,
2–5.30pm.* 🕒*Public holidays.*

A beautiful **Gothic colonnade★** is the outstanding feature of King Dinis' Audience Chamber, whose stellar vaulting dates from the Manueline period. Queen Saint Isabel and King Pedro I both died in this room.

Museu Municipal

🕒*Open Tue–Sat 9am–12:30pm,
2-5.30pm.* 🕒*Public holidays.* ⊜€1.50.
℘ 268 339 219.

Housed in a handsome old almshouse, this museum has some fine examples of Estremoz pottery, which was particularly important in gypsy weddings. As the bride and groom met in the town

square, the bride would suddenly make a dash for "freedom" hotly pursued by the groom. As he caught her and kissed her, several bowls would be thrown into the air. As they broke on hitting the ground, the couple were pronounced man and wife. In the courtyard you can often see artists at work who offer their ceramics for sale.

Museu de Arte Sacra

🕒*Open Tue–Fri 10am–noon,
3.30pm–5.30pm.* ⊜€1. *℘ 967 528 298.*
Located in a 16C convent, this small museum has some ornate examples of sacred art. You also get to see the marble church and some pretty views form the rooftop terrace.

Igreja de Nossa Senhora dos Mártires

2km/1.2mi south on the road to Bencatel.
The church dates from 1744 and has a monumental Gothic east end. The nave, which is preceded by a triumphal Manueline arch, contains noteworthy *azulejos (Flight into Egypt, The Last Supper, The Annunciation)* as does the chancel *(Nativity, Presentation in the Temple).*

Monsaraz★★

The old fortified village of Monsaraz occupies a strategic position in an outstanding **site★★** on a height near the Guadiana valley on the border between Portugal and Spain. When it lost its military role, Monsaraz also lost its importance in favour of Reguengos de Monsaraz. As a result, the town has retained much of its historic character. *Leave the car in front of the main gate to the town as vehicles are not allowed inside the village. It's a short walk through the Porta da Vila to Rua São Tiago, one of the two main streets in the village. Parallel to it is Rua Direita, which leads to the castle.*

Rua Direita★

The street retains all its original charm as it is still lined with 16C and 17C whitewashed houses, many flanked by outside staircases and balconies with wrought-iron grilles. All the village monuments may be seen in this street.

Monsaraz

©johnicopland/iStock

Igreja Matriz

Rebuilt after the 1755 earthquake, the parish church still contains an impressive 14C marble tomb carved with 14 Saints. Outside an 18C stone pillory is topped with a Manueline globe.

Casa da Inquisição

🕐Open Mon-Fri 10:30am–1pm, 4–10pm, Sat&Sun 10am–11pm, summer only. ⊛€1.

The former court building of the Inquisition hosts a small exhibition about the Jewish presence in Monsarraz, including traditions and persecutions.

Castle

Rebuilt by King Dom Dinis in the 13C, the castle was given a second perimeter wall with massive bastions in the 17C. Look especially for the Torre das Geiticeiras (Witches' Tower). The parapet walk commands a **panorama** of the Alentejo.

ADDRESSES

🏠 STAY

⊖ **Avis Guest House** – *Rua Avis, 154.* ☎*963 396 615. 6 rooms.* Excellent value for money. Clean, comfortable, simple rooms. Shared kitchen.

⊖ **Casa dos Teles** – *Rua Romão Ramalho, 27.* ☎*266 702 453. 9 rooms.* 🚫 *No breakfast.* Near the church of São Francisco, this house has a charming host. Some rooms have private bathroom, toilet and kitchenette. Request rooms 7 or 8, which overlook the small garden.

⊖⊖⊖⊖ **Hotel Solar de Monfalim** – *Largo da Misericórdia, 1.* ☎*266 703 529. www.solarmonfalim.com/solar-monfalim. 26 rooms.* 🅿 All the rooms in this peaceful hotel, set in a 16C mansion, are different, though the comfort level remains the same.

⊖⊖⊖ **Casa de São Tiago** – *Largo Alexandre Herculano, 2.* ☎*266 702 686. 7 rooms.* A delightful 16C house with its own inner garden and small orchard in the historical centre of the town. All the rooms are decorated with antique furniture.

⊖⊖ **Best Western Santa Clara** – *Travessa da Milheira, 19.* ☎*266 704 141. 41 rooms.* 🅿. Located in the heart of the old town, this comfortable hotel is quiet and has a lift. Some rooms have a small patio.

⊖⊖⊖ **Hotel Riviera** – *Rua 5 de Outubro, 49.* ☎*266 737 210. www.riviera-evora.pt. 20 rooms.* For lovers of modern comfort, this residence has little character but does have some nice rooms with private terrace.

⊖⊖⊖⊖ **Albergaria do Calvario** – *Travessa dos Lagares, 3.* ☎*266 745 930. www.adcevora.com. 22 rooms.* 🅿. North of the city, this ancient olive oil factory has been converted into a charming inn. The décor of the rooms is rustic with Moroccan terra-cotta wall tiles and marble bathrooms.

⊖⊜⊟ **M'Ar de Ar Muralhas** – *Tv. da Palmeira, 4/6. ☎266 739 300. www. mardearhotels.com/en. 85 rooms and 6 suites. ⊒⑆.* A modern hotel close to the city walls. Rooms are well furnished; those at the rear have balconies. The restaurant (⊖⊜⊟) serves Portuguese cuisine such as *porco preto do Alentejo* (stewed pork), as well as fish and duck.

⊖⊜⊟ **Pousada Convento de Evora** – *Largo Conde de Vila Flor. ☎266 730 870. www.pousadas.pt. 36 rooms. ⊒.* This elegant, luxurious *pousada* is situated in the buildings of the 16C Lóios convent. White-covered tables in the restaurant (⊖⊜⊟) surround a patio on which orange trees grow. The chef has chosen to prepare traditional dishes, which are delicious. There is a pool and solarium.

⑆ EAT

⊖ **Adega Alentejano** – *Rua G. V. do Monte Pereira, 21-A. ☎266 744 447. Closed Sun and holidays.* High vaulted and decorated with wine barrels and agricultural implements, this cheerful eatery has a noisy atmosphere, with a mixture of locals and tourists. The daily specials are displayed on the wall. The menu comprises vegetable soups, stews and pork. Service is a little slow.

⊖ **A Choupana** – *Rua dos Mercadores, 18–20 (just behind the Praca do Giraldo). ☎266 704 427. Closed Sun. Serves until 1.30am.* Varied menu at low prices, no frills but great food: grilled fish, pot-au-feu, steak and fries, *açorda de mariscos*.

⊖ **Restaurante O Templo** – *R do Escrivão da Câmara, 2B. ☎927 217 635. Sat and Sun dinner only.* Simple, homestyle, delectable fare: think grilled sardines with salad, lamb kebabs with potato and rice, and nice cheese and charcuterie boards.

⊖⊜ **São Luís** – *Rua do Segeiro, 30–32 (south, near the Porta do Raimundo). ☎266 741 585. Closed Sun.* Simple but authentic Alentejan food such as wild herbal soups and grilled pork is served here.

⊖⊜ **1/4 P'ràs 9** – *Rua Pedro Simões, 9-A. ☎266 706 774. Closed Wed.* Pleasant terrace in an alley. Specialities: rice and monkfish or lobster, açorda of mariscos (bread and seafood stew), rice and hare, clams and grilled pork.

⊖ **Restaurante Salsa Verde** – *R do Raimundo 93-A. ☎266 743 210. http://www. salsa-verde.org. Closed Sat dinner and Sun.* Healthy and toothsome vegetarian food,

available from a buffet or a la carte. Whole grains (pasta, barley), vegetables sauteed and roasted, tofu, and other bites. Free WiFi.

⊖⊜ **O Antão** – *Rua João de Deus, 5. ☎266 706 459. Closed Mon.* Regional cuisine at moderate prices is served: rabbit Alentejan-style, partridge with vegetables. Small patio.

⊖⊜ **Botequim da Mouraria**– *Rua da Mouraria,16-A. ☎266 746 775. Closed Sat, Sun and public holidays.* A cosy bistro where you eat perched on high stools, elbow to elbow along a narrow counter. Often crowded.

⊖⊜ **The Bakery Lounge** – *R de Burgos 6. ☎266 707 085. Closed Sun.* Nice little café for soup, salad, sandwiches, sweets, and coffee. Good for breakfast and lunch. Come early to snag a coveted terrace seat.

⊖⊜ **Quarta-Feira** – *Rua do Inverno, 16-18. ☎266 707 530. Closed Sun, Mon lunch.* Nice rustic tavern which serves a good soup and regional dishes such as pork marinated in red wine or lamb chops served with mashed spinach and coriander. Dining is around large communal tables in the shadow of towering wine jars.

⊖⊜⊟ **O Fialho** – *Travessa dos Mascarenhas, 16. ☎266 703 079. www. restaurantefialho.pt. Closed Mon.* Famous for its regional gastronomy, having won many awards during its 65-year history. Three rooms are decorated with plates and trophies. Among the specialties are dogfish soup, roasted cod with mashed potatoes and lamb stew. Good wine. Reserve for the evening.

⊖⊜⊟ **Luar de Janeiro** – *Travessa de Janeiro, 13. ☎266 749 114/5. www. luardejaneiro.com. Closed Thu.* One of the best restaurants in town, housed in an elegant building. Delicious ribs, stuffed ham and asparagus, and excellent fresh fish. Attentive service.

⊖⊜⊟ **Tasquinha d'Oliveira** – *Rua Cândido dos Reis,45-A. ☎266 744 841. Closed Sun.* The one room is tiny and full of charm. The young couple who own the restaurant serve *petiscos* (hot or cold appetizers): bean salad with mint, octopus salad, asparagus with scrambled eggs, artichoke hearts with smoked ham. The cuisine is regional and the wine is excellent.

Évoramonte★

The small fortified town of Évoramonte, along the A6 about 25km/15.5mi east of Évora, has a remarkable **setting**★ at the top of a high hill in the Alentejo. It was at Évoramonte on 26 May 1834 that the **Convention** was signed, which ended the civil war and under which the son of João VI, Pedro IV, Emperor of Brazil, compelled his brother Miguel I, an extremist whom he had vanquished at the Battle of Asseiceira, to abdicate in favour of his niece, Maria, and go into exile.

▶ **Population:** 600.

🜚 **Michelin Map:** 733.

🛈 **Info:** Tiny information office just behind the castle.

🕐 **Timing:** This is a place where you would stop for a coffee and a brief walk round en route to somewhere else.

🅿 **Parking:** No problems parking here.

⊘ **Don't Miss:** The castle and the house where the Convention was signed.

A BIT OF HISTORY

Born at Queluz in 1798, Pedro was the son of the man who later became King John VI of Portugal. The family escaped Napoléon's advance and went to Brazil, where Pedro was crowned King Pedro II and later Emperor. In 1831 he abdicated in favour of his son and returned to Portugal, planning to regain the crown that was rightly his, but which he had ceded to his daughter Maria. As she was still an infant, Pedro's brother Miguel had become Regent and *de facto* monarch. Arguments and later, battles, ensued but in May 1834 an agreement was reached restoring Pedro as King Pedro IV and banning Miguel. That agreement was signed in Évoramonte. Pedro had only a

few months to enjoy his throne, dying in October of the same year of tuberculosis in Queluz.

Access

1.5km/1mi from the modern village. Follow the signs to "Castelo de Évoramonte". After skirting the base of the 14C–17C ramparts, go through the entrance gate. 🚌 *Buses stop in the modern village; be prepared for a walk.*

SIGHTS

Castle of Évoramonte★

🕐*Tue–Sun Jun–Aug 10am–1pm, 2.30–6pm, Sep–May 10am–1pm, 2:30–5pm.* 🕐*1 Jan, Easter Sunday, 1 May and 25 Dec.* 🚫€2. 📞*268 950 025.*

Olives Groves with Évoramonte citadel

©marinzolich/iStock

The castle, which was first Roman, then Moorish, then radically remodelled in the 14C, emerges as a Gothic-style military monument in spite of further reconstruction in the 16C to repair damage caused by the 1531 earthquake.

The medieval keep is girdled by rope motifs that knot in the middle of each façade.

Inside, the central part of the castle consists of three superimposed storeys; each storey is covered with nine Gothic arches resting on sturdy central pillars, those on the ground floor being massive and twisted. Three vaulted chambers have intricately carved granite capitals.

From the top, there is a **panorama★** of the surrounding countryside speckled with olive trees and small white villages, and to the northeast, Estremoz.

Casa da Convenção

The house where the Convention was signed bears a commemorative plaque. It is said that the signing ceremony took so long that by the end of it there was only stale bread left to eat, though it was fashioned into what has since become a famed Portuguese dish, *açorda* – a soup of bread with water, coriander, garlic, salt and olive oil.

Vila Viçosa★

Vila Viçosa, on a hillside where orange and lemon groves abound, is a town of lush *(viçosa)* and bright flowers. It is a quiet town, making a living from various industries such as pottery, cork and tin, as well as marble-quarrying nearby. A few miles away, on 17 June 1665, the Battle of Montes Claros was fought, which confirmed Portugal's independence from Spain.

▶ **Population:** 8 400.
⚅ **Michelin Map:** 733.
🅱 **Info:** Praça da República; ✆ 268 889 310.
▶ **Location:** Vila Viçosa lies east of Évora, almost on the border with Spain, and 20km/12.4mi southeast of Estremoz.
🕐 **Timing:** Give yourself a day here, and have lunch too.
🚫 **Don't Miss:** The old town, the castle, the Ducal Palace.

A BIT OF HISTORY
The Ducal Court

Vale Viçosa, as this village was first called, was granted a charter in 1270 by Afonso III under its new name, Vila Viçosa. It was at one time the seat of the Dukes of Bragança and also the residence of several kings of Portugal. In the 15C the second Duke of Bragança, Dom Fernando, chose Vila Viçosa as the residence of his court.

The execution of the third duke, Dom Fernando, however, annihilated the ducal power, and it was only in the following century that court life became really sumptuous. In the palace, built by Duke Jaime, great seignorial festivals followed one after the other, as did gargantuan banquets and theatri-

cal performances, with bullfights in the grounds outside. This golden age ended in 1640, when the eighth Duke of Bragança acceded to the throne of Portugal as Dom João IV.

Execution of the Duke

On his succession to the throne in 1481, King João II instituted stern measures to abolish privileges granted by his father, King Alfonso V, to the nobles who took part in the Reconquest. The most powerful nobleman in the land, the Duke of Bragança, brother-in-law of the king, was guilty of plotting against the monarchy. After a summary trial, he was executed in Évora in 1483.

Cloister, Paço Ducal

© Laurent Marolleau/age fotostock

TERREIRO DO PAÇO★

Paço Ducal (Ducal Palace)★★

◐Jun-Sept Tue 2–6pm, Wed–Sun 10am–1pm, 2–6pm; Oct–May Tue 2–5pm, Wed–Sun 10am–1pm, 2–5pm. ◐Public holidays. ⊜€7. Palace ℘268 980 659; Castle ℘268 980 120.

The **Ducal Palace** overlooks the Terreiro do Paço (Palace Square), in the centre of which is a bronze statue of Dom João IV. The fourth duke, Dom Jaime I, began this palace in 1501.

The interior is now a museum. The well of the staircase to the first floor is adorned with wall paintings depicting the 15C Battle of Ceuta and the 16C Siege of Azamor. Much of the original furniture went to Lisbon when Dom João IV ascended the throne, and on to Brazil when the royal family went into exile, but there are still some very good items to see, especially the toiletries and clothes of Dom Carlos and his wife Marie-Amélie; these are left out as if the couple was due back any minute. A superb 16C Persian rug lies in the Dukes' Hall. The main wing is decorated with 17C azulejos, Brussels and Aubusson tapestries and Arraiolos carpets.

The rooms are embellished with finely painted ceilings representing a variety of subjects including David and Goliath, the adventures of Perseus and the Seven Virtues. There are also portraits of the Braganças by the late 19C Portuguese painters Columbano, Malhoa and Sousa Pinto, and paintings by the 18C French artist Quillard In the Sala dos Tudescos (Teutonic Hall). The west face looks over a boxwood topiary. The Transverse wing comprises the apartments of King Carlos I (1863–1908), who was a talented painter and draughtsman, and Queen Amelia. In the chapel an interesting 16C triptych, attributed to Cristóvão de Figueiredo, illustrates scenes from the Calvary. The 16C Manueline style cloisters are beautifully cool.

The **Armoury Collection** (◐same hours as the Ducal Palace; ⊜€3) is an assembly of rifles and pistols that belonged to the Bragança dynasty, attesting to the importance of hunting to the family. An exceptional collection of blue and white **Chinese porcelain** (◐same hours as the Ducal Palace; ⊜€2.50), dates from the 16C and 17C. The **Treasures Collection** (◐Oct–Jun same hours as the Ducal Palace weekdays only; ⊜€2.50) displays artefacts from the palace, the highlight being the Cruz (Cross) de Vila Viçosa, made between 1656 and 1673. Some 170 pieces illustrate the fine artistry of 18C and 19C goldsmiths in Portugal. You can also see examples of 15C Flemish paintings and tapestries, vestments in gold cloth and embroidered in gold, as well as ceramics.

♟♟ Museu dos Coches★

◷Same hours as the Ducal Palace. ◉€2.50.
More than 70 coaches, four-wheelers and carriages dating from the 18C to the 20C are displayed in four buildings including the **Royal Stables★**, built at the request of King José I in 1752. The stables, with room for hundreds of horses, are 70m long with a vaulted roof resting on marble pillars.

The condition and the variety of exhibits are outstanding; there are mail coaches, charabancs, phaetons, landaus, four-wheelers and state carriages. On leaving the museum the "Knot Gate" stands beside the Lisbon road.

Porta dos Nós★

The "Knot Gate" is one of the last remains of the 16C perimeter wall. The House of Bragança, whose motto was *Despois vós, nós* (After you, us), chose knots as emblems on account of the two meanings of the word *nós* (us or we and knots).

▷ Return to the Terreiro do Paço.

Convento dos Agostinhos

The **church**, rebuilt in the 17C by the future Dom João IV, stands at the east end of the Terreiro do Paço and is now the mausoleum of the Dukes of Bragança.

Antigo Convento das Chagas

The building on the south side of the Terreiro do Paço was founded by Joana de Mendonça, the second wife of Duke Dom Jaime I. The walls of the church, which serves as the mausoleum for the Duchesses of Bragança, are covered in *azulejos* dating from 1626.

OLD TOWN

🅿 Leave the car outside the ramparts.
The castle and ramparts built at the end of the 13C on the order of King Dinis were reinforced with bastions in the 17C. The crenellated walls flanked with towers still gird the old town.

Enter through a gateway cut into the ramparts. The alleys are lined with whitewashed houses, their lower sections painted with bright colours.

A narrow street leads to the **Igreja de Nossa Senhora de Conceição**, without doubt the best of the town's 22 churches, with an excellent collection of 18C *azulejos*.

Inside, the image of Our Lady of Conception is venerated, protected by silver white lattice-work and flanked by two 15C paintings from the Chagas Convent. In 1646, KIng João IV (João VIII of Bragança) dedicated the kingdom of Portugal to Our Lady of the Conception, crowning her queen and patron saint of the nation. Since then, this site has been a place of great devotion consecrated to the worship of Mary.

Castle

◆◞ Guided tour (1h30) Jun–Sept Tue 2–6pm, Wed–Sun 10am–1pm, 2–6pm; Oct–May Tue 2–5pm, Wed–Sun 10am–1pm, 2–5pm. ◷Closed public holidays. ◉€3. www.fcbraganca.pt.
In front of the castle stands a 16C **pillory** *(pelourinho)*. Modified since the earliest parts were built in the 13C, the castle is surrounded by a deep moat. The tour includes the original building's dungeons.

The **Museu de Caça e Arqueológico** *(Archaeology and Hunting Museum; ◷same times as Paço Ducal; ◉€3; ✆268 980 128)* on the first floor displays a collection of Greek vases as well as items from the sport of hunting in the nearby grounds.

Although you pay to enter the castle you can climb its walls free of charge. From the top are superb views around and over the surrounding countryside, speckled with olive trees and small white villages, and to the northwest, Estremoz.

Beyond the castle stretch the old hunting grounds (**Tapada Real**) of the Dukes. Enclosed by an 18km/11mi circuit of walls, this is a delightful place where wild boar and deer roam freely, though sadly it is not open to visitors.

Beja★

*Moura, Serpa and
Castro Verde*

Having been a thriving Roman colony *(Pax Julia)*, the town became the seat of a Visigothic bishopric and then fell under Muslim control for four centuries. Today the capital of the Baixo Alentejo is a flourishing agricultural market town of white houses and straight streets.

▶ **Population:** 35 000.
🚗 **Michelin Map:** 733.
ℹ **Info:** Rua Capitão Francisco de Sousa, 25; ℘284 311 913.
▷ **Location:** Beja is 80km/ 49.5mi south of Évora, on the main railway line south from Lisbon or along the E 802 by car.
🕐 **Timing:** You should see all you need within one day. You will need longer to take the excursions to the surrounding towns.
😊 **Don't Miss:** The cloisters in the old convent.

SIGHTS

Antigo Convento da Conceição★★

🕐 *Tue Fri and Sun 9.30am–12.30pm, 2–5.15pm.* 🚫 *Public holidays. www.museuregionaldebeja.pt*

The Poor Clares Convent was founded by Dom Fernando, father of King Manuel, in 1459. The graceful Gothic balustrade crowning the church and the cloisters recalls that of the Mosteiro da Batalha. During the occupation of the town by French forces in the early 17C, Sister Mariana Alcoforada, a young nun from this convent, fell in love with a young French officer, Count Chamilly. Her letters to him, published in 1669, caused a scandal.

Today the convent houses a regional museum, also known as the **Museu da Rainha Dona Leonor**. 🕐 *Tue–Sun 9.30am–12.30pm, 2–5.15pm.* 🚫 *Public holidays.* ✏️ *€2 (no charge Sun); ticket also gives you free entry to the Museu Visigótico nearby.* ℘*284 323 351 and 284 321 465.* The Baroque **church** is richly decorated with gilded and carved woodwork from the 17C and 18C. The walls of the cloisters on the right are covered with *azulejos*.

Alter in the church, Museu da Rainha Dona Leonor, Antigo Convento da Conceição

© Jon Arnold Images/hemis.fr

Whitewashed houses, Moura

© inaquim/iStock

The chapter-house is decorated with beautiful 16C Hispano-Moorish *azulejos* from Seville and the vaulting is adorned with 18C floral motifs. A collection of crucifixes is also on display. The rooms beyond contain paintings including a *St Jerome* by Ribera (17C) and a 15C *Ecce Homo*.

The first floor contains the Fernando Nunes Ribeiro archaeological collection of engraved flagstones from the Bronze Age and Iron Age epigraphic stelae. A second convent, that of São Franciso, has been turned into a *pousada*.

Castle of Beja

© *Tue–Sun Apr–Oct 9am–noon, 2–4:30pm; Nov–Mar 9:30–noon and 2–5:30pm.* © *1 Jan, 25 Dec and local holidays.* ≈ €1.50. ℘ *284 311 912. www.cm-beja.pt.*

The town is dominated by the 13C castle's crenellated perimeter wall (housing a military museum), flanked by square towers. At one corner a high **keep**★ is reached by 197 steps, topped by pyramid-shaped merlons. The views from the top over the surrounding countryside are magnificent. The first floor, reached by a spiral staircase, has fine star vaulting resting on Moorish-style veined corner squinches.

Igreja de Santo Amaro

This small Visigothic church, parts of which date back to the 5C, now houses the Visigothic art section © *Same opening times as the Museu da Rainha Dona Leonor in the convent (& left).*

Sé (Cathedral)

Beja's cathedral looks rather dull and dour from the outside, but the interior is richly decorated.

EXCURSIONS

Moura★

52km/32mi east of Beja.

Moura, the Town of the Moorish Maiden (she is said to have opened the gates to the Christians in 1223), stands grouped round the ruins of a 13C castle, 40km/24mi west of the Spanish frontier. It was once a small spa town, whose mineral waters were regarded for their healing properties, but no longer. A morning here should suffice.

Igreja de São João Baptista★ (Church of St John the Baptist) is entered through an interesting Manueline **doorway**. Inside an elegant twisted white marble column supports the pulpit; the chancel, with network vaulting, contains a beautiful Baroque crucifixion group and the south chapel is adorned with 17C *azulejos* representing the Cardinal Virtues.

The **Mouraria** is the former Moorish quarter, with the vestiges of that occupation, which finally came to an end in 1496.

The town is also home to the **Lagar de Varras do Fojo/Museu do Azeite** (© *open Tue–Sun 9.30am–12.30pm, 2.30–5.30 pm)*, an old olive pressing factory with giant stone-wheel presses that is well worth a quick visit.

Serpa★

28km/17mi east of Beja.

A market town in the Lower Alentejo east of the Guadiana river, Serpa crowns a hilltop overlooking vast plains of wheat fields interspersed with rows of olive trees. Visitors to Serpa are sometimes serenaded by the town's traditional singers, who are genuine descendants of medieval troubadours. The town has kept its ramparts, which partially surround the town, and there are the remains of an ancient **aqueduct**, with a chain-pump at one end.

The fortified gate, the **Porta de Beja**, leads through the ramparts into the narrow streets of this whitewashed town. The main square, the **Praça da República**, is delightful with its palm and cypress and a couple of restaurants. The Igreja de Santa Maria has an interesting 13C altarpiece surrounded by 17C *aluzejos*. A street on the right leads to the **castle**; the entrance looks like a romantic 19C engraving with its crumbling tower that now forms a porch. The aqueduct is closed to the public but at one end you can see an interesting chain-pump.

At nearby Capela de Guadalupe *(follow signs to the Pousada)*, excellent views extend over the surrounding countryside. You could spend the best part of a day here.

Castro Verde

44km/27mi south of Beja.

The vast golden plains of Castro Verde, known as "Campo Branco" (white field). for the whitened hue they take on in summer, are home to a wide variety of bird species.

Take your binoculars and follow one of several environmental circuits devised by the Vale Gonçalinho Environmental Education Centre. Alternatively, hire a professional guide, who will be able to explain the habitats of the birds in the special protection zone around the Vale Gonçalinho estate.

Many birds, such as the stone curlew and black-bellied sandgrouse, come from the cereal-growing steppes of the "Alentejan hinterland". Migratory birds include the crane from Northern Europe, the lesser kestrel, the bittern and the great bustard – the largest flying bird in Europe which can grow to the size of a turky. Of the 1 500 species found in Portugal, approximately 1 350 live here. Aquatic birds such as the great crested grebe and the gadwall are drawn to the streams and weirs that criss-cross the plains. One of the most unusual is the collared pratincole, whose bird song resembles laughter. You may find it at the Monte da Rocha Dam.

Away from nature, visit the Royal Basilica and admire the view and *azulejos* that tell the story of the Battle of Ourique.

Royal basilica decorated with azulejos, Castro Verde

© Jorge Duarte Estevao/iStock

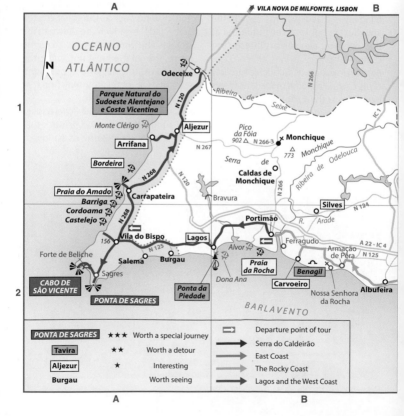

Guadiana Valley★

Between coastal Vila Real de Santo António, and Mértola (in the Alentejo), the calm waters of the Guadiana river meander through the lush valley past dazzling white villages and shores fringed with reeds and rosemary. The area, which marks the border between Portugal and Spain, is very sparsely populated. The Guadiana, one of the longest rivers of the Iberian peninsula (800km), rises in the arid plateaus of La Mancha in Spain. A lack of dams and pumping stations means that the water level can drop low so it is more navigable beyond Alcoutim.

SIGHTS

Mértola★

54km/33mi southeast of Beja.
Emerging from the middle of the vast Alentejo countryside, this town sits in the Guadiana Valley, rising in a tiered amphitheatre up a hillside overlooking the confluence of the Guadiana and the Oeiras rivers. Dominating the town are the restored keep and ruined walls of its 13C fortified castle.
Don't miss **Igreja-Mesquita**, a former mosque now converted into a church that testifies to Mértola's Moorish past.

- **Info:** Rua de São Sebastião, Castro Marim; ☎ 281 531 232.
- **Location:** Near the border with Spain, in the eastern Algarve.
- **Don't Miss:** A boat trip along the Guadiana River.
- **Timing:** Half a day is sufficient to visit the picturesque villages and to relax on the river.
- **Parking:** Easy to park in the villages.

The square plan and forest of pillars reveal the church's origin; look at the ancient *mihrab* behind the altar, the niche from which the Imam conducted prayers, and outside at the doorway leading to the sacristy.
Several museums throughout the old town catering for a different style or era. They include exhibits on Roman and Islamic periods, a sacred art museum and a museum on traditional weaving skills, as well as an ancient forge.

Alcoutim

41km/25mi southeast of Mértola.
This typical hill town, with its steep narrow streets and small whitewashed houses, some 100 years old, is best enjoyed on foot. The castle offers superb

Mértola overlooking the Guadiana

The Algarve

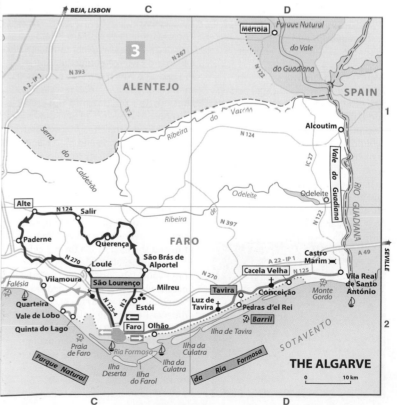

THE ALGARVE

0   10 km

The Algarve is Portugal's playground. It stretches across the whole of southern Portugal. Its name derives from the Arabic *El-Gharb* meaning "west". The terrain and climate, which is mild all year round, resemble that of North Africa, with almond trees, figs, carobs, bougainvillaeas, geraniums and oleanders. The beaches, which are extremely popular, have attracted extensive tourist development that doesn't always sit well with the landscape. The beaches in the east are excellent: long stretches of golden sand, many of which are on *ilhas* – reef-like islands, some of which you can reach only by boat. In the southwest there are more rocky little bays and coves. The west coast is wild and rugged, perfect for surfing. Of the towns, **Faro**, **Lagos**, **Albufeira** and **Portimão** are the main names you will come across, though you should also try to visit **Cabo de São Vicente** – the end of the world, or at least the most southwesterly point of mainland Europe.

Highlights

1 Feast on seafood in **Tavira's** famous fish restaurants (p204)
2 Cruise the **Ria Formosa** - spot rare birds on desert islands (p206)
3 Explore unusual sea caves from **Ponta da Piedad** (p215)
4 Climb **Cabo St Vincent** light- house for great views (p219)
5 Learn to surf on **Praia do Amado** (p220)

Along the Coast

The Algarve coastline is a split-person- ality of holiday delights: bustling resorts and beautiful sandy beaches backed by ochre cliffs in the west and tranquil, traditional villages and fishing towns in the east.

West of historic Faro, the popular coastal holiday resorts offer adrenalin- fuelled watersports, children's amuse- ment parks, street entertainment, boat trips and lively restaurants and bars. With seven golf courses, Vilam- oura is the Algarve's sporting capital; Albufeira is a nightlife mecca with clubs bursting at the seams until dawn. From Sagres and Cape St Vincent to Alzejur, the Atlantic coastline becomes much more rugged and wild. Surfers flock to the huge sandy beaches and rip-roaring curlers, while the tranquil natural park invites outdoor enthusiasts to explore its scented forests by bicycle, on foot or on horseback.

The coastline towards Faro is far less crowded and the towns more authentic. Olhão and Tavira celebrate their seafar- ing heritage with frantically noisy fish markets and fine seafood restaurants that bustle from dawn to dusk. Off its shores, the protected Ria Formosa Natural Park stretches 50km/30mi, its deserted lagoons and marshlands an important sanctuary for migratory birds, waders, flamingos, clams and oysters.

Inland Landscapes

Inland, the mood cools as the majestic mimosa-covered Monchique moun- tains and the Roman spa town, Caldas de Monchique, offer refreshing spring waters and fabulous views from the Foia and Picota peaks. As you head east, mountaintops give way to cork forests, whitewashed village houses with tra- ditional tiles and rolling countryside filled with almond, fig, olive, orange, lemon, pear and carob trees. The Gua- diana River meanders along the Spanish border, while locals weave baskets out of dwarf palm on its banks.

Cork trees, Monchique mountains
© HildaWeges/iStock

Lagoon, Ria Formosa Natural Park near Faro
© Jon Arnold Images/hemis.fr

Castro Marim

© PhotoLocation Ltd/Travel Pictures

views of the surrounding Serra da Caldeirao hills. Dating from the 14C, with a few modifications in the 17C, it served as a defence from potential Castile invasion.

The Church of Nossa Senhora da Conceição de Alcoutim dates from the 18C, but a 16C Manueline doorway remains. Other historic attractions include Roman remains and ancient copper, iron and manganese mines. Evidence of human presence dating back to the Neolithic and Chalcolithic period (around 4 000 BCE) has been found in the Alcoutim area.

Castro Marim
38km/24mi south of Alcoutin.

Castro Marim abuts a high point overlooking the marshy Lower Guadiana plain near its outflow into the Gulf of Cádiz. Facing the town across the estuary – and the border – is the Spanish town of Ayamonte. Castro Marim, which was in existence in Roman times, became the seat of the Knights of Christ on the dissolution of the Order of Templars in Portugal in 1321, until it was transferred to Tomar in 1334.

The ruins of Castro Marim's fortified castle (© *open daily 9am–1pm & 2–5pm, cm-castromarim.pt, ℘281 510746)* rth of the village, and the view parapet extends not only over sive salt marshes with their but also over the remains of

the 17C Forte de São Sebastião. Within the partly restored walls are the foundations of yet another castle dating back to the 12C.

Vila Real de Santo António
6km/3.7mi south of Castro Marim.

This border town, on the frontier with Spain in the far southeast corner of Portugal, was founded by the Marquis of Pombal in 1774 as a counterpoint to the Andalusian city of Ayamonte on the opposite bank of the Guadiana. The new town, which was built in five months, is a fine example of the town planning of the day, with its grid plan streets and whitewashed houses with distinctive roofs.

Don't miss the bustling port area, which is full of life and colour. Vila Real de Santo António has become one of the largest fishing and commercial ports on the Algarve and is also a considerable fish canning centre.

The Praça do Marquês de Pombal, the main square in the centre of the Pombaline quarter, is edged by orange trees and paved with black and white mosaics. The pedestrianised streets around the square are lined with shops selling cotton goods (table linen, sheets, towels, etc) popular with Spaniards who cross the border to buy them.

Have lunch at one of the good restaurants here before heading for the beach.

Faro★

and Around

The capital of the Algarve is sited on Portugal's most southerly headland. Faro is these days one of the most important tourist towns on the Algarve, though it manages to retain its original charm. Fishing (tuna and sardine), cork factories and marble works, food processing (beans) and canning, are still important. Faro's vast sandy beach, on an island, attracts many tourists.

> ▶ **Population:** 64 560.
> 👤 **Map:** p199.
> ℹ **Info:** Rua da Misericórdia, 8–12; ☎289 803 604. www.faroportugal.org.
> ▷ **Location:** On the Algarve coast, midway between east and west.
> ◔ **Timing:** An ideal place to be based for a week on the Algarve.
> Ⓟ **Parking:** Very difficult – stay outside the town at the Largo de São Francisco.
> ⊗ **Don't Miss:** The old town and the beaches.

OLD TOWN★

The old town lies south of the Jardim Manuel Bivar, a peaceful quarter resting in the shadow of the circle of houses that stand like ramparts around it. It has dozens of restaurants, bars, cafés and hotels though retains its charm.

The **Arco da Vila★** is the finest of the gateways in the old Alfonso wall. It has Italian-style pilasters and in a niche, a white marble statue of St Thomas Aquinas. The top of the bell tower above the arch has long been a nesting spot for a family of storks.

At the **cathedral** (◔ *open Mon–Fri 10:15am–5pm in winter/6:30pm in summer*; ◔ *closed public holidays*; ⊜€3; ☎ 289 823018), only the entrance's imposing tower-portico remains from the original church built on the site of an old mosque following the Reconquest in 1251. Today, it combines a mix of styles, including a panelled ceiling covered with 17C *azulejos* and a Renaissance altarpiece in the choir. It also preserves a medieval **bell tower**, which provides beautiful views of the town and the coast.

The **Museu Municipal** (◔ *open Jun–Sept Tue–Fri 10am–7pm, Sat–Sun 11.30am–6pm; Oct–May Tue–Fri 10am–6pm, Sat–Sun 10.30am–5pm;* ◔ *closed public holidays;* ⊜€2; ☎289 270829) is in the former Convent of Nossa Senhora de Assunção. It dates from the 16C. The archaeological collection (*Museu Arqueológico Lapilar do Infante Dom Henrique*), housed in the cloister galleries, contains various remains found at Milreu, capitals, mosaics, a Roman tomb from the 1C, a 15C sarcophagus, a 16C bishop's throne and ancient weapons and coins. Moorish earthenware jars and Mudéjar *azulejos* evoke the Muslim and post-Muslim periods of local art. The Ferreira de Almeida collection on the first floor includes sculptures, 18C paintings and Spanish and Chinese furniture. Highlights include a 3C *Mosaic of the Ocean*, found on a nearby building site in 1976 and a collection of Islamic artefacts.

The **Museu Marítimo** (◔ *open 9am–noon, 2.30–5pm;* ⊜1€, ☎289 894 990), housed in the harbour-master's office, exhibits model ships and displays of different types of fishing (tunny, sardines, octopus).

EXCURSIONS
Olhão

6km/4mi east of Faro. Allow as long as you like on the beach, but the city itself is only worth a couple of hours.
Don't miss the bell-tower of the parish church, or the Saturday market.
👪 *Kids will enjoy the beaches and safe swimming.*

Despite its very Moorish appearan the old town, Olhão is a fairly m community, having been fou fishermen in the 18C. It quickl

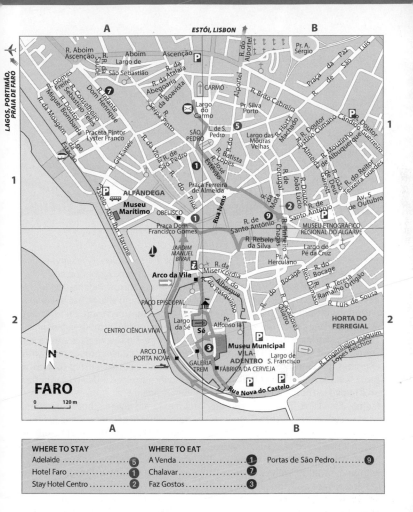

ESTÓI, LISBON

FARO

0 _____ 120 m

WHERE TO STAY		WHERE TO EAT		
Adelaide	⑤	A Venda	❶	Portas de São Pedro ....❾
Hotel Faro	❶	Chalavar	❼	
Stay Hotel Centro	❷	Faz Gostos	❸	

the busiest fishing port on the Algarve – sardines and tunny in particular – but has now been fairly extensively developed as a tourist resort with its beaches, in particular, being of major importance. Like many places in the eastern Algarve the beaches are found on *ilhas* – little reef-type islands offshore and reachable only by boat. Many visitors from nearby Faro use these beaches, which are excellent and safe.

A 17C **parish church** stands on the main street. From its belfry *(access through the first door on the right as you enter the church)*, an unusual **panorama★** of the whole town unfolds. At the back

of the church, outside, an iron grille protects the chapel of the **Nossa Senhora dos Aflitos** where, traditionally (but still today) the town's womenfolk pray for the safe return of their men from sea. A small museum, **Museu da Cidade** (⊙*open Tue–Sat 10am–5pm,* ☎*289 700103*) shows archaeological remains from Roman times to today. The beaches, reachable by ferries, are impressive: the best is **Praia de Farol**. Olhão is also the gateway for the **Parque Natural da Ria Formosa★★**, a 60km/37mi protected stretch of marshy coastline containing extensive fauna.

Aerial view of Faro and Ria Formosa Natural Park

Tavira★★

36km/22mi east of Faro. Try to spend a day here. Don't miss the Roman bridge and the fish restaurants. Kids will enjoy the beach on the Ilha da Tavira.

Tavira is a charming fishing town with whitewashed houses and numerous churches, pleasantly situated on an estuary of the Gilão river at the foot of a hill girded by the remains of ramparts built by King Dinis. The Roman bridge and Moorish walls testify to the town's long history.

The well-preserved centre is attractive with its narrow streets, river banks lined with gardens, and a lively covered market. From Praça da República you can see the **Roman bridge**. The town is full of old churches including the **Igreja da Misericórdia** and the **Igreja de Santa Maria do Castelo**, built over an old mosque. The choir holds the tomb of seven knights from the Order of St James. The 17C **Igreja de São Paulo** contains seven chapels with impressive Baroque gilded wood decoration dating from the 18C. Also see the 18C Baroque-style **Igreja do Carmo** in the Largo do Carmo, with its fine gilded wood altarpiece.

Carvoeiro★

67km/41mi west of Faro. It's the sort of place to stay, but not in July or August. Don't miss the beaches. Kids will enjoy the Slide & Splash, near Lagoa. Parking

can be difficult, especially in summer. There are car parks by the beaches.

Built into a narrow indentation in the cliff, this fishing village has become a pleasant seaside resort that has not yet been spoiled by modern buildings. The entire Algarve coast is a draw for golf and Carvoeiro is no exception with two 18-hole championship courses, a 9-hole course and a David Leadbetter Golf Academy.

A family-run diving school here offers both rental of equipment and lessons. Below Carvoeiro, the marine site of **Algar Seco★★** *(500m beyond the Miradouro de Nossa Senhora da Encarnação, plus 30min round trip on foot; leave the car in the car park)* with its dramatic rock formations, is reached through a maze (including 134 steps) of reddish rocks sculpted by the sea in the shape of peaks and arches.

On the right *(sign "A Boneca")*, a short tunnel leads under a conically formed ceiling into a cavern (converted into a refreshment room in summer) which has two natural "windows" from which there is a view encompassing the western cliffs. On the left, a path accesses a headland from which one can see the entrance to a deep underwater cave. Several blow-holes are dramatic when the sea is rough. The **sea caves** of Algar Seco can be visited by boat during the season.

🕐 *To visit, ask the fishermen in Algar Seco or on Praia do Carvoeiro.*

Cave of Benagil near Carvoeiro

Almancil

13km/8mi northwest of Faro, along the
N 125 that links Portimão to Faro.
An hour or so here to see the church is
sufficient.
This village just off the main road has a
lovely church just near it, in the hamlet
of São Lourenço, that is worth seeing.
The **Capela de São Lourenço**★★ (🕐
Oct–Apr open Mon–Fri 10am–1.30pm
& 2.30–5.30pm. May–Sep open Mon
3–6pm, Tue–Sat 10am–1pm & 3–6pm);
℘289 395 451), just 2km/1.2mi east of
Almancil, is the Romanesque chapel
of St Lawrence. Remodelled in the
Baroque period, it is decorated inside
with *azulejos*★★ dating from 1730, the
work of Bernardo, an artist known as
Policarpo de Oliviera Bernardes. The
walls and vaulting are covered with
tiles depicting the life and martyrdom
of St Lawrence: on either side of the
chancel, scenes depict the blind and
the distribution of money gained from
the sale of sacred vessels. In the nave,
on the south side, there is a meeting
between the saint and the Pope, the
saint in prison, and on the north side,
preparation for the martyr's torture
and St Lawrence being comforted by
n angel.
utside, on the church's flat east end,
ast panel of *azulejos* shows St Law-
ce and his gridiron beneath a
que scallop shell.
entro Cultural de São Lourenço
n Tue–Sun 10am–7pm; ℘289 395

475), located directly below the church
in a typical Algarve house, organises a
year-round music and arts programme
that includes performers from Portugal
and other countries.

Vilamoura

23km west of Faro. This is the sort of
place you might want to be based in for
a few days. Don't miss the marina at
night with its lively atmosphere and the
golf courses, if you are a golfer. There
are no problems with parking, other
than around the marina at night.
The resort and its southeast neighbour,
Quarteira, *are modern tourist resorts,*
with Vilamoura being one of the best
golf destinations in Europe. Quarteira's
high-rise blocks line a wide avenue beside
Vilamoura's holiday villages, hotels,
casino, seven golf courses and a vast
marina that can accommodate several
hundred yachts. The ruins of a Roman
city come as a surprise among all these
modern constructions.
The modern town of Vilamoura is a
completely man-made resort but quite
lovely with careful thought having gone
into the planning. High-rise apartments
and hotels dominate the scene but the
main feature in the town itself is the vast
marina, lined with dozens of shops, bars
and restaurants.
For famil]lies, **Aquashow Park** (*Semino*
EN 396, Quarteira: 🕐*open from 10am:*
until May 5pm, Jun and Sept 5.30pm, July
& Aug 6.30pm; 🎫*€29, child 6–10, €21.*

289 315 129; www.aquashowpark. com) is worth a visit; there are rides for adrenalin-junkies as well as gentler rides, and other ways to entertain the kids, such as the parrot show and the reptile show.

Seven golf courses include two recently designed by Nick Faldo and Christy O'Connor, Jr. The Old Course and the Victoria (designed by Arnold Palmer and host club to the 2006 World Cup of Golf) are among the best.

Silves★

18km/13mi inland from the coast road. midway between Albufeira and Lagos. Timing: To see it all you need almost a full day, including time for lunch. Don't miss the cathedral and the castle.

Of the ancient city of Xelb with its many mosques, the magnificence of the Moorish capital of the Algarve was said to eclipse even that of Lisbon. The red sandstone walls of the castle stand above the white-walled town, which rises in tiers up the hillside. Thanks to its protected position inland, in the foothills of the Serra de Monchique, Silves has managed to preserve its character with its steep, cobbled streets.

At the eastern exit of town on the N 124, the São Bartolomeu de Messines road, stands **Cruz de Portugal** (**Portuguese Cross**). On one side of this 16C Calvary is Christ crucified; on the other side is a Pietà.

The **castle** *(no parking by the castle; open mid Oct–Mar 9am–5.30pm; Apr–Jun & Sep–mid-Oct 9am–8pm; Jul & Aug: 9am–10pm; €2.80; 282 440 837)* was built in the 11C though on the site of a former Roman fortress and was occupied by the Moors. Attacked by the Crusaders, the Moors agreed to a truce and the gates were opened to let in the invading forces. Sadly the Crusaders did not hold to their word and slaughtered the Moors and their families. The gardens were spectacular at the time, and have been restored to their former glory in 2018. You can see the giant cistern from which water was fed to the town, and there are superb views from the walls.

The **cathedral★** was built on the site of a former mosque. The 13C Gothic nave and aisles have a striking simplicity; the chancel and transept are of the later Flamboyant Gothic style. The numerous tombs are said to include those of some of the Crusaders who helped to capture the town in 1242. Note the **Manueline door** opposite the cathedral's entrance. At the **Museu Arqueológico** *(open daily 10am–6pm. €2.10. 282 440 800; www.cm-silves.pt),* the collections retrace the history of the region including the Palaeolithic Age, the Iron Age and the Moorish period. Its ceramics and architectural displays are particularly well presented, although only in Portuguese!

🚗 DRIVING TOURS

EAST COAST AND OFFSHORE

From Faro to Vila Real de Santo António
65km/40.4mi. Allow a day.

From **Faro★** to the Spanish frontier the coast is broken up by several *ilhas* – sandy reefs that form the beaches of the area and are well developed with restaurants and campsites. They are linked to the mainland by boats as well as footbridges over the lagoon.

The entire coast from Ançao near Quinta do Lago to Manta Rota is a protected area, the **Parque Natural da Ria Formosa★★**, which is 60km/37mi long, and covers 18 400ha of dunes, channels and islands of great ornithological interest. There are many opportunities for deep-sea fishing expeditions and the fish restaurants are well-regarded.

▶ Continue to **Olhão**. *See OLHÃO.*

You next come to **Tavira★** *(see TAVIRA).* Before reaching **Pedras d'e Rei**, a holiday village of villas and attractive gardens with a rail link *(10min* the offshore sandbank and its be **Praia do Barril★★**.

The Renaissance church on the outskirts of **Luz de Tavira** has an attractive Manueline doorway and flame ornaments around the roof.

▷ Continue east to Cacela Velha.

Cacela Velha★

This pleasant hamlet is built around the ruins of a medieval fortress and a small church with an attractive doorway. From its rocky bluff a fine **view** unfolds over the lagoon and fishing boats below. During the summer, the main lake, with its two small restaurants, is a popular place to savour local Algarve delicacies.

Vila Real de Santo António
See VILA REAL DE SANTO ANTÓNIO.

THE INTERIOR

Circuit around Faro via the Serra do Caldeirão
107km/66.4mi. Allow a day.

This tour takes you into a relatively unknown area of the Algarve, between the limestone hills of the Serra do Caldeirão just a few kilometres (couple of miles) from the coast, yet far from its madding crowds. The flower-bedecked villages have managed to preserve their traditional appearance; handicrafts are still an important industry.

In January and February, the flowering almond trees carpet the mountains in a mass of white; spring heralds the appearance of the rock-rose with its white bloom, while in summer and winter, oranges stand out against the green backdrop of the cottage gardens. The year-round scents of almond trees, eucalyptus, pine, lavendar and rock-rose alone are worth the visit.

▷ Leave Faro on the N 2 heading northeast. After 10km/6.2mi, turn right along the Estoi road (towards Tavira).

Estoi
Estoi's main attractions are the Milreu Ruins and Estoi Palace.

Roman Ruins of Milreu
Open May–Sept Tue–Sun 10am–6pm; Oct–Apr 9am–5pm. €2. 289 997 823. http://monumentosdoalgarve.pt.
A square-shaped apse and two marble columns are all that remain of a 1C Roman settlement that was built around a temple. The brick foundations of the houses and baths surround the living quarters and pools, some of which still retain their mosaic designs. Particularly of note is the **mosaico dos peixes grandes**, a mosaic of large fish on the wall of one of the pools.

Gardens, Palácio de Estoi★★
From Estoi head 1km/0.6mi beyond Milreu.
The gardens are bordered with orange trees leading up to the Baroque façade of this small 18C palace, which is now a delightful *pousada* *See ADDRESSES.* The enclosed verandas, decorated with pools, statues, marble and earthenware vases, blue and multi-coloured *azulejos* give an overall atmosphere of romantic charm.

▷ Return to the N 2 and head north.

São Brás de Alportel
This peaceful small town is built on elevated ground dotted with white houses. The town used to be the country's main centre for cork extraction and still retains a few cork-related industries.

Museu do Traje (Costume Museum)
Open Mon–Fri 10am–1pm, 2–5pm, Sat, Sun and public holidays 2–5pm. €2. 289 840 100. www.museu-sbras.com.
This costume museum, housed in an attractive 19C bourgeois mansion, contains an interesting collection of old carts and carriages, dolls and typical local dress.
The beautiful garden of the former residence of the bishops of the Algarve can be seen in front of the museum.

Fonte Grande, Alte

© Associação Turismo do Algarve

Arbutuses abound in the surrounding fields, producing strawberry-like berries used to make the well-known **aguardente de medronho**, a local brandy.

▷ Retrace your route, then take the road to Aldeia da Tôr, close to the place where you will see a Roman bridge. Head towards Salir.

Salir

There is a fine view of the mountains from the ruined Moorish castle. To the northeast of this village, the Rocha da Pena sits atop a steep, rugged hill at an altitude of 479m with its two walls dating from the Neolithic period.

▷ Take the N124 toward Alte.

Alte★

The white houses of this attractive village with its narrow, winding streets cling to the sides of a hill in the *serra*. In the lower part of the town, two fountains, the Fonte Pequena (Small) and the Fonte Grande (Big) run as canals along shaded banks that provide a pleasant place in which to have a picnic.

▷ Rejoin the N 124. At Benafim Grande, turn right onto a small road leading to the N 270, which you join at the village of Gilvrazino. Then head towards Loulé.

▷ Continue along the N 2 for 14km/8.7mi. The road winds its way through groves of eucalyptus and pine before reaching Barranco Velho. Here, head towards Querença along the N 396.

Querença

The village nestles on the slope of a hill at an altitude of 276m. The foundation of the **Igreja de Nossa Senhora da Assunção** on the summit is attributed to the Knights Templar. Although the church was completely remodelled in 1745, it has retained its Manueline door. The interior contains some fine gilded carvings.

A Man of Wisdom

Prince Henry the Navigator, third son of King John I of Portugal, was born in Porto in 1394. (His wife Philippa was Henry IV of England's sister.) Soft spoken, devout and kind, he was sent by his father on several overseas voyages. He fell in love with the oceans and came to realise how important the sea could be to Portugal's trading interests. In 1415 he relocated to Sagres (ⓒ*see PONTA DE SAGRES*), where he founded a school of navigation, using the best Arab cartographers he could find. Theories were tested and put to practical use in expeditions that set out on voyages down the coast of West Africa. Improvements to the astrolabe and the sextant led to the prince's introduction of navigation by the stars: mariners learned to calculate their latitude from the height of the stars above the horizon and chart their positions with greater accuracy.

Loulé

The town, which was inhabited by the Romans, has preserved a few remnants from the walls of its Moorish castle. Loulé is also famous for its carnaval, reputed to be the predecessor of the famous carnival in Rio de Janeiro. Held every February, it attracts a large following with its fantastic costumes and dances. The Senhora da Piedade *romaria* held on the second Sunday after Easter originates from pre-Christian times.

▶ Return to Faro on the N 125-4.

THE ROCKY COAST

From Faro to Portimão
100km/62mi. Allow a day.

This is the Algarve's most famous stretch of coast. Ochre-coloured cliffs plunge down to the beach as far as Vilamoura, where the turquoise sea surges into coves and grottoes, some of which may be explored by boat. Unfortunately, the natural beauty has been marred in many places by extensive tourist development. Small harbours look lost among tall white apartment blocks, and in summer fishing boats are crowded out by beach umbrellas.

You arrive first in the hamlet of **São Lourenço** (*See ALMANCIL*) before going on towards **Quinta do Lago** and **Vale do Lobo**, two holiday villages with golf courses, country clubs and smart hotels around which are dotted villas among umbrella pines. There are footbridges across the lagoon to the beaches.

You next pass **Quarteira** and **Vilamoura** (*See VILAMOURA*) before reaching **Albufeira** (*See ALBUFEIRA*), **Carvoeiro** (*See CARVOEIRO*) and **Portimão** (*See PORTIMÃO*).

After Portimão comes one of the best beaches on the Algarve, Praia da Rocha.

ADDRESSES

🛏 STAY

FARO

Pensão Residencial A Doca – *Trv. Ivens, 21-1°. ℘289 823 349. 22 rooms.* Ideal location in the pedestrianised area close to the marina. The rooms are clean and light. The staircase leading to reception is a little narrow so don't take really big bags. Good value.

Adelaide Hotel – *R. Cruz das Mestras, 9. ℘289 802 383. 19 rooms.* A small hotel with big rooms (some with terraces) and pleasant furnishings. The only drawback is that many of the rooms overlook the street, which can be busy, particularly at weekends.

Residencial Avenida – *Avenida da República, 150. ℘289 823 347. 11 rooms.* Close to the bus station, so this hotel is convenient when arriving late. Rooms vary in size; some are tiny.

Hotel Afonso III – *Rua Miguel Bombardu, 64. ℘289 803 5342. http://hotelafonso.pt. 40 rooms.* A modern and central family-run hotel. Rooms are simple but are equipped with all comforts, including wi-fi. Good value.

Hotel Sol Algarve – *Rua Infante D. Henrique, 52. ℘289 895 700. www.hotelsolalgarve.com. 38 rooms.* Located, not far from downtown, but away from noise, this hotel provides every comfort (lift, WiFi, minibar, cable TV). The rooms on the third floor, with terrace are perfect. Moderate prices off-season.

Eva Senses Hotel – *Avenida da República, 1. ℘469 610 3608. http://hotel-eva-faro.h-rez.com. 134 rooms.* Close to the seafront of Faro, this hotel has some benefits, such as an on-site health club, which includes an outdoor pool and a fitness room, and balconies overlooking the sea.

Hotel Faro – *R. D Francisco Gomes, 2. ℘289 830 830. www.hotelfaro.pt. 90 rooms.* Simplicity and light are the two words that come to mind in describing the rooms at this hotel near the port. Breakfast is served on the top floor terrace, shaped like a boat and with a magnificent view over the marina and old town; rooftop bar and restaurant.

CARVOEIRO

O Castelo – *Rua do Casino, 59-61. 919 729 259. www.ocastelo.net. 12 rooms.* On the other side of the bay, a lovely castle-like guesthouse. All rooms have en suite bathrooms and WiFi.

ESTOI

Pousada do Palácio de Estói – *Rua São José. 210 407 620. www.pousadas.pt. 63 rooms.* This 18C palace 10km/6mi from Faro has been converted into a delightful hotel. The spacious rooms, furnished in traditional style in keeping with the period, exude comfort and good taste, and most have balconies from which you can look out onto Faro and the ocean. With Italian gardens, rococo tea rooms, a fine restaurant and a pool, this is the place to come for a treat.

⚥/EAT

FARO

Vivmar – *Rua Com. Francisco Manuel, 8. 916 145 584. Closed Sun.* This modest pub of the Association of Fishermen and Fishmongers of Faro is located at the foot of the ramparts, facing the harbour. Best to eat fresh fish.

Restaurante Zé Maria – *Avenida Nascente 18. 289 817 334.* A popular beach restaurant with spectacular ocean views and great sea food, including various octopus recipes and great desserts.

Adega Nova – *Rua Francisco Barreto, 24. 289 813 433. Closed Sun.* This Portuguese tavern consists of a long room, furnished with tables and wooden benches, so be prepared to share and enjoy the lively informal ambience. Portuguese specialities with fresh fish are popular, and there are giant TV screens in each corner so you need never miss a soccer match.

Sol e Jardim – *Praça Ferreira de Almeida, 22–23. 289 820 030. Closed Sun.* A good quality restaurant with a large dining room, good Portuguese food and live folk music Fridays.

Portas de Sao Pedro – *Largo do Dr. Silva Nobre 7. 289 095 433. Closed Mon & Sun.* This central restaurant serves fabulous fish-based appetizers including fried cod balls, and various bacalhao recipes. Gluten-free options available.

Dois Irmãos – *Praça Ferreira de Almeida, 15. 289 823 337. www.restaurantedoisirmaos.com.* This beautiful inn, founded in 1925, stands out as an institution. It is decorated in pleasant tiles and copper pots and serves succulent paellas, monkfish kebabs, cataplana and various meats.

Vila Adentro – *Praça Dom Alfonso III. 289 052 173. http://vilaadentro.pt.* This beautiful historical restaurant is decorated in gorgeous tiles and serves a delicious fish-based cuisine with dishes such as Cataplana or cod fillet with crab sauce. Pleasant outdoor space.

CARVOEIRO

Restaurante Boneca Bar – *Algar Seco. 282 358 391.* Situated by the rock formations at Algar Seco, this is a lively restaurant that serves good fish.

Don Carvoeiro –*Rampa do Paraiso. 282 357 830. www.doncarvoeiro.com.* Right on the cliffs overlooking the Carvoeiro beach, this this restaurant specializes in fish, but also serves its famous "Dracula Kebab," a huge skewer filled with various meats amd fish.

NIGHTLIFE

VILAMOURA

Along with Albufeira, Vilamoura has some of the Algarve's liveliest nightlife. The promenade along the **marina** has a large number of bars and restaurants to get your evening underway. Another possibility is the dinner-show at the **casino** in Vilamoura *(dinner 8.30pm; show 10.30pm; 289 310 000).* The **Dice** disco in the same building is one of the Algarve's most popular clubs *(daily).* Since clubs change frequently, it's best to check the Internet for the most popular venues.

Seafood Festivals

The delicious seafood served in the Algarve is testament to its close connections with fishing and the sea.

To witness this equation first hand, try to visit when one of the annual seafood festivals takes place.

In early August, the waterfront of Portimão comes alive when the Sardine Festival takes place. The air is filled with the smell of barbecued smoke from restaurants serving the Algarve's favourite fish with homemade bread, green peppers and boiled potatoes.

Cataplana

© Associação Turismo do Algarve

Meat eaters will find local specialities, sausages, cheeses, cured meats and regional confectionery served at stalls along the seafront. Plus there are Portuguese handicrafts to browse among and a colourful programme of entertainment, music and fireworks to enjoy.

In late July, the Fishermen Beach at Albufeira stages the Al-Buhera Festival (meaning Sea Castle, the ancient Arab name for the town). Steaming seafood and copious amounts of wine and beer are served to diverse sounds ranging from traditional Portuguese to Arab and Mediterranean music. An historical medieval re-creation and colourful parade along the streets also take place.

The Festival do Marisco (Seafood Festival), held in Olhão, six kilometres from Faro, is one of the Algarve's most important gastronomic events. Taking place every year in the first week of August, it provides an opportunity for locals and visitors to enjoy seafood served countless ways, from grilled sardines and fried shrimps to the traditional cataplana of clams, mussels, bacon, chorizo, garlic, onions and olive oil. Music and folk dancing add to the festive atmosphere.

In October and November, Alejur, on the west coast near the border with the Alentejo, celebrates the Sweet Potato and Goose Barnacles Festival.

Sardine festival

Associação Turismo do Algarve

Albufeira

Albufeira is a former Moorish stronghold that has kept its Arab name, meaning "castle on the sea". Situated midway between Faro and Lagos, it has become the most famous seaside resort in the Algarve over the past few decades, with its international visitors and fashionable nightlife. Mass tourism has altered the charm of the old fishing village in the centre. The beaches are packed all summer, and it is not the sort of place to go if you are seeking peace and quiet.

▸ **Population:** 40 828.
▸ **Michelin Map:** 733.
▸ **Info:** 5 Outubro; ☎289 585 278. www.visitalbufeira.pt.
▸ **Location:** On the Algarve coast, midway between Faro and Lagos.
▸ **Kids:** Krazy World theme park, and Zoo Marine.
▸ **Timing:** Set aside a week for this area. Try to get to all the local beaches – Praia da Galé, Praia da Oura, Praia da Falésia.
▸ **Don't Miss:** The beaches.

OLD TOWN

Relax over a freshly-squeezed orange juice in one of the many cafés in the lively town square. There are lots of shops to browse for souvenirs and street theatre to keep you entertained. The medieval centre is a maze of quaint white-washed houses and steep narrow streets. In Travessa da Igreja Velha, an old moorish arch stands on the place where a primitive mosque stood, later transformed into the town's first church

BEACHES

Huge swathes of golden sand dominate the town's three beaches. Access to the main Peneco or Túnel Beach is through a tunnel near the old town. This long stretch of sand runs the length of Albufeira and has a promenade at the far west corner which ends at the Xorino Grotto believed to have been used as a safe haven by Moors following the 13C Christian conquest of Albufeira.

Close by, Oura Beach has watersports, bars and restaurants, while Santa Eulália Beach is surrounded by craggy golden cliffs and covered with pine trees and gardens.

MUSEUMS

Worth visiting in Old Town are the **Museu de Arte Sacra** (*open daily: Winter, 10.30am–4.30pm; Summer 10.30am–4.30pm, 8–11pm; ☎289 585 526. www.cm-albufeira.pt; €2*) in the 18C church of São Sebastião, which

exhibits fine pieces of sacred art, and prints of Albufeira when it was a simple fishing village; and the **Museu Municipal de Arqueologia** (*open daily: Sept–Jun Sat–Sun, Tue and public holidays 9.30am–12.30pm, 1.30–5.30pm; Jul–Aug Sat–Sun, Tue and public holidays 9.30am–12.30pm, 1.30–5.30pm, Wed–Fri 9.30am–5.30pm; ☎289 599 508; www.cm-albufeira.pt; €1*) in the old town hall, which presents the region's history in an engaging style.

ADDITIONAL SIGHTS

▸ Krazy World Zoo

Open Jul–Aug 10am–6.30pm; rest of year, but check website for actual days, 10am–6pm. adult, €16.95, child, 4–10 €9.95, family, €43.85 (15% discount for tickets purchased online). ☎282 574 134. www.krazyworld.com.

Professional guided tours around the zoo give information about the animals' habitats. The animal shows with reptiles like alligators, iguanas and pythons are popular. A swimming pool, bouncy castles, pony rides and krazy karts also appeal to kids.

▸ Zoo Marine

Open daily from 10am, but check website for closing times, which vary. €29, children €21 children (cheaper if booked online). ☎289 560 300. www.zoomarine.pt.

Praia do Tunel, Albufeira

The focus at this enormous marine park is on fun. Kids can take part in the dolphin interaction programme after seeing a dolphin show. A huge aquarium houses 20 different ecosystems.

ADDRESSES

🏨 STAY

⊖⊖🛏 **Hotel Frentomar** – *Rua Latino Coelho, 36.* ☎289 512 005. *www.frentomar.com, 13 rooms.* Well located, in a quiet street overlooking the cliff, west of the city. Sympathetically decorated and comfortable.

⊖⊖ **Baltum** – *Avenida 25 de Abril, 26.* ☎289 589 102. *www.baltumhotel.com/en. 51 rooms.* This medium-class hotel is located centrally near the bar street. Although they lack charm, the rooms are comfortable and have balconies.

⊖⊖🛏 **Mansão Bertolina** – *Rua Joaquim Pedro Samora, 8.* ☎289 589 134. *www.cheerfulwaybertolinamansion.com. 12 rooms over 3 floors.* In a tranquil alley near the tourism office is this convivial hotel, whose well-kept rooms are simply decorated. Ask for a room overlooking the pool.

⊖⊖🛏 **Hotel Vila Recife** – *Rua Miguel Bombarda, 12.* ☎289 599 100. *Closed Oct–Mar. 92 rooms.* You will spot this large Belle Époque pension by the three white churches that surround it. Although some modern twists have been added, it maintains a calm pace

with its porch and driveway lined with palm trees.

⊖⊖🛏 **Villa São Vicente** – *Largo Jacinto Ayet.* ☎289 583 700. *www.hotelsaovicentealbufeira.com. 25 rooms.* In the centre of the old town, this luxuriously converted and peaceful 19C palace has great views over the sea and splendidly decorated rooms.

🍽 EAT

⊖⊖ **O Zuca** – *Travessa do Malpique, 6.* ☎289 588 768. Just behind the Largo Eng. Duarte Pacheco, this is one of those rare things in Albufeira – a restaurant that is not too touristy. Simple home cooking and a nice family atmosphere.

⊖⊖ **Três Coroas** – *Rua do Correio Velho, 8.* ☎289 512 640. At the top of the old city with a sea-view terrace, this restaurant serves a wide choice of dishes, with an emphasis on seafood.

⊖⊖🛏 **A Ruína** – *Cais Herculano (on the Pl. des Pescadores).* ☎289 512 094. *www.restaurante-ruina.com.* Fabulous location on the beach from where you can watch the sunset. The fish is excellent.

NIGHTLIFE

The places to be include Rua Cândido dos Reis, Rua São Gonçalo de Lagos, Rua Alves Correia or Largo Eng. Duarte Pacheco, where masses of tourists congregate. The most famous nightclubs is **Kiss** (on the beach at Praia da Oura) and Lick. Othe popular spots include **Sir Harry's Bar**, **Steps**, and **Central Planet**.

Portimão and Praia da Rocha★

Portimão is the second-largest town on the Algarve and is a fishing port nestled at the back of a bay. The best **view**★ is at high tide from the bridge across the Rio Arade at the end of the bay. The town specialises in the canning of tunny (small tuna) and sardines, but is also a major tourist resort – though that is more based on Praia da Rocha, very close by, which contains the town's famous beach.

OLD TOWN

Portimão itself is a large working town that has also succumbed to mass tourism. In summer it is mainly block-booked by holiday companies. But having said that, it still has its charm particularly in the back streets near the **Largo da Barca**, the old fishermen's and tradesmen's quarters.

The old town is dominated by the architecture of the late 19C and early 20C. The houses, with their wrought-iron balconies and ornate stonework around the windows and doors are decorated with balustrades of stone and ceramics and walls covered with tiles.

▶ **Population:** 55 614.
ⓒ **Michelin Map:** 733; p192-193.
🛈 **Info:** Avenida Tomás Cabreira. ☎282 419 132.
◖ **Location:** In the western part of the Algarve coast.
👥 **Kids:** The beaches; boat cruises to exciting sea-caves.
☺ **Don't Miss:** The *azulejos* on benches in the Largo 1° de Dezembro.

PRAIA DA ROCHA★

Portimão has its "own" resort in nearby Praia da Rocha, where the glorious three-kilometre Blue Flag beach stretches out, broken up by strange rock formations that the sea has carved out over tens of thousands of years.

There are plenty of restaurants and bars, and you can take cruises out either for the day (big game fishing is very popular) or for a couple of hours to nearby sea-caves. There are lots of good golf courses nearby, plus excellent water-sports and facilities for beach volleyball, basketball and football.

At night, the resort comes alive with a wide range of bars, clubs and restaurants serving local dishes and international cuisine. There is even a casino.

Praia da Rocha

© René Mattes/hemis.fr

🚗 DRIVING TOUR

LAGOS AND THE WEST COAST
From Portimão to Odeceixe
140km/87mi. About one day.

The south coast after the busy town of Lagos attracts fewer tourists. Its small fishing villages have managed to retain some of their character. The west coast heading north from Cabo de São Vicente is still quite wild with tall, grey cliffs. The hinterland is undulating, with eucalyptus, pine trees and aloes, while the bright white villages have remained unspoiled. The region is ideal for anyone seeking a quiet spot and is particularly popular with campers.

There are many golf courses along the southwest coast, normally less busy than those around Vilamoura, for example, and at Sagres and north of Vila do Bispo there are surf schools.

Lagos★
🚗*See LAGOS.*

Several roads lead southward between Lagos and Vila do Bispo to beaches and fishing villages such as **Burgau** and **Salema**.

Ponta da Piedade★★
The **setting★★** of this seaside resort, its **sea caves** and clear green sea make it especially attractive. You will find some of the most spectacularly stunning and sometimes bizarre **rock formations** and sandy coves here. Praia da Dona Ana, with its steep steps down to the beach, is one of the most photographed; Praia do Camilo is tucked away between high sandstone cliffs. The rock formations have created some spectacular sea caves that are most impressive when viewed from the sea. Local fishermen will take you by boat to explore them.

Vila do Bispo
The bright white village is a junction for roads to the north, the Algarve and Sagres. The Baroque **church** has a chancel in gilded wood and its walls are decorated with *azulejos*. A door to the left of the chancel opens into a small museum which contains a beautiful crucifix. You then reach the very western end of the Algarve.

Ponta de Sagres and Cabo de São Vicente★★★
🚗*See p219.*

▷ Return to Vila do Bispo.

The **Torre de Aspa**, *(6km/3.7mi west, take the Sagres road, then bear right and follow the signs)*, which stands at an altitude of 156m, has a good **view★** of Cabo de São Vicente and Ponta de Sagres.

Castelejo, **Cordoama**, **Barriga** and **Mouranitos beaches** may be reached by car from Vila do Bispo. The scenery is wild with tall, grey cliffs. At **Carrapateira** a road runs around the headland west of the village.

There are fine views of the steep rock-face and Bordeira's long sandy beach before you approach **Aljezur★**, which consists of white-walled houses with brightly painted borders.

A road from here leads west *(9km/5.6mi)* to **Arrifana** with its beach and fishing harbour nestling at the foot of a tall cliff. The whole of this coast is perfect for surfing and many surf camps, official and unofficial, can be found, especially in spring when the Atlantic surf is at its best. Finally you come into **Odeceixe** through eucalyptus trees. A road runs for 4km/2.5mi alongside the Seixe, a small coastal river and estuary with a **beach** at its mouth.

Monchique and its Spas – Inland a short distance from the west coast, you come to the mountain village of Monchique, in itself nothing much to speak of, though its twice-weekly markets are famed throughout the Algarve, especially for its smoked meats and sausages.

Near Monchique you'll find the natural spas at **Caldas de Monchique**, a village that has been totally renovated and now has hotels and other attractions surrounding its natural spa centre.

Lagos★

Lagos was the capital of the Algarve from 1576 to 1756. Today, in spite of great popularity with tourists, it has managed to preserve both character and charm with its fort, walls and old quarter. The most attractive approaches to Lagos are from Aljezur in the north along the N 120 or from Vila do Bispo in the west along the N 125. From both of these roads there are views★ of the town and the large marina that now lines the bay. Apart from being a seaside resort and a fishing port well sheltered by the Ponta da Piedade promontory, Lagos is also an important yachting centre organising international regattas.

A BIT OF HISTORY

Lagos was an important harbour at the time of the Great Discoveries, and it was from here that most of the African expeditions put to sea. It served as Prince Henry the Navigator's principal maritime base and as the port of registry to Gil Eanes who, in 1434, rounded Cape Bojador for the first time in history. This is a point on the west coast of the Sahara which, until then, had been the last outpost of the habitable world. On Prince Henry's orders, one expedition followed another down the coast of Africa, each time adding to the knowledge of ocean currents and improving navigational techniques.

▶ **Population:** 31 049.
⏱ **Map:** p213.
ℹ **Info:** Praça Gil Eanes; 𝒫 282 763 031; www.cm-lagos.pt.
▶ **Location:** On the Algarve coast, 23km/14mi west of Portimão.
🕐 **Timing:** Visit the sights in the morning and the beach in the afternoon.
👁 **Don't Miss:** The church of Santo António.

SIGHTS

Praça da República

A **statue** of Prince Henry the Navigator, erected in 1960 to commemorate the 500th anniversary of his death, stands in the middle of the square.

Slave Market

🕐*Open Mon–Sat 10am–6pm; times vary in winter.* 🕐*Closed public holidays.* 👓*€3.* 𝒫*282 762 301.*

The house with arcades (built after the earthquake in 1755) on the right of the square is the former slave market, **Mercado de Escravos**, home to a compelling exhibit. Lagos´ original slave market, built in 1444, was Europe's first. It was here during the 15C where enslaved people, who had been captured, and transported from Africa, were sold.

Old town viewed from the fishing port

© Jon Arnold Images/hemis.fr

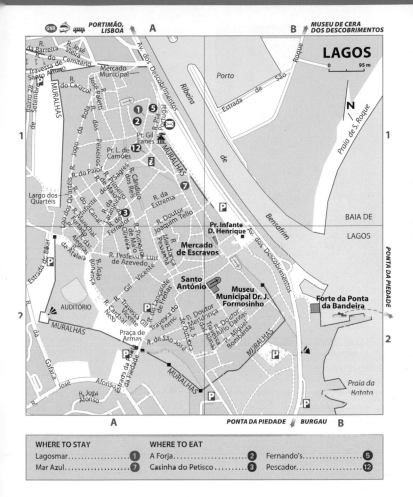

LAGOS

0   95 m

N

Porto

Praia de S. Roque

BAIA DE

LAGOS

PONTA DA PIEDADE

Forte da Ponta da Bandeira

Mercado Municipal

Pr. Gil Eanes

Pr. L. de Camões

Largo dos Quartéis

Pr. Infante D. Henrique

Mercado de Escravos

Santo António

Museu Municipal Dr. J. Formosinho

AUDITÓRIO

Praça de Armas

Praia da Batata

MURALHAS

PONTA DA PIEDADE   BURGAU

A   B

WHERE TO STAY		WHERE TO EAT		
Lagosmar	❶	A Forja	❷	Fernando's ❺
Mar Azul	❼	Casinha do Petisco	❸	Pescador ⑫

Museu Municipal

🕐 *Open Tue–Sun 9.30am–12.30pm, 2-5pm.* 🚫 *Closed public holidays.* ✆€3. 📞 282 762 301.

The regional museum adjoining the Igreja de Santo António contains an interesting archaeological collection (coins and fragments of mosaics) and an ethnographical section devoted to the Algarve (note the cork work).

Igreja de Santo António★

Access via Museu Municipal.

The plain façade gives no inkling of the exuberance and virtuosity of the **Baroque decoration★** inside. Outstanding are the ceiling painted in false relief, the Eucharistic symbols and statues of gilded wood in the chancel, the walls and the gallery ceiling.

Forte da Ponta da Bandeira

🕐 *Open Tue–Sun 10am–12.30pm, 2–5pm.* 🚫 *Closed public holidays.* ✆€2, €5 for combined ticket also incl. church and slave market. 📞 282 780 060.

The 17C fort juts out into the sea guarding a small harbour. There are boat trips from the harbour to Ponta da Piedade. Cross the drawbridge to enter the inner courtyard. The halls contain displays on the Great Discoveries. The chapel is decorated with 17C **azulejos**. There is a **view** from the terrace of the town and the coast.

Belfry of Igreja de Santo António

© Rene Drouyer/Bigstockphoto.com

ADDRESSES

🏠 STAY

🛏 **Hostel Caravela** – *Rua 25 de Abril, 16.* ℘*917 364 080. 4 rooms.* In the town centre, this lodging is simply furnished. Some rooms have a shower and wash basin, while others have a bath.

🛏🛏 **Pensao Dona Ana**– *Alameda Doutor Armando Soares Ribeiro.* ℘*967 550 622. www.pensaodonana.com. 13 rooms. Closed Nov–Mar.* The friendly staff and the location right next to te beach make this simple hotel an ideal stay in summer for no-frill travelers. The town is a 20-minute walk away.

🛏🛏🛏 **Lagos Atlantic Hotel** – *Estrada do Monte Carpineto, 9.* ℘*282 761 527. 18 rooms.* Just 750 m away from the beach of Porto de Mos, this 4-star hotel offers A/C, private bathroom in every room, wi-fi, and flat-screen TV. There's also a nice barbecue area that can be used by guests.

🛏🛏 **Hotel Mar Azul** – *Rua 25 de Abril, 13.* ℘*282 770 230. 18 rooms.* A central location is one of the benefits of this guesthouse, which offers small, but cheerful and comfortable rooms. Choose the ones with sea views. Internet access.

🛏🛏🛏 **Hotel Lagosmar** – *Rua Dr. Faria e Silva, 13.* ℘*282 763 523. www.lagosmar. com. 45 rooms.* Just a short walk from the beach and marina, this family-run hotel provides good service. The roof terrace affords great views. Rooms are much cheaper in low season.

🛏🛏🛏🛏 **Riomar** – *Rua Cândido dos Reis, 83.* ℘*282 770 130. www. hotelriomarlagos.com. 42 rooms.* This modern hotel resides on a calm street in the center of town. Most rooms have a balcony with sea views or views of the roofs of Lagos. The nearest beach is just five minutes' walk away.

🛏🛏🛏🛏 **Marina Club** – *Marina de Lagos.* ℘*282 790 600. www.marinaclub. pt. 141 apartments.* Self-catering studios and larger apartments are available here, some of which have great views onto the swimming pool. Fitness room, spa, and indoor and outdoor pools.

🛏🛏🛏🛏 **Quinta das Barradas** – *Odiáxere, 5km/3mi from Lagos, in the middle of the countryside.* ℘*282 770 200. www.quintadasbarradas.com. 15 rooms.* A very pleasant 19C *quinta* renovated and converted into a guesthouse. This is a rural place to stay, surrounded by lush vegetation and near the canal that leads to the dam. Close to the beaches.

🍽 EAT

🍴 **Padaria Central** – *Rua 10 de Maio.* ℘*282 763 994.* One of the best pastry shops in town. Also has a few savory tarts for a small lunch or snack.

🍴 **Millennium Jardim** – *Rua 25 de Abril, 78.* ℘*282 762 897.* Behind large railings, this restaurant has a delightful mezzanine and patio with a fountain. It serves classic Portuguese food and pizzas.

🍴🍴 **D Henrique** – *Rua 25 de Abril, 75.* ℘*282 763 563.* Perfect for a romantic dinner. Elegant room with Sienna-coloured walls, marble floors, and zealous service. The food (international menu and Portuguese dishes) is delicious and reasonably priced.

🍴🍴🍴 **Restaurante dos Artistas** – *Rua Cândido dos Reis, 68.* ℘*282 760 659. www.artistasrestaurant.com. Closed Sun.* A chic and refined restaurant for a special occasion. Beautifully presented food is inventive and inspired by Southeast Asia. The patio with trees is ideal for a romantic candlelight dinner. Prices are high but they are fully justified, and the service is professional.

Ponta de Sagres and Cabo de São Vicente★★★

The windswept headland falling steeply to the sea is the southwest extremity of mainland Europe. It was here, facing the Atlantic Ocean, the great unknown, that Prince Henry the Navigator retired in the 15C to found the Sagres School of Navigation, which would prepare the way for the Great Discoveries.

◔ **Michelin Map:** 733; p192-193

▤ **Info:** Rua Comandante Matoso, Sagres; ☏282 624 873.

◗ **Location:** The most southwesterly tip of mainland Europe.

◕ **Timing:** An afternoon excursion – Sagres first, then the Cape.

▣ **Parking:** No problems in Sagres or at Cabo de São Vicente.

◈ **Don't Miss:** The views from the Cape – especially at sunset.

PONTA DE SAGRES★★★

The headland is partially occupied by the remains of a 16C **fortress** *(◕open daily 9.30am–8pm, until 5.30pm from Oct–Apr; ◕closed 1 May and 25 Dec; ☏282 620 140).*

The entrance tunnel leads into a vast courtyard with an immense wind compass 43m in diameter. A cistern tower, former dwellings and barracks, and the old parish church of Nossa Senhora da Graça also remain. A temporary exhibit area, multimedia centre, shops and cafeteria are also on-site.

This meeting place for astronomers, cartographers and seamen offers spectacular views over the sea and the Cape of São Vicente. The area is, of course, very popular with surfers.

CABO DE SÃO VICENTE★★★

Continental Europe towers above the ocean at a height of 75m.

▨ There is an exhilarating walk along the top of the cliffs from Sagres, 6km/3.7mi each way, wild and windy but it's worth it (there are cafés along the way).

Otherwise, there is not much at the Cape, since most of the buildings were destroyed by Sir Francis Drake in 1587. A tall lighthouse guides hundreds of vessels as they pass by. With a range of 95km/59mi, this is one of Europe's most powerful beams. Watch fishermen land their catch as the sea rushes through the "blow holes" in cliffs.

Cliffs of the Cabo de São Vicente

© Neale Clark/age fotostock

Praia da Amado, Costa Vicentina

© Jon Arnold/hemis.fr

Costa Vicentina and Natural Park of SW Alentejo★★

One of the best preserved natural areas in Europe, the park stretches from Burgau in the southwest Algarve to Sines in the southern Alentejo. All along the coast, this wild protected area comprises sand dunes, pine forests and dramatic cliffs. To enjoy this remote area at its most peaceful, take the back roads, which are often bumpy and run between fragrant scrubland. They lead to huge and deserted beaches and small rocky coves where fishermen tease sea bass and bream from the waters. Away from the coast, small serene villages nestle in the valleys. Far away from the crowds, wilderness lovers can enjoy its rolling waves and the flight of migratory birds such as eagles, peregrine falcons and buzzards.

COSTA VICENTINA
Carrapateira
Close to this small town of whitewashed houses and a handful of shops and cafés are two fabulous surfing beaches. **Praia do Amado★**, a kilometre south, stretches along a beautiful sandy cove, where surf schools offer lessons to beginners and advanced surfers. It can be a little too windy for some sunbathers. A path to the north leads to the Pontal viewpoint, where people gather to watch fabulous sunsets.

▪ **Info:** LG do Mercado, Aljezur, &282 998 229; Rua Comandante Matoso, Sagres. &282 624 873.
▸ **Location:** Stretching along the far western coastline from Sagres to Aljezur.
▪▪ **Kids:** Surfing on the wide sandy beaches.
◔ **Timing:** You could easily spend a week or two here.

On the other side, **Praia da Bordeira★** *(also accessible by road)* is a large crescent beach lined with dunes. The silted river estuary forms a sheltered site for swimming. The **Museum of the Sea and Land** *(◔open Tue–Sat 10am–4:30pm. ⊛€2.70.)* traces the community's close ties with this protected area.

Aljezur and surroundings
This small market town is built on a hillside through which a river, probably of Arab origin, flows. The 10C castle, built on a peninsula, refers to an ancient Muslim presence in the region. From the ramparts, the view is magnificent. As you climb up to the castle, you pass the **Antoniano Museum** (◔open Jun–Sept Tue–Sat 10am–1pm, 2–6pm; Oct–May 9am–1pm, 2–5pm. ⊛€2.20. &282 991 011), the **Municipal Museum,** and

the **Museum of Sacred Art**. The Misericórdia church (16C) is next door.

Some 9km/5,5mi south of Aljezur, **Praia da Arrifana★** nestles between high cliffs. Farther north, 8km/5mi from Aljezur, **Praia Amoreira** is ideal for families.

Odeceixe

North of Aljezur 17km/10mi, this pretty village nestled beside the Seixe River has narrow streets around a tiny main square. The meandering river, which marks the border between the Algarve and Alentejo, leads to a beautiful beach, just 4km/2mi away, popular with windsurfers, and thanks to its being one of the most sheltered beaches on this stretch of coast, families. The mill offers views over the surrounding countryside.

COSTA ALENTEJANA
Zambujeira do Mar

This small fishing village is perched on a cliff above beaches and reefs battered by the waves. Every summer in early August, the resort is stirred from its slumbers by the Sudoeste rock festival, when nearly 35 000 fans descend on the town to hear reputable artists such as Massive Attack, Jamiroquai, Damian "Jr. Gong" Marley and Yellow Claw.

The main beach, below the village, is relatively sheltered. South of the beautiful Praia Carvalhal, there is a supervised swimming area in summer; 3km/1.8mi to the north, the small tranquil Porto das Barcas nestles in the hollow of a cliff. Farther on, the Cabo Sardão promontory provides spectacular views.

Vila Nova de Milfontes★

Located at the mouth of the River Mira, this lovely resort takes advantage of its white sand beaches and is busy in summer. Perched on a rocky hill overlooking the bay is the fort of São Clemente. This small 17C castle, now draped in ivy and redeveloped into a hotel, was originally built to defend the village from frequent pirate attacks.

© jcncopland/iStock

18C azulejo showing different types of caravel

The Caravel

One of Portugal's most significant contributions to maritime history was the **caravel**. Developed from 13C Portuguese fishing boats, that were based on the medieval Islamic qarib used in Spain, this type of light and highly agile sailing ship, was widely used in the 15C–17C in Europe, particularly for exploring uncharted seas. Caravels were rigged with lateen (triangular) sails, which enabled them to sail windward (using wind from the side of the ship to tack or turn against the wind). These elegant crafts superseded the oared galley, generally measured about 23m in length, with two or three masts (later versions added a fourth with square rigging for running before the wind). The caravel was capable of remarkable speed, and was well-adapted to long voyages. Two of the three ships under the command of Christopher Columbus in 1492, the *Niña* and the *Pinta*, were caravels. Sadly, the caravel is no longer in use, not even for exhibit purposes.

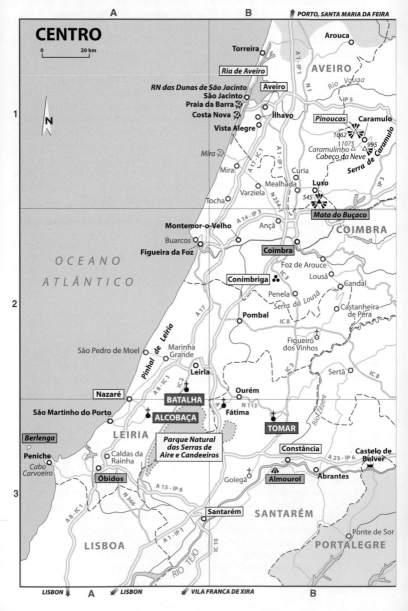

CENTRO

0   20 km

N

Arouca

Torreira

Ria de Aveiro

AVEIRO

A 1 - IP 1

Rio Vouga

N 1

IP 5

RN das Dunas de São Jacinto
São Jacinto
Praia da Barra
Costa Nova
Vista Alegre

Aveiro

Ilhavo

Pinoucas   Caramulo

1062

1075

995

Caramulinho △ △
Cabeço da Neve

Serra de Caramulo

IP 3

Mira

Mira

Curia

A 17 - IC 1

A 1 - IP 1

Mealhada

Varziela

N 234-1

Luso

545

Mata do Buçaco

Tocha

A 14 - IP 3

Ança

COIMBRA

Montemor-o-Velho

Buarcos

Figueira da Foz

Coimbra

OCEANO
ATLÂNTICO

Foz de Arouce

IC 3

Lousã

Conímbriga

Candal

Penela

Serra da Lousã

Castanheira
de Pêra

Pombal

IC 8

A 17

Figueiró
dos Vinhos

São Pedro de Moel

Pinhal de Leiria

Marinha
Grande

IC 3

Sertã

IC 8

Leiria

A 8 - IC 1

IC 2

Nazaré

Ourém

BATALHA

A 1

N 113

Fátima

Rio Tejere

São Martinho do Porto

ALCOBAÇA

TOMAR

Berlenga

LEIRIA

*Parque Natural
das Serras de
Aire e Candeeiros*

Constância

A 23 - IP 6

Castelo de
Belver

Peniche

*Cabo
Carvoeiro*

Caldas da
Rainha

Golegã

Almourol

Abrantes

Óbidos

A 15 - IP 6

A 8 - IC 1

N 366

Santarém

SANTARÉM

Ponte de Sor

IC 10

LISBOA

A 1 - IP 1

RIO TEJO

PORTALEGRE

Centro

» Coimbra and the Costa de Prata   p224
» Viseu and Serra da Estrela   p270

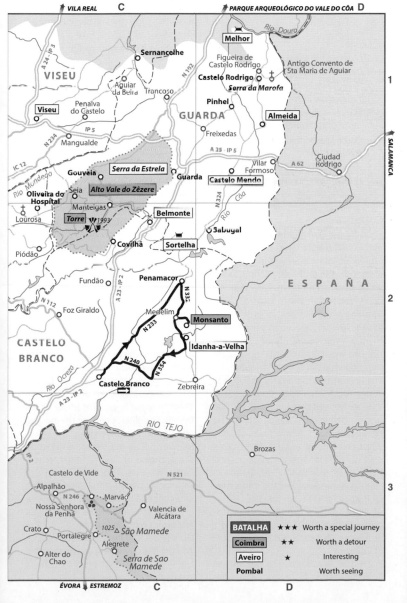

Coimbra is situated between Porto and Lisbon, inland from the coast. It boasts Portugal's oldest and most prestigious university, established in the 16C, and a wealth of historic monuments and academic traditions. The "Silver Coast" is known for its fabulous white sandy beaches, which extend from just beyond Aveiro in the north to Peniche in the south, and also for the size of its waves, especially around Nazaré. Impressive castles, 3C Roman ruins, convents, churches and museums are witness to the region's rich historical heritage. Curative springs, lush forests and prehistoric rock art dating back some 30 000 years provide a wealth of natural treasures. The region is also an important centre for porcelain, crystal and bobbin lace.

Highlights

1 Listen to the *fado* of **Coimbra** over a late-night drink (p234)
2 Picnic among 300 exotic trees at the **Buçaco Forest** (p235)
3 Marvel at amazing 3C Roman mosaics at **Conímbriga** (p237)
4 Cruise around the canals of **Aveiro** (p240)
5 Ride a jeep to the **Penascosa rock art engravings** (p247)

Coimbra

Coimbra is a fascinating university city and a great place to start exploring this region. Boasting a wealth of academic traditions, the entire city comes to life when students hit town. Early May is a great time to visit: the Queima das Fitas (Burning of the Ribbons) kicks off week-long festivities celebrating the end of the academic year. Different coloured ribbons worn on students' gowns are burned in the old cathedral square.

The university is famous for its Baroque library, commissioned by King Dom João V (1706–50) and housing some 250 000 books. Other must-sees include the New Cathedral, the Holy Cross Church, which contains the tomb of the first king of Portugal, Dom Afonso Henriques, and the Convento de Santa Clara-a-Nova. A short bus ride away are the impressive 3C Roman ruins at Conímbriga.

At night soak up the charged atmosphere in one of the many lively bars and listen to people singing the *fado* of Coimbra.

For nature, head north to the Buçaco Forest near the Luso spa, which has more than 700 trees, including impressive Mexican cedars. Take a picnic or enjoy a walking tour to Fonte Fria, a sparkling waterfall cascading down 144 stone steps.

Region

The fishing port of Aveiro, 39 miles north of Coimbra, provides a Portuguese twist on Venice, its charming small bridges criss-crossing the canals. Explore the old city by boat, bicycle or on foot, marvelling at its fine churches, cathedral and buildings, some in Art Deco style.

Just 2.5km/1.5mi south of Ílhavo, Vista Alegre has been an important centre of porcelain in Portugal; a small museum explains the development of the craft. Chill out on one of the glorious beaches nearby. The Reserva Natural das Dunas de São Jacinto has some of the best preserved sand dunes in Europe.

The Palaeolithic rock art discovered at the Parque Arqueológico do Vale do Côa in 1992 is certainly worth a detour. The long drive to this isolated area – situated on the River Douro close to the Spanish border – is well worth the effort. Dating back some 30 000 years, the three main sites provide an impressive artistic record from the Neolithic period to the modern age. Pre-book a guided tour.

Midway between Coimbra and Lisbon are a clutch of fascinating towns – Leiria, Batalha, Alcobaça, Ourém and Fátima – crowned with historic castles, churches and monasteries. The Sanctuary of Fátima is one of the world's most important religious sites.

Óbidos is a fine fortified medieval city, and the Ilha da Berlenga is worth a boat trip from the fishing port of Peniche to see its bird colony.

Coimbra★★

and Around

Under the watchful eye of the old university's tall tower, Coimbra majestically stands on a hillside, at the foot of which flows the Mondego. Many poets, inspired by the romantic setting★, have immortalised the charm of the city, an old capital of Portugal, and have helped to make it a centre of arts and letters. Although the town has spread substantially over recent decades, and has been surrounded by modern districts, the centre is still distinctly divided into the upper town (*A Cidade Alta*), the university and episcopal quarter, and the lower town (*A Cidade Baixa*) or shopping area.

▶ **Population:** 105 842.
◉ **Maps:** p226 and p229.
🅸 **Info:** Praça da Republica, ℰ239 488 120. www.turismodocentro.pt.
◐ **Location:** Midway between Porto and Lisbon, inland a little.
👥 **Kids:** Portugal dos Pequeninos.
◉ **Timing:** Allow a day.
🅿 **Parking:** There is a large parking area *(free)* on the south side of the Santa Clara bridge, along the banks of the Mondego river.

A BIT OF HISTORY

The University

The oldest university in Portugal was founded in Lisbon by King Dinis in 1290 and transferred to Coimbra in 1308. In 1537 Coimbra became its permanent home. Teachers from Oxford, Paris, Salamanca and Italy were drawn to it, making the town one of the most important humanist centres of the period.

Coimbra School of Sculpture

In 1530 several French sculptors formed a group of artists under the protection of their patron, Cardinal Georges d'Amboise. They were joined by a few prominent Portuguese artists of the day and created a school of sculpture in the town. Their art was inspired by Italian decorative forms: doorways, pulpits, altarpieces and the low reliefs surrounding altars in local churches were delicately carved out of Ança stone.

Student Life

The city, peaceful in the summer, reawakens at the beginning of the academic year and the return of the 20 000 students, many of whom live in groups known as "republics"*(◒see p231)*. Coloured ribbons denote their faculty.

Old Town, Coimbra

© José Antonio Moreno Moreno/age fotostock

Cloisters, Sé Velha

© LoisClare/iStock

OLD TOWN★
AND UNIVERSITY

The old town resides on the Alcáçova hill, reached by a tangle of narrow alleys cut by steps with expressive names such as Escadas de Quebra-Costas (Broken Ribs Steps).

Porta de Almedina

This gateway with an Arab name (*medina* means city in Arabic) remains from the medieval wall. It is topped by a tower and adorned with a statue of the Virgin and Child, which stands between two coats of arms.

Sé Velha★★

🕒*Open Mon–Fri 10am–5.30pm, Sat 10-6.30pm, Sun 11-5pm* ⊘*Closed public holidays.* ⊛€2.50. 🖉239 825 273.

The **old cathedral**, Portugal's earliest, was built between 1140 and 1175 by two French master craftsmen in a fortress-like style (the Moors were still a threat at the time). In the Interior a wide gallery above the aisles opens onto the nave by means of a graceful triforium with Byzantine capitals, which, like the lantern over the transept crossing, show Oriental influence. At the high altar, the Flamboyant Gothic **altarpiece★** in gilded wood is the work of Flemish masters Olivier de Gand (Ghent) and Jean d'Ypres. At the base, the four Evangelists support the Nativity and the Resurrection; above, surrounded by four saints, an attractive group celebrates the Assumption of the Virgin.

In the **Capela do Sacramento★** there is a fine Renaissance composition by Tomé Velho, one of Jean de Rouen's disciples. Below a figure of Christ in Benediction surrounded by ten Apostles, the four Evangelists face the Virgin and Child and St Joseph across the tabernacle.

The late 13C **cloisters** are an example of transitional Gothic architecture; they were restored in the 18C. Blind arcades are surmounted by round bays filled with a variety of tracery. In the chapter-house, on the south side, are several tombs, including that of Dom Sesnando, the first Christian governor of Coimbra, who died in 1091.

Museu Nacional de Machado de Castro★★

🕒*Open Tue 2–6pm, Wed–Sun 10am–6pm.* ⊘*Closed 1 Jan, Easter Sunday, 1 May, 25 Dec.* ⊛€6. *Sun from 2pm free* 🖉239 853 070.
www.museumachadocastro.gov.pt.

Listed as a National Monument, the museum building sits on a Roman **cryptoporticum**, the best preserved Roman building in Portugal.

Occupying what was once a medieval bishops' palace, this vast and fascinating museum was recently renovated and expanded to celebrate its 100th birthday (1911–2011). Named after the sculptor **Machada de Castra**, who was

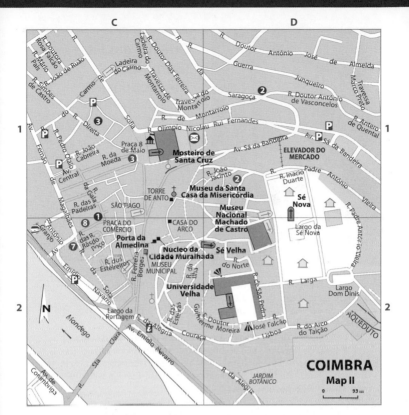

Universidade Velha

© Paulo Resende/iStock

born in Coimbra in 1731, the museum showcases exquisite sculptures, paintings, textiles, jewellery and furniture from the disbanded monasteries and convents in the diocese of Coimbra. The collections reflect the richness and high culture of the Catholic church and its patrons, especially during the Middle Ages and the Renaissance.

To peruse these collections is like once again living through the main artistic fashions that dominated Europe from

Queima das Fitas (Burning of the Ribbons)

The ribbons worn on the students' black capes indicate academic faculties: blue for arts, yellow for medicine, red for law. At the beginning of May, the old cathedral square is the setting for a festival marking the end of the university year, during which the ribbons are burned. A throng of students gather to hear the traditional serenade, the *Song of Coimbra*, that officially starts one vast, week-long party fuelled by free beer handed out by breweries. It can get pretty wild.

Countless cultural events are held during the week, the most well known being, among others, the Sarau Académico (Academic Social Gathering), the Baile de Gala (Gala Ball), the Garraiada (Bullock Fight) in Figueira da Foz, and the Chá Dançante (Tea Dance).

One of the most well-attended events takes place in the Largo da Feira. There, the *grelo* (student's badge consisting of a ribbon of the colour of his or her faculty) is burned in the chamber pot used during the initiation rites (*praxe*) that took place in students' first year at university. The burning symbolises the new status of the graduates.

Celebrations follow with students waving to the crowd from cars as they head towards the Baixa (downtown area), sharing their joy and exuberance with the city.

Join in the parties and celebrations – it's a wonderful, colourful spectacle. This is a week when Coimbra doesn't sleep!

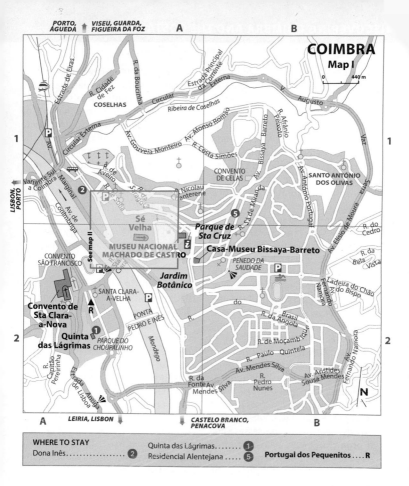

COSELHAS

Ribeira de Coselhos

CONVENTO DE CELAS

SANTO ANTÓNIO DOS OLIVAS

Sé Velha

Parque de Sta Cruz

MUSEU NACIONAL MACHADO DE CASTRO

Casa-Museu Bissaya-Barreto

PENEDO DA SAUDADE

CONVENTO SÃO FRANCISCO

Jardim Botânico

SANTA CLARA-A-VELHA

Convento de Sta Clara-a-Nova

Quinta das Lágrimas

PARQUE DO CHOUPALINHO

PONTA PEDRO E INÊS

Mondego

N

LEIRIA, LISBON   CASTELO BRANCO, PENACOVA

WHERE TO STAY

Dona Inês................... **2**	Quinta das Lágrimas........ **1**		
	Residencial Alentejana **5**	Portugal dos Pequenitos .... **R**

---

the 12C to 18C. Highlights include a small 14C **statue**★ of a medieval knight and the silver-gilded **chalice of Gueda Mendes** (1152).

Sé Nova

🕐 *Open Tue–Sat 9.30am–12,30pm, 2pm-6pm, Sun for services only.* ✆€1. 🕐 *Closed public holidays.* ✆ 239 823 138.

The **"new" cathedral**, the construction of which started in 1598, was part of the Jesuits' college of the "Eleven Thousand Virgins" until the order was disbanded in ˹59. The façade comprises two super-ˑosed sections; the four niches in the ˑˑr part house statues of saints from ˑˑociety of Jesus.

ˑˑt, single-nave interior is covered ˑˑrel vault topped by a high lan-ˑˑ Baroque style predominates ˑˑ chapels and the high altar,

where an imposing gilded wood altar-piece and a magnificent silver throne are of particular note. The baptismal font to the left of the entrance is Manueline in style and was part of the old cathedral.

Universidade Velha★★

🕐 *Open 5 Mar–28 Oct daily 9am–7pm; 10.30am-7pm rest of year.* 🕐 *Closed 24–25 Dec, 31 Dec–1 Jan.* ✆€2– €12. ✆ 239 859 884. www.uc.pt.

The old university is housed in buildings that once belonged to the royal palace and were restored and modified to become the Paço dos Estudos in 1540. The **courtyard** *(pátio)* is dominated by an 18C tower. To the left, the courtyard extends to a terrace that provides a fine view of the Mondego.

Opposite are the library and chapel and on the right, the graceful Paços da Universidade. This Manueline building was endowed with a colonnaded gallery called the Via Latina in the late 18C. The central body of the building is surmounted by a triangular pediment *(buy tickets at the entrance to this building)*. A staircase leads to the first floor and the loggia (formerly for women only) that gives on to the **Sala dos Capelos** (Ceremonial Hall) where formal events such as the inauguration of rectors, the defence of theses and the conferring of degrees take place. The name derives from the cap *(capelo)* given to students on graduating. The vast hall, once the palace assembly-room, has an exquisite 17C painted ceiling and is adorned with portraits of the kings of Portugal. Beside it is the private examination room, which was remodelled in 1701. It has a painted ceiling and is hung with portraits of former rectors.

An exterior balcony provides a **view★** of the city, the old cathedral and the more recent districts near the Mondego.

The Manueline **chapel★** *(capela)*, with an elegant door, is by Marcos Pires. It is decorated with 17C *azulejos* and a painted ceiling and also possesses a fine 18C **organ loft★★**. A small **museum of sacred art** adjoins the chapel.

The **Library★★** was built during the reign of João V in 1724 and consists of three large rooms, where precious wood furnishings are highlighted by Baroque decorations of gilded wood. Gilded Chinese-style patterns have been painted on green, red or gold lacquer work. The ceilings painted in false perspective are by Lisbon artists influenced by Italian art. Ladders have been fitted into the shelving itself for easy access. The 250 000 books and 5 000 manuscripts are classified according to subject matter. King John V' s portrait, painted probably in 1725 by an unknown artist, hangs in the library.

◗ On leaving the university, take Rua Guilherme Moreira to Almedina gate.

OUTSIDE THE OLD CITY
Mosteiro de Santa Cruz★
🕐*Open Mon–Sat 11.30am–4.30pm, Sun 2–5pm.* ✆€3 ✆*239 822 941.*
The Manueline ceiling of the **church★** is supported by twisted columns and brackets. The walls are adorned with *azulejos* depicting the life of St Augustine. The Renaissance **pulpit★** by Nicolas Chanterene is a masterpiece. Two bays on either side of the high altar contain the tombs of the first two kings of Portugal Afonso Henriques and Sancho I, surrounded by a late Gothic–early Renaissance decoration. A door at the back of the chancel leads to the **Sacristia** (sacristy), in which hang four early 16C Portuguese paintings. The **Sala do Capitulo** (chapter-house) has a fine Manueline ceiling and 17C *azulejos*. The

Parque de Santa Cruz, Coimbra

The Republics

Republics were created at the end of the 18C by students who wanted to introduce the French revolutionary ideas of the time into their communities. Although they were residences in which debate and protest flourished, as time passed they were also to become a cheap and practical form of accommodation. They generally number between 12 and 20 students, usually from the same region, who live together, renting vast apartments and managing the group budget in turn. Traditionally, they employ the services of a cook *(tricana)* to prepare meals, which are eaten communally. As you wander around the city you will probably come across some of these republics, which are recognisable by flags or paintings on the façades of their buildings. The **República dos Kágados** *(Rua do Correio, 98)*, which was founded in 1933, is currently the oldest republic in the city, while the **Real República Corsário das Ilhas** *(Couraça dos Apóstolos, 112)* is distinguishable by the pirates on its flag. Most of the republics have humorous names, often based on puns.

Claustro do Silêncio★ were designed by Marcos Pires in 1524. The galleries are decorated with *azulejos* of parables from the Gospel. Three low-relief sculptures illustrate scenes of the Passion after Dürer engravings. In the **gallery** *(coro alto – access through the sacristy)* at the entrance to the church are 16C wooden **stalls★** carved and gilded by French and Flemish artists.

Parque de Santa Cruz

The entrance to this delightful 18C garden is through two towers adorned with arches. A staircase leads to a grotto-like fountain decorated with statues. Picnic tables, a lake surrounded by sculpted boxwood creating a maze effect and exotic trees provide welcome cool and a haven of peace and quiet.

Jardim Botanico

◷Open Apr–Sept 9am–8pm; Oct–Mar 9am–5.30pm. ✆239 855 215. ⊜No charge. www.uc.pt/jardimbotanico.
The terraced botanical gardens *(jardim botânico)*, which were laid out in the 18C in accordance with reforms introduced by Pombal, have a wide variety of rare trees including many tropical species. Once one of the best-known of the world's botanical gardens, it is less renowned these days, but still an interesting place to visit. The **Museu Botânico** *(entry included in the greenhouse ticket)* is also well worth a visit.

Casa Museu Bissaya-Barreto

◷Open Tue–Fri 11am–1pm, 3–6pm year round; Sat–Sun 3–6pm in May–Sep only. ◷Closed Mon and public holidays. ✆239 853 800. www.cmbb.pt.
The former residence of Bissaya-Barreto (1886–1974), professor, surgeon, member of parliament and friend of Salazar, has preserved its original decoration. Built in 1925 in neo-Baroque style, it is surrounded by a small garden decorated with statues and *azulejos*.

The interior reveals the aesthetic tastes of its former owner: a 19C French lounge, *azulejos* from different periods, ceilings painted with frescoes, porcelain from the Indies company and from Saxony, silverware, Italian marble, a library with books dating from the 16C and 17C, a collection of paintings based on the theme of the mother and child (including a *Virgin and Child* by Josefa de Óbidos), and several canvases by José Malhoa, Sousa Pinto and António Vitorino.

SOUTH BANK

Convento de Santa Clara-a-Nova

✆239 441 674.
The chancel in this vast convent contains the 17C silver tomb of Queen St Isabel by Teixeira Lopes. At the end of the lower chancel *(coro baixo)*, behind the wrought-iron screen, is the queen's original **tomb★** (14C) of painted Ança stone made during her lifetime.

Holy Queen Festival

At the beginning of July in even-numbered years, the city pays homage to its patron saint. On Thursday evening, the statue of the saint is removed from the Convento de Santa Clara a-Nova and carried in procession across the bridge and through the city's streets to the Igreja da Graça, where it remains until the following Sunday, when it is returned to the convent. The streets are crowded with people, some of whom make the journey barefoot or on their knees, and the statue often takes several hours to travel just a few metres. The youngest members of the procession dress up as cherubs, King Dinis or Queen Isabel in memory of the miracle of the roses. When the queen, who was hiding bread in her lap to give to the poor, was asked by the king what she was carrying, she was said to have replied: "these are roses, my lord..."; when she went to remove the bread from the folds of her dress, a quantity of rose petals miraculously fell out. Today Coimbra's inhabitants throw rose petals onto the statue from their windows, which are draped with brightly coloured bedspreads and large flags for the occasion. At midnight, a huge firework display illuminates the Mondego.

The festivities last for the entire month of July and include a wide programme of performances, exhibitions, food and handicrafts fairs, sporting competitions and lots of entertainment.

Also in July, the Coimbra Art Festival, promoted by Inês de Castro Foundation, is held at the open-air amphitheatre in Quinta das Lágrimas. It gives voice to several art forms including music, painting, theatre, literature, cinema and photography. The Citemor Festival in Montemor-o-Velho is another popular cultural event taking place during the same month. It is an eclectic mix of theatre, dance, video, photography and other performances.

≗ Portugal dos Pequenitos

⊙Open Jan–Feb and mid-Oct–Dec 10am–5pm; Mar–May and mid-Sept–mid-Oct 10am–7pm; Jun–mid-Sept 9am–8pm. ⊙Closed public holidays.⊛€10.50, child, 3–13, €6.50. ℘239 801 170.
www.portugaldospequenitos.pt.
Especially appealing to children, this attraction features scale models of Portuguese monuments, including those of former overseas colonies. One of the houses contains a children's museum, the **Museu da Criança**.

Quinta das Lágrimas gardens

⊙Open mid-Mar–mid-Nov Tue–Sun 10am–7pm; mid-Nov–mid-Mar 10am–5pm. ⊛€2.50. ℘239 802 380.
www.quintadaslagrimas.pt.
The name of this wooded park, the Villa of Tears, recalls the legend described in verse by Camões of Inês de Castro's murder here on 7 January 1355 by King Afonso's chief justice and two of his henchmen.

EXCURSIONS

Miradouro do Vale do Inferno

1.7km/1mi from crossroads at Portugal dos Pequenitos, following Rua C. A. Abreu (the road on the right towards the Vale do Inferno is a steep climb); at a fork bear right.
The belvedere provides a good **view★** of Coimbra.

Figueira da Foz

On the coast close to Coimbra midway between Lisbon and Porto.
Due west of Coimbra, Figueira da Foz edges the mouth of the Mondego River beneath the Serra da Boa Viagem. Tourists are attracted by the vast beach of fine sand that lines the wide curve of Figueira bay.
This bay, previously known as Mondego bay, is overlooked by a fort of golden stone that was captured from the French by students of Coimbra University. Shortly before this momentous event, Wellington landed the first British troops here in August 1808. From Figueira

© José Antonio Moreno/age fotostock

Montemor-O-Velho castle.

began the advance south that was to bring the first battles of the Peninsular War, not far from Óbidos at Roliça and Vimeiro. Figueira, which was built in the last century, depends primarily on tourism, its fishing industry (sardines) and its shipyards.

Figueira is a beach resort and as such, the beaches close by are of major interest. There is plenty of room, even in mid-summer.

Apart from them, the headland of Serra de Boa Viagem, a heavily wooded headland, is a beautiful spot.

In the town itself the **Museu do Mar** (◷ *open Mon–Fri 9.30am–12.30pm, 2–5pm;* ☎*233 402 840*) and the **Museu Municipal Dr Santos Rocha** (◷*open Tue–Fri 9.30am–5pm, Sat 2–7pm.* ◉€2; ☎*233 402 840*) are worth a visit, the latter with its impressive archaeological selection. Also of interest near Figueira, in Armazéns de Lavos, is the **Núcleo Museológico do Sal** (Salt Centre and Museum: ◷*open May–mid-Sept Wed–Sun 10.30am–12.30pm, 2.30–6.45pm; mid-Sept–Apr Thu–Sun 10am–12.30pm, 2–4pm;* ◉€1; ☎*233 402 840; www.figueiradigital.pt*) where you can walk by the vast saltpans and learn about salt cultivation.

Montemor-o-Velho

Roughly between Coimbra and Figueira da Foz. Allow an hour to see the castle, which shouldn't be missed for its views of the Mondego river.

The town of Montemor-o-Velho in the fertile Mondego valley is dominated by the ruins of the citadel built in the 11C to defend Coimbra against the Moors. The **castle★** (◷*open Tue–Sun Apr–May 10am–7pm; Jun–Aug 9am–9pm; Sept–Mar 10am–6.30pm;* ◷ *closed 1 Jan, Good Friday, Easter Sunday, 25 Dec),* was originally built by the Romans, then re-fortified by the Moors. Little remains; a double perimeter wall, oval in shape, battlemented and flanked by many towers; the north corner is occupied by the church and the keep. From the top of the ramparts there is a **panorama★** of the Mondego Valley.

The **Igreja de Santa Maria de Alcáçova** is a Manueline church, designed by Diogo do Boitaca (who designed the Mosteiro dos Jerónimos at Belém), with wooden ceilings, twisted columns and some lovely Moorish *azulejos.*

The vast lawns outside the church are well maintained.

Once a month (the date varies between the second and fourth Wednesday), the town holds a huge market that completely fills its otherwise neat but tiny streets. There are plenty of restaurants and cafés.

Oliveira do Hospital

60km/37mi northeast of Coimbra.
The town is small but the countryside around it deserves a leisurely drive with several stops along the river.

Hills clad with vines, olive groves and pine trees form the setting of the town of Oliveira do Hospital, the name of which recalls the 12C Order of the Hospitallers of St. John of Jerusalem, now the Knights Templar of Malta (&see PORTO, Leça do Bailio). You will find it northeast of Coimbra along the N17. The surrounding countryside is beautiful.

The parish **church**, originally Romanesque, was reconstructed in the Baroque period and changed considerably in the mid-18C. The interior, covered by a fine ceiling painted in false relief, contains the late 13C tombs of Domingos Joanes and his wife. An equestrian **statue★** of a 14C medieval knight has been fixed to the wall above the tombs. Also noteworthy is a 14C stone **altarpiece★** of the Virgin.

ADDRESSES

🏨 STAY

🛏 **Residencial Larbelo** – Largo da Portagem, 33. ☎239829 092. 17 rooms. No breakfast. Very simple, family-run hotel located in a charming building in the city centre. Bright rooms, friendly staff.

🛏 **Hotel Jardim** – Avenida Emídio Navarro, 65. ☎239 825 204. 20 rooms. No breakfast. This beautifulbuilding, located opposite the park bordering the river, has a tiled facade and equally delightful interior. Ask to see rooms: some are more spacious than others, and have a new bathroom.

🛏🛏 **Hotel Vitória** – Rua da Sota, 9. ☎239 824 049. 20 rooms. The rooms at this small hotel are comfortable, if somewhat basic. It's in a good location.

🛏 **Casa Pombal** – Rua das Flores, 18. ☎239 835 175. www.casapombal.com. 7 rooms. This old house on three levels has a steep staircase. Rooms are all different, four with bathroom. Some have views over the rooftops. Nice garden and full buffet breakfast.

🛏🛏 **Astória** – Av. Emídio Navarro, 21. ☎239 853 020. www.astoria-coimbra.com. 64 rooms. The Astória is magnificently situated overlooking the Mondego River in an elegant, Parisian-style early 20C building. The hotel, which in the past was popular with artists and writers,

retains a certain charm, particularly in its dining rooms; an Art Nouveau-Art Déco masterpiece.

☝/EAT

🍽 **A Cozinha da Maria** – Rua das Azeiteiras, 65. ☎968 650 253. Grills are a speciality at this cosy eatery.

🍽 **A Toca do Gato** – Rua dos Gatos 8. ☎962 916 904. A typical Coimbra tavern serving snack-sized tapas (the bacalhau fritters are great!), as well as bigger dishes such as octopus with potatoes .

🍽🍽 **Jardim da Manga** – Rua Olímpio Nicolau Rui Fernandes. ☎239 829 156. jardimdamanga.net . Closed Sat. This peaceful self service hides behind what was the "Garden of La Mancha". Simple dishes vary at each meal, including suckling pig.

🍽 **O Pátio** – Pátio da Inquisição, 26. ☎239 828 596. Closed Sun. There are two small rooms and a large counter if you are in a hurry. The local specialty is chanfana, goat roasted in red wine.

🍽🍽 **O Zé Manel dos Ossos** – Beco do Forno, 12. ☎239 823 790. Closed Sun. A tiny room covered from floor to ceiling with African statues and plates. Try rustic Portuguese dishes such as the pork ribs that are eaten with your fingers.

🍽🍽 **Orpheu** – Rua Sargento Mor. ☎917 731 714. Closed Sun. A small self-service restaurant where dishes are written on blackboards: pies, quiches, soups, including the famous Pedra Stone – red bean and pork soup.

🍽🍽 **Salão Brazil** – Largo do Poço, 3. ☎239 837 078. A relaxed atmosphere with jazz concerts at the weekend. Varied selection of good, simple, low-priced dishes (pasta, fish, meat, salads, desserts).

🍽🍽 **Adega Paço do Conde** – Rua Paço do Conde, 1. ☎239 825 605. Closed Sun. A traditional Portuguese restaurant offering quality fish and meat dishes. You can eat in one of two small salons or in a larger dining room, the latter not quite as intimate. Good service.

🍽🍽 **Zé Neto** – R. das Azeiteiras, 8. ☎239 826 786. Closed Sun. An excellent family-run restaurant serving inexpensive local food with cabrito (kid) often on the menu. Very busy but with excellent, rapid service. You will find this place to be one of the best choices in town.

Buçaco Forest★★

Luso

The Mata Nacional do Buçaco lies to the north of Coimbra near the Luso spa, crowning the northernmost peak of the Serra do Buçaco. The forest is enclosed by a stone wall pierced by several gates, but can be explored by car as well as on foot.

ⓒ **Map:** p232.
ℹ **Info:** ☏231 937 000.
www.fmb.pt.
◐ **Location:** Due north of Coimbra, about 20km/ 12.4mi.
👥 **Kids:** An adventure and picnic in the heart of the forest.
◷ **Timing:** You should spend a day here, including a picnic.

THE FOREST

In the 6C, Benedictine monks built a hermitage in the forest at Buçaco. In 1628 the Carmelite monks built a community and surrounded the entire domain by a wall that stands to this day, totally enclosing the forest. They continued to develop the forest by planting new varieties of trees and other plants, and obtained a papal bull from Urban VIII threatening anyone damaging the trees with excommunication. Women were banned from the forest to protect the monks from any temptation.

In 1834 all religious orders in Portugal were abolished and the Carmelite friars had to leave Buçaco. The forest was taken into royal care and then came under the Water and Forest Department of the government.

Today of the 700 species of trees, the most impressive are some of the earliest, particularly the **Mexican cedars.** The 105ha forest harbours 400 native varieties of tree and about 300 exotic species, including ginkgos, monkey-puzzles, cedars, Himalayan pines, thuyas, Oriental spruces, palms, arbutus, sequoias and Japanese camphor trees, as well as tree ferns, hydrangeas, mimosas, camellias, magnolias, philarias and even lilies of the valley.

Palace-Hotel★

Visitors who just want to look inside are tolerated, or you could stop for a drink in the hotel bar.

The hotel, on the site of the monastery, was built by the Italian architect Luigi Manini between 1888 and 1907 as a hunting lodge for King Carlos. Inside, the walls are covered with huge *azulejo* panels depicting episodes from Camões' **The Lusiads**, and battle scenes from Portugal's history.

Buçaco forest

© Martin Bobrovsky/age fotostock

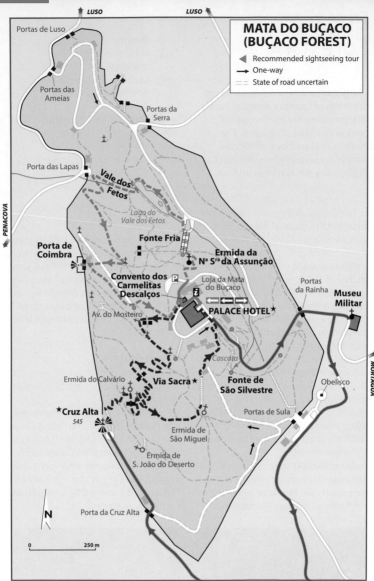

**MATA DO BUÇACO
(BUÇACO FOREST)**

◀ Recommended sightseeing tour
→ One-way
= = State of road uncertain

Convento dos Carmelitas Descalços

Below the hotel . ⏱*Open daily 10am–1pm, 2–4pm (Sat and Sun until 5pm).* ⏱*Closed public holidays.*

The remains of the Carmelite Convent completed in 1630, comprise a chapel, cloisters and a few monks' cells that were lined with cork for insulation against the cold.

👣 WALKING TOUR

1 FONTE FRIA AND VALE DOS FETOS★★

1hr 15min round trip on foot.

Ermida da Nossa Senhora de Assunção (Hermitage of Our Lady of the Assumption) is one of 10 hermitages in the forest to which the monks used to retire. After seeing it, move on to the **Fonte Fria.** The water of the Cold Fountain rises in a cave and spills out to form a cascade down a flight of 144 stone steps; at the bottom, hydrangeas and magnolias surround the pool into which the water flows and which also mirrors some majestic conifers nearby. The gate from the forest, the **Porta de Coimbra** (Coimbra Gate), was built at the same time as the 17C wall and has Rococo decoration.

◉ Return by way of Avenida do Mosteiro, an avenue of superb cedars.

2 VIA SACRA, CRUZ ALTA★★
By car (see map) or 1hr round trip on foot

◉ Take Avenida do Mosteiro below the convent, then turn left for the Via Sacra.

The **Via Sacra★** (Way of the Cross) was built in the Baroque style in the late 17C. The chapels along the way contain life-size terra-cotta figures enacting the road to Calvary. You then reach the **Cruz Alta★** at an altitude of 545m.

Conímbriga★

The Roman ruins of Conímbriga are among the finest in the Iberian Peninsula. A Celtic city stood on this spot as long ago as the Iron Age. The present ruins, however, are those of a Roman town situated on either side of an important road that connected Lisbon and Braga. In the 3C, threatened by Barbarian invasion, the inhabitants were compelled to build ramparts, leaving some of the houses outside the wall. Material from these houses was used in the construction of the fortifications. In spite of these measures, Conímbriga fell to the Suevi in 468 AD and the town declined.

VISIT
◉Open daily 10am–7pm.
◉Closed Jan 1, Easter Sunday, May 1, Dec 25; €4.50. ℘239 941 177.

◉ Return by the woodland paths that lead past various hermitages.

On your way back, a few hundred yards from the hotel, a waterfall *(cascata)* is fed by the **Fonte de São Silvestro**, amid ferns and hydrangeas. Driving to the Cruz Alta will take you past the **Museu Militar** (◉open Tue–Sun 10am–12.30pm, 2–5pm; ◉closed 1 Jan, Good Friday, Easter Sunday, 25 Dec; €2; ℘231 939 310), which features the Battle of Buçaco and campaigns of 1810.

EXCURSION
Luso★
A little outside the forest to the north you come across **Luso**, a charming little spa town that pulls in crowds eager to "take the waters" renowned for curing rheumatism and other complaints. Luso water, bottled, is sold all over the country, but you can fill up a small container here free of charge.

- **Map:** p233
- **Info:** Rua Emídio Navarro, 136, Luso. ℘231 939 133.
- **Location:** Just 14km/9mi south of Coimbra. You can get to Conímbriga either by car, or by bus from Coimbra. The bus takes 30 minutes. There is also a half-hourly service from Coimbra to Condeixa, but the walk from there to Conimbriga is about 2km/1.2mi and poorly signposted.
- **Kids:** A great place for them to begin to understand how people (including children) lived in an age now largely forgotten.
- **Timing:** About 3 hours.
- **Don't Miss:** Particularly the mosaics in the House of Fountains.

Mosaics in the Casa da Cruz Suástica

©José Elias/Dreamstime.com/iStock

www.conimbriga.pt. Leave the car in front of the museum and take the path towards the ruins, following the route marked on the map.

Visit the museum and its café first to see the information on display, which gives you a good overview of the site.

The first thing you notice on entering the site itself is the amazing **wall** that was put up literally overnight in 465 in a frantic, but futile attempt to repel a threatened Suevi invasion. The wall even cuts through the middle of several houses and was constructed of anything that came to hand. The inhabitants, fearing their own destruction, eventually fled the city and hid in the surrounding countryside, leaving the invaders to take control of the city without further destruction.

Cross the **Casa da Cruz Suástica** (House of the Swastika) and the **Casa dos Esqueletos** (House of the Skeletons), paved with fine mosaics, before reaching the baths and the interesting *laconicum* (a type of sauna) (1). You then come to the **Casa de Cantaber★**, which is one of the largest in the western Roman world and is said to have belonged to Cantaber, whose wife and children were captured by the Suevi during the attack on the town in 465. The tour begins

with the private baths: the *frigidarium* (2) with its cold baths, the *tepidarium* (warm baths) and the *caldarium* (hot baths) (3) over the *hypocaust* (heated space connected with the furnace). The hypocaust's layout gives an idea of the plan for the fireplaces and the underground system of warm air circulation; a few lead pipes remain.

You then arrive at the northern entrance to the house: a colonnade (4) preceded the *atrium* (entrance vestibule) (5). As you pass from the *atrium* to the central peristyle (6), you will note an unusual stone (7) in the pavement, cut away to a rose tracery through which the drain can be seen. The *impluvium* (a basin for collecting rain water) (8) is to the left of the peristyle. Leading off from the *impluvium* were the bedrooms.

From the *triclinium* (sitting and dining room) (9) you can see three pools. The most interesting of these pools (10) is encircled by columns, of which one has retained its original stucco painted in red. A suite of three rooms (11) adjoining the wall has a pool and flower beds in the shape of a cross.

Excavations northwest of the Casa de Cantaber have uncovered the centre of the **ancient town** *(cidade antiga)*, in particular the **forum**, a hostelry and baths. To the southwest, the craftsmen's quarter and the monumental baths have also been discovered.

You can also see the remains of the **aqueduct** *(aqueduto)*, which was some 3.5km/2mi long and brought water from Alcabideque to the supply tower by the reconstructed arch abutting on the wall.

Casa dos Repuxos (House of the Fountains)★★

Access by footbridge to the north.

The villa, which belonged to a Roman named Rufus, dates from the early 2C although it was built on the site of a 1C building. The layout of the rooms is easy to follow on account of the column bases and the paving which consists largely of wonderful mosaics.

Inside are the *atrium* (12), the peristyle (13) and the *triclinium* (14), which was bordered by a pool.

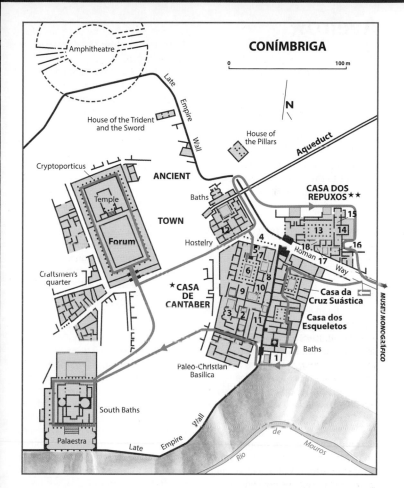

CONÍMBRIGA

Around these rooms were the living quarters and communal rooms. The **mosaics★★** covering the floors show extraordinary variety.

In a room to the left of the *triclinium*, a fine polychrome composition (15) shows hunting scenes, the Four Seasons and a quadriga. Another room (16) giving onto the *impluvium* presents some elegant figures at a deer hunt. A *cubiculum* (bedroom) (17) has ornamental tiling with geometrical designs and plant motifs surrounding Silenus astride an ass being pulled forward by its halter. Next door, a sitting room (18), opening on to the peristyle, is decorated with an outstanding mosaic: in the centre of an ornament representing wading birds, dolphins and sting rays, a marine centaur surrounded

by dolphins brandishes a standard and a fish. Lastly, in the southwest corner of the peristyle, Perseus stands, holding in his right hand Medusa's head.

Aveiro★

and Around

Canals, small bridges, colourful barges that evoke the gondolas of Venice, and a fine museum give Aveiro the feel of a city of culture. The centre has many fine buildings, some in an Art Nouveau style, but the surrounding areas are impressive as well, canals and marches to the north, dunes and the beaches to the west.

A BIT OF HISTORY
Loss and Reclamation

Aveiro was once a busy fishing port, with boats returning from cod fishing off Newfoundland. However, in 1575 disaster struck: a violent storm closed the lagoon; the harbour silted up and the city, deprived of its livelihood, fell into decline; more than 70 percent of its population left for work elsewhere. An effort to rehabilitate it in the 18C came to nothing, as did several plans to reconnect the town to the sea.

Finally in 1808, with the aid of breakwaters built from stones taken from the old town walls, a passage was reopened to the sea.

The porcelain industry developed locally (in nearby Ílhavo and Vista Alegre), bringing prosperity, and with it came expansion and artistic renown.

▶ **Population:** 78 455.
⚅ **Map:** p241.
🛈 **Info:** Rua João Mendonça, 8; ℘ 234 420 760.
◗ **Location:** 77.5km/48mi south of Porto, 63km/39mi north of Coimbra.
👪 **Kids:** Take them for an adventure cruise on the lagoon.
🕐 **Timing:** To get to know Aveiro stay a couple of days.
🅿 **Parking:** Difficult in town but there is a covered car park or you can use the road by the train station, 10min walk from the centre.
👁 **Don't Miss:** The Museu de Aveiro, the Art Nouveau Museum and a walk in the old town.

Aveiro Today

Saltpans, grazing, rice paddies and land made fertile with seaweed gathered from the sea floor are important, but Aveiro remains primarily a fishing town: lamprey are caught from the Vouga river, sea perch from the lagoon, eel, mackerel, bream, sea bass and other fish from the Ria de Aveiro. Aveiro is Portugal's third-largest industrial centre after Lisbon and Porto, yet has a

Painted prows of Moliceiros
© Lukasz Janyst /iStock

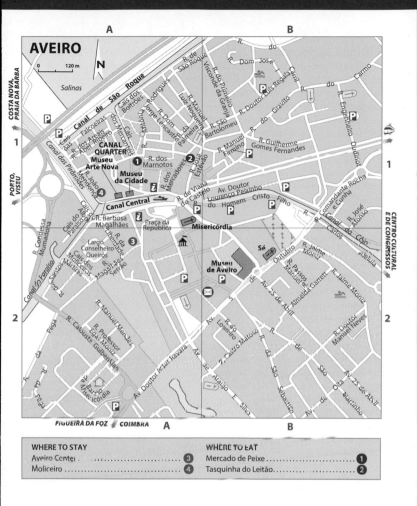

quiet charm. The best way to see it is either to walk or use the free bike service, *MoveAveiro*. Gourmets visiting the town should try the *ovos moles*, a type of egg dessert, usually served in miniatures or in painted wooden barrels. In July or August, during the Ria Festival, a competition takes place on the central canal to find the best painted prow from the fleet of wide-bottomed *moliceiros*.

Distinctive Features

Canals criss-cross the town spanned by small humpbacked bridges that give an almost Dutch feel to it, especially with the bicycles. Graceful *moliceiros* (flat-bottomed boats used for gathering seaweed), as well as their mooring posts, bring to mind Venetian gondolas. Some of the canal bridges have been decorated with bronze statues of traditional workers; prime among them is the *salineira* (the salt seller) with her tray of salt for sale. The Mercado do Peixe (fish market) is worth a visit, as are the *azulejo*-covered **railway station**, a pleasant park, the main avenue *(Avenida Dr Lourenço Peixinho)*, and the huge Forum Aveiro if you like to shop. Northeast of the city, the **Ecomuseu Marinha da Troncalhada** has displays on artisanal salt production, and you can view saltpans that have been in operation for more than a thousand years.

CONVENT AREA

Antigo Convento de Jesus★★

The Convent of Jesus was started in the 15C. Princess Joana, daughter of King Afonso V, wanted to become a nun, but her father forbade it; he wanted her married off for political reasons. To escape this fate, she "retired" here in 1472 and remained for the last 18 years of her life. She was later beatified for her determination to escape the material world. Her tomb and the chapel in which it rests are striking: the tomb is a masterpiece of early18C marble mosaic.

The **church★★** dates from the 15C, but the interior decoration was completed in the early 18C. The interior has some sumptuously carved and gilded wood, particularly in the **chancel★★**, a masterpiece of Baroque exuberance with its columns; scenes from the life of Saint Joana can be seen on *azulejos* panels. The **lower chancel★**(*coro baixo*), with its painted wood ceiling, holds **St Joana's tomb★★** (early 18C). This masterpiece by the architect João Antunes, a mosaic in polychrome marble, is supported by sitting angels, also in marble.

The Renaissance-style **cloisters** are surrounded by chapels, one of which contains the 15C **tomb** of João de Albuquerque. The refectory is totally covered with 17C *azulejos* decorated with floral motifs. A tour of the museum (*below*) includes a visit to the church gallery or **coro alto**, which is decorated with paintings and a 14C crucifixion in which Christ's expression changes according to the angle.

Museu de Aveiro★★

🕐*Open Tue–Sun 10am–12.30pm, 1.30-6pm.* 🕐*Closed 1 Jan, Good Friday, Easter Sunday, 1 May and 25 Dec.* €4, *free on Sun and public holidays until 2pm.* 📞*234 423 297.*

Highlighting the exuberance and richness of the Baroque period, this museum exhibits a superb collection of sacred art. It is Portugal's second-largest museum of sacred art after the Museu Nacional de Arte Antiga in Lisbon. Its various collections include sculptures of the Coimbra School (16C) and Portuguese Primitive paintings on wood. One

is a lovely **portrait★** of Princess Joana (late 15C), attributed to Nuno Gonçalves, remarkable for the severe sculptural features of the young girl dressed in court finery.

In the rooms devoted to Baroque art, there are statues in polychrome wood of the Aveiro angels, a strange Holy Family in earthenware from the workshop of Machado de Castro, and a lacquered wooden writing desk. The room where Saint Joana died in 1490 is now an oratory with altarpieces and gilded wood.

Cathedral

This cathedral (*sé*) is the only remaining vestige of the former Convento de São Domingos, founded in 1423, but it has been greatly modified since it was first built. It has a Baroque façade and, inside, a strange mixture of styles, with 17C and 18C polychrome *azulejos* on the walls of the nave and a 17C organ in the north arm of the transept. To the left of the entrance, there is an early Renaissance *Entombment*.

Cruzeiro de São Domingos

This Gothic-Manueline-style Calvary in front of the cathedral is an exact reproduction of the original, which is now housed inside the church.

Igreja da Misericórdia

The Church of the Misericord has an imposing, finely worked 17C doorway. Inside, the height of the nave and the 17C *azulejos* should be noted, as well as the churchwarden's pew opposite the pulpit.

Museu de Arte Nova★

🕐*Open Tue–Sun 10am–12.30pm, 1.30–6pm.* 🕐*Closed public holidays.* €1 (*includes a multimedia tour of the city*). €2. 📞*234 406 485.*

Opened in March 2012, this museum is housed in the gloriously ornate three-storey **Casa Major Pessoa**, a fine example of Art Nouveau architecture itself, and covers the story of Art Nouveau through the ages. One floor outlines a guided tour of the city's more than two dozen Art Nouveau buildings.

Equally awesome is the **Casa de Chá** tearoom on the first level. This charming café has an indoor room with bistro tables (◷*open Tue–Thu 10am–2pm, Fri 10am-3pm, Sat 12.30-3pm, Sun 12.30–9pm*).

CANAL QUARTER★ *2hr*

Some canals of the Ria de Aveiro continue right into the town; they are shored up by embankments that the water laps over at high tide.

Canal Central

Part of the canal is bordered by handsome old buildings, their Classical façades reflected in the water. The canal features a continuous spectacle of small boats called **moliceiros**; these flat-bottomed vessels, traditionally used for gathering seaweed in the lagoon, are distinguished by their prows curved like swans' necks and painted in vivid colours. They have either a sail or are propelled with a pole, similar to the gondolas of Venice. The best viewpoint is from the wide bridge-tunnel with balusters, which divides the canal at the halfway point; it is the main crossroads in the town (*Praça Humberto Delgado*).

Canal de Sao Roque

This canal borders the built-up area to the north, and is spanned (in front of Rua Dr. António Cristo) by an elegant stone humpback footbridge. It divides the salt marshes from the salt warehouses that line the embankment among the low-roofed houses of the fishing quarter.

Colourful houses, Costa Nova

© Kim Petersen/imageBROKER/age fotostock

RIA DE AVEIRO★

The Aveiro river empties into a vast lagoon marked by tides, dotted with islands and criss-crossed with channels. It is bordered by salt marshes and pine forests, behind an offshore bar some 45km/28mi long and not more than 2.5km/1.5mi wide, with a narrow bottleneck (*Estreito da Barra*) linking it to the ocean. The lagoon takes the shape of a triangle, and at high tide covers about 6 000ha, with an average depth of 2m. Rich in fish and fertile in the parts above high tide mark, the waters are particularly famous for their seaweed, which is used as a fertiliser, and is collected in the *moliceiros*. The rakes' prongs (*ancinhos*) for scraping or gathering up seaweed are hung around the tip of the prow. Unfortunately, the number of these boats is decreasing (some can be seen in front of the tourist office), although there is still an annual competition in July and August for the best-decorated vessel.

EXCURSIONS

Beaches

Although Aveiro itself has no beaches, there are plenty around, all very popular in summer. In fact the entire coast is

---

Vista Alegre

Vista Alegre, 5km/3mi west of Aveiro, has been a manufacturing centre of fine chinaware and glass since 1824. It acquired royal patronage shortly after opening and has since been regarded as the most important centre of porcelain in Portugal. A small **museum** (◷*open May–Sept 10am–7.30pm; Oct–Apr 10am–7pm; ⊚€6; ◷closed 1 Jan, Easter Sun, 25 Dec; ℘234 320 600; www.vistaalegre.com*) on the factory premises recounts the developments in production since its earliest days through displays of machines, tools and examples of most of the pieces produced since its foundation. There is both a shop and a factory outlet on site.

almost one continuous run of glorious sand.

The beaches closest to the town are **Barra**, about 9km/5mi west of Aveiro and then **Costa Nova**, 3km/2mi south of Barra. Both are reachable by bus from Aveiro. Both are good venues for surfing and there is a diving centre for scuba-diving. There are plenty of restaurants and beach bars along the edge of the beach.

Torreira, a small fishing port with numerous restaurants, is reached after crossing Murtosa. You can normally see many *moliceiros* tied up here. **Bico** is a small port on the *ria* where beautiful *moliceiros* may still be seen.

The Pousada da Ria, located between the two ports, sits on the water's edge. The Reserva Natural das Dunas de São Jacinto is situated 2km/1.2mi before São Jacinto.

Ílhavo

3km/1.8mi from Aveiro, down the coast road heading south.

This small former fishing port has become developed with some attractive early 20C villas such as the "Villa Africana", covered with *azulejos* in varying shades of yellow.

The modern **Museu Marítimo de Ílhavo★** (Ⓛ *open Mar–Sept Tue–Sat 10am–6pm, Sun 2–6pm; Oct–Feb Tue–Sat 10am–6pm; €6.50; ℘234 329 990; www. museumaritimo.cm-ilhavo.pt*) features three permanent exhibitions containing artefacts relating to the sea, including a comprehensive section on cod fishing. A documentary dating from the 1970s shows the harsh reality of the fishing expeditions, some of which would last six months in the fishing grounds off Newfoundland.

Santa Maria da Feira

33km/20mi north of Aveiro, just off the main A 1 highway.
Kids will enjoy the view from the castle's walls but probably more exciting are the secret passages and concealed entrances. An hour will suffice for a complete visit. Park near the castle.

North of the town of Aveiro, and about halfway to Porto (which is only another 30mins north), the castle of Santa Maria da Feira stands on a wooded height facing the town, which lies scattered over the opposite hillside. Feira itself is now becoming built up with commuters who travel by train each day to Porto, but its castle in the old section is one of the most spectacular in Portugal. It has been lovingly restored and is a good example of how to build an impregnable defence. At the foot of the hill is a shaded, wooded picnic area.

The 11C **castle★** (Ⓛ *open Tue–Sun 10am–12.30pm, 1.30–6.30pm; winter 9am–12.30pm, 1.30–5.30pm. ☞€3; ℘256 372 248*) was reconstructed in the 15C. A keep flanked by four tall towers with pepperpot roofs overlooks a fortified perimeter wall whose entrance is defended on its eastern side by a barbican.

Follow the wall walk; latrines can still be seen. Stairs lead to the first floor of the keep, where there is a vast Gothic hall; the upper platform (60 steps) affords a **panorama★★** of the castle's fortifications, the town, the surrounding wooded hills and the coastline, where one can make out the Ria de Aveiro in the distance.

Wits its coffered ceiling, the **Igreja da Misericórdia** is situated in the historical centre. Its chancel has a lovely gilded altarpiece. In a south chapel there are some unusual statues, one of which is a Saint Christopher, 3m/9.8ft high.

Reserva Natural das Dunas de São Jacinto

50km/31mi northwest of Aveiro.
The reserve is located at the southernmost tip of a sand-dune peninsula separating the northern branch of the Ria de Aveiro from the Atlantic Ocean. To ensure the preservation of this area, visitors are allowed to enter only between 9am and 9.30am, or between 2pm and 2.30pm. It is necessary to book at least one day in advance as the number of visitors is limited. You are permitted to stay only two-and-a-half hours.

This nature reserve, which covers 666ha of some of the best preserved dunes in Europe, is particularly interesting for its scenery, flora and fauna. More than 100 different types of birdlife can be seen here, including goshawks, and there are many hides along the trails. The **visitor centre** contains exhibits and details of the reserve, including a 7km/4mi walking trail with map, though you can also find someone who will be happy to give you a 🐾guided tour (*2h30: Fri–Sat, ℘234 331 282*).

São Jacinto

Located at the southernmost point of the Reserva Natural das Dunas de São Jacinto.

The small resort in the pine woods at the end of the northern offshore bar on the Estreito da Barra is also a busy little port with plenty of restaurants.

Arouca

70km/43mi northeast of Aveiro, and about an hour southeast of Porto on the N 224.
Holy Week celebrations are impressive in this town, culminating on Easter Saturday with a huge candlelit procession. Its church and monastery dominate the town, their walls towering above everything. Arouca Monastery and a few houses on its perimeter lie deep in the hollow of a small green valley surrounded by wooded hills. Founded in 716, but rebuilt in the 18C after a fire, the monastery forms an unadorned group. The **Igreja do Mosteiro** is an abbey church, whose single nave contains numerous gilded Baroque altars and several statues in Ançã stone carved by Jacinto Vieira. The 18C tomb worked in silver, ebony and quartz in the second chapel on the south side of the church contains the mummy of Queen Mafada (1203–52), daughter of King Sancho I; she retired here in 1217 after her marriage to Dom Henriques I of Castile was annulled. In 1792, 400 years after her death, the monastery was threatened by a huge fire and she is believed to have been seen dousing the flames. Her remains were exhumed and beatified shortly after.

The lower chancel *(coro baixo)* is ornamented with an 18C gilded organ loft, the choir stalls with richly carved backs and graceful statues of religious figures by Jacinto Vieira. If you have an opportunity to hear the organ played (sadly rare), you'll be quite impressed; it has a total of 1,352 stops.

The **Museu de Arte Sacra de Arouca** (🕐*open Tue–Sun 9am–noon, 2–5pm;* 🕐*closed 1 Jan, Good Friday, Easter Sunday, 1 May and 25 Dec*), an extensive museum on the first floor of the cloisters, contains many of the treasures of Queen Mafada, including an exquisite silver diptych dating from the 13C, several Portuguese Primitive **paintings★** dating from the late 15C to early 16C from the Viseu School, and works, including an *Ascension*, by the 17C artist Diogo Teixeira. There is also a statue of St Peter dating from the 15C.

ADDRESSES

🏨STAY

🛏🛏 **Tricana de Aveiro** – *Av. Dr. Lourenço Peixinho, 261, ℘234 428 792 6 rooms.* Situated in a gorgeous building, this charming hotel has clean and comfortable rooms. The owners also run a pastry shop, so breakfast is delicious.

🍽/EAT

🍽🍽 **Centenário** – *Praça do Mercado, 9-10, closed Mon, ℘234 422 798.* This restaurant has a large bay window, contemporary paintings on white panelled walls, wine cellar in white wood, and stylish lampshades. The kitchen is known to surprise diners with delightful dishes and presentation. Efficient service. Good value for money.

🍽🍽🍽 **Restaurant-Bar Salpoente** – *Canal São Roque, 83. ℘234 382 674. www.salpoente.pt.* Situated alongside the canal in a former salt warehouse, as is shown by several features which remind visitors of its original purpose. The cuisine is both well prepared and tasty, with the accent on fish specialities, such as eel *caldeirada* (a type of chowder) and a variety of cod dishes. From 11pm the restaurant becomes a bar, hosting regular concerts.

Parque Arqueológico do Vale do Côa★★

Guarda

The Parque Arqueológico do Vale do Côa is a World Heritage Site in the northeast of Portugal, near the border with Spain. The archaeological park was created to preserve one of the world's most important open-air sites for Palaeolithic rock art, and a new museum telling the story of the prehistoric carvings opened in 2010.

A BIT OF HISTORY

The landscape in this area has hardly changed since the age of Cro-Magnon man making rock engravings of animals living in nature. As a result of the area's isolation, the rock art in the Côa valley has been preserved; you could even say that it has been perpetuated over the course of history with every age leaving its mark engraved in stone as travellers passed through the region.

In 1992, during the construction of a dam at Canada do Inferno, rocks with engravings from the Palaeolithic period (between 30 000 and 10 000 years ago) were discovered. To date, about 1 000 rocks with engravings on them have

- **Michelin Map:** 733.
- **Info:** The park headquarters are at Rua do Museu, Vila Nova de Foz Côa; ℘279 768 260. You must pre-book your visit and take a guided tour in a jeep. In the summer it gets very hot, so bring a hat and sunscreen.
- **Location:** On the Douro inland from Porto.
- **Kids:** Kids will love the all-terrain jeep.
- **Timing:** Tours start at various times of day; check the website.
- **Parking:** There is ample parking at each site.
- **Don't Miss:** The Penascosa site.

been found in 70 different sites. Three sites are open to the public.

Other sites containing ornamented rocks have also been discovered (some of which are under water); as a result, and because archaeological work continues, the park is in a state of continual flux as more discoveries are being made. This extensive art gallery provides a record extending from the Upper Palaeolithic and Neolithic periods and Iron Age to the modern era.

Côa valley

© FredoLealGuerrero/iStock

PALAEOLITHIC ROCK ART

The Palaeolithic Age was the oldest, and longest (2.5 million years), era in the history of humanity and corresponds to the Stone Age. The oldest engravings in the Vale do Côa, identifiable by the species of animals represented, come from the Upper Palaeolithic, or Solutrean, Age and are 20 000 years old. Rock engravings can also be seen at Siega Verde in the Duero (Douro) valley in Spain, 60km/37mi north of the Vale do Côa site, although discoveries on this site mostly date from a later era.

Engraving techniques used in the Côa valley (where paintings may have been made as well) are of three main types: **abrasion**, which consisted of creating a deep groove through the repeated use of an instrument (a fragment of stone) along a marking; **pecking**, a succession of points hammered into the rock using a stone, occasionally finished off using the abrasion technique; and **fine line incision**, which resulted in finer markings that are more difficult to distinguish. The animals most frequently represented were the horse, aurochs, deer and mountain goat. In general, the same rock was used to depict various animals, with one drawing added on top of another.

What is special about art in the Côa valley is the exceptional beauty of the engravings, the representation of the shape and movement of the animals through the simple, firm lines.

VISIT

Coa Museum★★

Rua do Museu, Vila Nova de Foz Côa.
🕐*Open Mon–Sun: Oct–Feb 9am–5.30pm, Mar–May 9.30am-6pm, Jun-Sep 9.30am–7pm.* ✍€5.
🕐*Closed 1 Jan, 1 May and 25 Dec.*
Visit to the museum and one rock art site ✍€15. *℘279 768 260;*
www.arte-coa.pt.

One end of this massive, modern low-lying building juts out over a hill above the Coa River. Opened in 2010, the four-story museum provides an excellent introduction to the rock art you will see. The building is in fitting contrast

Palaeolithic rock art, Penascosa

to the prehistoric works of art on show. A restaurant and cafeteria are on-site.

Penascosa

🕐*Open 9am–12.30pm, 2–5.30pm.*
🕐*Closed Mon. Visit to rock art site in jeep* ✍€40 *. Night visits* ✍€17 *(minimum 4 persons; book in advance).*
The Reception Centre at **Castelo Melhor** (*⚲see GUARDA*) is located in an old schist house that is typical of the region. The jeep ride provides beautiful views of the surrounding hills planted with vines used for port, particularly the famous Quinta da Ervamoira (*⚲see p248*). Penascosa is the most accessible of the three sites and contains engravings that are the most legible in the park. These include a fish (one of only a handful of depictions of fish to be found worldwide) and some superimposed animals, the reason for which is not fully understood. It is located alongside the river, which has created a beach in this part of its course, and jeeps can park just a few metres from the rocks. The site is best visited in the afternoon, when the light is at its best for viewing the engravings. The movement of animals has been reproduced to an extraordinary degree here, particularly in a mating scene, in which a mare is mounted by a horse with three heads to interpret the downward movement of its neck. Seven rocks can be visited here at present.

ORGANISING YOUR VISIT

Guided visits to the rock art sites must be reserved at least one week (more in summer) in advance at the **Coa Museum**: *Rua do Museu, Vila Nova de Foz Côa; ℘279 768 260; www.arte-coa.pt.*
Archaeological Sites *open Tue–Sun. Exact times for visits are advised when reservations are made.*
Two days should be allowed for those wishing to see all three sites. If you have time to visit only one site, choose Penascosa. Transport to the sites is by 8-seater jeep. Children under age 3 are not allowed.
The visit to the Ribeira de Piscos site can also be arranged in conjunction with a Port tasting at the Quinta da Ervamoira where there is a museum devoted to the environment of the Côa valley.

DON'T FORGET

Suitable footwear, boots in winter, a hat and lots of sunscreen in summer, a bottle of water; keep your hands free (use a backpack) to make walking easier, particularly in Canada do Inferno and Ribeira de Piscos, where the uneven terrain and slopes mean you might need both hands to cling onto something.
Visitors who are sensitive to heat should avoid the summer months, when temperatures can reach 40°C.
The visits are not suitable for people with walking difficulties, and the park reserves the right to cancel visits during bad weather.

The village of Penascosa has a small restaurant and a ruined castle; it's an ideal place to have lunch before your afternoon visit to the cave paintings.

Ribeira de Piscos

Visit mornings only: 9.30am in summer, 10am in winter: 2h30, including 1hr round trip by jeep, but with 2.2km of walking. Closed Mon. €15.
The visit in itself is an extremely pleasant stroll along the river bank. The engravings, particularly fine line incisions, are dispersed over the hills and are not easily discernible. The main one is an engraving of two horses apparently "kissing" and you can also see some examples of the auroch bison, a species now extinct, as well as a rare engraving of a fellow man from the Palaeolithic period. The grace and purity of the engravings are moving in their beauty.

Canada do Inferno

Visit: 1h30 to 2h, including round trip journey by jeep and an 800m walk. Mornings only. Jeeps depart from the Coa Museum just outside Vila Nova de Foz Côa. Closed Mon. €15.
This was the first site to be found during construction work on the dam. This site is situated in the steepest part of the valley, where a canyon has formed, 130m deep, making access a little more difficult. From here the suspended work on the dam 400m downstream can be seen. The best time of day to see the engravings, the majority of which are fine line incisions, is in the morning. Although Canado do Inferno is the most interesting of the three sites, many rocks are under water, and only six are currently visible. These include engravings of several animals including horses and bison.
Near the Ribeira de Piscos site is a private site owned by the Ramos Pinto port producers, at **Quinta da Ervamoira** (*℘279 759 229; www.ramospinto.pt*), which offers vineyard tours with port tasting. The visit often includes a look at the engravings on their land, though times vary and the best place to enquire is at the tourist office in Vila Nova de Foz Côa as they will have the latest information. There is also a small museum on the estate displaying a collection of environmental, archaeological and oenological objects from the area. Documents relating to the production and export of wine dating back to the late 19C are archived in Vila Nova da Gaia.

Leiria

Pinhal de Leiria and Pombal

Leiria is pleasantly set at the confluence of two rivers, the Liz and the Lena, and at the foot of a hill crowned by a medieval castle. Its role as a crossroads near well-known beaches – notably Nazaré – the sanctuary of Fátima and the magnificent architecture of Batalha and Alcobaça, makes it a favoured stopping place.

▶ **Population:** 126 879.
⚅ **Michelin Map:** 733.
▦ **Info:** Jardim Luís de Camões; ℘ 244 848 771.
◯ **Location:** Midway between Lisbon and Coimbra on the A8 or A1 road.
◯ **Timing:** A full day is fine.
◉ **Don't Miss:** The castle, churches and museums.

LEIRIA CASTLE★

◯*Currently closed for restoration. Check castelodeleiria.wordpress.com.* ◉€2.50. ℘ 244 813982.

In an exceptional **site★**, inhabited even before the arrival of the Romans, Afonso Henriques, first King of Portugal, had a fortified castle built in 1135. This castle formed part of the defence of the southern border of the kingdom of Portugal, at the time, Santarém and Lisbon still being under Moorish domination.

After the fall of these two cities in 1147, the castle lost its significance and fell into ruin. In the 14C, King Dinis, who undertook the preservation and extension of the pine forest at Leiria, rebuilt the castle in order that he might live in it with his queen, Saint Isabel. The present buildings, modified in the 16C, have been restored. After entering the perimeter of the castle walls through a door flanked by two square crenellated towers, you reach a shaded garden courtyard. A stairway to the left leads to the centre of the castle. The royal palace is on the left, the keep is straight ahead, and on the right are the remains of the 15C chapel of Nossa Senhora da Pena, with a lanceolate Gothic chancel and an arcade decorated with Manueline motifs.

Paço Real (Royal Palace)

A staircase leads to a vast rectangular hall with a gallery adorned with depressed, three-centred arches resting on slender twin columns. The gallery, once the royal balcony, affords a good **view** of Leiria lying below. The narro streets of the town beneath the castle are pleasant for a stroll.

EXCURSIONS

Pinhal de Leiria

West of the town centre.

This vast pine forest, planted over 700 years ago by Dom Dinis, extends to the west of town and leads onto one of the most beautiful stretches of coastline in Portugal. Come here to walk and relax.

Craftsmanship and Folklore

The Leiria region has kept alive its tradition of art and folklore. The glazed and multicoloured pottery of Cruz da Légua and Milagres, the decorated glassware of Marinha Grande, the willow baskets and ornaments and the woven coverlets of Mira de Aire are among the best known crafts of the district.

The traditional festivals and customs have lost none of their spontaneity. The folklore of the Leiria region is closely associated with that of its neighbour, the Ribatejo. The women's costumes consist of a small black felt hat with feathers, a coloured blouse edged with lace, a short skirt and shoes with wide low heels. They differ from that of the Ribatejo only by the addition of a gold necklace and earrings. Folk dancing displays are held every year (◉*see CALENDAR OF EVENTS*).

Pombal

About 49.6km/31mi south of Coimbra on the main A 1 highway, on the western edge of the Serra da Lousã. Stop for an hour as you are passing through.

Sitting at the foot of its medieval castle, the town evokes the memory of the Marquis of Pombal. Born in 1699 as Sebastião de Carvalho e Melo, he began his career as a diplomat in London and Venice. In 1750, as a minister ,he oversaw the rebuilding of Lisbon after the 1755 earthquake and improved the country's finances. In 1769 he was given the title of Marquis of Pombal.

To visit the **castle** (○ *open 10am–1pm, 2–7pm;* ℘ *236 210 556*), take the Ansião road on the right at the corner of the Palácio de Justiça; at a cross, bear sharp right into a narrow surfaced road that rises steeply. Leave the car at the foot of the castle. Originally built in 1161 by Gualdim Pais, Grand Master of the Order of the Knights Templar, it was modified in the 16C and restored in 1940. From the top of the ramparts, overlooked by the battlemented keep, there is a view of Pombal to the west and the foothills of the Serra da Lousã to the east.

Mosteiro da Batalha★★★

Leiria

The Monastery of Batalha (Battle) is a mass of gables, pinnacles, buttresses, turrets and small columns standing majestically in a green valley. Although its setting is somewhat marred by the proximity of the N 1 road, vibrations from which are visibly damaging the building, the rose gold effusion of its architecture remains one of the masterpieces of Portuguese Gothic and Manueline art.

- ⟁ **Michelin Map:** 733.
- **Info:** Praça Mouzinho de Albuquerque; ℘ 244 765 497.
- ○ **Location:** On the N 1 road, 11.8km/7.3mi south of Leiria.
- ○ **Timing:** Allow a day.
- **Parking:** Plenty of parking at the Abbey.
- **Don't Miss:** The Tomb of the Unknown Warriors.

A BIT OF HISTORY

On 14 August 1385 on the plateau of Aljubarrota, 15km/9.3mi south of Batalha, two pretenders to the throne of Portugal faced each other and prepared to do battle: Juan I of Castile, nephew of the late king, and João I, Grand Master of the Order of Avis, who had been crowned king only seven days previously. The opposing forces were of very different strengths: against the organised forces and 16 cannon of the Castilians, the Constable **Nuno Álvares Pereira** could muster only a squad of knights and foot soldiers. João I of Avis,

knowing that defeat would mean Portugal's passing to Spanish domination, made a vow to build a superb church in honour of the Virgin if she were to grant him victory. The Portuguese troops resisted and were victorious. Three years later the Mosteiro de Santa Maria da Vitória, subsequently known as the Mosteiro da Batalha (Battle Abbey), began taking shape. The Portuguese Institute for Architectural Heritage classifies and protects the complex owing to its historical, cultural and architectural importance.

VISIT

○ *Open 16 Oct–31 Mar 9am–6pm; 1 Apr–15 Oct 9am–6.30pm.* ○ *Closed 1 Jan, Easter Sunday, 1 May, 24-25 Dec.*

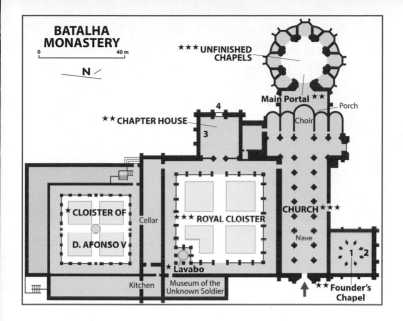

BATALHA
MONASTERY

0   40 m

N

★★★ UNFINISHED
CHAPELS

Main Portal ★★

Porch

4

★★ CHAPTER HOUSE

3

Choir

★ CLOISTER OF

D. AFONSO V

Cellar

★★ ROYAL CLOISTER

CHURCH ★★★

Nave

★ Lavabo

Kitchen

Museum of the
Unknown Soldier

1   2

★★ Founder's
Chapel

€6 (free 1st Sun of month); 244 765 497. www.mosteirobatalha.pt.

The **exterior** of the monastery, which in accordance with the Dominican rule has no belfry, possesses innumerable pinnacles, buttresses and openwork balustrades above Gothic and Flamboyant windows. The building is in fine-textured limestone, which has taken on a lovely ochre colour with time. The complicated structure at the east end of the church demonstrates the architectural problems arising from joining onto an earlier apse an octagonal rotunda which, by means of pillars, was to bear a vaulted ceiling.

The **Capela do Fundador★** (Founder's Chapel), off the south aisle, is surmounted by an octagonal lantern supported by flying buttresses. The main façade is divided into three: the central part, decorated with a network of lancet-shaped blind arcades, is pierced by a beautiful Flamboyant window; the main doorway is richly carved, bearing statues of Christ in Majesty, surrounded by the Evangelists, the Twelve Apostles on the sides, and angels, prophets, kings and saints on the covings. The doorway's proportions appeared to better

advantage when the church stood, as it did originally, below the level of the terrace outside.

Church★★

The church's vast **interior** is quite plain with strong English Perpendicular influences, the outstanding element being the upward sweep of the vaulting. In fact English architects were used in the design of the abbey following the marriage of King João I and his queen Philippa of Lancaster, the daughter of John of Gaunt. The chancel is lit by **stained-glass windows★** that date from the 16C and depict scenes from the Life of the Virgin and Jesus Christ.

Capela do Fundador★

This square chamber, known as the Founder's Chapel, lit by Flamboyant windows, on the right as you enter, is covered with an octagonal lantern topped by a star-shaped cupola.

In the centre are the tombs (1) of King João I and his queen Philippa of Lancaster, the two figures reclining beneath delicately carved canopies. They are depicted holding hands in an expression of the cordial relations between England

Main façade, Mosteiro da Batalha

and Portugal. The Avis and Lancaster coats of arms appear on the tomb. Bays on the south and west sides contain the tombs of the founder's four younger sons (Duarte, the eldest was buried in the sanctuary), Fernando, João, Pedro and Prince Henry the Navigator, whose tomb (2) is covered with a canopy.

Claustro Real★★★

The Gothic and Manueline styles mix most successfully in the Royal Cloisters, the simplicity of the original Gothic design not being obscured by Manueline detail. The fleur-de-lis balustrade and the flowered pinnacles provide a motif that harmonises well with the Manueline tracery backing the carved marble arcades.

Chapter-House★★

The chapter-house *(sala do capitulo)* contains the tomb (3) of the Unknown Soldiers, in which the bodies of two Portuguese soldiers lie. Both died during World War I, one in France, the other in Africa. The **vaulting★★★** is an outstandingly bold feat; after two unsuccessful attempts, the master architect Huguet managed to launch a square vault of some 20m without intermediary supports. The chamber is lit by a window containing early 16C **stained glass★** (4) representing scenes of the Passion.

Lavabo★

The lavabo in the northwest corner of the cloisters consists of a basin with a festooned curbstone surmounted by two smaller basins.

The light, filtering through the stone tracery between the arches, gives a golden glow to the stone and the water. The old refectory, which has a fine Gothic ceiling, houses the Museum of the Unknown Soldiers.

Claustro de D Afonso V★

The coats of arms on the keystones to the vaulting in these fine Gothic cloisters are those of King Duarte I and King Afonso V. Go round the outside of the chapter-house and through the porch to the Unfinished Chapels.

Capelas Imperfeitas★★

Dom Duarte commissioned a vast mausoleum for himself and his descendants, but he and his queen alone lie buried in the unfinished building open to the sky. A vast transitional Gothic Renaissance porch connecting the east end of the church with the doorway of the octagonal chamber was added later by Dom Manuel.

This **doorway★★**, initially Gothic in style, was ornamented in the 16C with Manueline decoration; it opens towards the church with a curved arch beneath a powerful multilobed arch.

Óbidos★★

Peniche and Ilha da Berlenga

Óbidos, which commands a vast sweep of countryside consisting of green valleys and heights topped by the occasional windmill, has managed to keep its proud medieval character through the ages.

The fortified city, protected by its perimeter wall, flanked by small round towers and massive square bastions, once commanded this part of the coastline.

The silting-up of its bay created a lagoon (Lagoa da Óbidos), which deprived the town of its coastal position and today Óbidos stands 10km/6.2mi inland. Óbidos is also known as the "Wedding City" having regularly been "given" throughout the ages as a wedding gift by the King to his new Queen.

MEDILVAL CITY★★

1hr 30min. Park outside the ramparts.

Porta da Vila

The inside walls of this double-zigzag gateway are covered with 18C *azulejos*.

Rua Direita★

A paved channel runs through the centre of this narrow main street bordered with white houses bright with flowers, shops, restaurants and art galleries.

Praça de Santa Maria★

The church square stands below the main street, forming an attractive scene.

Igreja de Santa Maria

It was here that the 10-year-old King Afonso V married his eight-year-old cousin, Isabella, in 1444. The **interior★** is noteworthy for its painted ceilings, and its walls, covered with blue and white 17C *azulejos*. In the chancel, a Renaissance (16C) **tomb★** is surmounted by a *Pietà*. This outstanding work is attributed to the studio of French sculptor Nicolas Chanterene.

▶ **Population:** 11 617.
Ⓜ **Michelin Map:** 733.
🅸 **Info:** Rua da Farmácia;
  ☏ 262 959 231;
  www.obidos.pt.
▶ **Location:** In Estremadura, about 100km/62mi north of Lisbon.
🕓 **Timing:** Spend the morning here, then have lunch.
✿ **Don't Miss:** A walking tour of the ramparts.

Museu Municipal

🕓*Open Tue–Sun 10am–1pm, 2–5.30pm;* 🕓*Closed 1 Jan, 11 Jan, Easter Sunday, 25 Dec.* ⊛€1.50. ☏ 262 955 500.

The small municipal museum next to the church houses a statue of St Sebastian dating from the 15C or 16C and also a 17C polychrome *Pietà*. The "Josefa de Óbidos" room, in the first basement, contains various works by this artist, including the remarkable *Faustino das Neves* (1670) while exhibits in another room include mementoes of the war against Napoléon.

▶ Go to the end of the main street to the ramparts. Follow the signs to the Pousada.

City Walls★★

Access near Porta da Vila or the Castelo. The walls *(muralhas)* date from the Moorish occupation but were restored in the 12C, 13C and 16C. On the north side, the highest, are the keep and the castle towers. The sentry path commands pleasant **views★★** over the fortified city and the surrounding countryside.

Castle

The 13C castle, built by Dom Dinis and converted into a royal palace in the 16C, is now a *pousada*. Its façade has paired Manueline windows with twisted columns and a Manueline doorway,

Óbidos with the ramparts and the castle

© René Mattes/hemis.fr

ADDITIONAL SIGHT
Santuário do Senhor da Pedra

🕐 *Open Tue–Sun 9.30am–12.30pm, 2.30pm–5pm, to 7pm in summer. www.obidos.pt. 🖉 262 959 633.*

In a glass case above the altar is a primitive stone cross (2C). The nave contains Baroque statues of the Apostles. The coach in the sanctuary transported the statue of the Virgin from Óbidos to the church of Nossa Senhora in Nazaré.

EXCURSIONS
Peniche

West of Obidos on a coastal peninsular. To see the island of Berlenga you need a morning, then have lunch and wander round Peniche for a few hours.
100km/62mi north of Lisbon, on the coast. 🔺🔺 *Kids will enjoy a cycle along the coast.* 🅿 *Park anywhere in the town at pay-and-display sites.*

Peniche, built to command access to the mile-long promontory, is today Portugal's second-most important fishing port (crayfish, sardines, tunny). The remains of ramparts and the citadel recall the former military role played by the city. A pleasant public garden planted with palm trees surrounds the Tourist Information Centre (Posto de Turismo) on Rua Alexandre Herculano.

Peniche has been trying to revive its former speciality of **bobbin lace**. An apprentice school has been set up at the town's Industrial and Business School *(avenida 25 de Abril)*. On the first floor there is an exhibit of samples from past and present production.

Lacemakers can also be seen working at the Casa de Trabalho das Filhas de Pescadores *(rua do Calvário)*, and handmade lace can still be bought in the town *(avenida do Mar)*.

The 16C **fortress** (🕐 *open Wed–Sun 10am–6pm.* 🖉 *262 780 116. www.cm.peniche.pt* 🖛 *€1.50 for museum)*, converted in the 17C into a Vauban-style citadel, stands proudly with its high walls and sharp-edged bastions topped with watchtowers. It dominates both the harbour to the east and the sea to the south with excellent views. Until 1974 it was a state prison, then it became an emergency city for refugees from Angola. A small museum inside displays a mix of history, archaeology and local crafts, and the top floor houses the old solitary confinement cells.

The **harbour** is situated southeast of the town. The esplanade *(Largo da Ribeira)* is always the scene of a highly colourful spectacle with the **return of the fishing fleet★**, when the catch of sardines, tunny fish or crayfish is unloaded. Hundreds of squealing seagulls hover overhead in the hope of finding some leftovers and it is a colourful scene. Peniche harbour is a departure point for trips to the island of Berlenga. 🕐 *See LEIRIA.*

There is one church of note in town. The **Igreja de São Pedro** has a 17C chancel, which was embellished in the 18C with gilded woodwork into which were incorporated four huge canvases from the 16C attributed to the father of Josefa de Óbidos.

Peniche is famed for its wide, spacious **beaches** where a wide variety of water sports activities can be found. It is the main centre of surfing in Portugal and World Championships have been held here. There are several surf schools and camps, particularly around the island-village of Baleal just to the north (4km/2.5mi) of Peniche. Enthusiasts of kite-surfing and diving are also well catered for here.

Ilha da Berlenga★★

An almost uninhabited island 12km/7.4mi off Peniche. Normally a half-day trip. Don't miss the grottoes as you approach the island by boat. 👥 *The bird colonies on the island will fascinate the kids.* 🅿 *Leave your car by the harbour in Peniche, park legally or you could get a steep fine. Regular boat service to the island from Peniche between May and mid-Sept. In July, August and September it leaves Peniche harbour at 9.30am and 12.45pm; other*

months 10am. It returns from the island at 2.30pm or 6.30pm in July and Aug; 4.30pm other months. Return (round trip) ticket: 💳€22.30 per person; crossing time: 30min. For bookings, contact Viamar ☎262 785 646; http://viamar-berlenga.com/uk. July and August are very busy. Other companies operate from the harbour in Peniche with "island trips" that include a brief stop on the island.

The Ilha de Berlenga, a reddish-coloured mass, which protrudes 12km/7.4mi out to sea from Cabo Carvoeiro (Peniche, close to Óbidos), is the main island in an archipelago consisting of a number of rocky islets, the Estelas, the Forcadas and the Farilhões. Berlenga, 1 500m long and 800m at its widest point, reaches a height of 85m. The major attractions of this block of bare granite lie in its numerous indentations and headlands and in its marine caves.

On a calm day the **boat trip★★★** is glorious, but if the sea is a bit on the rough side you could be a little uncomfortable Among the most striking sights of the trip are, south of the inn, the **Furado Grande**, a marine tunnel 70m long which ends in a small creek (**Cova do Sonho**) walled by towering cliffs of red granite; beneath the fortress itself is a

Fortaleza de São João Baptista das Berlengas, Ilha da Berlengas

cave known locally as the Gruta Azul or "Blue Grotto", where light refracts on the sea within, producing an unusual and most attractive emerald green pool. The island is almost uninhabited though there is an inn for overnight stays, but it is fairly basic. There is also a campsite, but you need prior permission to camp from the tourism office in Peniche.

The island is a **bird colony** and thousands of gulls screech and swoop.

If you take a picnic, guard it carefully. There is no shade on the island, so if it's a hot day make sure you have a hat at least, and some sun-cream.

The walk can be rough so take good boots – it is not recommended for those who find walking difficult.

The island and two other islands close by make a wonderful location for diving – there are diving operators in Peniche. Take the stairway from the inn to the lighthouse. Halfway up turn to look at the fortress (Forte de São João Baptista) in its **setting★**; on reaching the plateau take a path on the left which goes to the west coast or Wild Coast. There is a good **view★** from the top, of the rocks below. Return to the lighthouse and descend a path leading to a bay bordered by a few fishermen's cottages. Halfway down, the view of a creek is particularly impressive.

ADDRESSES

☞ STAY

Casa d'Óbidos – *Quinta de São José (1km/0.6mi south of town, near Senhor da Pedra church).* ✆*262 950 924. www.casadobidos.com. 6 rooms and 4 apartments.* ☰✗. Charming guesthouse in a 19C manor house with lovely gardens, a pool and tennis court.

Casa do Relogio – *Rua Porta do Vale* ✆*262 959 282. www.casadorelogio.com/ 8 rooms.* Just outside the walls, this ...ely little hotel in an 18C house has ...ll but cleanly furnished rooms and ...rooms. Not large, but friendly ...theless. Guests can use a ...ning pool 300m away.

Casas de São Thiago – *Largo de São Thiago.* ✆*262 959 587. www.casas-sthiago. com. 9 rooms.* Old family-run house full of flowers inside and out. Breakfast is served in a little courtyard overlooking the castle walls and although the rooms are not ultra-modern, they are comfortable.

Estalagem do Convento – *Rua D. João d'Ornelas.* ✆*262 959 216. 31 rooms.* An attractive inn set in an old convent. A rustic atmosphere, with pleasant and spacious rooms.

Casa das Senhoras Rainhas – *R. Padré Nunes Tavares, 6.* ✆*262 955 360. www.senhorasrainhas.com. 10 rooms.* An old house set at the foot of the ramparts, it has a simple though pleasing style, marble floored bathrooms and soothing colours. There might not be a grand view, although the rooms all open onto the terrace, but it has charm. It also has a good restaurant that is open to non-guests.

Pousada do Castelo – *Paço Real, Óbidos.* ✆*210 407 630. www.pousadas.pt. 17 rooms.* The former convent of Óbidos, set within the castle, today houses one of the best *pousadas* in Portugal.

☷/EAT

Petrarum Domus – *R. Direita.* ✆*262 959 620. www.petrarumdomus.com.* Old beams, leather armchairs, stone tables and soft lighting go to make this wine bar a place to relax. *Celta*, a local speciality, will delight you.

O Caldeirão – *Largo do Santuário do Senhor da Pedra (near the church of Senhor da Pedra).* ✆*262 959 839.* Opposite the church, this place is simple and a good value. Popular with locals.

O Alcaide – *Rua Direita.* ✆*262 959 220.* Its central location, beautiful views and simple traditional cooking make this a popular restaurant.

A Nova Casa de Ramiro – *Rua Porta do Vale.* ✆*967 265 945. Closed Jan.* Fine traditional cuisine served in an old country house outside the walls.

Adega do Ramada – *Trav Josefa d'Óbidos.* ✆*964 180 312. www. adegadoramada.com. Closed Mon.* Specialises in steaks, chops, pork and salmon, all cooked on an outside grill.

Alcobaça★★★

One of the most beautiful Cistercian abbeys dating from the Middle Ages stands in the heart of this small town. Alcobaça is set in an agricultural region at the confluence of the Alcoa and Baça rivers, which gave the town its name. Its main activities are fruit growing, wine-making and the production of a cherry liqueur called *ginginha*. Alcobaça is also an active commercial centre for local pottery, which is predominantly blue.

▶ **Population:** 15 800.
Ⓖ **Michelin Map:** 733.
🅸 **Info:** Rua 16 de Outubro; ☎262 582 377.
◑ **Location:** Inland from Nazaré, midway between Lisbon and Coimbra.
🕓 **Timing:** Spend at least a morning in the monastery and wander around in the afternoon.
◉ **Don't Miss:** The Monastery of Santa Maria.

MOSTEIRO DE SANTA MARIA★★

Allow 45min, 🕓*Open daily Apr–Sept 9am–7pm; Oct–Mar 9am–6pm.* 🕓*Closed 1 Jan, Easter Sunday and 25 Dec.* ☎*262 505 120.* ⌖*€6 (free 1st Sun of the month).*

The external appearance of the 18C Santa Maria Monastery belies the splendid Cistercian architecture within. Of the original façade, altered by successive 17C and 18C reconstructions in the Baroque style, only the main doorway and the rose window remain. It originally housed 999 monks who, by all accounts, enjoyed their life here to the full and were very hospitable to visitors, according to some early 19C reports.

Church★★

The abbey church *(igreja)*, the largest in Portugal, has been restored to the nobility and clean lines of its original Cistercian architecture. The **nave** is spacious; the quadripartite vaulting is supported on transverse arches which, in turn, rest on mighty pillars and engaged columns. By terminating the latter 3m above the ground, the architect increased the space available for the congregation considerably and gave the church a unique perspective. The aisles have striking vertical lines; they are almost as tall as the nave is long.

Sala dos Reis, Mosteiro de Santa Maria

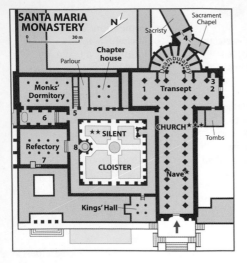

SANTA MARIA MONASTERY
N
0 — 30 m
Sacristy
Sacrament Chapel
Deambulatory
Parlour
Chapter house
Monks' Dormitory
1 — Transept — 3 — 2
6
5
★★ SILENT
CHURCH ★★★
Tombs
Refectory
7
8
CLOISTER
Nave
Kings' Hall
↑

Túmulo de Inês de Castro★★ (Inês de Castro's tomb)

In the north transept (1).

Inês de Castro was the maid of Constance, the wife of Prince Pedro, son of King Afonso IV. Pedro and Inês fell in love and on the death of Constance, secretly married. Afonso, who had other ideas for his son, had her murdered. On his succession, Pedro had Inês' body exhumed, dressed in Queen's robes and crowned, insisting that everyone paid homage to her by kissing her decomposing hand. Her reclining figure now lies upon a tomb on which the four panels depict scenes from the Life of Christ. *The Last Judgement*, which adorns the panel at the statue's feet, is particularly realistic; at the bottom on the left, the dead are standing in judgement before God.

...ulo de Dom Pedro★★ ...Pedro's tomb)

...uth transept (2).

...a severe reclining figure, Dom ...mb depicts, on its sides, the ...tholomew, the King's patron ...el at the foot depicts Dom ...oments. The **Transit of** ...a damaged terra-cotta ...h of the saint, stands ...south transept. It ...nks in the 17C. The ...l by a vast ambu-

latory off which open two beautiful **Manueline doors** (4) dating from the 16C, and nine chapels adorned with polychrome wooden statues from the 17C and 18C.

Abbey Buildings★★

The **cloisters★★** (**Claustro do Silêncio**), built in the early 14C, have an attractive simplicity of line; between buttresses slender twin columns support with great elegance three rounded arches which are surmounted by a rose.

A staircase (5) leads to the **Monks' Dormitory**, a vast Gothic hall over 60m long. Two rows of columns with capitals divide the room into three sections. The **Kitchens** (6), which were enlarged in the 18C, are flanked to the east by the storeroom. The white tiled chamber is 18m high and with enormous open fireplaces; water is provided by a tributary of the Alcoa river.

The Refectory is a large hall with ribbed vaulting. A stairway, built into the thickness of the wall and surmounted by a fine colonnade, leads to the reader's pulpit (7). Opposite the door, a **lavabo** and 17C fountain (8) jut out into the close. In the 18C **Sala dos Reis** (Kings' Hall) a frieze of *azulejos* illustrates the foundation of the monastery; the statues carved by monks represent the Portuguese kings up to Dom José I. Note also a beautiful Gothic Virgin and Child.

ADDITIONAL SIGHT

Museu Nacional do Vinho

1km/0.6mi along the N 8 towards Leiria, on the right. ⏱*Open Tue–Sun 10am–6pm with entry every hour.* ✆*968 497 832* ✆*€3.60.*

A wine **co-operative**'s warehouses are the setting for this wine museum with its collections of bottles (old Port and Madeira), wine vats, wine presses and stills.

Nazaré★

Nazaré

Nazaré lies in an exceptional site★★ with its long beach dominated to the north by a steep cliff. The town has three distinct quarters: **Praia** (the beach), the largest, which runs alongside the seafront, **Sítio**, built on the clifftop and **Pederneira**, on a hill. The name Nazaré comes from a statue of the Virgin brought back from the town of Nazareth in Palestine by a monk in the 4C.

PRAIA

Praia is the name of the lower town, with its geometrically laid out streets giving onto the beach of fine sand, and many hotels, restaurants and souvenir shops. Nazaré has long promoted itself as the best resort on this coast and obviously that has brought with it a lot of housing development, primarily apartment blocks which now line most of the seafront, as in many seaside towns throughout Europe and, in the height of summer, throngs of mainly Portuguese tourists. This popularity is obviously a double-edged sword but outside the main summer months it is a fairly pleasing place, with plenty to do in and around the town.

▶ **Population:** 15 158.
Map: p260.
Info: Av. Manuel Remígio; ✆ 262 561 194.
Location: 100km/62mi north of Lisbon on the A 8.
Kids: The beach of São Martinho do Porto.
Timing: Ideally, take a day – swim in the sea, explore Sítio, then relax with a glass of wine in the evening in the fishermen's area.
Don't Miss: The Sítio quarter of the town, or the beaches.

The **Bairro dos Pescadores**, the fishermen's quarter, stretches from Praça Manuel de Arriaga to Avenida Vieira Guimarães. Small whitewashed cottages line the alleys leading to the quayside though these days they are more likely to be used as B&Bs.

South of the beach, a **harbour** shelters the fishing boats. The catch normally comprises sole, whiting, perch, coalfish, hake, skate, mackerel and sardines.

Nazaré beach

Festivals

Nazaré is proud of its festivals. Each year, on 8 September and through the following weekend, is the **Nossa Senhora da Nazaré** pilgrimage and festival, with sombre processions to the chapel in Sitio (♿ *see main text*), followed by more temporal celebrations including fireworks, folk dancing and a bullfight (though in Portugal the bulls are not killed in the ring).

The most interesting festival, though, is Carnaval, which starts the week before Lent (February, normally) and ends on Ash Wednesday, with wildly extravagant costumes and dancers in long parades wending their way through the streets (*www.carnavaldanazare.com*).

SÍTIO

The Sítio quarter may be reached by car or on foot (up a flight of steps) although most enjoyable way is by the **funicular** ⏰*Funicular operates daily, 7am–midnight (until 2am in summer).* ⌨€2.40. ☎262 569 070.

The belvedere (**miradouro**), built on the edge of the cliff overlooking the sea from a height of 110m, affords a fine **view★** of the lower town and the beach. The tiny chapel of **Ermida da Memória**, near the belvedere, commemorates the miracle that saved the life of the local lord, Fuas Roupinho. One morning in 1182 Roupinho on horseback was giving chase to a deer which suddenly somersaulted into the air off the top of the cliff.

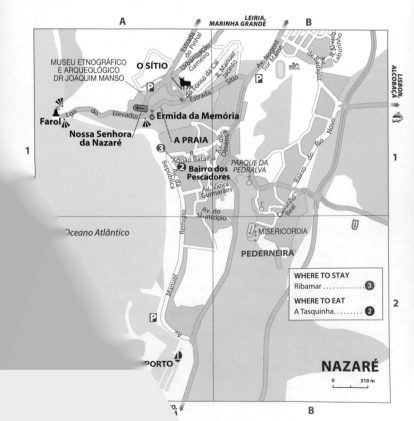

NAZARÉ

Belvedere, Sítio

© Kamilla V/iStock

Just as the horse was about to do the same, Dom Fuas implored Our Lady of Nazaré for help and the horse stopped. The façade, roof and the two floors inside the chapel are covered with *azulejos*: those of the façade on the side facing the sea evoke the knight's jump; those of the crypt, the miracle of the Marian Intercession. The footprint which the horse is said to have left on the rock face can still be seen in the cliff point next to the Ermida da Memória. The chapel is also the place where the long-lost statue of the Virgin, brought back from Nazareth in the 4C was found in the 18C.

The 17C **Santuário de Nossa Senhora da Nazaré** is on the main square and has a façade with a forepart forming a gallery, and a Baroque doorway opening at the top of a semicircular flight of steps. The interior has a profusion of Dutch *azulejos* depicting Biblical scenes. The **lighthouse** *(farol)* is built on a small fort at the farthermost promontory of a cliff. Behind, and lower down, a path with steps and a parapet wall and then an iron staircase leads to a point *(15min return)* overlooking a magnificent **seascape★★**: jagged rocks through which the sea swirls furiously.

On the right is wild Praia do Norte, famous for its big waves, a paradise for surfers.

EXCURSION

São Martinho do Porto

13km/8mi south via the N 242.
This seaside resort lies north of a saltwater lake linked to the sea by a narrow channel edged with tall cliffs.
Its **beach ♟♟** is one of the safest in the region for children.

ADDRESSES

🛏 STAY

◓◓◓ **Hotel A Cubata** – *Avenida da República, 6. ✆262 561 706. www. hotelcubata.com. 22 rooms.* Ideally located in the pedestrian area near the cliff and the are 4 bedrooms with balconies facing the beach.

◓◓◓ **Ribamar Hotel** – *Rua Gomes Freire, 9. ✆262 551 158. 5 rooms.* By the beach, this white building with yellow enhanced façade has a suitably outdated interior. Carpeted stairs and rooms with embroidered bed spreads and carved black furniture. The rooms at the front overlook the beach.

🍴 EAT

◓◓ **A Tasquinha** – *Rua Adrião Batalha 54. Closed Mon. ✆262 551 945.* Visiting tourists and eager fans wait patiently in the street, as this little restaurant is always full. Good home cooking is served on large rustic tables.

Fátima

and Around

The sanctuary at Fátima is one of the most famous in the world. Great pilgrimages numbering thousands of believers visit the shrine on the 13th of every month, especially in May and October, the dates of the first and final apparitions. Many travel to the shrine on foot and, along every road that crosses the plateau, an impressive number of pilgrims may be seen. Despite the souvenir shops around the sanctuary, the site has retained its atmosphere of spirituality. It is also a cosmopolitan place, with members of religious orders and visitors from around the world.

THE PILGRIMAGE

On 13 May 1917, three young shepherds, **Francisco**, **Jacinta** and **Lúcia**, were minding their sheep in the fields when the Virgin appeared before them. Her message was a call for peace. It was particularly apt since Europe had then been at war for three years. Leiria authorised the celebration of belief in Our Lady of Fátima (Nossa Senhora de Fátima). In May 2000 Pope John Paul II travelled to Fàtima to beatify two of the young shepherds, Jacinta and Francisco.

> ▶ **Population:** 11 596.
> ⚅ **Michelin Map:** 733
> ▤ **Info:** Av. José Alves Correia da Silva; ℰ 249 539 600.
> ◗ **Location:** Inland from Nazaré, halfway between Lisbon and Coimbra.
> ◷ **Timing:** If you arrive at the time of a pilgrimage, visiting the sights will take longer. At other times one day will be sufficient.
> ⊛ **Don't Miss:** The feeling of this place of pilgrimage.

The great pilgrimages include processions, nocturnal vigils, the celebration of solemn masses, the benediction of the sick and finally "farewell" processions. .

Basilica

Closing the end of the vast esplanade (540m x 160m) the neo-Classical **basilica** (capacity: more than 300 000 pilgrims) is extended on either side by a semicircular peristyle and dominated by a 65m tower. Inside are the tombs of Francisco and Jacinta who died in 1919 and 1920.

An oak grows on the esplanade, replacing the one in which the Virgin appeared. Nearby, the Chapel of the Apparitions (**Capela das Aparições**) contains a statue to Our Lady of Fátima.

Museu de Cera

◷*Open Nov-Mar 9am–6pm; Apr-Oct 9.30am-6.30pm.* ◷*Closed 25 Dec.* ◉€7.50 ℰ 249 539 300. www.mucefa.pt.

This wax museum contains a well rendered pageant of 28 tableaux telling the story of the apparitions.

PARQUE NATURAL DAS SERRAS DE AIRE AND DE CANDEEIROS★

This protected area in the Estremadura Limestone Massif encompasses two mountain ranges, three plateau and a large variety of caves and chambers.

Our Lady of Fátima pilgrimage

© G. Durand/Photononstop/Tips Images

Basílica da Santíssima Trindade, Fátima

Grutas de Mira de Aire★

In the village, to the right of the N 243 going towards Porto de Mós.
Guided tours (40min) daily from 9.30am: Oct–Mar until 5.30pm; Apr–May until 6pm; 7pm Jun and Sept; and 7.30pm in Jul–Aug. €6.90 (child, 5–11, €4.10). 244 440 322. www.grutasmiradaire.com.

About 20km/12mi southwest of Fátima, these **caves** are Portugal's biggest. Also called the Old Windmill Caves (**Grutas dos Moinhos Velhos**), they were discovered in 1947 and are now linked together by artificial tunnels with a total length of more than 4km/2.5mi and maximum depth of 110m.

They are impressive, especially the "Grand Salon" and the "Red Chamber". The reddish walls, due to iron oxide, the opalescence of the rock deposits with their evocative shapes ("jewels" from the Pearl Chapel; the Medusa, the Martian, the Organ etc), the sound of subterranean water, all exert their fascination. In the vast end gallery ,the "Great Lake" collects all the water from the streams and the "Black River" rises several days a year and floods the lower part of the caves. Dinosaur prints have been discovered here.

Grutas de São Mamede

Guided tours (25min) daily 16 Oct–15 Mar 9am–5pm; 16 Mar–15 Jul and 16 Sep-15 Oct 9am–6pm; 16 Jul-Sep 15 9am-7pm. €7 (child, 5–12, €4). 244 703 838. www.grutasmoeda.com.

Bandits were said to have hurled a traveller down here along with his purse, leading these spectacular caves to be called the Money Caves, **Grutas da Moeda**. There are nine "chambers", and the variety of colours, a waterfall, strange multi coloured calcareous deposits in the Shepherd's Chamber, are worth seeing.

Grutas de Alvados

Guided tours (35min) daily Jul–Aug 10am–6.30pm; Sept–Jun 10am–5pm. €6, children €3.80. 249 841 876. www.grutasalvados.com.

These caves were discovered in 1964 on the northwest flank of the Pedra de Altar hill. They extend for 450m across about 10 chambers linked by long tunnels, each having its own small limpid lake and colourful rock deposits. They have an additional attraction due to the golden colour of the walls, the number of stalactites and stalagmites joined together forming pillars, and the zigzag cracks in the ground.

Grutas de Santo António

Same as Alvados.
€6, children€3.80. 249 841 876.

The three chambers (the main one with an area of 4 000sq m is 43m high) and a short gallery have delicate rose-coloured concretions.

Tomar★★★

Tomar stretches along the banks of the Nabão at the foot of a wooded hill crowned by a fortified castle built in 1160 by Gualdim Pais, Grand Master of the Order of the Knights Templar. Within the castle grounds stands the Convento de Cristo, which is a UNESCO World Heritage Site.

A BIT OF HISTORY

Knights Templar to Knights of Christ

In the early 12C, at the height of the Reconquest, the border between Christian and Moorish territories passed through Tomar. The Order of the Knights Templar, founded in Jerusalem in 1118, built a convent-fortress in Tomar in 1160 which became the headquarters for the Order throughout Portugal. In 1312 Pope Clement V ordered the suppression of the Templars. A new Order, the Knights of Christ, was founded by King Dinis in Portugal in 1319. It took over the possessions of the Knights Templar and moved to Tomar in 1357. The golden period of the Knights of Christ was at the begin-

▶ **Population:** 19 168.
★ **Michelin Map:** 733.
Info: Av. Dr Cândido Madureira; ℘249 329 800.
Location: Inland from Nazaré, close to Óbidos.
Timing: Visit the convent early before the groups of tourists, then have lunch in Tomar and wander round before calling it a day.
P Parking: There are several large car parks in the town centre.
Don't Miss: The Convent of Christ (Convento de Christo).

ning of the 15C when Prince Henry the Navigator was Grand Master (1420–60). The town itself is a homely place with cobbled streets.

CONVENTO DE CRISTO★★

Open Oct–May 9am–5.30pm; Jun–Sept 9am–6.30pm. Closed 1 Jan, Easter Sunday, 1 May, 24-25 Dec. €6. ℘249 313 481. www.conventocristo. gov.pt.

The 12C walls crowning the summit of the hillock dominating the town enclose the **Convent of Christ** which was begun in the 12C but not completed until the 17C. The result is a mix of different Portuguese architectural styles.

Once inside, cross the garden of clipped box trees that precedes the convent. The **church★** doorway is by the Spanish architect Juan de Castilo, successor of Diogo de Arruda. To the former church of the Templars, which now forms the east end of this church, King Manuel added a nave.

The **Charola dos Templários★★** (Templar's Rotunda) was built in the 12C, modelled on the Holy Sepulchre in Jerusalem. The two-storey octagonal construction is supported by eight pillars. An ambulatory with a ring vault divides the central octagon from the exterior polygon which has sixteen sides. The paintings decorating the octagon are

Manueline window of Convento de Cristo

MICHELIN

by 16C Portuguese artists and the polychrome wooden statues date from the same period.

The **Claustro Principal★** (Cloisters) were built between 1557 and 1566. They are Renaissance in style with two storeys, the ground level gallery having Tuscan columns, the upper, Ionic. The most outstanding features of the decoration are on three windows of which only two are visible. The first may be seen to the right on entering the cloisters but the second, the most famous, is below, in the Claustro de Santa Bárbara.

Window★★★ (*see photo in Art and Culture, Introduction*). This window (*janela*) is the most amazing example of Manueline-style ornament in Portugal. It was designed by the architect Diogo de Arruda and sculpted between 1510 and 1513. The decoration that rises from the roots (1) of a cork oak, supported on the bust of a sea captain (2), climbs two convoluted masts. Among the profusion of plant and marine motifs can be seen coral (3), ropes (4), cork for use in the construction of ships (5), seaweed (6), cables (7) and anchor chains (8).

The whole is crowned with the royal emblems of Manuel I – a blazon and armillary spheres – and the cross of the Order of Christ, which recurs as a

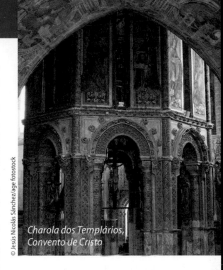

Charola dos Templários, Convento de Cristo

motif on the balustrades surrounding the nave. The window is "moored" by cables to two turrets that bear the same decorative stamp. These are encircled, one by a chain, representing the Order of the Golden Fleece, and the other by a ribbon, the Order of the Garter.

The 15C **Igreja de São João Baptista** has been restored with richly ornamented Manueline doorways. Leading 16C artist Gregório Lopes painted its six panels.

The **Aqueducto de Pegões** was built from 1593 to 1613 to bring water to the monastery for the monks. It is best seen from the Leiria road.

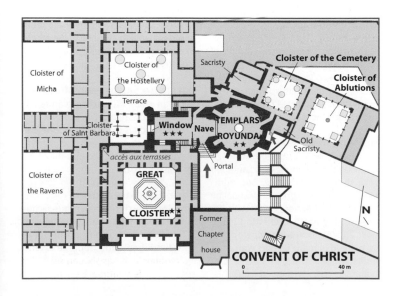

Santarém★

and Around

▶ **Population:** 29 929.
◔ **Map:** p267.
🅱 **Info:** Rua Capelo e Ivens, 63; ☏243 304 437; www.cm-santarem.pt.
▷ **Location:** About 80km/50mi northeast of Lisbon, on the Tagus.
🕐 **Timing:** An afternoon is best to enjoy the atmosphere.
◈ **Don't Miss:** The views over the surrounding countryside and the Tagus.

At some point in distant history Irene, a young nun in a convent near Tomar, was murdered by a monk whose advances she refused. Her body was thrown in the Tagus and washed up in the former Roman town of Scalabis. The town was renamed Saint Irene – Santarém – in her honour. On a hill on the north bank of the Tagus, the city overlooks the vast Ribatejo plain. It was an important Roman town, was recaptured from the Moors in 1147 by Alfonso I and later became a royal residence and seat of the Cortes. From this rich past, Santarém retains several monuments, mostly Gothic, dotted about the town's attractive old quarter.

OLD TOWN★★

The historical centre, with its mainly pedestrianised alleyways and steps, is a pleasant area for a stroll.

Igreja do Seminário★

The late 18C Baroque façade of this former Jesuit college has as its main feature the superimposition of several storeys outlined by cornices and pierced by windows and niches, which gives the church more the appearance of a palace than a church.

The **interior** remains austere in spite of the marble incrustations decorating the altar and the pilasters. The single nave is covered with a ceiling painted to represent the Immaculate Conception and Jesuit evangelical activities overseas.

Igreja de Marvila★

This church was founded in the 12C following the reconquest of Santarém from the Moors in 1147. 16C additions included the graceful Manueline doorway. The interior is lined with 17C *azulejos*, the most interesting being those known as carpet or *tapete azulejos*, painted in many colours with plant motifs, which date from 1620 and 1635.

Note the Manueline features in the three chapels and the Baroque gilded wood altar. The pulpit, made of 11 miniature Corinthian columns, is also interesting.

Igreja da Graça★

This Gothic church of 1380 has a fine Flamboyant façade with a spectacular rose window carved from a single block of stone. The **nave** has been restored to its original lines.

The church contains several tombs including, in the south transept, that of Dom Pedro de Meneses, first Governor of Ceuta. The 15C tomb, resting on eight lions, is carved with leaf motifs and coats of arms. On the pavement of the south apsidal chapel the funerary stone of the navigator Pedro Álvares Cabral, who discovered Brazil in 1500, can be seen.

Igreja do Santíssimo Milagre

Built in the 14C and subsequently modified on several occasions, this small church is well worth a visit. The sacristy contains the host that is said to have been transformed into the blood of Christ in 1247.

Igreja da Misericórdia

This 16C church had a Baroque façade added following the earthquake of 1755. The interior is noteworthy for its elegant ribbed vault supported by Tuscan columns.

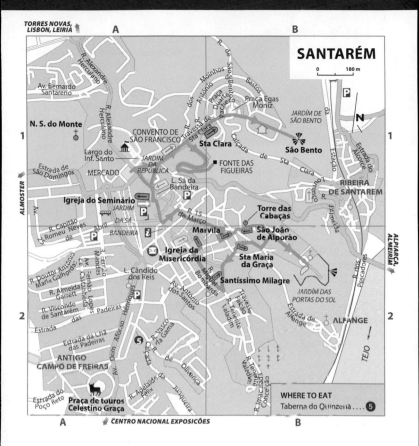

TORRES NOVAS, LISBON, LEIRIA

SANTARÉM

0   180 m

N. S. do Monte

CONVENTO DE SÃO FRANCISCO

Sta Clara

São Bento

JARDÍM DE SÃO BENTO

Praça Egas Moniz

Largo do Inf. Santo

JARDIM DA REPÚBLICA

MERCADO

FONTE DAS FIGUEIRAS

RIBEIRA DE SANTAREM

Igreja do Seminário

JARDIM DA SÁ

L. Sá da Bandeira

Torre das Cabaças

Marvila

São João de Alporão

BANDEIRA

Igreja da Misericórdia

Sta Maria da Graça

L. Cândido dos Reis

Santíssimo Milagre

JARDIM DAS PORTAS DO SOL

ANTIGO CAMPO DE FREIRAS

ALFANGE

TEJO

Praça de touros Celestino Graça

CENTRO NACIONAL EXPOSIÇÕES

WHERE TO EAT
Taberna do Quinzena .... ⑤

Igreja de São João de Alporão (Museu Arqueológico)★ ○Currently closed for restoration.
℘243 391 517.

To the left of the entrance of this Romanesque and Gothic church, built by the Knights Templar in 12C–13C, is the **tomb** of Duarte de Meneses, Count of Viana, which was erected by his wife in the 15C to contain a tooth, the only recoverable remains of her husband who had been killed by the Moors in North Africa. The stone balcony was carved by Mateus Fernandes.

Torre das Cabaças
○Open Tue–Sun 10am–1pm, 4pm–6pm (to 5.15 in winter).

There is a good **view** of Santarém from the top of Calabash Tower, a vestige of the old medieval wall, which faces

the church of São João de Alporão. The tower also houses an innovative Museum of Time with a collection of time-pieces.

ADDITIONAL SIGHTS
Igreja de Santa Clara

This vast Gothic church was once part of a 13C convent. The lack of a doorway on the façade intensifies the bare appearance of the church's exterior.

Inside, the narrow nave ends with a beautiful rose window above the 17C tomb of Dona Leonor, founder of the convent. The church also contains the original 14C tomb of Dona Leonor. On either side are Franciscan monks and Poor Clares, at the foot St Francis receiving the stigmata, and at the head the Annunciation.

Castelo de Almourol

© Patrick Frilet/hemis.fr

Miradouro de São Bento★

The belvedere affords a vast **panorama★** of the Tagus plain and Santarém where the main buildings can easily be distinguished.

Capela de Nossa Senhora do Monte

The 16C chapel stands in the middle of a horseshoe-shaped square. The façade is bordered on both sides by an arcaded gallery with capitals adorned with leaf motifs and heads of cherubim. At the east end stands 16C statue of Our Lady.

EXCURSIONS

Abrantes

Northeast of Santarém, 146km/90.7mi from Lisbon. Allow about a day to see everything worthwhile. Allow longer if you plan to visit Constância, the home to Portugal's great poet, Camões. Don't miss the castle and the church.

Abrantes occupies an open **site★** on a hillside overlooking the right bank of the Tagus. Its fortress had fallen into decay more than 200 years before the Peninsular War, when the town was entered, first by French troops in 1807 and later by Wellesley, who briefly made it his headquarters in 1809. The town is known for its delicious confections, "Abrantes straw" or *palha de Abrantes*, so called because the eggs from which they are made leave yellow straw-like streaks. The keep of the **Castle** *(Praça da República;* ◷ *open Tue–Sun 10am–6.30pm)* has been converted into a **belvedere** from which there are excellent views of the middle valley of the Tagus, the Serra do Moradal and the foothills of the Serra da Estrela.

There are three churches of note in Abrantes. The first, the **Igreja de Santa Maria**, was rebuilt in the 15C. It includes a small **museum** with a 16C carving of the Trinity in polychrome stone and, on the high altar, a beautiful statue of the Virgin and Child dating from the 15C. The tombs of the Counts of Abrantes date from the 15C and 16C. Also worthy of note on one of the walls are the 16C Hispano-Moorish *corda seca azulejos*.

The **Igreja e Hospital da Misericórdia**, built in 1584, contains six 16C oil paintings on wood. Attributed to Gregório Lopes, they evoke the life of Christ. Also see the 18C gilded wood altar and organ. The Sala do Definitório in the former hospital is decorated with attractive 18C *azulejo* panels beneath a coffered wood ceiling. The room also contains seven paintings representing the seven works of the Misericord. The collection of furniture includes a 16C *burra* (literally a she-ass) and an iron chest used to transport precious objects.

The **Igreja de São João Baptista,** located left of Igreja da Misericórdia, was founded in 1300 by Queen Saint Isabel and rebuilt at the end of the 16C. The interior contains gilded wood Renaissance altars.

Constância★

15km/9.3mi west of Abrantes.

Regarded as Portugal's national poet, Luís de Camões (1534–80) lived in this village from 1547–1550, having sought refuge from the king who was angry at him for having written love sonnets to a lady for whom the king himself had a passion. His house is now a centre for the study of his many works and there is a memorial to him: Casa Memória de Camões. Attractive with flower-bedecked cobbled streets, the village holds a huge fair every Easter Monday. It was at Constância that the British Army assembled in the Peninsular War to prepare their march into Spain for the Battle of Talavera.

Castelo de Belver in Gavião

37km/23mi east of Abrantes.

The Castelo de Belver is one of the prettiest castles in Portugal, looking out over the river far below. It dates from the 12C and was built to resist the Moors. The reliquary is of particular interest.

Ourém

About 7km/4.3mi northeast of Fátima. The fortified town is 2km/1.2mi south of the new town. Give yourself at least a couple of hours to explore.

The fortified city of Ourém was built round the top of a hillock, the summit of which is occupied by the remains of a castle. The town lived through a period of sumptuous richness in the 15C when the Count of Ourém, Dom Afonso, built several grand monuments and changed the castle into a palace. Napoléon's troops destroyed it but it has since been rebuilt.

In the **castle**, two advanced towers appear on either side of the road; note the unusual brick machicolations crowning the walls all round the castle. Go through the porch of the right tower. A path leads to a point where a former tunnel comes into view. Steps go up to a square tower commanding the entrance to an older triangular castle; in the courtyard is a Moorish underground cistern from the 9C. A path leads to the village and the collegiate church.

Enter the **collegiate church** through the south transept. A door immediately to the right opens onto a stairway down to the crypt with its six monolithic columns. The Gothic and highly ornate white limestone **tomb** of Count Dom Afonso in the crypt has a recumbent figure attributed to the sculptor Diogo Pires the Elder. Two lifting mechanisms are engraved on the tomb.

Castelo de Almourol★★

Located in the centre of a triangle formed by Santarém, Tomar and Abrantes. Access from the N 3, north of the Tagus (2km/1.2mi east of Tancos). Leave the car along the river bank opposite the castle. &Michelin Map: 733, Michelin Atlas Spain and Portugal p 47 (N 4).
Allow two hours to visit this castle. The castle is free to visit, but you can reach it only by boat (operates from 9am until sunset: €4. Closed Monday).

The fortress of Almourol, which stands with towers and crenellations on a small rocky island covered in greenery in the centre of the Tagus, was constructed by Gualdim Pais, Master of the Order of the Templars, in 1171 on the site of an earlier Roman fort.

The outstandingly romantic setting of this castle, set on a rocky island in the middle of the Tagus, has given way to many myths over the years – beautiful princesses being rescued by knights in shining armour and so on. It has been the fictional setting for many tales of derring-do (reckless courage) over the years and you can see why when you stand on its walls and look down.

The truth though is that, although the castle was built by the Knights Templar in 1171 to repel the Moors it has always been peaceful – no one has ever attacked it. But make sure you take a camera with you – wonderful photo-opportunity. From the landing stage, there is a good view of the castle in its attractive **setting★★**.

The double perimeter wall, flanked by ten round towers, all perfectly preserved, is dominated by a square keep *(access to the top by 85 steps and a low door)* commanding a panoramic **view★** of the river and its banks.

ADDRESSES

🛌 STAY

☺☺ **Hotel Umu** – *Av. Bernardo Santareno, 38. ℘234 377 240.* A modern hotel with bright and large rooms, furnished with minimalist decor. Nice art on the wall, and friendly staff. Parking available. Good value for money.

🍴 EAT

☺ **Taberna do Quinzena** – *Rua Pedro de Santarém, 93-95. ℘243 322 804. www.quinzena.com. Closed Sun.* The walls of three rooms are covered with posters of the old city, photos and drawings of bullfighters. The dish of the day is served on large tables.

Located in Beira Alta (Central Region of Portugal), this region is situated on a very large plateau of ever changing beautiful landscapes. Viseu is positioned half way between the Atlantic Ocean and the Spanish border, while Guarda, Portugal's highest city, is surrounded by the mountains of the Serra da Estrela. Covered in snow in winter time, they are ideal for skiing, plus walking and adventure activities once the ice has thawed. The landscape is dotted with ancient sites and historic fortified villages where local customs and arts are celebrated along with the famous Dao wine and Queijo da Serra cheese.

Highlights

1   Wander the alleyways to discover the craftsmen's shops of old **Viseu** (p272)

2   Spot rock sculptures in the **Serra da Estrela** Natural Park (p279)

3   Drive to the summit of **Torre** for magnificent valley views (p279)

4   Walk in the stunning glacial **Vale Glaciatio do Zezere** (p280)

5   Climb to the top of **Monsanto** keep for awesome views (p283)

Heart of Ancient Portugal

The heart of ancient Portugal, the Centro region, is one in which time has stood still. From the northeastern fortified villages, close to the border with Spain, to the beautiful Serra da Estrela National Park, you will find a huge variety of nature, history and culture celebrated here. It even has its own breed of dog – the stocky Serra da Estrela, which herds sheep and is resistant to the low temperatures of this central mountainous terrain. The largest protected area in Portugal with the highest peak, the Serra da Estrela is the country's biggest outdoor playground. In winter, skiers speed down the snow-covered mountains, while in summer, walkers hike along marked trails surrounded by rocky outcrops, boulders and crags. Pick up a Serra da Estrela Natural Park Tourist Map, which will take you on a circular route round the mountain starting in Lagoa da Torre.

Paragliding, canoeing, rafting, rock-climbing, abseiling and many other adventure sports can also be enjoyed.

While in the area, take a refreshing dip in one of the natural swimming pools such as the Serra da Lousã or the Serra do Açor. The glacial origin of the mountain range can be seen in the stupendous valleys of Zêzere and Unhais, and in the 25 natural lagoons. Several rocks have been sculpted by the weather, one of the most famous being the Old Man's Head in the Mondego valley, the source of the Mondego river, the longest flowing solely in Portugal.

The region offers genuine village tourism, generous hospitality and fine local cuisine. Queijo da Serra cheese, considered to be one of the very best in Portugal, is produced here, plus there are some excellent sausages and mountain honey to sample as well. Regional specialities include Lafões-style veal and egg chestnuts, a delicious dessert. Accompany your meal with a glass of Dão wine – you're right in the heart of the Dão demarcated wine region.

The area contains some of the oldest examples of Portuguese history including settlements that pre-date the founding of Portugal. An abundance of fortresses and castles define Europe's longest standing border. Belmonte and Monsanto are just two of the many historic villages worthy of a detour on a drive through the region.

Guarda, Portugal's highest city, as well as Viseu, offer some splendid monuments, museums and art collections. Wander around Guarda's Sé (cathedral) and old Jewish quarter. In Viseu, don't miss the magnificent art collection in the Grão Vasco Museum or the black clays of Molelos, nearby. Today, Castelo Branco is a trade centre for honey, olive oil and local cheeses, and is famous for embroidered bedspreads.

Viseu★

Caramulo, Pinoucas and Serra de Caramulo

The town of Viseu has developed in the region of the famous Dão vineyards in a wooded and somewhat hilly area on the south bank of the Pavia, a tributary of the Mondego. It is an important centre of agriculture (rye, maize, cattle and fruit) and crafts (lace, carpets, basket-making and black clay pottery). Its egg sweetmeats *(bolos de amor, papos de anjo, travesseiros de ovos moles, castanhas de ovos)* are a delicious speciality.

A CITY OF ART
Viseu School of Painting

Viseu had a flourishing school of painting in the 16C, led by two masters, Vasco Fernandes and Gaspar Vaz who, in their turn, were greatly influenced by Flemish artists such as Van Eyck and Quentin Metsys.

Gaspar Vaz, who died about 1568, developed his style at the Lisbon School. He was gifted with a brilliant imagination and could give great intensity of expression to forms and draped figures. The landscapes he painted kept their regional flavour.

His principal works, still showing considerable Gothic influence, hang in the Igreja de São João de Tarouca, although

- ▶ **Population:** 57 000.
- ♿ **Map:** p272.
- ℹ **Info:** Casa do Adro - Adro da Sé; ℘232 420 950.
- ◖ **Location:** Northeast of Coimbra; southeast of Porto, almost midway.
- ⏱ **Timing:** Between two and four hours will be enough.
- ⚑ **Don't Miss:** The Grão Vasco museum with its wonderful paintings; the Serra Caramulo.

The Last Supper hangs in the Grão Vasco Museum.

The early works of **Vasco Fernandes** (1480 c.1543), to whom legend has given the name of Grão Vasco (Great Vasco), reveal Flemish influence (altar pieces at Lamego in the regional museum and at Freixo de Espada-à-Cinta). His later work showed more originality, a distinct sense of the dramatic and of composition, a richness of colour and a violent realism inspired by popular and local subjects particularly in his portraits and landscapes. His principal works are in the Viseu museum, most notably St. Peter Enthroned.

The two masters probably collaborated in the creation of the polyptych in Viseu cathedral, which would explain its hybrid character.

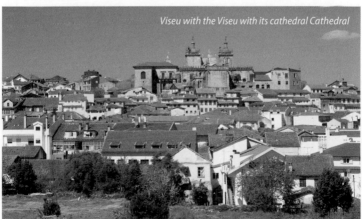

Viseu with the Viseu with its cathedral Cathedral

© nessaflame/iStock

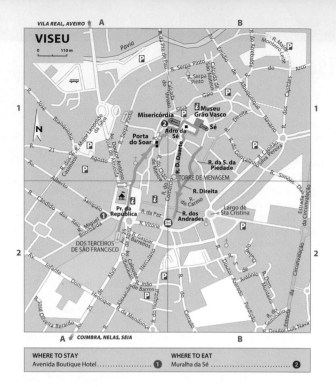

VISEU

0   110 m

WHERE TO STAY		WHERE TO EAT	
Avenida Boutique Hotel	**1**	Muralha da Sé	**2**

OLD TOWN★

(Cidade Velha) 2hr.

Follow the route marked on the map starting at Praça da República. Old Viseu is an ancient town with narrow alleys paved with granite sets and Renaissance and classical corbelled houses emblazoned with coats of arms.

Facing the town hall, the **Praça da República** (or Rossio) is a pleasant tree-planted square in the town's lively centre. From here you can climb up the Rua Soar de Cima to the Porta do Soar.

The **Porto do Soar** is a plain but impressive gateway built in the town wall by King Dom Afonso in the 15C. From here you enter the old town, a jumble of little alleyways and streets lined with an eclectic mix of modern boutiques and craftsmen's shops – printers, shoe-menders, key-cutters, florists, undertakers and grocers.

Adro da Sé★

The peaceful cathedral square in the heart of the old town is lined with noble granite buildings: the Museu de Grão Vasco, the cathedral and the Igreja da Misericórdia.

Museu Grão Vasco★★

🕐 *Open Tue–Sun 10am–1pm, 2pm–6pm.* 🕐 *Closed 1 Jan, Easter Sunday, 1 May, 21 Sept and 24–25 Dec.* ⌑€4 (no charge 1st Sun of the month). ℘232 422 049.

The museum is the former Palácio dos Três Escalões, which was built in the 16C and remodelled in the 18C, was originally designed by Vasco Fernandes (known as The Great Vasco).

The ground floor is devoted to 13C–18C sculpture. Outstanding are the 14C **Throne of Grace★**, of which only a representation of God the Father remains, and the 13C *Pietà*; some 16C Spanish-Arabic *azulejos* and Portuguese porcelain (17C and 18C) are also interesting.

On the **first floor** are several works by Portuguese painters of the 19C and early 20C. The **second floor**, with the exception of one room which contains paintings by **Columbano** (1857–1929) including a self-portrait, is devoted to the **Primitives★★** of the Viseu School. Particularly noteworthy is the painting of **St Peter on his Throne**, one of Vasco Fernandes's masterpieces. While it is a copy of the one in São João de Tarouca

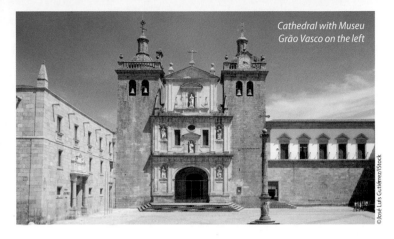

Cathedral with Museu Grão Vasco on the left

©José Luis Gutiérrez/iStock

attributed to Gaspar Vaz, it shows great originality. Another major work by Grão Vasco is the **Calvary**, in which the figures are depicted with forceful violence. The 14 paintings that comprise the altarpiece, which formerly stood in the cathedral, are by a group of artists from the Viseu School: the *Descent from the Cross* and the *Kiss of Judas* are among the best. In the *Adoration of the Magi*, the Black King has been replaced by an Indian from Brazil, as the country had just been discovered by Pedro Álvares Cabral in 1500. Also from the Viseu School are *The Last Supper* and *Christ in the House of Martha*.

Cathedral★

This Romanesque cathedral *(○ open Mon–Wed, Fri 8am–noon, 2–7pm; Sat 2–7pm; Sun 9am–noon, 2–7pm. ✆232 436 065)* was considerably remodelled between the 16C and 18C. The façade was rebuilt in the 17C, the central statue among the six which ornament the façade is of São Teotónio, patron saint of Viseu.

The roof, which rests on Gothic pillars, is supported by twisted **liernes★** that form knots at regular intervals; the keystones are decorated with the arms of the founder bishop and the royal mottos of Afonso V and João II (the latter's symbol is a pelican). The chancel is 17C; the barrel vaulting shelters a monumental Baroque **altarpiece★** of gilded wood; above the high altar is a 14C Virgin

carved in Ança stone. The north chapel is decorated with *azulejos* dating from the 18C.

Stairs lead from the north transept to the gallery *(coro alto),* where there is a wooden lectern brought from Brazil in the 16C. Go to the first floor of the cloisters where the chapter-house contains a **treasury of sacred art** including two 13C Limoges enamel reliquary caskets, a 12C Gospel in a 14C binding and a cross by Machado de Castro.

The **cloisters** are Renaissance. The ground-level gallery, where the arches rest on Ionic columns, is decorated with 18C *azulejos*. In the Chapel of Our Lady of Mercy, there is a fine 16C low relief of the Descent from the Cross which is said to be by the Coimbra School. A beautiful doorway in the transitional Gothic style leads from the cloisters back into the cathedral.

Igreja da Misericórdia

This Baroque building has an attractive rhythmic façade in contrast to its white walls and grey granite pilasters. The central section, focused beneath an elegant pediment, is pierced by a pretty Baroque doorway surmounted by a balcony.

Casas Antigas

The following old houses are worthy of note: in the **Rua Dom Duarte** a keep *(Torre de Menagem),* embellished with a lovely Manueline window; in the picturesque narrow, bustling **Rua Direita**,

273

18C houses with balconies supported on wrought-iron brackets and a very good place to buy souvenirs and many more items; in the **Rua dos Andrades** (south of the Rua Direita), corbelled houses; and in the **Rua da Senhora da Piedade**, houses built in the 16C.

▷ Take the Rua Direita before returning to Praça da Sé via Rua Escura.

Viseu has an huge street-market every day but Tuesday near Largo Castanheiro dos Amores and the ring road. The crafts market in the **Casa da Ribeira** manor (✆open Tue 2–6pm, Wed–Sun 10am–1pm, 2–6pm; ✆closed 1 Jan, Easter Sunday, 1 May, 25 Dec) often features potters at their wheels and is a short walk from the town centre across the river.

EXCURSIONS
Caramulo
Inland from Porto, close to Viseu.
Allow a day to see the highlights. Don't miss: The Museu do Caramulo.
Caramulo, a little to the southwest of Viseu, is a spa town at an altitude of 800m on a wooded hillside in the Serra de Caramulo. Parks and gardens enhance this town on the schist and granite massif that is wooded with pines, oaks and chestnuts and also has crops such as maize, vines and olives.

Museu do Caramulo★
✆*Open daily 10am–1pm, 2–5pm (until 6pm Mar–Sept).* ✆*Closed 24-25 Dec, the mornings of 1 Jan and Easter Sunday.* ≋€8. ✆ *232 861 270. www.museu-caramulo.net.*
This museum, named after its founder Abel Lacerda, comprises two sections. An Ancient and Modern Art Exhibition contains statues from the 15C Portuguese School including a Virgin and Child, a series of tapestries from Tournai representing the arrival of the Portugueuse in India and a large number of paintings: Picasso (still-life), Fernand Léger, Dufy, Dalí and Braque.
The other part contains an interesting **Automobile Exhibition★** with some

50 vehicles, all maintained in working order, on display. Among the oldest are an 1899 Peugeot and a 1902 Darraco; the most prestigious include Hispano-Suizas, Lamborghinis and Ferraris.

Pinoucas★
3km/1.8mi. Leave Caramulo heading north on the N 230; after 2km/1.2mi bear left on a dirt track that ends at the watchtower 1km/0.6mi farther on.
From the top (alt 1 062m) there is an impressive **panorama** over the Serra de Caramulo.

Serra de Caramulo
7.5km/4.6mi. Leave Caramulo heading west on Avenida Abel Lacerda, which becomes the N 230-3; 3km/1.8mi farther on you pass on your left the road leading to Cabeço da Neve.
The tip of the Serra do Caramulo (alt 1 075m; *30min round trip on foot, by a rocky path that has 130 steps cut into its face*) makes an excellent **viewpoint** over the Serra da Lapa in the northeast, the Serra da Estrela in the southeast, the Serra da Lousã and Serra do Buçaco to the south, the coastal plain to the west, and the Serra da Gralheira to the north. The **Cabeço da Neve (***Alt 995m)* summit has plunging **views** to the south and towards the east across wooded hillsides dotted with tiny villages, the Mondego basin and the Serra da Estrela.

ADDRESSES

⌂ STAY
⌸ **Avenida Boutique Hotel** – *Avenida Alberto Sampaio, 1.* ✆ *232 423 432. www.hotelavenida.com.pt. 29 rooms.* Facing Republic Square, the rooms are decorated in beautiful natural fabrics.

⍾ EAT
⌸ **Muralha da Sé** – *Adro da Se, 24.* ✆ *232 437 777. www.muralhadase.pt. Closed Sun eve and Mon.* The most beautiful place in Viseu. The food is fruity: picanha (grilled red meat with pineapple), cheese with fruit, etc.

Guarda★

and the Eastern Fortified Towns

Guarda, a pleasant health resort and the highest city in Portugal, stands at an altitude of 1 000m in the eastern foothills of the Serra da Estrela. Its name "protector" recalls that at one time it was the main stronghold of the province of Beira Alta near Spain. Medieval castles and fortresses are dotted throughout the region guarding the border. Over the last few years the town has sprouted modern quarters around its medieval centre, which is enclosed within the remains of ancient fortifications.

▶ **Population:** 42 541.
   Michelin Map: 733.
   Info: Praça Luis de Camões; 📞271 205 530.
▶ **Location:** East of Viseu, not far from the border with Spain.
   Timing: Allow a couple of days to explore the area.
   Don't Miss: The Eastern fortified towns that surround Guarda.

SIGHTS

Fortifications

Most of the once-impressive city walls have now fallen into decay, with the only preserved remains being the Torre dos Ferreiros (Blacksmiths' Tower), the 12C and 13C keep (Torre de Menagem) and the Porta d'El Rei and Porta da Estrela (King's and Star Gates). Public access is very limited and quite difficult, sadly.

Cathedral★

◷*Open Tue–Sun: Apr–Oct 10am–1pm, 3–5.30pm; Nov–Mar 9am–1pm, 2–5pm.* ◷*1 Jan, Easter Sunday, 1 May and 25 Dec.* 📞*969 330 910*

The cathedral *(sé)* was begun in 1390 in the Gothic style, but as it was only completed in 1540, Renaissance and Manueline elements are clearly visible in its decoration. The granite edifice is crowned with pinnacles and trefoils which give it a certain resemblance to the monastery at Batalha. The northern façade is embellished with an ornate Gothic doorway surmounted by a Manueline window. In the main façade, a Manueline doorway is framed by two octagonal towers emblazoned at their bases with the coat of arms of Bishop Dom Pedro Vaz Gavião, who aided completion of the cathedral.

The lierne and tierceron vaulting over the transept crossing has a key-stone in the form of a cross of the Order of Christ. In the chancel is a Renaissance altarpiece made of Ança stone in the 16C and gilded in the 18C. Attributed to Jean de Rouen, the high relief – which includes over 100 figures – depicts scenes from the Lives of the Virgin and Christ on four levels. A 16C altarpiece in the south apsidal chapel represents the Last Supper.

Museu da Guarda

◷*Open Tue–Sun 10am–6pm.* ◷*Closed 1 Jun, Easter Sunday, 1 May and 25 Dec.* ↪*€2 (no charge Sun or public holidays).* 📞*271 213 460.*

Housed in the former bishop's palace, the early 17C regional museum has preserved its Renaissance cloisters. Collections include displays of regional archaeology as well as painting and sculpture.

THE EASTERN FORTIFIED TOWNS

Distances indicated are from Guarda.

Medieval strongholds, built in the 17C–18C to protect the border, and numerous fortified small towns or villages still seem to mount guard at the top of a hillock or a steep headland, in the heart of the Beira Alta.

Almeida★

45km/28mi to the northeast.

Less than 10km/6.2mi from the border, the peaceful little town of Almeida, perhaps the most impressive of all the fortified towns of the region, crowns a hill

FORTIFICATIONS IN EASTERN PORTUGAL

0 _____ 15 km

BRAGANÇA

RIO DOURO

N 222

Meda

Penedono
N 229-1

★ **Castelo Melhor**

Castelo Rodrigo

Rio Águeda

Marialva
N 226
IP 2

Trancoso

Rio Massueime

Pinhel
N 221

Rio Côa

N 332

★ **Almeida**
N 340

S P A I N

CIUDAD RODRIGO

Celorico da Beira
IP 5

VISEU

N 17

COIMBRA

Castelo Bom

IP 5 - A 25

Linhares

Guarda
N 324

Castelo Mendo ★

Rio Mondego

A 23 - IP 2

N 233

Vila do Touro

Vilar Maior

★ **Belmonte**

★ **Sortelha**
N 233-3

Alfaiates

Sabugal

N 18-3

N

COVILHÃ, CASTELO BRANCO

729m high with its ramparts. Taken by the Spanish in 1762, then by the French under Massena in 1810, it has, nevertheless, kept intact its double **fortifications★**, in the form of a twelve-pointed star in pure Vauban style, which were completed in the 18C. Three arched gateways with monumental porches preceded by bridges, give access to the interior, the most important being the **Portas de São Francisco**. A medieval fortress dating from the time of King Dinis, this village clustered round a hill has only one ruined tower remaining, next to a Gothic gate.

The **Casamatas** (a stronghold that accommodated 5 000 men) is also well worth a visit.

Castelo Melhor★

77km/ 47.8mi to the northeast.
Visible from the N 222, the village clings to the flanks of a rocky peak dotted with olive trees. A medieval **wall★** reinforced with round towers encircles the grassy and bare summit.

Castelo Mendo★

35km/ 21.7mi to the east.
Cobbled alleys criss-cross on a rocky hillock among the remains of a Gothic wall, where the main gate is wedged between two towers. The village still has the marks of a flourishing past with a few Renaissance buildings, including a 17C church.

Celorico da Beira

28km/17.4mi to the northwest.
This busy small town is on the extreme north of a wooded ridge at the end of the Serra da Estrela. The square keep of the ancient castle rises up at the top.

Linhares

49km/30.4mi to the west (the last 6km/3.7mi after Carrapichana follow a winding road).
The outer wall of the castle, built at the time of Dinis I, with its two square crenellated towers, runs round the top of a granite spur dominating the upper valley of the Mondego. The village has a 16C pillory with an armillary sphere.

Marialva

69km/42.8mi to the north.
Marialva is dominated by its ancient castle. Within its walls, built in 1200, there is a complete, but deserted, village. A town hall, houses, prison, watchtowers, all standing desolate, are now

overgrown by olives and other plants. For some reason it was depopulated and the only buildings now standing that are visitable are the church (Igreja Matriz), the keep, the bell-tower and the pillory. Visits are organised daily between 10am and 5pm, though you are better off just going to the Turismo and asking for access.

Outside the walls a newer, populated village has taken hold and it makes a pleasing change with chapels, fountains, squares, cafés and restaurants. The change from one to the other is quite dramatic – and welcome.

Penedono

74km/46mi to the north.

The town of Penedono is perched on a rocky crest 947m high in the Beira Alta. It is overlooked on its northern side by a graceful and triangular fortified castle, the **Castelo Roqueiro** (◯open Mon–Fri 9am–5pm, Sat 10am–12.30pm, 2.30–5pm, Sun 2.30–5pm; ◯closed Easter Sunday; if closed, ask at the building next to the castle; ℘254 504 150), crowned with pyramidal merlons. A 16C **pillory** stands before the steps leading up to the castle.

Pass through the ramparts and turn left towards the simple entrance gate that is flanked by two battlemented turrets. ♿The climb up to the castle is difficult.

Sabugal

33km/20.5mi to the southeast.

The small city of Sabugal, on a hillock round its fortified castle, dominates the Côa valley. Founded by Alfonso X of León at the beginning of the 13C, it became Portuguese in 1282 on the marriage of Isabel of Aragon and King Dom Dinis of Portugal. The present appearance of the **castle** dates from the late 13C.

Sortelha★

45km/28mi to the south.

This 12C **stronghold★**, hemming in the old village with its picturesque granite houses, stands on a spur dominating the upper Zêzere valley. You enter it through one of the Gothic gates of the fortified wall, where the two existing square towers have their own surrounding wall with machicolated gateways.

Pinhel

29km/18mi northeast of Guarda. The village is small so you won't need much time here, though spend a day travelling around the countryside close by.

Pinhel, an old village and former fortified outpost on a mountainous shelf near to Spain, has many houses decorated with coats of arms and beautiful wrought-iron balconies. The road approaching Pinhel from the southwest (N 221) crosses a countryside covered

16C pillory and Castelo Roqueiro, Penedono

© Jon Arnold Images/hemis.fr

Ramparts of Sortelha

© PhotoLocation Ltd/Travel Pictures

with olive trees and vines; towards the end, near the town, there is a large group of wine vats, with very prominent white pointed domes.

The **Museu Municipal** (🕐*open Tue–Sun 10am–12.30pm, 2–8pm; 🖉271 410 000*) contains prehistoric and Roman remains, religious works of art, weapons and Portuguese pewterware. Upstairs, there is a collection of naive folk art.

🚗 DRIVING TOUR

Serra da Marofa
20km/12.4mi. About 1hr 30min.

▷ Leave Pinhel on N 221 going north.

The road linking Pinhel and Figueira de Castelo Rodrigo was known locally as the **Excomungada** (Accursed Road) because of the danger presented by its countless bends when crossing the **Serra da Marofa**, after which you reach the Figueira de Castelo Rodrigo plateau which is planted with fruit trees. To the left, the *serra's* highest peak, with an altitude of 976m commands an interesting view of the ruins of the fortified village of **Castelo Rodrigo**, an important city since the Middle Ages. Set high on a hill, Castelo Rodrigo has magnificent views across into Spain. Its history dates back to 500 BCE and it has recently undergone some much

appreciated renovation. Now, its cobblestoned streets and alleys have been restored, many shops have opened, but it is a pleasant enough place to stop for an hour or two. There is also the remains of a castle and fortifications, from where you have magnificent views.

The village of **Castelo Rodrigo** is surrounded by a new road and the entry to its ancient heart is via three monumental 13C gates – though make sure you park outside and walk in.

Local cheese, wine and smoked meats are famed throughout the region. It's well worth stopping to try them. About 20km/12mi north of Figueira is **Barca de Alva**, where the blossoming of the almond trees between late February and mid May provides a delightful spectacle with its sea of pink flowers. Douro cruises stop off at the modern wharf.

Estrada de Almeida★
25km/15.5mi to the southeast.

This route provides a picturesque link between Pinhel and Almeida. Take the N 324 southeast of Pinhel. The road comes to a desolate plateau strewn with enormous blocks of granite forming a lunar **landscape★**. After Vale Verde you cross a tributary of the Côa river by a narrow old humpback bridge. At a crossroads 2.5km/1.5mi farther on, turn left onto N 340: cross a bridge over the Côa river and rejoin the N 332; take the road to the left towards Almeida.

Serra da Estrela★

The Serra da Estrela *(Mountain range of the Star)*, **a great mountain barrier 60km/37mi long by 30km/18.6mi wide, is the highest massif in Portugal. Above the cultivated and wooded slopes, arid and boulder strewn summits appear, the tallest of which is Torre with an altitude of some 993m. Tourism is developing in this formerly isolated area: Penhas da Saúde has become a winter sports resort; Covilhã, Seia, Gouveia and Manteigas, small towns within reach of the plain, have become starting points for mountain excursions.**

🚗 DRIVING TOURS

MONTE DA TORRE ROAD★★

① FROM COVILHÃ TO SEIA
49km/30.4mi. About 2hr. This itinerary includes the highest road in Portugal.

On leaving **Covilhã**, the road rises rapidly before you arrive at **Penhas da Saúde**, a popular winter and summer spot though it is not exactly a town and has limited supplies of food and drink.

◐ Leave the Manteigas road on the right.

After a bend bringing the road parallel with the upper valley of the Zêzere, the **landscape★** becomes desolate. There is an interesting **view★** from a belvedere on the left, a short distance from the summit, of the glacial upper valley of the Zêzere. The river's source is hidden by a 300m-high granite cone.

◐ Bear left to Torre.

Torre★★
In 1817 King João VI decreed that an obelisk 7m high should be placed atop the Torre, bringing the official

- 🕭 **Michelin Map:** 733, Michelin Atlas Spain & Portugal pp 35 (K 6,7) and 48 (L 6,7); p277.
- 🛈 **Info:** Av. Frei Heitor Pinto; ℘275 319 560; www.rt-serradaestrela.pt.
- ◐ **Location:** In the triangle formed by Coimbra, Viseu and Guarda.
- ◕ **Timing:** A couple of days midweek to look around the region.
- ⊚ **Don't Miss:** The Zêzere glacial valley and the view from the summit of Torre.

"height" of Portugal to exactly 2 000m. The best thing about Torre, though, is the road leading up and back. Although from the summit the **panorama** includes the Mondego valley, the Serra da Lousã and the Zêzere valley, the top itself is marred by radar domes and a tacky souvenir shop. The "long lake", **Lagoa Comprida**, is the largest single expanse of water in the *serra*. The descent into the Mondego valley is swift and the **views★★** are magnificent. After **Sabugueiro**, a village of granite-walled houses, the road drops steeply into **Seia**, a small town pleasantly situated at the foot of the *serra*.

Road through Serra da Estrela

© Jacquesvandinteren/iStock

Vale Glaciário do Zêzere

© Cedric Pasquini/hemis.fr

ZÊZERE UPPER VALLEY★★

2 GOUVEIA TO COVILHÃ VIA MANTEIGAS

77km/47.8mi. About 2hr 30min.
This route crosses the massif by way of the upper valley of the Zêzere.

Gouveia is a small, attractive town built halfway up the side of the Mondego valley. The upper plateaux are soon reached; some of the granite boulders have been worn into astonishing forms, such as the Old Man's Head, **Cabeça do Velho**, which rises from a mass of rocks on the left of the road. The source of the Mondego (Nascente do Mondego – *signposted*), the longest river flowing solely in Portugal, rises to an altitude of 1 360mjust before Penhas Douradas.

The road runs past the Pousada de São Lourenço with a fine view of Manteigas and the Zêzere valley opposite. The descent becomes brutal as hairpin bends twist down to the Zêzere valley; a belvedere, not far from the *pousada*, affords an upstream **view★** of the valley that is commanded by **Manteigas** with its 17C houses with wooden balconies.

◗ At Manteigas leave the N 232 and turn right.

A short distance beyond the small spa of **Caldas de Manteigas**, with its still-functioning hot springs (well worth

a few hours to visit and sample), the mountain solitude takes over. However, cultivated terraces can be seen on the lower slopes. After the bridge over the Zêzere, the road (in poor condition) continues upstream until it reaches the rock face of the glacial valley; it then climbs to the top.

◗ Turn left into a narrow unsurfaced road to Poço do Inferno (6km/3.7mi).

Poço do Inferno★

The Well of Hell is a wild, wooded defile with a beautiful **waterfall★**. It is well worth walking through the oak and birch trees of the area to reach the waterfall, which makes for a pleasant picnic spot.

Vale Glaciário do Zêzere★★

This valley is a perfect example of glacial relief with U-shaped contours with steep slopes, hanging tributary valleys and connecting gorges, a cirque at the highest point, cascades, enormous erratic boulders strewn on the bottom, and scraggy vegetation on the slopes. The road bears westward and passes near the source of the Zêzere – signposted "Cântaros" (the source is not visible from the road, but it can be reached on foot through huge boulders). A little farther, at a fountain, there is an extensive **view★** across the glacial valley.

At the final pass, take the N 339 on the left towards Covilhã.

Covilhã

Covilhã, spread over the wooded foot-hills of the Serra da Estrela, is a health resort excursion centre, as well as the town for the Penhas da Saúde winter sports resort.

WESTERN SERRA★

3 FROM COVILHÃ TO SEIA VIA UNHAIS DA SERRA
81km/50.3mi. About 2hr.

This route goes round the *serra* by the west along a road that runs almost constantly at an altitude of between 600m–700m.

Leave Covilhã by the N 230 going south. The Serra da Estrela's high peaks come into sight beyond Tortosendo.

Unhais da Serra

This small spa and health resort enjoys a lovely **setting**★ at the mouth of a tor-rent-filled valley. **Alvoco da Serra**, situated half way up the hillside, and **Loriga**, perched upon a spur, come into view.

At São Romão turn right in the direction of Senhora do Desterro.

Senhora do Desterro

The road climbs the Alva valley to Sen-hora do Desterro. Leave the car and take the path on the left that will bring you *(15min round trip on foot)* to the Cabeça da Velha rock (Old Woman's Head).

Castelo Branco
Penamacor and Monsanto

This town was well fortified as it lay strategically close to the Spanish border, but nevertheless it suffered a number of invasions and occupations – events that have left few historic monuments. The maraudings of the Napoleonic troops in 1807 were among the most devastating. The scant ruins of a Templars' stronghold dominate the town. Today the capital of Beira Baixa is a peaceful, flower-bedecked city living on its trade in cork, cheese, honey and olive oil. It is particularly known for the fine bedspreads (**colchas**) embroidered in different colours in a tradition going back to the 17C.

▶ **Population:** 56 109.
✦ **Michelin Map:** 733.
🄸 **Info:** Avenida Nuno Álvares 30; ℘272 330 339.
◖ **Location:** The southern edge of the Serra da Estrela, just north of the Tagus as it spills into Portugal from Spain.
◷ **Timing:** Give yourself up to a full day here.
✿ **Don't Miss:** The Cargaleiro museum and the village of Monsanto.

SIGHTS

Museu Francisco Tavares Proença Júnior

🕓*Open Tue–Sun 10am–1pm, 2–6pm.* 🕓*Closed 1 Jan, Easter Sunday, 1 May and 25 Dec.* ⊛€3. ℘272 344 277.

This museum is housed in the old episcopal palace and contains an interesting collection of coins, earthenware, ancient weapons and Roman pottery on the ground floor, and 16C Flemish tapestries *(Story of Lot)* on the staircase. Perhaps of more interest to many visitors is the large collection of *colchas* (silk embroidered bedspreads) for which the town is famous.

Exhibits upstairs include more tapestries, paintings of the 16C Portuguese School (a **Santo António** attributed to Francisco Henriques) and antique Portuguese furniture.

Gardens, Antigo Paço Episcopal★★

🕓*Open daily 9am–5pm (7pm in summer).* 🕓*Closed 1 Jan, Easter Sunday and 25 Dec.* ⊛€2.

The 17C gardens belonged to the Episcopal Palace and now form an unusual ensemble of topiary, banks of flowers, *azulejo*-covered ornamental pools, fountains (one of which is activated by a clap – apparently one particular 18C bishop used to like "surprising" visiting ladies by clapping his hands as they passed the fountain, giving them a soaking) and Baroque statues.

An alley, which runs beside the Crown Lake and ends in two flights of steps, is lined by balustrades adorned with statues: the Apostles and the Evangelists on the right, Kings of Portugal on the left.

Convento da Graça e Museu de Arte Sacra da Misericórdia

☛*Guided tours (20min) Mon–Fri 9am–5pm.* 🕓*Closed public holidays.* ℘272 348 420.

Opposite the palace, the Convento da Graça has retained a Manueline door from its primitive early-16C construction. Inside the Santa Casa da Misericórdia, a small sacred art museum contains the statues of Queen Saint Isabel and St John of God with a pauper, a Virgin and Child, a 16C St Matthew and two marble statues of Christ on the cross.

Medieval Town

The medieval town, with its traditional stone-paved narrow streets, clothes and birdcages hanging from the windows, has preserved a few interesting buildings such as the former Paços do Conselho (Town Hall) on the Praça Velha, dating from the 1600s, but significantly remodelled since; the 17C Arco do Bispo

Gardens, Antigo Paço Episcopal

© Jon Arnold Images/hemis.fr

on the attractive Praça Camões; as well as several other delightful palaces.

Museu Cargaleiro★

⊙*Open Tue–Sun 10am–1pm, 2–6pm.*
℘*272 337 394.*

This is a museum of contemporary works by the Portuguese artist Manual Cargaleiro (who was responsible for the decoration of the Champs-Élysees-Clémenceau metro station in Paris). Works by his friends are also here, including a Picasso. Engravings, ceramics and paintings fill this interesting gallery.

🚗 DRIVING TOUR

TOUR VIA MONSANTO
150km/94mi.

▶ Leave Castelo Branco by N on map and follow the N 233 northeast to Penamacor.

This tour will take you through some of the most stunningly beautiful countryside in Portugal, via ancient terracotta-roofed villages perched on rocky outcrops and castles with amazing panoramic views.

Penamacor
Situated at an altitude of 600m, the village, which dates from Roman times, is crowned by a castle, the construction of which was ordered by Dom Sancho I

in 1209; parts of the wall and the keep can still be seen today. The panoramic view over the plains and surrounding hills is impressive, and the walk through the old part of Penamacor is particularly pleasant.

The **Igreja da Misericórdia** has a fine Manueline door and a high gilded wood altar.

The **Convento de Santo António**, founded in the 16C, contains a chapel with a roof and pulpit in lavish **talha dourada** style.

▶ Take the N 332 south as far as Medelim, and then the N 239 east.

Monsanto★★
Monsanto is the sort of place you pass through, pausing for an hour or two to take in the view, but it is worth the drive to get there. Don't miss the views from the top of the keep – they're worth the climb!

Monsanto clings to the foot of a granite hill in the middle of a plain. It is visible from afar in a chaotic mass of rocks which blends in with its castle. The origins of the village date from prehistory, when it was linked with pagan rituals; it was subsequently occupied by the Romans, and in 1165 was handed over by Dom Afonso Henriques to Gualdim Pais, master of the Knights Templar, who built the impregnable citadel. Every year in May (*⌚see CALENDAR OF EVENTS*), young girls throw pitchers of flowers from the ramparts to commemorate the defiant throwing out of a calf when the castle was once besieged and those inside wished to convince the assailants that they would never be starved into capitulation.

Steep and rough alleys cut across the village. The façades of the houses, many of them built with rough boulders from the surrounding countryside, are pierced by paired windows and, in some cases, Manueline-style doorways. In 1938 (some time ago it must be said) the village was voted as the "most Portuguese" in the country. An alley and a steep path lead to the **castle**, where it is not unusual to find hens or rabbits in openings formed in the rocks, and the odd pig or sheep sheltering within a Roman ruin. Although it was rebuilt by Dom Dinis, countless sieges have since reduced it to a romantic ruin. From the top of the keep, an immense **panorama★★** spreads northwest over the wooded hills of the Serra da Estrela and southwest over the lake formed by the Idanha dam, the Ponsul valley and, in the far distance, the town of Castelo Branco.

The **Capela de São Miguel**, a Romanesque chapel next to the castle, is now in ruins, yet it has preserved its four archivolts and historiated capitals.

▷ Return to Medelim and take the N 332 south.

Idanha-a-Velha★

This tiny village, once a prosperous Roman settlement, seems more like an open-air museum with excavations everywhere. By following the signposted path you will pass the 13C Torre dos Templários, a Templars' tower built on top of a Roman temple; the cathedral (sé), rebuilt five times on a site with paleo-Christian origins; a Roman bridge rebuilt during the Middle Ages; and many other historical remains.

▷ Rejoin the N 332 south to Alcafozes, then follow the N 354 towards Ladoeiro. From here, return to Castelo Branco on the N 240.

Belmonte★

Torre Romana de Centum Cellas

This delightful, isolated town is perched high on a line of hills near the Serra da Estrela. The great navigator **Pedro Álvares Cabral**, who discovered Brazil in 1500, was born here. His statue stands on the main street, which is named after him. An important Jewish community settled here in 1492.

▶ **Population:** 6 859.
🚗 **Michelin Map:** 733.
🚩 **Info:** Largo do Brasil – 6250 Belmonte; ℘275 911 488.
▷ **Location:** 29km/18mi south of Guarda.
🕐 **Timing:** A full morning spent here will be well rewarded.
😊 **Don't Miss:** The castle and as many churches as you wish to visit.

SIGHTS
Castle
🕐*Open Tue–Sun 9.30am–1pm, 2.30pm–6pm.*
Belmonte's castle was built in the 13C to the 14C by King Dom Dinis I.
Today, only the keep, the corner tower on the right with 17C balconies, and the section of the wall adjoining it on the left remain. A walk round the perimeter wall offers a fine **view★** of the countryside below.
Next to the castle, and of an earlier period but modified in the 16C, the church still has some interesting elements worth seeing.

Belmonte castle

© Abel Leão/iStock

Igreja de São Tiago★

This church has features that date from the Romanesque and Renaissance periods, such as a baptismal font, 16C frescoes in the chancel and 12C examples on the wall to the right. The Nossa Senhora da Piedade chapel, built in the 14C, contains a strange pulpit with a sounding-board and a polychrome Pietà carved from a single block of stone, as well as capitals which refer to the exploits of Fernão Cabral I, the father of Pedro Álvares Cabral, the man who "discovered" Brazil and had been born in the castle in 1467. The family mausoleum containing the tombs of his parents can be seen in the adjoining Panteão dos Cabrais though his own tomb is in Santarém rather than here.

Belmonte also has a restored Jewish Quarter just below the walls of the castle. This was one of the largest Jewish communities in Portugal. At the time of the Inquisition, many Jews fled though have since returned. Many pretended to convert to Catholicism, but practised their own religion in secret, right up to 1974. There is a **synagogue** *(which is open for celebrations but not to tourists)* and a **Museu Judaico** *(◕open Tue–Sun: mid-Sept–mid-Apr 9am–12.30pm, 2.30–5pm; mid-Apr–mid-Sept 9.30am–1pm, 2.30–6pm; ⊜€4; ℘275 088 698).*

Parish Church

The church, built in 1940, contains the picture of Our Lady of Hope, which, according to tradition, accompanied Pedro Álvares Cabral on his voyage of discovery to Brazil, as well as a replica of the cross used in the first mass celebrated there. The original can be seen in Braga Cathedral.

Torre Romana de Centum Cellas★

4km/2.5mi to the north.
Take the N 18 towards Guarda then, on the right, the road to Comeal (sign marked Monumento) where there is a road leading to the foot of the tower.
This impressive ruin is thought to be part of a 1C Roman villa which was connected to the tin trade along the road linking Mérida and Braga. Its square mass, made of pink granite blocks laid with dry joints, still stands with rectangular openings on three levels.
It is believed to have been the residence of a nobleman called Caecilius, according to an inscription found on the site, whose income came from agriculture and tin ore.

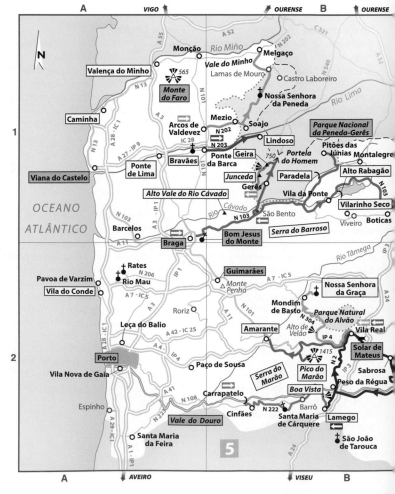

Porto and
the North

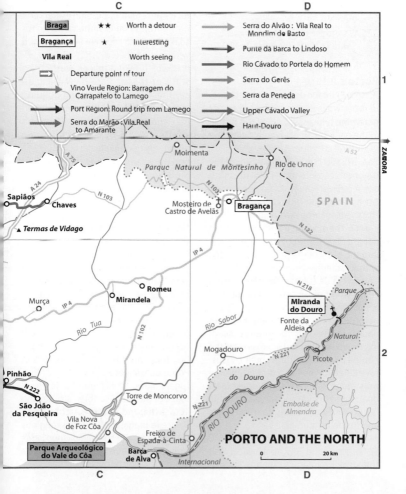

C | **D**

Braga ★★ Worth a detour
Bragança ★ Interesting
Vila Real Worth seeing

Departure point of tour

Vino Verde Region: Barragem do
Carrapatelo to Lamego

Port Region: Round trip from Lamego

Serra do Marão : Vila Real
to Amarante

Serra do Alvão : Vila Real to
Mondim de Basto

Ponte da Barca to Lindoso

Rio Cávado to Portela do Homem

Serra do Gerês

Serra da Peneda

Upper Cávado Valley

Haut-Douro

A 75

ZAMORA

A 52

Moimenta

Parque Natural de Montesinho

Rio de Onor

A 24

N 103

Sapiães

Chaves

N 103

Mosteiro de
Castro de Avelãs

Bragança

SPAIN

▲ *Termas de Vidago*

N 122

IP 4

Romeu

Murça

Mirandela

N 218

Parque

IP 4

Rio Tua

N 102

Rio Sabor

Miranda
do Douro

Fonte da
Aldeia

Natural

Mogadouro

N 221

Picote

Pinhão

N 222

São João
da Pesqueira

do Douro

Torre de Moncorvo

N 221

*Embalse de
Almenda*

Vila Nova
de Foz Côa

**Parque Arqueológico
do Vale do Côa**

Freixo de
Espada-à-Cinta

RIO DOURO

PORTO AND THE NORTH

Barca
de Alva

Internacional

0   20 km

C | **D**

Porto, the gateway to the north, is situated at the mouth of the River Douro and is a UNESCO World Heritage-listed city, world famous for the production of port wine. The Costa Verde, or Minho as it is sometimes known, is the greenest (hence the name) and northernmost province of Portugal, bordering Galicia in Spain. Some of Portugal's oldest towns are situated in this region, namely Guimaraes, christened the cradle of Portugal, Barcelos, Braga, and Ponte de Lima, famous for its Roman bridge. Valenca do Minho is situated on the pilgrim's route between Porto and Santiago de Campostela.

Highlights

1 Marvel at wacky art at **Serralves Museum** (p299)

2 Browse hand-painted crafts at **Barcelos** market (p313)

3 Step back in time at isolated **Vilarinho Seco** (p319)

4 Tuck into a Frenchie at the **Majestic Café** (p323)

5 Walk to the top of **Monte de Santa Luzia** for the views (p326)

Porto's Allure

Porto is a vintage destination for tourists in more ways than one. Famed for its port wine houses, set up by the British in the early 18C, it also has a multitude of cultural attractions.

The UNESCO World Heritage Site of the historical centre contrasts with the modern Serralves Museum of Contemporary Art and Casa da Música, built for the city's year as European Capital of Culture in 2001. The meandering River Douro is a delight for short trips or a longer cruise into the heart of the port wine country, with its steeply-banked vineyards.

This riverside is buzzing with inviting cafés, street musicians and traditional restaurants serving barbecued fish and octopus stews. Stroll around Ribeira's narrow streets with its houses cascading down the hillside, or cross over the Ponte Luis I metal bridge, built by Gustave Eiffel, to Vila Nova de Gaia, where port wine lodges and traditional *rabelo* boats, used to transport grapes from the Douro Valley, sit alongside trendy bars and fusion restaurants.

Take the funicular to the imposing 12C Sé Cathedral and Episcopal Palace. Visit the Stock Exchange to see the Golden Room's splendid gold leaf ceiling and the Arabian room's spectacular hand-painted mosaic windows and climb the Baroque Clerigos Tower's 235 steps for the best view of the city.

Enjoy coffee over a book at the neo-Gothic book shop, Livraria Lello, with its stained-glass windows and unusual bowed double staircase, or head to the Majestic Café, the city's oldest, famous for its large mirrors, bustling waiters and gargantuan Francesinha sandwiches soaked tomato and beer sauce, topped with melted cheese.

It is worth taking in a concert at the state-of-the-art Casa da Música, an asymmetrical poly-diamond building with seven sides, nine floors and curved glass panels which both reflect and absorb sound waves. Ticket prices are extremely reasonable.

Equally avant-garde is the Serralves Modern Art Museum and Art Deco Serralves House that displays work by contemporary artists.

Other Northern Draws

When tired of the city, drive north through the Minho, the greenest, northernmost province of Portugal. Explore woodlands, the Peneda-Gerês national park, beaches, Serra Amerela mountains and historic towns and villages where local festivals are celebrated and traditions enjoyed. Farmers markets sell everything from ox yokes to straw hats. Buy local produce at the markets in Ponte de Lima or Barcelos, two of Portugal's oldest; stroll around Guimarães' maze of medieval cobbled streets and 10C castle; and visit the Archbishop's Palace in Braga, the country's religious capital. Relax over a chilled *vinho verde* or head to one of Viano do Castelo's fabulous sandy beaches.

Porto★★

and Around

Porto (or Oporto in Portuguese) is Portugal's second-largest city, and has a reputation for working hard and playing hard. It occupies a magnificent site★★ where houses cling to the banks of the Douro, the legendary river that ends here after its long course through Spain and Portugal.

Not least among the city's claims to fame are its internationally celebrated port wines, which are matured in the **Vila Nova de Gaia** wine lodges across the river.

The best **general view★** of Porto is from the terrace of the former Convento de Nossa Senhora da Serra do Pilar. The historical city centre is a UNESCO World Heritage Site.

THE CITY TODAY

The city centre spreads across a network of shopping streets around Praça da Liberdade and São Bento station. The main street is **Avenida dos Aliados** (just known as Aliodos), which is very lively during the day with its crowds of people, pavement cafés and restaurants. Old-fashioned shopfronts can be found in Rua Miguel Bombarda (upmarket, with lots of art galleries), Formosa, Sá da Bandeira and Fernandes Tomás.

Near the Douro river, the working districts of **Ribeira** and **Miragaia** have been restored and renovated over the last few years.

Porto's **nightlife** is now centred in Rua Galeria de Paris (city centre, near the Clérigos Tower), with its many fashionable restaurants and bars that are lively on summer evenings, particularly Fridays. The quarter also provides a good selection of moderately priced restaurants and bars.

If you are fortunate enough to visit during one of the many colourful festivals, they are also held in Ribeira (along the river-front). All the famous port houses are located here, most of which you can visit and enjoy a tasting.

▶ **Population:** 216 405: Greater Porto 1.4 million.

◔ **Michelin Map:** 733. pp290-291 and 292-293.

▣ **Info:** Rua Clube dos Fenianos. ℘223 393 472. http://visitporto.travel.

◖ **Location:** Portugal's second city, Porto, is in the north, on the coast.

▲▲ **Kids:** Sea Life or Santo Inácio Zoo.

◕ **Timing:** Give yourself three days to get to know the city.

▣ **Parking:** Difficult. There are several large underground car-parks and these are recommended over street parking. ☺ Beware people who offer "private" parking You might not find your car when you get back!

☺ **Don't Miss:** Go over the D. Luís bridge (on metro or by foot) to Vila Nova de Gaia, where you can enjoy port-tasting. The views from the belltower of the Igreja dos Clérigos overlooking the city.

Porto's business centre has been moving gradually westwards around **Avenida da Boavista** between Porto and Foz. Major banks, businesses and shopping centres are springing up in modern tower blocks. If you are staying in the city for a couple of days, the best way to get around is by Porto's public transport with its reliable metro, bus and tram service. Make sure you buy a **Porto Card** (tourist office), which also provides free or reduced price entry to museums.

You will also probably want to go on a river cruise; these cruises depart from either Ribeira or Vila Nova de Gaia. The shortest cruises usually sail up to the mouth of the Douro, although a number of other options are available.

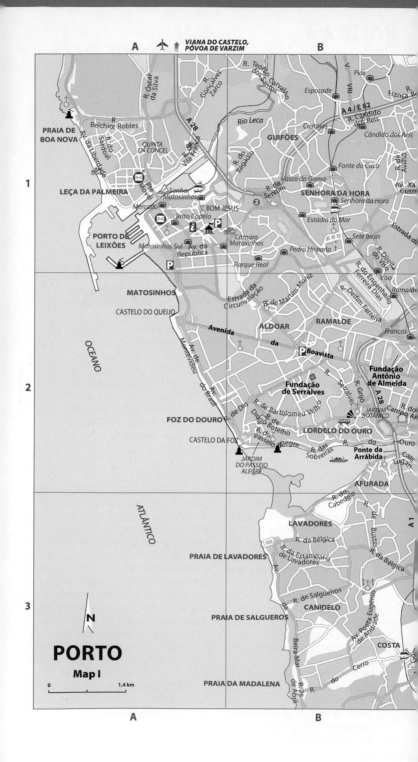

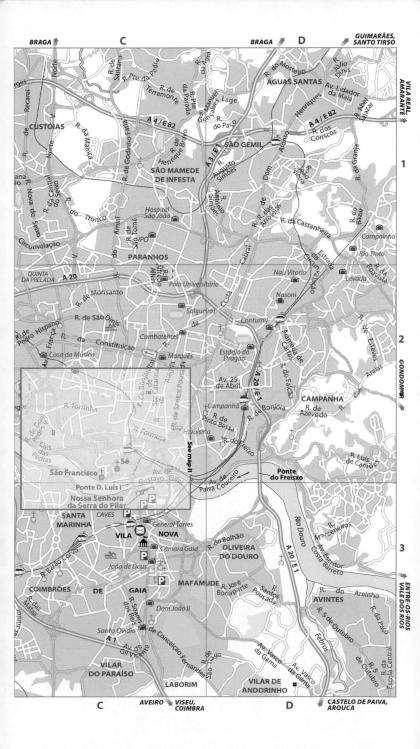

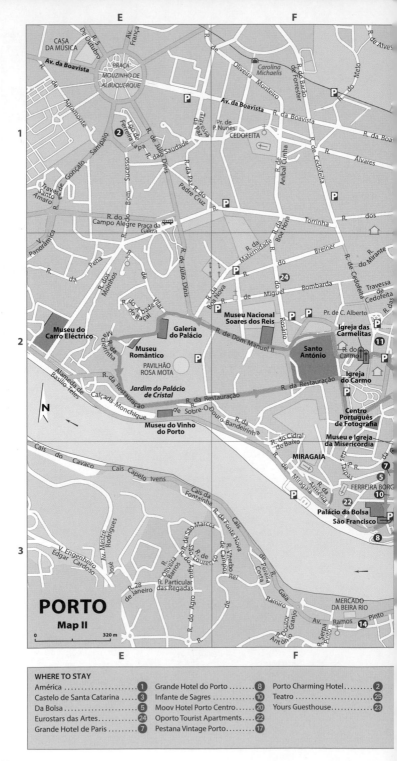

PORTO

Map II

0   320 m

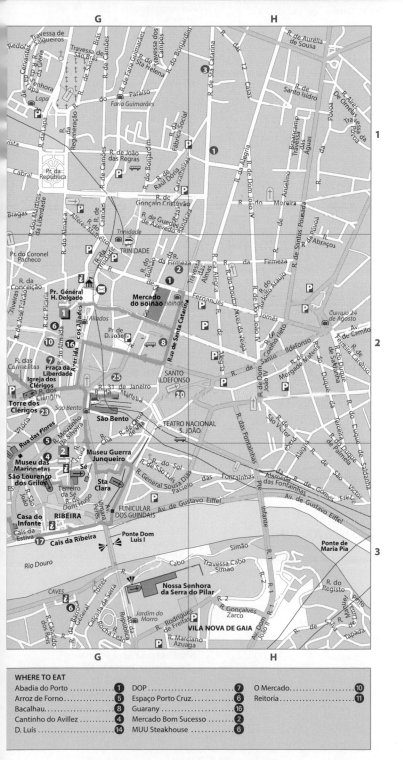

USEFUL INFORMATION

Porto Card – Tourist pass valid for one to four days (€6–€15), or including transport (€13–€33),with free or reduced entry to museums and monuments; free travel on the metro and buses; discounts in shops, visits to wine cellars or theatres and concert halls. *www.portocard.city*.

ARRIVALS

AIRPORT – Dr Francisco Sá Carneiro airport is on the EN 107 northwest of Porto. For arriving passengers, Porto airport has an information desk, InfoKiosk, inside the luggage claim area *(Open from 6am to midnight)*. Other than by taxi, the quickest and most efficient way to reach the city centre is by **metro** – line E-Violet (Aeroporto – Estádio do Dragão). This line operates daily from 6am–1am and takes 20–30 minutes to the centre (either Trindade or Bolhão station). *www.metrodoporto.pt*. To get to the city centre by **bus**, you can take line 601, 602, 604 or 3M lines (5.30am–11.30pm. *www.stcp.pt*. A **taxi** from the airport to the city centre will cost around €25. (*℡707 277 277; www.antral.pt*). There are six **airport shuttle** services available:

100rumos – hotel to hotel shuttle (*€6, www.100rumos.com, ℡960 426 692*). ◆ **Barquense** – www.facebook.com/barquense.pt. ◆ **Getbus** – ℡253 262 371; http://getbus.eu. ◆ **Goin'Porto** – budget shuttle service – www.goinporto.com. ◆ **Ovnitur Viagens** – ℡258 942 920; www.ovnitur.pt. ◆ **Transdev** – ℡225 100 100; www.transdev.pt/aeroportoporto.

GETTING AROUND

TRAIN – Two main stations: **Campanhá**, *R. da Estação* – both national and international services; **São Bento** – *Praça Almeida Garret* – serves the north of Portugal and local destinations. Train information on *℡707 210 220* or at *www.cp.pt*.
METRO – Oporto's state-of-the-art metro opened in 2002 and has expanded over the years. It covers most of the city both under and over ground, all the way to the surrounding suburbs. Trains run from 6am to 1am, and stations are marked with a wavy blue "M". For more information, obtain maps from any metro station or Tourist Information Centres or visit *www.metrodoporto.pt*.

BUSES – Porto has 78 different lines covering the entire city. If you're a night-owl, there are 13 lines that run all night. *www.stcp.pt. Buy tickets from the driver, and then validate them*.
TRAMS – There are two short tram routes still in operation in Oporto, No. 1 and No. 18. No.1 is a pleasant ride, passing along the riverfront to Foz. Tickets are bought from the driver.
TAXI – Taxis in Portugal are inexpensive compared to the rest of Europe. Most are beige, but there are also some older black and green ones. There are taxi stands by most main squares in Oporto, or you may call the following numbers to have one pick you up at a certain location at a scheduled time:
Raditaxis: ℡225 073 900
Taxis Invicta: ℡225 076 400
Taxis Unidos: ℡225 029 898

CITY TOURS

You can book all city tours, including cruises, sight-seeing bus, tram city tours, helicopter and more through **GetYourGuide** *(www.getyourguide.com)*.
Wine Cellar Visits – The port wine cellars are at Vila Nova de Gaia and you can visit and taste. They are easily identifiable by huge signs.
River Cruises – Departures are from the Quai Ribeira or Quai Amarelo every day from 10am. You can also take a full-day cruise upriver into the port wine country, normally returning by bus.

FUN ACTIVITIES

- Go for a **treetop walk** over the Serralves Park woods. www.serralves.pt/pt/parque/treetop-walk
- **Climb to the top of the Arrabida Bridge,** the largest concrete arch in the world, and enjoy breath-taking views. www.portobridgeclimb.com
- Learn about water at the **Pavilhao da Agua** exhibition *(www.pavilhaodaagua.pt)* or about biodiversity at the new **Galeria da Biodiversidade** *(www.mhnc.pt)*
- **Experience Porto in 5D** at Look at Porto *(www.lookatporto.pt)*
- **Visit the narrowest house in Portugal,** the Casa Escondida, between Igreja do Carmo and Carmelitas *(222 078 400)*

Azulejo decorations, São Bento station

THE BRIDGES

The river banks are linked by several outstanding bridges.

The **Ponte Ferroviária Marla★**, a railway bridge which is the farthest upstream and the most graceful, was designed by the French engineer Gustav Eiffel in 1877.

The **Ponte Rodoviária D. Luís I★★** is the most spectacular of Porto's bridges with two superimposed road tracks, serving both upper and lower levels of the town on both banks. It is a World Heritage Site with a span of 172m and was built in 1886.

The **Ponte Rodoviária Arrábida**, opened in 1963 and used by the IC 1 road that runs through Porto, is a particularly bold structure. It crosses the Douro in a single reinforced concrete span of nearly 270m. (You can book a bridge climbing adventure on *www.portobridgeclimb.pt*).

The **Ponte do Freixo** is situated to the east of Porto, providing motorists with an alternative route that avoids §the city centre.

🐾 WALKING TOUR

CITY CENTRE

Plan II. Follow the route marked on the map. Start your walk at the **Praça da Liberdade** and the **Praça do General Humberto Delgado**. These two squares in the city centre form a vast open space dominated by the Town Hall. Nearby is the pedestrian **Rua de Santa Catarina**, with the city's smartest shops and the famous Café Majestic. The **Mercado Muncipal de Bolhão**, the municipal market, located between Rua de Fernandes and Rua Formosa, is colourful. From the south side of Praça de Liberadade, you can head east to see the **Gare Sao Bento** and its stunning *azulejos*, which evoke traditional life in northern Portugal, or follow R. dos Clerigos west to **Igreja dos Clérigos**,

Torre dos Clérigos

295

a Baroque church built by the architect Nasoni between 1735-1748. The oval plan of the nave bears out the Italian influence. Dominating the church is the 75.60m high **Torre dos Clérigos★** (*tower and belfry open daily 9am–7pm; €5; 222 001 729; www.torredosclerigos.pt/en*), Porto's most characteristic monument, which in the past served as a seamark to ships. The **panorama★** from the top takes in the city, the cathedral, the Douro, and the wine lodges across the river. There are 225 steps to climb though!

Continue on R. das Carmelitas towards the **Igreja do Carmo** and **Igreja das Carmelitas**. The two Baroque churches stand side by side. The Igreja do Carmo is decorated on the outside with a large panel of *azulejos* showing Carmelites taking the veil. The older and rather less ostentatious Igreja das Carmelitas, is more sombre but just as interesting. An ancient law stated that two churches could not share the same wall (in this case to keep the monks from one and the nuns from the other apart to thwart any amorous liaisons), so they are divided by the narrowest house in Portugal, no wider than a letter-box. Incredibly it was inhabited until the 1980s.

Pass around the imposing Palladian-style **Hospital of Santo Antonio**, built by the English architect John Carr in 1770 to visit the **Museu Nacional Soares dos Reis★** (*open Tue–Sun 10am–6pm; closed 1 Jan, Easter Sunday, 1 May and 25 Dec; 223 393 770; www.museusoaresdosreis.gov.pt*). Housed in the 18C Palácio dos Carrancos, this museum, one of the best in Porto, exhibits permanent collections of Portuguese paintings and sculpture from the 17C to 20C, in particular a gallery of works by Portuguese sculptor António Soares dos Reis, after whom the museum is named. Portuguese painting between 1850 and 1950 is represented by canvases by Silva Porto, Henrique Pousão, who was influenced by the Impressionists and Symbolists, José Malhoa, João Vaz and Columbano. Older paintings on display include Portuguese works by Frei Carlos, Gaspar Vaz, Vasco Fernandes and Cristóvão de Figueiredo, and international works by Francis Clouet (portraits of *Marguerite de Valois* and *Henri II of France*), Quillard, Pillement, Teniers, Troni and Simpson. Particularly worthy of note are two 17C Namban screens illustrating the arrival of the Portuguese in Japan. The decorative and applied art section is perhaps the best exhibit on display, with a collection of old ceramics, gold articles and sacred art.

The walk continues around the **Jardim do Palácio de Cristal★** (*Crystal Palace Gardens; open daily Oct–Mar 8am–7pm; Apr–Sept 8am–9pm*). This garden provides a haven of peace in its tree-lined paths, its beautiful flowers, lagoons, grottos and fountains. Animals roam freely; it is the ideal place for a picnic while watching the children play. There are some spots with lovely views over Vila Nova da Gaia, the Douro and the coast. A crystal palace was built here similar to that used for the Great Exhibition of 1865 in London, but it has since been demolished and replaced by a rather uninspiring sports pavilion, to the chagrin of many locals.

At one part of the garden, you will find the **Galeria do Palácio**, which has regular exhibitions and also houses the **Biblioteca Almeida Garrett**. Nearby is the Quinta da Macieirinha, a small house where the King of Sardinia spent his final days in exile. Part of the house has been turned into the charming **Museu Romântico** (*open Tue–Sun 10am–5.30pm; €2.20; 226 057 000*), which contains his belongings and furniture. Nearby, the **Museu do Vinho do Porto** (*open Tue–Sun 10am–5.30pm; 226 057 000*) is a small museum that tells the history of the city and its development around the wine trade, as well as the interesting **Museu do Carro Eléctrico** (*Alameda de Basílio Teles, 51; open Mon 2–6pm, Tue–Sun 10am–6pm; closed 1 Jan, 24 pm only–25 Dec; 226 158 185; www.museudocarroelectrico.pt*), which charts the story of Porto's electric trams and has the oldest tram in Iberia (1872). The walk back to the Torre dos Clerigos takes you past the **Centro Português de Fotografia**, which has a permanent

Douro excursion boat, Cais da Ribeira and Torre dos Clérigos in the background

collection of photographic artifacts, housed in the sinister former jail for the Court of Appeal.

OLD PORTO★★

The Old Town, which comprises the medieval borough located inside the 14C Romanesque wall, was classified a UNESCO World Heritage Site in 1996. It includes the oldest buildings in the city, as well as typical streets, attractive public areas and famous buildings.

Cathedral

Open Summer: Cathedral: 9am–6.30pm, to 5.30pm in winter. Museum and cloisters 10am–5.30pm. 222 059 028.

The cathedral *(sé)*, begun as a fortress-church in the 12C, was considerably modified in the 17C and 18C. The main façade is flanked by two square, domed towers; there is a 13C Romanesque rose window and a Baroque doorway. Inside, the narrow central nave is flanked by aisles on a lower level.

The transept and chancel were modified in the Baroque period. The Chapel of the Holy Sacrament, which opens off the left arm of the transept, contains a fine **altar★** with a silver altarpiece worked by Portuguese silversmiths in the 17C.

The 14C **cloisters** are decorated with **azulejos★** panels, illustrating the Life of the Virgin, and Ovid's *Metamorphoses*, made by Valentim de Almeida between 1729 and 1731.

The original Romanesque cloisters containing several sarcophagi can be seen from these cloisters. A fine granite staircase designed by Nicolau Nasoni in the 18C leads to the chapter house, which has a coffered ceiling painted by Pachini in 1737.

Behind the cathedral is the delightful **Museu Guerra Junqueiro★**.

The Mannerist-style **Igreja de São Lourenço dos Grilos**, built by the Jesuits in the 17C, is the headquarters of the Grand Seminary. It also houses the **Museum of Sacred Art and Archaeology** (open Mon 2-6pm; Tue–Fri 10am–6pm, Sat 10am–12:30pm, 1.30–6pm; closed public holidays. 223 395 020.) with its rich collection of art, especially religious sculpture, from the 13C to the present day.

Rua das Flores

This narrow street leading to São Bento railway station is bordered by traditional shops and 18C houses with coats-of-arms adorning the façades. It was once the main street for jewellers as well as gold and silversmiths.

Opened in 2013 at no. 22 is a delightful puppet museum, the **Museu das Marionetas do Porto** (open daily 11am–1pm, 2–6pm; €2; 222 108 224; www.marionetasdoporto.pt).

The **Museu da Misericórdia** (open Apr–Sept 10am–6.30pm; Oct–Mar 10am–5.30pm; €5; 220 906 960; www.mmipo.pt), beside the Baroque Igreja

Tram in front of Igreja de Santa Clara

da Misericórdia, contains the Gallery of Benefactors, an example of the architecture of iron and glass in the city. The collections embrace romantic paintings depicting a Bourgeois family of Porto, and the **Fons Vitae**★★, an outstanding painting from the Flemish School. It has been attributed to different people including Holbein, Van der Weyden and Van Orley: perhaps it was the work of a Portuguese artist who drew his inspiration from Flemish painters.

Igreja de São Francisco★★

This Gothic church *(no longer in use for services)* has kept its fine rose window and 17C doorway. The original restraint of the building was in keeping with the Franciscan order's ideal of poverty. However, in the 17C the order became extremely powerful with the result that privileges and material possessions were bestowed upon it. This status is borne out by the **Baroque decoration**★★ inside: altars, walls and vaulting disappear beneath a forest of 17C and 18C carved and gilded woodwork.

The **Tree of Jesse**★ in the second chapel on the left is particularly noteworthy, as is the high altar. Beneath the gallery, to the right on entering the church, is a polychrome granite statue of St Francis dating from the 13C.

Begin your visit at **Casa dos Terceiros de São Francisco** (House of the Third Order of St Francis). The building houses a permanent collection of sacred art with objects from the 16C–20C. The crypt contains the sarcophagi of Franciscan friars and nobles. An ossuary is also visible in the basement through an iron railing.

On nearby Rua da Alfândega is the **Casa do Infante**, where Prince Henry the Navigator is believed to have been born. It was the city's Customs House from 14C–19C.

Palácio da Bolsa

🕐*Open daily Apr–Oct 9am–6.30pm; Nov–Mar 9am–1pm, 2–5.30pm.*
🕐*Closed public holidays.* ⊛€10. ℘223 399 013. www.palaciodabolsa.com.
This 19C Neoclassical building is decorated in opulent style, the highlight being the sumptuous **Arab Room** and the wooden marquetry. It's a working building, housing the Commerical Association of Porto, so you'll need to take a tour *(given in several languages)*.

Cais da Ribeira★★

The quayside dominated by the tall outline of the D. Luís I bridge is the most picturesque spot in Porto. Ancient houses look down from a great height on the waterfront with its fish and vegetable market and lively nightlife. Several old boats lie moored at the water's edge. This section of the old city is a World Heritage Site, and has undergone major restoration work over the past few years. Cross the Douro by the D. Luís I bridge to reach the wine lodges.

Igreja de Santa Clara★

The church, which dates from the Renaissance, has kept its original granite doorway with figures in medallions. The rather austere exterior contrasts with the profuse decoration of 17C **carved and gilded woodwork**★ inside. The ceiling is Mudéjar in style. 🕐*The church is currently closed for restoration.*

Fundação de Serralves

AVENIDA DA BOAVISTA

This wide avenue is lined with shops, galleries, upmarket hotels and the poly-hedron-shaped Casa da Música, which was built by the Boavista roundabout in 2001 as part of the city's plans for its year as European Capital of Culture.'

Fundação de Serralves★★

Plan I, B1. ⏱*Open Apr–Sept Mon–Fri 10am–7pm, Sat–Sun 10am–8pm; Oct–Mar Mon–Fri 10am–6pm, Sat–Sun 10am–7pm.* ▣*Museum and park €20; museum or park only €12; free 1st Sun of month 10am–1pm.* ✆*226 156 500.* www.serralves.pt.

The Casa de Serralves complex, which stands in a magnificent **park★**, is an outstanding example of 1930s architecture with an Art Nouveau interior. Inside, note the architecture, decoration, graceful **forged iron grilles★** designed by Lalique and the luxurious inlaid parquet floors on the first floor.

Museu de Arte Contemporânea★

This vast building was designed by one of Portugal's best known architects, Álvaro Siza Vieira, who was born in Porto. It's an impressive sight, strikingly modern with clean lines and pure white stone. The museum is dedicated to modern art, with cutting edge exhibits and a strong permanent collection of works since 1960. Concerts, dance performances and talks are also held here.

Fundação Engenheiro António de Almeida

🎧*Guided tours (30min) Mon–Fri 2.30–5.30pm.* ⏱*Closed public holidays.* ✆*226 067 418.* www.feaa.pt.

Throughout his lifetime, the rich industrialist António de Almeida put together a fine collection of **gold coins★** (Greek, Roman, Byzantine, French and Portuguese) which is exhibited in the house where he lived. The interior decoration includes some handsome antique furniture and porcelain from various countries.

EXCURSIONS
Leça do Bailio

Just 8km/5mi north of Porto. Allow a day for this trip out from the city. Don't miss Lamego and the Mateus Palace near Vila Real.

It is said that after the First Crusade, the domain of Leça do Bailio was given to brothers of the Order of the Hospital of St John of Jerusalem who had come from Palestine, probably in the company of Count Henry of Burgundy, father of the first King of Portugal. Leça was the mother house of this Order (now the Order of Malta) until 1312 when this was transferred to Flor da Rosa.

The fortress church, **Igreja do Mosteiro★**, built in granite in the Gothic period, is characterised outside by pyramid-shaped merlons emphasising the entablature by the tall battlemented tower surrounded with balconies and watchtowers and by the plain façade adorned only with a door with carved capitals below and a rose window above. The historiated capitals portray scenes from Genesis and the Gospels – of particular note are Adam and Eve with the serpent and the angel. In 1372, the church hosted the royal wedding of King Fernando and Leonor Teles.

Several of the Hospitallers are buried here. The chancel, which has stellar vaulting, contains the 16C tomb of the bailiff Frei Cristóvão de Cernache, which is surmounted by a painted statue (16C) while the north apsidal chapel houses the tomb of the prior Frei João Coelho, with a reclining figure by Diogo Pires the Younger (1515). The Manueline-style **font**★ in the lateral apse is carved in Ança stone (⧯see COIMBRA) by the same artist.

Paço de Sousa

Inland from Porto on the A 4, halfway to Vila Real. It's no more than a brief stopping place along the road to or from Vila Real, but the church is worth a visit. Don't miss Lamego and the Mateus Palace near Vila Real.

Paço de Sousa was the headquarters of the Benedictines in Portugal and has retained its monastery, founded early in the 11C, a vast Romanesque church (restored) in which lies the tomb of Egas Moniz, the companion in arms of Prince Afonso Henriques.

The 10C church, **Igreja do Mosteiro de São Salvador**, is fairly dark inside but its façade has a tiers-point doorway with recessed orders ornamented with motifs, repeated on the surround of the rose window. The tympanum is supported on the left by a bull's head and on the right by an unusual head of a man.

On the tympanum on the left is a man carrying the moon, on the right one carrying the sun. Inside, the three aisles with pointed arches shelter, on the left, a naive statue of St Peter and, on the right near the entrance, the 12C tomb of Egas Moniz. Low-relief sculptures carved somewhat crudely on the tomb depict the scene at Toledo and the funeral of this loyal preceptor. A battlemented tower stands to the left.

Póvoa de Varzim

About 35km/25mi north of Porto, on the coast, the last stop on the local train along the coast from Porto, about an hour's ride. Soak up some sun (the kids will love the beach), but see the two churches nearby. Don't miss the Fishermen's quarter, south of the main beach.

Póvoa de Varzim is an old fishing port and also an elegant seaside resort. It is also the birthplace of the great novelist Eça de Queirós (1845–1900).

Use the resort as a base for visiting the Romanesque Churches of **Rio Mau** and **Rates**. This 15km/9.3mi drive will take about an hour. Leave Póvoa de Varzim by the Porto road (N 13) going south; after 2km/1.2mi turn left onto the N 206 towards Guimarães. In Rio Mau, turn right opposite the post office onto an unsurfaced road. The small Romanesque **Igreja de São Cristóvão** is built of granite; the rough decoration of the capitals contrast with the more detailed ornamentation on the **capitals**★ in the triumphal arch and in the chancel which is later in date.

2km/1.2mi beyond Rio Mau, take a turning to the left to Rates (1km/0.6mi). Here, the granite **Igreja de São Pedro** was built in the 12C and 13C by Benedictine monks from Cluny. The façade is pierced by a rose window and a door with five arches, and capitals decorated with animals; on the tympanum a low-relief sculpture presents a Transfiguration.

The **beaches** around Póvoa de Varzim are excellent, being just after the Rio Mau empties into the Atlantic. There are about 8km/5mi of open beaches.

Vila do Conde★

About 36km/22mi north of Porto, on the coast. On a normal day a couple of hours to stroll around and buy some lace; but if arriving at festival time, plan to spend longer. Don't miss the lace museum. Children will enjoy watching lace being made, and of course the beach.

Vila do Conde at the mouth of the Ave, birthplace of the poet José Régio, is a seaside resort, fishing harbour and industrial centre (shipbuilding, textiles and chocolate). The town is also well known for its pillow-lace and for its festivals. The Feast of St John (&see CALENDAR OF EVENTS) is the occasion for picturesque processions by the mordomas adorned with magnificent gold jewellery and by the rendilheras, the town's lacemakers in regional costumes.

Pillow-lace has been manufactured in Vila do Conde since the 16C. The **Museu das Rendas de Bilros** (Qopen Tue–Fri 10am–6pm; ℘252 248 468) lace museum-school has been created to revitalise this manual activity, which requires great skill on the part of the lace-makers, who use a cylindrical cushion to produce the designs for the models. Onto these they then insert pins, between which they pass the spindles containing the threads of cotton, linen or silk. The museum provides visitors with an introduction to the different aspects of this activity through an exhibition of old and modern lace, photos, and the presence of the lace-makers.

The **Convento de Santa Clara★** rises above the Ave river. Behind the 18C façade are 14C buildings. Today the convent is a reformatory and only the church is open to the public.

The **church**, founded in 1318 and designed as a fortress, has retained its original Gothic style. In the west face is a beautiful rose window. The interior, with a single aisle, has a coffered ceiling carved in the 18C. The Capelada Conceição (first chapel on the left), built in the 16C, contains the Renaissance **tombs★** of the founders and their children. The low-relief sculptures on the sides of the tomb of **Dom Afonso Sanches** represent scenes from the Life of Christ.

The reclining figure on the tomb of **Dona Teresa Martins** is dressed in the habit of a nun of the Franciscan Tertiaries. Scenes of the Passion are depicted on the sides and St Francis receiving the stigmata is shown at the head. The children's tombs have the Doctors of the Church (left tomb) and the Evangelists (right tomb) carved upon them. A fine grille divides the nave from the nun's chancel.

The arches of the 18C cloisters can still be seen to the south of the church; the fountain in the centre of the close is the terminal for the 18C aqueduct from Póvoa de Varzim.

On Rua do Cais da Alfândega is the **Museu da Construão Naval** (Qopen Tue–Sun 10am–6pm; ℘252 248 468). Housed in the imposing former Customs House, this small museum details the history of the construction of ships here in Viano. It also has information on cartography, navigations and details of life on board ship during the 17 and 18C. Close by you will see the imposing white dome with a small cross on top of the **Capela do Socorro**, where Moorish tradesmen were "converted" to Catholicism in order to keep working. The chapel was built in 1599 by Gaspar Manuel, professed knight of the Order of Christ and is situated beside the river Ave. Beautiful tiles depict various religious scenes and landscapes. The altarpiece is carved in white and gold.

ADDRESSES

STAY

⊜⊜⊜ **América** – Rua Santa Catarina, 1018. ℘223 392 930, or ℘936 729 073. www.hotel-america.net. 22 rooms and 1 suite. ⚒🅿. This hotel has wood floors and lovely furniture. 15min walk from the city centre.

⊜⊜ **Castelo Santa Catarina** – Rua de Santa Catarina, 1347, (metro: Marquês, line D). ℘225 095 599. www.castelosanta catarina.com.pt. 26 rooms. 🛏🅿. This astonishing fairy-tale villa complete with a crenellated tower, extensive terraced gardens and massive reproduction furniture provides reasonably priced, comfortable accommodation only 10min-walk from Porto's centre.

⊜⊜⊜ **Hotel Vera Cruz** – Rua Ramalho Ortigão, 14. ℘222 323 396. www. veracruzportohotel.pt. 35 rooms. Pleasant small hotel with beautifully styled bedrooms and from the 8th floor, where breakfast is served, a view over the city.

Hotel Peninsular – *Rua Sá da Bandeira, 21. ℰ222 003 012. www.hotel-peninsular.pt. 53 rooms.* Just blocks from the São Bento railway station, this quaint hotel retains traditional decor. Large rooms, some with a balcony. Attentive service and pleasant Portuguese-style restaurant.

Grande Hotel de Paris – *Rua da Fábrica, 27–29. ℰ222 073 140. www.hotelparis.pt. 43 rooms.* This hotel, opened in 1888, has regained its past splendor. Antique objects decorate the living room. Windows open onto a garden planted with a lemon tree. The rooms have old furniture, but modern bathrooms. Opt for those overlooking the back – bigger and with a view.

Da Bolsa – *Rua Ferreira Borges, 101. www.hoteldabolsa.com. ℰ222 026 768. 36 rooms. &.* On the lively Ribeira riverside district, Da Bolsa has a 19C façade, although the interior has been completely refurbished in a rather dull modern style. The top-floor rooms are more expensive but have good views.

Grande Hotel do Porto – *Rua de Santa Catarina, 197. ℰ222 076 690. www.grandehotelporto.com/pt. 94 rooms. &.* This landmark hotel retains much of its former splendour, its public areas exuding an old-fashioned charm. Rooms are basic modern style. Its location on a bustling pedestrian shopping street in the centre is a plus for walkers.

Infante de Sagres – *Praça D. Filipa de Lencastre, 62. ℰ220 133 115. www.hotelinfantesagres.pt. 72 rooms.* This centrally located hotel sitting close to the Praça da Liberdade, is the most prestigious hotel in Porto with a charm all of its own. Its interior contains wood-panelling, period furniture and stained glass.

Hotel Aliados – *Rua Elísio de Melo 27. ℰ222 004 853. www.hotelaliados.com. 41 rooms and 2 suites. ▣.* This beautiful Beaux-Arts building located in the centre of town boasts polished wood floors and newly furnished rooms (though the rooms at the front can be a bit noisy at night). Best to request one at the back.

ⵏ/ EAT

Tentaçoes no Prato – *Rua da S.ra Luz 97. ℰ222 618 2738. Closed Mon.* Rustic, informal place serving traditional cuisine.

Restaurante Conga – *Rua do Bonjardim, 314-318. ℰ222 000 113.* At 314 is the snack bar. At 318, the restaurant serves the famous sandwich of *bifanas* (pork cooked in fat and served with bread). By midday, the counter and the room are packed.

D. Luis – *Av. Ramos Pinto, 264–266. ℰ223 751 251. Closed Mon.* Attractive décor makes this little restaurant in Vila Nova de Gaia a cosy place to spend the evening, with room for only 20 guests. Fish plays a big part on the menu. Reservations essential at weekends.

Abadia do Porto – *Rua Areneu Comercial Oporto. ℰ222 008 757. www.abadiadoporto.com. Closed Sun.* Large brasserie popular with residents, in the back streets of Santa Catarina. Large choice of fish (sole, hake, mackerel, whiting) and meat (pork, veal, goat) cooked on the grill, baked, grilled or fried. Service fast and efficient.

O Buraquinho da Sé – *Rua Ponte Nova 5. ℰ919 107 398. Closed Mon & Tue.* Small but very popular restaurant serving excellent sea food dishes, including delicious octopus and bacalhau varieties. Kids' and vegetarian menus available.

Filha da Mãe Preta – *Cais da Ribeira, 39-40. ℰ222 086 066. www.filhadamaepreta.com/pt.* Simple food to eat on the terrace of the most beautiful pier of Porto, facing the bridge Dom Luis I. Order stuffed octopus and sardines.

Tapabento – *Rua da Madeira, 222. ℰ912 881 272. www.tapabento.com. Closed Mon.* This bi-level space next to the Sao Bento station serves buzzworthy share plates alongside dynamic wines from the Douro region.

Enoteca 1756 – *Alameda de rua Serpa Pinto, 44B, Vila Nova de Gaia. ℰ229 448 500. Closed Mon & Tue. www.enoteca1756.pt.* A veritable wine temple. A modern restaurant and wine bar uniting the very best of contemporary Mediterranean cuisine with the world of wine, with tastings and creative recipes.

Port Wine

The city's **wine lodges★** cover several
acres (a couple of hectares) on the
south bank of the Douro in the lower
quarter of **Vila Nova da Gaia**. More
than 50 port companies are established
in the area, including all the famous
international names such as Taylor's,
Dow, Sandeman and Croft.

In bygone days, boats known as *barcos
rabelos* would transport the wines of the
Upper Douro some 150km/90mi along
the river to lodges where they would be
transformed into port.

Several wine lodges offer tours with
tastings. There is normally an entrance
fee, though the amount is credited
against the price of any bottle you buy
to take away.

Some lodges have exhibits on display
outlining how the white and red port
wines are made, from the harvesting of the grapes on the banks of the River
Douro to the treading of grapes in large stone tanks called *lagares*, fortifying
the liquid with grape spirit of 77° alcohol, and finally storing it in huge oak
barrels. Being fortified, port is capable of ageing in wood for much longer than
most other wines – from two years to many decades.

To get your bearings in the area, visit the **Antigo Convento de Nossa Senhora
da Serra do Pilar** *(across Luís I bridge in Vila Nova de Gaia)*. The old convent has
one of the finest views of Porto that includes the remains of the 14C walls to
the right of D. Luís I bridge. It is a curious building, erected in the 16C and 17C in
the form of a rotunda and designed by Filippo Terzi.

Valença do Minho★

*Monte de Faro and
Vale de Minho*

Valença, on a hillock overlooking the south bank of the Minho, has stood guard for centuries over Portugal's northern border. The town is situated on the main highway linking Santiago de Compostela with Oporto, as well as on the northerly and westerly pilgrims' route to the shrine of St James. The road crosses the river by a metal **bridge** built by Gustave Eiffel in 1884. The old town is an unusual double city, consisting of two fortresses and a single bridge spanning a wide ditch and continuing through a long vaulted passage.

VILA FORTIFICADA★ (FORTIFIED TOWN)

Access by car from the south on a shaded road off N 13.

Each of the two fortresses in this double town, unchanged since the 17C, is in the shape of an irregular polygon with six bastions and watchtowers, in front of which are the defensive outworks and two monumental doorways. Old cannon are still in position on the battlements. From the north side of the ramparts there is a fine **view★** over the Minho valley, Tui and the Galician mountains. Each stronghold is a self-sufficient quarter with its own churches, narrow cobbled streets, fountains, shops, and houses.

EXCURSIONS

Monte do Faro★★

7km/4mi. Leave Valença on N 101 going towards Monção; bear right towards Cerdal and shortly afterwards left to Monte do Faro.

Leave the car at the last roundabout and walk up the path to the summit (565m) which lies to the left of the road. The **panorama★★** from the summit is extensive: to the north and west lies the Minho valley, scattered with white houses grouped in villages, and domi-

▶ **Population:** 14 127.
◔ **Michelin Map:** 733.
🛈 **Info:** Loja de Turismo, Portas do Sol
    ✆251823329.
▶ **Location:** The very north of Portugal on the border with Spain.
👫 **Kids:** The town's huge gates.
🕐 **Timing:** Two hours or so are needed to visit.
👁 **Don't Miss:** The fortified town and the Minho valley.

nated in the distance by the Galician mountains; to the east is the Serra do Soajo and southwest the wooded hills of the coastal area and the Atlantic.

Vale do Minho

From Valença to São Gregório 52km/32mi; leave Valença on N 101, to the east.

The Portuguese bank of the Minho on the east side of Valença is the most interesting. The river, which at the beginning is majestically spread out, becomes hemmed in until it is practically invisible between the steep green slopes. The road winds through trees and climbing vines which produce the well-known *vinho verde* (green wine).

Monção

This attractive little town overlooking the Minho is also a natural spa whose waters are used in the treatment of rheumatism. The **parish church**, which has preserved some of its Romanesque features, the **belvedere★** over the Minho and surrounding countryside, and the well-known local Alvarinho wine make Monção a pleasant place to stop for a while.

About 3km/1.8mi south on the road towards Arcos de Valdevez, the early-19C **Palácio da Brejoeira** can be seen. Below the road vines, fields of maize and pumpkins grow on terraces facing the verdant slopes of the Spanish side, dotted with villages.

Parque Nacional da Peneda-Gerês★★

Peneda-Gerês, Portugal's only national park, was established in 1971 and covers 72 000ha in the northern districts of Braga, Viana do Castelo and Vila Real. The valleys of the Lima, Homem and Cávado rivers divide the region into *serras* – da Peneda, do Soajo, da Amarela and do Gerês. The park is designed to protect the natural sites, archaeological remains, and the outstanding flora and fauna – many of which cannot be seen elsewhere. Endemic species include the blue-violet Gerês lily. Wildlife includes the roe deer, Iberian wolf and garrano ponies – small wild horses that roam across the hills. For the energetic, there is canoeing, and walking trails include the winding path of the Roman road or *geira*.

Map: p306.

Info: Rua D. Manuel, Ponte da Barca; ℘258 452 250; www.adere-pg.pt.

Location: Northern Portugal, on the border with Spain. Nearest large town is Braga.

Kids: Get them looking for wildlife – otters, badgers, boar, deer and ponies.

Timing: Each driving tour has approximate times.

Don't Miss: The wonderful journey from Mezio to Lamas de Mouro.

🚗 DRIVING TOURS

RIO CÁVADO TO PORTELA DO HOMEM★★

① NORTHWARDS FROM THE N103
20km/12.4mi. About 3hr.

The N 304 branches north from the N 103 between Braga and Chaves and winds downhill through a landscape of rocks and heather. After 2km/1.2mi you pass the beautifully situated São Bento *pousada* with its panoramic view of the Caniçada reservoir (have the camera handy). Two bridges cross, successively, the Cávado and its tributary, the Caldo, turned into reservoir-lakes by the Caniçada dam. The first bridge crosses a submerged village which appears when the water level drops. Here you are close to the **Rio Caldo** water sports activity centre.

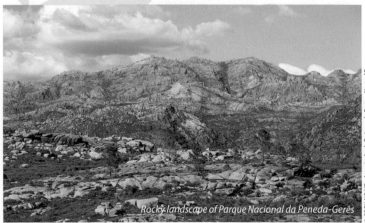
Rocky landscape of Parque Nacional da Peneda-Gerês

Trekking near Pitões das Júnias,
Parque Nacional da Peneda-Gerês

© Jon Arnold Images/hemis.fr

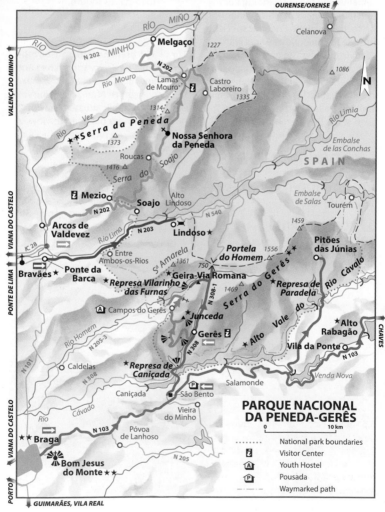

OURENSE/ORENSE

RÍO MIÑO

RÍO MINHO

VALENÇA DO MINHO

Melgaço

N 202

Rio Mouro

Lamas
de Mouro

Castro
Laboreiro

1227

1086

Celanova

N

Rio Limia

Rio Vez

Serra da Peneda

1373

1314

1335

Nossa Senhora
da Peneda

Roucas

Soajo

1416

Serra do

Embalse
de las Conchas

SPAIN

Mezio

VIANA DO CASTELO

Soajo

Alto
Lindoso

N 540

Embalse
de Salas

Tourém

Arcos de
Valdevez

N 202

Rio Limo

N 203

Lindoso

1459

IC 28

Entre
Ambos-os-Rios

Sª Amarela

Portela
do Homem

1556

Pitões
das Júnias

PONTE DE LIMA

Bravães

Ponte da
Barca

1361

750

Represa Vilarinho
das Furnas

Geira-Via Romana

N 308-1

1469

Serra do Gerês

Represa de
Paradela

Rio Cávalo

CHAVES

Campos do Gerês

Junceda

Alto

Vale

do

Gerês

Rio Homem

N 205-3

N 308

Alto
Rabagão

Vila da Ponte

N 103

Caldelas

N 308

Represa de
Caniçada

Salamonde

Venda Nova

N 101

VIANA DO CASTELO

Rio

Cávado

Caniçada

São Bento

Vieira
do Minho

PARQUE NACIONAL
DA PENEDA-GERÊS

0   10 km

Braga

Póvoa
de Lanhoso

N 205

.... National park boundaries

Visitor Center

Youth Hostel

Pousada

Waymarked path

Bom Jesus
do Monte

PORTO

GUIMARÃES, VILA REAL

306

◐ From the first bridge onto the peninsula between the two lakes, take N 308 on the right at the intersection, and then cross the second bridge. Head for Caldas do Gerês (also called Vila do Gerês or just Gerês).

Caldas do Gerês, as its name implies, is a pleasant little spa at the bottom of a wooded gorge. Its waters, rich in fluorine, are used in the treatment of liver and digestive disorders.
After **Gerês**, the road is lined first with hydrangeas, then winds up through woods of pines and oaks. Some 8km/5mi from Gerês you reach the nature reserve. The road climbs gently and crosses the Homem river, which races through a rocky course.

◐ Turn back and take the track on the right towards Campo do Gerês (unpaved road). The track crosses the remains of a Roman road at two points: after 1.3km/0.8mi and 2km/1.2mi.

Remains of the Roman Way (Geira)★ – The milestones on the side of the road are the remains of the Roman Way (Via Romana), which stretched some 320km/198.8mi between Braga and Astorga in Spain via the Homem Pass. The path continues, affording lovely views of, and then skirting, the **Represa de Vilarinho das Furnas★**, a blue-water reservoir set in a wild, rocky landscape, before you reach the mountain pass and customs post at **Portela do Homem**.

② SERRA DO GERRÊS★★
Gerês to the Vilarinho das Furnas reservoir. 15km/9.3mi. Allow 2hr.

From Gerês take the N 308 south then turn right to **Campo do Gerês★★**, where there is an interesting local museum, picnic area and adventure sports centre. This road has tight hairpin bends and offers good views of the Caniçada reservoir and of the superb rock falls. When the road stops climbing, turn right towards the **Miradouro de Junceda★**, which offers a bird's-eye view of Gerês and its valley. Return

to the main road and continue on to Campo do Gerês.
In the centre of a crossroads, note an ancient Roman milestone bearing a sculpture of Christ. Continue along the road to the right to reach the Vilarinho das Furnas reservoir.

SERRA DE PENEDA★★

③ ARCOS DE VALDEVEZ TO MELGAÇO
70km/43.5mi. Allow half a day.

This itinerary takes you through the north, the wildest part of the park. From **Arcos de Valdevez**, where the towers of two churches dominate this little town on the banks of the Vez, you reach **Mezio**: a village at the entrance to the national park. The road to Peneda begins 2.5km/1.5mi farther on, but continue towards **Soajo**, an isolated village with a group of 18C granaries or **espigueiros★** (⊙see LINDOSO) and some good accommodation options.

◐ Return to the junction and take the Peneda road.

The **Mosteiro de Nossa Senhora da Peneda** stands in a fine **setting★** preceded by 300 steps climbed by pilgrims in early September each year.

Barrosã cattle in Parque Nacional da Peneda-Gerês

© Daniel Rodrigues/CC BY-NC-ND - Associação de Turismo do Porto e Norte, AR

© Jacobo Hernández/age fotostock
Granaries in Lindoso

Continue past Castro Laboreiro, a village that has preserved several traditional stone houses and the ruins of a castle.

Return to Lamas de Mouro and take the Melgaço road.

4 PONTE DA BARCA TO LINDOSO

31km/19mi via the EN 203.

Ponte da Barca belongs to the vinho verde demarcated wine region. It is believed to have taken its name from the boat (barca) that connected the two banks before the bridge (ponte) was built in the 15C.

The town's historical centre has a number of manor houses, some of which have been converted into tourist accommodation, and beautiful monuments dating from the 16C–18C. Also worth a visit is the Romanesque São Salvador de Bravães church at nearby Bravães, recognised as a masterpiece of Portuguese Romanesque art.

Lindoso★ is a small village in the Serra Amarela mountains, part of the Parque Nacional da Peneda-Gerês. It is the type of place you will pass through, stopping for an hour or so. Don't miss the granaries, which look like huge tombs.

Built like an amphitheatre against the southern flanks of one of the last mountains in the Serra do Soajo, Lindoso, in the far north of Portugal, on the border with Spain, sets out its austere granite houses in tiered rows up to a height of 462m. The village is perfectly integrated into the rocky landscape – despite the presence of a few recent constructions – and surrounded by cultivated terraces (maize, vines).

The castle stands on a hillock where there is also an unusual group of *espigueiros* (*see below*).

Covering a rocky platform at the foot of the castle, the 60 or more *espigueiros*, or **granaries★**, are grouped together, resembling a cemetery. They are small granite buildings, perched on piles, most with one or two crosses on the roof. Their construction dates back to the 18C and 19C. They are still used today for drying maize.

Lindoso's **castle** (*open Tue–Sun 10.30am–12pm, 2–5pm*) faces the border. It was attacked several times by the Spanish during the War of Independence in the 17C. Restored, it appears again as a crenellated feudal keep in the middle of a small 17C square with a surrounding wall with bastions and watch turrets.

From the watchpath there are views over the Lima valley and the surrounding Portuguese and Galician mountains. The castle was originally thought to have been named by King D. Dinis who described it as "so bright and exquisite that he called it Lindoso (beautiful)".

In reality, the name is more likely to have been derived from the Latin Limitosum, which in Portuguese means boundary.

Guimarães★★
and Around

Guimarães, north of Porto, was
Portugal's first capital – its motto is
'Portugal was born here'. In 2012 it
was European Capital of Culture, and
it made the most of its year in the
spotlight, opening major new arts
spaces in former textile factories and
at the old market. The city's highlight
is its perfectly preserved medieval
centre, but a young population
keeps things lively, with bars and
restaurants buzzing until late.

A BIT OF HISTORY
The Cradle of Portugal – In 1095
Alfonso VI, King of León and Castile,
bestowed the County of Portucale on his
son-in-law, Henry of Burgundy. Henry
had the tower at Guimarães converted
into a castle and installed his wife, the
Princess Teresa (Tareja), there. In about
1110 Teresa bore Henry a son, Afonso
Henriques, who succeeded his father
in 1112. He vanquished the Moors at
Ourique on 25 July 1139 and was proclaimed King of Portugal by his troops.
Gil Vicente (1470–1536), a poet and
a goldsmith, was born in Guimarães.
Later, living at the courts of King João
II and King Manuel I, he wrote plays to
entertain the King. He wrote 44 plays
that satirised Portuguese society.

CASTLE HILL
This hill is the place to go for a panoramic view over the town and to visit the
castle, small 12C São Miguel do Castelo
Renaissance church and the Palace of
the Dukes of Bragança, where the foundation of Portugal began.

Castle★
○*Open daily 10am–6pm (winter closed
12.30–2pm).* ○*Closed 1 Jan, 1 May and
25 Dec.* ≈€2 (keep). ℘253 412 273.
In the 10C Countess Mumadona had
the 28m/91.8ft keep built to protect the
monastery and small town in its midst.
The castle was later built under Henry
of Burgundy and reinforced in the 15C.
Seven square towers surround the keep

▶ **Population:** 158 124.
Ġ **Map:** Below.
🛈 **Info:** Praça de S. Tiago;
℘253 421 221.
◐ **Location:** Northeast of
Porto about 22km/13.6mi
southeast of Braga.
◐ **Timing:** A full day at least.
🅿 **Parking:** To visit the old
town, leave your car in
the underground car park
at Largo da Mumadona,
near the Town Hall, or
at the stadium. You
can also park near the
castle or at the cable car
in the town centre.
🕙 **Don't Miss:** Make sure you
stop for a glass of wine at
one of the terrace cafés on
the Largo da Oliveira or
the Praça da São Tiago.

and although you can walk to the top
you should take care as the stonework is
not as secure as it might be. Afonso was
born in the keep of this castle.

Igreja de São Miguel
do Castelo
This small 12C Romanesque church
contains a font in which Afonso Henriques was baptised, in addition to a
great many funerary slabs.

Paço dos Duques de
Bragança★
○*Open daily 10am–6pm;* ○*closed
1 Jan, Easter Sunday, 1 May, 25 Dec.*
≈€5 (no charge 1st Sun of month).
℘253 412 273.
The palace was built in the early 15C
by the first Duke of Bragança, Afonso I,
illegitimate son of King Dom João I. The
architecture shows a strong Burgundian influence, particularly in the roof
and the unusual 39 brick chimneys. The
palace was one of the most sumptuous dwellings in the Iberian Peninsula
until the 16C when the court moved
to Vila Viçosa (*see VILA VIÇOSA*). The
vast rooms were heated by huge fire-

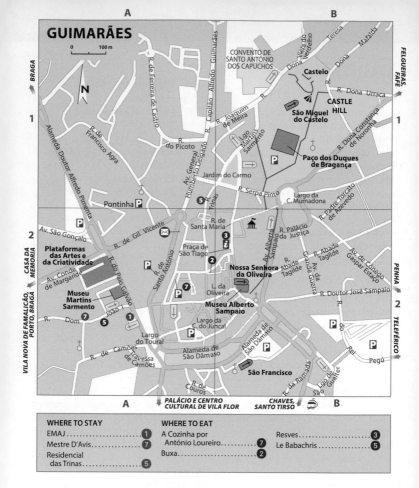

GUIMARÃES

places. On the first floor the **ceilings★** of oak and chestnut in the dining and banqueting halls and the 16C and 18C **tapestries★** are special. The Tournai tapestries depicting the capture of Arzila and Tangiers are copies of the series woven after cartoons by Nuno Gonçalves.

Other decoration includes Persian carpets, 17C Portuguese furniture, Chinese porcelain, weapons and armour, as well as Dutch and Italian paintings.

HISTORICAL CENTRE★★

Wide avenues mark the limits of the well-preserved historic quarter, which makes a pleasant stroll with its maze of streets, squares and old houses. The Largo da Oliveira lies at the very heart of the UNESCO-listed historical centre. The **Centre for Art and Architecture** (*Open Tue–Fri 2.30–7pm; Sat 3–6pm.*

Rua Padre Augusto Borges de Sá; ℘253 088 875; www.centroaaa.org), a factory turned co-operative, stages art exhibits and concerts and hosts a digital and multimedia lab. The former city market has been transformed into the visually stunning **Plataforma das Artes e da Criatividade** (*Open Tue–Sun 10am–1pm, 2–7pm. €4. Avenida Conde Margaride 175; ℘253 424 715; www.ciajg.pt*), a multi-functional space for art exhibits and cultural events. Both these sights were inaugurated in June 2012 as part of Guimarães 2012 European Capital of Culture.

Colegiada de Nossa Senhora da Oliveira

The main doorway of this collegiate church is surmounted by a 14C Gothic pediment. Inside, note the silver altar in the Chapel of the Holy Sacrament.

Paço dos Duques de Bragança

A Gothic **shrine** in front of the church contains a *padrão* commemorating the victory over the Moors at the Battle of the Salado in 1340.

Museu Alberto Sampaio★

⏱*Open Tue–Sun 10am–6pm (until midnight in Aug).* ⏱*Closed 1 Jan, Easter Sunday, 1 May and 25 Dec.* ✆€3. ☎253 423 910; *www.culturanorte.pt. www.facebook.com/museu.sampaio/.*
The museum is housed in three conventual buildings. In a Gothic chapel to the right on entering is the fine **recumbent figure★** in granite of Dona Constança de Noronha, wife of Dom Afonso, first Duke of Bragança.

Statues on the first floor include the 15C alabaster statue of Our Lady of Pity. The galleries that follow contain **church plate★**. Much of the collegiate church treasure was donated by Dom João I. In addition to the tunic worn by João I at the Battle of Aljubarrota, the room of the same name also contains the silver-gilt **triptych★**, which shows the Nativity, Annunciation, Purification and Presentation at the Temple on the left and, on the right, the Shepherds and the Magi.

Among other pieces of the treasure, note a silver-gilt Gothic chalice, a Manueline monstrance attributed to Gil Vicente and an engraved 16C Manueline **cross★**.

Largo da Oliveira

Cable Car

○ *Open Nov–Mar: Fri–Sun 10am–5.30pm. Apr, May, Oct, daily 10am–8pm (until 7pm Mon–Thu), Aug: daily 10am–8pm. Sep: daily 10am–7pm. . ○ Closed last Mon of each month.* ∞ *€4 one-way, €7.50 return. Departs from Parque das Hortas.* ℘ *253 515 085. www.turipenha.pt.*

The cable car whisks you up the Peñha Mountain to an altitude of 400m. From here there are fabulous views over the city and surrounding landscape. It takes about 10 minutes to reach the top.

OUTSKIRTS

Museu Martins Sarmento

○ *Open Tue–Fri 9.30am–noon, 2–5pm, Sat 9.30am–noon, 2–5pm, 2–5pm, Sun 10am–12pm, 2-5pm. ○ Closed public holidays.* ∞ *€3.* ℘ *253 415 969. www.csarmento.uminho.pt.*

The museum, housed partly in the Gothic cloisters of the Church of São Domingos, includes a large collection of archaeological exhibits from the pre-Roman cities of Sabroso and Briteiros.

Igreja de São Francisco

The capitals of this 15C church (remodelled in 17C) in the main doorway represent the legend of St Francis. The chancel, with a Baroque altar carved in wood and gilded, is decorated with 18C *azulejos★* depicting the life of St Anthony. In the **sacristy★** is a fine coffered ceiling ornamented with grotesques and an Arrábida marble table standing against an elegant Carrara marble column.

The chapter-house, which gives onto 16C Renaissance cloisters, is closed by a fine Gothic grille.

ADDRESSES

🛏 STAY

⌂ **Hotel Mestre d'Avis** – *Rua D João I, 40.* ℘ *253 422 770. www.hotelmestredeavis.pt. 16 rooms.* Near the historic centre of town, this imposing building hides behind it well-appointed rooms, though some are a little on the small side. The proprietor is very knowledgeable about the town and makes a good guide.

⌂ **Pousada de Juventude** – *Largo da Cidade.* ℘ *253 512 050. www. pousadasdejuventude.pt. 14 rooms. 5 dormitories.* Located a 10 minute walk from the train station, this spacious 19C mansion combines modern and antique charm. The dorm rooms are colourful in contemporary style.

⌂ **Residencial das Trinas** – *Rua das Trinas, 29.* ℘ *253 517 358. 11 rooms.* This small, welcoming *pensão* in the old town has rooms that are furnished in traditional style and look out over the street, though the view to the rear is better. TV, air-conditioning.

⌂⌂🍽 **Hotel da Oliveira** – *Rua de Santa Maria.* ℘ *253 514 157. www.hoteldaoliveira. com. 16 rooms.* This elegantly furnished and welcoming inn at the heart of the city's historical centre has a good restaurant serving regional specialities.

🍴 EAT

⌂⌂ **Vira Bar** – *Rua do Colegio Militar 480.* ℘ *911 006 641. Closed Mon night.* Cosy restaurant serving delicate monkfish rice with prawns, octopus grilled over a wood fire and lobster.

⌂⌂ **Cafe Oriental** – *Largo do Toural, 11.* ℘ *253 414 048. Closed Sun.* A cosy restaurant, opened in 1925, with informal atmosphere. Grilled fish and seafood, cataplana.

⌂⌂ **El Rei Dom Afonso** – *Praca S. Tiago, 20.* ℘ *253 419 096. Closed Mon.* The terrace is the place to sit here, contemplating the corbelled houses and arcades of the old city hall. Classical Portuguese food and friendly service.

⌂⌂🍽 **Histórico by Papaboa** – *Rua de Valdonas, 4.* ℘ *253 412 107; www.papaboa. pt.* Located in the historical centre of Guimarães, this restaurant offers classic dishes of the region with an international touch. Sit under the wisteria outside, and enjoy octopus, monkfish or médaillon of pork, which are some of the house specialities.

⌂⌂ **Solar do Arco** – *Rua de Santa Maria, 48–50.* ℘ *253 035 233. Closed Tue.* A gourmet restaurant. Specialties are fish: creamy seafood shrimp with black beans *(feijoada* of Camarão) and skewered shrimp.

Barcelos

Barcelos is an attractive town on the north bank of the Cávado. It was the capital of the first county of Portugal and residence of the first Duke of Bragança, who was also the Count of Barcelos. It is now a busy agricultural centre and is well known for the production of pottery, ornamental crib figures, carved wood yokes and decorated cockerels.

▶ **Population:** 120 391.
  Michelin Map: 733.
  Info: Largo Dr. José Novais, n.º 27. ☎ 253 811 882. www.cm-barcelos.pt.
▶ **Location:** 65km/40.3mi northeast of Porto.
  Timing: Spend Thursday morning at the market.
  Don't Miss: The market on Thursdays.

MARKET

Barcelos' **market★**, held on Thursdays (most lively in the mornings), is one of Portugal's oldest and largest, with agricultural products on one side and arts and crafts from the region, and farther afield (pottery, baskets, hand-embroidered household linen, leather goods, harnesses) on the other. They come mainly from the region which is more based on cottage industries and small-holdings than anything more industrialised. Like most markets across Portugal there's a fair selection of "branded" goods that are not quite the real thing.

OLD QUARTER

The main sights are centred on the **medieval bridge** over the Cávado in the southern part of the town.

The **Torre de Porta Nova** tower, part of the remains of the 15C ramparts, now houses the Tourist Information Centre, where visitors can also purchase a range of arts and crafts.

The 13C **parish church**, which was modified in the 16C and 18C, has a plain façade, flanked on the right by a square belfry, and a Romanesque doorway. The **Interior★** is glittering with gold and bordered with Baroque chapels. The walls are decorated with 18C *azulejos*. Some of the capitals are historiated.

The **Solar dos Pinheiros** is a beautiful 15C Gothic manor house built of granite and is adorned with three-storey corner towers.

The 15C **Ruínas do Paço dos Duques de Bragança ou Condes de Barcelos** are the setting for a small open air **Museu Arqueológico** (*open daily Summer: 9am–7pm; Winter: 9am–5.30pm; closed 1 Jan, Easter Sunday, 1 May and 25 Dec;* ☎ 253 809 600).

Souvenirs in the town of Barcelos

© Henrique NDR Martins/iStock

Of particular interest are the steles and coats-of-arms of the House of Bragança, as well as the 14C monument set up in honour of the Barcelos cockerel.

The **ceramics museum** (*Museu da Olaria; ₰253 824 741; ⊙ open Tue–Fri 10am–5.30pm, Sat–Sun and public holidays 10am–12.30pm, 2–5.30pm; ₰253 824 741; www.museuolaria.pt*) in the basement of the palace contains one of the largest collections of its kind in Portugal, with pride of place given to the city's colourful emblem. An entire section is also devoted to the black tableware from the village of Prado, with illustrations of this age-old technique that is no longer used today.

The museum is an ideal place in which to purchase the work of modern-day ceramists at reasonable prices. The best known include Mistério, who is continuing his family's traditions, and Júlia Ramalho, the grand-daughter of the already famous Rosa Ramalho.

CAMPO DA REPÚBLICA

This vast esplanade in the centre of the town is the scene of the famous **market** held on Thursday mornings.

The **Igreja do Bom Jesus da Cruz** (Church of Jesus), which is built in the Northern Baroque style, has an interesting plan in the shape of a Greek cross. According to legend, on 20 December 1504 a cross appeared on this very spot, following which a church was built to commemorate this miracle.

On the north side of the campo is the **Igreja de Nossa Senhora do Terço★**, The Church of Our Lady of Terço, which was formerly part of a Benedictine monastery from 1707.

The walls of the nave are covered with beautiful 18C *azulejos★* depicting events in the life of St Benedict. The coffered ceiling is painted with 40 scenes of monastic life. The pulpit of gilded wood is richly ornamented.

Braga★★

Santuário do Bom Jesus do Monte

Braga is regarded as the religious capital of Portugal, equivalent, in Portuguese eyes, to Rome. There are dozens of churches to go alongside its cathedral, and a short distance outside the centre, you will find the impressive sanctuary of Bom Jesus. Yet it is also an important and lively metropolis, so the sacred and secular live comfortably together. Holy Week here is a time of major celebration.

▶ **Population:** 136 885.

⚙ **Map:** p316.

▯ **Info:** Av. da Liberdade, 1. ₰253 26 25 50.

▷ **Location:** About 54km/ 33.5mi northeast of Porto.

⊙ **Timing:** Allow one full day.

▯ **Parking:** Difficult. Use the underground parking in the city centre.

☻ **Don't Miss:** Holy Week, when the entire city is richly decorated with flowers and filled with processions.

A BIT OF HISTORY

A Most Religious City

Bracara Augusta, an important Roman town, was made into their capital by the Suevi when they advanced upon the area in the 5C. The town was subsequently captured by the Visigoths (who built the Igreja de São Frutuoso) and then by the Moors and only regained prosperity after the Reconquest when

it became the seat of an archbishopric. From this time onwards the influence of the Church became paramount, a feature now particularly apparent in the richness of the architecture; in the 16C the archbishop and patron Dom Diogo de Sousa presented the town with a palace, churches and calvaries in the Renaissance style; in the 18C the two prelates, Dom Rodrigo of Moura Teles and Dom Gaspar of Bragança, made Braga the centre of Portuguese Baroque art. Braga, once the seat of the Primate of All Spain, is still strongly ecclesiastical in character. Holy Week is observed with devotion and is the occasion for spectacular processions. The Feast of St John the Baptist on 23 and 24 June attracts crowds of local people and even many from as far as Galicia; they attend the processions, folk dancing and firework displays in the highly decorated town.

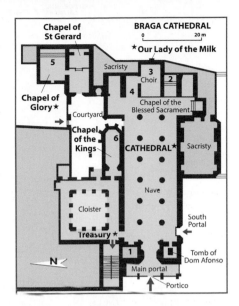

CHAPEL OF ST GERARD · BRAGA CATHEDRAL · ★ Our Lady of the Milk · Sacristy · 5 · 3 · 2 · Choir · 4 · Chapel of Glory★ · Chapel of the Blessed Sacrament · Courtyard · Chapel of the Kings · 6 · CATHEDRAL★ · Sacristy · Nave · Cloister · South Portal · Treasury★ · 1 · Tomb of Dom Afonso · N · Main portal · Portico

CATHEDRAL★

🕐 *Open daily 9.30am–12.30pm, 2.30–5.30pm (until 6.30pm in the summer). www.se-braga.pt*

Only the south doorway and the arching over the main doorway remain from the original Romanesque cathedral. The portico with festooned Gothic arches is by Biscayan artists brought to Braga in the 16C by Diogo de Sousa. The moulded window frames date from the 17C. This same archbishop is responsible for the cathedral's east end bristling with pinnacles and balusters. The graceful **statue★** of the Nursing Madonna (Nossa Senhora do Leite) beneath a Flamboyant canopy which adorns the east end exterior is said to be by Nicolas Chanterene.

Interior★

The interior, which was transformed during the 18C, is striking in its contrast between the richness of the Baroque woodwork and the simplicity of the nave. The font (1) is Manueline: to the right, in a chapel closed by a 16C grille, lies the bronze tomb (*túmulo*, 15C) of the Infante Dom Afonso. The Chapel of the Holy Sacrament (Capela do Sacramento) contains a fine 17C polychrome wooden altar (2) representing the Church Triumphant after a picture by Rubens.

The chancel, covered with intricate ribbed **vaulting★**, contains a Flamboyant **altar★** (3) of Ançã stone carved on

the front with scenes of the Ascension and of the Apostles. Above the altar is a 14C statue of St Mary of Braga. To the left of the chancel is a chapel (4) decorated with 18C *azulejos* by António de Oliveira Bernardes depicting the life of St Pedro de Rates, first bishop of Braga. A harmonious Baroque group is formed by the two 18C **cases★** on either side of the balustraded organ loft.

Treasury★

🕐 *Open daily 9am–12.30pm, 2–5.30pm.* 💶 €3.

The cathedral treasury (*tesouro*) is the most magnificent in Portugal and has a fine collection of 16C–18C vestments as well as a Manueline chalice, a 14C cross in rock crystal, a 17C silver-gilt

TRANSPORT

Railway station – *Largo da Estação* 📞 *253 153 707. www.cp.pt.* Trains for Porto (1hr) every hour during the day. **Buses** – *Praça da Estação Rodoviária* 📞 *253 209 400.* There are extensive services with connections to many towns, particularly in the region. The company **Getbus** runs buses to and from the airport (📞*see p294*).

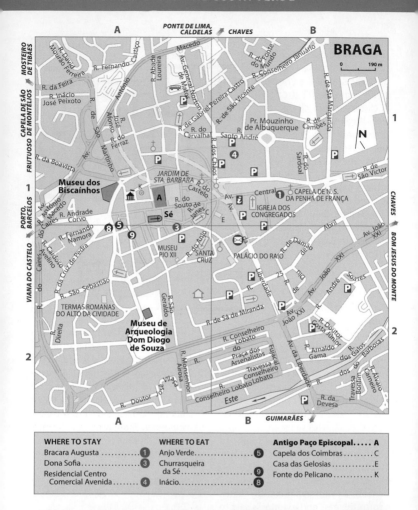

BRAGA

0 ____ 190 m

PONTE DE LIMA, CALDELAS • CHAVES

MOSTEIRO DE TIBÃES
CAPELA DE SÃO FRUTUOSO DE MONTÉLIOS
PORTO, BARCELOS
VIANA DO CASTELO

CHAVES
BOM JESUS DO MONTE

GUIMARÃES

Museu dos Biscaínhos

Sé

MUSEU PIO XII

TERMAS ROMANAS DO ALTO DA CIDADE

Museu de Arqueologia Dom Diogo de Souza

CAPELA DE N. S. DA PENHA DE FRANÇA
IGREJA DOS CONGREGADOS
PALÁCIO DO RAIO

WHERE TO STAY	WHERE TO EAT	
Bracara Augusta .... ❶	Anjo Verde .... ❺	Antigo Paço Episcopal ..... A
Dona Sofia .... ❸	Churrasqueira	Capela dos Coimbras C
Residencial Centro	da Sé .... ❾	Casa das Gelosias .... E
Comercial Avenida .... ❹	Inácio. .... ❽	Fonte do Pelicano .... K

Braga cathedral

reliquary cross, a 10C Mozarabic chest made of ivory, a 16C chalice, a 17C monstrance, Dom Gaspar of Bragança's 18C silver-gilt monstrance adorned with diamonds. Statues include a 13C Christ and St Crispin and St Crispinian. One room is dedicated to the treasures of Dom Rodrigo de Moura Telles, who commissioned 22 monuments (including Bom Jesus) during his years in office. He was a popular Archbishop remembered mostly for his height – he was less than four feet tall and had shoes built so he would look taller.

A tour of the treasury includes the **Capela de São Geraldo** and the **Capela da Glória★**, the walls of the former decorated with 18C *azulejos*. The Gothic Chapel of Glory is decorated with 14C mural paintings in the Mudéjar style. The sides of the Gothic **tomb★** (5) of the founder, Dom Gonçalo Pereira, in the centre of the chapel, bear reliefs of the Crucifixion and the figures of the Apostles, the Virgin and Child and clerics at prayer.

Capela dos Reis

The Kings' Chapel, with Gothic vaulting resting on beautiful brackets sculpted with human heads, contains the 16C tombs (6) of Henry of Burgundy and his wife Teresa, parents of Afonso Henriques, the first king of Portugal, and the mummy of Dom Lourenço Vicente (14C), archbishop of Braga, who fought at Aljubarrota.

ADDITIONAL SIGHTS

Antigo Paço Episcopal

The former Episcopal Palace is made up of three buildings dating from the 14C, 17C and 18C. The library, (◔*open daily 9am–noon, 2–8pm*) whose reading room has a gilt coffered ceiling, contains many exquisite books and some 9C documents. The medieval north wing looks out over the pleasant Santa Bárbara Gardens, including the 17C fountain of St Barbara. In the gardens is a 200-year-old Virginian magnolia tree.

Stairway of the Five Senses, Santuário do Bom Jesus do Monte

©Alexandre Fagundes De Facundes/Dreamstime.com

Museu dos Biscainhos★

◔*Open Tue–Sun 9.30am–12.45pm, 2–5.30pm.* ◕€2. ☏253 204 650.
This 17C and 18C palace with its painted ceilings adorned with stuccowork and its walls decorated with panels of *azulejos* has been arranged with Portuguese and foreign furniture dating from the same period. There are carpets from Arraiolos, Portuguese silverware, porcelain and glassware. The graceful suite of rooms leads onto beautiful gardens with an ornamental pool and 18C-style statues.

Museu D. Diogo de Sousa

◔*Open Tue–Sun 9.30am–6pm (to 5.30pm in winter).* ◕€3. ☏253 273 706.
Opened in 2007, the D. Diogo de Sousa Archaeological Museum preserves innumerable remains, the most impressive being a large mosaic from the late 5C–6C.

EXCURSION

Santuário do Bom Jesus do Monte★★

6km/3.7mi east. Leave Braga by ① *marked on the edge of the town plan.*
The Baroque flight of steps to the Bom Jesus sanctuary is one of Portugal's most famous monuments. It is carved from granite set off by whitewashed walls,

an example of the Northern Baroque style. The Stairway of the Three Virtues is Rococo, while the church, which was built by Carlos Amarante between 1784 and 1811, is neo-Classical.

Escadaria dos Cinco Sentidos

🕐*Funicular to the top, Apr–Sept 9am –8pm, Oct–Mar 9am–7pm; departures every 30min.* ⊛*€1.50 (single), €2.50 (return).*

The Stairway of the Five Senses is a double staircase with crossed balustrades; the base consists of two columns entwined by a serpent; water pours from the serpent's jaws, flowing back over the length of its body.

Above the Fountain of the Five Wounds (where water falls from the Portuguese coat of arms), each level is embellished by a fountain modeled after one of the five senses. Water springs from the eyes representing sight, the ears for hearing, the nose for the sense of smell, and the mouth for taste. The sense of touch is shown by a person holding a pitcher in both hands and pouring water.

On your visit here, you should also take time to look at the **view** of the church from the bottom of the stairway. Looking upwards, you will see the church towering over the ornate fountains and the white, chalice-shaped outline of the various landings. The Museum of Brotherhood next door contains a collection of religious artefacts.

🚗 DRIVING TOUR

Upper Cávado Valley★ (Alto Vale do Rio Cavado)

In the very north of Portugal just below the Parque Nacional da Peneda-Gerês – the lakes form part of the frontier with Spain. You could spend a couple of days here. 😊 Don't miss Montalegre, Braga or Chaves. 235km/146mi.

The course of the Cávado river above Braga is steeply enclosed between the Serra do Gerês and the Serras de Cabreira and do Barroso. In this rocky upper valley, as in its tributary, the Rabagão, a series of dams control reservoir lakes of a deep blue colour which are surrounded by wooded mountain slopes crested by bare peaks – altogether a highly picturesque landscape. The Cávado, which is 118km/73mi long, rises to 1 500m in the Serra do Larouco not far from the Spanish frontier; after crossing the Montalegre plateau, the river drops sharply as it follows a series of rock faults running northeast–southwest. The hydro-electric development of this upper valley began in 1946. There are dams at Alto Cávado, Paradela, Salamonde and Caniçada on the Cávado, at Alto Rabagão and Venda Nova on the Rabagão and at Vilarinho des Funas on the Homen.

On leaving Braga, the Cávado valley becomes deep and wild; the road climbs along the south slopes which are covered with pine and eucalyptus. 11km/6.8mi further, the castle of Póvoa de Lanhoso can be seen. After this village, the Cávado valley is hidden, while on the right the parallel valley of the Rio Ave appears. Then the road climbs up through a bare and rocky landscape.

A little before Cerdeirinhas, the N 103 turns and descends following the Cávado river, running along the edge of the Parque Nacional da Peneda-Gerês. The road then twists and turns, with stunning **views★** of two reservoirs: 15km/9.3mi-long **Represa de Caniçada★** and the Salamonde. Both are dominated by the bare summits of the Serra do Gerês.

▷ Bear left off the N 103 on the Paradela road over the crest of the Vanda Nova dam; at the next crossroads bear right.

As the road rises rapidly, the **views★★** of the Serra do Gerês become even more beautiful.

A little before Paradela, on the left, there is a village built on a rocky projection at the foot of a shale hillock, which has been hollowed out at the back by a gigantic quarry.

Barragem do Alto Rabagão

▷ The road crosses Paradela and arrives at the dam of the same name.

At Paradela you enter the eastern part of the **Parque Nacional da Peneda-Gerês★★**, known as the Barroso region, where life seems to have stood still, before reaching **Represa da Paradela★**. This reservoir lake, sitting at an altitude of 112m above the Cávado river, has a lovely mountain **setting★**.
Pitões das Júnias, a village 15km/9.3mi north of Paradela, has some Romanesque ruins belonging to a Benedictine monastery which dates back to the Visigothic period. Several arches indicate where the cloisters once stood.

▷ Return to N 103. The road runs alongside the Venda Nova reservoir.

Vila da Ponte
This village, one of several small towns situated in the region of Montalegre, perches upon a rock spur.

▷ After Pisões, a path to the right leads to the Alto Rabagão dam.

Barragem do Alto Rabagão★
The dam stands as a massive concrete wall. Go to the crest, where there is a good **view** over the reservoir-lake.

▷ Return to N 103; the road skirts the lake before turning left to Montalegre.

Montalegre
Montalegre was built at an altitude of 966m. Old red-roofed houses encircle the walls of the ruined 14C castle, the keep of which looks out over the wild and mountainous plateau.
The pine and heather-lined N 308 on the plateau returns to the N 103. Then the road crosses arid rock-strewn moors covered with heather.
The plateau suddenly disappears as the **view★★** extends dramatically to take in a vast green and cultivated basin at the far end of which the low-lying old villages of **Sapiãos** and **Boticas** can be seen.

Serra do Barroso★
Continuing along the N 311, pass through **Carvalhelhos**, famous for its spa waters. On the next summit, with access via a dirt road, you find the **Castro de Carvalhelhos**, a settlement dating from the Iron Age, with its foundations, doors and walls still clearly visible. A road leads from Carvalhelhos to **Alturas do Barroso**, a traditional village in these harsh, isolated mountains. From there, head to **Vilarinho Seco★**, the most traditional mountain village in this area. It has no modern buildings,

and the rural two-storey dwellings of loose, dark stone with wooden veranda and staircase and thatch roof appear not to have changed in centuries. Hens and goats run loose, with the most frequent traffic on the street the pairs of the impressive breed of Barroso oxen.

▶ Rejoin N 311 at Viveiro towards Sapiãos; then N 103 to Chaves.

Chaves

Half a day should be enough but if you are 'taking the waters' you'll need a few days. Don't miss the natural spas while you're here. 🅿 *Parking is difficult in the town centre but there is plenty of space around the Forte de São Francisco.*

Chaves is one of the most attractive little towns in Trás-os-Montes. Built on the banks of the Tâmega, the small town of Aquae Flaviae was known to the Romans for its thermal springs, and became an important stopping point on the Astorga-Braga road when Trajan built a bridge over the Tâmega. In 1160, after being recaptured from the Moors, Chaves was fortified to ensure its command of the valley facing the Spanish fortress of Verín. Today the old castle and dozens of picturesque white houses with wooden verandas give the quiet spa town considerable style.

The massive square tower of the **Torre de Menagem**, with battlements at the corners, is all that remains of the castle. Built by King Dinis in the 14C, it was the residence of the first Duke of Bragança, illegitimate son of Dom João I.

With the passing of the years, the **Ponte Romana** bridge has lost its stone parapets and even some arches, but adds a considerable charm to the town.

You can trace the town's history at the **Museu da Região Flaviense** (🕙*open Mon–Fri 9am–12.30pm, 2–5.30pm;* 🚫*closed public holidays;* 𝄢*276 340 500).* This museum's collection, housed in a fine 17C building, includes prehistoric stone relics – the main piece in the display is a megalithic **figure in human form** (about 2000 BCE) – and Roman remains including sculptures and military columns. Exhibits also include

ancient coins, a banknote plate, a magic lantern and radio receivers dating from the early wireless days (pre-1930).

The **Igreja da Misericórdia★** is worth a look. The façade of this small 17C Baroque church is embellished with verandas and twisted columns. The inside walls are covered with *azulejos* showing scenes from the Life of Christ attributed to Oliveira Bernardes. There is a large gilded wooden altarpiece; the ceiling is decorated with 18C paintings, one of which is a Visitation.

Chaves has its own spa with waters rich in minerals, recommended for digestive disorders and rheumatism. Alternatively, the **Termas de Vidago** *(11km/6.8mi from Chaves)* are set in a top-class hotel situated in a beautiful park. The water from the spa is also bottled and sold throughout Portugal. Another spa worth visiting is the **Caldas Santas de Carvalhelhos** *(30km/18.6mi from Chaves),* surrounded by mountains.

ADDRESSES

🍽 STAY

😊😊 **Hotel Dona Sofia** –*Largo São João do Souto, 131.* 𝄢*253 263 160. www.hotel donasofia.com. 34 rooms.* This comfortable hotel close to the cathedral is housed in an old mansion. Its modern furnishings give the interior a sleek, minimalist feel.

😊😊😊 **Bracara Augusta** – *Av. Central, 134.* 𝄢*253 206 260. www.bracaraaugusta.com. 19 rooms.* A pleasant hotel in a beautiful building. The rooms are comfortable, well-decorated and contemporary. The garden at the rear is ideal for breakfast.

🍴 EAT

😊 **Restaurante Vegetariano Anjo Verde** – *Largo da Praça Velha.* 𝄢*253 264 010. Closed Sun.* Lovely décor, a lively crowd, and fresh vegetarian food. The portions and flavours will leave you delighted. A warm welcome.

😊😊 **Inácio** – *Campo das Hortas, 4.* 𝄢*253 613 235. Closed Mon, Christmas, Easter, 2 weeks in Mar and Sept.* A restaurant where typical menus are served with exquisite care. The restaurant enjoys a high reputation and it is well deserved.

Ponte de Lima★

The charming town of Ponte de Lima is in the far north of Portugal. Its Roman bridge was part of the main road north to what is now Spain. In the early 12C, Queen Tareja (Teresa), mother of the first king of Portugal, came to live in Ponte de Lima and granted it local privileges. Its streets are lined with Romanesque, Gothic, Manueline, Baroque and neo-Classical constructions while its environs are particularly rich in manor houses *(solares)* and country estates *(quintas)*.

▶ **Population:** 2 800.
◉ **Michelin Map:** 733.
🖫 **Info:** Passeio 25 de Abril; ℘258 942 335.
◖ **Location:** About 30km/22mi north of Braga, midway between Viana do Castelo and the Peneda-Gerês National Park.
◷ **Timing:** A couple of days is ideal.
◉ **Don't Miss:** The Roman and medieval bridges: the Igreja Matriz (main church), Museu dos Terceiros, Museu do Brinquedo Português (Portuguese Toy Museum) and the fountain.

TOWN

The town is beautiful and well worth a couple of days looking around the area. The **Roman bridge★**, several arches of which are still standing, is a focal point but there are beautiful manor houses dating from the 16C–18C, adorned with coats-of-arms, many with covered galleries. Some of them have been turned into visitor accommodation as part of the country's rural tourism programme. The town, which is situated in a rich farming region, is also a major centre in the production of *vinho verde*, a young lightly sparking white wine. It is home to Portugal's oldest **market** *(alternate Mondays on riverbank)*, which dates back to 1125 when its first charter was granted. There lots of green areas to walk around including the two plane tree lined streets along the Lima river. The town is particularly colourful in summer when it comes alive with festivals, such as the garden festival *(May–October)*. In September, the town bursts once more into life with the Feiras Novas (New Fairs) festival which includes fireworks and a carnival parade.
The **Igreja Matriz** dates from the 15C but more famous is the **fountain** in Largo de Camões, which dates from 1603.
There are two museums worth visiting. **Museu dos Terceiros** (◷*open Tue–Sun 10am–12.30pm, 2-6pm. ℘258 240 220; www.museuspontedelima.com)*, in a lovely setting in two churches with cloisters and a garden, houses a strong collection of mostly 18C sacred art. The **Museu do Brinquedo Português** *(◷open Tue–Sun 10am–12.30pm, 2-6pm; ℘258 240 210)* in Largo da Alegria is the toy museum.

EXCURSION

Bravães★

15km/9mi east from Ponte de Lima.
Bravães is a tiny village in a secluded spot along the road between Ponte da Barca and Ponte de Lima. Its church is one of the finest Romanesque buildings in Portugal. The façade of the small 12C Romanesque **Igreja de São Salvador★** has a remarkable **doorway★**, whose arching is covered in an intricate decoration representing doves, monkeys, human figures and geometrical motifs; richly historiated capitals crown naively carved statue columns.
The tympanum, resting on the stylised heads of a pair of bulls, is ornamented with two angels in adoration of Christ in Majesty. A low relief of the Holy Lamb is carved into the tympanum of the south doorway. There are two magnificent medieval murals of St Sebastian and the Virgin Mary.

Caminha★

The fortified town of Caminha was part of Portugal's northern frontier defences against Galician aspirations. It occupied a key position at the confluence of the Coura and the Minho and also controlled the Minho estuary, overlooked on the Spanish side by Monte Santa Tecla. Caminha is now a fishing village and craft centre for coppersmiths.

▶ **Population:** 16 684.
⚙ **Michelin Map:** 733.
🛈 **Info:** Praça Conselheiro Silva Torres. ℘258 921 952.
▶ **Location:** On the northern border, on the main road towards Vigo (Spain).
🕐 **Timing:** A few hours will allow you time to see everything.
👁 **Don't Miss:** The Igreja Matriz.

TOWN
Praça do Conselheiro Silva Torres

The square, locally referred to as *Largo Terriro*, is still largely medieval in character with ancient buildings grouped round a 16C granite fountain. You can clearly see that the town was once very prosperous and although a little sleepy now it still has its charm and its pride.

The 15C **Casa dos Pitas** is Gothic and its emblazoned façade is elegant with curved windows.

The battlemented town hall (**Paços do Concelho**) has a lovely coffered ceiling in the council chamber. It was built in the 17C in Romenesque style.

The **clock tower** (Torre do Relógio) was once part of the 14C fortifications.

Igreja Matriz

©Luis Pedrosa/iStock

▶ Go through the gate to Rua Ricardo Joaquim de Sousa, which leads to the church.

Igreja Matriz

Built towards the end of the 15C – when Caminho rivalled Porto and was the main shipping point for the export of port wine – this parish church has recently undergone extensive renovation, and stands tight in against part of the old city walls. Inside is a magnificent *artesonado* inlaid **ceiling★** of maplewood. Each octagonal panel, framed in stylised cabling, bears a rose at its centre. On the right, stands a statue of St Christopher, patron saint of boatmen. The Chapel of the Holy Sacrament, to the right of the chancel, contains a 17C gilded wood tabernacle illustrated with scenes from *The Passion* by Francisco Fernandes. There is a magnificent granite carved pulpit. There are some wonderful figures carved on the Renaissance doorways.

There is a small **museum** in the nearby library (🕐*open 9.30am–5pm. ℘258 921 952)* with a motley collection of items found in nearby archaeological sites.

FERRY TRIP TO LA GUARDIA
From Caminha you can take a ferry across the river Coura to La Guardia in Spain (👁with a one-hour time change). *Ferries operate daily 8am–7pm (from 10am Sun and until 8pm May–Jul);* ⇔€3 or €4 per car; €1 on foot.

Northern Nibbles

Whatever your tipple, you will find a surprisingly diverse array of culinary and wine specialities in Porto and the north of Portugal.

Porto is famous for the Francesinha – known as the **little Frenchie** – the Portuguese take on a croque monsiuer, a monster sandwich filled with steak (or porkloin), sausage and ham, coveredwith melted cheese and a rich tomato and beer sauce. The grand and ornately-mirrored *Majestic Café*, Portugal's oldest eatery, is famous for them.

Bacalhau (salted cod), the country's national dish, is served countless ways

Salt cod fish cakes

at restaurants all over the region. Try it au gratin (with cheese), as *pataniscas* (fried patties), stuffed with smoked ham or even with a poached egg on top. Rows and rows of large dried salt codfish can be spotted hanging in shop windows all over the city. Some restaurants have even given their names to famous Portuguese cod recipes, such as Bacalhau à Narcisa in Braga and Margarida da Praça in Viana do Castelo.

In addition to port wine, the region also produces international wines – perhaps the two most well known are the lightly sparkling Mateus rosé and the young and white vinho verde (green wine).Mateus is produced just outside Vila Real in the Douro River valley at the enchanting Casa de Mateus, which is featured on the bottle label. North of Porto, vinho verde is produced at Ponte de Lima in the heart of this farming region.

For port wine aficionados, the **Port Wine Route**,visits some of the main estates by car, train or boat. The river is navigable from Porto to Barca d'Alva, on the border with Spain, or you can take a traditional *rabelo* (flat-bottomed, square-sailed boat) from the quay at Gaia in Porto to Ruler and take the old steam train from there.

Francesinha

Viana do Castelo★★

Viana do Castelo, lying on the north bank of the Lima estuary at the foot of the sunny hillside slope of Santa Luzia, is perhaps the nicest holiday resort on the Costa Verde. Until the 16C Viana was a humble fishermen's village but it attained prosperity when, following the Great Discoveries, its fishermen set sail to fish for cod off Newfoundland. It was during this period that the Manueline and Renaissance houses, palaces, churches, convents and fountains were built, and that today make the old town so attractive.

▶ **Population:** 88 725.
◔ **Map:** p325.
▤ **Info:** Praça do Eixo Atlantico; ☎258 098 145.
▷ **Location:** On the coast midway between Porto (80km/50mi) and the northern border of Portugal.
🏃 **Kids:** Take them to the beach at Cabedelo, south of the town.
🕐 **Timing:** A half day is plenty, unless you're here for the *Festa*.
👁 **Don't Miss:** The old quarter and the views from Santa Luzia.

THE OLD QUARTER★
(Bairro Antigo)

Praça da República★
Everything in this charming town revolves around the beautiful main square. The 16C buildings, including **Casa dos Sá Soutomaior**, make up a graceful, picturesque ensemble. Built in 1554, the **fountain** has several basins with sculptured decoration supporting an armillary sphere and a cross of the Order of Christ.

Only the façade of the former **town hall** has retained its original 16C appearance. It bristles with merlons above,

has pointed arches at ground level, and on the first storey has windows crowned with the coat of arms of Dom João III, the armillary sphere or emblem of Dom Manuel I and the town's coat of arms which features a caravel, as many sailors from Viana do Castelo took part in the Great Discoveries.

The former Bank of Portugal building now houses the **Museu do Traje** (🕐*open Tue–Thu 10am–6pm, Sat and Sun 10am–1pm, 3–6pm; ⊜€2, ticket also gives access to the Museu de Artes Decorativas; ☎258 809 306)*, exhibiting folk costumes from the Alto Minho region.

Filigree jewellery worn over traditional costume of Minho

© Jon Arnold/hemis.fr

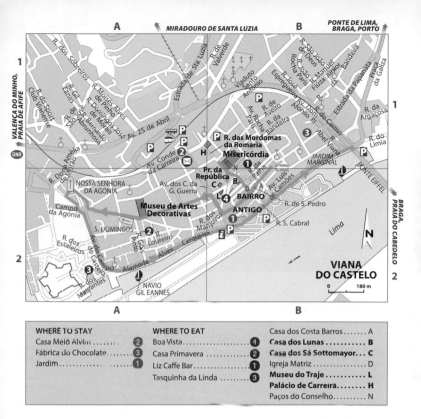

A unique collection of traditional gold jewellery is on display in the museum's vault.

Hospital da Misericórdia★

This 1589 Renaissance hospice, with Venetian and Flemish influence in its style, was designed by João Lopes the Younger. Its noble façade, to the left of the monumental doorway, rises from a massive colonnade with Ionic capitals as two tiers of loggias supported on atlantes and caryatids.

The adjoining **Igreja da Misericórdia** was rebuilt in 1714. It is decorated with *azulejos* by the master craftsman António de Oliveira Bernardes and gilded woodwork dating from the same period.

Museu de Artes Decorativas★

⊙*Open Tue–Thu 10am–6pm, Sat and Sun 10am–1pm, 3–6pm;* ⊙*Closed public holidays.* ✆€2. ☎258 809 305.
The museum is housed in a former 18C palace and bears testament to Viana's rich and opulent past. The interior walls

are covered with lovely *azulejos*★★ depicting distant continents, hunting and fishing scenes and receptions painted by Policarpo de Oliveira Bernardes in 1721. These *azulejos*, together with some fine wooden ceilings, decorate the rooms on the first floor which contain an outstanding collection of **Portuguese glazed earthenware★** said to be the largest in Portugal.

The rooms on the ground floor, with coffered ceilings of varnished wood, contain some fine pieces of 17C Indo-Portuguese furniture, carved or inlaid, including a sumptuous cabinet made of ivory and tortoise shell.

Passeio das Mordomas da Romaria

Some of the houses fronting this street have Manueline façades. Particularly noteworthy is **Palácio de Carreira** which houses the present Town Hall. Its beautiful Manueline front is strikingly symmetrical. The **Casa dos Lunas**, Italian Renaissance in style, also has some Manueline features.

Basilica de Santa Luzia with a view of the Lima estuary

ADDITIONAL SIGHTS
Praia do Cabedelo
The main beach for Viana lies across the river, reachable by a boat that crosses about every hour between 9am and dusk or you can take a circuitous bus ride. The beach is wide and ideal for swimming and also for watersports – there are several outlets that hire out surfboards, kitesurfs and give lessons.

Monte de Santa Luzia★★
4km/2.5mi on the road from Santa Luzia.

The belvedere, on the hill of Santa Luzia, north of the town, is topped by the imposing **Basilica de Santa Luzia** that has developed into a place of pilgrimage. Neo-Byzantine in style, the basilica opens onto a vast church square and a monumental staircase.

Lit by three rose windows, the interior features domes adorned with frescoes. The upper lantern of the central dome provides a magnificent **panorama★★** over Viana do Castelo and the Lima estuary. You can see wooded heights dotted with the white villages of the Barcelos region and endless beaches of fine sand. By car the approach is via a cobbled road with a series of hairpin bends that climbs through pines, eucalyptus and mimosas. The **funicular** makes this journey an easier one.

ADDRESSES

🛏 STAY
Casa Melo Alvim Hotel – *Ac Conde da Carreira, 28.* ℘*258 808 200. www.hotelmeloalvim.com. 20 rooms.* P ⚹. An old country mansion converted into a beautiful hotel with contrasting and artistic styles. The rooms have every comfort and particularly fine bathrooms.

Pousada Viana do Castelo – *Monte de Santa Luzia.* ℘*258 800 370. www.pousadas.pt. 51 rooms.* P. One of Portugal's most popular pousadas, this elegant hilltop lodging provides magnificent views of the ancient city and the coastline. On-site pool. Town and beach are a drive away.

🍽 EAT
Liz Caffe Bar– *Rua Gago Coutinho, 17.* ℘*967 869 198. Closed Wed.* Excellent toasts and tapas for a quick lunch or dinner.

Restaurante Tasquinha da Linda – *Doca das Mares, A-10.* ℘*258 847 900.* Serving incredibly fresh fish and seafood dishes, this eatery is a popular choice with locals.

Os Tres Potes – *Beco dos Fornos, 7 (near the Praça da República).* ℘*258 829 928. Closed Wed.* A typical restaurant with live music and *fado* on summer Saturdays.

RIVER CRUISES
A river cruise is particularly good here and can be taken from the beach at Cabedelo. ℘*962 305 595. www. passeiofluvial.com*

The Douro valley is the oldest and first officially designated wine-growing region in the world, dating from the mid 18C. The vineyards are situated in the Upper Douro, the nursery of Portugal's port industy. The River Douro rises in Spain and flows to Porto and into the Atlantic. The landscape is dotted with *quintas* (old country villas and estates), and whitewashed villages and towns whose museums and churches contain historical artefacts. Vila Real stands at the foot of the Serra do Marao, close to the Palácio de Mateus, after which the renowned rosé wine is named. To the east is Mirandela with its beautiful Roman bridge, as well as the medieval city of Bragança.

Wine and Wildlife

The Douro valley is the ideal place to escape the hustle and bustle of Porto and journey back in time. *Quintas* and wine estates that have belonged to port wine familles such as the Ferreiras, Sandemans and Dows for generations dot the rolling landscape, which rises steeply alongside the mighty river as it winds its way from Spain to the Atlantic. Vine-terraced hillsides form a patchwork of colour, their vineyards still harvested by local people and the grapes trodden by foot.

There are three different ways to journey into the Upper Valley – by luxury cruise ship from Porto, by train or by car. The Linhe du Douro railway line follows all 160 kilometers/100 miles of the river to Pocinho, while cruise ships operate a variety of different itineraries, stopping at riverside villages and towns along the way.

Travelling by car provides the greatest freedom, enabling you to drive south from *vinho verde* country outside Porto and Amarante into the Lower Valley to vist Lamego, where the champagne-like sparkling wine called espumante is produced. The Museu de Lamego houses the most amazing 16C Brussels tapestries depicting mythological scenes. While in Amarente, stroll around its 16C and 18C houses and sample its famous and delicious pastries such as lerias and foguetes. North of the river in the upper valley, Peso da Régua and Pinhão sit in the heart of the demarcated Douro region. Pinhão's beautifully tiled railway station is certainly worth a detour, as is a ride on the 1924 steam train that runs to Regua and Tua *(p334)*.

If you are only going to visit one palace or museum, it should be the magnificent

Highlights

1 Tread grapes with locals during harvest at a **vinhedo** (p334)

2 Sail in a traditional *rabelo* boat from **Pinhão** (p334)

3 Ride in a 1924 steam train along the **Douro River** (p334)

4 Sample chilled rosé wine at **Mateus Palace** (p336)

5 Marvel at the **Museu das Curiosidades do Romeu** (p339)

Mateus Palace close to Vila Real. You will recognise it from the label of the Mateus rosé wine.

To really get up close to the wine-making process, arrange a stay in a quinta or luxury wine estate along the way – several have opened up in the region. Enjoy the peace and tranquillity, perhaps taking a trip in a traditional rabelo boat from Pinhão – once used to transport port wine to the lodges in Porto - to enjoy a panoramic view of the stunning countryside from the river itself.

Upstream towards the Spanish border, the river gets narrower and the countryside wilder. Birdlife becomes more abundant with blue and yellow kingfishers flitting along the surface of the river and eagles soaring high.

Wolves and wild boar roam in the Douro International Nature Park. One of the last packs of wolves lives in Carrazeda de Ansiães, a few miles from the river. To the northeast, the medieval city of Bragança stands on high overlooking the modern town and remote border villages. Miranda do Douro even has its own dialect.

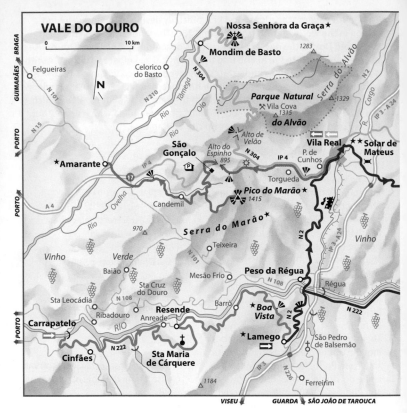

Douro Valley★★

The Douro, which rises in Spain, flows in an erratic course before reaching the Atlantic near Oporto. Its valley is fertile, with vineyards, orchards and olives growing in abundance as they have done for centuries. The valley itself is quite steep and can be very hot in mid summer, though cooler at high temperatures and farther downstream. The landscape has been enhanced by beautifully built *quintas* (country villas or estates). Port is the main wine produced here.

VALLEY

The Douro was the first officially designated wine-growing region in the world, predating even the great regions of France. The valley of the river Douro is

◖ **Location:** The valley runs across the northern part of Portugal from the Spanish border to the Atlantic, emptying into the sea at Porto.

◷ **Timing:** Two or three days of peace and quiet.

◉ **Don't Miss:** Wine route!

beautiful and one of the most interesting (though not cheap) ways of seeing it is on an all-inclusive river cruise. Cruises normally start in Porto on a Sunday, returning the following Saturday. The hills climbing from the valley floor are lined with vineyards from which both red and white wines are made, and not just port, though obviously it is very important. The higher altitudes as well as the vineyards farther downstream are

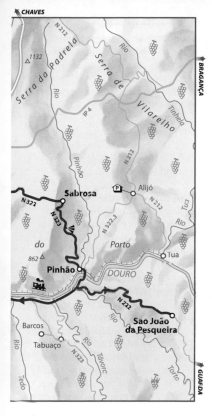

by successive dams, runs hemmed in by steep hills and winds round in great twists and turns. The shale and granite slopes, more wooded on the north bank and more cultivated on the south bank, where little white villages seem to hang between the vines, terraced olive groves and corn fields, with the river below, have created a delightful landscape, despite the reminders of industrial civilisation evidenced by the railway line, the Carrapatelo dam *(barragem)*, a few factories, and the installations for transporting coal from the Pejão mines on the south bank.

Barragem do Carrapatelo

This dam measures 170m long. A hydroelectric station and a fish ladder occupy its south bank. On the north bank, a lock with the greatest displacement in Europe drops 43m.

Cinfães

Cinfães is the commercial centre for *vinho verde,* but apart from that, there is nothing much of interest to see.

◖ Continue along N 222 to Anreade; turn right on the road towards Ovadas, heading south; 5.5km/3.4mi on, bear left.

Priorado de Santa Maria de Cárquere

Only the church and the funeral chapel of the Lords of Resende remain, linked by a monumental arch. The church, restored in the 13C, 14C, 16C and 17C (the square crenellated tower and chancel are Gothic, the façade and nave Manueline) still has a Romanesque doorway decorated with small columns and capitals with interlacing. The chancel, under diagonal ribbed vaulting, has a door on the left with a high pediment and a double string course of billets. The chapel, which has a remarkable Romanesque window with capitals of sculpted pelicans, contains four stone sarcophagi carved with animals and inscriptions.

best for white wines, while the intense summer heat of the upper part of the valley is perfect for full-bodied reds.

🚗 DRIVING TOUR

VINHO VERDE REGION

1 BARRAGEM DO CARRAPATELO TO LAMEGO
62km/38.5mi. About 2hr 30min.

The lower valley of the river, near Oporto, is not the domain of the great wine of that name but that of the well-known **vinho verde** (green wine), so-called because the local climate is such that the grapes cannot fully ripen here. The description of the wine reflects its youth rather than its colour. Port is made much farther east, between Régua and the Spanish border. The Douro, widened

Santuário de Nossa Senhora dos Remédios, Lamego

▶ Return to N 222 and turn right.

Resende is an important wine production centre. From the village of Barrô, there is a good view of the valley's wooded slopes; the 12C Romanesque church has a richly carved tympanum and a rose window.

▶ After 6km/3.7mi, turn right on N 226.

Miradouro da Boa Vista★
There is a magnificent view from this belvedere of the Douro valley. High up, cut out against the sky, are the whitish summits of the Serra do Marão.

▶ Continue until you arrive at Lamego (&See LAMEGO).

Lamego★
Allow two hours. Don't miss Santuário da Nossa Senhora dos Remédios
Lamego is an attractive small episcopal and commercial town known for its sparkling wine called espumante and

its smoked ham. It lies near the Douro Valley in a landscape of green hills covered with vines and maize. The town, which is rich in 16C and 18C bourgeois houses, is overlooked by two hills on which stand respectively the ruins of a 12C fortified castle and the Baroque Santuário de Nossa Senhora dos Remédios, famous for the annual pilgrimages held in late August and early September. It hosted Portugal's first Parliament in 1143.

Museu de Lamego★
○*Open Tue–Sun 10am–6pm.*
○*Closed 1 Jan, Easter Sunday, 1 May, 8 Sept and 25 Dec.* ▨€3 *(no charge 1st Sun of each month).* ☎254 600 230. *www.museudelamego.gov.pt*
The museum is housed in the former episcopal palace, a majestic 18C building. The right-hand section of the ground floor contains mainly religious sculpture from the Middle Ages to the Baroque period and a fine collection of coats of arms which adorned the façades of mansions belonging to the nobility. On the first floor two series of works (paintings and tapestries) are particularly noteworthy. The five **paintings on wood★** (early 16C) by Vasco Fernandes were part of the altarpiece in Lamego's cathedral (&*see VISEU: Viseu School of Painting*). From left to right they show the Creation, Annunciation, Visitation (the most outstanding in the series), the Presentation at the Temple and Circumcision. The six 16C Brussels **tapestries★** are of mythological scenes (note the myth of Oedipus and the rich composition of the Temple of Latone). On the first floor are two Baroque chapels of carved and gilded wood, one of which, São João Evangelista from the Convento das Chagas, has statues and niches. There is also a Chinese room, gold and silver plate and ceramics.
The second ground-floor section contains another Baroque chapel and some fine 16C and 18C *azulejos*, in particular polychromed ones from the Palácio Valmor in Lisbon.

Capela do Desterro

This chapel, built in 1640, is decorated inside with 18C carved and gilded woodwork and 17C *azulejos*; outstanding is the coffered **ceiling★**, with painted scenes from the Life of Our Lord.

Santuário de Nossa Senhora dos Remédios

The 18C façade, on which stucco serves to highlight the elegant granite curves, overlooks the crossed ramps of the **staircase** ornamented with *azulejos* and bristling with a multitude of pinnacles which recalls that of Bom Jesus near Braga. The view from the church parvis *(access by car possible: 4km/2.5mi)* extends over Lamego to the heights on the horizon which border the Douro.

PORT REGION★★

② ROUND TRIP FROM LAMEGO

112km/69.5mi. About 3hr.

As the local saying goes: *"God created the Earth and man the Douro"*. You have to see the way the steep banks of the Douro have been shaped meticulously into terraces, each one comprising several rows of vines, to understand the enormous amount of work man has put into these hillsides for more than 20 centuries. The sight is particularly fascinating between mid-September and mid-October when the terraces are invaded by thousands of grape-pickers. The vineyards cover an area of 42 500ha and it is their grapes, which ripen in the shelter of the valley, where the temperature in summer can easily reach 40°C, that produce port wine.

There are many opportunities to taste port (and other wines) at some of the *quintas* along the way, though take care if driving. In **Peso da Régua** you will find the **Instituto do Vinho do Porto** (R. dos Camilos), where you can taste various wines, and pick up brochures with full details.

Leave Lamego and take the picturesque N 2 above the Corgo valley to Vila Real.

Vila Real

See *VILA REAL*.

▷ Leave Vila Real on N 322 and continue east towards Sabrosa (the town is Magellan's birthplace), passing, on the way **Solar de Mateus★★**. See *VILA REAL*.

Road from Sabrosa to Pinhão★★

After Sabrosa, the N 323 descends towards the Douro and overlooks the deep valley of the Pinhão. About 7km/4mi before Pinhão, there is a fine **view★** of a bend in the Douro and its confluence with the Pinhão River.

Pinhão

Pinhao, which stands at the junction of the Douro and Pinhão rivers, is an important port production centre and is said to produce the very best port. Nowadays, all the wine is transported by road rather than on the flat-bottomed boats that look like Venetian gondolas – some of which can still be seen on the river in Porto.

Pinhão's **railway station** is decorated with *azulejos* illustrating the sites and the traditional costumes of the valley.

By making an excursion eastwards to **São João da Pesqueira** *(18km/11mi of hairpin bends on N 222)*, you will see the terraced hillsides of vineyards in the Torto valley.

São João da Pesqueira is a large village on the plateau with an arcaded main square around which stand white balconied houses. After Pinhão, N 222 follows the valley westwards between shale slopes terraced and contained by small drystone walls.

An important diversion is to take the train from Peso de Régua to Vila Real on the Corgo Line, renowned as one of the most picturesque **train rides** in the world.

SERRA DO MARÃO★

③ VILA REAL TO AMARANTE

70km/43.5mi. About 1hr 30min.
This driving tour will take a couple of hours, though along the way you can

stop as many times as you choose.
Don't miss a diversion on the train ride
from Livração to Amarante.

The Serra do Marão is a block of granite and shale bounded to the east by the Corgo, to the west by the Tâmega and to the south by the Douro. The dislocations caused by the range's upheaval in the Tertiary Era are the reason for its variation of altitude; the wildness and desolation are due to intense erosion.

Vila Real &See VILA REAL.

⊳ Leave Vila Real by the Porto road (IP 4/E 82), heading west.

As soon as the road reaches the slopes, maize, pine and chestnut trees replace the vineyards and olive groves. At Parada de Cunhos there are fine views of the serra's foothills and of Vila Real.

⊳ After Torgueda leave the N 304, the Mondim de Basto road on your right.

The road continues to climb and shortly, to the left, the view of the summit of the **Marão**, the highest of the serra's peaks.

⊳ At the Alto do Espinho pass leave IP 4 and take the road south towards Pico do Marão. You pass the Pousada de São Gonçalo. Continue for a short while then bear left. The road rises through a landscape of crystalline rocks and ends on a ledge near the summit of Nossa Senhora da Serra.

Pico do Marão★
Alt 1 415m. The summit, topped by an obelisk, commands a magnificent **panorama** of the serra's bare peaks.

⊳ Return to the road and continue westwards to Amarante via Candemil.

Amarante★
Spend the morning here and then have lunch. Don't miss the churches.
Amarante is a picturesque riverside town, with its 16C, 17C and 18C houses, complete with wooden balconies and

wrought iron grilles, on a hillside overlooking the Tâmega. The town, well known for its pastries *(lérias, foguetes, papos de anjo)* and its *vinho verde* wine, has become popular with weekenders from Porto.

The **Igreja e Convento de São Gonçalo**, erected in 1540, and modified in the 18C, has some lovely gilded wooden Baroque furnishings: an altarpiece in the chancel, two pulpits and the superb **organ case★** (early 17C) supported by three Tritons.

The 18C **Igreja de São Pedro** has a Baroque façade decorated with statues of St Peter and St Paul. The nave is decorated with 17C bands of blue and yellow *azulejos*; the chancel has a gilded wooden altar. There is a coffered chestnut wood **ceiling★**, with elegant carving in the sacristy.

④ VILA REAL TO MONDIM DE BASTO
61km/38mi. About 1hr 30min –
Itinerary on the VALE DO DOURO map.
Leave Vila Real westwards on IP 4
described above, then bear right
after Torgueda onto N 304.

The road climbs to the Alto de Velão pass from where there is a **view** to the left of the upper basin of the Olo river. You cross the western end of the beautiful **Parque Natural do Alvão** dotted with jumbled granite rock formations, then begin the **descent★** to Mondim de Basto in the Tâmega valley.

⊳ Leave Mondim de Basto on N 312 to the north and then bear right on a forest road that climbs between rocks and pine trees.

Capela de Nossa Senhora da Graça★
Leave the car at the bottom of the majestic staircase (68 steps) which leads to the chapel.
From the top of the steeple (reached by 54 steps and rungs; take great care), there is a **panorama** of the Tâmega valley, Mondim de Basto and the Serra do Marão.

Igreja e Convento de São Gonçalo, Amarante

© Franck Guiziou/hemis.fr

EXCURSIONS

São João de Tarouca

South of Lamego, easily accessible from the Douro Valley. Allow a couple of hours to visit.

The former monastery of Tarouca, overlooked by the heights of the Serra de Leomil, lies in a hollow In the Barossa valley. The **church** erected in the 12C by Cistercian monks, was remodelled in the 17C. Built in 1169, this Romanesque church remains pretty much intact. Of interest are the choir and the Baroque organ, dating from 1766 and whose central figure beats time during Mass. *Azulejos* in the transept depict the life of St Bernard, one showing him standing in a barrel of wine! A side chapel contains paintings attributed to Gaspar Vaz, notably a superb **rendition of St Peter★**. The monumental 14C granite tomb contains the remains of Dom Pedro, Count of Barcelos, illegitimate son of King Dimis. Pedro was the author of the Great Chronicle of 1344, and was considered one of the greatest Portuguese writers of the Middle Ages.

Sernancelhe

Just north of Viseu. Worth a few hours to look around and have lunch. ▣Park on the outskirts of the village. Don't miss the old Jewish quarter with the houses of the "converted" marked with a cross.

The old town of Sernancelhe, off the beaten track about 50km/31mi northeast of Viseu, occupies a rocky height in the Beira Alta. It has been occupied by the Romans and the Arabs, who have each left behind traces of their presence. It was also once a commandery of the Order of Malta, which built the castle that now lies in ruins. It had a sizeable Jewish quarter and still has some magnificent 16 and 17C mansions, one of which is reputedly the birthplace of the Marquis de Pombal.

The façade of the 13C Romanesque **church**, flanked by a vast square belfry, is pierced by a rounded doorway, in which one of the arches is adorned with an unusual frieze of archangels. The tympanum is carved with plant motifs. Two niches on either side of the door shelter six granite statues of the Evangelists St. Peter and St. Paul. They are the only free-standing Romanesque statues in Portugal.

Sernancelhe is also famous for its chestnut production, farming being the most important activity in this region.

Douro Valley vineyards

© AbelC/Getty Images

Port Wine Route

The Douro River Valley is the oldest wine producing region and also one of the most beautiful. Neatly-terraced vineyards (vinhedos) in the Upper Douro, the nursery of Portugal's port industry, descend steeply towards the meandering river. Terra-cotta-tiled white houses, chestnuts and pines dot the landscape.

Early September is an ideal time to visit to hear the locals sing as they tread the harvested grapes in large stone tanks. Throughout the year, *quintas* with famous names such as Taylor, Ferreira and Croft open their doors to visitors.

Port was first developed in this region in the 17C when British merchants, keen to build trade with Portugal, laced Douro wine with brandy to stop it going sour in transit. Traditional flat-bottom *rabelo* boats, made from pine, transported barrels of wine from the *quintas* down river to the port wine lodges in Vila Nova da Gaia, Porto, to mature in oak casks.

Rabelo is not the quickest way to explore the river nowadays, although these boats can still be hired from Pinhão, which sits in the heart of the demarcated Douro region. For a longer trip, take a luxury cruise from Porto, or explore by car, staying at *quintas* along the way. The Douro railway line (Linha do Douro), which follows the river 160km from Porto to Pocinho, is cheaper and quicker than by boat.

On Saturdays, a 1924 steam train runs from Regua to Pinhão and Tua and back again. Passengers are serenaded with Portuguese folk music and refreshed with port wine and olive-filled bola bread along the 1.5 hour journey. Pinhão station is worth a visit in its own right. Thousands of blue and white tiles (azulejos) depicting harvest scenes from the early 20C decorate the walls and it still has a separate waiting room for first, second and third-class passengers.

Pinhão railway station

© Luso/iStock

Vila Real

Vila Real is a lively small town enhanced by numerous houses dating from the 16C and 18C. It stands on a plateau among vineyards and orchards at the foot of the Serra do Marão. Fine black pottery is made in the surrounding countryside and can be bought in the town, particularly on 28–29 June at St Peter's Fair *(Feira de Sâo Pedro)*.

> ▷ **Population:** 50 252.
> 👌 **Michelin Map:** 733.
> 🚩 **Info:** Av. Carvalho Araújo, 94; ℰ259 322 819.
> ▶ **Location:** 120km/74.5mi east of Porto along the A 4.
> 🕐 **Timing:** A morning in the Mateus mansion and park, then lunch in the town.
> 😩 **Don't Miss:** The Manor-house at Mateus; and the train to Peso da Regúa.

🐾 WALKING TOUR

The main sights are to be found in the vicinity of Avenida Carvalho Araújo. From the central crossroads by the cathedral, walk down the avenue on the right.

Cathedral

The cathedral, a former 15C conventual church built at the end of the Gothic period, has preserved some of its Romanesque details, particularly noticeable in the treatment of the capitals in the nave.

Casa de Diogo Cão

At No. 19 (door-plate).
The casa owes its name to tradition: the well-known navigator, Diogo Cão, was born here. The façade was remodelled in the 16C in Italian Renaissance style.

Town Hall

Built early in the 19C, the town hall has a lantern pillory in front, and a remarkable monumental stone staircase with balusters in the Italian Renaissance style.

▷ Continue along towards the cemetery, which you skirt round on the right.

Esplanada do Cemitério

This shaded walk along the cemetery esplanade, on the site of the old castle, overlooks the junction of the Corgo and Cabril rivers. In direct line with the cemetery and behind it, there is a **view** looking steeply down into the Gorges of the Corgo and its tributary. Farther to the left, there is an extensive view over the Corgo ravine and the houses that overhang it.

Ministry of Justice, Praça Luís de Camões and Avenida Carvalho Araújo

© Arco/J. Moebes/age fotostock

Palácio de Mateus

© Bruno Barbier/Photononstop

▶ Return to Avenida Carvalho Araújo, turn right and climb upwards.

Tourist Information Centre

At No. 94. The Tourist Information Centre *(Poste de Turismo)* occupies a 16C house that has a lovely Manueline façade.

▶ From here take the first road on the right (by the law courts) to the Igreja de São Pedro.

Igreja de São Pedro

St Peter's Church is decorated in the chancel with 17C multicoloured *azulejos* and a fine coffered **ceiling★** of carved and gilded wood.

PALÁCIO DE MATEUS★★

3.5km/2mi to the east on N 322 towards Sabrosa. ⏱Open 9am-5pm daily. ⏱Closed 25 Dec. ☞€13 (gardens only €9.50). ⓘIf you drive, park outside the walls as it is free; inside you pay. ☎259 323 121.
www.casademateus.com.
Chestnut trees, vines and orchards herald the approach to the village of Mateus, famous for the manor belonging to the Counts of Vila Real.
Dating from the first half of the 18C, this manor by Nicolau Nasoni is a perfect example of Portuguese Baroque architecture. Behind lawns planted with

cedars, followed by a garden laid out with clumps of boxwood and a tree-covered walk, appears the **façade★★** of the manor, preceded by a mirror of water. The central section of the manor is set back, and has a beautiful balustraded stairway and a high emblazoned pediment, surrounded by allegorical statues. The main courtyard is protected by an ornamental stone balustrade. The windows upstairs are topped with moulded gables. Beautiful pinnacles top the roof cornices. To the left of the façade there is a tall elegant Baroque chapel built in 1750, also by Nasoni.
Inside the palace there are magnificent carved wooden ceilings in the main hall and the salon, a rich library, furniture from Portugal, Spain, China and 18C France, and in two rooms which have been made into a museum **copperplate engravings** by Fragonard and Baron Gerard, precious fans, liturgical objects and vestments, a 17C altar and religious sculptures, one of which is a 16C ivory crucifix. The library has a remarkable edition of the epic poem *Os Lusíadas*.
The palace is owned by the Mateus Foundation, which sponsors a number of cultural activities in areas such as music, literature, sculpture and ceramics and hosts a variety of seminars, workshops and exhibitions.

Bragança★

Miranda do Douro, Mirandela and Romeu

The medieval city within Brangança's ramparts stands on high overlooking the modern town. The best view★ is from the São Bartolomeu *pousada* or from the chapel look-out point beside it *(2km/1.2mi southeast).*

- **Population:** 35 341.
- **Michelin Map:** 733.
- **Info:** Av Cidade de Zamora – 5300-111; ℘273 381 273.
- **Location:** 90km/60mi east of Chaves, close to the border with Spain.
- **Timing:** Allow a day for the park and the town.
- **Don't Miss:** The park at Montesinho and the border villages.

MEDIEVAL CITY★

Castle

At the heart of the Cidadela, the Medieval city, the **castle** was built in 15C. It comprises a tall square keep 33m/108ft high, flanked by battlemented turrets, and several towers, which house a small **military museum** *(open Tue–Sun 9am–noon, 2–5pm; closed public holidays; €2; ℘273 322 378)*; two halls are lit by paired Gothic windows. There is a wonderful view from the keep platform over the old town, the lower town and the surrounding hills.

Domus Municipalis

Open Tue–Sun, 9am–6pm. Closed public holidays. ℘273 381 273.

This pentagonal-shaped building, erected in the 15C, is the oldest town hall in Portugal. It is pierced on every side by small rounded arches. A frieze of carved modillions runs beneath the roof. The interior consists of a vast chamber and, below, a basement with a former cistern. By the side of the Domus you will find the Igreja de Santa Maria. The origins of the church date from the Romanesque period, although it was totally remodelled in the 18C. It has an elegant façade with a door which is framed by two twisted columns decorated with vine plants; inside a fine ceiling painted in *trompe-l'œil* depicts the Assumption.

LOWER TOWN

The lower town was built in the 15C and 18C. The **Largo da Sé** (Cathedral Square) is adorned with a large Baroque cross. The cathedral is decorated with *azulejos* and features Baroque carved and gilded altars. This church is, in fact, no longer the cathedral, as that honour is now con-

Walled city of Bragança

© Jon Arnold Images/hemis.fr

ferred on the **Igreja de Nossa Senhora Rainha**, a short distance to the west.

The **Igreja de São Vicente** (St Vincent's church) is Romanesque in origin, but was totally reconstructed in the 18C. The interior contains a profusion of *talha dourada* work from the 17C, and the chancel is topped by a gilded vault. According to tradition, it was in this church that the secret wedding between Dom Pedro and Dona Inês de Castro took place (&see ALCOBAÇA).

Another church of note, the 16C Igreja de São Bento, has a single-nave and a Renaissance-style painted wooden ceiling. The chancel, with its attractive **Mudéjar ceiling**, contains a valuable 18C gilded wooden altar screen.

Museu do Abade de Baçal★

Open Tue–Sun 9.30am-12.30pm, 2-6pm. Closed 1 Jan, Good Friday, Easter Sunday, 1 May and 25 Dec. €3 (no charge on Sun and public holidays until 2pm). 273 331 595.

The museum is housed in the former Episcopal Palace. The collections include archaeological displays, paintings, items of local ethnological interest, coins and religious art. At the entrance, a video provides an insight into Trás-os-Montes costumes, and an interactive computer provides information on the museum, the region and its monuments. The ground floor contains a fine collection of funerary steles and milestones. On the second floor, the chapel of the former palace, with its painted ceiling, displays a set of 16C and 17C ecclesiastical vestments and polychrome pictures of saints. In Room 7, a 15C Virgin with Child in gilded and polychrome wood is worthy of particular note.

EXCURSIONS

Miranda do Douro★

Southeast of Bragança. Allow a couple of hours for the town.

Miranda is an old town perched on a spur above the Douro valley. It has its own dialect, somewhat similar to Low Latin, known as *mirandês*. Guarding the entrance to the village from a hillock are the ruins of a medieval castle which was destroyed by an explosion in the 19C. This place has had an interesting history, having been vital to the rise of Afonso Henriques, the first King of Portugal as he fought off his Spanish masters at the start of the 12C. The Independence, Spanish Succession and Seven Year wars were all fought out across the region and the explosion in 1762 left the town a desolate mass of ruins. Yet that desolation allowed the local dialect, Mirandês, to flourish: today, local road signs are in both Portuguese and Mirandês.

Façade, Igreja de Santa Maria, Bragança

© curtoicurto/iStock

Cathedral, Miranda do Douro

Mirandela

Halfway between Vila Real and Bragança. Normally the place you'd drive past, but worth a half day to walk through the town and along the river bank. Don't miss the Roman bridge – the most beautiful in Portugal

Although Mirandela is Roman in origin, the town visible today was founded by Dom Afonso II. It looks down upon the Tua, which is spanned by a long Romanesque bridge, rebuilt in the 16C, which is 230m long and has 20 different arches. It is an elegant, flower-decked town with many gardens and lawns and various options for visitors, such as a boat trip on the Tua river, a journey by train along the old railway line connecting Mirandela with Carvalhais, or a visit around the city by mini-train.

The 18C **Palácio dos Távoras**, now occupied by the town hall, stands at the top of a hill. Its three-part granite façade (with the middle part the highest) is topped with curved pediments and crowned by spiral pinnacles. A statue of Pope John Paul II sits in the middle of the square, with a more recent church to one side.

The **Museu Municipal Armindo Teixeira Lopes★** (○open Mon–Fri 9am–12.30pm, 2–5.30pm, Sat 2.30–6pm; ℘278 201 590), housed in the town's cultural centre, is devoted to sculpture and painting. It has been created from donations from the children of Armindo Teixeira Lopes, and contains more than 400 works by 200 predominantly Portuguese artists from the beginning of the century to the present day. These include Vieira da Silva, Tapiès, Cargaleiro, Nadir Afonso, Graça Morais, José Guimarães, Júlio Pomar and Teixeira Lopes.

The narrow gauge **Tua Railway** from Mirandela is beautifully scenic and well worth a detour, taking 90 minutes to reach Tua.

Romeu

11km/6.8mi to the northeast of Mirandela.

In the heart of the Trás-os-Montes, Romeu together with **Vila Verdinho** and **Vale do Couço** form a group of colourful villages bedecked with flowers, in a landscape of valleys wooded with cork oaks and chestnuts. Restoration work has provided a new lease of life.

The **Museu das Curiosidades do Romeu** (○open Tue–Sun: May–Sept noon–5pm; ⊜€1.50; ℘278 939 133) contains the personal collection of Manuel Meneres, the benefactor of all three villages. In one room are early machines such as typewriters, sewing machines and a phenakistoscope (predecessor to the cinema); in another are a music box, dolls and clocks; also some old cars and motorbikes.

Trail leading to Pico Ruivo from Pico do Areeiro, Madeira
© Francisco Correia Photos/Associação de Promoção da Madeira

The Madeira Archipelago

MADEIRA ARCHIPELAGO

The Madeira Archipelago consists of the main island, which has the greatest area (740sq km/286sq mi) and the largest population (267 785); the island of Porto Santo (42sq km/16sq mi), lying 40km/25mi to the northeast; and two groups of uninhabited islands, the Ilhas Desertas (The Deserted Isles), 20km/12.4mi from Funchal and the Selvagens (The Wild Islands), 240km/150mi away, and closer to the Canary Islands than to Madeira.

GETTING THERE

Access by Air – There are direct flights from London (Heathrow and Gatwick) and from several other UK cities; some are seasonally direct, others go via Lisbon (*see PLANNING YOUR TRIP*).

WHEN TO GO

The temperature is mild throughout the year with an average of 17°C in January and 25°C in July. Rain usually falls in March, April, October and November. There is an abundance of hotel accommodation of all standards on Madeira. To choose a hotel or restaurant in Madeira, consult the red-covered *Michelin Guide Spain and Portugal*. Funchal has most of Madeira's hotels, although on the island of Porto Santo, beautiful and calm, the building of quality hotel accommodation is an on-going development.

GETTING AROUND

Madeira by Car – Madeira can be explored by following the routes outlined here. **Taxis** may be used for short distances and cars hired for longer ones, but there are many English-speaking taxi drivers who can be booked for a full day's tour at reasonable prices – ask at your hotel. There are also numerous **bus services**, although they are tailored to the needs of local people rather than tourists.

Madeira on Foot – Madeira offers a wide choice of walking potential. Some paths

Highlights

1 Ride a cable car to **Monte** (p351)
2 Explore the **Old Town** (p351)
3 Wander **Monte Palace Gardens** (p352)
4 Thunder down the **Monte** toboggan run (p352)
5 Visit **Curral das Freiras** (p355)
6 Take in the view from **Cabo Girão** (p363)

follow the *levada* network, while others take mountain routes around Pico Ruivo. A number of popular walks are described in this guide.

ACTIVITIES

Madeira island itself has only dark-sand beaches, except at Calheta and Machico, where golden sand has been imported. Porto Santo, however, has a long stretch of natural golden beach. Sports on Madeira include angling, deep-sea fishing and golf. Diving, surfing and paragliding are increasingly popular.

Madeira★★★

Funchal

Madeira rises from the Atlantic Ocean, a volcanic island mass high above the ocean swell. The "Pearl of the Atlantic" is 900km/559mi southwest of Lisbon, and due west of Morocco. The island offers visitors a climate that is mild, as well as vegetation that is subtropical, transforming the land into a blossoming garden all year round. The landscape, beautiful and varied, opens out into vast panoramas.

A BIT OF HISTORY

Discovery and Colonisation

In 1419 the leaders of an expedition dispatched by Prince Henry the Navigator, **João Gonçalves Zarco** and **Tristão Vaz Teixeira**, landed first on the island of Porto Santo, and later on Madeira itself. The island appeared to be uninhabited and entirely covered in woodland; they therefore named it the wooded island, *a ilha da madeira*.

The navigators reported their discovery to Prince Henry, who commanded them to return the following year. He also divided the territory into three *captaincies*: Zarco received the land centred on Funchal and extending south of an imaginary line drawn from Ponta do Oliveira to Ponta do Tristão; Tristão Vaz Teixeira received Machico and all the rest of the island, and **Bartolomeu Perestrelo** the island of Porto Santo. The islands are volcanic having been thrust up from the Atlantic during a period of volcanic eruption in the Tertiary Era, and climb to heights culminating in Pico Ruivo (1 862m).

Madeira, which is almost at the same latitude as Casablanca in Morocco, enjoys a temperate climate. Mild with no extremes, the average temperature only varies from 16°C to 24°C from winter to summer. The rainy season is usually short, though in the mountains, mist and some drizzle are possible on many days, even in summer.

▸ **Population:** 267 785.

⏣ **Michelin Map:** 733 fold 43.

🄸 **Info:** Avenida Arriaga nº16, Funchal. ✆291 211 902. www.visitmadeira.pt.

▶ **Location:** 900km/559mi southwest of Lisbon, on the same latitude as Casablanca in Morocco.

⚇ **Kids:** The Madeira Aquarium in Porto Moniz; the Madeira Story in Funchal. A boat trip on the *Santa Maria* to watch dolphins. The golden beaches at Machico and Calheta.

🕐 **Timing:** Stay a week and really explore Madeira; be sure to take a few day trips, including to Porto Santo.

🅿 **Parking:** Parking in Funchal is a problem, but elsewhere on the island you will encounter no major difficulties.

✲ **Don't Miss:** The Monte Palace Gardens; the Monte toboggan; Porto Santo if you have the opportunity – if not, go out on a sea-watch cruise from Funchal.

Flowers

The entire island of Madeira is a mass of flowers; every hillside, every garden and roadside verge is covered with hydrangeas, geraniums, hibiscus, agapanthus, bougainvillea, fuchsia and euphorbia. Certain species such as orchids, anthurium and strelitzia (Birds of Paradise) are grown in large quantities for export. There are also several species of flowering trees – mimosa, magnolia, sumaumás and jacaranda. Bananas are the island's major export crop.

Madeira Wine

Vines were introduced to Madeira in the 15C from Crete and planted in the rich and sunny volcanic soil along the south coast. In 1660 a commercial

Monte toboggan – wicker basket sledge ride from Monte

treaty between England and Portugal encouraged the export of the wine and increased production. Overseas buyers, for the most part English (Blandy, Leacock and Cossart Gordon), were drawn to Madeira by the prosperous trade, which reached its height in the 18C and 19C.

There are four principal wines. **Sercial**, made from grapes whose vines originally came from the Rhine valley, is a dry wine with a good bouquet; it is amber in colour and is served chilled and drunk as an aperitif. **Boal** originates from Burgundy; the rich, full-bodied flavour of this red-brown wine makes it primarily a dessert wine. **Malvasia**, also known as Malmsey, is a dessert wine, honey in flavour with a deep-red, almost purple colour. A medium sweet, all-purpose wine, **Verdelho**, a Muscatel and *Tinto* or red wine are also produced.

Vintage Madeira made from the best wines in exceptionally good years may be consumed up to and over 150 years later.

Madeira Embroidery

Embroidery used to be a mainstay of the island's economy. Madeira embroidery owes its origin to an Englishwoman. In 1856 **Miss Phelps**, the daughter of a wine importer, started a workroom where women embroidered designs after the manner of *broderie anglaise*. The work was sold for charity. Samples of the embroidery reached London and were received with such enthusiasm that Miss Phelps decided to sell the work abroad. In less than a century, embroidery became one of Madeira's major resources; today 30 000 women are believed to be employed making embroidery. The embroidery on linen, lawn or organdie is very fine and varied.

FUNCHAL★★

The island's capital rises in tiers up the slopes of a natural amphitheatre around the bay. When the early settlers arrived, they found the heights covered in wild fennel, hence the name Funchal. The luxuriant vegetation, the *quintas*, hotels, shopping, night-life and sports facilities combine to form a popular city resort, attracting visitors from many countries year round. The harbour faces central Funchal. East of this stretch are the lively alleyways of the old town, bustling with locals in the mornings and early evenings.

In February or March each year, Funchal comes alive with its fantastic **Carnaval**, a lively procession of brightly-coloured dancers and musicians who parade through the streets. It's not quite as spectacular as Rio de Janeiro's in Brazil, but great fun. Also well worth seeing is the Flower Festival each April or May when the entire town is perfumed with the rich fragrance of fresh flowers. A flower-bedecked Wall of Hope is decorated by children.

🐾 WALKING TOUR

THE CENTRE

The heart of Funchal is a delightful mish-mash of architectural styles; the main street, Avenida Arriaga, is largely pedestrianised and offers strolling in the main shopping centre. Follow the route marked on the map on p348–349.

Avenida das Comunidades Madeirenses / Avenida do Mar

This wide promenade was remodelled following devasting floods in 2010, and today features an extensive flower garden with walkways, and even a new breakwater that generates a sheltered if bouldery beach. Many of the original cafés and bars remain, but gone are the floating restaurants of old.

Avenida Arriaga

The jacaranda trees along this street are covered in purple flowers throughout the spring. The **Jardim Público de São Francisco** is a small but interesting botanical garden with a wide variety of plants. Between the garden and the tourist information centre (Turismo) is the the **Old Blandy Wine Lodge★** (🐾guided tours – 30–60min including wine-tasting at various times Mon–Sat ◷ closed Sun and public holidays; ⊚€9.50–€24.30), housed in a former 16C Franciscan monastery. Opposite the cellars is **Palácio de São Lourenço**, which still serves as residence for the Prime Minister of the Autonomous Region and the Military Command.

Cathedral (Sé)★

◷Open daily 7am–noon, 4–7pm.
𝄕291 228 155.
www.sefunchal.com.

The first Portuguese cathedral to be constructed out of the mainland dates from 1514. The apse, decorated with open-work balustrades and twisted pinnacles, is flanked by a crenellated square belfry, the roof of which is tiled with *azulejos*. In the nave, slender columns support arcades of painted lava rock while above, and also over the transept, extends a remarkable *artesonado* **ceiling★** in which ivory inlays in the cedar have been used to emphasise the stylistic motifs. The floor is made of wood.

Praça do Município

The square is bordered to the south by the former episcopal palace, now the Museu de Arte Sacra (Sacred Art Museum – ◷see below) and to the east by the town hall.

Avenida Arriaga

© Francisco Correia/Associação de Promoção da Madeira

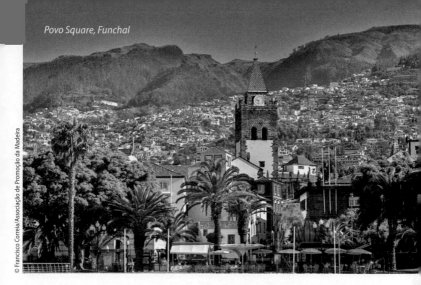

Povo Square, Funchal

Town Hall

The town hall, formerly the 18C palace of Count Carvalhal, is surmounted by a tower that dominates the area. The inner courtyard is decorated with *azulejos*. There is also a small museum inside the town hall with items relating the history of Funchal.

Parque de Santa Catarina

Attractively linking central Funchal with the hotel zone, the Parque de Santa Catarina is a lovely place to stroll or have a coffee, dotted, as it is, with exotic plants and sculptures. A statue of Henry the Navigator looks out across a busy roundabout at the centre of which a bronze globe is borne by seahorses rising from the fountain. Elsewhere, a statue of Christopher Columbus vies for attention with an early 20C bronze called *The Sower*.

Museu de Arte Sacra

ⓞ*Open Tue–Fri 10am–5pm, Sat 10am–1pm.* ⓞ*Closed public holidays.* ⬤€3. ✆291 228 900.
In the 15C and 16C much of the Madeiran economy was based on the production and export of sugar, most of it to the Netherlands. Some of the profits were used to commission and purchase Flemish art; many such works are now in the Museum of Sacred Art, housed in the former episcopal palace. It contains fine religious items and liturgical ornaments, but its main interest lies in a collection of **paintings★** on wood from the 15C and 16C Portuguese and Flemish Schools. From the Portuguese School, see particularly the triptych depicting *St James and St Philip*. From the Flemish School are a *Descent from the Cross* attributed to Gérard David; a full-length portrait of *St James the Less*; a triptych attributed to Quentin Metys of *St Peter*; an *Annunciation*, a portrait of *Bishop St Nicholas*, a *Meeting between St Anne and St Joachim*, a *Crucifixion*, and an *Adoration of the Magi*.

Igreja do Colégio

The Jesuit Church of St John the Evangelist was built early in the 17C, extended and changed over the years and has undergone a major renovation (which lasted 70 years). The austere white façade has also been hollowed out to form four statuary niches. These contain marble figures on the upper level of St Ignatius and St Francis Xavier, and on the lower of St Francis Borgia and St Stanislas. Carved birds, vines, barley-twist columns and *azulejos* make for a fascinating sight.

⚹⚹ Museu Municipal

ⓞ*Currently closed for restoration. Call for info.* ✆291 229 761.
The former mansion of Count Carvalhal now houses an aqarium and a natural history museum, the oldest in Madeira. The aquarium contains various sea creatures from the waters around Madeira,

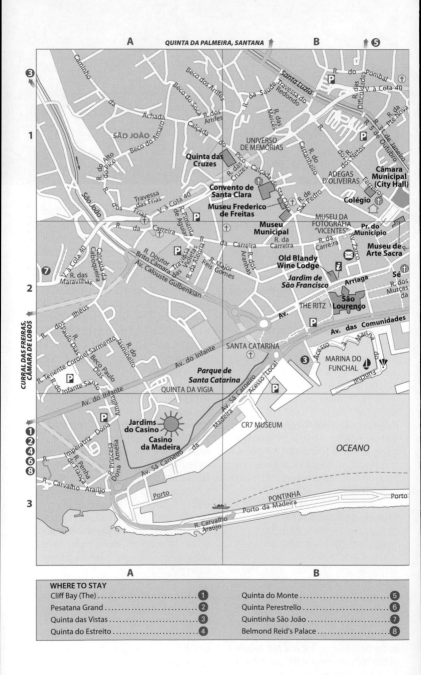

C   MONTE   CAMACHA, MACHICO, JARDIM BOTÂNICO   D

SANTA LUZIA
R. Doutor Gaspar Frutuoso
R. Silvestre Quintino de Freitas
ROCHINHA
V. à Cota 40
R. Lomba da Boavista
R. Elias Garcia
Travessa do
R. Nogueira
R. João de Deus
MUSEU HENRIQUE E FRANCISCO FRANCO
Beco do Lombo da Boavista
R. do Bom Jesus
R. Conceição
MUSEU DO BORDADO E DO ARTESANATO
Carmo
R. Magdalena Oudinot
R. Ribeirinho de Baixo
R. do Seminario
R. das Pretas
R. 31 de Janeiro
R. dos Ferreiros
R. do Aljube
NÚCLEO MUSEOLÓGICO DA CIUDAD DO AÇÚCAR ❶
H. Alfândega
João Gomes
R. Conde Carvalhal
Av.
Nova
Conde
Coronel
Carvalhal
Santiago
Menina
São
R. de São Filipe
Alegria
R. de Santiago
R. Bela Santiago
R. Padre Laurindo
SOCORRO
SANTA MARIA MAIOR
Mercado dos Lavradores
Madeira Story Centre
MUSEU DE ELECTRICIDADE
TELEFÉRICO
ZONA VELHA ❹ ❷
Carlos
Largo do Corpo Santo
Sta. Maria
São Tiago ❺
❻
Madeirenses ou Av. do Mar
Praça da Autonomia
PRAÇA DO POVO
PRAIA DA BARREIRINHA
Museum of Contemporary Art

ATLÂNTICO

N

da Madeira

FUNCHAL

0   150 m

C   PORTO SANTO   D

SÃO GONÇALO   QUINTA DA SOA VISTA

1

2

3

Reid's Palace Hotel

The most famous hotel on Madeira, Reid's Palace has about the best location on the island, on a promontory jutting out overlooking the bay. It is a beautiful place identifiable by its red-ochre roofs and whitewashed walls.

Non-residents can enjoy the tradition of afternoon tea (3–5.30pm) on the terrace overlooking the sea (€34.50). Winston Churchill wrote much of his war memoirs here and also painted. George Bernard Shaw learned to tango in its ballroom.

including red scorpion fish, mantis shrimps and morays. Among the stuffed and mounted animals are sharks, rays and white-bellied seals.

Museu Frederico de Freitas★

○Open Tue–Sat 10am–5.30pm. ○Closed public holidays. ⊛€3. ℘291 202 570/℘291 202 576.
The former mansion of Dr Frederico de Freitas contains art illustrating Madeira through the centuries. The more intimate first floor shows the interior of a 19C middle-class home. Its English furniture has been preserved, as have its

'sugar chest' cupboards, musical instruments and cabinets adorned with ivory and whalebone.

Convento de Santa Clara

☛Guided tours (20min) Mon–Sat 10am–noon, 3–5pm. ○Closed public holidays. ⊛€2. ℘291 742 602.
The convent was built in the 17C on the site of a church founded in the 15C by Zarco. His Gothic tomb, supported by lions, is at the far end, and his two granddaughters, who founded the original convent of the Order of St Clare, are buried here. The Sisters still in residence are always happy to show you round. Take a look at the stunning gardens.

Quinta das Cruzes★★

○Open Tue–Sun 10am–12.30pm, 2–5.30pm. ○Closed public holidays. ⊛€3. ℘291 740 670.
http://mqc.madeira.gov.pt/en/.
Zarco's former mansion has been converted into a museum of decorative arts (Museu de Artes Decorativas).
The ground floor contains 16C Portuguese furniture. There are many 17C cabinets and chests known as caixa de açucar or sugar chests made with wood taken from boxes in which Brazilian sugar was transported.
At the back of one room stands a 15C Flemish altarpiece of the Nativity. The rooms on the first floor contain a rich

Quinta das Cruzes

© Associação de Promoção da Madeira

Mercado dos Lavradores

collection of 18C and 19C English furniture in the Hepplewhite and Chippendale style.

ZONA VELHA (THE OLD TOWN)

The original town was founded in the 15C. Today, the narrow streets are a multitude of boutiques, taverns, bars and restaurants. It has a wonderful atmosphere, especially in the early evenings when everyone seems to be out on the streets.

Mercado dos Lavradores

The town's main market is particularly lively in the morning when you can buy (or just look at) all types of fresh fish, fruit and vegetables. At the entrance are the flower sellers who stay all day. The main market is a delight to explore, housed on two floors, and crammed with stalls. Market folk offer you a taste of everything on offer, although it is good to buy something.

The fish market is an amazing if gory display of fresh fish and seafood. Get up close and personal with the fiercesome-looking scabbard fish, and then try them later at a restaurant, where they are often served with fried bananas.

Madeira Story Centre

Rua D Carlos, 1. 27/29.
⊙Open daily 9am–7pm.
⊚€5; child, €3. ☎291 000 770.
www.madeirastorycentre.com/en.

Located in the old part of Funchal, near the cable cars that go from Funchal to Monte. The centre gives an overview of 14 million years of the history of Madeira in a visit lasting 1h30.

There are re-creations of Madeira's history, exhibits of authentic historical objects and an interactive, multimedia experience. Volcanic Origins, the Discovery of Madeira, Turmoil and Trade, The Development of Madeira, and Explore Madeira.

Museum of Contemporary Art - Forte de São Tiago

⊙Open Mon–Fri 9.30am–5.30pm.
Guided tour (30min). ⊙Closed public holidays. ⊚€3.
☎291 213 340.

The fort was built in 1614. Its yellow walls rise above the shore where fishing boats lie moored beside small blue and white striped huts. It also houses the exciting **Museum of Contemporary Art** with a rich collection of European art from the 60s, 70s and 80s.

WESTERN FUNCHAL
Jardims do Casino

Funchal's **Casino da Madeira** (⊙open Sun–Thu 3pm–3am, Fri–Sat 4pm–4am; closed on 24-25 Dec. ☎291 140 424; www.casinodamadeira.com) was built in 1979 by the Brazilian architect Óscar Niemeyer, and stands in a park of beautiful exotic trees in the grounds of the

Pestana Casino Park Hotel on Avenida do Infante.

ABOVE FUNCHAL
Quinta Palmeira

The Palmeira Estate and the surrounding gardens are located on the Rua da Levada de Santa Luzia in Funchal, just below a section of the Cota 200 motorway. Take a yellow town bus No. 26, or a taxi.

The terraces of this well-kept park overlook Funchal. There are fine *azulejo* benches and a Manueline Gothic-style stone window which, it is claimed, was formerly in the house in which Christopher Columbus stayed when he lived in Funchal.

The Quinta Palmeira itself is a large white-walled building with wooden shuttered windows. Tourists can visit the gardens, but the Estate house is closed to the public.

Monte★

7km/4.3mi. About 1hr.

Monte, at an altitude of 600m, is an area developed as an escape for its well-off traders from the heat and bustle of Funchal. The **Quinta do Monte**, which lies above the former Belmonte Hotel, is a luxury hotel. Just before entering Monte is the **Quinta do Imperador**, the house of the last Emperor of Austria when he was exiled to the island in 1921. Karl I died in the house the following year.

You can reach Monte by **cable car** from the old town of Funchal *(15min trip;* **◷**open daily 9am–5.45pm; **◷**closed 25 Dec; **⊜**€16 round trip; €11 one way, children €8 and €5.50; www.madeira cablecar.com). The **Monte Palace** (with a permanent exhibition of 1950s and 60s Zimbabwean sculpture) **and Tropical Gardens** are well worth seeing if you adore beautiful flowers and plants (**◷**open: garden 9.30am–6pm; museum 10am–4.30pm; **⊜**€12.50; ℘291 742 650; www.montepalace.com). For an amazing experience, try the "**Monte toboggan**" (**⊜**€25 per basket) – a huge wicker basket on runners steered by two drivers in traditional dress and boaters. It's fun but bumpy.

☻ However, the ride does not descend all the way to Funchal, but only to Livramento, from which you will need to take a taxi down into town or back up to Monte; bear this in mind when buying your cable car tickets. Walking down is very steep and not recommended.

Igreja de Nossa Senhora do Monte – The church was built on the site of a chapel erected in 1470 by Adam Gonçalves Ferreira. He and his twin sister Eva were the first children to be born on the island. The Baroque façade is highly decorative. In a chapel to the left is the iron tomb of Karl I of Austria. A tabernacle worked in silver above the high altar shelters a small cloaked statue of Our Lady, the patron saint of Madeira. The figure, discovered in the 15C at Terreiro da Luta at the spot where the Virgin appeared to a young shepherdess, is the subject of a popular pilgrimage held on 14 and 15 August each year.

Jardim Botânico★ (Botanical Garden)

From the top of the Monte cable car, turn right and walk a short distance to a new cable car that takes you down to the botanical garden.
◷Open daily 9am–6pm. **◷**Closed 25 Dec. **⊜**€16.50 for cable car from Monte plus admission to botanical garden. ℘291 211 200.

Many outstanding examples of Madeiran flora can be viewed. The elegant white house with green shutters contains a small museum showing botanical, geological and zoological collections; note the vulcanised wood. There is a fine **view★** of Funchal harbour.

EAST OF FUNCHAL
Quinta do Palheiro Ferreiro★★

Leave Funchal on Rua Dr Manuel Pestana towards the airport. Take the first road towards Camacha. After several bends, turn right on a narrow cobbled road signposted Quinta do Palheiro Ferreiro.
◷Open daily 9am–5.30pm. **◷**Closed 1 Jan, 25 Dec. **⊜**€11, children up to 15 years old free. ℘291 793 044. www. palheironatureestate.com.

The immense mansion is set in a well-maintained **park** approached by paths lined with camellias. More than 3 000 plant species including exotic trees and rare flowers can be found in the park. There is also a golf course here that is open to the public.

🚗 DRIVING TOURS

SOUTH COAST

EIRA DO SERRADO★★
AND CURRAL DAS FREIRAS
Round trip of 34km/21mi, 2hr.

▶ Leave Funchal on Av. do Infante.

Garden, Quinta do Palheiro Ferreiro
© brytta/iStock

São Martinho
In São Martinho the parish church stands on a "peak" 259m high.

▶ As you come to the cemetery, turn right.

Pico dos Barcelos★
The viewpoint (alt 355m) gives a great view of Funchal set at the foot of the mountain ranges, the ragged outlines of which can be seen to the north. **Santo António** sits snugly in its valley clustered round its village church.

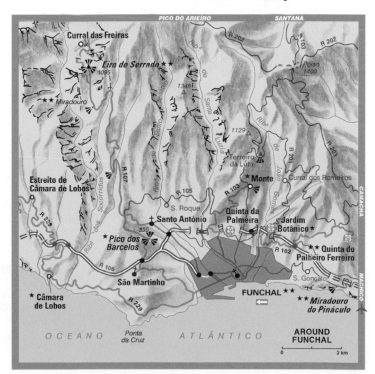

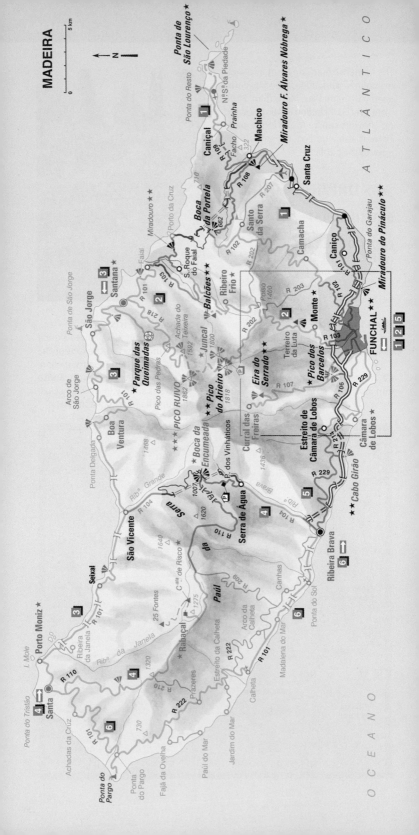

MADEIRA

N

0 5 km

O C E A N O   A T L Â N T I C O

Ponta de São Lourenço ★★
Ponta do Resto
N.ª S.ª da Piedade
Prainha
Caniçal
Facho
322
R 109
Machico
Miradouro F. Álvares Nóbrega ★
R 108
R 207
Santa Cruz
Santo da Serra
R 102
R 202
Camacha
Caniço
Ponta do Garajau ★
Ponta do Pináculo
Miradouro do Pináculo ★★
R 101
Miradouro ★★
Porto da Cruz
710
Boca da Portela
662
S. Roque do Faial
Faial
R 103
Ribeiro Frio
Balcões ★★
Santana ★
Ponta de São Jorge
São Jorge
R 101
R 218
Achada do Teixeira
1592
Juncal
1800
Pico do Arieiro ★★
1818
R 203
Poiso 1460
Monte ★
Terreiro da Luta
R 103
Eira do Serrado ★★
Pico dos Barcelos ★
R 107
FUNCHAL
Estreito de Câmara de Lobos
Câmara de Lobos ★
R 214
R 229
Arco de São Jorge
Boa Ventura
1468
PICO RUIVO ★★★
1862
Parque das Queimadas ★
Pico das Pedras
Boca da Encumeada ★★
P. dos Vinháticos
Curral das Freiras ★
1436
★★ Cabo Girão ★★
Ponta Delgada
Ribª Grande
Serra
1007
1620
da
1640
São Vicente
R 104
Serra de Água
R 110
R 229
Ribeira Brava
Ribª Brava
Seixal
Paul
da
C.ca de Risco
1275
25 Fontes
Ribeira da Janela
Ribª da Janela
Rabaçal ★
1320
Porto Moniz ★
R 110
R 101
I. Mole
Ponta do Tristão
Santa
R 101
Achadas da Cruz
730
Ponta do Pargo ★
Ponta do Pargo
Fajã da Ovelha
Paúl do Mar
Jardim do Mar
Madalena do Mar
Ponta do Sol
Calheta
R 101
Estreito da Calheta
Arco da Calheta
R 222
Canhas
R 209
R 210
R 222
Prazeres

1
1
2
3
2
2
3
3
4
4
4
5
5
6
6
6
1 2 5

Eira do Serrado

▷ Continue along the road towards Eira do Serrado.

Several kilometres (a few miles) on, beyond a wood of eucalyptus trees, the road nears the Ribeira dos Socorridos (River of Survivors). There is an impressive **sight**★ of the deep defile caused by a volcanic fracture through which the stream flows. A magnificent **view**★★ unfolds from here.

▷ A right fork takes you to Eira do Serrado where you temporarily leave the car.

Eira do Serrado★★

A path *(10min round trip on foot)* goes round the Pico do Serrado (1 095m) on the right to a viewpoint. The view is outstanding: the white houses of the village of Curral das Freiras lie scattered around mountain ravines a long way below.

▷ Drive to the main Funchal road, and turn left through a tunnel and then follow the winding road down to Curral das Freiras.

Curral das Freiras

Curral das Freiras lies in an enclosed **setting**★ at the foot of a great circle of extinct volcanoes. The valley served as a refuge for the sisters of the Convent of Santa Clara, who took shelter here when French pirates pillaged Funchal in 1566.

The event was commemorated in the name of the village, which in Portuguese means the "Nuns' shelter".
As you return uphill take a moment, on leaving the village, to take in a stunning **view**★ of the circle of mountain peaks.

▷ Return towards Funchal, but later leave the Pico dos Barcelos road by branching left for Santo António.

Santo António

This is Funchal's smart residential quarter. It has an 18C Baroque church.

▷ Return to Funchal by Caminho de Santo António which drops rapidly into the town centre.

① EAST COAST★
90km/56mi. About 4hr.

▷ Leave Funchal on the Via Rapida to speed you along in the direction of the airport; most of the drive destinations are well signed from the highway. ⊘ *It is compulsory to use headlights on the Via Rapida at all times.*

This itinerary is along one of the sunniest of Madeira's coasts. Rivers flowing from the mountains have formed ravines and inlets along which villages have grown, and offer a less frenetic experience than around Funchal.

Road leading to the beach of Ponta do Garajau

© Günter Gräfenhain/Sime/Photononstop

Miradouro do Pináculo★★

2km/1.2mi beyond São Gonçalo.

A belvedere on a rocky promontory *(pináculo)* gives a wonderful view of Funchal, lying spread out at the end of its beautiful bay. Cabo Girão stands out to the west. The Desertas islands form misty shapes out to sea.

Caniço

Caniço is a small town whose inhabitants live from fishing. On Ponta do Garajau stands a tall statue of **Christ in Majesty** raised by a Madeiran family.

Santa Cruz

Santa Cruz, a fishing village, possesses several Manueline monuments. The **Igreja São Salvador★** borders the main square and dates back to 1533. The interior, divided into three aisles, is covered with a painted ceiling. The chancel contains a metal memorial plaque to João de Freitas. The tomb of the Spínolas is in the north aisle. The former **Domus Municipalis**, with beautiful Manueline windows, stands on the other side of the square.

The small street on the east side of the square leads to the present **town hall** *(Câmara Municipal)*, a fine 16C building.

Miradouro Francisco Álvares Nóbrega★

A road to the left leads to this viewpoint named after a Portuguese poet, known also as the Lesser Camões (1772–1806), who sang Madeira's praises. From the belvedere there is a view of Machico and the Ponta de São Lourenço.

Machico

The town of Machico, situated at the mouth of the Ribeira de Machico valley, is divided by a river: the fishermen's quarter, the Banda d'Além, lies on the east side, the old town on the west. It was at Machico that Zarco and his companions landed.

The island's first settlement, modern Machico now has a golden sandy beach (best at low tide), and a growing number of fine hotels and modest restaurants.

Parish Church

The 15C Manueline parish church stands in a square shaded by plane trees.

The façade is pierced by a lovely rose window and a doorway adorned with capitals carved with the heads of animals. The side doorway, a gift from King Manuel I, consists of paired arches supported on white marble columns.

A Manueline arch in the north wall leads to the Capela de São João Baptista.

Capela dos Milagres

As ruler, Tristão Vaz Teixeira had a chapel constructed in 1420 on the east bank of the river. This Chapel of Miracles was destroyed by floods in 1803. The original Manueline doorway was reinstalled when it was rebuilt.

▷ Take the Caniçal road.

There are views, as the road rises, of the valley of Machico dominated by mountain summits. The road leaves the valley through a tunnel under Monte Facho. *It is worth diverting briefly, just before*

The Lovers of Machico

There is a legend that in 1346 an English ship sank in a tempest at the mouth of the river. Robert Machim and Ana d'Arfet, who had fled from Bristol to get married in spite of their parents' opposition, survived the shipwreck but died a few days later. Their companions took to sea again on a raft, were captured by Arab pirates and taken to Morocco. The story of their adventure was told by a Castilian to the King of Portugal who decided to equip an expedition to find the island. When Zarco landed at Machico, he found the lovers' tomb at the base of a cedar tree and named the village after the young Englishman, Machim.

entering the tunnel, to visit Pico de Facho, which has a splendid view of the airport runway.

Caniçal

After whaling was banned in 1981, Caniçal stagnated for a few years. It regained its status as a major port, this time for tunny fishing, which has become an important activity as the port facilities and canning factory testify.

▷ Continue to Ponta de São Lourenço.

Ponta de São Lourenço★★

The headland of red, black and ochre-coloured volcanic rocks stretches far out into the sea and is the only place on the island with a natural sand beach, **Praínha**. The beach, tiny and popular as it is, lies sheltered at the foot of a hillock on which stands the hermitage of **Nossa Senhora da Piedade**.

There are impressive **views★★** from the **Miradouro Ponta do Rosto** viewpoint *(narrow road to the left at roundabout)* of the sheer cliffs on the island's northern coast.

▷ Return to the roundabout and turn left.

The road continues to a large parking area near Abra bay, from where a footpath leads to a rocky spot overlooking amazing rock formations (not for anyone suffering from vertigo).
There is a good path (PR 8) along the narrow peninsula, with some spectacular views along the way. But there is virtually no shade, and you should carry supplies of food and drink

▷ Return to Machico and take the road to Portela.

Machico viewed from Pico do Facho

As you climb, the valley floor of agricultural terraces gives way to pine and eucalyptus trees.

Boca da Portela

At the Portela Pass (alt 662m) crossroads, go up to look at the view from the belvedere overlooking the green Machico valley.

Santo da Serra

Santo da Serra, built on a forest-covered plateau (pines and eucalyptus) at an altitude of 800m, has become popular with the residents of Funchal as a country resort with a cool climate in a restful setting.

From the main square by the church, go into the **Quinta da Junta park**. At the end of the main drive lined with azalea, magnolia and camellia, a belvedere provides a view of the Machico valley; in the distance can be seen the Ponta de São Lourenço and, in clear weather, Porto Santo.

Camacha

Surrounded by woodlands at 700m, the village of Camacha is famous for its basketwork and its folk dancers and musicians. The dances are accompanied by chords from a *braguinha*, a four string guitar, while the rhythm is accentuated by an amusing looking stick adorned with a pyramid of dolls and castanets, known as a *brinquinho*.

▷ Follow the signs back to Funchal.

CENTRE AND NORTH COAST

Itineraries ②, ③ *and* ④ *on the Island map (p354). Starting from Funchal – 220km/137mi. Allow two days.*

The following tours of the island cover Madeira's main sights. It can be done in a day but if you wish to go on some of the walks, it's best to allow at least two days with a stopover in Santana.

② FROM FUNCHAL TO SANTANA VIA PICO DO AREEIRO

This section of the itinerary describes the journey north from Funchal up to the island's highest peaks and then the descent to the north coast.

▷ Leave Funchal by Rua do Til.

Beyond Terreiro da Luta the road, lined with flowering hedges, rises in steep hairpin bends through pine and acacia woods becoming more barren.

Ponta de São Lourenço

© Andre Carvalho/Associação de Promoção da Madeira

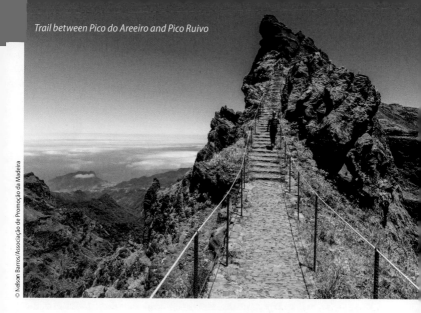

© Nelson Barros/Associação de Promoção da Madeira

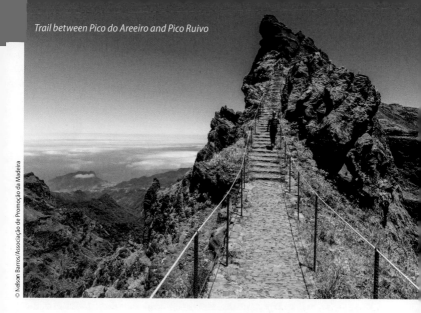 At Poiso (Boca do Poiso), take the road (left) to Pico do Areeiro.

The road follows the crest of the mountains with views of both Funchal, and the southern and northern coasts. The road ends near the Pousada do Pico do Areeiro. Keep an eye open for a domed ice house on the left just below the road.

Pico do Areeiro★★

There is a magnificent view from the Areeiro belvedere on the very summit of the mountain at 1 818m.
The landmarks include the Curral das Freiras crater, the distinctive outline of the crest of the Pico das Torrinhas (turrets) and, standing one before the other, the Pico das Torres and Pico Ruivo. To the northeast are the Ribeira da Metade, the Penha d'Águia (Eagle's Rock) and the Ponta de São Lourenço.

A good path has been constructed from Pico do Areeiro to Pico Ruivo (PR 1, Vereda do Areeiro). The walk (one-way) will take around 4 hours, and will require a pick-up at Achada do Teixera. Only seasoned walkers should contemplate the journey to Pico Ruivo and back (*Torches will be needed for the tunnels*).

Miradouro do Juncal★

A path goes round the summit of Pico do Juncal – 1 800m – to the belvedere *(15min round trip on foot),* from which there is an attractive view along the full length of the Ribeira da Metade valley to the sea below Faial.

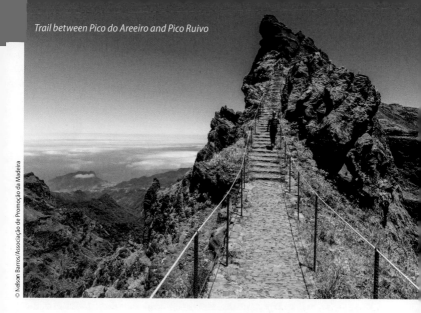 Return to Poiso and take the road on the left going to Faial. The road descends in a series of hairpin bends through pines and laurel.

Ribeiro Frio★

Near a little bridge over the Ribeiro Frio (meaning cold stream) stand a few small bars and restaurants, settled in a pleasant site amid the greenery at an altitude of 860m.
The **Levada do Furado**, which irrigates these slopes as far as Porto da Cruz and Machico, passes through Ribeiro Frio. It is possible to walk along it eastwards, on the PR 10, to Portela *(3h30),* or more gently and much shorter, westwards to the viewpoint at Balcões.

Balcões★★

1hr round trip on foot along the PR 11, the Vereda dos Balcões. Take the signed path to the left of the bend below Ribeiro Frio.
The path runs alongside the Levada do Furado through passages hewn out of the basalt rock to the Balcões belvedere.

Santana houses

© Francisco Correia/Associação de Promoção da Madeira

The view extends from the upper valley, which begins among jagged peaks (Pico do Areeiro, Pico das Torres and Pico Ruivo) to the open valley with its richly cultivated slopes that run down to the coast.

▶ Return to the road and head for Faial.

Continuing along the valley you will come to **São Roque do Faial**, a village perched on a long crest between two valleys. The houses with roofs covered in vines are surrounded by small, terraced gardens, willow plantations and orchards scattered with straw-thatched byres *(palheiros)*.

▶ Turn right towards Portela.

From the bridge over the Ribeira de São Roque there is an attractive view of the Faial valley and the village perched on the clifftop. Bananas, sugar cane and vines are grown on the sunny slopes.

▶ Head for Porto da Cruz.

A belvedere built on the left of the road has a fabulous **view**★★ of Porto da Cruz, a village nestled at the foot of a cliff. Autumn and winter are the best times of year for surfing here.

▶ At Porto da Cruz turn round and make for Faial.

About 4km/2.5mi from Faial, two belvederes on the right provide a **view**★ of Faial, the Penha d'Águia, the village of São Roque at the confluence of the Metade and São Roque valleys and, on the horizon, the Ponta de São Lourenço.

▶ Continue to follow the Via Espresso towards Santana.

Santana★

Santana, on a coastal plateau at an altitude of 436m, is one of the prettiest villages on the island. It is renowned for its brightly painted A-framed houses, a traditional style of architecture.

The **Madeira Theme Park** features attractions relating to the history and culture of Madeira (◷ *open Tue–Sun 9am–6pm.Nov-Mar 10am-6pm;* ∞€6, *child, 5–14 years* €4; ☏*291 570 410; www.parquetematicodamadeira.pt*).

Parque das Queimadas★

Bear left off the main road onto Caminho das Queimadas.
The road leads to some thatched cottages, at 883m. In a peaceful **setting**★ at the foot of the Pico Ruivo slopes is a beautiful park where the trees stand reflected in a small pool.

Pico das Pedras and Achada do Teixeira
10km/6.2mi.

The road from Santana runs to Pico das Pedras (**viewpoint★★**) and then continues to Achada do Teixeira. From a viewpoint at the far side of the car park you can see Faial and, in the foreground, a basalt formation known as **Homem em Pé** (the Man Standing). A path winds down to this feature from the car park. A paved path (PR 1.2, Vereda do Pico Ruivo) leads from the car park to Pico Ruivo. A short distance along and above this path there is a fine **view★★** of the Pico Ruivo massif and of Pico Areeiro.

③ FROM SANTANA TO SANTA
70km/44mi.

As you leave Santana, there is a splendid panorama to your left of the mountains. The road, lined with hydrangea, arum and canna lilies, crosses coastal valleys where a variety of crops are grown.

São Jorge
São Jorge's 17C **church** is unusually rich in its Baroque ornament, recalling the sumptuous period of King João V.
Before beginning the descent to **Arco de São Jorge**, a belvedere to the right of the road affords a wide **vista★** of the coast as it curves to form São Vicente bay. This is a region that produces Sercial wine.

Boa Ventura
This small village lies among vineyards in a pretty setting on a hill dividing two valleys. About 3km/1.8mi on, there is a beautiful **view★** to the right over the coastline which, beyond the nearby Moinhos river, sweeps away in a series of headlands and inlets.

São Vicente
São Vicente stands in a protected site at the mouth of the river of the same name, grouped in a cliff hollow a little way from the sea. It makes a pleasant stop with its renovated houses huddled around the church. Close by, the **Grutas de São Vicente** (volcanic caves, essen-

tially lava tubes) are a brief but interesting diversion (*open daily 10am–6pm; €8, child, 5–14 years, €6; ✆291 842 404; www.grutasecentrodovulcanismosaovicente.com*).

Road from São Vicente to Porto Moniz★★
The falls that drain the Paúl da Serra can be seen cascading down the slopes. 3km/1.8mi from Seixal the road passes through a long tunnel over which a waterfall cascades. A belvedere at the far end provides a good **viewpoint★**.

Seixal
This village has a pleasant **setting★** surrounded by vineyards on a promontory. Three small islands *(ilhéus)* rise out of the sea at the mouth of the Ribeira da Janela, the largest pierced by a sort of window *(janela)* that has given its name to the river and village. At a distance from the bridge the unusual shape of this rock islet can be clearly seen.

Porto Moniz★
The splendid village of Porto Moniz provides the only sheltered harbour along the north coast. Here you will also find swimming pools carved out of the volcanic rock filled with sea water.
North of the village the coast is strewn with a mass of pointed **reefs★**.

Parque das Queimadas

© Francisco Correia/Associação de Promoção da Madeira

Rock pools, Porto Moniz

© Greg Snell/Associação de Promoção da Madeira

On leaving Porto Moniz the road winds up the cliff, which dominates the village. Two successive belvederes afford **views★** of the village.

Santa

At Santa, short for Santa Maria Madalena, a curious belfry resembling a minaret flanks the white church.

▶ Beyond Santa bear left onto the 204 towards Paúl da Serra and Encumeada, or take itinerary G to follow the coast in the opposite direction.

4 SANTA TO RIBEIRA BRAVA VIA PAÚL DA SERRA
55km/34mi.

The 204 road, which is quite pleasant and a good deal faster than the coast road, links the west of the island, near Santa, to the Boca da Encumeada. It crosses the high plateau pastures of the Paúl da Serra, the only flat surface on the island, where small numbers of cattle can be seen grazing. Between Santa and Rabaçal the road follows the mountain crests affording fine views of both sides of the island.

Rabaçal★

A narrow (closed) road *(4km/2.5mi)* twists and turns through the shrubs to the Rabaçal forest huts (Casas de Rabaçal) set in a wild and remote spot.

⚡ Risco Waterfall★
50min walk round trip from the hut.

A path (PR 6.1) alongside the Levada do Risco leads to a waterfall that drops about 101m into a pool in the Ribeira da Janela valley. Another path (PR), which branches off the Risco, leads to the **25 springs** along the Levada das 25 Fontes *(allow at least 3hr round trip on foot).*

Paúl da Serra

This vast plain, unusual for Madeira, is grazed in summer by flocks of sheep and cows. Some parts of the road between Paúl da Serra and Encumeada overlook the south side of the island with fine views of the mountains dominating the coast and its banana plantations.

⊙ *The road down to Encumeada is prone to rockfall, so stay alert for debris in the road. Occasionally it is closed altogether; check at your hotel (or with a taxi driver) to ensure that the road is open and safe.*

Boca da Encumeada★

The Encumeada Pass at an altitude of 1 007m looks down over both sides of the island and of Madeira's two central valleys between the Paúl da Serra plateau and the mountain ranges near Pico Ruivo.

Serra de Água

The village of Serra de Água is in a pretty **setting★** halfway up a slope in the Riviera Brava valley.

The river flows through a narrow valley with rich plant life, mostly willow and black poplar along the water's edge.

From Ribeira Brava to Funchal
35km/22mi. Drive described in itinerary ⑤ *going in opposite direction.*

SOUTHWEST COAST★
Tour of 145km/90mi. Allow one day – Itineraries ⑤ *and* ⑥ *on the map of the island.*
Southwest Madeira has a much sunnier climate than the northern coast, and its slopes are thick with banana trees.

⑤ FROM FUNCHAL TO RIBEIRA BRAVA VIA CABO GIRÃO★
30km/18.6mi west. About 1hr.
Leave Funchal on Avenida do Infante.

Câmara de Lobos★
Câmara de Lobos was named after the great number of seals (*lobos marinhos* in Portuguese) on the shores when Zarco first arrived. Along the harbour you have a view of the town **setting★**. The white houses stand scattered on terraces among banana trees. Below, on the beach, fishing boats lie drawn up in the shade of palm trees with their nets suspended on willow frames to dry.

▷ Continue along the road.

Banana plantations give way to vineyards and cherry trees. Above 500m in the Jardim da Serra region, vines are grown on espaliers.

Estreito de Câmara do Lobos
This small bustling village is dominated by its white parish church. A narrow road beside the church leads to the upper village and the Levada do Norte.

▷ Return to R 101 and continue westwards, and then bear left towards Cabo Girão.

Cabo Girão★★
This belvedere offers a breathtaking Skywalk. From the belvedere there is an extensive view of the coastal plain as far as Funchal, and the sea 580m below. The cliff is often erroneously described as the second highest in Europe; it isn't, but is is mightily impressive nonetheless.

⑥ FROM RIBEIRA BRAVA TO SANTA
70km/44mi.

Ribeira Brava
This small town was built at the mouth of its eponymous river. In the town centre, in a square laid with a mosaic of cobbles, stands a 16C **church** flanked by a belfry with a blue and white tiled roof.

▷ Leave Ribeira Brava on the road, west along the coast.

The road passes near the headland, **Ponta do Pargo**, the westernmost tip of Madeira.

▷ Continue along the west coast to the junction with the 204. Return to Funchal via Paúl da Serra – the itinerary E is described above.

PICO RUIVO★★★
Pico Ruivo, Madeira's highest point, stands at 1 862m. Its volcanic slopes are covered in giant heathers and from the summit there is a glorious view over most of the island. 🔼 *From Pico do Areeiro.*
From Pico do Areeiro to Achada do Teixeira allow 4hr (minimum) walking time. This is the best-known excursion and a most rewarding mountain walk. ⊙ *However, the route is potentially hazardous, particularly for anyone who suffers from vertigo, and during high winds (⊙ Torches essential).*
The path begins by descending steps along a narrow rock crest which, on the left, overlooks the Curral das Freiras valley and, on the right, that of the Ribeira da Metade.

Espada - scabbard fish

© Th. Stankiewicz/Associação de Promoção da Madeira

Madeiran Cuisine

Mainstream Madeiran cuisine makes the most of the island's vegetable produce, grown in a fertile soil and superb climate. In addition, the seas around Madeira are rich in marine life, so fish, in one guise or another features on every menu. Perhaps oddly, it is one of the ugliest fish, the scabbard fish (espada), that takes pride of place everywhere. Despite its fiercesome appearance, this big-eyed, needle-toothed fish from the depths produces the most delicate flesh and is often served with fried banana.

Madeira has very good speciality meat dishes, including *espetada*, made with large chunks of beef rubbed in garlic and salt, then put on a skewer along with bay leaves, onions and peppers and grilled over wood chips. Another popular dish, especially at festival time, is *carne vinha d'alhos*, pork cooked slowly in a casserole with garlic and wine.

It's not hard to eat very well in Madeira. One restaurant – Il Gallo d'Oro in the Cliff Bay Hotel – has been awarded a Michelin star. Most of the luxury hotels and quintas have talented chefs, but elsewhere across the island food is wholesome, well cooked, excellent value and so fresh you can hear it still growing as it comes to your table.

Traditional Madeiran wines have a long pedigree. But increasingly the island is producing its own table wines from vineyards around Estreito de Câmara de Lobos, Seixal and Arco de São Jorge. Almost 30 percent of the vineyards are dedicated to producing red and white wine, which since 1999 has held the denomination VQPRD Madeirense.

Desserts are excellent too; chefs are able to make use of the wide variety of fresh fruit grown on the island, and also local products such as sugarcane honey. The most typical desserts are *queijada*s and *bolo de mel*.

Madeira barrels

© Olga_Anourina/iStock

A viewpoint after half an hour offers the most stunning mountain images. The trail winds on splendidly, and after a brief tunnel through the Cabo de Gato peak, more tunnels avoid the alternative climb around the Pico das Torres.

The continuation to Pico Ruivo is a delight and has spectacular scenery before finally easing up towards the summit. There is a small bar/tea house near the summit, but it cannot be guaranteed to be open, or stocked. From here a clear, paved path descends to Achada do Teixeira.

⚑ From Achada do Teixeira

This is a much easier, faster and less demanding route along PR 1 Vereda do Areeiro.

It takes less than 1hr on foot along on a paved pathway to the tea house at Pico Ruivo. From here there is a 15min climb to the summit.

A good plan is to book a taxi to Pico do Areeiro, do the walk to Pico Ruivo and then descend to Achada do Teixeira, having arranged for the taxi to meet you there.

ADDRESSES

🏠 STAY

The Cliff Bay – *Estrada Monumental, 147, Funchal. ☎291 708 750. www.portobay.com. 200 rooms.* This sumptuously appointed hotel offers every modern comfort. Perched on a natural promontory, the hotel is surrounded by gardens with innumerable secluded corners and centenary palm trees extending to the very edge of the cliff face. Indoor and outdoor pools, private sea access, diving centre, tennis court, fitness room and spa. The Cliff Bay is also home to **Il Gallo d'Oro**, which has two Michelin stars.

Pestana Grand – *Ponta da Cruz, São Martinho, Funchal. ☎291 707 400. www.pestana.com. 177 rooms plus 12 suites.* This luxury high-rise hotel offers the highest standards of comfort. Large, heated salt water pool, indoor jet stream pool linked to health club and spa. Bars and restaurants offer Moroccan, Italian and Portuguese fare.

Quinta Perestrello – *Rua Dr Pita, 3, Funchal. ☎291 706 700. www.quintaperestrellomadeira.com. 36 rooms.* Part of a select chain of Madeiran hotels, the Quinta Perestrello offers 12 double rooms in the main house and the rest, all with terrace or balcony offering garden or pool view, in the modern wing. All rooms are equipped with marble bathrooms (bath/shower and hairdryer), air conditioning, private safe, direct dial telephone, cable TV.

Belmond Reid's Palace – *Estrada Monumental, 139, Funchal. ☎291 717 171. www.belmond-com. 128 rooms and 35 suites.* Renowned for old world charm and exacting service, it was here that Sir Winston Churchill wrote his war memoirs, and where George Bernard Shaw learned to tango. All 163 rooms and suites are individually decorated with luxurious furnishings. Pool.

Quinta das Vistas – *Caminho de Santo António, 52-A, Funchal. ☎291 750 007. www.quintadasvistasmadeira.com. 71 rooms, including 3 junior suites, 4 suites and 1 presidential suite.* A most classy hotel in an excellent position above Funchal. You'll find a full range of facilities, including a beautiful south-facing swimming pool. A heated indoor pool features a passage leading to a hanging outdoor pool that has a waterfall linking to a second heated outdoor pool.

Quinta do Monte – *Caminho do Monte,192 194, Monte. ☎291 780 100. www.quintadomontemadeira.com. 42 rooms.* Set high above Funchal in the village of Monte, this peaceful and most agreeable hotel offers well appointed rooms and a gourmet restaurant. Pool.

Quintinha São João – *Rua da Levada de S. João, 4, Funchal. ☎291 740 920. www.quintinhasaojoao.com. 40 rooms.* Perched on the slopes above Funchal, this family-owned hotel is ideal for anyone wanting to be away from the bustle of Funchal. Sumptuous rooms and apartments, along with Wellness Spa and Treatments, 2 swimming pools, fitness and games rooms, and a gourmet restaurant serving Goan as well as traditional Madeiran cuisine makes this a perfect and peaceful place.

Quinta do Estreito – *Rua José Joaquim da Costa, Estreito de Câmara de Lobos. ☎291 910 530. www.quintado estreitomadeira.com. 44 rooms and 2 suites.*

At an altitude of 400m, in the hill village of Estreito de Câmara de Lobos, this charming hotel is a real find. Foodies will love the on-site gourmet **Restaurant Bacchus** and the more informal **Adega da Quinta** restaurant serving traditional Madeiran cuisine; in fact, it's worth making the journey from Funchal for espetada at the adega.

⫙/EAT

◎◎ **Armazém do Sal** – *Rua da Alfándega, 135, Funchal. ℘291 241 285. www.armazemdosal.com.* Tucked away in a quiet back street, this former salt warehouse offers high quality Madeiran cuisine, an excellent range of wines, and attentive service.

◎◎ **Arsénio's** – *Rua de Santa Maria, 169, Funchal (Old Town). ℘291 224 007.* Renowned for its fish kebabs and excellent steak, and for *fado* performances that take place most evenings. Generous portions.

◎◎ **Gavião Novo** – *Rua de Santa Maria, 131, Funchal (Old Town). ℘291 229 238. www.gaviaonovo.com.* Renowned for its fish dishes, serving only the freshest food according to the day's catch. A family owned and run enterprise; small but a real find.

◎◎ **Beerhouse** – *Avenida Sa Carneiro. verlooking the west end of Funchal marina. ℘291 229 011. www.beerhouse.pt/web/.* Looking rather like a tented village, the Beerhouse is famed for its beer, brewed on the premises, as much as for its excellent but simple cuisine.

◎◎ **Riso** – *Rua de Santa Maria, 274, Funchal (Old Town). ℘291 280 360. www.riso-fx.com/en/.* The food and service get mixed reviews but the location is great. Part of the restaurant is partially open above the crashing waves; ideal on a warm evening, but ask for an indoor table on a breezy one.

◎◎◎ **Restaurante Do Forte** – *Av. Santiago Menor 14 - Forte de Santiago, Funchal (Old Town). ℘291 215 580. https://en.forte.restaurant.* Considering its rather isolated location, this restaurant is a firm favourite, serving modern twists on national and regional cuisine. Well worth visiting.

SHOPPING

Funchal has transformed in recent years from a centre where shopping mainly targeted locals to one holding interest for visitors, too. A number of shopping malls have introduced modern chains of shops, notably:

Dolce Vita – in an excellent central location, next to Santa Caterina Park, and has almost 70 shops as well as a food court.

Forum Madeira – located within the tourist and hotel zone on the west of Funchal (Lido/Ajuda), this mall has over 86 shops, including 17 restaurants, cafés and snack bars, 6 cinemas and a hypermarket.

Madeira Shopping – This is another large shopping centre away from Funchal, in Santa Quitéria. Built in an attractive modern style blending with typical Madeiran features, this spacious shopping centre offers 83 shops, 20 restaurants, coffee shops, snack bars and 7 cinemas.

Souvenir Shopping – Wicker products are offered everywhere in Funchal – one of the biggest shops is in 'Rua do Castanheiro' . The main centre for wicker products with the biggest choice is the village of Camacha.

Embroidery shops – are found everywhere in the centre of Funchal.

There are several **Wine Lodges and Shops** in Funchal and surrounding areas where Madeira Wine tasting is offered and where your purchases will be professionally packed for safe transport home (such as Diogos Wine Shop, Madeira Wine Company, Oliveiras).

Madeira flowers, such as orchids, birds of paradise, king proteas, flamingo flowers etc… are the favourite souvenir to take home. These flowers can be purchased anywhere in Funchal; at the local market, the flower stands in the city centre or the flower shops. All these selling points will pack your flowers in special boxes for safe transport home.

Porto Santo★

A Pedreira

The island of Porto Santo, though only 40km/25mi to the northeast of Madeira, could not be more different. With an area of 42sqkm/16sq mi, it is much less densely inhabited, and geographically consists of a large plain edged to the northeast and southeast by a few so-called "peaks", of which the highest, Pico do Facho, has an altitude of only 517m.

SIGHTS

Vila Baleira

Vila Baleira is a fitting capital for the island. At the centre of the town is the **Largo do Pelourinho★**, an attractive square shaded by palm trees. Around it stand fine white buildings including the church and an emblazoned edifice that houses the town hall. An alleyway to the right of the church leads to the **Casa de Cristóvão Colombo** (the House of Christopher Columbus) *(⊙open Mon-Sat 10am–6pm, Sun 10am-1pm; ⊙closed public holidays; ∞€2; ℘291 983 405; www.museucolombo-portosanto.com/*

▶ **Population:** 5 483.
◉ **Michelin Map:** 733 fold 43; and below.
⊟ **Info:** Av. ManuelGregorio Pestana Junior. ℘291 985 244.
◖ **Location:** Just north-east of Madeira.
⚎ **Kids:** The ferry ride across can be fun on a calm day.
◕ **Timing:** A day trip by ferry from Funchal.
⊛ **Don't Miss:** The beach, but touring the island is easy, fun and peaceful.

home.html). You can see two rooms where he lived with his wife and, in an annexe, engravings and maps recalling events from his life including his many voyages.

To tour the island and take in all the main sights is easy. Take the road from Vila Baleira round **Pico do Facho**.

There are good views over the entire island and shepherds looking after sheep and cattle. **Pico do Castelo** is

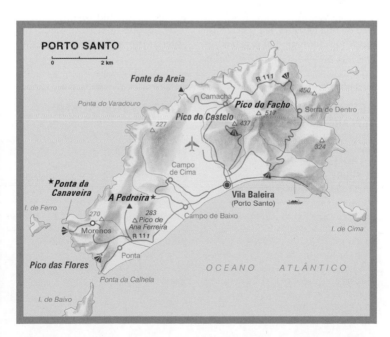

Praia do Combro, Porto Santo

© Francisco Correia/Associação de Promoção da Madeira

reached next before you come to the **Fonte da Areia**. This fountain in the sands flows near cliffs that overlook a wild and rocky coast, worn into strange shapes by erosion.

A Pedreira★

Take the road parallel to the beach towards the headland, Ponta da Calheta. Beyond the Porto Santo Hotel, bear right onto a track which after 2km/1.2mi leads to a quarry.

A Pedreira, which stands on the slope to **Pico de Ana Ferreira**, is a spectacular basalt rock formation of organ pipes soaring skywards. You reach **Pico das Flores** and then **Ponta da Canaveira★** with wonderful views and a lighthouse.

Sport on Porto Santo – There is a golf course on Porto Santo designed by Seve Ballesteros. Very close to the airport, so easily reachable, it has a fairly flat front nine but the back nine is played along the edge of the cliffs and across some huge ravines, making it quite a test for the average player, though good fun. From the beach in Vila Baleira, you can parasail and kite-surf. **Diving** is increasingly popular from Porto Santo; the water is warm and visibility up to 30m.

GETTING THERE

BY PLANE – A number of small airlines operate daily flights both ways between Madeira and Porto Santo. The flight takes about 15min.
BY FERRY – By Porto Santo Line (℘291 210 300; www.portosantoline. pt). Sailing time between Funchal and Porto Santo is 2hr 45min. A ferry leaves Funchal at 8am and sets out on the return journey from Porto Santo at 7pm; the frequency of service may vary according to the time of year, best to check online. Day return (round trip) ticket ☞€47.50–58.10 according to season.

TOUR OF THE ISLAND

As a complete tour takes 3–4hr, it is possible to make a day trip to Porto Santo from Madeira. You can tour the island by taxi, hired car or by bicycle. If you plan on spending several days on Porto Santo, why not visit the island on foot?
The island's main interest is its beautiful long sandy **beach,** which attracts tourists and Madeirans alike. During summer the beach can be crowded, so it is vital to book a hotel ahead of time.

For many people the Azores are largely unknown, and often confused with the Canary Islands or Madeira. Situated way out in the Atlantic, this archipelago of nine islands, three-and-a-half hours' away by plane from London, is not unlike Madeira, but spreads across 640km/400mi of ocean and two continental plates. In spite of their remote location, the islands are part of Europe and of Portugal, to which they belong; indeed, the Azores boast both the highest and westernmost points of the Portuguese Republic. These nine islands are united by unspoiled nature, a relaxed pace of life, and unique traditions and festivals.

Highlights

1 Don't miss an opportunity to go **whale watching** (p373)

2 Take a trip to **Sete Cidades, São Miguel** (p377)

3 Trek to the **Furnas do Enxofre, Terceira** (p387)

4 Visit the Interpretative Centre at **Capelinhos, Faial** (p393)

5 Try **Cozido das Furnas** (p404)

Geography

There are three distinct groups of islands between latitudes 36°55 N and 39°43 N. The eastern group consists of São Miguel and Santa Maria, the central one of Terceira, Graciosa, São Jorge, Faial and Pico, and the western group of Flores and Corvo. The total surface area is 2 335sq km/902sq mi.

Santa Maria, the easternmost island, is 1 300km/808mi from Portugal, and Flores, the westernmost, is 3 750km/2 330mi from North America.

Formation

Geological origins of the Azores are difficult to date. Like other islands belonging to archipelagoes in the Atlantic, they are volcanic. Their formation dates from the Quaternary Era, except for Santa Maria where Tertiary soil from the Miocene period has been found. The islands, which emerged from ocean depths of over 6 000m, are among the youngest in the world. The archipelago originated from a weak zone where the Atlantic rift meets the fault line that separates the African and Eurasian continental blocks. Apart from Corvo and Flores, which belong to the American Plate and have a north-south relief line, the Azores form part of the Eurasian Plate with an east-west relief line.

Ever since the islands were settled in the 15C, they have been subject to intense seismic and volcanic activity, including the upheaval of the Sete Cidades caldeira in 1440, eruptions in the Lagoa do Fogo crater in 1563, lava flows known as **misterios** on Pico (in 1562, 1718 and 1720) and Faial (in 1672), as well as

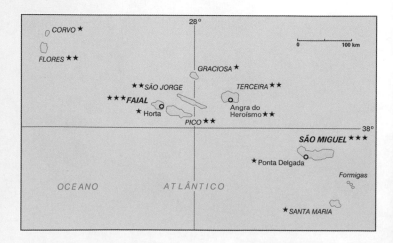

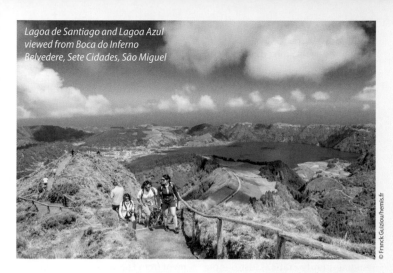

Lagoa de Santiago and Lagoa Azul
viewed from Boca do Inferno
Belvedere, Sete Cidades, São Miguel

eruptions on São Jorge (1808). Volcanic activity continues in the form of fumaroles and hot springs. From time to time a volcano erupts (as at Capelinhos on Faial in 1957) or an earthquake strikes (Terceira in 1980).

A great many eruptions have also been noted beneath the sea, their presence marked by a bubbling of the water, emissions of gas and clouds of steam. The most spectacular of these occurred in 1811 when an islet 90m high appeared briefly off the coast of São Miguel. A prolonged period of seismic activity preceded the emergence of what was named Sabrina Island, which vanished under the ocean a few months later.

Physical Appearance

Volcanic activity on the islands has given rise to large amounts of ash and the formation of **caldeiras** or vast craters formed either by explosion or in larger cases, collapse. Further explosions inside and around these *caldeiras* have formed small cones. Unusual examples of lava flows resulting from effusive types of eruptions can be seen on the islands of Pico and Faial, where they are known as **misterios**.

As for the island's coastlines, most consist of black cliffs dropping sheer to the sea. One of the most characteristic features of erosion is the **fajãs**, collapsed sea cliffs that then form a shoreline platform, the most striking of which can be seen along the north coast of São Jorge, and are now put to good use as farmland.

A Bit of History

In the 14C the islands were mentioned in several accounts of voyages and appeared in various navigation manuals. By the time Prince Henry the Navigator had founded the School of Navigation at Sagres in the early 15C, he had heard reports about far flung "sea islands" and decided to send an expedition to investigate. Santa Maria is said to have been the first to be discovered, in 1427. By 1452 all the islands had been discovered, but not all were settled immediately: Terceira in 1450, Pico and Faial in 1466, Graciosa and São Jorge in 1480 and Flores and Corvo as much as a century later.

In the 16C, the Azores were involved in the succession to the throne after King Sebastião's death. One of the pretenders to the crown, **Dom António, Prior do Crato**, had taken refuge in Terceira, where he obtained such support from the islanders that he was proclaimed king in 1582, in spite of the fact that Philip II of Spain had been reigning over Portugal for the last two years. In 1583 the Spanish troops got the upper hand, and the Prior of Crato fled to France.

The Azores Today

Population

The Azores have a mixed population. Early settlers were heterogeneous: Portuguese, Moorish captives, and Flemings sent by the Duchess of Burgundy, the daughter of King Dom João I. In the 19C many Americans came to settle in Faial and São Miguel.

Today the estimated population is a little under 250 000; in 1960 it was 327,000. A large proportion of each new generation has tended to emigrate. In the 17C people mostly went to Brazil, and later to the US and Canada. More than 130 000 islanders emigrated to North America between 1955 and 1974. In recent times the population has remained fairly static. Most people live in such towns and villages as there are, with the rest pursuing an agrarian lifestyle.

Economy

The main source of livelihood in the Azores is **farming**, particularly dairy farming, which accounts for a quarter of Portugal's total production. Dutch cattle are a common sight throughout the islands. São Miguel has also specialised in the large-scale cultivation of tea, tobacco, sugar beet, and especially pineapples, which are grown under glass. Crops are grown according to the altitude: potatoes, bananas and vines up to 150m; maize and fodder crops between 150m–400m, and pastures above 400m. Submarine cables linking Europe and the US and passing through the Azores were laid in the 19C; these were used considerably after World War II. The islands also continued to be used as a main refuelling point for transatlantic aircraft.

Although **fishing** has diminished, it is still an important activity. Almost 90 percent of Portuguese tuna is fished in these waters.

São Miguel and Terceira, the archipelago's two most densely populated islands, are the centres for most of the administrative and economic bodies. There has been considerable investment from Europe, and many (but not all) of the roads, for example, are now in good condition; new hotels are appearing, too.

The Azores Anticyclone

The Azores Anticyclone is a major weather system that affects continental Europe and the UK. In the mid 19C, the French geographer Elisée Reclus predicted that the cable, "which will link the Azores with European observatories will be of immense importance to meteorologists." In 1893 Reclus' prediction was realised: an underwater cable was laid between Faial and the European continent to transmit information from

Tea plantation with hydrangeas, Porto Formoso, São Miguel

© ARoxoPT/Shutterstock

Whale off Pico

© Herner Damke/Shutterstock

the weather stations in Faial, Flores, São Miguel, Terceira and Santa Maria to the Paris observatory.

The Azores Anticyclone arises because the Azores archipelago lies in the contact zone between cold currents from the North Atlantic and warm ones from the tropical Atlantic. It is at this point that the two high atmospheric pressures merge – the warm, subtropical ones on the one hand and the Arctic intensified ones on the other.

Climate and Vegetation

The weather changes quickly in the Azores; it is commonly said that each of the four seasons can be experienced in a single day. Clouds tend to settle thickly over highland regions, leaving the coast in full sunshine. Surrounded by a huge ocean warmed by the Gulf Stream, the Azores have a climate that is mild and very humid throughout the year, with a humidity rate that can reach 80 percent and average temperatures of 14°C in winter and 23°C in summer.

About 60 plants are unique to the Azores. Vegetation is very dense and varied on account of the humidity, latitude and volcanic soil. Tropical species thrive beside European plants, giving a surprising combination of sequoia, dragon tree, tulip tree, jacaranda, pine, beech, monkey-puzzle tree, palms and cedar. The variety of flora is even more striking in the case of flowers. The most emblematic of the Azores is the **hydrangea**, either pink or blue depending on the season.

Whale Watching

From the 17C onwards, whaling was carried out around the Azores, organised first by the English and then by the Americans. In 1870, when oil was discovered and replaced whale blubber as fuel, American whalers became scarce and the Azoreans decided to hunt from their own shores.

Whaling continued until 1981, and many Azoreans still look back nostalgically to those days. It was an important source of income for the islanders. While it has been partly replaced by tuna fishing, the gap it left in the economy has caused many of the islanders to emigrate.

Today, whale watching has taken over, and the Azores make a very good base from which to head out into the Atlantic to watch whales and dolphins. In the prime whale-watching season (May to September), boats set out each morning from Faial and São Miguel. More than 20 different species can be seen, though not normally all on the same day. Minke, bottlenose, fin, pilot and blue whales are regular visitors to this part of the Atlantic on their north-south journeys, as are huge groups of dolphins – up to 900 have been spotted in one pod.

WHEN TO GO

The most pleasant season is between May and September when there is less rain, and the temperatures are mild. The Azores enjoy a mild temperate climate, and benefit from the Gulf Stream. Whatever the season, it is best to take a raincoat, good walking shoes and a pullover. Warm clothes are required in winter. It is never cold in summer except at high altitudes; light trousers and dresses are ideal. Festivals for village patron saints are held throughout the year. All the islands celebrate the well-known feast of the Holy Ghost, when a gift-bearing emperor is elected. Brightly coloured buildings known as *impérios* – Empires of the Holy Ghost – are used to house symbols for the festival. **Time Zone:** The Azores are 1hr behind London (GMT): when it is 8am in London (and Madeira), it is 7am in the Azores. They are 4hr ahead of the East Coast of the US (EST).

GETTING THERE

BY AIR - TAP Air Portugal *(www.flytap. com)* or SATA Internaçional *(www.sata. pt),* which has flights to Ponta Delgada (São Miguel), Lajes (Terceira) and Horta (Faial). Ryanair *(www.ryanair. com*) offer direct flights from London Stansted. **Archipelago Choice** in the UK have an excellent record of arranging all-inclusive, customised trips to the Azores *(www.azoreschoice.com*).

GETTING AROUND
INTER-ISLAND

BY AIR - SATA Air Açores *(Av. Infante D. Henrique, 55, Ponta Delgada; ☏707 22 72 82, or ☏296 209 720; www.sata.pt)*, the local airline, has flights to all the islands. You may not have a direct flight, so take this into account when organising your trip if you wish to visit several islands. Terceira acts as a hub for most flights.
BY SEA - In the summer there are boat connections between the islands in the central group several times a week. Crossings can be slow:

4h between Terceira and Graciosa, 3h30 between Terceira and São Jorge and 1h15 between São Jorge and Pico. Boats link Faial and Pico several times a day *(30min crossing)*, Santa Maria and São Miguel, and Flores and Corvo daily in the summer *(2h both ways).* Island-based tourist offices provide boat timetables. See also *www.atlanticoline.pt.*

ISLAND-BASED

TAXIS - Each of the islands has English-speaking taxi drivers who offer day-long excursions – ask at your hotel.
CAR RENTAL - There are car rental firms on all the islands, except Corvo.
BUSES - The main islands have a regular bus service, but it is geared to local needs rather than tourists.
ROADS - On the whole, the roads are in fairly good condition, though not always well signposted.

TELEPHONES

To call the Azores from the United Kingdom, dial 00 351 and then the number being called, which will begin with 292 (Pico, Faial, Flores, Corvo), 295 (Terceira, Graciosa, São Jorge), or 296 (São Miguel and Santa Maria). To make an international call from the Azores, dial 00 then the country code (44 for the UK, 353 for Ireland, 1 for the US and Canada), the area code (excluding the first 0, where applicable) and the number. Mobile and cell phones can be used on the major islands.

LANGUAGE

The language of the Azores is Portuguese. Staff in all tourist information centres, hotels, restaurants and car rental firms generally speak English, French and German.

BANKS

There are banks on all the islands except Corvo. ATMs can be found on most islands at ferry or airports and in the larger towns. Smaller guesthouses may not accept credit cards.

São Miguel★★★

Ponta Delgada

São Miguel, the largest of the Azorean islands with more than half of the total population, forms the eastern group of islands with Santa Maria. It is known as the green island or *ilha verde*. In spite of a certain amount of modernity, you can still see traditional scenes such as milk churns being transported on donkey-drawn carts.

GEOGRAPHY

São Miguel, known by many as the "Green island" for its abundant vegetation, consists of two volcanic mountain massifs divided by a depression, which is covered in lava from recent volcanic eruptions between Ponta Delgada and Ribeira Grande. The oldest massif, in the east, is dominated by **Pico da Vara** at 1 103m. The island's most impressive features are its craters, which contain lakes: Sete Cidades, Lagoa do Fogo and Furnas. Volcanic activity is still abundantly apparent today in the form of fumaroles and bubbling mud springs (*sulfataras*) at Furnas, Ribeira Grande and Mosteiros. The jagged coastline, particularly in the north and east, consists of sheer cliffs at the foot of which are sometimes narrow beaches of black sand. The gentler, southern coast has wider beaches at Pópulo, Água de Alto, Ribeira Chã, Vila Franca do Campo and Ribeira Quente.

PONTA DELGADA★

Ponta Delgada is the main town in São Miguel, home to the Regional Government and the University for all the islands in the Azores. It became the capital of the island in 1546; fortifications were built in the 16C and 17C to protect the town from pirates.

The town is a bustling place, busy by day and with several good and relatively inexpensive hotels in its tightly packed streets (making parking overnight difficult if you have rented a car). Walking along the road by the water's edge is a pleasant way to spend an evening, and

▶ **Population:** 137,856.
🚗 **Michelin Map:** p373 Michelin Atlas Spain and Portugal.
ℹ **Info:** Av. Infante Dom Henrique, Ponta Delgada; ℘296 308 610. www.visitazores.com.
◗ **Location:** The largest island, to the east of the main group, 1 300km/800mi from the mainland.
◷ **Timing:** Spend a few days on the island with several day trips to its various parts. If you wish to visit any of the other islands, you can do day trips to a couple of them by air from Ponta Delgada.
🅿 **Parking:** Difficult in Ponta Delgada, but no problems anywhere else.
⌖ **Don't Miss:** Sete Cidades, Lagoa do Fogo and Furnas.

GETTING THERE

ACCESS: There are direct flights daily to and from London and Lisbon, and the other islands in the Azores archipelago to São Miguel. Inter-island boat travel is not recommended in winter.

LENGTH OF STAY: If you are short of time, it is possible to see Ponta Delgada, Sete Cidades and Furnas in two days. However, you should allow four days for a more worthwhile visit.

you will find many restaurants where excellent dishes can be enjoyed. Summer evenings tend to be fairly lively, especially if there are several yachts in the marina en route between Europe and the Caribbean.

The **historical quarter** of Ponta Delgada is set back from **Avenida do Infante Dom Henrique**, a wide boulevard that runs alongside the harbour. The quarter is a tight network of streets,

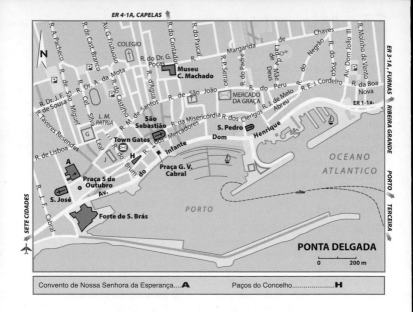

Map labels:
ER 4-1A, CAPELAS
R. A. Pacheco
R. de Cast. Branco
Av. G. Frutuoso
COLEGIO
R. do Contador
R. do Pascal
R. do D. G. Poças
Margarida
de
Chaves
R. Negrão
Av. João III
R. Moinho de Vento
ER 3-1A, FURNAS
Museu C. Machado
R. P. Serrão
Lado
da Mãe de Deus
R. do Poço
R. do Padre
R. do Peru
R. E. J. Cordeiro
R. da Boa Nova
RIBEIRA GRANDE
R. de São João
MERCADO DA GRAÇA
R. J. de Melo Abreu
ER 1-1a.
R. Dr. J. F. São Miguel
R. de Sousa
R. Cel.
R. Dr. A. da Mota
R. do Castilho
R. d'Água
R. dos Clérigos
PORTO
L. M. PATRIA
São Sebastião
R. da Misericórdia
R. dos Mercadores
S. Pedro
Henrique
Dom
TERCEIRA
R. Taveres Resendes
R. M. de Santos
Silva Leal
Town Gates
R. dos Infante
R. do Brum
Praça G. V. Cabral
OCEANO ATLANTICO
R. de Lisboa
A
Praça 5 de Outubro
AV.
S. José
PORTO
R. J. F. Cabral
SETE CIDADES
Forte de S. Brás
PONTA DELGADA
0   200 m

Convento de Nossa Senhora da Esperança....**A**   Paços do Concelho.....................**H**

along which stand fine 17C and 18C mansions. Open spaces are provided by squares and public gardens shaded by monkey-puzzle trees.

Praça Gonçalo Velho Cabral

On the square stands the statue of Gonçalo Velho, who allegedly discovered the island. The 18C **town gates** consist of three archways set in basalt. Extending from the square is the **Largo da Matriz**, dominated by the tall façade of the 16C

Café terrace in front of Igreja Matriz de São Sebastião

© Brian Jannsen/age fotostock

church of São Sebastião and the 17C Baroque **Town Hall** *(Paços do Conselho)*.

Igreja Matriz de São Sebastião

The 16C parish church, built on the site of a former chapel, is famous for its graceful **Manueline doorway★** in white limestone. The stone was brought from the Alentejo in mainland Portugal. The interior is noteworthy for the vaulting in the chancel and the gilded Baroque statues of the Evangelists on the high altar. The sacristy to the left of the chancel is decorated with *azulejos* and has 17C furniture made of jacaranda. The **treasury** to the right of the chancel contains gold and silver plate as well as some extremely precious 14C vestments that were brought over from Exeter Cathedral in England.

Forte de São Brás

This fort was first built in the 16C and remodelled in the 19C. The vast park, **Praça 5 de Outubro** (also known as Largo de São Francisco), has a bandstand and a huge tree stretching out in front of the fort. Two large churches give onto the square: the Igreja de São José, which was part of a former Franciscan convent, and the Igreja de Nossa Senhora de Esperança.

Convento de Nossa Senhora da Esperança★

The convent houses the statue of **Senhor Santo Cristo dos Milagres** (Christ of Miracles), believed to have been given by Pope Paul III to nuns who petitioned in Rome for the setting up of their convent near Ponta Delgada in the 16C.

Inside, the long narrow church is divided by a wrought-iron grille, behind which are the church treasures, including the statue of Santo Cristo, gold and silver plate and polychrome *azulejos* by António de Oliveira Bernardes.

Outside the church, beneath an anchor carved in the wall and inscribed with the word *Esperança*, is the spot where the Azorean poet **Antero de Quental** (1842–91) committed suicide.

Igreja de São José

The church belonged to a 17C Franciscan monastery, and is now a school. Inside, the vast nave is covered in wooden vaulting painted in false relief. The late 18C chapel of Nossa Senhora das Dores has a Baroque façade.

Igreja de São Pedro

This 17C and 18C church overlooks the port and faces the **São Pedro Hotel**. Behind the church's graceful façade is a rich Baroque interior with gilded altarpieces and ceilings painted in false relief. The chapel to the right of the chancel contains the 18C **statue of Our Lady of Sighs★**, one of the most beautiful statues in the Azores.

Carlos Machado Museum

◷*Open Tue–Sun 9.30am–5pm.* ℘*296 202 930. www.parqueterranostra.com.* Founded in 1880 and since 1930 installed in the former 16C Convento de Santo André, this museum houses one of the most notable collections of the Azores. Begun originally with natural history (particularly zoology), botany, geology and mineralogy specimens, the collections were extended to jewellery, glazed tiles, porcelain, toys, paintings, sculptures and folk art when the museum was moved to the former

convent. Of particular importance is a group of **oil paintings** from the Portuguese school from the 16C, as well as a collection of contemporary art.

🚗 DRIVING TOURS

☐1 THE WEST★★
80km/50mi. Allow half a day.

▶ Take the airport road from Ponta Delgada and then the road marked Sete Cidades.

Pico do Carvão★

A lookout point dominates a large area of the island affording views of the centre, the northern coast and Ponta Delgada. The road runs past a moss-covered aqueduct and then some small lakes, including **Lagoa do Canário**, which is surrounded by botanical gardens.

Sete Cidades★★★

Sete Cidades, the natural wonder of the Azores, is a volcanic crater with a circumference of 12km/7.4mi. It is best seen from the **Vista do Rei★★★** viewpoint to the south. The view takes in the twin lakes, one green, the other blue, and the village of Sete Cidades at the bottom of the crater.

▶ A road (marked Cumeeiras) leads from Vista do Rei along the edge of the crater (🚶 allow 2h to walk). There are views of both sides of the crater, inside and out. The road crosses another one leading down to Sete Cidades. Beyond that are the lakes.

The road runs across a bridge built between the two lakes. On the other side of the bridge a path to the left leads to a picnic area beside the blue lake, Lagoa Azul.

Miradouro da Vista do Rei★★★

The "King's Lookout" might be the best translation of this, and when you stand here, on the side of the southern (green) lake and look at the surrounding sea, land and sky, you'll understand why. A view fit for a king, indeed. It was named after the visit of King Carlos I and Queen D. Amélia in 1901. The route back to Ponta Delgada depends upon the amount of time you have:

If you have about 1hr, take the road round **Lagoa de Santiago**, and back up to Vista do Rei, then the road which begins near Monte Palace. This route descends between banks of glorious flowering hydrangeas to join the road to Ponta Delgada.

If you have 3hr or more, head northwest to **Miradouro do Escalvado★** on the coast, which has a fine view of the village of Mosteiros and its rocks, then continue along a winding road to Capelas where you head south to Ponta Delgada via Fajã de Cima.

THE CENTRE★★

2 NORTHERN ROUTE FROM PONTA DELGADA
71km/44mi. 4hr.

Take the Lagoa road east of Ponta Delgada. Beyond Lagoa head north towards Remédios and Pico Barrosa.

Lagoa do Fogo★★
An eruption in the 16C formed a crater lake that was given the name "Fire Lake". Today this is a peaceful, beautiful spot with the clear water of the lake covering the crater floor. A white sand beach (an ideal place for a picnic) borders the lake on one side, a sheer cliff face on the other.

The road continues uphill towards Ribeira Grande.

Ribeira Grande
Ribeira Grande, the second-largest town on the island, is an ideal place to stop for lunch with several good, inexpensive restaurants. It has fine 16C–18C mansions, including **Solar de São Vicente**, which houses the arts centre. The vast garden square in the middle of town, alongside which flows the Ribeira Grande, is surrounded by interesting

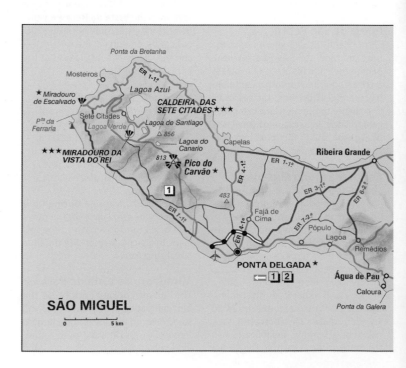

buildings including the 16C **Town Hall** with its double staircase and square tower, and the **Igreja do Espírito Santo** with its elaborate Baroque façade.

The church is also known as the Dos Passos Church as it contains the statue of Christ (Senhor dos Passos) which is carried in traditional processions on Saints' Days and at the great church festivals throughout the year.

The large 18C **Igreja de Nossa Senhora da Estrela** stands at the top of a wide flight of steps.

Inside, the walls and ceilings are painted and, as elsewhere on the island, the gilt altarpieces are richly decorated.

◯ Head south from Ribeira Grande following signs to Caldeiras.

Caldeiras

This is an active volcanic area heralded by a group of small fumaroles. There is a natural spa centre and some springs that produce a well-known mineral water that is bottled and sold throughout Portugal.

Birds of Prey

The origin of the name Azores was derived from the archaic Portuguese word "azures", the plural of the word blue. Some say that it was named after the goshawk bird ("açor") because the first Portuguese to discover the islands saw many birds that reminded them of this type of sparrow-hawk. The birds were in fact buzzards, but the association has remained. One of the islands, Corvo, is certainly named after a bird, the crow.

◯ Return to the coast road and head east.

The coast is a series of headlands and bays within which are found small secluded beaches, like that of **Porto Formoso**.

◯ Take the Furnas road.

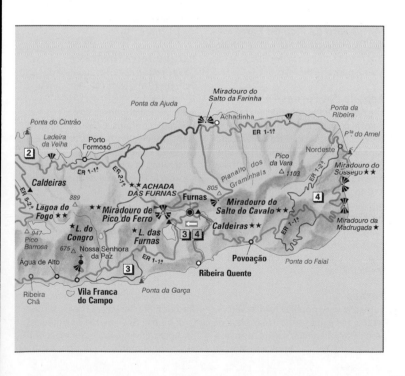

Making Cozido, Furnas valley

Ribeira Quente
8km/5mi from Furnas.

The road between Furnas and Ribeira Quente is one of the most attractive on the island. At a point between two tunnels an impressive waterfall cascades down to the right. The village of Ribeira Quente (Hot River) is mainly known for its beach warmed by the hot springs after which the place is named.

Miradouro de Pico do Ferro★★

The view stretches across the whole Furnas valley, taking in the village, Terra Nostra park and the lake.

Achada das Furnas★★

The **Achada valley** is an idyllic site set in a crown of hills and mountains. The best views of it are from the Pico do Ferro and Salto do Cavalo viewpoints. The name Furnas derives from the hollows in the ground from which spurt hot springs and sulphurous, bubbling mud fumaroles that can be seen from a distance by their jets of steam. The vegetation surrounding the charming, whitewashed town of Furnas is exceptionally luxuriant thanks to the area's warm, moist soil and the humidity.

Furnas

Furnas is very popular for its waters, which are used in the treatment of respiratory ailments, rheumatism and depression. You can book a treatment here, ideal also for easing aches and pains and an overall detox.

Terra Nostra Park, begun in the late 18C by wealthy American merchant Thomas Hickling, is a delightful series of lakes set in lush gardens surrounding a hotel (&see below).

Caldeiras★★

The sulphurous waters in the area with their volcanic eruptions and vapours boil at temperatures of around 100°C. Known as *caldeiras*, they punctuate the landscape with their boiling water from deep in the earth.

Parque Terra Nostra★★

🕐*Open daily: Apr–Sept 10am–7pm; Oct–Jan 10am–6pm; Feb–Mar 10am–5.30pm.* ⊚€8. 𝒫296 584 706. www.parqueterranostra.com.

The park contains a diverse range of plant species with hibiscus, azalea, hydrangea and tropical plants and flowers thriving in the shade beneath Japanese larch. The avenues are bordered by magnificent royal palms.

Lagoa das Furnas★

Clouds of steam rising up from the northwest shores of the lake at the foot of steep slopes mark the presence of fumaroles. The warm earth has been hollowed out and cemented to form underground ovens with large wooden lids. Traditionally the villagers would cook their food in this way, burying the pots for hours on end while the meat and fish gently simmered in the hot earth.

3 SOUTHERN ROUTE FROM FURNAS
52km/32mi. 3hr.

▶ Leave Furnas on the Ponta Delgada road. After 16km/10mi turn right and 3km/1.8mi farther on turn left. After 300m you reach a fork; turn right and continue for another 450m.

⚑ Lagoa do Congro★
To reach Lagoa do Congro, which is an emerald green lake at the bottom of a large crater, you leave the pastureland with its hydrangea hedges and follow a footpath *(40min round trip)* that leads rapidly down the crater slopes through thick vegetation and magnificent trees.
⊛ *Wear good walking shoes.*

▶ Return to the road and travel west for a few kilometres (couple of miles).

Vila Franca do Campo
The town, the island's early capital, was partly destroyed by an earthquake in 1522. Facing the town is a volcanic **islet** that appeared when the sea bed erupted. In the town centre is a beautiful square with a public garden dominated by the Gothic **Igreja de São Miguel**.
Standing on a rise above Vila Franca is the **Capela de Nossa Senhora da Paz**, a chapel that is approached by a flight of steps rather like a small-scale version of that of Bom Jesus at Braga. There is a fine **view★** of the coast, Vila Franca and the sea of white hothouses in which pineapples are ripened.
Once past the long **Água D'Alto beach** turn south to the headland, **Ponta da Galera**, with the delightful little harbour of Caloura and attractive holiday homes.

⚑ Água de Pau
Follow the signs to Ermita and Miradouro (20min round trip on foot).
The lookout point gives an interesting **view★**, to one side, **Ponta da Caloura** and a volcanic cone covered right to the top in a patchwork of fields, and to the other, the **hermitage** which stands out against a mountain background. The road continues along the coast past a series of beaches including those of Lagoa and Pópulo to Ponta Delgada.

4 THE EAST
85km/53mi. About 4hr.

The road climbs from Furnas eastwards onto the Graminhais plateau. There is a beautiful view of the Furnas valley from **Miradouro de Salto do Cavalo★★**. The road continues to the **Salto da Farinha** viewpoint beyond Salga, which affords a good view of the north coast. It is always worth stopping at the several viewpoints; they are not placed haphazardly, but in such a way that you get the best vistas across the island.

The East Coast★★
The eastern part of the island has a strikingly beautiful coastline. In most parts it is rocky with some wonderful places to stop and look out over the sea, though none of the other islands visible from this side of the island – Santa Maria is too far south. The most spectacular views are from viewing points on the cliffs south of the village of Nordeste: **Miradouro da Ponta do Sossego★★** and **Miradouro da Ponta da Madrugada★**. Along much of this coast cliffs drop sheer to the sea. Beyond Miradouro da Madrugada a narrow winding road 2km/1.2mi long leads to the beach at Lombo Gordo. This coast is dominated by **Pico da Vara**: at 1 100m, it is the high point here and makes a wonderful viewing point.
It is also the site of a terrible air crash. On 27 October 1949 an Air France Constellation aircraft flying from New York to Paris was attempting to land at Ponta Delgada to refuel, but on its third attempt to land in bad weather, it crashed into the mountain, killing everyone on board. Among them was Marcel Cerdan, the 1948 world middleweight boxing champion who was the lover of Edith Piaf.

Povoação
This is the first place on the island to have been settled (*povoação* means population). The village stands at the mouth of a picturesque valley under intense cultivation.

Santa Maria★

Santa Maria is one of the least visited islands of the Azores, and yet it is one of the most pleasant, with a warm climate, **beaches** and delightful countryside dotted with white, terra-cotta-roofed houses. These houses have tall cylindrical chimneys painted with brightly coloured borders to outline the façades. The landscape you first see on arrival in Santa Maria is somewhat unexpected: a dry plateau of yellow grass that looks more like Texas than the Azores. Several kilometres beyond the airport, the landscape changes to the green countryside typical of the Azores.

▶ **Population:** 5 550.
◔ **Michelin Map:** p383.
   Michelin Atlas Spain
   and Portugal.
🗊 **Info:** Aeroporto de
   Santa Maria, Vila do
   Porto; ℘296 886 355.
◖ **Location:** The southern-
   most island in the Azores,
   88km/55mi south of
   São Miguel.
◷ **Timing:** Book a taxi for a
   full day tour of the island,
   even though this may
   involve two nights' stay.
◉ **Don't Miss:** The view
   from Pico Alto; also Baía
   de São Lourenço.

A BIT OF HISTORY

The original wealth of Santa Maria came from the cultivation of woad and the gathering of orchil (a lichen that gives a brown dye), both used in the dyeing industries in Flanders and Spain. The discovery of indigo in Brazil put an end to this industry and the island reverted to agriculture, which today employs most of its inhabitants. The island is popularly regarded as the "Yellow Island" primarily due to the crops grown here, but the entire island is ablaze with colour, the yellow fields contrasting with the deep blue of the ocean and the azure of the sky above, interrupted by the whitewashed houses.

GETTING THERE

ACCESS: There are regular flights between Santa Maria and São Miguel.

SIGHTS
Vila do Porto

The town is in the south of the island between Cabo Marvão and Cabo Força. It stretches along a strip of basalt plateau between two ravines that join to form a creek. Among the buildings dating from the 16C and 17C are the **Convento de Santo António**, now the public library and the Franciscan mon-

astery, now the **Town Hall**. Attached to the convent is **Nossa Senhora da Vitória** (Our Lady of Victory), with its beautiful 17C panel of tiles depicting the miracles of St Anthony. Other notable buildings include the **Igreja da Nossa Senhora da Assunção" (Our Lady of Ascension Church)**, whose construc-

Baía de São Lourenço with terraced vineyards

tion began near the end of the 15C: the **Igreja da Misericórdia**, constructed in 1536 which has an altarpiece of Saint Isabel, and an image of Senhor dos Passos, regarded as one of the most beautiful in the Azores.

It is also worth seeing the **São Brás Fort**, constructed to defend the town, and the **Santa Maria Museum**, which exhibits interesting pottery works.

The chapels of **Nossa Senhora do Pilar** (Our Lady of Pilar) and **Nossa Senhora de Fátima** (Our Lady of Fátima), are also religious sites of historical importance on the island.

Almagreira

Below the village lies **Praia Formosa**, literally "beautiful beach", and it certainly is one of the finest in the Azores.

Pico Alto★★

Take the road to the left and drive for 2km/1.2mi.

The **view★★** from the top of Pico Alto (590m/1,936ft) takes in the whole island. It is one place you should not miss, and one that provides a rewarding view of the island.

Santo Espírito

In the village is the **Igreja de Nossa Senhora da Purificação** (Our Lady of Purification); with its baroque façade and country tiles from the 16C, it is the most beautiful on the island.

Beyond Santo Espírito the road descends to **Ponta do Castelo** through a dry landscape dotted with aloes and cacti, in the middle of which stands a lighthouse. Lower still is **Maia**, a former whaling station.

Return to Santo Espírito and head towards Baía do São Lourenço. Go right just before you get there and go to the **Miradouro do Espigão★★**, which has a most beautiful view of the bay.

Baía do São Lourenço★★

The bay, once a crater long since invaded by the sea, is an outstanding site with concave slopes covered in terraced vineyards. Bordering the narrow beaches around the turquoise water are houses occupied only in summer.

Santa Bárbara

Houses are scattered over the hills and along the steep coastline bordering Tagarete bay. The **church** was rebuilt in 1661.

Anjos

The small fishing harbour is mainly known for its history. A statue of **Christopher Columbus** recalls that the Genoese explorer is believed to have stopped here on his return from his first voyage of discovery across the Atlantic and to have attended Mass in the **Capela da Nossa Senhora dos Anjos.**

Terceira★★

Angra do Heroísmo

Terceira, the Portuguese word for third, was the third island in the archipelago to be discovered. It is also the third-largest island, after São Miguel and Pico. While its landscape is less striking than those of the other islands, Terceira is more interesting in terms of architecture, traditions and festivals.

Terceira is a tableland overlooked in the east by the Serra do Cume, the remains of Cinco Picos, the island's oldest volcano. The central area is demarcated by a vast crater known as Caldeira de Guilherme Moniz, which is surrounded by other volcanic formations. To the west is the Serra da Santa Bárbara, the island's most recent and highest (1 021m) volcanic cone with a wide crater. The islanders make a living essentially from farming, cultivating maize and vines, as well as stock rearing. Terceira is the granary of the Azores.

▶ **Population:** 56,062.

🖥 **Michelin Map:** p388. Michelin Atlas Spain and Portugal.

🈺 **Info:** Rua Direita,74; 📞295 213 393 &204 810.

◐ **Location:** The easternmost of the five islands grouped centrally in the Azores – about 161km/100mi northwest of São Miguel

🕐 **Timing:** Stay here at least for a couple of nights to enjoy all this lovely island has to offer.

🅿 **Parking:** Not too bad, even in the main town. Elsewhere, no problems.

🕲 **Don't Miss:** Make a special effort to seek out some of the "Impérios" – the small chapels dedicated to the Holy Spirit. You'll find them in every village.

A BIT OF HISTORY

Impérios

The Azorean tradition of worshipping the Holy Ghost is particularly strong in Terceira. Every quarter in each village has its little chapel known as an *império* or "empire" of the Holy Ghost. The chapels look like salons, their picture windows adorned with net curtains; they are maintained by brotherhoods whose chief task is to organise festivals. The festivals follow a ritual that dates from the early days of settlement when the islanders would call upon the Holy Ghost in times of natural disaster. They were originally intended to be charitable events and one of their main functions was to provide meals for the poor.

During today's festival, an "emperor" is still elected by the people. He is presented with a sceptre and crown on a silver platter and is crowned by a priest. He is then accompanied to the *Império*

Império do Espírito Santo de Santa Cruz, Praia da Vitória

© Jon Arnold Images/hemis.fr

GETTING THERE

ACCESS: There are regular flights between Terceira and Lisbon, and the other islands in the archipelago. In summer, the boat connecting the central group of islands calls at Terceira several times a week.

TOURING THE ISLAND: Allow at least two days to tour the island and spend some time in Angra do Heroísmo.

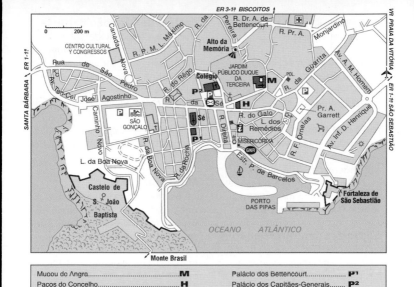

Muoou do Angra	**M**	Palácio dos Bettencourt	**P¹**	
Paços do Concelho	**H**	Palácio dos Capitães-Generais	**P²**	

do Espírito Santo, where he receives the gifts to be distributed to the poor and then invites the whole village to take part in the feast which is followed by a traditional *Tourada da corda (see below).*

The Island of Bulls

Terceira is known for its **touradas à corda** that take place during village festivals. A bull with a long rope about its neck is allowed to rush at crowds of men who jump out of the way leaving the bravest to taunt the bull by opening a large umbrella beneath its muzzle.

ANGRA DO HEROÍSMO★★

The town, set in the curve of a wide bay or *angra* and dominated by Monte Brasil on a little promotory, is without doubt the most beautiful harbour in the archipelago and is home to a branch of the University of the Azores.

On 1 January 1980, a violent **earthquake** shook the town and demolished a large part of it without taking any lives. In 1983 Angra do Heroísmo was given World Heritage status by UNESCO, and the outstanding work carried out has since restored its former beauty.

The architecture is a mix of Portuguese, Brazilian, English and American styles.

Beyond the Bahía de Angra lies the **historical quarter** with its geometric street plan that follows the original layout. The houses in the square of streets bordered by the harbour, Rua Direita, Rua da Sé and Rua Gonçalo Velho, have wrought-iron balconies and window and door frames made of stone and pastel-coloured façades.

Cathedral

The cathedral *(Sé)* is the Episcopal See of the Azores. Building began in 1570 on the site of a 15C church and was completed in 1618. The austere design is in keeping with the architecture prevalent during Philip II's reign. The cathedral was badly damaged by the 1980 earthquake. Inside, there is fine carved wooden vaulting and a beautiful silver altarpiece in the chancel.

The collection of 17C sculptures by Masters of the Cathedral of Angra show a Spanish and Oriental influence, a sure sign of the voyages undertaken by the Portuguese.

Palácio dos Bettencourt

Open Mon–Fri 9am–5pm. Closed public holidays. 295 401 000.
The 17C Baroque mansion houses the public library and the city archives.

Azulejos inside illustrate episodes from the history of Terceira.

Praça da Restauração or Praça Velha

The 19C **Town Hall** or Paços do Concelho looks onto the square.

Igreja do Colégio

The collegiate church was built by the Jesuits in the middle of the 17C. Of particular interest are the carved cedarwood ceiling, the delft earthenware in the sacristy and the many altarpieces and Indo-Portuguese ivory statues.

Palácio dos Capitães-Generais

The former Jesuit college was converted into the Palace of the Captain-Generals after the expulsion of the Society of Jesus by the Marquis of Pombal. The palace was largely rebuilt in 1980 and painted white and yellow.

Today, it houses the offices of the Regional Government of the Azores. It was in this palace that President Pompidou of France held a meeting with President Nixon in 1971.

Convento de São Francisco: Museu de Angra

ⓉOpen Apr–Sept Tue–Sun 10am–5.30pm; Oct–Mar Tue–Sun 9.30am–5pm. ⊚€2. ☏295 213 147/8. http://museu-angra.azores.gov.pt.
The museum houses collections of weapons, musical instruments, ceramics, porcelain, furniture and paintings, including some 16C panels of St Catherine. The gardens are of particular interest.

Igreja de Nossa Senhora de Guia

This vast church with painted pillars forms part of the São Francisco Monastery. It was built in the 18C on the site of a chapel where Vasco da Gama buried his brother Paulo who died on his return from a voyage to the Indies.

Alto da Memória

The obelisk was erected on the site of the castle to honour Dom Pedro IV.

Castelo de São João Baptista

The fortress stands at the foot of Monte Brasil and commands the entrance to the harbour. Built during the Spanish domination of Portugal, it was first called the St Philip Fortress and is one of the largest examples of military architecture from 16C and 17C Europe. The Igreja de São Baptista inside the fortress was built by the Portuguese to celebrate the departure of the Spanish.

Monte Brasil★★

It is worth climbing to the Pico das Cruzinhas, passing the fortress of São João Baptista for a view of the Monte Brasil crater.

A **panorama**★★ of Angra is possible from the commemorative monument or *padrão*.

Fortaleza de São Sebastião

This fortress was built during the reign of King Sebastião and dominates the harbour.

🚗 DRIVING TOURS

① TOUR OF THE ISLAND: FROM ANGRA DO HEROÍSMO
85km/53mi. Allow one day.

The coast road between Angra do Heroísmo and the village of São Mateus is lined with country estates with fine houses *(quintas)*. From the road there is a beautiful view of São Mateus.

São Mateus

The picturesque fishing village is dominated by its church, the tallest on the island. The west of the island is dotted with charming little villages such as the summer resorts of **Porto Negrito** and **Cinco Ribeiras**. There are views of the islands of Graciosa, São Jorge and Pico.

Santa Bárbara

The 15C village **church** contains a statue of St Barbara in Ançã stone (which comes from mainland Portugal).

Angra do Heroísmo viewed from Alto da Memória

Serra da Santa Bárbara Road

Head towards Esplanada then bear left onto a forest road which climbs to the summit.

The road affords wonderful panoramas of the island. From the top there is a view of the vast crater of the **Caldeira de Santa Bárbara**.

▶ Return to the road, bear left, continue to the junction with the road between Angra do Heroísmo and Altares. Turn left.

Biscoitos★

The name *biscoitos* has been given to the strangely shaped layers of lava which flowed up from the earth during volcanic eruptions and formed a lunar landscape. Biscoitos is famous for its vines, protected by stone walls beneath which they grow, called *curraletas*. A wine museum, **Museu do Vinho** (open May–Sep Tue–Sun 10–11am, 1–5.30pm; Oct–Apr Tue–Sat 1–4pm. ℘295 908 404), displays the equipment in which generations of wine-growers have made *verdelho*, a sweet aperitif wine, produced and bottled by the museum itself.

▶ Take the Angra road from Biscoitos and bear left towards Lajes.

The terrain in the centre of the island has suffered from volcanic upheaval which has left craters like the vast **Caldeira de Guilherme Moniz**.

▶ Follow signs to Furnas do Enxofre.

🏃 Furnas do Enxofre★

Follow the path to the left (after taking the Estrada do Cabrito at the Pico da Bragacina crossroads) until you reach a small car park 🅿. 10min round trip on foot.

You soon reach a wild landscape where fumaroles rise up from sulphur wells in the ground. The air is hot and smelly. The sulphur crystallises into beautiful bright yellow flowers; in some places a red colour dominates, spreading over the ground and rocks.

Caldeira de Guilherme Moniz

As the road descends between Furnas do Enxofre and Algar do Carvão you catch glimpses of the immense crater with its 15km/9.3mi perimeter.

Algar do Carvão★★

Open daily 24 Mar–31 May, 2.30–5.15pm; 1 Jun–14 Oct, 2–6pm; 16 Oct-22 Mar, Thu-Sat 2.30-5.15pm. ⊛€6. Contact "Os Montanheiros", Rua da Rocha 6/8, Angra do Heroísmo. ℘295 212 992. www.montanheiros.com.

A tunnel some 45m long leads to the base of a volcanic chimney, a sort of moss-covered well of light 45m high. You continue down into an enormous cave that was formed by escaping gases when the lava cooled. Above is a series of majestic overlapping arches of different colours: beige, obsidian black and ochre. Several siliceous concretions have formed milky-white umbrella shapes on the cave walls. The arches can be seen reflected in a pool.

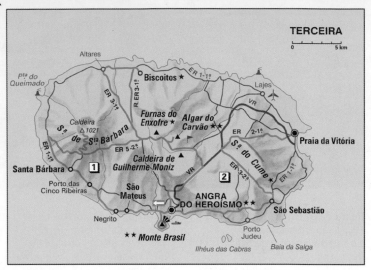

TERCEIRA

0   5 km

Altares

Pta do Queimado

Biscoitos ★

Lajes

ER 1-1ª

R. ER3-1ª

ER 3-1ª

VR

Furnas do Enxofre ★

Algar do Carvão ★★

ER 2-1ª

Caldeira △1021

ER

Praia da Vitória

Sª de Sta Bárbara

ER 5-2ª

Sª do Cume

ER 1-1ª

Caldeira de Guilherme Moniz

ER 3-2ª

ER 1-2ª

Santa Bárbara

1

2

Porto das Cinco Ribeiras

VR

São Mateus

ANGRA DO HEROÍSMO ★★

São Sebastião

Negrito

Porto Judeu

★★ Monte Brasil

Ilhéus das Cabras

Baía da Saiga

▶ The road connects with the Via Rápida which leads back to Angra do Heroísmo. You could also follow itinerary ② in the opposite direction to return to Angra.

② ANGRA DO HEROÍSMO TO PRAIA DA VITÓRIA
35km/22mi. 2hr.

The strange rocks, Ilhéus Cabras, a short distance beyond Angra, look as though they have been sawn through the middle.

São Sebastião
The village was the first site to be settled on the island and has preserved some old monuments.

Igreja de São Sebastião★
The Gothic church built in 1455 has a graceful doorway and chapels with Manueline and Renaissance vaulting. The nave has some interesting 16C frescoes. Opposite the church is the **Império do Espírito Santo** decorated with romantic paintings.

▶ Beyond São Sebastião take ER 3.2 left to Serra do Cume, then a road right which climbs to the top.

Serra do Cume★
The gentle slopes of this eroded volcano form a patchwork of fields divided by low stone walls where Dutch cows can be seen grazing. At certain times of the day, particularly in the evening, the countryside takes on a lush bucolic air.

Praia da Vitória
The "Praia" in the name derives from the beautiful white sand **beach** which stretches the full length of the bay, and the "da Vitória" commemorates the battle in 1829 between Liberals and supporters of Dom Miguel. The Lajes air base nearby, which was established by the British in 1943 and enlarged by the Americans in 1944, was used extensively during and after World War II as a refuelling stop on the transatlantic routes. Praia da Vitória is a lively place when the weather is fine and the beach and the surrounding cafés fill with people. The town centre has been preserved and has a 16C **Town Hall** and an old church.

Parish Church
This large church was founded by Jácome de Bruges, the island's first donee-captain. Its main doorway was a gift from the King, Dom Manuel. The rich interior decoration includes *azulejos* and gilt altarpieces.

Graciosa★

Santa Cruz da Graciosa

Graciosa is the second-smallest island after Corvo and has the lowest altitude (the highest point, Pico Timão, rises to just 398m). The whole of the eastern part of the island is occupied by a vast crater. Graciosa or "gracious" island owes its name to its attractive main town, Santa Cruz, its countryside of well-tended vineyards and fields of maize, and its villages bright with flowers set at the foot of gently rolling hills dotted with windmills.
These Dutch-style windmills with their red, pointed, onion-shaped tops that pivot in the direction of the wind are a rather surprising feature of the island's landscape. There are not so many as there once were, but they are still an interesting attraction and would make a good subject for a painting.

▶ **Population:** 4 391.
◔ **Michelin Map:** p390. Michelin Atlas Spain and Portugal.
▯ **Info:** Rua D. Joao 28, Santa Cruz da Graciosa. ℰ 295 712 430.
◑ **Location:** A small island just north of São Jorge and Pico.
◔ **Timing:** Being such a small island, a day tour will suffice.
◓ **Don't Miss:** The cave at Furna de Enxofre.

GETTING THERE

ACCESS: There are regular flights between Terceira and Graciosa, and boat connections (3h) between the two islands several times a week.
TOURING THE ISLAND: You can tour the island in a few hours, although it is pleasant to spend time strolling through Santa Cruz or driving along narrow country roads.

SANTA CRUZ DA GRACIOSA★

Santa Cruz is a delightful small town with bright white house façades set off by volcanic stone and several older fishermen's cottages.
There are also two small reservoirs in the town, originally intended to provide drinking water for cattle and people, though today they just reflect lovely views and provide a nice change of colour.

Churches

Built in the 16C and reconstructed two centuries later the **Igreja de Santa Cruz** has some **panels★** at the high altar illustrating the Holy Cross.
A chapel has Flemish statues of St Peter and St Anthony. See also the **Santo Cristo** church, and the **Nossa Senhora da Ajuda** (Our Lady of Charity), **São**

© Mauricio Abreu/age fotostock.com

Graciosa windmills

João and **São Salvador** chapels along with the **Cruz da Barra** (Iron Cross).

Museu Etnográfico

🐚 *Guided tours: summer Tue–Sun 10am–5.30pm, winter 9.30am–5pm* ✆€1. ☎295 712 429.

The collections housed in a former mansion show traditional island life through various displays including tools, clothes and pottery, as well as items from the cultivation of wine.

Ermidas do Monte da Ajuda

The three hermitages devoted to São João, São Salvador and **Nossa Senhora da Ajuda** dominate the town. There is a beautiful **view★** of Santa Cruz.

EXCURSIONS
Farol da Ponta da Barca★

4.5km/3mi west of Santa Cruz.

There is a view from the lighthouse of the headland of red rocks plunging to a bright blue sea.

Praia

The old village stretches along its harbour and the beach after which it is named.

Furna do Enxofre★★

🕐 *Open Nov–Mar Wed–Sat 10am–1pm, 1.30–5pm. Apr–Oct daily 10am–1pm, 2–6pm.* ✆€5. ☎295 714 009 or 295

730 040. *The best time to visit is from 11am to 2pm when the sun shines into the cave.*

Furna de Enxofre is in the middle of a vast caldeira or crater. A tunnel has been dug through one of the sides of the crater giving access by car. Once inside the crater the road zigzags down to the entrance of the chasm. From here a path and then a spiral staircase lead down to the chasm. The cave itself is immense and contains a lake of hot sulphurous water.

Furna Maria Encantada

Leave the caldeira. Once through the tunnel take the first road left. About 90m farther on there is a sign on the right to Furna de Maria Encantada. A path reinforced by logs leads up to a rock above the road (5min).

A natural tunnel in the rock about ten yards long opens onto the crater with a good overall view.

The road continues around the crater. There are views over Graciosa island with Terceira in the distance.

Carapacho

Carapacho is a small spa as well as a seaside resort. The hot springs that rise from the sea-bed are used for therapeutic purposes, particularly in the treatment of rheumatism.

Faial★★★

Horta

The "Blue Island", as Faial is also known, owes its name to the mass of hydrangeas that flower there in season. There is a magnificent view from Faial of Pico's volcano, while Faial itself has some interesting volcanic features such as the Caldeira crater and the Capelinhos volcano. The island's particular charm derives from Horta, the main town and harbour, its attractive villages, windmills and beaches (Porto Pim, Praia do Almoxarife and Praia da Fajã).

A BIT OF HISTORY

The headland on the west of the island is covered in ashes from Capelinhos, the volcano that rose up from the depths of the ocean in 1957. On 27 September, there was a huge eruption under the sea accompanied by gaseous emissions and clouds of steam that reached a height of 4 000m. A first islet surfaced only to disappear a short time afterwards. Then a second islet-volcano formed and was joined to Faial by an isthmus of lava and ash. For 13 months, until 24 October 1958, volcanic activity continued in the form of underwater explosions, lava flows, eruptions and showers of ash that covered the village of Capelo and the lighthouse. As Capelinhos volcano rose, so the water level of the lake inside Faial's crater or caldeira, fell. By the end of the eruption, the volcano had increased the size of Faial by 2.4sq km/0.9sq mi, although marine erosion has since reduced this to 1sq km/0.38sq mi.

HORTA★

Horta stretches out alongside a bay that forms one of the rare sheltered anchorages in the archipelago.

Anglo-Saxon influence is apparent in Horta's architecture. This heritage comes down from the **Dabneys**, a family of wealthy American traders in the 19C. When they left, American presence in Faial continued through transatlantic

▶ **Population:** 14 875.
◉ **Michelin Map:** p392. Michelin Atlas Spain and Portugal.
▯ **Info:** Rua Vasco da Gama, Horta; ℘292 292 237.
▷ **Location:** Just west of Pico, on the edge of the main group of islands.
◷ **Timing:** Stay a ccouple of nights and get to know this peaceful island.
⊛ **Don't Miss:** The volcano – it's spectacular!

GETTING THERE

Access: There are direct flights from Lisbon to Horta and regular flights between Faial and the other islands. Boats connect Faial and the port of Madalena on Pico Island (30min) several times a day, and Faial, São Jorge and Terceira several times a week in summer.

Touring the Island: Allow at least two days to fully explore Horta and enjoy a relaxing tour of the island.

cable companies. In the 1930s Faial was a port of call and a refuelling station for sea-planes and it was not uncommon to see one or more of these in Horta harbour.

The historical quarter is dominated by the imposing façades of its churches that face the sea. It comprises the area around **Rua Conselheiro Medeiros**, **Rua W. Bensaúde** and **Rua Serpa Pinto**, which are lined with 18C and 19C shops and houses surmounted by unusual wooden upper storeys. This main thoroughfare leads to **Praça da República**, a charming square. The striking façade of the **Sociedade Amor da Pátria** building (1930) and decorated with a frieze of blue hydrangeas, can be seen in the northeast corner of the square on Rua Ernesto Rebelo.

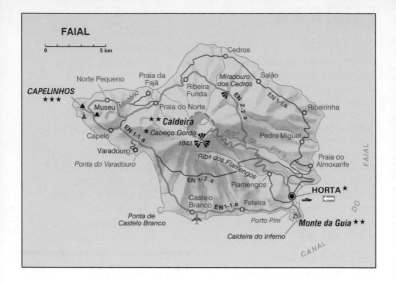

Marina da Horta★

Yachtsmen on their journeys across the Atlantic congregate at this marina. It has become a kind of open-air art gallery, since each crew leaves a visual trace of its stay; otherwise, as the superstition goes, some mishap will befall it.

Churches

The 18C **Igreja Matriz de São Salvador**, which formerly belonged to the Jesuit College, has some fine *azulejos* and interesting Baroque furniture. The **Nossa Senhora das Angústias** (Our

Lady of Anguish), the **Nossa Senhora do Carmo** (Our Lady of Carmo), and the Church of St.Francis which is presently integrated with the **Museu Arte Sacra**, are also worth a visit.

Museu da Horta

◷*Open summer Tue–Sun 10am–5.30pm; winter 9.30am–5pm*⊙*€2.* ☎*292 392 784.*
The museum is in the former Jesuit College. It traces the history of the town, particularly the laying of the underwater cables. There is also a collection of

Horta viewed from Monte da Guia

© cinoby/iStock

© zodebala/iStock
Capelinhos

miniatures★ made of fig-tree pith by Euclíades Rosa from 1940–1960.

Forte de Santa Cruz
The fort was begun in the 16C, enlarged at a later date and now houses an inn.

Peter Café Sport
The café, a popular meeting place for visiting yachtsmen, contains the **Museu do Scrimshaw** (🕐 *open daily 10am–noon, 2–4pm;* 🕐 *closed 1 Jan and 25 Dec;* 🎫 *€2,50;* ✆ *292 292 327*).
Among the items on display are sperm-whale teeth engraved by whalers and newer portraits of well-known yachts-men such as Sir Francis Chichester and the Frenchman Eric Tabarly.

Monte da Guia★★
A road leads up to the summit of Monte da Guia.
Horta bay is sheltered by two volcanoes linked to the mainland by isthmuses. The first volcano, Monte Queimado, dominates the harbour and is linked by an isthmus to the second, Monte da Guia. From the top of Monte da Guia, beside the **Ermida de Nossa Senhora da Guia**, there is a view of **Caldeira do Inferno**, a former crater that has been filled in by the sea.
As you return to Horta, there is a good **view★** of the town and the beach at Porto Pim inlet which was originally protected by fortifications – **Portão fortificado do Porto Pim** (large iron gate of Porto Pim); and the **Muralhas de São Sebastião** (walls of St.Sebastian).

It is also worth taking a little detour to climb to the top of **Mount Carneiro** from where you have some wonderful views over the Flamengos valley and, in the opposite direction, of the island of Pico, its volcano standing proudly against the blue sky.

🚗 DRIVING TOUR

TOUR OF THE ISLAND
80km/50mi from Horta. Allow 5hr.

Take the airport road from Horta and drive along the southwest coast. The road leads past **Castelo Branco** head-land, named on account of its white cliffs, and continues to **Varadouro**, a small spa.

▶ Follow signs to Capelinhos.

Cross Capelo village with the ruins of houses destroyed by Capelinhos in 1957.

🚶 Capelinhos★★★
The best way to explore the volcano is to see it on foot. Park below the lighthouse and then allow for a walk of at least 1hr.
The landscape of the volcano, so recent it is still almost devoid of vegetation, is fascinating. The volcano's structure, with its ash, bombs (solidified lava) and scoria, is gradually being eroded by the sea, and the different mineral colours of ochre, red and black stand out. In places you can see the roof tiles of bur-ied houses poking through the ash.

An **interpretative centre** 👥 (🕐open 1 Nov–31 Mar, Tue-Fri 10am–5pm, Sat–Sun 2–5.30pm; 1 Apr-31 Oct, 10am-6pm. ✆€10; children €5, under 6 free; 🕐closed public holidays; 𝒫292 200 470) has been opened at Capelhinos, and traces the different phases of the eruption from 1957 to 1958. The building itself is subterranean, allowing visitors to enjoy the volcanic scenario.

Between Capelinhos and Praia do Norte the road passes through Norte Pequeno with houses still buried in ash, then crosses a *mistério* or lava flow covered in thick vegetation: hydrangeas, cedars and mango trees. The coast beyond Praia do Norte becomes steep with a succession of lookout points.

▶ Beyond Ribeira Funda go right onto the road for Horta and Caldeira.

There is a fine view from the **Miradouro dos Cedros**. After entering the **Ribeiro dos Flamingos,** join the road that rises in zigzags to Caldeira and its crater.

Caldeira★★

Walk through a short tunnel to the crater.

Caldeira's vast crater is 400m deep with a diameter of 1 450m. It is a nature reserve covered in cedars, ferns, junipers and moss. The floor of the crater is flat and the contours of the former lake, which emptied during the eruption of Capelinhos, can be clearly seen.

▶ A path leading round the crater takes about 2hr. A second path, which is for experienced walkers, leads down into the crater (allow at least 5hr round trip).

Beside the crater is **Cabeço Gordo★** *(45min round trip)*, a lookout point at an altitude of 1 043m, with fine views of the islands of Pico and São Jorge.

▶ Return via Ribeira dos Flamengos.

Pico★★

Madalena

Pico is a long island only 7km/4.3mi east of Faial. It is the second-largest island in the archipelago after São Miguel and is dominated by the volcano after which it is named. The small population is spread among the different coastal villages.

A BIT OF HISTORY

This volanic island was formed relatively recently, a mere 300,000 years ago, which makes it the newest of the islands in the Azores.

At 2 351m, the island's summit, also called Pico, is the highest point in the whole of Portugal. Recent volcanic activity is visible in the form of **mistérios** or "mysteries" as the islanders did not know what caused them.

These are lava flows that occurred during eruptions after the island had

▶ **Population:** 15 761.
🚗 **Michelin Map:** pp396-397. Michelin Atlas Spain and Portugal.
🏛 **Info:** Gare Maritima da Madalena, 9950 Madalena; 𝒫292 623 524.
◐ **Location:** The southernmost of the main group of islands, and lying close to Faial, a short ferry ride away.
🕐 **Timing:** A day trip is possible, but more time is needed if you intend to climb the volcano. If you do stay make sure to pre-book your accommodation, especially in summer.

been settled, and so destroyed various cultivated areas. The most striking and recent of the *mistérios* are those of

Pico Volcano

GETTING THERE

ACCESS: There is a boat shuttle service between Horta on Faial and Madalena on Pico several times a day. In summer, boats call in at Cais do Pico from Terceira and São Jorge several times a week.

LENGTH OF STAY: It is possible to tour Pico island in a day from Faial. However, if you wish to climb the volcano, allow at least two or more nights on the island.

Prainha (15/2), **Santa Luzia** (1718) and **São João** (1720).

PICO WINES

The vines growing on volcanic rock produced a wine known as **verdelho**, which was appreciated in England, America and Russia. Then the vines were attacked by vine-mildew in the mid-19C. The wine trade is slowly being built up again on the island today.

PICO VOLCANO★★★

Taxis from Madalena can drive you to the beginning of the path. By car, take the central road and turn right after 13km/8mi. A narrow road climbs for 5km/3mi up to the path.

Allow at least 7h for the walk (3h to climb to the crater, 30min to walk round it, 1h to climb up to and down from Pico Pequeno and 2h30 to come right down again). Strong climbing shoes are an absolute must. It is a good idea to take

at least 1l of drinking water per person (1.5 litre if the weather is hot).

Pico's greatest attraction is the ascent of its volcano, a perfect cone, sometimes snow-capped in winter, but more often than not hidden by clouds that gather on the top, or ring the volcano like a scarf. No matter the weather, Pico is rarely completely cloud-free.

The walk is fairly difficult and tiring on account of the difference in altitude and terrain. Most walkers like to climb at night to be able to reach the summit as the sun rises. In this case it is best to have a guide *(list of guides available at the Tourist Office)*. Otherwise, during the day and when the weather is fine, the path is easy to follow.

After a 3h climb you reach the crater, which is 30m deep. It is impressive – a bare landscape forming a circle with a 700m perimeter. **Pico Pequeno** (70m) rises at the far end to form the mountain summit. The fumaroles and smell of sulphur at the top are a reminder that a volcano is never completely dormant. On a clear day the **panorama**★★★ takes in São Jorge and Faial with its volcano, Capelinhos. In the far distance are Graciosa and Terceira.

The central crater of Pico, called Pico Grande, is hugely impressive, a bleak landscape with a diameter of around 700m. On the way back to Madalena, the cave at **Furnas de Frei Matias** *(5min walk)* has a series of long underground galleries stretching out between mossy wells of light.

🚗 DRIVING TOUR

1 MADALENA TO SÃO ROQUE
28km/17mi. 2hr.

Madalena
The harbour is protected by two rocks, Em Pé (meaning upright) and Deitado (meaning recumbent), which are home to colonies of sea birds. Madalena is a pleasant little town centred around the **Igreja de Santa Maria Madalena**.

Cachorro★
After Bandeiras bear left off the main road and follow the signs.
The small village built of lava stretches out behind the airport landing strips beside black rocks and cliffs that have been eroded into caves.
The road continues through the villages of **Santa Luzia** and **Santo António**.

Convento and Igreja de São Pedro de Alcântara
The Baroque building has an interesting façade and, inside, the chancel is adorned with *azulejos* and an abundantly decorated altarpiece.

Igreja de São Roque
The church is a large 18C building decorated inside with statues, jacaranda wood furniture inlaid with ivory, and a silver lamp donated by Dom João V.

São Roque–Lajes do Pico
There are two possible itineraries:

2 VIA THE COAST
50km/31mi. Allow 2hr 30min.
This itinerary is for those who have the time and who don't mind winding roads.

The villages along this route include **Prainha**, which is well-known for its *mistério*, **Santo Amaro** with its ship-building yard, and **Piedade** and the attractive countryside at the end of the island. The itinerary continues along the southeast coast and the fishing villages of **Calheta de Nesquim** and **Ribeiras**.

3 VIA THE CENTRE OF THE ISLAND
32km/20mi including an excursion to Lagoa do Caiado . Allow 1hr.

Take the Lajes road which soon rises to cross the centre of the island. After 10km/6.2mi take the road left marked Lagoa do Caiado and continue for 5km/3mi. The centre of the island, at an altitude of 800m–1000m, is often covered in cloud. There are many small crater lakes amid indigenous vegetation. A road crosses the island from east to west affording good views of beautiful countryside. After visiting Lagoa do Caiado, return to the main road and continue towards Lajes.

Lajes do Pico
This was the first settlement on the island. The main activity from the 19C, up until 1981, was whaling. Lajes, a small, quiet, white town in the middle of maize fields, extends into a lava plateau known as a **fajã** (♿*see SÃO JORGE.*

Museu dos Baleeiros★

Open 1 Apr-30 Sep, Tue–Sun 10am-5.30pm; 1 Oct-31 Mar, 9.30am-5pm.
Closed public holidays. ✆292 679 340. www.museu-pico.azores.gov.pt/
The whalers' museum is housed in a former boat shelter in the harbour. The fine **scrimshaw collection** contains engraved sperm-whale teeth and ivory walrus tusks.

Ermida de São Pedro

By continuing along the quayside, you reach a white chapel, the oldest on the island. Beside the chapel stands the **Padrão** monument, commemorating the 500th anniversary of the settlement of the island.

Vineyards divided by lava walls

© HeadSpinPhoto/Shutterstock

④ LAJES TO MADALENA – MISTÉRIOS AND VINEYARDS★★

35km/22mi. Allow 1hr 30min.

The road crosses the *mistérios* on either side of **São João** that date from an eruption in 1718.

São Mateus

The road passes through vineyards closed off by low lava walls. The countryside is striking with the black of the lava walls contrasting sharply with the soft green of abandoned vines and the deep blue of the sea beyond.
The road passes through **Candelaria** and **Criação Velha**, the village in which *verdelho* wine originated, before reaching Madalena.

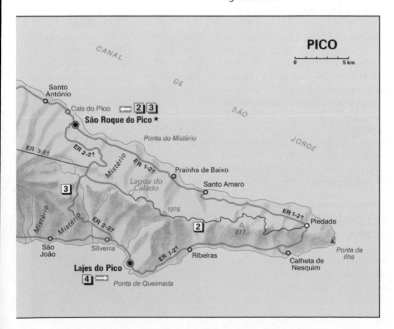

São Jorge★★

Velas

This cigar-shaped island stretches out parallel to Pico. It is almost entirely a plateau with 700m cliffs, and its wild, landscapes are splendid for walking.

VELAS

Velas, a neat settlement backed by a steep cliff, has preserved several old buildings including the 16C **Paços do Concelho** (Town Hall), of Azorean Baroque style with twisted columns on either side of its doorway. The 16C **church** of São Jorge has an interesting façade. Visitors will find a large **supermarket** here along with a number of small shops selling everyday items.

The area around the harbour is attractive in an unkempt kind of way, and here you find the 18C **Portão do Mar**, the "Gate of the Sea", a gateway remaining from the old ramparts.

Velas to Ponta dos Rosais

14km/9mi west. The road runs alongside Baía de Entre-Morros, crosses the village of Rosais and continues to **Sete Fontes Forest Park★★** 👥, a splendid place for a picnic, where the forestry department has also created a small pets' corner. Above the centre of the park, a dirt track leads up to a stunning viewpoint, **Pico da Velha★★**, from which you gaze down on Ponta dos Rosais.

You can continue to **Ponta dos Rosais** by car although it is better to walk *(2h30 round trip)*.

The sea cliffs and sea stacks are important breeding grounds for birds; the nearby lighthouse was abandoned after the 1980 earthquake.

GETTING THERE

ACCESS: There are flights between São Jorge and the other islands throughout the year. In summer, the boat that serves the islands in the central group of the archipelago calls at São Jorge several times a week.

▶ **Population:** 9 500.
Michelin Map: p399. Michelin Atlas Spain and Portugal.
Info: Rua Conselheiro Dr. José Pereira, Velas. ℘295 412 440.
Location: Almost at the centre of the main group of islands.
Timing: Allow a couple of days, minimum.
Don't Miss: The Pico da Esperança, the centre of the island.
Timing: Allow a full day to tour the island by car.

🚗 DRIVING TOUR

NORTH COAST
83km/52mi. 4hr.

▷ Take the Santo António road out of Velas.

Fajã do Ouvidor★★

The *fajã* with its hamlet is the largest on the north coast with an elevated view of a flat stretch of land covered in cultivated fields and houses, dominated by a sheer cliff. Potatoes, sweetcorn, beans and vines grow well here, the grapes producing a palatable *vinho de cheiro*.

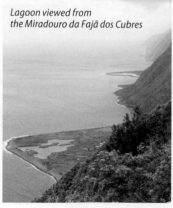

Lagoon viewed from the Miradouro da Fajã dos Cubres

© QUILLE/iStock

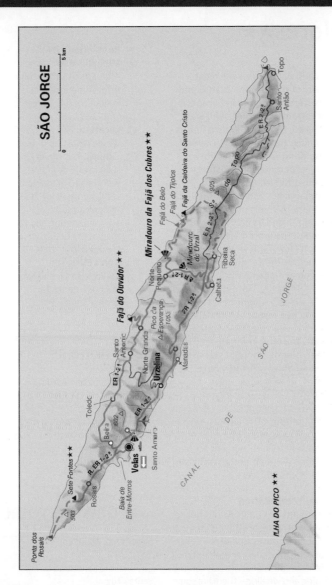

Miradouro da Fajã dos Cubres★★

The landscape viewed from this lookout point, on the road beyond Norte Pequeno, is highly characteristic of São Jorge. The most impressive, **Fajã da Caldeira do Santo Cristo**, is occupied by a lagoon that has been made into a nature reserve to protect its clams, a particular type of scallop-shell only found here. The road from the north coast to Ribeira Seca village on the south, crosses beautiful woodland criss-crossed by hedges of hydrangeas. The **view★★** from the **Miradouro da Urzelina** is good.

Urzelina

The village, rebuilt after the volcanic eruption in 1808, was named after the island's brown lichen or orchil *(urzela)*. A tower emerges out of the lava beneath which the church lies buried. Small working windmills stand out against Pico island in the background.

Flores★★

Horta

The island of flowers is the most westerly of the Azorean islands and the westernmost point in Europe. It is not certain when the island was discovered, but it was known first as São Tomás, and only later became Flores. Along with its sister Corvo, Flores lies at quite some distance from the other islands in the archipelago. It is 236km/147mi from Faial. Flores is thinly populated, very rugged and its wild landscapes are among the most majestic in the Azores. Its luxuriant vegetation is explained by the very high rainfall; it rains on average nearly 300 days a year. Geologically, Flores (and Corvo) sit on the North American tectonic plate and as a result, neither island experiences earthquakes. Flores is arguably the most tranquil of all the Azorean islands. Those in search of peace and quiet will find it here.

SANTA CRUZ DAS FLORES

Santa Cruz is a quiet, pleasant town with a small harbour. The airport runway seems to run straight into the centre of town, and such settlement as there is lies spread out around a haphazard arrangements of streets.

Museu Etnográfico

The museum, set up in an old house, displays several reconstituted interiors of traditional houses as well as a collection of items illustrating the inhabitants' way of life on the island. Life was centred on fishing and whaling – there are some scrimshaw pieces – as well as work in the fields.

Convento de São Boaventura

The 17C building, once a Franciscan monastery, has been restored to house part of the museum. The Baroque chancel in the church shows a Hispano-Mexican influence.

▶ **Population:** 3 907.
Michelin Map: Michelin Atlas Spain and Portugal.
Info: Câmara Municipal, Santa Cruz das Flores; ℘292 592 369.
▶ **Location:** This really is the westernmost tip of Europe.
Timing: This island can be seen in one day, though if you are also planning to see Corvo, you will need to book a couple of nights' accommodation and take the boat to Corvo, which is a day trip in itself.
Don't Miss: The Convent and the Church of Christ (Igreja do Senhor Santo Cristo).

GETTING THERE

ACCESS: Flores is accessible only by air from the other islands.
TOURING THE ISLAND: It is possible to tour the island in a day although it is well worth taking the time to explore Flores on foot. An extra day is required for an excursion to the island of Corvo.

🚗 DRIVING TOUR

68km/42mi. About 4hr.

▶ Take the Lajes road out of Santa Cruz.

The road twists and turns with the relief, dipping into deep ravines and running alongside mountain ridges with views above the banks of bright red and yellow cannas and blue hydrangea that line it.

Fazenda das Lajes

The **Igreja do Senhor Santo Cristo**, with its *azulejo* decoration on the façade, is one of the most representative examples of Azorean religious architecture.

Ribeira Grande Waterfall

Lajes das Flores

The island's second-largest town, and inhabited since the 15C, **Lajes das Flores** thrives on its harbour activities and a major radio station. The port is capable of receiving container ships that bring weekly supplies to the island. The **Island of Flores Museum** occupies an old Franciscan convent and houses a notable collection of ceramics and agricultural implements (*open summer Tue–Sun 10am–5.30pm, to 5pm in winter* 𝄢*292 592 159. www.museu-flores. azores.gov.pt*).

▷ Once past Lajes, take the road south. Turn right towards Lagoa Funda.

Lagoa Funda★★

Lagoa Funda is a crater lake stretching for several kilometres below the road. After 3km/1.8mi you reach an area where, to the right, and at a great depth, you can see the end of Lagoa Funda and, to the left, at road level, **Lagoa Rasa**.

▷ Return to the road; 600m beyond the 25km marker, look up to admire the Rocha dos Bordões rock formation.

Rocha dos Bordões★★

Masses of flowers can be seen bursting from these dramatic basalt organ pipes. These high, vertical strata were formed when the basalt solidified.

▷ Take the Mosteiro road.

The road passes **Mosteiro**, set in enchanting countryside with the sea in the background.

▷ Farther on, take the road to Fajãzinha and Fajã Grande.

Fajãzinha

As the road approaches Fajãzinha there is a beautiful **view★★** of the village, and its white and terracota houses. Overlooking it on a hill is the **Church of Nossa Senhora dos Remédios** (Our Lady of Remedies).

Ribeira Grande Waterfall

Turn right towards Ponta da Fajã. Continue for 400m and stop at the first bridge. Take the path on the left of the bridge as you stand looking towards the cliff. 🚶 *20min round trip on foot.*
The track follows the stream and passes three water-mills. The 300m **Ribeira Grande waterfall★** plunges from the top of the cliff onto a ledge where it divides into a multitude of smaller cascades.

▷ Return to the main road and head for Santa Cruz. Turn left towards the lakes.a

Corvo★

Horta

A large, black, sea-battered rock rises out of the water 15 nautical miles northeast of Flores. This is Crow Island, the visible part of Monte Gordo (718m), a marine volcano. As there is no protected bay, access is difficult. In 1452 Corvo was the last of the islands in the archipelago to display the Portuguese flag; settlement began only in the middle of the 16C. A remote community of farmers and herders began to develop. In winter, for weeks on end, it was impossible for boats to dock, so communication with Flores was made by lighting fires on a hill.

▶ **Population:** 470.
Michelin Map: Michelin Atlas Spain and Portugal.
Info: Caminho dos Moinhos. ℘292 596 227
Location: The most northwesterly island, just above Flores.
Timing: Plan no more than half a day to see the Caldeirão. Other than to fly out, the only way to see the island is to take a boat trip from Flores, taking you back the same afternoon. Be sure to check the times.
Don't Miss: The Caldeirão.

SIGHTS

Vila Nova do Corvo

The **Igreja de Nossa Senhora dos Milagres** has preserved a 16C Flemish statue. Vila Nova do Corvo may well be the smallest and least populated district in Portugal, yet it possesses an airport. Walk alongside the landing strip and you reach some disused windmills and a restaurant.

Caldeirão★

6km/3.7mi from Vila Nova.
You might be able to hitch a lift (ask at the town's restaurant, the only one on the island) with one of the locals

GETTING THERE

ACCESS: You can fly to Corvo from Terceira (the only way if you have baggage), or take a day trip by boat from Flores (up to 1hr). The boat leaves Santa Cruz harbour in the morning, and returns between 4-6pm depending on sea conditions. It is advisable to book in advance once you arrive in Flores as the boat holds only 20 passengers. Make sure you check the return time of the boat. Cost is negotiable, but about €30.

Caldeirão

© Mauricio Abreu/age fotostock

to the Caldeirão, which is also accessible on foot along the road *(3hr round trip)*. There is a difference in altitude of 550m. Bring warm clothes as the uplands are often covered in cloud and can be cool. The road crosses beautiful countryside brightened by hedges of hydrangeas. The crater has a perimeter of 3.4km/2mi and is 300m deep, in the bottom of which are two blue lakes with two islets at the bottom. Tradition has it that these islets have the same layout as the islands in the Azores (without Flores and Corvo). The slopes of the crater were once cultivated.

ADDRESSES

STAY

Tourist accommodation varies from island to island. São Miguel (Ponta Delgada and Furnas), Terceira (Angra do Heroísmo and Praia da Vitória) and Faial (Horta) are well equipped, while the smaller islands have fewer than two or three hotels. It is best to book ahead of time it you are planning a visit during the tourist season. Prices are comparable to those on the Portuguese mainland. See www.visitazores.com for more on accommodation, and www.casasacorianas.com for rural areas.

SÃO MIGUEL

The Lince – *Avenida D. João III, 29, Ponta Delgada, São Miguel. ℘296 630 000. www.thelince-azores.com. 154 rooms.* Formerly the Holiday Inn, this impressive modern hotel stands on a hill overlooking Ponta Delgada. The rooms are generous and fully equipped. Swimming pool, gymnasium, jacuzzi, pool table, bar and restaurant serving island cuisine.

Azoris Royal Garden – *Rua de Lisboa, Ponta Delgada, São Miguel. ℘296 307 300. www.azorishotels.com. 193 rooms.* Located just a few minutes' walk from the centre of Ponta Delgada. Set around an Asian-style garden with interior Aztec and African themes. Spacious, with integral restaurant. Minor drawback is that it lies directly below the flight path from the airport: only a problem for light sleepers.

Terra Nostra Garden Hotel – *Rua Padre José Jacinto Botelho, Furnas, São Miguel. ℘296 549 090. www.terranostra-garden.com. 86 rooms.* Justly popular hotel with 12ha garden, to which hotel guests are admitted free. Panoramic restaurant – arguably the best place to try *cozido das Furnas* – bar, gymnasium, indoor and outdoor swimming pools.

SÃO MIGUEL, PONTA DELGADA

Azor Hotel – *Avenida Dr. João Bosco Mota Amaral, Ponta Delgada 9500-765. ℘296 2499; www.starwoodhotels.com. 123 rooms and suites.* This new hotel, opened in 2016, is vibrant and cosmopolitan, and located overlooking the marina and within easy walking distance for the city centre. Swimming pool, spa, gym, restaurant, wine and cheese shop and private parking on site.

SANTA MARIA

Hotel Colombo – *Rua Cruz Teixeira, Vila do Porto, Santa Maria. ℘296 820 200. www.colombo-hotel.com. 85 rooms.* Not the most imaginative building design, and with something of a spartan restaurant, the hotel is nevertheless comfortable and quiet. It is a 20min walk from the centre of Vila do Porto.

TERCEIRA

Hotel Caracol – *Estrada Regional, Silveira. ℘295 402 600. www.hoteldocaracol.com. 100 rooms.* Located west of Angra do Heroísmo (10min away) overlooking the Atlantic and close by Monte Brasil. Cable TV, telephone, Internet, air conditioning, Wellness Centre and 5-star PADI Dive Centre.

Azoris Angra Garden Plaza – *Praça Velha, Angra do Heroísmo. ℘295 206 600. www.azorishotels.com. 120 rooms.* At the centre of the city, this hotel backs on to the Angra Gardens. Restaurant, bar, lounge and Health Club with gym, sauna, Turkish bath, jacuzzi and indoor pool.

TERCEIRA, ANGRA DO HEROISMO

Pousada Forte Angra do Heroismo – *R. do Castelinho, 9700-045 Angra do Heroísmo. ℘295 403 560; www.pousadas.pt/en/hotel/pousada-angra. 29 rooms.* This remarkable hotel is situated in a fortress commonly known as the Castelinho de São Sebastião. The rooms have a modern decor and furnishings.

The suite and few of the bedrooms have balconies with a seaside view. Restaurant; 2 swimming pools.

GRACIOSA

🜨 **Pensão (Residencial) Ilha Graciosa** – *Ave Mouzinho de Albuquerque 49, Santa Cruz da Graciosa. ☎295 712 675. 15 rooms.* Restored manor house, 10 minutes' walk from the town square. Spacious grounds and 2 tennis courts Comfortable lounge and bar/breakfast room, all rooms en suite, with cable TV and wireless Internet.

🜨🜨 **Graciosa Resort Biosphere Island Hotel** – *Porto da Barra, Santa Cruz da Graciosa. ☎295 730 500. www. graciosaresort.com. 44 rooms and villas.* The only "hotel" on Graciosa, built on the coast. The standard rooms are ample and with a balcony, Pay TV, air conditioning, mini-bar, work desk, internet and amenities. Bit of an odd design, but perfectly functional.

SÃO JORGE

🜨🜨 **São Jorge Garden Hotel** – *Avenida dos Baleeiros, Velas. ☎292 430 100. 58 rooms.* A smart, up-market place in the centre of town. Although there is no restaurant, there are many good restaurants nearby. Swimming pool, bar, Internet access, and excellent views.

🜨🜨 **Guesthouse Jardim do Triângulo** – *Terreiros 91, Velas. ☎295 414 055. www. oceanohoteis.com.* Not so much a guesthouse as a small group of independent cottages, little more than a bedroom and a bathroom, all set in a palmy garden with a wonderful view over the ocean.

PICO

🜨🜨🜨 **Pocinho Hotel** – *Pocinho-Monte, Madalena do Pico. ☎292 629 135. www.pocinhobay.com.* An outstanding hotel offering a blend of modern and traditional influences of the Azores. Its rooms include telephone, mini-bar, cable TV, and Internet connection. The hotel overlooks the bay, with a natural beach.

🜨🜨🜨 **Hotel Caravelas** – *Rua Conselheiro Terra Pinheiro 3, Madalena, Pico. ☎292 628 550. www.oceanohoteis. com. 50 rooms and 17 apartments.* Just a short walk from the ferry port. All accommodation has telephone and TV; bar, solarium and swimming pool.

FAIAL

🜨🜨🜨 **Azoris Faial Resort Hotel** – *Rua Cônsul Dabney, Horta. ☎292 207 400. www.azorishotels.com. 131 rooms.* An excellent and popular hotel, central to Horta, and about 10km/6mi from the airport; good view over Horta and to Pico. All rooms fully equipped, air conditioned, cable TV, Internet. Restaurant, bars, swimming pool, jacuzzi, sauna, gymnasium, laundry.

🜨🜨🜨 **Hotel do Canal** – *Largo Dr Manual de Arriaga, Horta. ☎292 202 120. www.bestazoreshotels.com. 103 rooms.* Located in the historic area of Horta on the main ocean front avenue in the centre of town, and across the street from the port and marina.

FLORES

🜨🜨 **Servi-Flor Hotel** – *Antigo Bairro dos Franceses, Santa Cruz das Flores. ☎292 592 453. www.servi-flor.com. 32 rooms and 1 apartment.* A somewhat basic, but clean and welcoming hotel just a short distance from the airport (hotel pick up); the restaurant serves appetising regional dishes.

FLORES, SANTA CRUZ

🜨🜨 **Hotel das Flores** – *Zona do Boqueirão, 9970-390 Santa Cruz Das Flores. ☎292 590 420; www.inatel.pt. 26 rooms.* Opened in 2009, this is the first 4-star hotel on the island of Flores, built on the Boquierão promontory, just to the north of the main town Santa Cruz, and has spectacular views over the Atlantic and Flores' neighbour, Corvo. The hotel has a lovely swimming pool, bar and restaurant.

CORVO

🜨🜨 **Guesthouse Comodoro** – *Caminho do Areeiro s/n, Ilha do Corvo, Corvo. ☎292 596 128. www.comodoroazores.com. 6 rooms.* The only hotel on the island. Air conditioning, cable TV, Internet. Clean, simple and very welcoming.

⌾/EAT

Grilled fish served with chilled *vinho verde* is delicious, as are local specialties such as the *cozido das Furnas*, a kind of meaty (and tasty) casserole baked slowly in underground ovens hollowed out of the hot volcanic earth. But it's very filling.

SÃO MIGUEL

⊜⊜⊜ **A Colmeia Restaurant** –
Travessa do Colégio, Ponta Delgada.
℘296 306 600. In the Hotel do Colégio;
a stylish restaurant serving traditional
cuisine cooked to the highest standards,
supported by an excellent array of
Portuguese wines.

TERCEIRA

⊜⊜ **Restaurante Caneta** – *Às Presas,
Estrada Regional, Altares. ℘295 989 162.
www.restaurantecaneta.com.* Altares is
on the north coast of the island, but this
restaurant is worth the journey, serving
fish and meat dishes (upstairs) and basic
bar food (downstairs). Specialities include
grilled octopus and black pudding, but
try the house steak (*hifa da casa*).

GRACIOSA

⊜ **Marlsqueira Jose Joao** – *Rua Fontes
Pereira de Melo 148, São Mateus, Praia.
℘295 732 855.* Hugely popular eatery
serving traditional cuisine. You may have
to wait for a table at weekends, but it is
well worth it. The wine list has excellent
Portuguese and Azorean wines.

SÃO JORGE

⊜⊜ **Cafe Restaurant Açor** – *Largo
du Matriz 11, Velas ℘795 432 463.*
Fast, friendly service in this small
restaurant opposite the church. Rather
more international cuisine than other
restaurants, mainly Italian.

PICO

⊜⊜ **Fonte Cuisine** – *Aldeia da Fonte,
Caminho da Fonte/Silveira, Lajes do Pico.
℘292 679 500. www.aldeiadafonte.com.*
A bit out of the way, but the best place
on the island to eat. Within the hotel
Aldeia da Fonte.

FAIAL

⊜⊜ **Medalhas Taberan and Casa de
Pasto** – *Rua de Serpa Pinto 22c, Horta.
℘292 391 026.* Well worth seeking out; a
rustic eatery in a lovely setting, serving
spicy sausage, blood sausage, rib-eye
steak, blue jack mackerel and yams.

FLORES

⊜⊜ **Casa do Rei** – *Rua Peixoto
Pimentel/Monte, Lajes das Flores. ℘292
593 262. Closed Tue in winter. www.
restaurantcasadorei.com.* Excellent local
cuisine, with lots of fresh fish and tasty
meats.

SPORT AND LEISURE

WALKING

Walking is one of the most popular
pastimes in the Azores. The most
pleasant islands in which to walk are
Pico for the climb up the volcano, São
Jorge with its wonderful coastal rambles,
Flores and Corvo for their caldeira and
São Miguel, which has a wide choice
of walking itineraries. ⊚ Ask at local
information centres for free leaflets
about walking routes on each island.

SWIMMING

There are not many beaches in the
Azores apart from those on São Miguel,
Santa Maria, Faial and Terceira. Swimming
is possible on the other islands in natural
swimming pools hewn out of the lava.

DIVING

The coastal waters around the Azores are
very beautiful, so this is a popular place
to come for diving. Diving centres for all
levels, from beginners to advanced, have
been set up in almost all of the islands.

GOLF

The climate is ideal for playing golf,
provided you pack waterproofs. There
are three golf courses in the Azores – an
18-hole course on Terceira near the
airport, another 18-hole course at Furnas
(São Miguel) and a 27-hole course at
Batalha (São Miguel).

SPAS

Several spas have been developed to
take advantage of the therapeutic
waters from hot springs. There are baths
at Furnas and Ferraria on São Miguel and
Carapacho on Graciosa.

FESTIVALS

5th Sunday after Easter, São Miguel –
Santo Cristo Festival at Ponta Delgada.
29 June, São Miguel – São Pedro
Cavalcade at Ribeira Grande.
Last week in June, Terceira –
Midsummer's Day (St John) Festival with
processions and bullfights.
22 July, Pico – Madalena Festival. **Week
of 1st to 2nd Sunday, August, Faial** –
Sea Festival at Horta harbour with boats.
15 August, Santa Maria – Island Festival.
Election of Holy Ghost emperor.
August, Terceira – Festas da Praia takes
place every year during the first week
of August, and combines leisure, musical
performances, parades and gastronomy.

INDEX

INDEX

INDEX

INDEX

🏨 STAY

INDEX

♟/EAT

INDEX

MAPS AND PLANS

MAP LEGEND

	Sight	Seaside resort	Winter sports resort	Spa
Worth a special journey	★★★	초초초	✳✳✳	⸙⸙⸙
Worth a detour	★★	초초	✳✳	⸙⸙
Interesting	★	초	✳	⸙

Tourism

◉━▷	Sightseeing route with departure point indicated	AZ B	Map co-ordinates locating sights
⛪⛪⛪⛪	Ecclesiastical building	ⓘ	Tourist information
🕍🕌	Synagogue – Mosque	⚔ ∴	Historic house, castle – Ruins
⬛	Building (with main entrance)	◡ ⚙	Dam – Factory or power station
■	Statue, small building	☆ ⌒	Fort – Cave
†	Wayside cross	⊤⊤	Prehistoric site
◎	Fountain	▼ ⚐	Viewing table – View
●━■━▪	Fortified walls – Tower – Gate	▲	Miscellaneous sight

Recreation

🏇	Racecourse	🚶	Waymarked footpath
⛸	Skating rink	◆	Outdoor leisure park/centre
≋ 🖼	Outdoor, indoor swimming pool	🎡	Theme/Amusement park
⛵	Marina, moorings	🦌	Wildlife/Safari park, zoo
⌂	Mountain refuge hut	❀	Gardens, park, arboretum
▫━■━▫	Overhead cable-car	🐦	Aviary, bird sanctuary
🚂	Tourist or steam railway		

Additional symbols

══ ══	Motorway (unclassified)	✉ ☎	Post office – Telephone centre
❶ ❶	Junction: complete, limited	✉	Covered market
▭▭	Pedestrian street	⋅✕⋅	Barracks
‡═══‡	Unsuitable for traffic, street subject to restrictions	⚠	Swing bridge
▥ - - -	Steps – Footpath	∪ ✕	Quarry – Mine
🚆 🚌	Railway – Coach station	B F	Ferry (river and lake crossings)
▫┼┼┼┼┼┼▫	Funicular – Rack-railway	🛥	Ferry services: Passengers and cars
—•— ⏺	Tram – Metro, underground	⛴	Foot passengers only
Bert (R.)...	Main shopping street	③	Access route number common to MICHELIN maps and town plans

Abbreviations and special symbols

A	Agricultural office (Chambre d'agriculture)	P	Local authority offices (Préfecture, sous-préfecture)
C	Chamber of commerce (Chambre de commerce)	POL.	Police station (Police)
H	Town hall (Hôtel de ville)	🎖	Police station (Gendarmerie)
J	Law courts (Palais de justice)	T	Theatre (Théâtre)
M	Museum (Musée)	U	University (Université)
		ⓐ	Hotel
		🅿	Park and Ride
		🏖	Beach

COMPANION PUBLICATIONS

travelguide.michelin.com
www.viamichelin.com

MAPS

Portugal and Spain

Michelin Portugal Map 733 at a 1:1 000 000 scale covers the whole of the Iberian Peninsula, as does the **Michelin Atlas Spain and Portugal** (scale: 1:400 000). Map 733 at a 1:400 000 scale covers Portugal and includes an index and an enlarged inset map of Lisbon. **Michelin plan 39** with a scale of 1:11 000 covers the city of Lisbon, with details on one-way streets, main car parks and public buildings.

Michelin Spain & Portugal National Map 734. A 1:1 000 000 scale map of the Iberian Peninsula.

Map of North West Spain 571 (Galicia, Asturias-León). A 1:400 000 scale map of northwest Spain and the northern half of Portugal.

ROUTE PLANNING

Michelin is pleased to offer a route planning service at **www.viamichelin.com**.

Personalised route plans, comprehensive maps, addresses of hotels and restaurants featured in *The Red Guides* and practical and tourist information.

YOUR OPINION IS ESSENTIAL TO IMPROVING OUR PRODUCTS

Help us by answering the questionnaire on our website:
satisfaction.michelin.com

Michelin Travel Partner

Société par actions simplifiées au capital de 15 044 940 EUR
27 cours de l'Ile Seguin - 92100 Boulogne Billancourt (France)
R.C.S. Nanterre 433 677 721

No part of this publication may be reproduced in any form
without the prior permission of the publisher.

© Michelin Travel Partner
ISBN 978-2-067243-18-7
Printed: February 2020
Printed and bound in France : Imprimerie CHIRAT, 42540 Saint-Just-la-Pendue - N° 202002.0149